CW00542866

Shades of the Prison House

Shades of the Prison House

A History of Incarceration in the British Isles

HARRY POTTER

THE BOYDELL PRESS

First published 2019
The Boydell Press, Woodbridge

ISBN 978 1 78327 331 7

The Boydell Press is an imprint of Boydell & Brewer Ltd
PO Box 9, Woodbridge, Suffolk IP12 3DF, UK
and of Boydell & Brewer Inc.
668 Mount Hope Ave, Rochester, NY 14620–2731, USA
website: www.boydellandbrewer.com

A catalogue record for this book is available
from the British Library

The publisher has no responsibility for the continued existence
or accuracy of URLs for external or third-party internet websites
referred to in this book, and does not guarantee that any content
on such websites is, or will remain, accurate or appropriate

This publication is printed on acid-free paper

Printed and bound in Great Britain by TJ International Ltd, Padstow, Cornwall

Contents

Illustrations

All illustrations are from the author's collection unless otherwise attributed.

Abbreviations

Behan	*Borstal Boy*
Chesterton	*Revelations of Prison Life*
Clay	*The Prison Chaplain*
Clayton	*The Wall Is Strong*
Defoe	*Tour of the Whole Island of Great Britain*
Du Cane	*The Punishment and Prevention of Crime*
EHD	*English Historical Documents.*
Ellwood	*The History of Thomas Ellwood*
EPBS	Fox, *The English Prison and Borstal Systems*
Extracts	*The Third Report of the Inspectors of Prisons for the Home District*
Fry	*Memoir of the Life of Elizabeth Fry with extracts from her Journals and Letters*
Grew	*Prison Governor*
Griffiths	*Fifty Years of Public Service*
Gurney	*Notes on a Visit made to some of the Prisons in Scotland and the North of England in company with Elizabeth Fry*
H&B	Hobhouse and Brockway, *English Prisons*
HMBI	Her Majesty's Borstal Institution
HMP	Her Majesty's Prison
HO	Home Office
Howard	*Prisons and Lazarettos*
Letters	Oscar Wilde, *Complete Letters*
M&B	Mayhew and Binny, *The Criminal Prisons of London*
NOMS	National Offender Management Service
OED	*Oxford English Dictionary*
OHLE	*Oxford History of the Laws of England*
OHP	*Oxford History of the Prison*
Paterson	*Paterson on Prisons* (ed. S.K. Ruck)
PD	*Parliamentary Debates*
POA	Prison Officers' Association
Radzinowicz	*The Emergence of Penal Policy*

Report (date)	Reports of the commissioners of prisons or reports on prisons
Rich	*Recollections of a Prison Governor*
SIPD	Society for the Improvement of Prison Discipline and Reformation of Juvenile Offenders
Smith	*Works*
Webb	*English Prisons under Local Government*
YOI	Young Offender Institution

Foreword

There can be few subjects about which so many people hold stronger views, many of which are either prejudiced or ill-informed, than imprisonment. Of course, victims of crime are entitled to view perpetrators differently from others; but there is no justification for those frequently referred to as 'hangers and floggers', who, not knowing anything about the circumstances of those who find themselves in prison, regard every prisoner as a combination of mass murderer, paedophile, rapist and arsonist, who deserves nothing more than being locked up and the key thrown away.

Their attitude is far from the truth and distorts the purpose of imprisonment. It is often said that there are three types of people in prison – the mad, the bad and the sad – of which by far the fewest number (15% maximum) are incorrigibly bad. There have always been prisons in this country, initially holding people awaiting sentence, which, because it was corporal or capital, meant that they were not incarcerated for very long. Prisons were local, paid for by local taxes. The use of imprisonment has changed over the years, as the number of capital offences decreased, including the period when transportation was in vogue, the introduction of convict prisons, nationalisation under a Prison Commission, the abolition of the death penalty and, finally, putting it under the control of a government Ministry, first the Home Office and currently the Ministry of Justice.

The great thing about Harry Potter's book is the way that he sets about correcting the ill-informed and, by recounting the history of imprisonment and explaining the motivation and ideas of some of the giants of penal reform, educating the prejudiced. But, by deliberately bringing the history of imprisonment up to date, he is also informing the public about current issues. I am particularly pleased that he tells us so much about one of those giants, Alexander Patterson, who uttered one of the inalienable truths about imprisonment, when he said that 'prison was punishment, it was not for punishment'. The only punishment involved is the deprivation of liberty, for a specified time, awarded by the courts following conviction for a crime. We do not practise double jeopardy in this country, and therefore it is not the job of prison officers, or prison conditions, to inflict further punishment.

I must admit that I have often wondered whether successive Home and Justice Secretaries have thought through the position of imprisonment in the Criminal Justice System before setting out on the route that they did. Inspired by Patterson's observation, I did just that on taking up the appointment of Chief Inspector of Prisons for England and Wales in 1995, concluding that it was analogous to the position of hospitals in the National Health Service. Both are the acute part, to which people should only be sent if they needed the treatment that only these Services can give, which, in the case of prisons, includes the protection of the public. Neither has any control over who comes in, and has got to try to make them better, conscious that that process will never be completed in either prison or hospital but will have to be continued in the community in the form of aftercare. Choke either with people who should not be there, and their staff will be prevented from being able to do all that they could for the people who should.

Harry Potter clearly appreciates that prisons are places of opportunity. Tony Blair, on becoming Prime Minister in 1997, gave one unifying aim to the four parts of the Criminal Justice System – police, courts, prisons and probation – namely 'to protect the public by preventing crime'. Unfortunately he gave it to the wrong people, because the Criminal Justice System only clicks in when a crime has been committed – police investigate, courts sentence and prison and probation administer that sentence either in custody or the community. Much better had he said 'preventing re-offending', which would have given a unifying aim to prisons and probation. Each should identify what has prevented a convicted person from leading a useful and law-abiding life, which leads on to assessment of their educational, work and social skills, any physical or mental health needs and whether they are abusing any substance. Armed with this assessment, they can then make an individual sentence-plan, prioritised according to the severity of the symptom and the time available. At the end of a prison sentence, an aftercare plan must be made, which must be passed on to whoever is responsible for actioning it in the community. As Harry Potter identifies, if this is done, time spent in prison is nothing less than an opportunity that the Prison Service must not miss, of protecting the public, by helping all those sentenced to live useful and law-abiding lives.

By concentrating on people, Harry Potter emphasises the key importance of staff. I have lost count of the number of times that I have said that unless things are right for staff, nothing will be right for prisoners, which makes the deliberate cut of a third in their size, imposed by Chris Grayling when he was Secretary of State for Justice, seem all the more reprehensible. Behind every example of a person who makes the decision to turn his or her life around is often an individual member of staff, who by their attitude or understanding has been responsible for the change. Without sufficient numbers, prisoners will not be escorted to courses and other training, leading to their being unable to develop life-changing skills. It is nothing short of a tragedy that, today, far too many prisoners are victims of the very double jeopardy which Alexander Patterson warned against, because of the additional punishment inflicted by being left for far too many hours in a day, sitting in what is little better than a shared lavatory.

Clearly Harry Potter has researched his subject with considerable care, and I wish that his book had been published before I took up my appointment. He is to be congratulated and thanked for doing so much to lift the veil on a subject that affects us all, because all readers are members of the public, whom it is the task of imprisonment to protect. I hope that it will be widely read.

GENERAL LORD DAVID RAMSBOTHAM GCB, CBE
Her Majesty's Chief Inspector of Prisons
for England and Wales (1995–2001)

Introduction

> Prison is variously regarded ... as a cloakroom for trial prisoners, a
> dustbin for nuisances, and limbo for those whom society is reluctant
> to see again. The word merely connotes a place of confinement, where
> men have to be kept in custody for many different reasons. As a result
> the prison is apt to become an *omnium gatherum*, a convenient receptacle
> into which a puzzled court may put anyone for whom no alternative
> method of disposal is very obvious.
>
> Alexander Paterson

> The humanitarian theory wants simply to abolish Justice and substitute
> Mercy for it ... Mercy, detached from Justice, grows unmerciful. All I
> plead for is the prior condition of ill desert; loss of liberty justified on
> retributive grounds before we begin considering the other factors.
>
> C.S. Lewis

Prisons, like prostitutes, have always been with us but, over time and place,
have changed radically in conditions, attributes and functions, as well
as in their name, character and rationale. The period of our consideration
spans the Anglo-Saxon era to the present day; the place is largely confined
to the constituent parts of the British Isles.

Du Cane Road in West London, which bisects the lower-middle-class
area of East Acton, serves a highly symbolic function. Named after the
most famous of Victorian prison administrators, it divides the homes of
the respectable and law-abiding residents of suburbia from the refuse
tip in which the vermin who offend against the law and their mores are
exiled and immured. That refuse tip, or 'penal dustbin' as it was described
by one of its own governors, is Her Majesty's Prison Wormwood Scrubs.[1]
With its massive walls and fortress gates embossed with the faces of those
great penal reformers John Howard and Elizabeth Fry, it is an enduring
and intimidating reminder of the Victorians' moral certainty and of
their indomitable determination to enforce the law and to punish, deter
and reform the criminal. The great surviving castellated institutions of
incarceration – or their modern monolithic equivalents – that stand like
citadels in our major cities or outside our county towns, or are clustered

---

1 John McCarthy, letter to *The Times*, 19 November 1981.

on islands or dotted throughout some parts of our countryside, appear so monumental in design and so intrinsic to the criminal justice system that it is tempting to think of them as permanent and fixed features of the British legal landscape, immemorial, immutable, immovable. Punishment and imprisonment are almost synonyms. Yet the forbidding edifices we see today were the outcome of an evolutionary process. The history of prisons is much more than merely a tale of the Victorian Gothic.

Indeed, it is anything but static. Until the modern period, the change was primarily in the number of places of imprisonment, rather than any alteration in their purpose. People were held in custody for well-defined and straightforward reasons: felons pending trial and punishment; debtors as an inducement to pay their dues; minor offenders, guilty of a few specified offences, as a 'short sharp shock'. There was no penological theory, and no need for one. Since the eighteenth-century Enlightenment, however, there has been almost constant flux as one penological purpose has been replaced by another, or, at least, different emphases have ebbed and flowed.

The term 'prison', or its synonym 'gaol', is generic,[2] encompassing a wide range of institutions of confinement. In medieval castles 'dungeons' denoted dark, deep and damp depositories for rebels, traitors and others who had fallen foul of nobleman or monarch. By contrast, 'lock-ups', 'pounds' or 'cribs' were found in the smallest towns for the overnight detention of drunks, prostitutes and minor offenders, while in the larger towns and cities gaols held prisoners pending trial or debtors pending payment. The term 'Bridewell' originated in the City of London in the sixteenth century when a reformatory for misdemeanants, nuisances and orphans was established in the former royal palace of that name. 'Houses of Correction' were county institutions modelled on Bridewell. 'Penitentiaries', so fashionable in the early nineteenth century, were government-funded and state-controlled and were designed to induce penitence through a quasi-monastic discipline. Gaols, run by the county or municipality to hold pre-trial prisoners and those serving short sentences, were amalgamated with houses of correction in 1865 and

---

[2] Or near synonym. In the middle ages there may at times have been some distinction, as Richard son of Nigel in 1225 claimed that he had escaped from a prison but not from a gaol (Christopher Harding *et al.*, *Imprisonment in England and Wales* (Beckenham, 1985), p.xiii). Peter Spierenburg also makes 'an analytical distinction between jails and prisons'. Medieval jails – as he calls them – were primarily holding pens where the incarcerated were largely left to themselves, while prisons were 'punitive institutions' where the inmates were 'to be chastised or corrected', and they had 'a specific regime – forced labour, a system of solitude, or a rehabilitative program' ('The Origins of the Prison', in *The Persistent Prison*, ed. Clive Emsley (London, 2005), pp.27–48, at p.28). I remain unconvinced.

were called 'local prisons'. 'Convict prisons' were for those serving sentences of penal servitude. By the early twentieth century, all places of short and long detention for adults, on remand or convicted, were called 'prisons'. In addition, for young offenders, there have been 'approved schools', 'borstals', 'detention centres' and 'young offender institutions'.

The history of incarceration is marked by extraordinary changes. Before the eighteenth century, prisons were only one part, and a peripheral one, of the system of punishment. There was no need of any theory behind them. Although imprisonment was imposed for some offences, and so served a retributive or deterrent purpose, and was a means of coercing debtors or the contumacious, the primary aim of imprisonment was detention *before* punishment and not detention *as* punishment. Prisons were antechambers to the courts, and the task of the judges was to empty them periodically by a process known as 'gaol delivery' and not, as in later days, to fill them to capacity. Gaols were noisy, packed, and brutal, but human for all that, with all the vices of drink, gambling and sex to make living in them more tolerable. 'Let us eat and drink for tomorrow we shall die' – on the gallows or of the pox – was the Isaianic motto above their gates.

Then things began to change. Prisons, for the first time, were becoming primarily places of secondary – non-capital – punishment, the prime impetuses in this being the decline in capital punishment and the ending of transportation. Criminals who could no longer be executed or exiled had to be confined, and confined for prolonged periods. But was punishment and deterrence imprisonment's sole rationale? Could prisons also be used for reform and rehabilitation? And could these disparate purposes be combined, or would they inevitably jar? A theory of punishment, an ideology of incarceration, was needed. Deplorable conditions alleviated by debauchery, crimes compounded with sins, aggravated Christian concern for criminals and their redemption, for their bodies and their souls. In the late eighteenth and early nineteenth centuries, prison conditions and regimes became the target of reformers, not just the ardent evangelicals, Howard and Fry, but the ardent atheist, Jeremy Bentham. Under a religious and utilitarian imperative to burnish the soul, remould the mind, repair the character and remake the miscreant, prisons were radically reorganised, and the stern principles of penitence and submission were imposed on the sinners or defectives sent there.

Order was to replace chaos. Prisons became places of both punishment and reformation and were reorganised around principles of discipline, regularity and control. The sterile monotony and utter futility of the crank and tread-wheel deployed in county gaols symbolised the penal aspect. Custom-built penitentiaries in which prisoners were isolated from each other in separate cells, and where rules of total silence were strictly enforced, incarnated the reformatory approach. The abject failure of these moral factories to reap rehabilitative results led to the abandonment of their ideals.

When penitence failed, punishment triumphed. From the mid-nineteenth century prisons became almost wholly penal, and those imprisoned therein were subjected to retributive regimes of hard labour: climbing the tread-wheel, breaking stones or picking oakum. From 1877 the entire penal estate was placed under State control, and the State appointed Edmund Du Cane to create and administer a uniform and uniformly deterrent system. Punishment, inexorable and exact, was to the fore, and prisons were places for punishment. This period was very much the exception and was relatively short-lived. A Christian country ultimately could not tolerate this affront to humanity.

Late Victorian philanthropists and, crucially, Liberal politicians, thought the Du Cane system brutal and immoral, and drove change, humanitarian rather than utilitarian. The early and mid-twentieth century saw many attempts to improve both prisoners and prison conditions, with a greater emphasis on education and skills and with experiments in treatment, training and rehabilitation. Penal institutions modelled themselves more on the outside community, encouraging constructive association, affording inmates the opportunity to work and socialise together, providing a parade-ground for release. Work was no longer pointless and craft skills were encouraged, with prisoners being taught fine bookbinding or how to render books into braille.

The two most interesting, influential and partially successful initiatives were the attempts to reform young offenders by sending them to the carceral equivalent of the English public school, the borstal, and to treat the psychologically damaged in a purpose-built psychotherapeutic prison, Grendon. The borstal system, in particular, is given a lot of attention in this book since it constituted the most imaginative, innovative and successful experiment in British penal history. It was a very British beacon of hope until it was casually extinguished.

In the 1960s and 1970s, with criminologists calling into question the effectiveness of treatment and training, and the idealism engendered by the religious impulse diminishing as the country became ever more secular, penal optimism began to erode and the number imprisoned rose inexorably. In the last half-century or so security has been the predominant factor in prison design and cost. Perceived public safety is paramount. In recent years we have had one Home Secretary imposing a penal policy based on 'just deserts', with a concomitant drop in the prison population, and a host of others increasing the numbers in prison on the ground that 'prison works' – as a punishment, as a deterrent, for containment. Prisons are primarily to incapacitate, not rehabilitate, the offender: to contain the problem, not solve it. Yet ideals of reform and rehabilitation persist, sitting uneasily, where they have always sat, alongside retribution and deterrence. None of our current debates on imprisonment is new. The same issues in prison discipline have been regurgitated for two centuries or more – cleanliness, godliness, overcrowding, contamination and contraband, even if gin has been replaced by 'spice' as the anaesthetic of choice. And so too the arguments about the purpose of imprisonment. The arrow of penal progress does not fly straight, but the tread-wheel of penal theory inexorably turns. There is nothing new under the sun.

The major present threat to any and all penological purposes is the persistent and exponential growth in the numbers imprisoned. The prison population in Great Britain has soared as more and more criminals are imprisoned, and those who are serve ever longer and longer terms. All the while there are increasing budget constraints, coupled with public indifference to the fate and fortune of those we imprison. Out of sight, out of mind. Good riddance.

In this book I do not intend to analyse in great depth the differing perspectives on the nature and ideology of incarceration put forward by historians and sociologists. My own views will be abundantly clear in the text, but a few paragraphs on the matter of the historiography of imprisonment are appropriate for an introduction.

In the late twentieth century, taking their lead from the Americans Gertrude Himmelfarb and David Rothman and the French sociologist Michel Foucault, revisionist historians such as Michael Ignatieff and Marxist ideologues such as Melossi and Pavarini postulated a sharp break in penal practice taking place in the late eighteenth and first half of the nineteenth century whereby physical punishment was largely replaced by body- and mind-control in panoptic-style penitentiaries.[3] These were just one of an

---

3   Gertrude Himmelfarb, *Victorian Minds* (London, 1968); David Rothman, *The Discovery of the Asylum* (Boston, 1971); Michel Foucault, *Discipline and Punish*, English trans. (London, 1975); Michael Ignatieff, *A Just Measure of Pain* (London, 1978); Dario Melossi and Massimo Pavarini, *The Prison and the Factory*, English trans. (London, 1981). Foucault's work is largely based on the French experience, but Ignatieff's comprises a detailed study of Pentonville itself. Both are engaging books from which much can be learnt even if the premises and conclusions are rejected. Indeed Ignatieff revised his own position about the prevalence of penitentiary practice (as opposed to propaganda about its extent) in 'State, Civil Society and Total Institutions: A Critique of Recent Social Histories of Punishment', in *Social Control and the State*, ed. Stanley Cohen and Andrew Scull (New York, 1983), pp.75–105.

array of 'total institutions' which included workhouses, factories, barracks and asylums used to confine, control and discipline deviant and unruly members of the working class or instil habits of industry and discipline in the proletariat of a burgeoning industrial society.[4] Penitentiaries were mills, to paraphrase Bentham, for grinding dissidents into submission. The capitalist agenda required a carceral State. Concomitant with this view went a scepticism towards, or downright dismissal of, the motives of reformers such as Howard and Fry. Their humanitarian endeavours were merely a subterfuge to subject all and sundry to panoptic surveillance, to ensnare them in the tentacles of the State, and in particular to subjugate or suborn the dissident leaders of the masses. An iron fist in a velvet glove.

To postulate such a strategy of totalitarian control is to credit a greater degree of Machiavellian sophistication to the governing elite than is warranted and flies in the face of the serendipitous nature of much penal change. The English, it has been said, are 'suspicious of system', tend 'to deal with the situation confronting them', and only then discover 'on what principles they have done so'.[5] Trial and error and muddling through were more the British way, and the reality of remedial incarceration rarely lived up to the rhetoric, and never to the expectation. Until 1877 there was no 'prison system' but a variety of institutions for incarcerating offenders, many of which were old and ill-designed for novel purposes. And those purposes varied from place to place and were subject to vagaries of local interpretation and resources. The history of prison reform will no more fit into a Marxist strait-jacket than a Whig one. It is a rather more interesting 'story of mixed motives, intractable problems and unintended consequences'. The motives of individual reformers could vary and their motives would not necessarily be those of the local worthies who ran the gaols and bridewells.

---

[4] Roy Porter in *Mind-Forg'd Manacles* (London, 1987) comprehensively debunked the notion of a 'great confinement' of the insane, at least so far as eighteenth-century England is concerned (pp.141, 168). Margaret DeLacy, in her detailed study, *Prison Reform in Lancashire, 1700–1850* (Stanford, CA, 1986), demonstrated that the condition of a prison derived from the nature of its inmates, the quality of the staff, and the extent of outside supervision (as it does today!). She persuasively argued that 'the story of prison reform ... is not simply the story of the repression of one group' by another, since it was often 'working men' who 'prosecuted other working men for thefts', and many prisoners welcomed greater regulation, security and privacy (pp.8–12). One of the best re-assessments of Foucault *et al.* is that of Peter Spierenburg in chapter 4 of *Violence and Punishment* (Cambridge, 2013). He sees more virtue in the original than in his acolytes.

[5] William Temple, *The Ethics of Penal Action* (Rochester, 1934), pp.14f.

Further, the Foucaultian perspective, asserting a sudden transformation in the late eighteenth century, failed to account for the existence of the Rasphouse in Amsterdam and Bridewell in London in the sixteenth century as a prelude to the penitentiary, and from whose acorns the reformative oak would grow. And not all would grow to fruition. 'English society persistently baulked at adopting' Bentham's all-invasive panopticon, whatever it represented. Millbank and Pentonville were both prestige government projects and were not typical of what was going on outside the capital. Indeed between 1838 and 1854 the average period of confinement in the county prisons of England and Wales was under fifty days, hardly enough time to crop, clean, clothe and classify prisoners let alone to institutionalise or indoctrinate them.[6]

The revisionist project also failed to account for the reactionary attack on reformist endeavours as undermining deterrence and mollycoddling felons and, upon their failure, the advent of Du Cane's austere imperium whereby physical punishment was again to the fore – although it had never gone away, as even in the high days of panoptic optimism the tread-wheel still turned, flogging still persisted, and hanging survived as a popular public spectacle until 1868. Indeed the Bloody Code in England, whereby over two hundred offences, many of them against property, carried the death penalty, with imprisonment only for those whose sentences were commuted, was contemporary with the development of reformist penal theories, and, along with transportation, provided a rival counterpart to them. Vast expenditure on building penitentiaries cannot be explained as a desire to coerce, as the much cheaper alternatives of eradication, exile, or mere repression would have sufficed. Du Cane's prisons were far less expensive to construct or run than the likes of Millbank and Pentonville. They were also arguably more effective. The money was there for the penitentiary experiment because reformatory hopes were high and the public conscience about the state of prisons was stirred.

Most importantly, revisionist theses displayed a complete lack of interest in, or understanding of, the strength and universality of the religious and humanitarian impulses which motivated not only active reformers but many ordinary concerned Christians, not just in the eighteenth and early nineteenth centuries but in the twentieth as well. Indeed the eighteenth century witnessed not only an industrial revolution but another of considerable import – the great religious revival inspired by the preaching of George Whitfield and John Wesley and energised by the hymns of

6   DeLacy, *op. cit.*, pp.3, 11–14, 193–7.

Charles Wesley, which led to the advent of Methodism, and reanimated fervour even in the somnolent Anglican Church. Indeed it was to the industrial working class that the efforts of Whitfield and Wesley were primarily directed, the former reducing twenty thousand Bristol black-faced miners to tears by the passion of his preaching. A fresh spirit of moral zeal was the result, and a new philanthropy galvanised Whig and Tory alike to address a whole number of social evils, from the reform of the Bloody Code to the abolition of slavery.

It was this same religious fervour that spurred on Howard and Fry and others like them to tackle the cancer of contemporary incarceration, and reach out to the poor souls languishing in filthy, anarchic gaols. They did the best they could to alleviate suffering and to preserve the human dignity and worth of all. Neither they – nor Bentham for that matter – can be held responsible for the later extremes of which they would not have approved. It was not their intention and it was not inevitable that their ideas should have produced Millbank or Pentonville.[7] Even their advocates were striving for the good. Reformers may sometimes have been misguided but they were not acting out of self-interest nor conspiring to protect the elite to which they belonged. The urge to inculcate the religious and moral values of their class and confession into those individuals deprived of them, and to elevate 'the fallen' to a respectable role within their own community so as to become 'useful' members of society, did not equate to a desire to enforce societal gradations, merely an acceptance of them, as was usual in their day. Although the great and the good offering a helping hand could be accompanied by condescension, this did not mean that reformers wanted to keep the imprisoned downtrodden. They wanted to elevate them from the mire in which they found themselves, and reintegrate them into the community. They should have a place in society even if they should know their place.

It was duty, 'stern daughter of the voice of God', not a need to dominate or subjugate that constituted the driving force motivating the reformers. The whole history of England, its laws and its penal system, has been far more determined by Christianity and its ethical demands and by the common law and its maxims than by secular forces and class struggle. Even the Labour Party, the political arm of the working class as it set out to be, owed more to Methodism than to Marx. Thus its moral fervour and thus its moderation.

---

[7] Janet Semple, *Bentham's Prison* (Oxford, 1993), pp.132f.

Conversely, those following David Garland's lead[8] saw in the late nineteenth and early twentieth century positivism, eugenicism, and the new social sciences becoming the dominant influences behind a model which dramatically broke with the past by discarding culpability and resorting to treatment, again as a means of defanging dissent. Between 1895 and 1914 the 'penal-welfare' complex came into being. This theory too goes against the British experience, as prison administrators, who had become the major instruments of change, were on the whole dismissive of these trends; imprisonment remained largely rooted in the classical and common law view that individuals were responsible for their actions, that those who committed crimes merited punishment, and that punishment should be proportionate to their offending, and not tailored to their needs. Even the most influential reformer of all, Alexander Paterson, despite approving of preventive detention for habitual criminals – the 'incorrigible' – and espousing indeterminate sentences to ensure enough time for effective treatment, never saw offenders as less than moral agents and was motivated far more by his Christian faith and experience of working-class life than by any other factors. The inter-war reformist thrust harked back to the evangelical impetus of a century before.

It is also striking that in liberal and democratic Britain in the first half of the twentieth century, unlike in totalitarian states such as Nazi Germany, Soviet Russia or Maoist China, the number imprisoned fell dramatically, prisons were closed, and strenuous efforts were made to find alternative means of punishing and reforming criminals. Britain in this period led the way in decarceration, not the reverse. It was no penal archipelago, no gulag.

There are many generic histories of imprisonment, so why another? Where they are largely academic and erudite, this should be as entertaining as it is informative. I embarked on an eclectic survey in the hope of making an important subject an engaging one. This volume will follow a largely chronological order, and whenever possible the nature and quality of

---

8 David Garland was one of the later revisionists to enter the lists, but whatever value *Punishment and Welfare* (Aldershot, 1985) might have is vitiated by the impenetrable prose which renders much of it unintelligible. The author inhabits a world in which 'knowledges' and 'logics' are words, 'discourses' are as prevalent as bacteria, there are 'politico-discursive struggles', descriptions are 'privileged', responses can be 'theoretically innocent', and there can be a 'theoretical determination of historical periodisation', and – wait for it – 'the transformation of complex ideological configurations comes about through the discursive revision of signifiers, the gradual production of new connotations and the restructuring of the existing representational practices'. Make of that what you will!

imprisonment at any given time and place will be enlivened by the accounts of those who experienced it. Inevitably the earliest period is that for which we have least human content of imprisonment, mere snatches from contemporary historians, law reports or letters. In the early modern period, when many literate Dissenters and debtors ended up behind bars, we have a wealth of first-hand accounts. From the eighteenth century to the present day we have even more material, in the form of treatises and reports by individuals and officials, accounts of imprisonment written by the imprisoned, histories of imprisonment and of individual prisons, and studies of prison architecture and design.

I myself have extensive experience of prison life. In 1978, as part of my vocational education, I opted to become a 'borstal boy' for two weeks, living in, being locked up alongside, and experiencing the life of, young men serving their sentence in Hollesley Bay borstal. From 1984 to 1987 I was a part-time assistant chaplain in Wormwood Scrubs, and, for a year, deputy-chaplain. Following that, I was appointed chaplain at Aylesbury Young Offender Institution where I worked from 1989 to 1993. Both were maximum security establishments holding life-sentence and long-term prisoners, although the former also served as one of the remand prisons for London. Some of the later chapters will draw on my own recollections of life on the inside: 'out of the depths have I called unto thee'.

PART I

IN THE BEGINNING
600–1500

The earliest evidence of imprisonment from Anglo-Saxon times to its development under the Normans and Angevins, including prison escapes and attacks on prisons as symbols of oppression. The plethora of places of incarceration in London and Southwark, and the proliferation of gaols of all sorts elsewhere. The gradually increasing use of imprisonment as a punishment, although gaols remained largely as a holding-bay or, in the case of debtors, a means of coercion.

CHAPTER 1

Bonds of Iron

Bonds of iron encircle me; a halter of chain yokes me, I am powerless, such hard hell-fetters have fast laid hold of me. Fetter of links, a cruel chain, have impeded my movements, deprived me of my motion. My feet are shackled, my hands tethered.

Genesis B poem, possibly mid-ninth-century

Prisons are for confinement and not for punishment.

Bracton

We cannot say when the first place of imprisonment was established in England. It is unlikely to have been created for that specific purpose and more likely to have been an improvised expedient: a piece of rope tied to a pillar; manacles forged by a blacksmith and fastened to a floor; stocks erected on the village green or in the churchyard; or the cellar of a substantial house; whatever and wherever needs must.[1] Headmen, landowners and bishops would have been the gaolers.

As royal power grew, and royal control over the administration of justice with it, local expedients would become more regularised. When the early Anglo-Saxon kings promulgated law codes and established courts in shire and hundred to try criminal offences, the necessity arose for means and places to detain and restrain the small number of those awaiting judgment who could find no sureties or were too dangerous to be let loose, or perhaps the rather larger number of those who were in danger of the lynch-mob. In the early tenth-century law codes of Edward the Elder and Aethelstan and early eleventh-century ones of Canute, detention pending trial was specifically reserved for strangers or for those who had neither friends willing to stand surety nor property that could be held as security.[2] Prison was thus the preserve of those who had no ties to the locality and every incentive to evade justice by going elsewhere, and of those who could evade

---

[1] Eighth-century wooden stocks found in a well at Barking Abbey are the earliest known 'instrument of confinement' (Andrew Reynolds, *Anglo-Saxon Deviant Burial Customs* (Oxford, 2009), p.13).

[2] *OHLE*, II, p.73; *EHD*, I, p.420.

justice without leaving recompense. The poor, the alien, and the unpopular were 'held for judgment' – pending trial by ordeal.

> If a friendless man, or a stranger from a distance, becomes so afflicted by his friendless state that he has no surety he is then, at a first charge, to go to prison and stay there until he goes to God's ordeal and experience there what he may.

If, later, sureties were provided, release would ensue for even quite serious offences. This beneficence was too late for some, since those who fell under universal suspicion and who could find no surety were to be killed by the king's reeve and buried in unconsecrated ground, damnation clasping retribution.[3]

With few exceptions, imprisonment was not for punishment but for safe custody. In a tale related in Lantfred's *Miracles of St Swithun*, the slave of a Winchester merchant called Flodoald was seized by the royal reeve Eadric for some offence and was held in chains by some of the king's thegns, pending trial. Should he fail the hot iron, his punishment would not be a further period in the manacles but death.[4] In this particular slave's case the prayers of his master were heard, the marks of ordeal were made invisible to the reeve, and the servant was released. For those with intercessors less devout, prison was not the punishment but a portal to something else and often something worse. Compensation, fines, flogging (primarily used on slaves), enslavement, castration, mutilation, exile, execution: these were the primary punishments exacted on offenders in Anglo-Saxon times. They were swift, salutary and far more effective and less expensive than locking people up for prolonged periods.

But penal imprisonment did exist and persist. Significantly for later developments there is some suggestion that in specific cases prison could be the appropriate place for punishment in the form of penance and for penitence. The Latin word carcer – prison – first appears in a law code of Alfred the Great dating from 892–893. The king ordained that those who broke their oath and pledge should 'with humility' surrender their weapons and possessions into the keeping of friends 'and be for forty days in prison at a king's estate'. Forty days was no arbitrary number: it was the same period as Lent. There 'let him endure what penance the bishop prescribes for him, and his kinsman are to feed him if he has no food himself'. Those without kinsmen were to be fed by the king's reeve. Those who refused to

---

3   Laws of Cnut, ss.33.1, 35 (*EHD*, I, p.460).
4   *OHLE*, II, pp.68f.

go peacefully were to be bound and dragged to the place of incarceration, and their weapons and possessions forfeited. Those who escaped before the end of the period were to be returned to prison to complete the full forty days. Those who made good their escape were to be outlawed and excommunicated – subject to both secular and sacral damnation.[5] Thus the penal purpose of imprisonment dates back at least to the first use of the word 'prison' in an English document.

There were other instances of prison being deployed for both punishment and deterrence. There is reference in the Laws of Wihtred to those freemen working on Sundays being liable to healsfang, originally a proportion of the wergild, the monetary impost for an offence, but which is thought by Wihtred's time to mean in effect a 'fine to avoid imprisonment'.[6] King Athelstan, at the very start of his ordinance issued at Grately c.926–930, decreed that no thief caught with stolen goods could be spared execution if he were over twelve years of age and the value of goods was over eight pence. A lucky, lesser-offending minor who escaped the noose was to be imprisoned for forty days – the earliest example of the 'short, sharp, shock' – before being redeemed on payment of 120 shillings and after kinsmen gave surety 'that he will desist for ever' from such deeds. Parents had to pay up for their chastened prodigal offspring and keep them in check in the future. Similarly those found guilty, after ordeal, of witchcraft or arson should serve 120 days before being freed on the same terms as for juvenile thieves.[7] In a later ordinance, Athelstan, learning that everywhere mercy was not being extended to the young, declared that it was too cruel to kill those under fifteen for theft and that they should be imprisoned instead, if such were available, or released on surety and pledge of good behaviour if not.[8] Prisons, where provided, had become a punishment for certain crimes and certain criminals.

At least before the ninth century, it does not seem that specific buildings were built or designated as prisons. They would be too costly and they were unnecessary. On the rare occasions imprisonment was needed, it could be improvised. The means of restraint would be stocks, ropes or iron fetters; the places of detention the houses of the shire-reeves – royal administrators – or the cellars of the manor houses of ealdormen – local noblemen.

---

5   Laws of Alfred, ss.1.2–6 (*EHD*, I, p.409).
6   Laws of Wihtred, s.8.2 (Lisi Oliver, *The Beginnings of English Law* (Toronto, 2002), pp.157, 171).
7   II Athelstan, ss.1.3, 6.1–2 (*EHD*, I, pp.417f.).
8   VI Athelstan, ss.12.1–2 (*EHD*, I, p.427).

Imprisonment was usually of short duration. There were no 'state' prisoners as there would be under the Normans. Political enemies or rivals were killed or exiled, not incarcerated. In any case, with a few late exceptions, castles were not a feature of Anglo-Saxon England and so there was nowhere to detain such dangerous individuals for prolonged periods and in adequate security.

As time went on, and the extent of monarchical power and involvement in the localities grew, royal estates were required to have prisons. In Mercia two early ninth-century charters of King Coenwulf for the first time refer to malefactors, thrice apprehended, being handed over to the royal vill where it was likely that a designated prison would exist.[9] By Alfred's time, royal control of the apparatus of justice was very much in the ascendancy and kings were increasingly avid legislators. Consequently, and not surprisingly, it seems that by then all royal manors – in Wessex at least – had prisons.

The king, however, was not alone in supplying structures converted into prisons. From 860 the bishop of Winchester was known to have imprisoned thieves, perhaps in the gaol known to exist in the city in Edward the Confessor's time. The Winchester prison was, however, known as 'the king's beam-house', suggesting that the structure itself had been provided by the king, if utilised by the bishop. It comprised a strong timber cage originally standing in the open street before being incorporated into an adjacent property.[10]

Whether in a specified structure or not, custody had to be secure and escape prevented. The accused for whom prison was deemed necessary should not be able to evade justice. As a deterrent to errant gaolers, those who failed in their duty could be made to pay for their negligence, and if the gaoler was an ealderman he could forfeit his office, unless pardoned by the king.[11]

The Norman Conquest upended England. New masters arrived in triumph and dispossessed the English, but for some time their hold on the spoils was precarious. It was necessary to subdue the kingdom, not just defeat it, and the former took longer than the latter. Symbolism and the perception of permanence were vitally important. William the Conqueror and his successors stamped their authority on their new realm. It was as though the country were a map, spread out on a table, subject to winds, liable at any

[9] A royal vill was the centre for the administration of a subdivision of a kingdom.
[10] Reynolds, *op. cit.*, pp.12f.
[11] Laws of Ine, ss.36 and 36.I (*EHD*, I, p.403).

moment to blow over or blow off. Cathedrals, keeps and castles were the paperweights, festooning the land and keeping it firmly in its place. These new castles could be made as hard to get out of as to get into, and made perfect prisons.

None of these Norman statements in stone was to prove more imposing or more enduring than the Tower of London, an immense edifice that did indeed tower over the City as it was meant to. It was an impregnable royal palace in which to house the Conqueror safe from 'the inconstancy of the numerous and hostile inhabitants' of London and 'the fickleness of the vast and fierce populace', and an intimidating stronghold with which to cow his new subjects. It would also serve as the first royal prison within which to confine his enemies.[12] This was something new. William had adopted the chivalric code which discouraged the use of political murder and assassination. He rarely killed his captured foes; he regularly imprisoned them, often for long periods. It was the earliest example in England of life imprisonment replacing the death penalty.

Fortifications on Tower Hill began immediately after the Conquest but were temporary, probably consisting of a motte with a surrounding wooden palisade, and were soon superseded by something more robust. Construction of the great keep began around 1078 and was completed some twenty years later in the reign of William I's son, William Rufus. In both position and design it mirrored the Conqueror's keep in Rouen. It was constructed of fine Caen limestone, both beautiful and durable, and its walls were fifteen feet thick and ninety feet tall. Turrets reinforced its corners and windows were high up, small and easily defensible. It was first called the Great Tower until it was whitewashed in the thirteenth century when it became known as the White Tower. Dank dungeons were constructed beneath for those in close confinement and rather lavish suites on its upper floors for the use of distinguished detainees. Around it was built a curtain wall, and the entire castle complex took its simple but distinctive name from its keep. The Tower of London was placed under the charge of Geoffrey de Mandeville by William I. As its first constable Geoffrey commanded an edifice of enduring Norman intent.

It first came to note as a prison in 1100 when, on the death of William Rufus, his younger brother, Henry, in effect usurped the throne from his older brother, Robert, duke of Normandy. One of the new king's early acts was to imprison his predecessor's rapacious regent, Ranulf Flambard,

---

12 William of Poitiers, *Gesta Guillelmi*, ed. R.H.C. Davis and Marjorie Chibnall (Oxford, 1998), ii.34.

bishop of Durham, in the commodious Great Tower, hardly 'in the darkness of the prison-house' as one chronicler put it. The first prisoner was also the first escapee. After less than a year's less than onerous detention, he resorted to techniques which would be emulated by bold escapees, in reality and fiction, for the next thousand years. As an important state prisoner, Ranulf could command large quantities of wine. One of the flagons concealed a rope, while its liquid contents were liberally dispensed to the gaolers invited to a lavish dinner by their generous guest. They happily imbibed, and drank themselves into stupefaction. When they were snoring soundly, the prelate, whose agility rivalled his ingenuity, tied the rope to a window column of his chamber and, taking his pastoral staff with him, clambered down to his accomplices and their waiting horses. He only just made it as the rope was not long enough and he had to jump the last few feet. A little battered and bruised he fled to Normandy to seek succour with Robert. Despite escaping from Henry I's clutches and aligning himself with the king's sibling and rival, the bishop was soon rehabilitated and returned to his see.[13]

Less fortunate was his gaoler, William de Mandeville, who had succeeded his father to the prestigious post of constable. For his folly over Ranulf he was fined the enormous sum of £2,200 with three of his most lucrative manors held as guarantee of payment, one Anglo-Saxon tradition willingly carried on by the Normans.[14] The king also spent money on the Tower, but whether to further enhance security is not known. It may have been futile, since even the most secure prison is susceptible to human frailty.

The Tower was not the only prison built in Norman times in London, but it was the only royal one, and the only prison 'for state-delinquents of rank'.[15] The other long-lived places of incarceration which originated in this period were the City's responsibility, and were to accommodate a wide variety of inmates from London, Middlesex and even further afield. Over time and through custom they were differentiated in the type of detainee they housed, but differentiation was rarely absolute.

---

[13] William of Malmesbury, *Gesta Regum Anglorum*, I, ed. R.A.B. Mynors, R.M. Thomson and M. Winterbottom (Oxford, 1998), 393.2, 394.2.

[14] Stephen Porter, *The Tower of London: The Biography* (Stroud, 2012), p.20.

[15] Howard, I, p.212. Some were of the very highest rank and their confinement could be commensurably comfortable. For instance John Balliol, King of Scots, after his defeat at the battle of Dunbar in 1296, spent, along with his large retinue, three leisurely years in the Tower, during which time he could go hunting outside London with his own pack of dogs. The grandest prisoner was the French king, John the Good, who had been captured at Poitiers in 1356 and lodged in some resplendence with his son and retainers in the White Tower, dying there in 1364.

The Fleet dates back to Henry I's reign and was erected on a moated site in the ward of Farringdon Without, north of what is now Ludgate Circus, near the mouth of the river Fleet from which it got its name. It was the first structure in London, and possibly even in all England, to be purpose-built as a prison, and by 1172 was being called 'the gaol of London'. For a time it was the only prison other than the Tower. The City paid for its construction and upkeep. It was built of stone and had a moat, which in time would become less a protection and more a cesspit. As early as 1155 the sheriffs of London and Middlesex secured an allowance to cover repairs and refurbishment.[16] Initially it held prisoners pending trial, and curfew-breaking drunks as well as the king's political foes, but by the second half of the twelfth century it specialised in holding those owing money to the Crown, as an account of the functioning of the Exchequer makes clear. Written between 1177 and 1179 by Richard FitzNigel, the bishop of London, it relates that the impecunious who could not, or more likely would not, pay their dues to the Exchequer were liable to arrest by the marshal who was empowered to send them to the 'public gaol' for safe-keeping until the sheriff distrained their goods or they were induced to pay up. One robust defaulter was the chamberlain of Chester who was imprisoned in the Fleet for a year on account of a debt he owed Edward I.[17] But a distinction was made: the insolvent did not deserve to 'be numbered with the transgressors'. They were not to be put in chains or imprisoned in dungeons, but housed apart, by themselves, 'or over the lower gaol', isolated from contagion, and free from contamination by the reprobate. Imprisonment for them was purely coercive: pay up or stay put. Social distinctions were maintained inside prison as without. Knights unlucky enough to end up in gaol were merely confined within the precinct under parole, while barons were not imprisoned but had to swear not to leave the suburbs of the town.[18] The Fleet remained 'the gaol of London' until shortly after Newgate prison was built.

In Henry I's reign a prison may have been constructed within the new gate in the old Roman wall to the north-west of St Paul's Cathedral and due north of Ludgate. Certainly in 1188 a piece of adjacent land was purchased upon which a prison was built, perhaps separate from the gatehouse or perhaps attached to it. From then until 1219 there are many references to work being carried out on 'the gaol of Newgate', as the structure was known. In 1236 Henry III ordered that a proper prison be built in one of

---

[16] R.B. Pugh, *Imprisonment in Mediaeval England* (Cambridge, 1968), pp.4, 114.

[17] Arthur Griffiths, *The History and Romance of Crime* (London, 1905), I, p.17.

[18] *The Dialogue of the Exchequer*, Book I, v, II, xxi (*EHD*, II, pp.537f., 601f.).

its turrets. Owned by the City, Newgate replaced the Fleet as the primary municipal gaol for felons from both London and Middlesex – of which it was the county gaol – and for debtors from the latter. But its remit was wider and served a national purpose. Although relatively small and cramped, it was thought particularly secure, and over the years security was enhanced.[19] Thus, at the behest of the Crown, it held prisoners of importance from all over the country. It boasted among its amenities the Press Yard for the use of the better off and the Press Room for the use of *peine fort et dure* on those who refused to plead.

On land granted him by Henry I in 1127, William Giffard, bishop of Winchester, built a magnificent palace for himself on the southern bank of the Thames in the borough of Southwark. To serve both ecclesiastical and secular purposes the bishop incorporated a double lock-up in the grounds between the river and his fish-ponds. One part was for men and the other for women, primarily petty offenders, drunkards, 'bawds and whores' and others guilty of breaking the rules governing the bishop's brothels. There they were held manacled or in fetters in dark, damp, and squalid cells far removed from the apartments enjoyed by the owner. The name 'Clink' seems to have been attached to the prison in the fourteenth century and may have derived from the sound of the blacksmith's hammer closing the irons around the wrists or ankles of the prisoners. Whatever the etymology, the prison subsequently bequeathed its notorious nickname to other gaols which were colloquially known as 'Clinks'. It was under episcopal jurisdiction or 'Liberty', and so by 1180 the land nearby was called, with no sense of irony, 'the Liberty of the Clink'.[20]

London was unique in the number of its prisons, but it was not alone in having them. Sheriffs, the king's officers in the counties, were expected to be responsible for the safe-keeping of those suspects awaiting trial, but had to rely on a hodgepodge of provision. They could provide their own places of detention or persuade others to do so. Not all were persuadable and not all complied. Such remissness persisted until the time of Henry II and beyond. Throughout the land there were franchise gaols belonging to ecclesiastics and noblemen whose newly built abbeys and castles provided convenient places of detention. In York, for instance, in addition to the castle, each of its 'liberties' had some sort of secure accommodation, and major provision

[19] Pugh, *op. cit.*, pp.103f.; Anthony Babington, *The English Bastille* (London, 1971), p.14.
[20] Originating from medieval sanctuaries, liberties were geographical areas outside, and outside the control of, the City, claiming judicial independence, and nominally governed by the monarch.

was made for confinement on church property. In most towns of any size there operated a swarm of lock-ups. Gateways were frequently utilised, such as the fortified Monkbar in York which was put to use as a prison for freemen.

And what was built to enforce justice could be abused to subvert it. During the nineteen lawless and turbulent years when Stephen and Matilda vied for the throne, barons, with impunity, utilised their gaols for personal profit or revenge. The Anglo-Saxon Chronicle related that they 'filled the country full of castles' which they filled with 'devils and wicked men':

> Then both by night and day they took those people they thought had any goods – men and women – and put them in prison and tortured them with indescribable torture to extort gold and silver ... they hung them up by the feet and smoked them with foul smoke ... they put knotted strings round their heads and writhed them till they went into the brain. They put them into dungeons crawling with adders and snakes and toads.

It was not surprising that men said 'Christ and his saints slept'.[21]

Even when the carceral provision was not subverted by the powerful and avaricious Norman aristocracy it varied in both quality and quantity and was completely unregulated. Prisoners could languish in dire conditions indefinitely and unprotected. There was no system to imprisonment, no philosophical underpinning, and no uniformity either in provision or regime. There was also no redress, no judicial oversight. Everything was *ad hoc*, make-do, and local, a little like justice itself. But things were about to change.

---

[21] *EHD*, II, p.210.

CHAPTER 2

Gaols Ordained

A gaol is nothing else than a common prison. And as leprosy is a malady which disgraces the body of a man so that he may not be suffered to dwell among healthy folk, so mortal sin is a kind of leprosy which makes the soul abominable to God and severs it from the community ... In order that the innocent may not be tainted with their sins, gaols were ordained in all the counties so that mortal sinners might be put therein to await their judgments.

Mirror of Justices

Five jayles or prisons are in Southwark placed,
    The Counter once St Margaret's church defaced
The Marshalsea, the King's Bench, and White Lyon,
    Then there's the Clink where handsome lodgings be.

John Taylor, the Water Poet

Henry II was only twenty-one when he came to the throne in 1154, but, young as he was, he was a fully-formed Plantagenet: energetic, irascible and interventionist. He was a veritable force of nature and his tempestuous character was felt throughout the kingdom. He took control. It was in his reign, and as a result of his actions, that the common law was forged, beginning with the Assize of Clarendon in 1166.[1] Enforcement of the king's law required the apparatus of justice. Among other royal diktats on this subject issued that year, Henry ordered that 'in the several counties where there are no gaols, let such be made in a borough or some castle of the king at the king's expense and from his wood ... to the end that in them the sheriffs may be able to guard those who shall be arrested' for felony. Lest their evil infect others, they were effectively quarantined from respectable society until they could be tried by the newly created itinerant royal judges called 'justices in eyre'.[2]

This was the first attempt to establish a regional system of common prisons as an adjunct of the king's common law, the essential infrastructure for the imposition of royal justice. County gaols, commissioned and paid for by the king, were under the authority of his sheriffs. The rest were the responsibility

---

[1] Harry Potter, *Law, Liberty and the Constitution* (Woodbridge, 2015), ch.4.
[2] S.7 (*EHD*, II, pp.441f.).

of municipal corporations and local dynasts. It took a long time, and further kingly intervention, for such a diverse constituency to produce results. Even his own officials could be laggard. Some complied at once, Norwich castle, for instance, being used as the county gaol from about 1165 and Bedford boasting a gaol from the same date.[3] Others dallied. As late as 1301 Edward I had to order 'for the easement of the men of the county ... that a prison should be made in Leicester for prisoners from the same county'. Eight years later another royal edict commanded that the still unfinished prison should be completed, 'well and securely' and as soon as was possible, so that thereafter no one should be sent from Leicester to the prison in Warwick which had been the normal recourse up until then. Towns could also be dilatory. In 1285 the Statute of Merchants laid down that those who failed to pay their debts should be sent to the town's prison, 'if there is one'.[4]

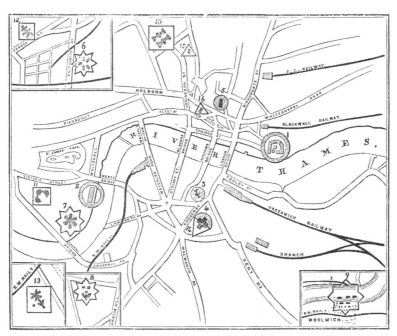

MAP ILLUSTRATIVE OF THE LOCALITY OF THE SEVERAL PRISONS OF THE METROPOLIS.

I.	II.	III.	IV.	V.
STATE PRISONS.	DEBTORS' PRISONS.	CONVICT PRISONS.	CORRECTIONAL PRISONS.	DETENTIONAL PRISONS.
Tower. 2. House of Commons.	3. Queen's Bench. 4. Horsemonger Lane (Surrey). 5. Whitecross Street (London and Middlesex).	6. Pentonville (Government). 7. Millbank (ditto). 8. Brixton (ditto). 9. Hulks (ditto).	10. Coldbath Fields (Middlesex). 11. Tothill Fields (ditto). 12. Holloway (City). 13. Wandsworth (Surrey).	14. Horsemonger Lane (Surrey). 15. House of Detention (Middlesex). 16. Newgate (City).

1. London's principal prisons, 1100–1900

3 R.B. Pugh, *Imprisonment in Mediaeval England* (Cambridge, 1968), p.77.
4 *EHD*, III, pp.458, 575.

Nonetheless, the proliferation of gaols continued. The grandest were the property of the Crown. During the reign of Henry III York castle was used as a prison to house all and sundry from peasants to peers, from common felons to Crown debtors. This was a royal bastion, strong, secure, and capable of indefinite detention.[5] At the other extreme, royal authority could be used to commandeer private property as makeshift lock-ups, never intended for more than a day or two's incarceration. For instance a room atop Chelmsford's Crown Inn served as the sheriff's temporary prison, holding even the most serious offenders overnight before execution.[6]

So far as franchise gaols were concerned, the brash new castles of the aristocracy were an obvious resource as most had dungeons and all had towers, courtyards, high walls and resident guards. Chester castle served several custodial functions, having four separate places of confinement within it, from a gaol called 'Gowestour' for common criminals to the crypt of the Agricola Tower that would hold King Richard II. Cellars in the manor houses of the lesser nobility were also utilised. In the municipalities, gatehouses or tolbooths on bridges were requisitioned for carceral use.

The Church too had the buildings and the money, and had long pioneered the use of imprisonment for errant clerics and some lay people *as* punishment as well as *pending* punishment, although even then clerical punishment had a higher purpose, as was demonstrated in 1217 when Bishop Poore of Salisbury prescribed 'penitence in prison' for clerks who had deserted their orders. In 1261 the archbishop of Canterbury was instructed to provide one or two prisons within his diocese. By 1343 every monastery housed a prison or what was sometimes even called a 'penitentiary'.[7] Monasteries already had cells, identical enclosures where monks would seek salvation in silence, solitude and the contemplation of their sins. Such cells were easily turned into places of confinement and enforced contrition, as can be seen at Fountains Abbey where the foundations of three connecting penal cells adjacent to the abbot's chambers are extant. It is no surprise that the term 'cell' would later be used to designate the accommodation afforded criminals. Upon occasion the ordinary convict and errant cleric could be housed together, although their ultimate fates might diverge. In York there was a prison within the precincts of St Mary's Abbey, once the richest in the north, for the detention of clerics and probably for some of the laity

---

5   A.W. Twyford and Arthur Griffiths, *Records of York Castle* (London, 1880), p.45.

6   F.G. Emmison, *Elizabethan Life: Disorder* (Chelmsford, 1970), pp.5, 51.

7   A cell in Flaxley, Gloucestershire, was so called, and in 1303 the abbot of Abingdon converted the infirmary in the priory of Earl's Colne in Essex into a 'penitentiary' (Pugh, *op. cit.*, pp.379f.).

since until 1379 the place of execution for criminals was 'the gallows of the Abbot of St Mary's'. In the same city, beneath the church of St Sepulchre, there was a dungeon equipped with iron staples and stocks.[8]

Prisons holding criminals were still not primarily places of punishment, although for those who escaped a worse fate by successfully pleading benefit of clergy, or who had committed petty offences, such as violating municipal trade laws, or serious infractions against the system of justice, such as giving false verdicts or perjury, imprisonment was the penalty. Often, but not always, release could be procured by payment of a fine or 'ransom'.[9] In other cases those defaulting on fines would be locked up until they paid up. The penalty for the crime was a fine; the penalty for not paying the fine was prison. The notion of using secular gaols to reform offenders, however, was yet unknown and would have been thought bizarre. The only exceptions were attempts by the clergy to induce repentance, almost exclusively in wayward clerics or in those awaiting the noose.

Castles, monasteries and lock-ups could serve the limited needs of rural communities and provincial towns. Cities were a different matter. The concentration of people in urban areas required dedicated prisons. London in particular added greatly to its carceral repertoire, mainly utilising the city gates and large town houses within its walls.

The Lud Gate was rebuilt about 1215 and by 1383 had become a prison, the rooms above the entrance being used for the detention of freemen of the City for debt, trespass, and contempt. Ludgate proved rather a cushy number – or so it was supposed – and gave rise to gripes about 'soft' prison conditions that persist to this day. In 1419 citizens complained that it was too comfortable, the management too tolerant, and the inmates more willing to abide there than pay their debts. The prison was closed and its inmates decanted to Newgate. Such was the mortality rate in 'the hateful gaol of Newgate, by reason of the fetid and corrupt atmosphere' there, that Ludgate was soon reopened and those of its prisoners who had survived returned.[10]

The City also had compters or counters – large town houses converted into gaols more substantial than lock-ups – for holding petty offenders and

---

8   Twyford and Griffiths, *op. cit.*, pp.133ff. The Church provided the same facilities in Scotland. Most notably, in the twelfth century, a castle was built in St Andrews to serve as an episcopal palace and as an ecclesiastical prison. It still boasts the infamous 'bottle dungeon'. Prisoners would be lowered – or thrown – down the narrow neck into a wide chamber below and would find it impossible to escape unassisted.

9   Pugh, *op. cit.*, pp.10ff., 30f.

10 *Ibid.*, p.107; Charles Creighton, *A History of Epidemics in Britain* (Cambridge, 1891), p.375.

debtors. There was the Bread Street counter and the nearby Poultry counter, both likely dating from the fourteenth century.[11] Owing to its vicinity to Old Jewry, the latter had a ward set aside for Jews. Each counter was under one of London's two sheriffs but rented out to keepers. They were subdivided into 'wards' or 'sides'. Accommodation varied according to the amount of money the inmate could put up. Comfort, if not luxury, could be obtained on the Master's Side where prisoners enjoyed furnished single cells, adequate accommodation on the Knight's Ward, and much less than adequate on the Common or Twopenny Ward. The longer you stayed the more likely you were to become indigent and end up in the aptly named 'Hole'. The longer you stayed in that dark and dank dungeon, dependent on charity for food, the more likely you were to die there. Many did.

In contrast to these conversions there was one custom-built and distinctive novelty: the Tun. This barrel-shaped building with one large room on each of its two storeys was erected in 1282 by the then Lord Mayor, as a bastion of public morality to house curfew-breakers, drunks, whores, pimps and their clients, and somewhat later for incontinent clerics and adulterers.[12]

All of these were prisons for profit, and great profits could be made out of housing prisoners. All gaolers had to make money, and theirs was a commercial concern rather than a custodial vocation. They had no training and were merely those who had bought their keeperships. Some were pardoned criminals themselves. Many were mercenary rogues and some would end up as inmates of the prison they previously owned. They knew all the scams, and money could be made from fleecing their charges. Much could be made by levying extortionate fees from the inmates for entry and for discharge and for everything from lodgings and bedding to food and water. Even alcohol could be purchased from the 'taps' – alehouses provided for prisoners and visitors. Cheating prisoners out of their own possessions was commonplace, and cheating justice could also be lucrative. At times active thieves and busy prostitutes would pay for a safe haven inside a prison. Great criminals on the run might commit minor crimes to get inside a gaol, the last place pursuers would look. They could easily pay for the best accommodation with their ill-gotten gains.[13] They could also bribe

---

[11] Compter is an old spelling of counter, the name deriving from the keeping and counting of official records in the king's counting houses. From the seventeenth century there was a reversion to compter as the official term. The Bread Street counter was replaced with that of Wood Street in 1555 which itself was replaced with the Giltspur compter in 1791.

[12] Pugh, *op. cit.*, pp.43, 112. It survived until 1546.

[13] Gamini Salgado, *The Elizabethan Underworld* (London, 1977), pp.171ff.

their keepers. Officials, be they sheriffs or gaolers, who allowed prisoners to escape could end up behind bars themselves, while those who let out debtors could have their dues imposed on themselves.[14]

Keepers devolved their responsibilities onto turnkeys – rough, tough, savage types, of whom the only attribute required was immunity from compassion. To enhance profitability most prisons were grossly under-staffed, and where manpower was lacking, manacles made up. Disease was an indiscriminate killer and a constant accompaniment to the squalid and crowded conditions of most prisons. Inside prison, as without, the indigent were prone to die of hunger while the more affluent could call upon many a creature comfort. There was no convict uniform, no forced labour, no prison diet. Food could be brought in. Family and servants could move in. Children could be born and live there. Games and recreations were unhindered. Prisoners were pretty much left to their own devices so long as they paid their bills.

As more and more gaols were created, more and more they were filled to overflowing, sometimes literally so. In 1269 the chief forester, Peter de Neville, imprisoned Peter son of Constantine for two days and nights at Allexton on suspicion of taking a rabbit in Eastwood. The dungeon in which he was kept was so full of water that poor Peter paid two pence to his gaolers for a bench to sit on. In another case the feet of a Norfolk deer-stalker were so putrefied by the dank dungeon of Norwich castle that he could not walk to his trial. Such treatment was not sanctioned by law. Indeed according to an author writing a few decades later, 'the law wills that no one be placed among vermin or putrefaction, or in any horrible or dangerous place, or in water, or in the dark, or any other torment'.[15] This suggests that humanitarian concerns, even for those in prison, have a long history. Felons could not be left indefinitely to fester in ever more fetid conditions. Pressure on prison places has proved to be an age-old and persistent problem. So too has the ill-treatment of those held there.

Edward I, 'the English Justinian', took action on both fronts: by bringing speedy justice to those detained pending trial, by regulating and making bail more available, and by punishing those who abused their carceral authority.

Speedy justice had not always been done. In one case, William of Leake, who had been accused of horse-stealing, was held for two years before a

---

14 Pugh, *op. cit.*, pp.21ff.
15 *EHD*, III, p.565; *Mirror of Justices*, ed. W.W. Maitland (London, 1895), c.IX. It was also 'lawful for gaolers to put fetters upon those whom they suspect of trying to escape; but the fetters must not weigh more than twelve ounces'.

jury exonerated him. In another a woman in Guildford was kept in prison for twenty years over the death of her husband.[16] Gaol delivery had taken place before Edward's reign, but on an *ad hoc* basis, when the king or the king's justices in eyre visited the locality. As these eyre visitations became less frequent it became necessary to commission justices to go on circuit with the specific task of emptying both the common and private gaols by putting those held there on trial. This began in 1220. At first the commissions were issued separately for each gaol and varied from county to county as well as in their frequency. With Edward's creation of assize circuits, commissions of gaol delivery became more frequent and more systematic, until prisons were emptied, in theory at least, thrice a year: in the spring, summer or autumn, and winter.[17]

In 1274–5 Edward instigated inquests into the behaviour of sheriffs and bailiffs, royal agents in counties and hundreds, many of whom had become a law unto themselves in their localities, scorning the king's commands and 'obstruct[ing] common justice and overturn[ing] the king's power'. Royal authority was once more to be imposed with a firm hand or even an iron fist. In particular, thorough investigations were to be made into those corrupt officials who by their actions were undermining the legal system. Sheriffs who took bribes to suborn justice by concealing felonies or by fabricating evidence, or to let imprisoned felons escape 'free and unpunished', or who extorted money for releasing their charges on bail, were to be held to account.[18] The king did not dally. Shortly after the results of the inquests were known, the Statute of Westminster was enacted. So that there could be no excuses and no doubt, it clarified the position, decreeing that those arrested for serious offences, such as high treason, counterfeiting, and breaking out of the king's prison, were 'in no wise replevisable [bailable] by the common-law writ or without writ'. Excommunicates arrested at the request of the bishop were also to be denied bail. One group, approvers (accomplices who had implicated others), were to be detained to ensure that their evidence was protected and preserved, and those accused by approvers were to be kept in custody 'as long as the approver is alive'. If he died, his evidence died with him and the accused should be granted bail. So too should the many more arrested for petty offences not meriting loss of life or limb. Sureties were required to secure release, but payment to gaolers

---

[16] B.A. Hanawalt, *Crime and Conflict in English Communities, 1300–1348* (Cambridge, MA, 1990), p.39; R.F. Hunnisett, *The Mediaeval Coroner* (Cambridge, 1961), pp.130f.

[17] For the definitive account of the development of gaol delivery see Pugh, *op. cit.*, pp.255–314.

[18] *EHD*, III, pp.392ff.

was prohibited. Those officials empowered to detain prisoners who freed those in the interdicted category would lose their positions, while underlings acting on their own account were to be fined and imprisoned themselves for three years, a clear example of prisons being used for both punitive and deterrent purposes.[19]

The Statute of Westminster was to prove a milestone in the development of penal imprisonment. It stipulated that those guilty of rape or of the forcible abduction of a woman against her will or of an under-age girl, with her consent or not, should be imprisoned for two years and fined. Those unable to pay the financial penalty should suffer 'longer imprisonment, according to what the offence demands'.[20] It also ordered that known felons and those of ill-repute were to be remanded to '*prison forte et dure*' – secure confinement in harsh conditions in which the prisoner lay half-naked upon bare earth, sustained only by bread and water provided on alternate days.[21] It was small comfort that this ill-treatment was by royal command and not at the gaoler's whim.

Other imprisonable offences were added later in Edward's reign and proliferated in the reigns of his successors. Trespassers on royal demesne, hawk thieves, poachers, jurors accepting bribes, those guilty of unlawful land seizure, those contravening 'the great charter of liberties' – Magna Carta – or the Charter of the Forest, and even those playing illicit games of football and dice all became liable to imprisonment. Although some of those offences carried sentences of two years or more, the commonest sentences laid down in statutes were either one year or a year and a day. In 1285, for instance, it was decreed that one year's imprisonment should be the fate for lawyers deceiving the court.[22]

And then there were debtors. Those who owed money to the Crown had been detained as far back as Henry II's time at least. But now mercantile default was proving a serious economic problem. Because redress under the existing law was slow and cumbersome, merchants were being put off coming to England with their merchandise. Trade was affected. Edward, as was his wont, took decisive action. For those owing money to merchants and whose property was insufficient to satisfy their debts, imprisonment was

---

[19] Imprisonment was not the worst fate that could befall an errant gaoler. In 1290 a turnkey at Newgate was hanged for murdering one of his charges (Anthony Babington, *The English Bastille* (London, 1971), p.6).

[20] Chs 12–15, *EHD*, III, pp.400f. In our own day those who fail to repay their ill-gotten gains receive a further period in prison in default.

[21] *Fleta*, ed. G.O. Sayles (London, 1984), II, p.85.

[22] *EHD*, II, p.497; Pugh, *op. cit.*, pp.26–47; Babington, *op. cit.*, p.8.

laid down as the last resort in the Statute of Acton Burnell in 1283. Those incapable or unwilling to pay their dues, even after their goods had been distrained, could be imprisoned, even though the effect was to pile debt on debt. Those unable to support themselves in prison, so that they 'would not die of want', had their bread and water provided by their creditors, but the cost had to be repaid along with the original debt before they were released. Two years later these small mercies were removed by the Statute of Merchants. Defaulting debtors should be immediately imprisoned and were made to pay for their own upkeep. It is not clear how the genuinely indigent could.[23]

In 1352 a statute of Edward III extended to private individuals the right to imprison debtors. The number increased and so too did their places of confinement. By the fourteenth century the Fleet in the City and the King's Bench and the Marshalsea in Southwark were dedicated to the coercive task of inducing debtors to pay their creditors. To die within their walls was easier than to secure release. To prove no debt was owed was an expensive business and debtors were often impecunious rather than obdurate. The only alleviation of their distress was the donation or bequest of money for their relief.

In the space of three score years and ten imprisonment for debts of all kinds had become a first resort. It had also become more common and much more harsh. It was 'productive of untold misery to enormous numbers of innocent people' and would remain a rancorous injustice for centuries to come. Its use would escalate. In the late eighteenth century John Howard found that three-fifths of those in prison were debtors.[24]

Rancour and injustice, affecting so many poor 'innocents' and suppurating over the years, would generate a widespread detestation of gaols and could burst into attacks upon them when civil disorder erupted.

---

[23] *EHD*, III, pp.420ff., 457ff.

[24] Arthur Griffiths, *The History and Romance of Crime* (London, 1905), I, p.10; Howard, I, p.17. It was not until the nineteenth century that legislation drastically reduced the number of debtors in gaol.

CHAPTER 3

Prisons, Peasants and Pastons

> The confinement ... of any man in the sloth and darkness of a prison, is a loss to the nation and no gain to the creditor. For of the multitudes who are pining in those cells of misery, a small part is suspected of any fraudulent act by which they retain what belongs to others. The rest are imprisoned by the wantonness of pride, the malignity of revenge, or the acrimony of disappointed expectations.
>
> Dr Johnson

> Stone walls do not a prison make,
> Nor iron bars a cage
> Minds Innocent and quiet take
> That as an hermitage.
>
> Richard Lovelace[1]

The middle of the fourteenth century saw the arrival in Europe of a cataclysmic pandemic known forever as the Black Death, during which great swathes of the population were scythed down by the Grim Reaper. Those huddled together in squalid prisons in crowded towns were especially susceptible. They could even be exploited, as the example of Bedford shows. When the Black Death reached there on 23 May 1349, the mayor, Henry Arnold, summoned Johanne Warderare, the keeper of the town gaol, and told him that as he had 'three sturdy vagrants in custody to die betimes at Gallows Corner, and four prisoners awaiting trial for felony before the Court of Pleas', he should tell them that they should have 'life and liberty' if they agreed to 'drive the death cart at the stated hours and dig a great pit in Bury Field and stand by to bury the dead'.[2] They had nothing to lose, and they found ready employment as the town was devastated.

London in particular was an ideal setting for the spread of disease. Many people living in close proximity in cramped, filthy dwellings in cramped, filthy streets meant that every household was prey to fleas and vermin, and the transmission of infection from person to person was easy. While

---

[1] Lovelace wrote 'To Althea, from Prison' when he was incarcerated in the Westminster Gatehouse in 1642.

[2] C.F. Farrar, *Old Bedford* (London, 1926), p.104.

palaces and priories were not exempt,[3] London prisons were incubators of disease. Newgate and Ludgate were situated near London's great open sewer, the ditch that ran by the Fleet prison. It was ten feet wide and deep enough to carry a boat laden with a tun of wine, but it was so choked with the effluence of eleven latrines and three sewers that no water from the river Fleet could flow around it. Smelly sludge, deep enough to drown in, surrounded the unhappy inmates. And that was not all. At the time of the Black Death the butchers of St Nicolas Shambles near Newgate cleaned carcasses and disposed of the entrails in Seacoal Lane, adjacent to the Fleet prison, creating 'an abominable and most filthy stench'. In 1361, fearing that their presence 'corrupted and infected' the air, the slaughterhouses were removed by royal command far from the City to Stratford or Knightsbridge.[4] Over three centuries later that witty cleric, Jonathan Swift, would hymn this festering pustule in his 'Description of a City Shower':

> Sweepings from Butchers' Stalls, Dung, Guts and Blood;
> Drown'd puppies, stinking Spratts all drench'd in Mud;
> Dead Cats and Turnip-tops come tumbling down the Flood.

Rat heaven.[5]

Even the Tower, isolated as it was, was not spared the ravages of disease. Insanitary conditions contributed, just as they did in other prisons. In 1295 the pool which supplied drinking water for the inmates of the dungeons was described as a place 'where rats drown themselves'.[6] While French hostages were evacuated and paroled 'for their health's sake', Sir Thomas of Moray, a Scot held for four years, was left to perish along with some of his guards during a second outbreak of plague in 1361.[7] This unorthodox form of gaol delivery at least eased overcrowding.

The plague, devastating in its consequences, was a major catalyst for change. Workers were at a premium and competition for them was fierce. Yet villeins were kept to service, and wages were restricted by statute. In England civil unrest not just among the poor and landless but also among

---

3   In 1361 so many of the benefactors of Bethlehem priory died of the plague that the Pope was informed (E.G. O'Donoghue, *The Story of Bethlehem Hospital* (London, 1914), p.49).

4   Philip Ziegler, *The Black Death*, Folio Society edn (London, 1997), pp.130f.; Barney Sloane, *The Black Death in London* (Stroud, 2011), p.127.

5   It was not until 1731 that the Fleet from Holborn to Ludgate was arched over to form Farringdon Street, and in 1766 the remainder of its route through the City was culverted. Highgate Ponds are now all that remains above ground.

6   Anthony Babington, *The English Bastille* (London, 1971), p.13.

7   Sloane, *op. cit.*, pp.131f.

their better-off neighbours was simmering, with unrequited demands for higher wages, and detestation at unfair imposts to fill an impecunious treasury, keeping it at the boil. Crimes against property – mainly by those who had little or none – rose apace.

That was the economic reality. Official rhetoric failed to recognise it. Both Church and State attributed the crime-wave, no less than the pestilence itself, to sinfulness and godlessness. It had to be stamped out and 'the malice of labourers' had to be constrained with the full force of law. Some lesser offenders could be dealt with peremptorily by public disgrace and deterrence and by 1351 stocks were to be found in every town. Others were detained in gaols and lock-ups in ever more cramped and squalid conditions. There was no inspection and no oversight. It was not until a statute of Henry IV in 1403 that justices of the peace would be directed to commit all accused to the common gaol which was under the authority of the sheriff of the county, a small step towards government regulation. Meanwhile abuse was rife, and death by neglect, disease or malnutrition commonplace. Eight men died in Northampton gaol from hunger, thirst and want.

The indignation of Langland's rustic hero, Piers Plowman, was roused for 'prisoners in pits' as well as for poor peasants in hovels. The plague was seen by many as a divine judgment on a society rotten to its aristocratic core. The noble elite was oppressive, the Church collusive. Ordinary folk, reduced to debt or criminality by social conditions, incarcerated alongside felons and political prisoners, and villeins imprisoned under the Statute of Labourers for daring to demand higher wages, were seen as the victims of oppression. While perpetrators should be punished, victims should be set free. Prison breaks were to be a regular part of popular uprisings for four hundred years, from the Peasants' Revolt of 1381 to the Gordon Riots of 1780.

In 1381 rural discontent at low remuneration and high taxes, successive poll taxes in particular, led to uprisings across England, beginning with and centring on Essex and Kent. It was the only way in which the disenfranchised, many of whom were prosperous town-dwellers, could demonstrate their discontent. Among the very first acts of what became known, rather inaccurately, as the Peasants' Revolt, were gaol breaks. The very spark that ignited the whole conflagration in Kent may have been the unjust imprisonment in Rochester castle of Robert Belling, a respected Gravesend resident whom a knight of the king's household claimed as his serf. According to the *Anonimalle Chronicle* this occasioned such local outrage that the commons in Kent marched on Rochester where they rendezvoused with the commons of Essex who had already risen. Together the rebel bands forced the constable to surrender the castle on 6 June, and set free not just Belling but all his prisoners.[8] The archbishop's gaol in Maidstone was another target. Languishing in it – not for the first time – was a maverick, radical, and dangerously popular priest called John Ball, who had been imprisoned on account of his subversive and heretical preaching. He had predicted, so it was said, that 'he would be set free by twenty thousand of his friends'. This prophecy was fulfilled when on 11 June the gaol was torn down and he was liberated by the Kentish rebels, some of whom wanted to elevate him to archbishop of Canterbury. He vowed bloody vengeance on the current holder of that office. All the other prisoners there were also set free, as were the few held in fetters in Canterbury castle and town hall.[9]

The exultant rebels were led by Ball and their lay 'captains', Wat Tyler and Jack Straw, to Blackheath near London, and from there to Southwark, an independent borough but almost a suburb of the City that had grown up on marshy land on the south bank of the Thames. Perhaps on their way to the nearby brothels on Bankside, the mob destroyed the new royal prison of the Marshalsea – though not it seems the Clink – recruiting to their ranks those they had set free, many of whom eagerly participated in the depredations to come.[10] Only eight years before, Edward III had empowered the 'good men of Southwark' to rebuild on the main north–south road leading to London Bridge a certain house for the safe custody of prisoners of the court of the Marshall of the Royal Household, to replace a building in Westminster which may have been used as a prison as early as 1332.[11] This migration done, the Marshalsea was to be used as a state prison second only to the Tower, as well as holding debtors and felons sent from the shires. It proved to be a bone of contention with the City, the jurisdiction and privileges of which it infringed. It was not only a particular target of the rebels' animus,

---

8   R.B. Dobson, *The Peasants' Revolt of 1381* (London, 1983), pp.126f.

9   Dobson, *op. cit.*, pp.136f., 374; Juliet Barker, *England Arise* (London, 2014), p.187. According to John Froissart (*Chronicles of England*, trans. Thomas Johnes (London, 1855), I, ch.LXXIII), the 'crazy priest', for 'his absurd preaching, had been thrice confined in the prison of the Archbishop of Canterbury', and so it may have been assumed he was on this occasion too. A recently discovered Essex indictment suggests that Ball may in fact have been sprung from the bishop of London's prison at Bishop's Stortford, which housed mainly convicted clerics on a farthing a day each for food, with resultant high mortality rates (Barker, *op. cit.*, pp.212f.). If this is so, Ball may not have been in Blackheath the following day and his famous Adam and Eve sermon may be a transposition from another occasion. Froissart states that it was a common refrain of Ball. Be it in Maidstone or Bishop's Stortford, however, he was freed from prison on 11 June.

10   Dobson, *op. cit.*, p.155.

11   R.B. Pugh, *Imprisonment in Mediaeval England* (Cambridge, 1968), p.119.

but an easy and vulnerable one, being unprotected by defensive walls.[12] Its buildings were demolished along with the houses of jurors, paid informers and the Marshall himself, Richard Imworth. He had already fled and had taken sanctuary in Westminster Abbey. It would not be enough to save the gaoler's skin. Sacrilege was a prelude to murder. He was dragged from the abbey by the rabble, and taken to Cheapside where he was beheaded.[13]

The 'commons' – which included many Londoners as well as prison escapees – may not have 'broken open all the prisons' but they did their level best 'specially to break up the king's prisons'.[14] They breached the King's Bench prison which had been in Southwark since at least 1368; the Westminster Gatehouse, built by the abbot in 1370 to hold, in separate wings, both lay and clerical offenders and state detainees on trial at Westminster Hall. Moving on they attacked the Milk Street counter[15] and the Fleet and Newgate prisons in the City, liberating their inmates and 'offering the iron chains' of the last 'in the church of the Friars Minor' – Greyfriars – which was adjacent to the prison.[16] Thanksgiving prayers accompanied successful acts of excarceration.

Even the impregnable Tower itself was infiltrated, as its portcullis had been raised and drawbridge lowered in expectation – it was said – of King Richard II's entry. The rebels took their chance, charged into the royal palace-fortress, searched its recesses and dragged out Simon Sudbury, the archbishop of Canterbury who had imprisoned Ball, and Sir Robert Hales, the Treasurer, both of whom they had found at prayer in the chapel of the White Tower. These grandees were beheaded on Tower Hill.

The usual recipients of popular prejudice – lawyers and Flemings – were also liable to be murdered. Flemings were foreigners who could not pronounce 'bread or cheese' but why this defect resulted in their murder is far from clear.[17] Lawyers were a different matter. They were a particular

---

[12] Froissart, *op. cit.*, ch.LXXV.

[13] Dobson, *op. cit.*, p.163. This did not set a precedent. Oppressive turnkeys and keepers had been killed in the past. The keepers of Cambridge gaol must have been either a very bad lot or suffered very bad luck, as two were killed in 1346 and 1349 respectively (Babington, *op. cit.*, p.6).

[14] Froissart, *op. cit.*, ch.LXXV.

[15] This was probably still a counting house rather than a prison and may have been mistaken for the nearby Wood Street counter.

[16] Dobson, *op. cit.*, pp.206, 228, 374.

[17] The most recent description of the persecution of Flemings and an explanation for it (not in my view wholly convincing) are to be found in Erik Spindler's 'Flemings in the Peasants' Revolt' in *Contact and Exchange in Later Mediaeval Europe*, ed. Hanna Skoda *et al.* (Woodbridge, 2012), pp.59–78.

target, along with 'old justices and all the kingdom's jurors'. The insurgents
believed 'that the land could not be fully free until the lawyers had been
killed', and court rolls and old muniments destroyed.[18] The Temple, which
housed many of them, was sacked, and law books and legal records were
burnt.

Outbreaks of revolt occurred in many places other than London, and
often involved attacks on gaols, such as the abbey prison of Bury St
Edmunds, the bishop's prison in Ely, and that in Great Yarmouth where
an Englishman was released but the three Flemings incarcerated with him
were beheaded. Gaol was too bad for a native but too good for foreigners.

Eventually the authorities in London regained the initiative as the orgies
of destruction and killing discredited the movement. When Wat Tyler was
stabbed to death during a parley, the leaderless rebels were first duped
and then dispersed and many, including Straw and Ball, were pursued and
despatched. Many others were imprisoned, some returning whence they
had sprung. Gaols were not designed for such numbers and were soon
filled. Improvisation was essential. In some counties indicted felons had to
be bailed. Such lenity was soon stamped upon and orders given that none
arrested in connection with the Revolt should be released, and those who
had been bailed should be rearrested. Not more bail, but more buildings to
serve as prisons were what was needed. Guildford castle, for instance, 'the
chief gaol of the counties of Surrey and Sussex', was deemed insufficient
'for the safe custody of all the late insurgents indicted' before the earl of
Arundel and 'his fellow justices', and so permission was given on 9 July for
the earl to house the excess in his own castles of Arundel and Lewes. Simple
and effective.

The Revolt was crushed, the rebels emasculated, and over the following
decade any threat of future insurrection was rapidly countered. In Norfolk
in 1382 beheadings followed the betrayal of a plot to kill the bishop
and all the great men of the county. In Suffolk, Yorkshire and Cheshire
isolated acts of insurrection were suppressed. In 1390 sixteen men, mainly
workmen, were captured at Croydon and imprisoned in the Marshalsea
for fomenting rebellion in Kent. Three of these were hanged. In October
1413 Sir John Oldcastle, a leading Lollard condemned to death for heresy,
managed to escape from imprisonment in the Tower to lead a rebellion,
the supposed aim of which was to murder King Henry V and his lords at
Eltham. London stood by its new king and this king was one for decisive
action. The rebels were dispersed, thousands captured, and hundreds put to

18 Dobson, *op. cit.*, pp.125, 133.

death. Oldcastle fled the carnage only to be apprehended four years later. He was returned to the Tower, pending his second appointment with the hangman, an appointment which this time he punctiliously, if reluctantly, kept.[19]

These were but trifles. In June 1450, less than eighty years after the Peasants' Revolt, a second major rising broke out in the south-east of England and to similar effect to the first. It was led by Jack Cade, 'John Amend-All' as he called himself or 'the Captain of Kent' as others called him, after whom the rebellion is known. His followers – petitioners turned insurgents – arrived in Southwark in July, and broke into the Marshalsea and King's Bench prisons, releasing and recruiting their inmates. This was no surprise. Both were vulnerable as being south of the river, and both were prisons. One of the spurs to revolt, along with widespread discontent with the weak and feeble Henry VI, years of cumulative and disastrous mismanagement of foreign and domestic policy, and the oppressiveness of the king's noble favourites, was the high-handedness and outright corruption of petty royal officials, especially those in charge of prisons. A particular object of ire in Kent was the 'great extortioner and traitor' Robert Est, the keeper of Maidstone gaol, who often resorted to prising money from those he had wrongfully seized and kept under lock and key. Another was William Crowmer, who as sheriff of Kent was in charge of the gaol in Canterbury castle, the least of whose sins was allowing the escape of eleven prisoners under his watch in 1445. Whether this was through negligence or for gain is not known, but the latter is more likely. Est and Crowmer were both in effect criminals running gaols as money-making rackets. They were local examples of a national system of justice which had not merely broken down but had been corrupted. Their punishment was one of the express demands of the rebels.[20]

The proposed cure, however, was as bad as the disease. Cade's Rebellion followed a trajectory strikingly similar to that of the Peasants' Revolt. The bloodletting began on 4 July. Lord Saye, the corrupt and incompetent treasurer and father-in-law of the odious Crowmer, had sought refuge in the Tower, but his timorous keeper handed him over to the rebels. He was beheaded and his naked corpse dragged through the streets. The same day the same fate befell his son-in-law who was found in the Fleet – though

---

[19] Dobson, *op. cit.*, pp.334f.; Barker, *op. cit.*, pp.372f., 398f.; *EHD*, IV, pp.863f.
[20] I.M.W. Harvey, *Jack Cade's Rebellion of 1450* (Oxford, 1991), pp.39ff., 102, 191.

why he was there is not known – from which he was seized, taken to Mile End, and despatched.[21]

Blood-lust and love of loot took over. Demands for the redress of grievances and the punishment of 'false traitors' degenerated into indiscriminate murder and widespread pillaging, alienating the inhabitants of London who promptly turned against the rebels and barred them from the City. Frustrated of their prey and profit, and offered a general pardon, they dispersed. Cade – on the pretext that he had given a false name – was exempted, hunted down and mortally wounded, dying before he could be brought to trial. He escaped the terrible punishment of traitors. Not so his corpse. It was ritually decapitated at Newgate and the severed head placed on London Bridge.

In both popular uprisings, prisons – the Marshalsea and Newgate, later to be dubbed 'the English Bastille', in particular – were obvious targets.[22] Prisons may have been ordained to hold malefactors awaiting just judgment, but their purpose had been corrupted. Their inmates were often perceived as being the victims of authority, not villains. Some of those 'victims' were those who had been involved in insurrection and who had been lucky enough to be imprisoned rather than executed. Prisons were seen as the very epitome of oppression, stone symbols of all that rebels rebelled against.

Prisons were a microcosm of life at its largest. They were not merely the depository of the criminal class. For both sexes, and all manner of people, spells in gaol, especially over civil disputes and debts, were commonplace. Sometime after 1432 William Paston, a Norfolk worthy and judge, had Julian Herberd, a widow with whom he had a dispute over an inheritance, imprisoned in the King's Bench where she lay for a year 'in hard pain and

---

21 *Ibid.*, pp.93f. One source places Crowmer in the Tower with Saye (*EHD*, IV, p.265). Est survived and returned to his old ways. In September 1450 he told the justices sent to deliver Maidstone gaol that a particular prisoner was no longer there. He was, of course, and duly rewarded his complicit gaoler handsomely. The law almost caught up with the 'great extortioner' when jurors in Kent indicted him on eleven counts. He was convicted of none and resumed life as a county official (pp.115, 133, 179).

22 The appellation 'Bastille' would be promiscuously awarded to many a prison in the tumultuous years straddling the late eighteenth and early nineteenth century. Newgate in the heart of the capital was merely the first candidate for such an accolade. Coldbath Fields was also so named, and the radical demagogue, Henry Hunt, called the prison in which he had been incarcerated for two and a half years the 'Ilchester Bastille'. It was a most inapt analogy as the Bastille was a state prison where a small number of primarily political prisoners were held in no great privation. It had, however, come to symbolise reactionary state oppression.

distress, nigh dead from cold, hunger and thirst'.[23] She was later committed to the Fleet where she was kept for another year, 'beaten, fettered and stocked'. If she was not exaggerating, and there is a suspicion she was, her time in prison was far longer and far more arduous than that of the descendants of the man with whom she had had the dispute. In 1464 and 1465 William's son, John Paston, was himself thrice committed to the Fleet as a result of local disputes in Norfolk. He died the following year at forty-five, but whether his end was hastened by his period of imprisonment is not known. His son, also called John, survived a similar experience. It left him with almost fond memories as he recalled in 1472 that the 'Fleet is a fair prison but ye had but small liberty therein for ye must needs appear when ye were called'. Loss of liberty, being at another's beck and call, were what irked him, not the conditions within the gaol itself. He must have lacked all sense of smell. In the following century, John Hooper, the heretic bishop of Worcester, was put in a 'vile and stinking' chamber having the 'stink and filth' of the house on the one side and 'on the other the town ditch so that the evil smells have affected me with sundry diseases'.[24]

But for some the Fleet did seem to provide a productive respite. It may be that we owe the existence of two near-contemporaneous legal treatises to the enforced leisure occasioned by a sojourn within its confines. 'The Fleet Book' or *Fleta* in Latin (which also means 'tears'), an epitome of, and commentary on, Bracton's *Laws and Customs of England*, was completed around 1290. The Elizabethan and Jacobean jurist, Sir Edward Coke, suggested, perhaps ironically, that it was written 'by some learned lawyer who, being committed to the Prison of the Fleet, had leisure to compile it there'.[25] It was a short step for those who followed to identify this person as one of the judges imprisoned by Edward I as a result of the 1289 inquiry into their behaviour. One candidate stood out: Matthew of the Exchequer, who spent two years in the Fleet from 1290 until 1292, and who is known

---

23 *Paston Letters*, ed. James Gairdner (London, 1904), I, pp.331ff.

24 *Ibid.*, V, 139. Hooper was held in the Fleet for seventeen months from September 1553 to January 1555, pending his burning at the stake. His account of the conditions he experienced there and the treatment he received at the hands of his gaoler is to be found in the third volume of John Fox's *The Ecclesiastical History Containing the Acts of Monuments of Martyrs* (London, 1684), p.123.

25 Edward Coke, *Preface* to the *Tenth Report*, p.xv. Sayles disputes this ascription, observing that Coke was 'the sublimely confident originator of so many unhistorical statements' (*Fleta*, IV, p.xxiv).

to have had a copy of *Bracton* with him.[26] Whoever the author was, naming his own *magnum opus* after his gaol shows he had more of a sense of humour than of self-importance. Andrew Horn, the author of *The Mirror of Justices* and chamberlain of the City of London, equally shows no shame but rather boasts in his preface that he,

> the prosecutor of false judges and falsely imprisoned by their order, in my sojourn [in gaol] searched out the privileges of the king and the old rolls of his treasury ... and there discovered the foundation and generation of the customs of England which are established as law ... and as briefly as I could I set in remembrance what is essential.

Prisons may have always been sinks of sin and universities of crime but they could, upon occasion, be seed-beds of scholarship.[27]

For others, however, the sound of the clanging door did signal the end of a career. In 1454 the Speaker of the Commons, Sir Thomas Thorpe, was committed to the Fleet until he paid damages due on an action taken against him for trespass. The Lords took advice from the Chief Justice on the point of parliamentary privilege. He declined to give it as 'the high court of parliament is so high and mighty in its nature that it may make law ... and the determination and knowledge of the privilege belongeth to the Lords of Parliament, and not to the justices'.[28] The Lords left the Speaker to rot in prison and the Commons insouciantly appointed a replacement.

Not all forgot those society imprisoned. Nor should they forget. That society was, after all, Christian, and it was a Christian imperative to visit the least of Christ's brethren in prison. A near brush with, and thankful escape from, the clutches of the Black Death seems to have inspired charitable giving to outcasts: physical lepers forcibly isolated in lazar-houses, and social lepers confined to gaols. Such beneficiaries had time enough to pray and the greater their afflictions or suffering, the greater the efficacy of their prayers. Bequests for the relief of prisoners in London are first recorded in 1346, but rise sharply after the first outbreak of the Black Death and even more so after the recurrences, so that by the end of the fourteenth century about

---

26 N. Denholm-Young, *Collected Papers on Mediaeval Subjects* (Oxford, 1946), pp.68–79; Jean Dunbabin, *Captivity and Imprisonment in Mediaeval Europe, 1000–1300* (Oxford, 2002), p.164.

27 *Mirror of Justices*, ed. W.W. Maitland (London, 1895), p.2. On account of the number of poets, dramatists, and pamphleteers imprisoned there over the years, Pope in *The Dunciad* dubbed the Fleet 'the Haunt of Muses'.

28 *Paston Letters, op. cit.*, I, pp.134–7.

ten per cent of those making wills were leaving money for that cause.[29] One such was the sheriff and fishmonger, John of Croydon. In 1378 he bequeathed money 'to the leper in the lazar-house and to the prisoner in Newgate' to pray for his soul.[30]

Richard II set an example of pious giving when in 1388 he paid the debts of all those imprisoned in Newgate. Dick Whittington went further when in 1423 he bequeathed money to rebuild it, in commemoration of which a depiction of his cat was carved upon the entrance gate. There was a new central hall for meals, a new chapel, and the creation of additional chambers and basement cells. Locals thereafter dubbed the prison 'Whit's palace'. In this bequest he was following a tradition of mayors of London to whom, after all, Newgate belonged. For instance, one of his predecessors, Sir John de Pulteney, in 1349 had left the sizeable sum of four marks annually for the prisoners there. Others, less publicly prominent, played their part, some more willingly than others, and some discriminating between types of prisoner. John Scorfeyn, an armourer who died in 1389, was concerned for the relief of 'poor prisoners, more especially women, in Ludgate and Newgate'.[31] In 1487 Dame Elizabeth Browne left in her will 20 pennies that prayers might be said 'for the prisoners of Newgate and Ludgate, King's Bench and Marshalsea', but not it would seem for those in the other principal debtors' prison, the Fleet.[32] In the same year William Littlesbury, another London mayor, bequeathed ten shillings 'in victuals' at Christmas and Easter for the prisoners of Newgate, Ludgate, Marshalsea and the King's Bench in perpetuity, although his wishes were frustrated.[33] Bequests of the wealthy and powerful are well documented. Such donors had the resources to be generous and the status for their munificence to be recorded. There may in addition have been many poor widows putting in their mites but of these we do not hear. Their charity was known unto God, as it was meant to be.

Recourse was made to other methods of raising money or getting food for those imprisoned. Some parishes employed paupers to beg on the street for scraps for the poor prisoners. Poor prisoners themselves were sometimes allowed to beg with arms outstretched through the bars of their cells. Pupils at Westminster School, caught with coin during school hours, were marched to the Gatehouse. There by the door they had to put the money in the

29 Sloane, *op. cit.*, p.167. The Canterbury records indicate that in the period 1400–1530 a quarter of those making wills were leaving money for the benefit of prisoners.

30 O'Donoghue, *op. cit.*, p.45.

31 Sloane, *op. cit.*, p.167.

32 *Paston, op. cit.*, VI, p.202.

33 John Stow, *A Survey of London* (1603), ed. Charles Kingsford (Oxford, 1908), I, p.246.

alms-box for the prisoners.[34] It was a salutary lesson for the young to learn: the love of money is the root of all evil.

But *squalor carceris* was a dominant theme, and for many apologists a necessary adjunct both for the punishment and deterrence of delinquents and for the coercion of debtors. Close confinement in overcrowded and filthy institutions was also the perfect incubator for infection. Malnutrition and diseases such as smallpox and pneumonia were the constant companions of the incarcerated, and, at least from the early fifteenth century, 'gaol fever' – typhus – a disease usually associated with poverty, was easily transmitted by lice and ticks which thrived on dirt. It was a major killer not only of the imprisoned but of those with whom they had contact. In 1414, the first instance recorded, an epidemic 'of the sickness of the house' struck the London prisons, killing sixty-four inmates of Newgate along with their gaoler and that of Ludgate as well. Between 1573 and 1579 one hundred prisoners died in the Queen's Bench prison.[35] And this was one of the more sanitary of the London prisons, being later described as 'a neat little regular town surrounded by a very high wall'.[36] Provincial towns were not exempt. 'Gaol sicknesse' reputedly caused the death of senior judges, court officials and members of the public at the notorious 'Black Assizes' held in Cambridge in 1522, Oxford in 1577, and Exeter in 1586, although in the last city 'men of foreign breed, the Portugals' were held primarily responsible for the spread of the contagion.[37] Referring to these forensic fatalities, Francis Bacon observed:

> The most pernicious infection, next to the plague, is the stress of the jail, when prisoners have been long, and close and nastily kept; whereof we have in our time experienced twice or thrice, when both the judges that sat upon the jail, and numbers of those that attended the business or were present, sickened upon it, and died.[38]

'Let them rot' was a rationale for neglect, and a justification for indifference to the plight of the wrongdoer and debtor. It was only when diseases of the poor infected the rich and powerful that concerns about the insanitary conditions of incarceration were voiced.

---

[34] Richard Byrne, *Prisons and Punishment of London* (London, 1989), p.79.
[35] Stow, *op. cit.*, I, pp.36f.
[36] J.P. De Castro, *The Gordon Riots* (Oxford, 1926), p.28.
[37] Charles Creighton, *A History of Epidemics in Britain* (Cambridge, 1891), pp.375–6.
[38] Francis Bacon, *Sylva Sylvarum, or A Natural History in Ten Centuries* (London, 1627), Cent.10, paras.914–15.

PART II

SQUALOR CARCERIS
1500–1750

The first shoots of an ideology of reform in houses of correction. Conditions in the counters and the Clink. Imprisonment as experienced by John Bunyan in Bedford and by Quakers throughout England. The exploitation of the incarcerated by gaolers whose prisons were a private enterprise. Disease and disaster struck prisons. Newgate and its most notorious inmates were celebrated on the page and on the stage. Popular detestation of prisons grew, culminating in their destruction during the Gordon riots.

CHAPTER 4

Bridewells, Counters and the Clink

Fear not! I do not exact vengeance for evil, but compel you to be good.
My hand is severe, but my heart is benevolent.
Inscription over the entrance of Spinhuis prison, Amsterdam, 1607

It is enough to know, too much to see,
That in the Counter there is room for thee.

William Fennor

Prisons *ought to be* so conducted as to produce reform: they too often
are so conducted, as to be the very seminaries of crime.

Joseph Gurney

The first feeble shoots of a new plant – the ideology of imprisonment – emerged above ground in the sixteenth century. By 1520 there were at least 180 imprisonable offences at common law. Now that imprisonment as a punishment for crime was becoming commonplace, some thought was given to its purpose. Was it purely penal, with the unwanted result that those ultimately discharged were more embittered and more ingrained in criminality, or could it have another function and be of advantage both to the individuals enduring it and to society at large? A development that began in 1556 was to put England at the very forefront of penal reform. Retribution, deterrence, containment, correction and training were put into the carceral cauldron and mixed. Punishment by imprisonment with multiple – and often conflicting – purposes was the result.

In that year, with the blessing of Edward VI and in response to the influx of a host of country people, dispossessed by the dissolution of the monasteries or the breakup of feudal retinues, and the resultant increase in vagrancy, the City authorities transformed the dilapidated Bridewell, Henry VIII's castellated palace situated on the left bank of the Fleet Ditch opposite the western City walls, into a unique institution serving a multiplicity of complementary ends.

Of lavish dimensions, as well as accommodating a granary and a coal store, it could combine a school for poor boys, a prison for refractory apprentices, a reformatory for 'harlots' and 'vagbonds', a workhouse for the unemployed, and a place of refuge for the relief of the poor. It boasted medical facilities far superior to those in any gaol, with a surgeon, a physician and an infirmary and with inmates being regularly checked for disease. Later Bridewell was incorporated with Bethlehem, the hospital for 'lunatics', and the two institutions shared the same governors, president, treasurer, clerk, physician and apothecary.[1]

Bridewell was denoted a House of Correction – or by some a 'House of Corruption' – and was designated not merely to punish petty offenders by confinement but, through education, training, industry and apprenticeships, to reform orphans, poor children and those perceived to be idle and indigent who were resorting to petty criminality or were just cluttering up the streets. Idleness, gaming, swearing, drinking and fornicating were perceived to be the causes of crime – not poverty or destitution which were considered merely to be by-products of the same vices – and these vices should be countered with the instillation of habits of industry, sobriety, and decency. It was the first institution specifically created for penal incarceration and correction and the first attempt to improve the prospects of those imprisoned, and it and its offspring remained the only type until the end of the eighteenth century. But it was not for all. Courts and legislators declined to extend its remit to felons. Their crimes were too serious and they were beyond redemption. Papist recusants seemingly were not, as some of them were held in the Bridewell in 1594.[2]

The incarcerated were largely the poor, the penniless and the friendless, those who were both malleable and impotent in the face of authority. They remained vulnerable to abuse inside the institution. Prostitutes and vagrants were whipped on entry and for infractions while resident. Despite these ostensible efforts to beat out sin, some governors took advantage of their charges and ran a highly profitable brothel, encouraging or compelling women to prostitute themselves.[3] Whippings, especially of semi-naked women, became a spectator sport for the curious and lecherous. A balustraded gallery was erected for their delectation.

Nonetheless, Bridewell was deemed to be a success and those who passed through its gates, young men in particular, were considered to be redeemable and able to become motivated and desirable employees. It was time to expand the correctional experiment. By the 1572 Act for Relief of the Poor, 'rogues,

---

[1] Defoe, I, p.371. The nearby Christ's Hospital, a school for indigent orphans, also owed its foundation to the brief reign of Edward VI.

[2] F.G. Emmison, *Elizabethan Life: Disorder* (Chelmsford, 1970), p.61.

[3] *OHP*, p.329.

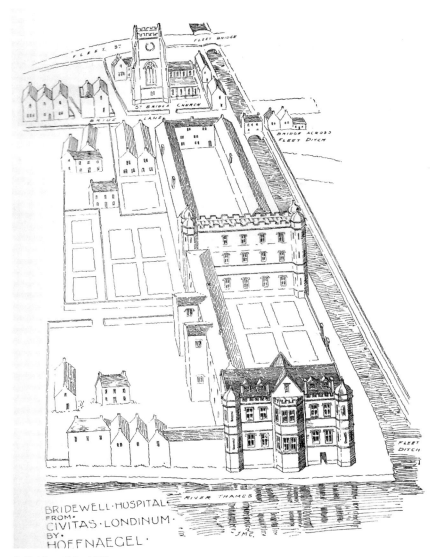

2. Bridewell in 1572

vagabonds and sturdy beggars' throughout the land were to be put in the common gaol 'or such other places as shall be appointed' in each county for 'setting on work and punishing'.[4] Four years later those places so appointed were to be designated houses of correction. They were incorporated in the Poor Law system on its inception in 1597, and from then on they were utilised not just for their intended purpose but for the disposal of the aged

---

4   *EHD*, V(a), pp.675f. In law, rogues were those burnt on their shoulders for some notorious offence, vagabonds had no place of abode, and sturdy beggars were able-bodied individuals capable of working for a living.

and infirm, classified as the 'deserving poor'. In 1609 James I made houses of correction obligatory for all counties, but they were to be self-supporting, the 'rogues, vagabonds, idle and disorderly persons' paying their way through work, and the 'master or governor' having power to 'punish them by putting fetters on them, and by whipping'. They were also put under the control of local justices of the peace rather than the sheriffs responsible for county gaols. Regional authorities needed little encouragement to comply. The 'Bridewell System' had begun and was still flourishing a century later. In each county these institutions targeted idleness, deploying hard work to induce reform. Even when this failed, justices still found merit in short periods of custody as an effective way to deter vagrants. Deterrence deputised for and often displaced reform.

As time went on, bridewells came to look more and more like ordinary prisons, and concern was expressed at the legality of locking up those whose only offence was to be poor. Sir Francis Bacon considered such detention to infringe Magna Carta. Right or not, he was ignored. The original Bridewell remained a functioning institution until it was closed in 1855 and its inmates transferred to Holloway.

Bridewells were something new, but their buildings were not, as institutional architecture was two centuries away. They complemented but did not replace the plethora of prisons that dotted the land. Many were ramshackle affairs and seemed to leak like sieves. Escapes, with or without the gaoler's assistance, were commonplace, and from franchise gaols not even illegal as no offence had been committed against the monarch. Although, particularly in tempestuous times, religious or political sympathy could play their part, it was usually the persuasive power of money, or a complacency bred out of an easy familiarity between inmates and their keepers, that was to blame. Prisoners in Hertford could meet with their friends for drinks in the gaoler's house, and two burgesses in Reading complained that 'there is great disorders in the [county] gaol by reason of the gaoler's keeping a common alehouse there'.[5] The deputy-warden in the Fleet made a door in the prison wall through which paying prisoners could pass freely to and fro. One of them, Thomas Dumay, made several trips to France at the behest of the turnkeys to get wine at wholesale rates.[6] Their own ingenuity or the empathy of others came to the aid of prisoners of conscience. Catholic priests, helped by sympathisers or by Heaven, were beneficiaries. So too were state prisoners.

---

5   Emmison, *op. cit.*, p.56; Peter Southerton, *The Story of a Prison* (Reading, 1975), p.63.
6   Gamini Salgado, *The Elizabethan Underworld* (London, 1977), p.171.

An escape often led to suspicion falling on the gaoler. In 1578 Robert Mantell *alias* Bloys was found guilty of treason by making out he was Edward VI. Pending further trial, he was held in Colchester castle gaol from which he duly escaped the following year with two others. The gaoler, the aptly named Richard King, was indicted for treason despite, or because of, the fact that the escapees had made off on horses that they had taken from him. He contested the charge but admitted negligence and exchanged his gaoler's house for a cell in his former prison, where he was to languish for two years. Mantell in the meantime was recaptured and thrown into Newgate, from which he emerged only to meet a traitor's fate. In 1600 the keeper of Colchester, William Eyres, was indicted for feloniously allowing the escape of a woman convicted of arson. He too was found guilty of negligence, but not of felony. The following year yet another prisoner escaped, but whether this was due to the repeated negligence of the reinstated Eyres or a similar failing of his replacement is unclear.[7]

Even the Tower had its share of embarrassment. One incident in particular stood out. In October 1597 John Gerard made a daring and dangerous escape, and lived to tell the tale. Owing to his extensive sojourn in the Elizabethan prison system he gives invaluable accounts of life – at least for a gentleman – in the Poultry counter, the Clink, and the Tower.

Gerard was a Jesuit priest sent to England 'to bring back wandering souls to their Maker' in his words, or 'to seduce people from the Queen's allegiance to the Pope's' in those of his inquisitors. In April 1594, after six years of clandestine work, he was betrayed to the authorities and initially put under arrest in a room of a house. Gerard was an escapee born. He noticed that his 'cell' was not far from the ground and could easily be vacated using a rope made from the bedclothes provided. The chance, not taken immediately, then eluded him, as the next night his arms were manacled. It was a salutary lesson and one he learnt well.

The following day, after interrogation, Gerard was placed in 'close confinement' in the Poultry counter but with instructions to the gaolers 'to treat him well – he is a gentleman'. His place of confinement turned out to be a small, damp garret next to the communal privy. The 'gentleman' recalled years later that 'the stench from it often kept me awake at night or even woke me up'. Heavy leg-irons were added to his manacles. His only exercise was by shuffling 'from side to side with short steps', a great mercy in Gerard's eyes as 'when the prisoners below started singing lewd songs' and worse, Geneva Psalms, he 'was able to drown their noise with the less

---

7 Emmison, *op. cit.*, pp.40f., 99, 286.

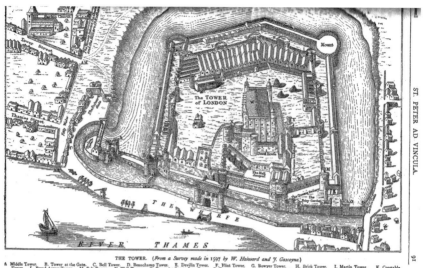

THE TOWER. *(From a Survey made in 1597 by W. Haiward and J. Gascoyne.)*

A Middle Tower.   B. Tower at the Gate.   C. Bell Tower.   D. Beauchamp Tower.   E. Devilin Tower.   F. Flint Tower.   G. Bowyer Tower.   H. Brick Tower.   I. Martin Tower.   K. Constable Tower.   L. Broad Arrow Tower.   M. Salt Tower.   N Well Tower.   O. Tower leading to Iron Gate.   P. Tower above Iron Gate.   Q. Cradle Tower.   R. Lantern Tower.   S. Hall Tower.   T. Bloody Tower.   V. St. Thomas's Tower.   W. Cæsar's, or White Tower.   X. Cole Harbour.   Y. Wardrobe Tower.   A B. House at Water Gate, called the Ram's Head.   A H. End of Tower Street.

3. The Tower in 1597

unpleasant sound of [his] clinking chains'. This was to be his home and these his home comforts from spring until summer. Then orders came that he be held under closer confinement in the Clink, his abode for the next three years. First he had to pay his prison bill, 'which did not amount to much since all I had was a little butter and cheese with my bread'.[8]

The move to Southwark proved a boon – 'a translation from purgatory to paradise' – both because conditions were better in that gaol – at least for those such as Gerard who could pay for 'handsome lodgings' to avoid the lot of paupers held in the common side – and there were more of his co-religionists occupying it, so that 'I no longer heard obscene and bawdy songs, but, instead, I had Catholics praying in the next cell'. A hole in the wall enabled Gerard to hear confessions and smuggle out letters. Since his associates had managed to make their own keys for their doors, every morning before the warder was even awake Gerard would go to another part of the prison and say Mass for those confined in that section. He introduced many inmates to the Spiritual Exercises at the heart of Jesuit practice. Able to perform as a Jesuit priest once more, a shepherd to the persecuted, Gerard had such 'a quiet and pleasant time' that 'provided only I could have stayed in this prison, I should never have wanted to have my liberty again in England'.

[8]   John Gerard, *The Autobiography of a Hunted Priest*, trans. Philip Caraman (New York, 1952), pp.67f., 77.

His first gaoler had a fierce temper and was a stickler for the rules but 'God took him from the custody of the prison and from the prison of his own body at the same time'. Whether it was gaol fever that whisked him off to meet his Maker is not stated, but prison was rarely good for health. His replacement was a much more pleasant young man, one who 'with bribes and a little coaxing' could be induced 'not to pry too closely' into Gerard's affairs. He agreed to do his rounds at set times, and posed so little inconvenience to his 'apostolic work' that Gerard was able to turn an upstairs room into a chapel. He even converted one of the gaolers, who would eventually end up imprisoned in the Clink himself.[9] Another gaoler, though no convert, became a good friend and was to do Gerard sterling service later.

While thus presiding over the Clink, Gerard learnt that William Wiseman, a close friend who had harboured him, had been imprisoned in the Wood Street counter in such close confinement that for the first three or four months no visitors had been allowed. Solitude at least provided Wiseman the time and opportunity to write *A Triple Farewell to the World or Three Deaths in Different States of Soul*, an addition to the corpus of mawkish spiritual allegory but, alas, not a contribution to legal or penal literature, unlike that of his erstwhile guest.[10]

After three years Gerard's happy respite in the Clink came to an end when a fellow priest betrayed him to the authorities for corresponding with Henry Garnet, a fellow Jesuit and 'enemy of the state', considered to be the most dangerous Catholic in England. Gerard's cell was searched but nothing incriminating was found – it was too well hidden. Nonetheless his easy days in the Clink were over and Gerard was transferred to the Tower. He was following in his father's footsteps as he had spent two years imprisoned there for his role in a plot to rescue Mary Queen of Scots from her captivity in Tutbury castle.

Gerard was housed in the Salt Tower at the south-east corner of the Inner Ward. It was three storeys high with lock-ups in each storey. His cell was on the first floor, and had previously held another Catholic priest – and martyr – Henry Walpole. Comforted by his predecessor's spiritual presence, Gerard slept well on 'the little straw' provided. The following day, however, the warder assigned to him, a man called Bonner, moved him to a cell on the floor above which, by prison standards, was large and comfortable. Bonner promised Gerard that he would allow him to return from time to time to

9   *Ibid.*, pp.111f.
10   *Ibid.*, p.87.

pray in Walpole's former cell. The warder also offered to bring him in a bed if Gerard's friends would provide it, for neither beds nor other furniture were provided in this prison. At Gerard's behest, Bonner went to the Clink where the priest's former parishioners provided him with money, a coat and 'with the kind of bed I liked – a simple mattress stuffed with wool and feathers in the Italian style'.[11]

This little luxury would be needed in the days to come as Gerard was 'put to the manacles' in an attempt to get him to divulge the whereabouts of Garnet. After the first day of this procedure, Gerard was escorted back to his cell, where his compassionate warder laid a fire and brought some food. After the second day of the same procedure, tears welled up in the eyes of Bonner as he hand-fed his ward. For reasons unknown there was to be no more torture, just time and opportunity. The formidable Tower was to prove porous: Gerard escaped it six months after his incarceration there began.

He did so by patiently biding his time, allowing the injuries to his arms and legs to heal, and ingratiating himself with his already empathetic warder. After a few weeks and much importuning, Gerard had been allowed to have a Bible brought over from the Clink. He sought and got some money. With that he purchased large oranges to supplement the very good food provided at royal expense for a prisoner of his class. As Gerard acerbically noted, the grades of diet, varying as they did according to social rank irrespective of religious persuasion, put 'first what ought to be esteemed last'.[12] Oranges, however, were not just a frivolity amidst misery. They would serve other purposes altogether. The peel he made into little crosses and strung them on silk thread to make rosaries. The juice he preserved in a jar.

He wound a web around Bonner. First he asked a little thing: that the warder take the rosaries to his friends in the Clink. Bonner agreed. Then Gerard asked for a quill as a tooth-pick. He sharpened the end and cut it off, making a pen. He got paper on the pretence it was for wrapping his hand-made rosaries. So he secured the means to carry on a clandestine correspondence with his friends in the Clink. Using the orange juice he penned invisible messages on the paper in which the rosaries were distributed. For each little favour done, Bonner was remunerated. For each little favour done, Bonner was compromised.

A further favour was asked: that Bonner let Gerard visit John Arden, a fellow Catholic priest whose cell was in the nearby Cradle Tower, a squat edifice overlooking the moat. Escape from there was feasible. Before such

---

11 *Ibid.*, p.105.
12 *Ibid.*, p.117.

a hazardous attempt was made, Gerard offered Bonner a thousand florins and a pension of a hundred florins if he would let them escape in borrowed clothes. This hefty bribe the warder declined, fearing that he would be an outlaw on the run for life or hanged if caught. He did not, however, betray his ward. That ploy having failed, Gerard contacted his servant Richard Fulwood and an erstwhile fellow gaol-bird from the Clink. They agreed to come by boat to the Tower in the dead of the night, wearing white handkerchiefs as identification. On the first attempt, the boat, steered by his former gaoler in the Clink, capsized. The following night the conspirators tried again, bringing with them a rope which they tied to a stake opposite the roof where Gerard and his co-religionist were stationed. The escapees then threw down a metal ball with a 'stout thread' attached. Hearing the thump, their accomplices found the ball and tied the cord to the rope which Gerard then pulled up to the roof where he was standing. He and Arden, using hands and legs, gingerly clambered down the rope and into the welcoming arms of their friends.

Considerately Gerard had left letters behind exonerating Bonner of all blame, and offering him a chance to seek safety with them if he wished. The warder took up the offer and later turned Catholic: 'My escape from prison, was, I hope, in God's kind disposing, the occasion of his escaping hell.' Bonner at least escaped temporal punishment.[13] So happily ended the best-documented escape from the Tower.

Gerard's description of his earlier incarceration in the counter and Clink was not the only contemporary account of life inside London's more mundane prisons. In Elizabethan and Jacobean times the capital boasted fourteen different gaols, three of which were counters. Many a Londoner would end up in one of them, at least for a short while but sometimes for years, for all manner of minor offences and, of course, for debt. Inmates of the counters included several well-known but impecunious playwrights such as Christopher Marlowe, Philip Massinger, and Thomas Dekker, the last being imprisoned in the Poultry counter in 1599 and later spending seven years in the King's Bench prison, both times for debt.[14]

In 1616, one lesser writer, the rhymester William Fennor, was imprisoned in the Wood Street counter for assault. He used his time there to write a

---

13 *Ibid.*, pp.128–9.
14 In 1620 Dekker published *Dekker, His Dreame*, a long poem describing his confinement. A contemporary, Geffray Mynshul, also wrote an account of life there in this period in his *Essayes and Characters of a Prison and Prisoners* (London, 1618).

pamphlet detailing his experience in rich hyperbole, and on his release the following year he published it under the title *The Counter's Commonwealth, or a Voyage Made to an Infernal Island discovered by many Captains, Seafaring Men, Gentlemen, Merchants and other Tradesmen.*

In it he recounted that after an altercation in the City, during which he had struck a clumsy tradesman on the head, he was seized by 'a brace of bandogs belonging to one of the Counters' and taken off to that abode, a commonwealth where 'jailors and officers feed upon the poor prisoners', like sharks in the sea. Fennor's name was entered in the Black Book and he opted for a cell on the Master's Side, the best accommodation the counter could offer, but the most expensive. He was conducted upstairs and had to pay a shilling for entry through the door and into a gallery decorated with an edifying tapestry depicting the Prodigal Son. There he had to pay a further two shillings in 'garnish', a euphemism for what Fennor deemed extortion, a profitable racket since he estimated that over five thousand prisoners were committed and discharged in a single year. Even bequests for poor prisoners and 'the liberality of the City' at Christmas and Easter would be misused and end up in the pockets of the mercenary staff.

For his two shillings Fennor was locked in a cell, with two dirty sheets for comfort and a candle-end for illumination. The following morning he met his fellow guests, one of whom, an attorney, assured him that for forty shillings he could get a writ of *habeas corpus* for his release. Fennor declined the offer and spent the day eating dainties and drinking claret with the other detainees. After a month, and with his own resources depleted and the kindness of his friends exhausted, Fennor was demoted to the Knight's Ward, a cavernous hall filled with men pacing aimlessly up and down. They could still buy drink if they had the money but only the poor, watered-down, over-priced variety sold by the counter tapsters. Any bottles sent in by friends were smashed. Nonetheless it was far preferable to 'the Hole' to which the indigent were confined in unspeakable and almost airless conditions deep below ground. It stank, was a propagator of disease, and was the death of many an inmate. Starvation and even thirst stalked the place. It brought out the worst in gaoler and gaoled alike. Fennor heard of one poor sick prisoner who was left to die, the turnkeys ignoring his cry for water. He was but one of many. The prisoners lay 'together like so many graves ... In this place one man is ready to prey upon the other, so that they walk up and down like so many ghosts from want of food to relieve them.' Fennor was finally set free, but could not forget what he had seen and endured. He put down his experiences and condemnations on paper for posterity. Others would do the same.

One such was destined for literary immortality. A son of the soil, literate but with only a rudimentary education, a voracious reader, he spoke and wrote with an imaginative simplicity that would beguile future generations. His personal pilgrimage led to him spending over a decade in gaol. His name was John Bunyan.

CHAPTER 5

Higher than the Stars

For though men keep my outward man
Within their locks and bars,
Yet by the faith of Christ I can
Mount higher than the stars.
Their fetters cannot spirits tame
Nor tie up God from me;
My faith and hope they cannot lame,
Above them I shall be.

John Bunyan

The Restoration of the monarchy in May 1660 saw the return of the Stuart dynasty in the person of Charles II. Soon the persecution of religious non-conformity intensified. The Act of Uniformity, which became law on 24 August 1662, was part of a comprehensive process of suppression known as the Clarendon Code. It required that the Book of Common Prayer be used in all services, and that all clergy and teachers subscribe to the Thirty-Nine Articles of the Church of England. It banned extemporary prayers and unlicensed preaching, mainstays of Puritan worship. Long-term imprisonment, or even transportation, would be the fate of many who, by their righteous obduracy and refusal to submit, prolonged their confinement or exile. It was not, however, the first piece of legislation designed to enforce religious conformity.

Among the many Dissenters stuffed into the county gaols in the early years of Charles II, one stood out, the radical Puritan preacher and prolific writer, John Bunyan. He was also one of the first, as his offending behaviour pre-dated the Restoration. His first brush with the law came when he was thirty, during the Protectorate. In 1658, he was arrested 'for preaching at Eaton', but it seems that the grand jury dismissed that case.[1] His luck would soon run out. On 12 November 1660 Bunyan, with a Bible in his hands, was arrested under an Act of 1593 on a warrant issued by Francis Wingate,

[1] Eric Stockdale, *A Study of Bedford Prison 1660–1877* (London, 1977), p.2.

G. F. Langley.]   THE GREAT BRIDGE.

4. Bedford Bridge with its protruding lock-up as John Bunyan would have known it

the local justice of the peace. The charge was that he refused to attend Anglican services and had attended unlawful assemblies or conventicles. The real threat he posed was by his preaching.[2] If convicted, the Act decreed that he should remain in prison until he conformed. Should he not do so within three months then worse would befall. Bunyan was taken, 'with God's comfort in my poor soul', to the county gaol on the corner of the High Street and Gaol Lane (as Silver Street was sometimes known) to await his hearing at the quarter sessions.[3]

2   Christopher Hill, *A Tinker and a Poor Man: John Bunyan and His Church, 1628–1688* (London, 1989), p.107.

3   John Bunyan, *A Relation of the Imprisonment of Mr John Bunyan* in *The Pilgrim's Progress and other Select Works by John Bunyan* (London, 1874), p.693. Legend has it that the place of incarceration was the Stonehouse, the tiny town or borough 'clink' situated on the bridge straddling the Ouse. Originally a chapel, it was converted, 'both for strength and sweetness of the air', into a tolbooth and lock-up, surviving as such until 1765 when it made way, initially for a temporary structure under the town hall, and ultimately for a newly constructed gaol. However, as Bunyan's was a county offence he would have been imprisoned in the county gaol. Further, the clink could hold only a handful of prisoners and not the dozens held with Bunyan. Finally, before the end of his lengthy detention, the 'bridge-dungeon was swept away by a great flood' and remained out of use from 1671 until the town council sanctioned its rebuilding in 1675 (John Brown, *John Bunyan*, Tercentenary edn, revised by Frank Harrison (London, 1928), pp.151f.).

The gaol had two storeys and a basement, with two day-rooms and sleeping quarters for felons on the ground floor, two dank and dark night-dungeons beneath, and, on the first floor, four sleeping rooms for debtors and another which served as a chapel. There was also a small courtyard for use of all the prisoners. The entrance consisted of a massive barred door made of three transverse layers of oak, fastened through with iron bolts. Iron-grated windows overlooked Silver Street.[4]

The gaol housed a motley assortment of drunks, drifters, and debtors of both sexes who were to form Bunyan's coerced congregation. He would preach in prison. To these, over time, were added another sixty Dissenters, 'by which means the prison was very much crowded'.[5] As state-sanctioned religious repression increased, sanctified sinners would come greatly to outnumber secular ones. All would endure the same primitive gaol conditions, some with more equanimity than others. There was no heating, merely straw for a bed, poor food and worse sanitation. Pestilence stalked the land, and in 1665 it raged around the gaol, in the course of a year carrying off forty persons in St Paul's parish where the prison lay. Forty is relatively few. Aylesbury prison, in nearby Buckinghamshire, was badly affected by the plague but there is no such record for Bedford and so it may have escaped the worst.

Nor, in general, was it was one of the worst county gaols. It was certainly not as hideous as some of those, Launceston in particular, into which George Fox was flung. As Bunyan later observed, Satan could make a 'gaol look like hell itself'.[6] So could his minions.

Bunyan's appearance before the Sessions took place in January 1661. The hearing was presided over by Serjeant John Kelyng of Southill, a future Chief Justice of the King's Bench, but immortalised in infamy as Lord Hategood of Vanity Fair. A bill of indictment was preferred against 'John Bunyan, labourer'. Labourer or no, Bunyan stoutly defended himself before

---

4   Howard, I, p.283. It was demolished in 1801. The Bunyan Museum houses what is left – the oak entrance door – along with artefacts associated with Bunyan's incarceration: an earthen jug believed to be the one that his blind daughter Mary used to bring in broth to her father; and the chair-leg flute he was supposed to have carved. C.F. Farrar, a local man, states in 1926 that two other doors were preserved, one at Howard Chapel (now Howard Memorial Church) in Cardington, Bedfordshire, and the other in F.C. Fuller's St Peter's Brewery in Lurke Lane, Bedford.

5   Brown, *op. cit.*, p.152, quoting an account by one of Bunyan's visitors.

6   'Old Nick' may be the origin of the term 'the nick' for a prison. Or it may come from the phrase 'in the nick of time' since prisoners 'do time', or from the slang term 'to nick', meaning to steal, or 'to be nicked', meaning to be arrested, since prisons are dens of convicted thieves.

the hostile tribunal, refusing to plead but admitting the basic facts of the charge. He was in effect convicted on his own testimony. The condescending Kelyng told him that as he had 'the gift of tinkering' he should 'follow his tinkering ... cease his canting' and refrain from preaching. Bunyan would not be silenced, until the judge informed him that as he had confessed the indictment he would be sent back to prison for three months and, if by the end of that period he should not submit to hearing the divine services of the Established Church and desist from preaching, he would be brought before the assizes, banished the realm, and hanged as a felon if he returned. As he was led away he defiantly retorted that 'if I am out of prison today, I will preach the gospel again tomorrow – by the help of God'.[7]

Shortly before the expiry of three months, he received a visit from Paul Cobb, the not unsympathetic clerk to the justices who repeatedly called him 'Neighbour Bunyan' and 'goodman Bunyan'. Cobb exhorted him to 'submit and, notwithstanding, do as much good as you can in a neighbourly way, without having such meetings'. Bunyan refused to compromise, even for a short time to weather the political storm, and so his incarceration continued. It did so without the necessity of release, re-arrest for another offence and the inevitable transportation. It was a mercy of sorts. He would await the Midsummer assizes.

Efforts were made to free him. The coronation of the new king, Charles II, in April 1661 held out a prospect of pardon. It did not come. An alternative, pursued by his indomitable young wife Elizabeth, was to question the legality of his imprisonment. He had never pleaded to the indictment, nor had he confessed to it. The conviction was void. Bunyan appeared before the assizes in August, the judges of which included Sir Matthew Hale, another, eminent, future Chief Justice, who, unlike 'Lord Hategood', had a certain sympathy for Dissenters. But nothing could be done. The other justices maintained the validity of the conviction which had been recorded. There could be no redress. The judges were powerless to free such a man ... unless he left off preaching. All Hale could do was to suggest that Elizabeth apply to the king himself for a pardon or seek a writ of error to overturn the conviction. The procedure was all very odd. Why was Bunyan produced if not to be indicted and transported? Instead the irregularity of his conviction and his eligibility for pardon were discussed. Nothing was done to re-sentence him. Instead he was returned to prison

---

7   Bunyan, *op. cit.*, p.696. The sentence was irregular as it was only for a third offence that the case would go to the assize. Perhaps the tribunal, not unreasonably but unlawfully, assumed that he had committed many offences before this.

determined to attend the next assizes in the following January, an attempt deliberately stymied by Cobb, again probably engaging in a sabotage of mercy. Bunyan was being saved from himself.

He was to remain in Bedford prison, languishing in a sort of legal limbo, for a further eleven years. Despite the squalid and harsh conditions, the prison regime was rather relaxed. His family could visit and provide him with nourishment for soul and body: a Bible and *Fox's Book of Martyrs* along with food and drink. There was no shortage of opportunity for pastoral care. One visitor recorded:

> There also I surveyed his library, the least and yet the best I ever saw consisting of only two books ... He rises from his knees and walks out into a small courtyard which was common to all prisoners, where he enters into a long and earnest talk with one John Bubb ... lying under sentence of death. Bunyan preached in the day room to his fellow prisoners with the spirit of Faith and Plerophory [certainty] of Divine assistance.[8]

After a while he would even get furlough for a few hours at a time during which he attended dissenting religious meetings and continued to preach. Whether his temporary release was sanctioned by a gaoler who sympathised with the man or his cause is not known, although many in Bedford were well-disposed to both and the under-gaoler, John White, got into trouble himself for refusing to pay the church rate.[9] Such sympathy with 'prisoners of faith' was not unusual. The gaoler of York castle was indicted for granting parole to Quakers, and in Hampshire they were also allowed to be at large.[10] In Bunyan's case it was not to last. When word got out that he was on the loose and had even strayed as far as London, his gaoler was threatened with dismissal, and his prisoner more closely confined than before so that he 'must not look out of the door'. Close confinement continued until he was unofficially paroled on the cusp of his ultimate release.

Alongside the Dissenters with Bunyan in Bedford gaol was a dissident of a rather different ilk. He was a man called Jones and he was accused of treason. What little is known of him is tantalising. In 1666 William Goodman, the former gaoler at Hertford, was imprisoned in the Westminster Gatehouse, charged with being part of a plot to free Jones. Goodman disclaimed any

---

8   Bubb had killed George Edwards in a drunken brawl not of his own making. He spent two years in custody but was reprieved and then pardoned. His petition refers to 'this dismal place' where he had 'long remained in a calamitous condition' (Brown, *op. cit.*, p.157n.).

9   *Ibid.*, p.201.

10   Stockdale, *op. cit.*, p.7.

involvement and counter-claimed that 'all the imputations arise from the spleen of the gaoler at Aylesbury'.[11]

Bunyan 'did not Eat the Bread of Idleness', but provided for his bereft family by making and selling thousands of leather bootlaces. Further financial and practical support came from his co-religionists. For recreation he may even have fashioned a flute out of the leg of a stool, bamboozling his gaolers who could not find the source of the music.[12] The carceral midden in which he found himself, a 'slough of despond' to many, proved fertile ground for one such as Bunyan. He had pen and paper and a small table given to him by the rejected rector of Pertenhall, John Donne,[13] but little peace to write, given the overcrowding, noise, and the behaviour of other inmates including the deranged, such as Elizabeth Pratt, who had been charged with witchcraft but was probably schizophrenic. Bunyan nonetheless found inner tranquillity. Tranquillity and inspiration. His imagination none could trammel, and it soared. The burning intensity of his vision could not be quenched. He called himself 'a prisoner of hope'. He had never had 'so great an inlet into the Word of God as now'. The Scriptures 'that I saw nothing in before are made plain in this place to shine upon me ... Jesus Christ was never more real'.

During this fertile period he was to publish numerous works, including *Profitable Meditations* (1661), *Praying in the Spirit* (1662), *Christian Behaviour* (1663), *One Thing is Needful* (1664–5), *The Holy City* (1665), a book of verse called *Prison Meditations* (1665), and above all his magnificent spiritual autobiography *Grace Abounding to the Chief of Sinners* (1666), this last referring to the agony of separation from his family 'as the pulling the flesh from my bones'. Some of these writings were based on sermons he had preached in gaol. All were but a prelude to his greatest work and the one which required the longest gestation.

Bunyan was pardoned and freed in May 1672 under the provisions of the Declaration of Indulgence which suspended, by royal prerogative, the execution of parliament's penal laws against Non-Conformists and Recusants.

---

11 Probably Nathaniel Birch, the splenetic official mentioned by Ellwood – see p.74.

12 Samuel Pepys visited Bedford on 8 June 1668 and merely notes in his diary that he rode through the town. Nothing more. Further information he was intending to insert he never did. C.F. Farrar does the job for him. As Pepys would undoubtedly have passed the gaol, Farrar imagines him encountering Bunyan selling shoe-tags at the gate of the town gaol and singing sweetly, his little blind daughter at his side. Well maybe. Farrar is certainly right in observing what 'a strange contrast' these two literary giants would have made 'within a stone's throw of each other' (*Old Bedford* (London, 1926), pp.194f.).

13 Brown, *op. cit.*, p.160; Monica Furlong, *Puritan's Progress: A Study of John Bunyan* (London, 1975), p.86.

He was but one of the 491 who benefited from this royal derogation from the law. Quakers had led the way in seeking inclusion in the dispensation, and one of their leaders, George Whitehead, wryly but rightly commented that Bunyan, 'whose first book [*Gospel Truths Opened* (1656)] had been directed against the Quakers, now owed his liberty to their assistance'.[14] In 1675, after the Declaration's abrogation and the subsequent passing of the Test Act, Bunyan again became a wanted man, although he eluded arrest for a while. In late 1676, however, the law – if not justice – caught up with him, and he was imprisoned as an excommunicate for a further six months.

It was long thought that this time he was put in the Stonehouse clink. The learned and meticulous Dr John Brown, the pastor of Bunyan Meeting and Bunyan's greatest biographer, who had proved that his subject's earlier imprisonment must have been in the county gaol, maintained nonetheless that the later incarceration was in the town lock-up. This accorded with all the evidence he had at hand, and was consistent with the local tradition which in turn seemed to emanate from Bunyan's immediate descendants. In particular he noted that a Congregational minister, William Bull, whenever he crossed the town bridge would pause and bare his head at the spot he had been told Bunyan was imprisoned. Bull had known Bunyan's great-granddaughter personally and was a friend of a friend of Bunyan's son John, who had been eighteen at the time of his father's last incarceration. Similarly, Bedford's chronicler, C.F. Farrar, who had vast local knowledge and connections, agreed, maintaining that the tradition was well authenticated. However, a copy of the June 1677 cautionary bond given to bishop Barlow of Lincoln (in whose diocese Bedford lay) to secure Bunyan's release has come to light which shows that if the sheriff followed the normal procedure the second imprisonment would also have been in the county gaol.[15] Perhaps the sheriff did, perhaps he did not.

Six months' imprisonment, wherever it was, was long enough for another glorious harvest. The fruit, germinated in his twelve years in custody and his four years of freedom, ripened. This was his great allegory, *Pilgrim's Progress*, one of the most influential and memorable books ever written, certainly so

---

14   An anecdote goes that when a Quaker told him that he had been sent by the Lord to find him and had sought in vain through several counties, Bunyan doubted that his mission was divine, 'for the Lord well knows that I have been in prison for some years, and if He had sent thee, He would have sent thee here direct' (John Roberts, *Memoir of John Bunyan* (London, 1874), p.36).

15   Brown, *op. cit.*, pp.239–45; Farrar, *op. cit.*, pp.188ff; Joyce Godber, 'The Imprisonments of John Bunyan', *Transactions of the Congregational Historical Society*, XVI, 1 (April 1949), pp.23–32. The date of his release certainly shows that the six months began in 1676 and not 1675 as was hitherto thought.

from a gaol cell, although publication had to await his release.[16] It was very much a prison book and owed its 'motive force to an heroic assertion of the inner man against the blind injustice of confinement'.[17] Bunyan, in his own words, had entered a 'den' – in the margin he placed the explanatory words 'the Jail' – and 'laid down in that place to sleep: and as I slept I dreamed a dream'. And such a dream. Farrar waxed lyrical:

> As with St Peter in his cell, so with Bunyan in the Stonehouse, 'behold the angel of the Lord came upon him and light shined in the prison'. Bunyan's spirit was set free and he was walking with Christian and Hopeful in the Delectable Mountains, a prisoner of the Lord on parole.[18]

Another, shorter work, impressive in its honesty, remained unpublished in his lifetime. It was handed down in his family and was not to appear in print until 1765. It is his prison memoir: *A Relation of the Imprisonment of Mr John Bunyan*. It formed a fitting coda to his spiritual autobiography. From it much of the above derives. From it our knowledge of county gaols in the seventeenth century is greatly enhanced.

---

16 That it was published in 1678 is highly suggestive that the work originated from his latter period in custody, although it may have been finished after his release.

17 Roger Sharrock, *John Bunyon* (London, 1968), pp.70ff.

18 Farrar cites several passages in the work that he believes were influenced by a sojourn in a cell placed over the river.

CHAPTER 6

Treason in the Cheese

Some men are free while they in prison lie;
Others, who ne'er saw prison, captives die.

Thomas Ellwood

Your jails and prisons we defy
By bonds we'll keep our liberty

William Penn

Bunyan was not the sole incarcerated Dissenter who put pen to paper. Quakers, in particular, were frequently imprisoned and often recounted their ordeals. They were considered to be members of a dangerous cult, the disseminators of dissident views, but famed for their integrity, obstinacy and literacy.

In Bedfordshire their persecution had begun in 1655 when three Quakers were arrested on frivolous charges but detained in prison for a month for refusing to remove their hats in court. The following year Isabel Parlour 'for exhorting the people to ... repentance and amendment of life' was detained for a month in the bridewell where she was whipped. In 1658 a couple were imprisoned for 'living in sin': they were married but according to Quaker rites. In March 1661 fifty-two Quakers appeared before the Bedford assizes for refusing to conform. Despite appealing to the grand jury to do justice to those who, for conscience sake, had endured 'nasty prisons, holes and dungeons, under the custody of cruel and unmerciful jailors', they were indicted.[1]

Bedford was far from unique. Throughout the land, and no more so than in London, thousands of Quakers were subject to persecution and prosecution. Their movement thrived under chastisement. If they could not be indicted for sedition, in that they refused to remove their hats they could always be imprisoned or fined for contempt of court. Peripatetic as they tended to be, the same individuals often experienced incarceration in several different gaols. As the political wind blew, so their lot would change from

---

[1] Eric Stockdale, *A Study of Bedford Prison 1660–1877* (London, 1977), p.13f.

day to day, and England from the time of the Protectorate to the period of the Restoration was experiencing a political hurricane.

George Fox, their founder, was the most notable of the Society of Friends to be immured, and he was so repeatedly, his experience comprehending gaols throughout England. In his journal he gives us a vivid depiction of many provincial prisons.

His first taste of imprisonment was in 1649. The year before, the twenty-four-year-old fanatic from Leicestershire had begun an itinerary around the country. When he got to Nottingham he began preaching in 'the steeple-house', as he habitually called the parish church since God's people constituted the Church not buildings. He was outspoken, and could easily come across as a self-righteous prig, but his personality was magnetic, his courage considerable, and his ardour unquenchable. He was never discreet, he was never temperate, he was never moderate. Words were his weapons and he wielded them well. The fact that he knew his brief and argued brilliantly was all the more unsettling for those on the receiving end. He was arrested and put 'into a nasty stinking prison; the smell whereof got so into my nose and throat, that it very much annoyed me', until John Reckless, the 'friendly' sheriff, lodged him in his own house. The magistrates, angered by the influence he was having on the official, committed Fox once more to the common gaol where he was held for some time before being sent on his way. In Coventry he visited religious dissidents held in the prison, but as they were blasphemous 'Ranters' he left them to it. In Chesterfield, Fox was threatened with the 'correction house', but was merely expelled from the town.

On to Derby where he was not so fortunate. In 1650 he ended up in its bridewell for six months accused of blasphemy. John Fretwell had been imprisoned with him, but he 'got in with the gaoler and by him made way to the justice to have leave to go and see his mother, and so got his liberty'. It was reported that Fox had 'bewitched and deceived' the runaway, and from then on the gaoler, Thomas Sharman, hoping to ensnare the wily Fox, would often question him. He, of course, turned the tables, brought his persecutor to repentance and ended up as a guest in his keeper's lodgings. Twelve years later Sharman wrote to Fox with thanks and told him that he had been turfed out of his job and was like to become a prisoner himself.[2]

---

2   All the material relating to Fox on the following pages can be found under the date or place in *The Journal of George Fox*, ed. John Nickalls (Cambridge, 1952), or in any other edition.

Justice Bennet, the first to call Fox and his followers 'Quakers' – 'because we bid [him] tremble at the word of the Lord' – wanted rid of this nuisance. Fox was allowed to walk within a mile of the house of correction in the hope that he would break parole and 'ease them of their plague'. Of course he 'was not of that spirit', but he did take the opportunity to stroll around the market and streets preaching repentance before dutifully returning to confinement. This life of relative liberty was soon ended as his enduring recalcitrance riled the authorities.

He was transferred into the town prison which stood at the corner of the corn-market where it overhung a branch of the Derwent, exposing its inmates to cold, damp and dirt. Fox was put 'into the dungeon amongst thirty felons in a lousy, stinking low place in the ground without any bed'. Yet even as a 'close prisoner' he was allowed to walk in the garden as the gaoler knew he would not try to escape. He may have been subversive but he had already gained a reputation for probity. His subsequent behaviour prolonged his confinement. The 'tender youth' was irrepressible, being 'moved to write to the judges concerning their putting men to death for small matters', and for using 'bad language'. He lectured them on their duties, reminded them of the laws of God, warned them against pride and peculation, and told them to fear God and show mercy. Few judges would take kindly to such admonitions, especially when they came from an imprisoned son of a weaver. He made one plea that still resonates, namely 'what a sore thing it was that prisoners should lie so long in gaol, and how that they learned badness one of another in talking of their bad deeds, and therefore speedy justice should have been done'. Finally in late 1651, after being detained for a year, he was released.

'Being at liberty, I went on as before' chirped this callow zealot for the Lord. As he traversed the country he managed to keep out of gaol, if not out of trouble, until he came to Carlisle in 1653. There he was committed 'to prison as a blasphemer, heretic and seducer'. To Fox, the gaolers 'looked like two bear-herds'. He told them to expect no money from him and he would neither lie in their beds nor eat their 'victuals'. He was confined in an isolated room with three musketeers guarding him until the next assize where he was like to be sentenced to death. 'Great ladies and countesses' were allowed into the prison to gaze on a man about to die, and clergy were admitted to berate him, including a 'company of bitter Scotch priests and Presbyterians made up of envy and malice, who were not fit to speak of the things of God'. On a procedural technicality he could not be indicted and his fate was left to the magistrates. They ordered that he be put in among the 'moss-troopers [border brigands], thieves and murderers' in the gaol. He draws a stark portrayal of life among the riff-raff.

> A filthy, nasty place it was, where men and women were put together in a very uncivil manner; one woman was almost eaten to death with lice ... the gaoler was cruel and the under-gaoler very abusive both to me and to Friends that came to see me; for he would be at Friends with a great cudgel, who did but come to the window to look in upon me. I could get up to the grate, where sometimes I took in my meat, at which the gaoler was often offended. Once he came in a great rage and beat me with his cudgel.

Not all in authority approved of such brutality. The governor of the castle and Justice Pearson came into the prison to see for themselves the conditions in which Fox was kept. They were appalled at what they found and decried the magistrates for allowing the gaolers to behave so. They demanded that the gaolers find sureties for their good behaviour and put the particularly cruel under-gaoler into the dungeon with Fox 'amongst the moss-troopers'. Fox was soon released.

Not all his disciples were so fortunate. While in Carlisle he had persuaded a teenage boy called James Parnell to follow the true path. This he faithfully did, embarking on a ministry in Essex, until his short life ended in 1656. Having been committed to Colchester castle, Parnell 'endured very great hardships and sufferings; being put by the cruel gaoler into a hole in the castle wall, called the oven'. This was so high from the ground that the ladder fell short and the last six feet had to be scaled using a rope. To get food he had to climb down and then up again, until one day he lost his grip and fell to his death on the flagstones below. The gaoler's wife had threatened to have the boy's blood. She certainly had it on her.

Fox continued on his way, preaching, admonishing, hectoring, and irritating more souls than he saved. He even secured a meeting with Oliver Cromwell, who granted him liberty to go where he pleased. Not all were so indulgent. In 1656 Fox and two others were arrested in Cornwall for handing out pamphlets and taken to Launceston gaol where they were kept for nine weeks awaiting the assize. Brought before the Chief Justice, additional charges of treason were levelled against Fox which were both ridiculous and unsubstantiated. In the event he and his co-accused were fined for not putting off their hats in court and were sent back to prison until they had paid.

Not only would they not pay the fine, they would not pay the head-gaoler, as a result of which 'he grew very devilish and wicked and ... put us into Doomsdale, a nasty stinking place, where they said few people came out alive; where they used to put witches and murderers before their execution; where the prisoners' excrements had not been carried out for scores of years'. It was all 'like mire and in some places to the top of the shoes in water'. They were not allowed to clean the fetid place nor have any straw to lie upon. Townspeople brought them some straw which they foolishly burnt to take away the stench. When the smoke rose into the gaoler's room, he threw 'pots of excrements' through a hole upon their heads so that 'the stink increased upon us', so that 'what with the stink and what with smoke we were like to have been choked and smothered'. They had to stand all night as it was too dirty to sit. When one young girl from the town brought them some food, the gaoler, to discourage any others, sued her for trespass. Fellow prisoners tried to scare the Quakers with tales of ghosts haunting Doomsdale and of those who had died there. Fox and his friends were unmoved.

Launceston gaol was one of the very worst. It and the lands belonging to the castle had been bought by Colonel Bennet, a Baptist teacher, and he had appointed the keeper. His singular choice brutally demonstrated that his sole aim was to make money out of misery. The head-gaoler, his wife and the underkeeper were all former thieves and had been branded accordingly. In their new station they meted unto others what had been done unto them. Fox had endured enough and he petitioned the justices, who ordered that the dungeon door be opened and that the occupants be allowed to clean it and buy food in the town. Fox also wrote to Cromwell, as a result of which their grievances were looked into and the conditions of their imprisonment materially improved. The visits of solicitous Friends also eased their lot, although some of them were arrested and joined their co-religionists in gaol. The wife of one of his confederates sent in a cheese which the gaoler seized and took to the mayor to search for treasonable correspondence 'and though they found no treason in the cheese, they kept it' for themselves. Finally Bennet offered to free them if only they would pay their fees, but Fox was obdurate, not deigning to pay fees to the gaoler for suffering inflicted by that gaoler. The colonel gave up and freed them anyway.

Fox left his tormenters to the Lord, and the Lord worked his mysterious way, as Fox, with a tinge of satisfaction, perhaps even of unchristian glee, related:

> This gaoler might have been rich if he had carried himself civilly but he sought his own ruin which soon after came upon him; for the next year he was turned out of his place, and for some wickedness was cast into the gaol himself, and there begged of our Friends. And for some unruliness in his behaviour, he was by the succeeding gaoler put

down into Doomsdale, locked in irons, beaten, and bid to remember how he had abused those good men, whom he had wickedly, without any cause, cast into that nasty prison; and told that now he deservedly should suffer for his wickedness, and the same measure he had meted to others he should have meted out to himself. He became very poor, and died in prison. His wife and family came to misery.

The next time Fox was incarcerated a new age had dawned. The Protectorate was gone, King Charles was come, and the attitude of the authorities towards Quakers was changed, at least temporarily. Some seven hundred of them, imprisoned under Cromwell, were set free. There seemed 'an inclination and intention in the government to grant Friends liberty'. Nonetheless in 1660 while travelling round the north Fox was charged with 'embroiling the nation in blood and raising a new war and being an enemy of the king'. Although he was imprisoned for more than twenty weeks in Lancaster castle and was made a 'close prisoner' in 'the dark-house' there, he gave no detailed description of it, suggesting it was less awful than those he had previously experienced. He did mention the 'very wicked' and cruel under-gaoler, one Hardy, who would not allow him to have food brought in, but would let tormenters visit him: two 'abusive young priests' and a woman who taunted him with the gallows. For her impiety 'the Lord God cut her off, and she died in miserable condition'.

The king himself intervened, issuing a writ of *habeas corpus* for him to be produced before the justices in the King's Bench. Again Fox refused to pay any fees, post bail or pay for his transfer and, despite the treason charges, stubborn as ever, he was allowed to leave the prison and make his own way to London. The judges could find nothing against him and on the king's command he was set free.

It was at this point that the actions of wilder millenarian religious sects, in particular the insurrection of 'the Fifth-monarchy-people', jeopardised everything. Quakers fell under suspicion and again filled the prisons. Most were soon set free, but persecution persisted and meetings were disrupted. Friends, for whom their word was their bond, would not swear and so could not take the oaths of allegiance and supremacy demanded by parliament. This made them suspect, and several died in prison. One such was the prominent Quaker, Francis Howgill, who spent five years in Appleby gaol, Westmorland, dying there of disease in 1669. In Cornwall, as a result of the 'fanatic hunting' of Colonel Thomas Robinson, many Friends ended up in custody, and when it was discovered that their gaoler had let them out to visit their families he was fined and they were closely confined. Robinson got his just reward when he was gored to death by a bull.

Fox himself in 1662, for refusing the oath, was arrested and sent to Leicester gaol. He could have stayed in an inn but preferred to be with other Friends who had already been imprisoned. The gaoler, 'a very wicked cruel man', had cudgelled them as they prayed and crammed several of them into the dungeon amongst common felons. Fox remained in the prison-yard but was denied straw for a bed. It became apparent that the gaoler's wife was the real power and 'though she was lame, and sat mostly in her chair, not being able to go except on crutches, yet she would beat her husband when he came within her reach, if he did not do as she would have him'. She proved more accommodating and allowed Fox to have a room so he could receive visiting Friends and those Quakers she released from the dungeon. The gaoler, however, wanted money and refused to let them buy beer from the town but only from him. Fox said water would suffice. At the quarter sessions the Quakers were convicted, but nonetheless set free.

Two years later, for the same refusal to swear allegiance, Fox once again ended up in Lancaster castle. As he was to be kept in isolation, he was put into the tower 'where the smoke of the other prisoners came up so thick, it stood as dew upon the walls, and sometimes it was so thick that I could hardly see the candle when it burned ... so that I was almost smothered'. It was winter and the tower was high and exposed to the wind and the elements. Besides the smoke, it rained upon his bed and he was drenched when he tried to stem the leak. Cold and wet he lay all winter, his body swollen, his limbs benumbed. Weak as he was he continued to write.

In 1665 Fox was transferred to Scarborough castle on the Yorkshire coast where he was kept for over a year. Again he suffered from both smoke from the little fire and rain from the open window. To prevent both he had to lay out fifty shillings. No sooner done than he was moved into another room which had neither chimney nor fire-hearth and where the North Sea wind blew rain over his bed and clothes. He had no means to dry them and he suffered from both cold and wet. His fingers swelled. He survived on water and a three-penny loaf which had to last three weeks or more. Friends were not allowed to visit or alleviate his suffering, but Catholics and Presbyterians were admitted to harangue or argue with him. To try to refute George Fox seemed an estimable pastime and many partook of it. Finally in September 1666 the king, being informed of his predicament, again intervened and ordered his release.

His travails were not yet over. In 1673 he was held for a short time in Worcester gaol before being sent to the King's Bench at Westminster. The judges there sent him back to gaol where he remained for over a year. Again his health suffered badly, and again he wrote prodigiously, both books and letters. It was time to take stock, and Fox enumerated the terrible misfortunes that befell all those who had persecuted or ill-treated him in prison. 'I did not seek revenge upon them', asserts Fox, 'yet the Lord had executed His judgments upon many of them.' Fortunately for us, by his travels and travails, he had given detailed first-hand descriptions of life in gaols throughout the length and breadth of England in the mid-seventeenth century.

Fox's most famous disciple, William Penn, also suffered for his faith. In December 1668, for publishing a supposedly blasphemous book, he was placed in solitary confinement in a small, cold room in the Tower. The son of an admiral, Penn was 'a gentleman of quality' and unusually well-connected at Court. His publisher ended up with the riff-raff in the Gatehouse prison. Penn was offered the option of recanting or being locked up indefinitely. He replied that 'the Tower is to me the worst argument in the world', and declared 'my prison shall be my grave before I will budge a jot'.[3] After eight months it was the authorities who gave way to this adamantine resolve and he was released.

Prison had done for him what it did for Bunyan, forcing him to pause and take stock. His biographer and eulogist waxed lyrical: 'the onrushing river of Penn's magnificent mind met a dam and accumulated into a deep lake, and while its waters were forcibly stilled their impurities settled out, leaving his thoughts and direction crystal clear'.[4] The increasing clarity of his thought was expressed in his writing, and the essay *No Cross, No Crown* was both the proof and the result.

From being a prisoner himself he was soon to become an advocate for other imprisoned Quakers. Visiting Ireland he was appalled to find as many as eighty Friends in Cork prison, confined in a small enclosure with no food or drink except that which could be pushed through a hole, and children and servants who had tried to bring in tools and bedding put in the stocks. He immediately set about trying to secure their release or ameliorate their lot, and as he had persistence, a ready wit, and access to the highest in the land, he met with considerable success. But for the next twenty years Quakers were to be a staple of the prison population, and it was this common and traumatic experience of going in and out of prison, as inmates or their visitors, that ignited their enduring passion for, and commitment to, prison reform.

---

3 William Hepworth Dixon, *William Penn* (London, 1851), pp.69f.
4 Catherine Peare, *William Penn* (London, 1956), p.84.

Another early disciple of Fox and editor of his journal, as well as being Milton's secretary and friend, produced an equally vivid and moving account of conditions in a number of prisons of his acquaintance, both provincial and metropolitan. Thomas Ellwood, fifteen years younger than Fox, was a Quaker convert repeatedly detained by the authorities on account of his new-found faith. He was first imprisoned in 1660 at the age of twenty-one for refusing to take the oath of allegiance and supremacy. It was an easy confinement in Oxford. Not for him the rigours of the castle where conditions in this 'unwholesome and nasty place' were dreadful.[5] Possibly out of deference to his father, the authorities decided on another disposal. Ellwood, as a result, was to spend several months in the house of the city marshal, 'a genteel, courteous man, by trade a linen-draper', until he was freed and committed into paternal care.[6]

Two years later in London he was arrested again, along with thirty-one other Quakers who were attending a forbidden meeting, and taken to Bridewell. Ellwood was directed to ascend a staircase at the south-west corner of the outer court which led to a dismal court-room on the second floor which opened into another room draped in black, the sole furnishing of which was a 'great whipping-post'. This was for the punishment of 'ill people who for their lewdness were sent to this prison, and there sentenced to be whipped'. But 'the way to Heaven lay by the gate of Hell'. On the floor above was 'one of the fairest rooms' Ellwood 'was ever in' – Henry VIII's erstwhile sixty-foot dining-room – and into it came the fellow-prisoners, other Friends apprehended when their meetings had been raided. In expectation of this mass incarceration Friends in the City had appointed individuals to have oversight of specific prisons to ensure that care and sustenance would be provided to those of their order committed there. Meat, broth, beer, bread and cheese were all provided, primarily for those unable to pay for the provisions available in the chandler's shop. The dining-room served as a dormitory and the inmates snuggled up as best they could, keeping on their clothes and using the rushes provided. Ellwood found work with a hosier in Cheapside, making night-waistcoats of red and yellow flannel for women and children. Not so fortunate was a poor Quaker who, for finishing a shoe-

---

5   The tower in Oxford castle was particularly bad and the space so small that prisoners were forced to lie on top of each other. Conditions there during the civil war and the treatment meted out by the venal and sadistic gaoler, William Smith, are set out in 'The Inhumanity of the King's Prison-keeper at Oxford', in *A Collection of Scarce and Interesting Tracts tending to Elucidate Detached Parts of the History of Great Britain Selected from the Sommers-Collections* (London, 1795), pp.281–91

6   Ellwood, pp.53, 59.

repair on the Sabbath, was committed to Bridewell where he was to be kept to hard labour beating hemp. For refusing this work he was whipped. The procedure was savage:

> The manner of whipping there is to strip the party to the skin from the waist upwards, and having fastened him to the whipping-post, so that he can neither resist nor shun the strokes, to lash the naked body with long but slender twigs of holly, which will bend almost like thongs, and lap around the body; and these having little knots upon them, tear the skin and flesh, and give extreme pain.[7]

Ellwood and his friends tended to his wounds and ensured that the poor man was properly fed during the rest of his incarceration.

Eventually Ellwood and the others were taken to the Old Bailey, where they refused to swear the oath of allegiance. They were then committed to Newgate and 'thrust into the common side'. This was the worst part, 'not so much from the place as the people'. It was 'stocked with the veriest rogues and meanest sort of felons and pickpockets, who not able to pay chamber-rent on the master's side, are thrust in there', not to mend their ways but to learn their trade: 'if they come in bad, to be sure they do not go out better, for there they have the opportunity to instruct one another in their art and impart to each other what improvements they have made therein'.[8]

During the day these matriculands in the University of Crime shared with Quakers, prisoners of conscience, the inaptly named Justice Hall on the first storey over the gate. There the latter could perambulate, and the former beg. In addition the Quakers had access to two other rooms above the hall. At night all the Newgate prisoners shared one large, round room, the central pillar of which supported the chapel above and the three tiers of hammocks upon which the men slept. During the day the hammocks were hung up by the walls. On the rough floor beneath was space for another layer, largely given over to the weak and sick who were unable to get into hammocks and had to make do with pallets. The noxious vapours that filled the room were conducive neither to sleeping nor to good health. Disease ran rampant. Ellwood found it particularly disgusting when the gaolers parboiled the heads of three dead traitors so that they could be displayed on spikes at various points in the City.

Because Newgate was badly overcrowded, some Quakers, who for all the suspicions they aroused posed no threat to prison discipline, were transferred

---

7   *Ibid.*, pp.80–7.
8   *Ibid.*, p.94. Howard would later state that 'half the robberies committed in and about London are planned in the prisons' (Howard, I, p.10).

back to Bridewell. Ellwood and his fellows were allowed to make their own unescorted way from one prison to the other, as it was assumed that none would abscond. None did. Life in Bridewell was less than onerous. The returnees were housed together in a low room 'in another fair court which had a pump in the middle of it'. They were not shut up as before but could walk around the court and use the pump for washing and drinking. Escape would have involved but a stroll down a passage that led from the court to the street. The Quakers remained 'steady and true prisoners' confined only by 'conscience and honour'. Ellwood 'under this easy restraint' was granted parole to visit his less fortunate co-religionists left in Newgate. Finally he was released but continued visiting Friends in prison.

Later he was to experience the very different regime in a typical county prison, Aylesbury. It was suffering under a tyrannous gaoler, Nathaniel Birch, who behaved with 'great rudeness and cruelty'. Many a Quaker had been in his charge, and had suffered for it, and in particular Ellwood's friend and mentor, Isaac Pennington. He had been committed to Aylesbury gaol for 'worshipping God in his own house' (holding a conventicle). Like other Quakers he was kept in an old room behind the gaol, a former malt-house 'now so decayed that it was scarce fit for a dog-house'. It would have been easy to escape, but that was not the Quakers' way, and the gaoler knew it.[9] So porous was the malt-house that Ellwood chose to join his friends and stayed a day or two. Over the winter months Pennington remained 'in a cold and incommodious room, without a chimney' and his 'tender body contracted so great and violent a distemper that, for several weeks after, he was not able to turn himself in bed'. Pennington was lucky to survive a year-and-a-half's detention in such conditions, as well as the plague which during the later stages of his incarceration carried off other inmates. When at last he secured his release by writ of *habeas corpus*, the court granting it wondered that he had been detained for so long for no good reason.

Indeed many an inmate endured longer in prison than the law required. This was due to unpaid fees. In Aylesbury Birch contrived to detain Quakers discharged in court, 'using great violence and shutting them up close in the common gaol among the felons because they would not give him his unrighteous demand of fees'. They turned down the offer of expensive lodgings and demanded a 'free prison'. The gaoler, perhaps impressed

---

9   Ellwood, pp.95, 98, 99, 115. Less trustworthy prisoners suffered a different fate. Over a century later Howard noted that 'the prison not being strong, the men were in irons' (II, p.127). It was an argument often deployed: weak prison security necessitated individual restraint.

despite himself with the moral strength of his captives, relented. They had more or less free rein to enjoy their bread and cheese and chat beside the prison well, and after a month's detention in lieu of the fine imposed by the justices, Birch set them free without further charge. It was a victory for integrity over iniquity.

Ellwood's own freedom was short-lived. In March 1665 he was sent to the house of correction at Wycombe where he was kept in close confinement for several months 'with friends, prison-fellows and bed-fellows'. He was not idle, making 'nets for kitchen service, to boil herbs etc', which he gave away or sold and 'pretty well stocked the Friends' in Buckinghamshire. Thereafter he seems to have kept out of gaol, but without in any way compromising his stance or moderating his outspoken views. He died in 1713 and was buried in the Friends' burial place at New Jordan, Chalfont St Giles.[10]

Bunyan had predeceased him by a quarter of a century, dying in 1688 in Snow Hill, under the shadow of Newgate. He too had sought out like-minded bed-fellows, being buried alongside many another Dissenter in Bunhill Fields burial ground in the City of London. Bunyan died of pneumonia. Many who were buried there before him had also suffered imprisonment for their beliefs but had died not in their beds of pneumonia or old age but in prison of the plague.[11]

---

10 Ellwood, pp.120f. He was not by any means the last Quaker to be imprisoned for conscience and to write about it. In 1814 three young Friends refused to serve in the militia or pay the fine incurred. They were sent to the Wakefield bridewell and spent a whole month in the undifferentiated company of thieves and prostitutes. 'They employed themselves ... in minutely observing the scene which was passing before them', and gained a far better insight into prison life than any mere visitor could. On release one of them wrote a memorandum for the magistrates, describing prison conditions and proposing reforms 'of a very enlightened kind' (Gurney, pp.88–92).

11 Some 5,000 Dissenters are thought to have died in prison between 1660 and 1672 (Richard West, *The Life and Strange Surprising Adventures of Daniel Defoe* (London, 1997), p.3).

CHAPTER 7

Plague, Pudding and Pie

London was a city of prisons, the locked and guarded dwellings of citizens into which Plague had entered. A watcher stood before each door, ready to fetch the bare necessities for sustaining life for the stricken prisoners within, but never loosening the bolts.

Walter Bell

The Black Death was the worst pandemic to strike England but not the only one. Nor was the plague the only killer disease, but it was the most deadly. It was endemic for long periods in major towns, Norwich and London in particular, biding its time, awaiting the arrival of a more virulent strain from the Continent to burst into a full-blown epidemic. Outbreaks recurred over the years, in one place or another, erupting in the spring and summer months, their character never understood.[1] The last major blast was the Great Plague of 1665 which in April struck the land, 'leaving hardly any place free from its insults'.[2]

A town was more in danger than a village, a city than a town, and a big city most of all. London in particular – the City and Westminster, the liberties and out-parishes, Southwark and the suburbs – with its enormous population largely herded into confined and cramped tenements amidst teeming streets festooned with the dirt and detritus of an urban life virtually devoid of sanitation, was devastated. Of its perhaps 450,000 inhabitants well over 70,000 – some say over 100,000 – were to die in less than a year. The rich, or many of them, the king included, escaped the City and Westminster, the poor being left largely to their own devices and the care of some devoted and often dissenting clerics and a few officials, schoolmasters and medical men, to face the wrath to come. The mayor stayed on but

---

[1] Paul Slack, *The Impact of the Plague in Tudor and Stuart England* (London, 1985), *passim*. Some blamed the Scots for the outbreak in 1603, King James I having brought it from Edinburgh along with his entourage and baggage. York was particularly badly affected by this visitation and it is reasonable to suppose that those prisoners huddled in its cramped castle were prime targets (A.W. Twyford and Arthur Griffiths, *Records of York Castle* (London, 1880), pp.121ff.).

[2] Nathaniel Hodges, *Loimologia Or An Historical Account of the Plague in London in 1665*, English trans. (London, 1720), p.7.

transacted all his business from a specially constructed glass cage, a prisoner by his own design.

In an attempt to stop the spread of infection, the authorities had recourse to a simple, long-tried and wholly disastrous strategy in terms of plague prevention and public health. When one member of a household exhibited plague symptoms, the building was sealed off, a red cross, like a stigma, daubed on their door, and all those inside – sick or sound – were shut in for forty days, consigning them to almost certain death, prisoners encoffined in their own homes. It was a crime to break bounds. Plague killed its thousands but this immuring tens of thousands. Some thought the wrong people were suffering: the poor in their hovels rather than the princes in their palaces. Yet the rich were exempted from quarantine, and had the resources to flee, leaving the plague to flourish in the poorer parts of the metropolis. 'The meaner sort', its prime target, became the human fuel upon which it fed. The City became a prison. The inhabitants were incarcerated therein either in their individual domestic cells if ill, or within the perimeter of the City and its parishes and suburbs if indigent. Few of the poor could get out and fewer still would be let out.

This metaphor of London as a prison has a pedigree that goes back to Daniel Defoe or before. In his faux reportage, *A Journal of the Plague Year*, Defoe's narrator, H.F., never describes an actual prison nor the effects of the plague on it. Rather he considers the whole of London to be a place of confinement where the sick are guarded under quarantine. There 'were just so many Prisons in the Town, as there were Houses shut up; and as the people shut up or imprison'd so, were guilty of no Crime, only shut up because miserable, it was really the more intolerable to them'.[3]

Those already segregated – for their sins – in the City's or Southwark's gaols, where conditions were atrocious and flight not an option, must have stood little chance of survival. Mortality was at its highest where urban squalor was at its worst. Pestilence was incubated in overcrowded tenements and subdivided houses.[4] Contemporaries themselves attributed incidences of plague to 'many people being packed together', and 'the corrupt keeping' of houses – especially by European immigrants – while 'stench and nastiness' were known at the time to be 'the Entertainers of Infection'. A doctor who gallantly ministered to the sick during the Great Plague and lived to write about it urged that 'the Streets, Sinks and Canals should be daily cleared of all Filth', and that 'Dogs, Cats and other domestic Brutes' be killed to stop

---

3   Daniel Defoe, *A Journal of the Plague Year* (1722), Norton edn (New York, 1992), p.47.

4   Slack, *op. cit.*, pp.116–43, 152.

the propagation of the plague.[5] He might have given a thought to rat- and flea-infested gaols as incubators of infection. They were pestilential places at the best of times, but these were the worst. Gaol delivery took on a different connotation when Death extra-judicially depleted the prison population. If Death had 'pitched his tents ... in the sinfully polluted suburbs' he must have established his headquarters in Newgate.[6]

To what extent plague infested and decimated London prisons we can readily surmise but do not actually know as that invaluable resource, the Bills of Mortality, compiled every week to enumerate deaths in the parishes, does not specifically cover prisons or any institution that had a private burial ground as distinct from the parochial churchyard.[7] Nor does Pepys help other than noting numerous deaths in the parish of St Sepulchre, adjacent to Newgate.[8] We have only the odd titbit about individual prisons to assist.

Newgate, the most notorious, is the best-documented of all the London prisons. It was fetid and overcrowded, a death trap for many incarcerated there. In ordinary years if the gallows did not get you, gaol fever or smallpox probably would. Keeping prisoners in was all that seemed to matter, and the cells and rooms in the old prison 'were so close, as to be almost constant seats of disease, and sources of infection, to the destruction of multitudes, not only in the prison, but abroad'.[9] Ellwood had observed of the communal sleeping arrangements that 'the breath and steam that came from so many bodies of different ages, conditions, and constitutions, packed up so close together, was enough to cause sickness amongst us ... There were many sick and some very weak.' Although he did not remain long there, during his incarceration one of his fellow-prisoners died. The coroner's jury, come at night to see the conditions in which this had occurred, had not been able to enter the room for lack of space. The foreman had exclaimed:

> Lord bless me! What a sight is here! I did not think there had been so much cruelty in the hearts of Englishmen to use Englishmen in this manner. We need not now question how this man came by his death;

---

5   *Ibid.*, pp.71f., 140; Hodges, *op. cit.*, p.51. Extermination of the thousands of dogs and cats that inhabited the streets proved another disastrous policy since it destroyed the best means of rat-control.

6   Thomas Dekker, *The Wonderful Yeare*, 1603.

7   Walter Bell, *The Great Plague of London in 1665*, revised edn (London, 1951), p.190, n.1. Other cities are no better served, and nowhere is there specific information about prisons.

8   Samuel Pepys, *Diary*, ed. Robert Latham and William Matthews (London, 1970–83), VI, p.225.

9   Howard, I, p.213, commenting on the original structure.

we may rather wonder that they are not all dead, for this place is enough to breed an infection among them.[10]

Similarly, Colonel Turner, who had been briefly imprisoned in the worst conditions Newgate had to offer, had described them thus:

> I was put in the Hole: it is the most fearful sad, deplorable place; Hell itself in comparison cannot be such a place; there is neither bench, stool nor stick for any person there; they lie like swine upon the ground; one upon another, howling and roaring.[11]

That was two years before the Plague, and 'it may be imagined how Plague fed fat in such quarters'. In 1665 the last gaol delivery at Newgate occurred, in June, but was soon abandoned when one of those brought up to the adjacent Old Bailey for trial was found to be plague-ridden. No deliveries were to be held before February in the following year. The cessation of justice in this and other courts 'eliminated one cause of death from the Bills of Mortality': hangings ceased.[12] Those spared the gallows, however, may have had only a short reprieve as they were confined in gaol throughout the months the plague raged. It swept through Newgate, killing its keeper, a Mr Jackson, in July.[13] He was far from the only victim. When the Old Bailey Sessions began again eight months later they were shorter than had been expected, given the accumulation of prisoners. Of those who had been committed in July 1665 only six survived to be tried in February 1666, of the August intake three, of September five: gaol delivery had already taken place.[14]

Quakers independently documented their dead, and many of their number died in gaols. When others fled, Quakers had remained in the City. They were conspicuous in their humanitarian work among plague victims. They were conspicuous in general, and were always liable to arrest. George Whitehead carried a night-cap in his pocket, just in case. Fox referred to 'many Friends' in 1665 being 'crowded into Newgate and other prisons, where the sickness was' and many dying there.[15] The burial ground at Bunhill Fields holds over ninety Quaker 'martyrs who were carried to this spot on the shoulders of their brethren from the crowded prisons in which they expired'. Of these, fifty-two, including women and children, had succumbed

---

10 Ellwood, pp.90ff.
11 T.B. Howell (ed.), *State Trials* (London, 1809–26), IV, p.628.
12 Bell, *The Great Plague*, pp.63f., 311f.
13 *Ibid.*, p.189.
14 *Ibid.*, p.174.
15 Catherine Peare, *William Penn* (London, 1956), p.51; *The Journal of George Fox*, ed. John Nickalls (Cambridge, 1952), p.493.

in Newgate. Added to them were 'the sufferers who died on board the ship that was to have transported them to the western plantations', and together they made up more than a tenth of all Quaker fatalities from the plague buried there.[16] The high mortality among incarcerated Quakers, who were well tended by other Friends, suggests that an even higher death-rate would prevail among other groups.

Presumably, all London's prisons were infected. The parishes around them were. The Fleet, with its pestilential ditch, certainly harvested its dead. A Mr Bastwick, who preached to the prisoners in the Poultry compter, died of plague. Whether he contracted it as a result of his prison ministry is unknown, but not unlikely. Bridewell too suffered, hardly surprising given its location and the fact that it served as a granary housing fifty tons of corn and hundredweights of rats. To what extent, however, is hard to say as its 'court-books' for that specific period are missing, as are the registers of its sister foundation, Bethlehem Hospital. Its surgeon, Edward Higgs, did not desert his post, and yet survived.[17] It is significant, however, that Daniel Defoe in 1722, when the threat of the pestilence's return was taken seriously, proposed that no one should be 'arrested for debt, so as to be put in prison above a certain time', that those unable to put up bail or already imprisoned should be moved at least fifteen miles away, and 'all criminals, felons and murderers should be forthwith tried, and such as are not sentenced to die, should be immediately transported or let out, on condition of going forty miles from the City, not to return on pain of death'.[18] This recommendation is strongly suggestive that prisons were seen as incubators of infection.

The Great Plague finally burnt itself out even if life did not yet return to normal as plague deaths, while petering out, continued sporadically into the following summer. One disaster would succeed another. In 1665 Londoners had died; London had survived. In 1666 – the ominous year of the number

16 Beck and Ball, *The London Friends Meetings* (London, 1869), p.330. Some county gaols were likewise infected. Aylesbury for instance had the plague not only in the town but in the gaol (Ellwood, p.118); so too, in Colchester, Dutch prisoners-of-war, already infected, spread the disease in their cramped prison quarters.

17 E.G. O'Donoghue, *The Story of Bethlehem Hospital* (London, 1914), p.192; *Bridewell Hospital* (London, 1923 and 1929), II, pp.135, 138.

18 Defoe, *Due Preparations for the Plague* (London, 1722), pp.21f.

of the Beast – far fewer of its inhabitants would perish but its very fabric would be consumed, not by disease but by fire.[19]

In the early hours of Sunday 2 September 1666 a fire began in a bakery in Pudding Lane. The flames carried down to the nearby Thames Street where they eagerly devoured the provender provided by the warehouses: tar, tallow, oil, hemp and other flammable items stored there. Still ravenous, it turned into an inferno which raged until the 5th, first stalling at Pie Corner, and sputtering out soon thereafter. When it eventually expired, the medieval City had been reduced to charcoal. The summer had been hot and dry, and the City, its houses built largely of 'Timber, Lath and Plaister or, as they very properly call'd Paper Work', and its many buildings and warehouses holding combustible materials, was especially vulnerable to any spark. Narrow streets, with overhanging roof-tops forming an arboreal canopy, did not help. Additionally, Londoners had a reputation as being 'the most careless people in the World about Fire'.[20] Above all, strong winds carried and nurtured the resultant flames. It was a perfect firestorm.

The fire 'wad[ed] through the streets', the buildings burned, the debris scattered, and the populace scurried around trying to save life and limb and property. There was no stopping the infernal progress. Eventually Old St Paul's, the medieval cathedral dominating the skyline, in whose vaults publishers had placed their entire stock of books for safety, would go up with the rest, leaving scarred ruins under which a furnace had raged, feeding off the learning of the age, seeking to devour and erase the very literary soul of the City. If St Paul's was its soul, the Royal Exchange and the Guildhall were its heart and mind. They too were destroyed. Familiar landmarks were erased, books burned, authors despaired, and people fled from the swift flames, if they could. Some were forcibly immured and impotently immobile: those held in gaols. Their number was swollen with supposed 'incendiaries', incarcerated either to prevent their activities or to protect them from mob hysteria.[21]

---

19 The number of Fire fatalities is hard to estimate. One casualty was the press which printed the weekly Bills of Mortality. It fell victim to the flames and so no bill was published for three weeks. Estimates of the number of the dead have varied from the nine recorded to several hundreds or even thousands, though the last is implausible. Whatever the number it was as nothing to the toll taken by the Plague.

20 Defoe, I, pp.327, 351. Paper Buildings in the Temple to this day provides an echo of the combustible nature of pre-pyric London.

21 Walter Bell, *The Great Fire of London*, revised edn (London, 1951), pp.74, 122.

By the Monday the firestorm was raking the north side of Poultry and engulfed its compter. Whether it had been evacuated or its inmates had been left to roast we do not know, but given what happened elsewhere the former is likely. The Wood Street compter likewise went up in flames. The compters were to cost £8,845 and £7,705, respectively, to replace and improve. The previous edifices had been valued at only £3,000 each.

On the morning of Tuesday 4 September the fire approached Bridewell and its flammable stores. Despite concerted efforts to pull down all the houses and sheds on the nearby quay and tip the timber, coal and hemp into the Thames, the torrent of fire could not be staunched. It struck first the southern quadrangle. About noon the 'high wind carried great flames of fire and set Salisbury Square alight and several houses between it and Bridewell Dock', and 'waves of flame' from Blackfriars and Cheapside were blown into the granary which 'indeed, became a funeral pyre'. The City grain had been stored there and 40,000 quarters of corn were consumed in the fire. The quadrangle was incinerated. The northern courtyard was gutted but not burnt down. The massive walls and battlements, thirty-six feet high, survived the conflagration but brick was shattered and metal melted and fused. In Hollar's drawing of the devastated City, the walls of Bridewell are depicted standing but they form merely a shell. Molten lead poured into the Fleet Ditch, making the water boil. So intense was the heat that corpses – many of them plague victims – buried in the chapel yard were cremated in their graves 'or robbed of their reverent covering of earth'. The chapel warden, Hugh Knowling, reverently re-covered the remains with earth and sand at a cost of £8.[22] The living had all been evacuated to safety. The palace was uninhabitable and so its inmates were rehoused, the children lodging with their art-masters, until Bridewell rose again from the ashes. The damage was assessed at £5,000 but the repairs – and presumably improvements – cost £8,523.[23]

The Old Bailey was burnt. Next to it was Newgate. The prison then standing was largely down to Dick Whittington, the famous lord mayor who had paid for its 're-edification'. Perhaps as a result it was the most expensive of the City prisons, being valued at £15,000. The repairs it had to undergo after the fire cost only £8,000, demonstrating that the thick stone walls had withstood the intense heat, although both wings were set ablaze, and, as John Evelyn observed, in his peregrination through the desolation, iron hinges, bars and manacles had melted, and the gates had been reduced

---

[22] *Ibid.*, pp.150f.; E.G. O'Donoghue, *Bridewell Hospital* (London, 1923 and 1929), II, pp.143–7.

[23] Bell, *The Great Fire*, pp.224f.

to cinders.[24] The gaolers evacuated the prison, and attempted to march their charges to alternative accommodation in the Clink. The escort was inadequate, the chaos all-enveloping, escape was easy. Similarly, as the fire approached Ludgate the gaolers freed the debtors imprisoned there. They scarpered. At least the City gaolers had done the decent thing, unlike the keepers of Bedlam who had fled as the fire approached, leaving their charges to God's mercy. An east wind diverted the flames.[25]

Just north of Newgate at Pie Corner on Cock Lane the inferno was checked but not yet stopped. St Bartholomew's Hospital was spared. St Sepulchre's church, downwind of Newgate, was not so fortunate. Its tower survived but its bells did not, except for one small handbell used under charitable bequest since Elizabethan times to sound the death knell before the cells of condemned Newgate felons. It was reprieved for future use for the prisoners 'within, who for wickedness and sin', were 'appointed to die'.[26]

The Fleet too was engulfed, but at least its occupants were allowed to flee their horrid underground cells, ironically known as Bartholomew Fair. The 'Rules' around it, where debtors who could afford it dwelt, were also consumed. The warden, Sir Jeremy Whichcote, charitably housed the homeless debtors, and bought with his own money a house in Lambeth as temporary accommodation pending the rebuilding of his prison. He proved an exemplary public servant.[27]

Such servants would be sorely needed in the weeks, months and years to come as they laboured to ensure that London would rise, like a phoenix, once more. The rubble would be cleared, St Paul's would be resurrected and transformed, and the City's prisons, all destroyed, would renew their dispiriting work, rejoining those that survived in Southwark and Westminster whose work had never ceased. But it would take time. Four years after the fire Newgate and Ludgate were still unfinished.

That did not prevent them resuming their vital function. Roofless though it was, in October 1666 Newgate, speedily patched up but without a water supply, was used to house a few felons. These included Robert Hubert, transferred there from Surrey's county gaol, the White Lion in Southwark, pending his hanging at Tyburn. A French fantasist who had confessed to starting the Fire (though his judge disbelieved it), Hubert was an innocent victim, a sacrifice made to public paranoia. Other suspected arsonists were

24 *EHD*, VIII, p.501.
25 Bell, *The Great Fire*, pp.147, 181; O'Donoghue, *Bethlehem Hospital*, pp.192f.
26 Howard, I, p.215; Bell, *The Great Fire*, pp.146f., 158.
27 *Ibid.*, p.149.

detained, but after exhaustive inquiry the Privy Council concluded that 'nothing hath yet been found to argue [the Fire] to have been other than the hand of God upon us, a great wind, and the season so very dry'.[28]

Evanescent incendiaries apart, more generally, crime proliferated. There were rich pickings amongst the rubble. 'Vagrants and sturdy beggars, loose and idle persons' were everywhere. Thefts, robberies, even murders amidst the ruins were easy to perpetrate and hard to prevent. Restraint and deterrence were all that remained. A wooden structure was raised amidst the ruins of the Guildhall and the Old Bailey so that the judges could resume hearing cases and carry out the all-important gaol delivery. But secure gaols were in short supply.

The governors of Bridewell saw it as their first duty to build on their site prison rooms to detain the human vultures who were descending on the corpse of the City. These vultures included jerry-builders who, in the reconstruction, were flouting the provisions of the Rebuilding Act. They were subjected to a fine or a few months' imprisonment. Similarly, workers refusing the set wage or failing to complete work started were liable to a £10 fine or one month's imprisonment. Improvisation was essential. The Aldersgate lodging of the Common Crier was used to make room for prisoners from the compter in Poultry while Bishopsgate took those from Wood Street. Westminster and Southwark prisons were fully utilised to take in the increasing number of debtors – some erstwhile merchants of substance – impoverished as a result of the devastation of buildings, destruction of stock and disruption of trade occasioned by the calamities of plague, fire and the Dutch wars.[29]

Newgate was a cesspit. Water had been finally restored in November 1666, but in the following March the common sewer broke into the still ruinous prison. Water there was aplenty, but all contaminated. That did not preclude the accommodation – if not the detention – of felons there. Newgate was porous. Eleven months after the Fire, Pepys recorded that thieves had broken out of their confinement. Walter Cowdrey, the keeper of 'the College', as it was later called by Defoe, seems to have acquiesced as he was accused of making 'his house the only nursery of rogues, prostitutes and pickpockets and thieves in the world, where they were bred and entertained'. The University of Crime is an ancient foundation.[30]

---

28 State Papers (Domestic), 1666–7, p.175; Bell, *The Great Fire*, p.202.

29 Bell, *The Great Fire*, pp.190, 286, 288.

30 Pepys, *op. cit.*, VIII, p.562. Once again, in all his descriptions of the effects of the Fire, Pepys, just like John Evelyn in his diary, makes no mention of prisons. Prison was a university of which Pepys himself would be a graduate. In 1679 during the Popish

Alongside ordinary criminals, Quakers, as ever, were imprisoned in Newgate during the period of its reconstruction. William Penn was the most famous, being held there in 1670 while on trial at the Old Bailey for seditious preaching and holding a riotous assembly. His acquittal occasioned a lasting development in the law: the unequivocal right of jurors to bring in whatever verdict they wished, however perverse. Nonetheless the following year he was back in Newgate, this time under a six months sentence. As with so many of his forebears, Penn's time in what he called 'a common, stinking gaol' enabled him further to consolidate and articulate his thoughts. 'Being in prison, he shortened the *Hours of Confinement*, which Inactivity would think tedious, by a Continual Employment, and writ several treatises' as well as finishing a major literary work of long gestation, appropriately titled *The Great Case of Liberty of Conscience*.

Only by 1672 was Newgate fully finished, ready to begin the period of its greatest notoriety, a notoriety best illustrated by the literary work of one of its former inmates, also of dissenting stock. The work was Moll Flanders, the Dissenter Daniel Defoe.

Plot he was imprisoned in the Tower and King's Bench on trumped-up charges of treason. In 1689, after the Glorious Revolution and the accession of William and Mary, he spent several anxious weeks in the Gatehouse, as he did the following year. To the new regime this servant of the old was suspect. He was bailed and the charges against him were dropped.

CHAPTER 8

A Newgate Pastoral

> There are in London, and the far extended Bounds ... notwithstanding
> we are a Nation of Liberty, more public and private Prisons and Houses
> of Confinement, than in any City of Europe, perhaps as many as in all
> the Capital Cities of Europe put together.
>
> Daniel Defoe

> Time partially reconciles us to anything. I gradually became content –
> doggedly contented, as wild animals in cages.
>
> Charles Lamb

In 1703 Daniel Defoe was imprisoned in Newgate both before and after
his conviction at the Old Bailey for seditious libel, the publication of
The Shortest Way with Dissenters, an outrageous satire on High Church Tories.
Dissenting pamphleteers were prone to punishment. A few months earlier
another such, one William Fuller, had been sentenced to three days in the
pillory, fined 1,000 marks, and forced to endure a whipping followed by hard
labour in Bridewell until he finally paid his dues. It was not the first time
Defoe had been in gaol, but this experience was both the most traumatic
and most fecund.

In 1692 he had been committed to the Fleet, having run up the colossal
debt of £17,000. It was not a good place to be confined, if the account given
of it by Moses Pitt, a bookseller imprisoned there three years before Defoe,
is to be believed. His *Cry of the Oppressed from Prison*, published in 1691,
recounted the 'unparalleled sufferings of multitudes of poor imprisoned
debtors in most of the gaols of England under the tyranny of the gaolers
and other oppressors', and in particular 'the barbarities of Richard Manlove
Esq, the present warden of the Fleet'. Fortunately, while the claims of his
numerous creditors piled up, Defoe was transferred to the King's Bench
prison in Southwark whence he managed to get to 'the Mint' which offered
a safe if insalubrious haven for debtors because of its status as a 'Liberty'.
Along with the notorious 'Alsatia' which lay in Whitefriars between Fleet
Street and the Thames, it was the last of the infamous little 'bastard
sanctuaries' that had ringed the City, offering a safe haven from the law.
They were the sites of monasteries which, after the Dissolution, retained

their ancient rights. The others had been progressively closed down in the seventeenth century, and 'Alsatia' would be in 1697. The Mint alone was to survive into the next century, a medieval relic, finally losing its sanctuary status in 1723. Defoe was soon set free but remained for the rest of his life a prey of those to whom he owed money.

Neither of the debtors' prisons he had experienced could prepare him for what was to come: Newgate, 'that wretch'd Place', as Defoe called it in his novel, *Moll Flanders*.[1] It had a fearsome reputation, possibly exaggerated, but largely justified. The gaol rebuilt after the Great Fire was externally far more ornate than its predecessor. Statues of Justice, Mercy and Truth adorned the entablatures inside the entrance gate, while in the niches between the Tuscan pilasters on the west front were placed Peace, Security, Plenty and Liberty, the last and most prominent having the word *Libertas* inscribed on her cap and with a cat lying at her feet. Dick Whittington was not forgotten. One critic observed that 'Newgate ... is a structure of more cost and beauty than was necessary; because the sumptuousness of the outside but aggravates the misery of the wretches within.'[2]

The prison straddled both sides of the street, and consisted of a warren of cells, store-rooms, strong-rooms, staircases, passages and the Press Yard where wealthier prisoners could 'take the fresh air'. By contrast there was little air – and none of it fresh – in the Hole, the underground dungeon whose only joyous inhabitants were flea-ridden rats, fat white lice and cockroaches, the shells of which lay deep on the floor, crunching under every footstep. The Hole was Hell. A former resident, the 'popish midwife', Elizabeth Cellier, bore witness to this in her *Malice Defeated* of 1680. In it she recounted that a Captain Cooke, who 'being a prisoner [in this "Mansion of Horror"] only for debt, was locked up in a little dark hole for two days and two nights having no other company but the Quarters of two Executed persons, the extream stench of which perhaps had kill'd him, had he not took the miserable relief of holding a foul Chamber Pot to his Nose'. The prison had to be made lucrative. The keepership cost £5,000. Redundant iron frames, used from the reign of William III until that of Anne to hold

---

1   Published in 1722 it purported to be an account written by Moll herself in 1683. Moll, a derivative of Mary, was a name often bestowed on young women of disreputable – and alluring – character. Hogarth's harlot, Moll Hackabout, is committed to Bridewell. In *The Beggar's Opera* 'Black Moll' is a 'very active and industrious' wench who 'educated' Filch and ended up behind bars. This usage probably derived from Mary Frith, a seventeenth-century pickpocket and fence known as Moll Cutpurse, who was said to have escaped Newgate and Tyburn by paying a £2,000 bribe.

2   *The Universal Magazine of Knowledge and Pleasure*, vol.XXXIV (April 1764), p.169.

convicts' heads as they were branded, were deployed as instruments of persuasion to extract garnish, the entry fee. Corruption was rife. Anything could be bought, even bespoke fetters. In *The Beggar's Opera*, Lockit, the Newgate turnkey, welcomes back the highwayman MacHeath:

> Noble Captain, you are welcome. You've not been a lodger of mine this year and a half! You know the custom sir. Garnish, Captain, garnish. Hand me down those fetters there. They'll fit as easy as a glove, and the nicest man in England might not be ashamed to wear them.[3]

Having been fleeced by the keepers, new arrivals were prey to further predation – at the hands of their fellows. John Howard condemned 'the cruel custom [which] obtains in most of our gaols, which is that of the prisoners demanding of a newcomer *Garnish*, footing, or (as it is called in some London jails) chummage'.

> 'Pay or strip', are the fatal words. I say *fatal*, for they are so to some, who having no money, are obliged to give up part of their scanty apparel, and then if they have no bedding or straw to sleep on, contract diseases which I have known to prove mortal.

He noted with satisfaction that in 1730 four inmates of the New prison were indicted for extracting money from a John Berrisford 'under the pretence of garnish', and, to deter others 'from the infamous and inhuman practice', they were sentenced to death.[4]

One of the main sources of profit for the gaolers came from the tap-room, the prison tuck-shop which sold tobacco, beer and spirits, especially gin which was known as 'Kill-Grief'. One keeper maintained that the more drink was available the better discipline would be, as 'when prisoners are drunk they tend to be docile and quite free of rioting'. Not all observers were so sanguine or complacent. In 1751 parliament interdicted the sale of 'spirituous liquors', and each prisoner was restricted to one bottle of wine or one quart of ale a day 'at the bar of the prison'. A parliamentary committee ruefully noted that this regulation 'little tends to promote sobriety and order'. Profiteering from the sale of alcohol which also tended to encourage consumption was also prohibited.[5] Doubts remained about how effective these measures were, especially in keeping out spirits. Where profits were

---

3   Act 1, scene 7.
4   Howard, I, pp.12f.
5   *Report from the Committee of the House of Commons on the State of the Gaols of the City of London*, 1814 (*EHD*, XI, pp.377f.).

to be made by the gaolers, pleasures to be had by the gaoled, and life made more tolerable for both, this was hardly surprising.

The day of first entry into any prison is always the worst. Time inures. The senses dull. The mind adapts. This is the truism that Defoe reiterates at length with respect to Newgate. As it was for Moll, so it must have been for her creator.

> 'Tis impossible to describe the terror of my mind, when I was first brought in ... the horrors of that dismal Place ... the hellish Noise, the Roaring, Swearing and Clamour, the Stench and Nastiness, and all the dreadful crowd of Afflicting things I saw there, joyn'd together to make the Place seem an Emblem of Hell itself, and a kind of Entrance into it.

Defoe received a similar but somewhat less severe sentence than William Fuller: three days in the pillory, a 200 mark fine, and 'to remain in prison till all be performed'. But there was to be no whipping. The public punishment was bad enough. Unlike Fuller, whose period in the pillory proved more injurious than the thirty-nine lashes in Bridewell, Defoe deflected the animus of the mob into amusement with his *Hymn to the Pillory*, and 'if he was pelted it was with flowers'.[6]

This would be the last fragrance he would enjoy for some time. In Newgate between July and November 1703 it was stench that he would smell. Stench would pervade his nostrils, noise penetrate his ears, fear populate his mind. Yet he, like any other, 'after the first Surprize was gone', acclimatised. Hell became 'natural' to him and he would soon come not to 'disturb [himself] about it'. Defoe observed that for prisoners 'Time, Necessity, and Conversing with the Wretches that are there Familiarizes the Place to them'; and 'how at last they become reconcil'd to that which at first was the greatest Dread upon their Spirits in the World, and are as impudently Cheerful and Merry in their Misery, as they were when out of it'. A favourite pastime was to stage mock trials where the judges tied white towels around their heads as wigs and spoke in language that made mockery of the courts. This was one of 'the Liberties of Newgate'.[7]

The sentiments Defoe attributed to Moll, the 'meer Newgate-Bird', the thief caged in Newgate, came from his own bitter experience:

6   Richard West, *The Life and Strange Surprising Adventures of Daniel Defoe* (London, 1997), p.83.

7   Bernard Mandeville, *An Enquiry into the Causes of the Frequent Executions at Tyburn* (London, 1725), p.17; Henry Fielding, *The Life of Mr Jonathan Wild the Great*, Folio edn (London, 1966), p.140.

> I can not say, as some do, this Devil is not so black, as he is painted; for indeed no Colours can represent the Place to the Life; not any Soul conceive aright of it, but those who have been Sufferers there: But how Hell should become by degrees so natural, and not only Tolerable, but even agreeable, is a thing Unintelligible, but by those who have Experienc'd it, as I have ... Conversing with such a Crew of Hell-Hounds as I was, which had the same common Operation upon me, as upon other People, I degenerated into Stone; I turn'd first Stupid and Senseless, then Brutish and Thoughtless, and at last raving Mad as any of them were; and in short I came as naturally pleas'd and easie with the Place, as if indeed I had been Born there.

Newgate's 'cold embrace' left an indelible impression. Defoe, like so many before and after him, was both changed and inspired by his prison sojourn. But before he would utilise his experiences in fiction, he would let them gestate.

On the second anniversary of his arrival into Newgate, Defoe, released so that his abilities could be used in government service, embarked on an extensive tour around England on behalf of his political masters. Having escaped the narrow confines of a London prison, he traversed, untrammelled, the wide spaces of the not yet united kingdom. During the subsequent debate over the Union he was sent to Scotland to inform his patrons and help facilitate the desired outcome. Again he travelled widely there, all fodder for his great *Tour Thro' the Whole Island of Great Britain* which he published between 1724 and 1727. The proliferation of prisons in London fascinated and appalled him. No other city in all Europe could compete. In the section on the capital he enumerated under public gaols twenty-three items including 'Five Night Prisons called Round-houses', and 'the Clink, formerly the prison to the Stews'. Alongside these he listed places of private detention, or 'tolerated prisons', including Bedlam, 'fifteen private mad-houses, three pest-houses', and 'one hundred and nineteen Sponging Houses' where debtors were held until their committal to prison, noting that all these

> private Houses of Confinement are pretended to be like little Purgatories, between Prison and Liberty, places of Advantage for the keeping of Prisoners at their own Request, till they can get Friends to deliver them and so avoid going into Public Prisons; tho' in some of them the Extortion is such, and the Accommodation so bad, that Men choose to be carried away directly.[8]

8   Defoe, I, p.356.

Defoe recognised that prisons could be the seed-bed of criminality, and the more there were, the greater the crop. He said of Jonathan Wild, the notorious 'thief-taker' and monstrous progenitor of Fagin, that he had in his employ seven thousand 'Newgate-Birds'. Wild himself would have agreed with Moll's mother that prison made thieves. Along with the renowned thief and thief-mistress, Mary Frith, the 'Moll Cut-purse' mentioned by Moll Flanders, Wild served as a model for Defoe's 'Mother Midnight', a recruiter and trainer of thieves and receiver and retailer of stolen goods. But, along with vice, redemption could also be found within Newgate's dark walls. Moll Flanders had been both born and reborn there. Abandoned at the age of six months, she was taken into the care of the parish, and, after traversing every depravity from incest, bigamy and prostitution to the capital crime of larceny, she ended up once more within the walls of Newgate. In the shadow of the gallows, it became the gateway to life. Moll underwent a spiritual awakening and, having been transported to the isles of the blessed, through her faith and self-reliance, was born anew in 'Virginia' to innocence and respectability at the last. Her life was a moral fable; a fiction of progression from initial deprivation, through degeneration, to final regeneration.

Defoe also penned short, real-life moral fables about the lives of the two most notorious inmates of Newgate: Jack Sheppard and Jonathan Wild. Sheppard was the classic romantic rogue, hard to like in person, but hard not to admire for his daring escapades; Wild the infamous blackguard and murderous hypocrite of whom nothing good could or would be said. Their lives of crime would overlap, and both would endure the same fate on 'Tyburn's fatal tree'. How they lived in popular memory was to be very different.

Sheppard was born in Spitalfields in 1702. A cheeky, cheerful cockney, he was a caricature criminal, an able but idle apprentice, seduced into crime, so he said, by his assignation with a pickpocket, the dissolute Edgware Bess. Given that his brother had been in Newgate and had introduced him to some of his thieving friends, she was not the first or only bad influence upon him.

The couple lived by theft, burglary and robbery. In May 1724 they were apprehended and placed in heavy irons in the Newgate ward, the most secure area of New Prison, Clerkenwell, pending transfer to Newgate itself. Sheppard was a known escape risk. In February he had been arrested in the Seven Dials, a notorious thieves' 'rookery' near Covent Garden. Confined overnight on the uppermost floor of St Giles's Roundhouse – a temporary place of detention for suspected criminals – he escaped within two hours.

With only the help of a razor, a piece of broken chair, and a sheet and blanket, he broke open its roof, lowered himself into the churchyard and got away. Somewhere more secure was needed to hold this desperado. But even the 'safest apartment' in New Prison was not enough to hold Sheppard. With implements brought in by visitors he managed to saw off his fetters, dislodge the bars from the window, and lower both Bess and himself to the ground, again using a sheet. They had escaped into the yard of the contiguous Clerkenwell bridewell. Undaunted, he improvised a scaling ladder to get over the twenty-two-foot wall and both got away. So miraculous was their escape considered that the broken chains and bars were kept at New Prison 'to testify and preserve the memory of this extraordinary villain'.[9]

Enter Wild, the 'thief-taker'. In July he was employed by one of Sheppard's victims to catch the thief. This would prove no problem as Wild knew Sheppard well, possibly having encouraged, and profited by, the latter's 'villainies'. But now Sheppard was a rival. Wild soon seized Bess in a brandy shop near Temple Bar and 'she being much terrified, discovered where Sheppard was'. He was taken back to New Prison and confined in the dungeon and was then committed to Newgate to await trial. Acquitted of two matters, he was finally convicted of housebreaking and sentenced to die.[10] In the condemned hold he was visited by Bess and another girl. With their help he dislodged a bar in the door leading from his cell into the lodge, and squeezed through. Accompanying the two girls and wearing a woman's cloak that they had brought in, he walked out of the prison and away. For her efforts Bess was apprehended by Wild and put in the Poultry compter. The Newgate keepers were stigmatised and accused of taking bribes.

They spared no effort to regain the cause of their embarrassment. A man-hunt ensued, and after ten days they succeeded in retaking Sheppard. They would take no chances with him. He was placed in the 'Castle', a supposedly escape-proof strong-room half-way up the gatehouse, and chained to the floor with two large iron staples. He was subjected to repeated searches. A small file was found in his Bible, and two files, a hammer and a chisel in the rushes of a chair. He told Mr Wagstaffe, the chaplain, that 'one file's worth all the Bibles in the world'. He improvised and unpicked the padlock with a nail. For want of a file, however, he could not get past the bars in the chimney. Nonetheless, his example inspired the felons on the Common side of Newgate who sawed off their fetters and cut through

---

9   *A History of the Remarkable Life of Jack Sheppard* (1724), in Richard Holmes, *Defoe on Sheppard and Wild* (London, 2004), p.11. Its attribution to Defoe is uncertain.
10   *Ibid.*, pp.14ff.

several iron bars, muffling their efforts by singing and shouting. They too were discovered and their designs frustrated.

Sheppard, however, was not finished. On the night of 15 October, taking advantage of the uproar occasioned the previous day by a murderous attack on Wild by another prisoner whom he had betrayed, he again picked the padlock, took an iron bar out of the chimney and broke through the 'Castle' into another strong-room. He forced six barred doors, gained the roof of the tower and lowered himself down with a blanket. ''Tis questioned whether fifty pounds will repair the damage done to the jail.' He became the talk of the town. The papers and populace loved the 'frolicsome and desperate adventures of the famous house-breaker and gaol-breaker', and his cocking a snook at the authorities. Not so the authorities. Mr Austin, the keeper of Newgate, was not gratified to receive a missive from his erstwhile charge apologising for the loss of the gaoler's irons. So astounding was this third 'miraculous' escape that 'the only answer is ... that the Devil came in person and assisted him'.[11]

Demonic assistance did not last long. Ten days later his luck finally ran out. He was found drunk, arrested, and placed under constant watch in the Middle Stone Room next to the 'Castle'. It was not just his guards who kept watch: all London wanted to see him. He was a celebrity. Hundreds of visitors besieged his cell paying the eager turnkeys 3s 6d as the cost of admission. Many of them gave money to Sheppard, which he passed to prisoners more needy than himself. Several clergymen – 'Gingerbread Fellows', as Sheppard called them – attended on him, intent on saving his soul or at least getting titbits out of him for their moralising tracts. Sir James Thornhill, Hogarth's father-in-law and serjeant-painter to George I, sketched him for a portrait, and even Hogarth himself may have paid his respects. The king ordered two prints of this 'martyr in mezzotint', showing the manner of him being chained to the floor.[12] James Figg, the prize-fighter, was another famous visitor. Despite his frenetic social life Sheppard managed to find time to give an account of his life to 'Applebee's Man', the ever-assiduous and opportunistic Daniel Defoe.[13]

It was a life Sheppard was not anxious to renounce and he took the chance on being produced in court to establish his identity of pleading for

11 *London Journal*, 7 (November 1724); Holmes, *op. cit.*, p.36.

12 Jenny Uglow, *Hogarth: A Life and a World* (London, 1997), pp.103f. The portrait does not survive but a mezzotint engraving does.

13 *A Narrative of all the Robberies, Escapes, etc of Jack Sheppard* (1724), in Holmes, *op. cit.*, pp.47–68. John Applebee was a publisher who had bought the rights to Sheppard's confessional and 'dying speech'.

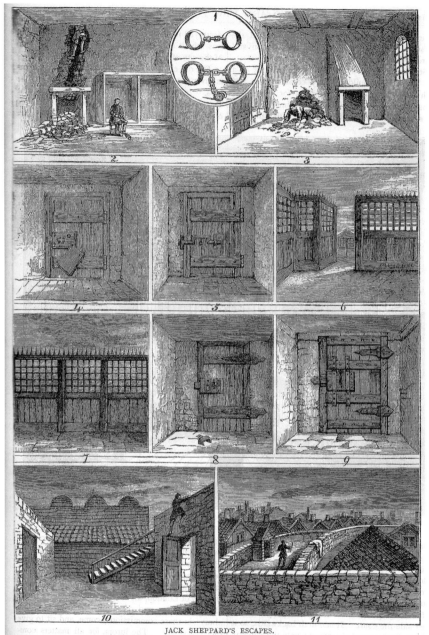

JACK SHEPPARD'S ESCAPES.

1. Handcuffs and Feetlocks, and Padlock to Ground.   2. Cell over the Castle, Jack Sheppard fastened to the floor. Climbing up the Chimney, where he found a bar of iron.   3. Red Room over the Castle, into which he got out of the Chimney.   4. Door of the Red Room, the lock of which he put back.   5. Door of the Entry between the Red Room and the Chapel.   6. Door going into the Chapel, which he burst open.   7. Door going out of the Chapel towards the Leads.   8. Door with a Spring Lock, which he opened.   9. Door over the same Passage.   10. The Lower Leads.   11. The Higher Leads, the walls of which he got over, and descended by the staircase off the roof of a turner's house into the street.

5. The ingenuity of the 'Cockney Sparrow'

clemency on the grounds that he had informed on all his accomplices. His plea fell on deaf ears, and his cause was not helped when he implicated God Almighty as the sole abetter of his 'miraculous' escapes. Sheppard, as usual, resorted to self-help. A final bid for freedom, on the way to the gallows, was frustrated when a turnkey found a pen-knife concealed in his pocket. The game was finally up and the twenty-two-year-old desperado would finally swing. Before a large and admiring crowd he was 'launched into eternity' on Monday 16 November 1724. Sheppard died well, and Defoe helped deify him, the ghosted 'autobiography' being available for sale at the gallows. His apotheosis came later in the year when Drury Lane put on a pantomime, 'Harlequin Sheppard'. He had become a popular hero, a lovable rogue. In reality he was a vicious brigand who would betray his friends and accomplices, and demeaningly plead for his own life. All that was forgotten by a public enchanted by the bravado and dash of this 'London Legend', this 'Cockney Sparrow', and by his extraordinary escapes which had made mockery of the authorities. He had lived fast and died young, and he had lived and he had laughed and he had loved. Better such a short but full life ending on the gallows, than a long, dull, drab, dreary existence ending in the gutter.

Defoe's only half-concealed admiration of Sheppard did not extend to his nemesis, that 'infamous creature', Jonathan Wild, whose 'every step was criminal'. He ran gangs who stole goods and he then purported to find and return them to the losers for a reward. He sacrificed men of his who displeased him or when justice needed propitiation. The term 'double-cross' comes from his meticulous marking in his ledger of two 'x's next to the name of the person he had betrayed. Thus he induced others into crime and ensured some would die for his, as well as their own, sins. He was a public detective and a private thief:

> By detecting some criminals he assumed a kind of power to protect others ... he did the first publicly and the last privately ... [and] thought his being useful in the first would protect him in being criminal in the last; but here he was ... mistaken and fell into a snare which all his pretended merit could not deliver him from.[14]

A Wolverhampton man, Wild was born in 1683 and came to London in his mid-twenties to seek his fortune. He lived beyond his means, and soon got

---

[14] *The True and Genuine Account of the Life and Actions of the late Jonathan Wild* (1725), in Holmes, *op. cit.*, pp.69–117.

into debt with at least five creditors. At their instigation he ended up in the Wood Street compter in March 1710.

By the eighteenth century the compter, in addition to some four hundred debtors, held all those arrested in the City prior to their being admitted into Newgate, as well as 'rats' – drunks, street-walkers, street-children, and other 'nuisances' picked up by City marshals or the Watch. There was no attempt to separate the inmates, debtors from criminals, or children from adults. It was a fertile nursery for criminality. Like other gaols it was privately run, office-holders buying their position. To recoup their costs and make a profit, the keepers and their turnkeys, known in the argot as 'Quod-Culls', exploited those in their charge, charging fees for basic necessities and little luxuries. An indication of how much could be gained from this recourse in Wild's day is the fact that in 1716 the keeper of Newgate, William Pitt, was estimated to have made £1,000 a month.

With no friends to help him, and no money, Wild was put on the Common side where initially he 'fared badly', possibly ending up in the 'Hole', crammed in with some seventy others into a space thirty-five feet long, fifteen feet wide and twelve feet high. There was little light, and little air. It was cold and wet, with up to a foot of water on the floor. Rats scurried and lice thrived in such surroundings. Human beings were lucky to survive.

After two years, by ingratiating himself with the keepers, who employed privileged inmates as 'partners' to assist them, Wild got 'the liberty of the gate', becoming a trustee who checked in the new arrivals at night, and assisted the 'Javelin Men', as the gaolers were called, in guarding and escorting them to the magistrate the following morning. Wild himself looked back on his time in the compter as his introduction into the world of crime. He learnt much of the ways of criminals and made many underworld contacts. One such was 'a jade of some fame', Mary Milliner or Molyneux,[15] the archetypal *femme fatale* who recruited him into her own gang of 'thieves and whores', and led him deep into the London underworld. Taking advantage of an Act of parliament for 'the Relief of Insolvent Debtors' which became law in September 1712, Wild petitioned for his 'deliverance', and secured his release in December. He would never get into debt again. Indeed he would become a man of substance.[16]

---

[15] Gerald Howson, *Thief-Taker General* (London, 1970), p.18.

[16] Despite this Act, insolvent debtors could be immured for years. In 1761 Millicent Rasby died in York castle having spent thirty-eight years there for debt, and she was far from the only example (A.W. Twyford and Arthur Griffiths, *Records of York Castle* (London, 1880), p.119).

He moved in with Mary and quickly assimilated all that she could teach. He learnt also from a fellow Wolverhamptonian, Charles Hitchen, who as the under-marshal of the City was a regular visitor to the compter as well as being a well-known recoverer of stolen goods and 'thief-taker'. He was also a thief-recruiter, who asked Wild to be his assistant in his enterprise. Wild soon realised that it was much safer and more profitable to run gangs than to run with them. Having learnt the trade, he set up on his own. At arm's length he received stolen goods, and, purporting to be acting as an honest broker, set up a lost property office in a tavern in a lane called Little Old Bailey, and advertised his services for their restitution. For his endeavours a retaining fee was exacted. When the items were returned, their owners gratefully, or grudgingly, paid a finder's fee. His reputation for integrity was enhanced when he gave up 'every now and then, one or two of his clients to the gallows', proclaiming all the while 'his own credit in bringing offenders to justice'. What incensed Defoe most was that Wild under the guise of charity had corrupted street-children and exploited them and then consigned them to the gallows when they had served their use. Those adults most liable to be sacrificed were those who had crossed him or double-crossed him or posed as rivals. He also fabricated evidence, or induced accomplices to testify, against those whom he had lured into 'the thieving trade', and then 'detected'. As a result many malefactors went to the gallows, but he had murdered them.[17]

Over-confident, over-greedy, the gangster over-reached himself, continuing in his trade even after it had been outlawed by parliament. By a clause inserted into the 1718 Transportation Act it became a felony to receive payment for returning stolen goods without at the same time arresting the thief and giving evidence against him. This clause became known as the 'Jonathan Wild Act'. The provisions were not put into effect for a further two years, and there were loopholes in the legislation. Wild continued in his wicked ways.

Eventually justice – or at least retribution – caught up with him. He had made many enemies. He was increasingly brazen. And he had done for Sheppard. As Sheppard's reputation was soaring across the firmament, Wild's star was crashing to earth. He was vulnerable. On 15 February 1725 he was arrested on a holding charge of receiving stolen goods and was committed to Newgate prison, detained under a warrant denouncing him as the 'Head or Director' of a 'Corporation of Thieves', the very 'Moriarty of crime'.[18]

---

[17] Holmes, *op. cit.*, pp.89f.,110.
[18] Conan Doyle made this comparison.

Shaken, but undeterred, he carried on his business from Newgate, which proved 'a castle very far from being an improper or misbecoming habitation for any great man whatever'.[19] He had wealth enough to secure a single cell, and he employed one or two servants to tend to his needs. He received visitors, including 'Applebee's Man' who sought biographical information. One visitor came by invitation and on business. On 10 March a Mrs Stetham arrived, bringing ten guineas with her. Her lace had been stolen and Wild had 'found' it for her. By taking the money from her he had played into the hands of his persecutors. Tried on Saturday 15 May, when several of his confederates gave evidence against him, he was convicted of receiving stolen goods under the 'Jonathan Wild Act', and sentenced to death.

Wild, like so many of those he had 'detected', ended up in the condemned hold 'under the greatest Horrors and Agonies of Mind'. There he was prepared for 'the approaching Change' by the ministration of the Revd Mr Nicholson, Lecturer of St Sepulchre's. The cleric admonished him that 'he ought to have taken Warning when he was first committed Prisoner to the Compter, where he should have observed the Misery of vicious People, instead of learning their Ways ... and afterwards associating with them'. For fear of the abuse he would receive at the hands of the other prisoners or spectators, Wild refused to attend chapel at all, not even on the day before his execution. Those 300 or 400 people who had paid handsomely to be admitted to Newgate to gaze on the fallen thief-taker, were sorely disappointed.

On 24 May, self-drugged with laudanum, and crying, Wild was taken from Newgate to Tyburn, under an escort of his old comrades, the 'Javelin Men', jeering crowds attending him all the while. He died badly and to the execrations of the mob, but he found a grim sort of immortality in Henry Fielding's biographical novel and as Mr Peachum[20] – alongside Sheppard's MacHeath – in *The Beggar's Opera*, the effervescent and wildly popular 'Newgate Pastoral, set among the whores and thieves there', written two years after Wild's execution by an acquaintance of his from happier days, John Gay.[21]

---

19 Fielding, *op. cit.*, p.132.

20 The name 'Peachum' derives from 'impeach', to accuse.

21 Wild's notoriety, and Sheppard's allure, lived on long in art and literature. Hogarth painted the climactic and comedic scene in Newgate. In 1743 Fielding, following in Gay's vein of satirising Walpole and comparing the corrupt to the criminal, produced his ironical *Life of Jonathan Wild the Great*. Brecht continued this trend into the twentieth century with his 1928 *Threepenny Opera*, a 'socialist' rehash of Gay's satire. Dickens based aspects of Fagin on Wild and of the Artful Dodger on Sheppard.

Defoe died in 1731. Appropriately he was buried in Bunhill Fields, alongside that other Puritan 'jail-bird' and writer, John Bunyan.[22] By the time of his death, Defoe's literary output had made him the most popular writer on crime and criminals in the land, his works rivalling even the pot-boilers produced by the Ordinaries of Newgate who attended – or tormented – those condemned to die.

[22] The two not only shared a Puritan heritage, but were coupled by Robert Louis Stevenson as the two modern writers who left an indelible imaginative impact.

CHAPTER 9

The Ordinary and Extra-Ordinary

There are six men to be hanged, one of whom has a wife near her
confinement, also condemned, and several young children. Since the
awful report has come down, he has become quite mad, from horror
of mind. A strait waistcoat could not keep him within bounds – he had
just bitten the turnkey, I saw the man come out with his hand bleeding,
as I passed the cell.

Elizabeth Fry

The law locks up the man or woman
Who steals the goose off the common
But leaves the greater villain loose
Who steals the common from the goose.
The law demands that we atone
When we take things we do not own
But leaves the lords and ladies fine
Who takes things that are yours and mine.

Seventeenth- or eighteenth-century ballad

As the eighteenth century wore on, and as capital statutes proliferated,
blossoming into what became known as the Bloody Code, more and
more prisoners in Newgate would be awaiting trial for crimes for which
the punishment was death, and more and more spent their last days in the
condemned cell. Judges in black caps passed the death sentence; chaplains
ministered to the doomed; hangmen duly dispatched them; governors kept
busts of their more prominent executees as macabre trophies.[1]

In the few days between sentence and execution the condemned were
left to the tender care of the Newgate chaplain, the 'ordinary' or 'the great
bishop of the cells' as he was called. The title 'ordinary' dates from 1544
when one of the four chaplains at St Bartholomew's Hospital was delegated
to 'visit all the poor and miserable captives ... and minister unto them such
ordinary service at time convenient, as is appointed by the King's majesty'.[2]
In 1620 the first resident ordinary was appointed. Newgate was unusual in

---

[1] In 1937 when Major Grew was posted to Durham prison he found to his horror the
casts of five executed criminals stored in a cupboard (Grew, p.99; Clayton, p.30).

[2] Norman Moore, *The History of St Bartholomew's Hospital* (London, 1918), II, p.152.

Pugin & Rowlandson, delt. et sculpt

NEWGATE
CHAPEL.

6. The condemned sermon in Newgate chapel, a coffin prominently displayed

this provision. It was not until an Act of 1773 that justices of the peace were permitted, but not compelled, to appoint chaplains to their prisons and to pay them from the local rates, and not until 1824 that they had to. Before that, county gaols and town lock-ups made do with such visitations as the local clergy cared to make. Of these, Dissenters were the most dedicated and diligent.

A primary function of the prison chaplain was inducing repentance and, most importantly, getting a confession from the condemned. Moll observed that when the Newgate ordinary visited her, 'all his Divinity run upon Confessing my Crime ... without which he told me God would never forgive me; and he said so little to the purpose, that I had no manner of Consolation from him'. Later she found

> the poor Creature preaching Confession and Repentance to me in the morning ... drunk with Brandy and Spirits by Noon: this had something in it so shocking that I began to Nauseate the Man more than his work, and his Work too by degrees, for the sake of the Man; so that I desir'd him to trouble me no more.[3]

---

3 This portrait may have been based on Paul Lorraine, the ordinary who died in October 1719.

Prison chaplains, such as the ordinary encountered by Moll, both justified the penalty imposed by the court and gave religious sanction to the proceedings. The State with the imprimatur of the Established Church was carrying out what, after all, was a sentence of Scripture: 'whoso sheddeth man's blood, by man shall his blood be shed' (Genesis 9:6). But the Bloody Code went far further than that. Instead of an eye for an eye, the law, in deference to deterrence, demanded death for any number of property offences. Thus many saw this trinity of judge, chaplain and hangman, the chief participants in this drama of death, in a far from hallowed light. Edward Gibbon Wakefield, the cousin of Elizabeth Fry, and an abolitionist pamphleteer, lampooned them as business partners who imposed, sanctified and performed monstrous punishments for minor offences. The judge provided 'the animals for the slaughter', and the ordinary 'broke their hearts, so that they might stand quiet without kicking or bellowing' while Jack Ketch 'butchered them'.[4] Wakefield had himself served a three-year stretch in Newgate which he considered 'the very best place to form a second opinion on the efficacy of capital punishment'. There he chronicled aspects of the existence of the condemned. 'A batch of convicts [was] sentenced to death every six weeks in London' for crimes other than murder. The average age was twenty. Not all would perish, and in the condemned cell they would await the decision of the Privy Council. When the result of the lottery was known, the condemned were assembled together and made to kneel while the chaplain communicated to each his fate. Then over the five to seven days the unspared had left to live the penitential work would really begin:

> As soon as a man is ordered for execution, the great increase of his danger produces extraordinary exertions on the part of those who administer the offices of religion to the inmates of Newgate ... the ordinary and his assistants visit the press-yard frequently every day, and indeed almost live with the condemned men, exhorting them to repentance, prayer, and faith.[5]

Before the sacrifice itself, a purificatory liturgy had to be performed. On the Sunday prior to the execution, a special service was held in the chapel. The ordinary preached the condemned sermon, an opportunity to appal those about to die and admonish those who had so far escaped the noose.

---

4   Edward Gibbon Wakefield, *The Hangman and the Judge or a Letter from Jack Ketch to Mr Justice Alderson* (London, 1833), p.2. Jack Ketch was a notoriously brutal hangman in the reign of Charles II whose name was later used of hangmen in general.

5   Wakefield, *Facts Relating to the Punishment of Death in the Metropolis* (London, 1832), pp.155f., 173.

A coffin was placed on a table in full view of the condemned as a *memento mori*. Fashionable visitors were eager to join the congregation. Not all the flock would be decorous. Felons would cut the tassels off the pulpit cushions, and, during the sermon, shout abuse at the preacher. At midnight the bellman of the nearby St Sepulchre's church would disturb the repose of those awaiting execution by tolling the salvaged bell twelve times with double strokes, in accordance with Robert Dow's charitable bequest, while singing the comforting lines:

> All you that in the condemn'd hold do lie,
>   Prepare you for tomorrow you shall die.
> Watch all, and pray, the hour is drawing near,
>   That you before the Almighty must appear.
> Examine well yourselves, in time repent,
>   That you may not t'eternal flames be sent.
> And when St Sepulchre's bell tomorrow tolls,
>   The Lord have mercy on your souls!
> Past twelve o'clock.[6]

For much of the eighteenth century such care was not bestowed on those convicted of murder. Under the Murder Act of 1752 they were rushed to their doom within forty-eight hours of being sentenced. The offices of religion were denied them; if a chaplain visited he did so by stealth. They were led to the scaffold without any religious ceremonies. Not for them a Christian burial, as their corpses would end up publicly displayed on the gibbet or dissecting table.

Newgate chaplains came to be considered as 'an adjunct of the executioner' and it was generally thought that the 'main business of the ordinary [was] to break the spirits of capital convicts so that they might make no resistance to the hangman'.[7] It was also in their self-interest. Ordinaries were recruited from the lower fringes of the church and were not well remunerated. The sale of pamphlets containing the last speeches and confessions of the condemned which the ordinaries induced, and often penned, were an important additional source of income, and one they guarded jealously. In 1745 James Guthrie complained to the aldermen who supervised Newgate that John Applebee, the printer, had infringed his copyright by printing his own version of these macabre utterances.

Not all were venal and some were exceptional. One such, by all accounts, was Dr Brownlow Forde, ordinary from 1799 to 1814. He was a kindly and

---

6   BM Add. MSS. Francis Place Papers, 27,826, fol.14.
7   Wakefield, *Facts Relating to the Punishment of Death*, p.167.

effective minister, and got into trouble for his outspokenness. The noted reformer Basil Montagu, who had cooperated with him for many years in his work in Newgate, wrote a lengthy and persuasive apologia on his friend's behalf. Many prisoners when tended by such as these received their ministrations with gratitude and went to the gallows with resignation and fortitude. One woman, before her imminent execution, wrote to Elizabeth Fry expressing her gratitude to her for her ministration as well as to Horace Cotton, the ordinary, and to Benjamin Baker, another lay visitor.[8]

The ordinary was not the only source of divine solace. The condemned proved an irresistible magnet to Christian philanthropists, ordained or otherwise, who welcomed the opportunity to minister to prisoners *in extremis* with the marvellous possibility of bringing to salvation these most miserable of sinners. The Quaker, Elizabeth Fry, and the Methodist brothers, John and Charles Wesley, were among the most assiduous ministrants in Newgate. John echoed the views of them all when he wrote that of 'all the seats of woe on this side hell few, I suppose, exceed or even equal Newgate'.[9] The ordinaries did not always welcome these intrusions into their infernal regions. The inadequate or uncaring were threatened by the influx of inexhaustible evangelists; the venal feared rivalry for the rich rewards from published 'confessions'; the more dedicated found the approach of some 'enthusiasts' crass and insensitive. In the first category, John Taylor, in post from 1747 to 1755, tried unsuccessfully to obstruct the ingress of Silas Told, who had been introduced to prison work by John Wesley, and regularly attended Newgate.[10] The immediate effectiveness of Told's ministry and that of his mentor must have been a manifest and standing reproach. One who fell into the last category, Dr Forde, criticised the dissenting ministers who 'haunted the gaol', harassed and worried his flock, and even demanded entry into cells when he was ministering to the inmates.[11]

Some would resort to almost anything to get the desired result. It was by ruse that two visiting clergymen in 1810 induced 'contrition and repentance'

---

8   Fry, I, p.306. Cotton, who served in Newgate from 1814 to 1839, had tried in vain to end the practice of placing a coffin on a table in full view of the condemned during chapel services.

9   Letter to the Editor of *The London Chronicle*, 2 January 1761 (*The Letters of John Wesley*, ed. John Telford (London, 1931), IV, pp.84, 127). One 'region of horror' that did exceed it was Newgate in Bristol. John Wesley had preached both there and in Oxford castle, and dispensed money, clothes and food to poor prisoners in the Poultry compter and Whitechapel debtors' prison, so knew whereof he spoke.

10   Silas Told, *Life of Mr Silas Told Written by Himself* (London, 1786), p.177.

11   Basil Montagu, *An Inquiry into the Aspersions of the late Ordinary of Newgate, with some Observations upon Newgate and upon the Punishment of Death* (London, 1815), p.65.

in an obdurate child killer, Richard Faulkner, who was incarcerated in Norwich castle gaol. After all normal means of persuasion failed – and he had even threatened to murder them when they tried to minister to him – they dressed a little boy in the dead child's clothing and led him by twilight into the condemned cell. Faulkner, who was only fifteen himself, was so startled and terrified by the apparition that he broke into a cold sweat, begged the clergy to stay with him, confessed his crime and implored divine forgiveness. 'In this happy transition he remained' until his execution two days later.[12]

Fry was far from being alone among women in preparing the condemned for death. Saving the souls of the most wretched appealed to women of affluence and religious enthusiasm. Miss Richards, Miss Unwin and Miss Tomlinson worked a miracle of salvation on the distraught and inconsolable Mary Voce who, in Nottingham gaol, was awaiting execution for the murder of her child. After her condemnation at least two of the women were constantly with her. After hours of prayer, Mary suddenly pronounced that God had saved her, her prison had become her Bethel, and her fate was the happiest conceivable, a brand plucked from the burning.[13]

The ministrations of ardent young women, like those of their male colleagues, were more appreciated by the felon than by the chaplain. In 1832 a Miss Payne and Miss Owston decided to visit a young man called James Cook who had been sentenced to death for murder. They had read of the terrible case and began a correspondence with him, with the end of achieving 'this grievous sinner's conversion'. They sent him religious tracts including a little book of verse called 'Sunbeams'. He wrote back, his missive falling 'on the Holy Bible which lay open before my friend – she pushed it off the Book with horror, exclaiming "What! A dreadful murderer's letter on the Bible!"' But the letter invited them to visit him in Leicester gaol.

Armed 'with a new large Bible, having marked some hundreds of verses peculiarly suited to such a wretched criminal's case', they entered his cell. There, to their obvious surprise and pleasure, they found a youth 'of most interesting, handsome countenance, heavily ironed, leaning over "Sunbeams"'. Miss Payne assured him that one drop of Christ's blood would wash him clean, but first he had to repent, 'the first proof of which is, your

---

12   *The Complete Newgate Calender*, ed. J.L. Raynor and G.T. Cook (London, 1926), V, pp.62f.

13   *An account of the Experience and Happy death of Mary Voce, Bury and Norwich Post*, 25 November, 1801, reprinted as appendix 2 of the Penguin edition of George Eliot's *Adam Bede* (London, 2008), pp.589ff. This story provided the germ of the novel, and of her depiction of the condemned-cell contrition of Hetty Sorel.

own open and full confession of your crime. This is what I am most anxious to procure.'

> – I did confess when I was examined before the magistrates ...

She pressed him hard:

> – Yes, I did see it; but that confession was false; you know it was.

He remained silent. She earnestly continued:

> – Are you not wretched?
> – I don't enjoy myself as much as if I had nothing on my conscience, certainly.
> – Enjoy yourself! You know that there does not breathe in existence a more miserable creature than you are at this moment.

He was again silent.

Miss Payne's persistence paid off. A few days later he was 'much improved'. He prayed and then confessed to her in full. She consoled him with the thought that she believed him worthy of death, and through death, eternal life. Their sole desire was to be able to worship God with their young protégé, but the chaplain, Dr Fancourt, refused them permission to attend the communion service in the prison chapel. He would not let them further usurp his role. They had failed to observe the usual courtesies of asking his permission to visit prisoners in his care. They agreed to inform him of their intentions and went to see him.

> Alas! Instead of beholding the calm and unruffled meekness which shone forth so brilliantly in the character of the great pattern of all excellence, we were ushered into the presence of one whose age might have commanded respect, but whose irritability of temper was strikingly perceptible even after a few words had escaped our lips.

He said that the soul of the prisoner was admitted to his charge. This they doubted, firmly believing that they were the instruments chosen by God for Cook's conversion. He forbade their entry; they withstood him. The newspapers shared Fancourt's opposition. Five days after the hanging, a Leicester paper criticised Miss Payne for pampering 'the murderer with all sorts of delicacies'. The editor thought that 'three clergymen of the Established Church were quite sufficient to convince, if not convert, a murderer without the interference of females'. Along similar lines, *The Age of Sunday* found 'something infinitely disgusting in the interference of women in the case'. In contrast two evangelical clergymen who had witnessed the effect that they had had on Cook commended the women and their ministry.[14]

Though the parties might quarrel, these varied means of caring for the condemned served the interests of both State and Church. Confessions induced by subterfuge, cajolement or caress were an essential adjunct to the whole process of punishment in Georgian England and an essential prelude to penitence and salvation. The judge in the court and the minister in the cell were servants of both the temporal kingdom and the heavenly. Some, less charitably, saw them as Pilate and Caiaphas.

With the development of penal philosophy, with the greater involvement of the State in the prison estate, with every town and county vying with each other to be at the forefront of the new thinking, the role of the amateur evangelists would decline, while that of salaried prison chaplains would grow. Procuring penitence would become a profession.

Meanwhile, not only did the agents of execution displace the recipients as objects of execration, so too did the structure and symbols. The Bloody Code, protecting the property of the rich with the blood of the poor, was perceived to epitomise the partiality of a legal system designed not to uphold equity and justice but the injustice of a state controlled by men of money and standing. Prisons symbolised this injustice. They were the receptacles in which the poor were held by the rich, and those that were rebuilt and reordered in the eighteenth century to be more imposing and permanent came more and more to be seen as merely intimidatory and oppressive.

At least the prisons of the metropolis, bad as they were, were better regulated than any others. The Corporation of London took their responsibilities seriously. The main courts those prisons served were situated in Westminster, or, in the case of the Old Bailey, right beside Newgate. Although there was no prison department or inspectorate, supervision and surveillance, deficient as they were, were more obvious in the capital than elsewhere in the country. Elsewhere, as had been the case for centuries, chaos reigned. There was nothing approaching a national or even local 'prison system', but a medley of *ad hoc* arrangements, each county, and often each town within a county, going their own way. Not much had changed since medieval times. Any strong-room could be utilised as a lock-up. For instance in John Howard's time Wallingford's town gaol was accommodated under the council chamber, while Reading's consisted of two rooms in a

---

14   *Mrs Lachlan's Narrative of a Conversion of a Murderer in Letters addressed to a Clergyman* (London, 1832).

public house.[15] More permanent structures existed for the county. Anyone who paid for a concession could run them. To ensure a profit they would employ a minimal number of untrained turnkeys noted for their brawn rather than brain. Where money was to be made out of prisoners, money talked. Those with it could have a relatively untrammelled existence, although in the Reading county gaol they had to forgo keeping dogs or pigeons, and felons could share a bed with a debtor only with the latter's permission.[16] Those without lived in deplorable conditions, mired in filth, immured in exploitation.

Houses of correction were the only exception to this motley medley, as they had a reformatory purpose and county justices were responsible for their construction and operation, but as time went on even these institutions degenerated from their ideals and became largely indistinguishable from ordinary gaols. In 1750 Henry Fielding, who as chief magistrate in the metropolis had had many 'impudent and flagitious wretches' brought before him, all of whom had 'been acquainted with the discipline of Bridewell', opined that 'whatever these houses were designed to be, or whatever they first were ... they are at present, in general, no other than schools of vice, seminaries of idleness, and common bearers of nastiness and disease'.[17] Since vice and idleness were the main causes of crime, prisons should not be perpetuating them!

The infrequency of prisoner petitions and inmate insurrections suggests the occupants of gaols were in some measure reconciled to their habitat. For many poor inmates, conditions inside prison were little worse than outside, and in any case prisons were porous, discipline non-existent, and self-government the norm. It has been said that 'life in an eighteenth-century prison could be tumultuous, but it would be a mistake to confuse disorder with anarchy'.[18] Anarchic or not, prisons run by prisoners – not as some utopian commune, but for the benefit of bullies, could be just as bad as, or worse than, those run by venal keepers. People, however, became habituated to their circumstances and made the best of it. Keepers could be conned, bullies bribed, cohesive groups could grow for self-protection or the sharing of resources.

---

[15] Howard, I, pp.338ff.

[16] Peter Southerton, *The Story of a Prison* (Reading, 1975), p.13.

[17] *Inquiry into the Causes of the Late Increase of Robberies etc*, in *Works*, XIII (London, 1903), pp.71f.

[18] *OHP*, p.83.

But no one could escape the filth. Disease thrived in such insanitary conditions. Gaol fever continued to be a perennial problem. It was endemic. In 1759 it was estimated that each year a quarter of prisoners nationally died from typhus. They were not the only ones. In 1730, for instance, gaol fever spread from Dorchester gaol to the nearby assize, killing the judge, the sheriff and some jurymen.[19] Twenty years later in London, the Lord Mayor, two judges, an alderman and many others died of the fever when it spread from Newgate to the Old Bailey. Death was carried 'from the seat of guilt to the seat of justice, involving in one common catastrophe the violator and the upholder of the laws'.[20]

The evangelical revival inside and outside the Church of England directed spiritual energy and practical attention to the sources of misery and vice. As we have seen, philanthropists – many of whom were Dissenters and Quakers – began ministering to those in gaol. Their first-hand experience, and the conditions they found and deplored, led to the first moves for penal reform. In 1702 the Society for the Promotion of Christian Knowledge conducted an investigation into Newgate and the Marshalsea, listing abuses, condemning profiteering, and promoting the idea of keeping prisoners in separate cells. To discourage such wanton exploitation as that of William Pitt, the keeper of Newgate, profiting by several thousand pounds from the Jacobites incarcerated there, an Act of 1728 required gaolers to post a schedule of fees. At least prisoners would know the cost of their keep, even if it remained exorbitant: in 1736 the keeper of New Prison was charging a shilling daily for board and lodging, more than a day's wage for a labourer.[21] In 1751 the sale of liquor in prisons was forbidden, further curbing keepers' profits but removing prisoners' palliatives.

The first major parliamentary investigation came in 1729 when the Tory MP James Oglethorpe moved for the appointment of a select committee 'to inquire into the state of gaols of this kingdom'. Oglethorpe had a personal stake in penal reform. A friend of his, the architect Richard Castell, who had been committed to the Fleet for debt, refused to pay the warden's extortionate fees for airy lodging, and died as a result of being put in a smallpox-ridden 'sponging house'. Despite its ambitious remit, the committee quickly decided that it would only be possible to concentrate on London's main debtor prisons. Its members, under Oglethorpe's chairmanship, met daily, investigated

---

19 Arthur Griffiths, *Memorials of Millbank* (London, 1875), I, p.3.

20 Jeremy Bentham, *Panopticon Writings*, Verso edn, introduced by Miran Bozovic (London, 1995), pp.46f.

21 James Sharpe, *Dick Turpin: The Myth of the English Highwayman* (Bungay, 2004), p.131.

thoroughly, and made visits to the gaols, Hogarth capturing the moment when they interviewed the warden of the Fleet, Thomas Bambridge, amidst the squalor and filth of his prison.[22] Its report led to the well-publicised prosecution of Bambridge, for exploiting and ill-treating the debtors in his charge. Indignant and dedicated as the members of the committee were, except in the face of the most egregious exploitation, their effect was largely ephemeral, the monopoly of the keepers was undisturbed and debtors would continue to be treated like felons. For gaolers the only categorisation of prisoners that mattered was between those who could pay through the nose and those who could not. Fifty years were to elapse before parliament would begin to replace the contract system of prison management.[23]

As would later be the case, the aim of increasing the deterrent effect, security, and capacity of prisons trumped the amelioration of conditions, while rehabilitation was as yet not even an afterthought. 'A new architecture and landscape of authority were constructed in these years from the familiar and homely fabric of London.'[24] From 1767 a massive prison building programme began to replace the old, cramped lock-ups with large stone edifices designed to intimidate and overawe those held within as well as those walking without. Newgate, along with its adjacent court-house, the Old Bailey, was the first to undergo such a transformation. At a cost of £50,000, the celebrated architect, George Dance, replaced the gateway gaol with a massive stone keep. Other prisons followed. Between 1772 and 1775 New Prison was rebuilt at a cost of £3,500, its neighbouring house of correction was projected for a make-over, while the Surrey one was demolished and rebuilt at a cost of £2,682.

What transpired in the last quarter of the century was the creation of a large and stable prison population for the first time. Many of those incarcerated had not chosen a life of crime out of cupidity or vice but in preference to a life of abject poverty. Most were desperate, a few were desperadoes. Hundreds of villains and thousands of venial offenders were locked up for long periods in atrocious conditions and with time on their hands, and so a new culture of unrest and solidarity was created. Similarly those passing by these carceral citadels, especially those who might through the exigencies of a hard life end up in one of them themselves, viewed them not only as objects of terror but as symbols of hypocrisy and oppression. At

---

[22] Hogarth's father was confined for five years in the Fleet and as a child Hogarth must have lived within its precincts.

[23] John Bender, *Imagining the Penitentiary* (Chicago, 1987), pp.17f., 111ff.

[24] Ian Haywood and John Seed (eds), *The Gordon Riots* (Cambridge, 2012), p.187.

the end of the century as at the beginning, the moral of *The Beggar's Opera* held resonance.

First performed in January 1728, Gay's subversive burlesque depicts the criminal under-world as a reflection of the corrupt upper-world. As the Beggar states at the end of Act III, 'Through the whole piece you may observe such a similitude of manners in high and low life, that it is difficult to determine whether (in the fashionable vices) the fine gentlemen imitate the gentleman of the road, or the gentlemen of the road, the fine gentlemen.' The rogues in their cells in Newgate are more lovable and less culpable than the rogues in their seats in parliament. The main difference is not in what they are, but in how they are treated. Gay's 'most excellent moral' is an elegant and ironic inversion, showing that 'the lower sort of people have their vices in a degree as well as the rich: And that they are punish'd for them'. The greater criminals ruled the land; the lesser ended up in gaol or on the gallows. It was not fair.

For many ordinary Londoners prisons were the ultimate institutions of class distinction and the harshness and inequity of the law. This view was hardly new, but more held it. From the mid-eighteenth century the introduction of an elementary police force in the form of the Bow Street Runners, the rise of paid informants and thief-takers in securing convictions, the construction or reconstruction of prisons to hold more and more inmates for longer and longer periods, and the increasing imposition of the death penalty and of the public dissection of the hanged, hardened the perception that tyranny had supplanted justice.[25] Prisons incarnated popular disquiet. They held the desperately poor, many of whom would be condemned to death under the Bloody Code for trivial property offences committed out of dire need; they held others seduced into larceny by the prominent display in shops of luxury goods they could not dream of buying and by dwellings exuding an opulence they could scarcely imagine; and they held the indebted who, often through no fault of their own, had fallen on hard times and on hard creditors. They also held tough swaggering rogues whose numbers could and would swell any insurgency. They held, in short, those who had to peer through grates 'to polish the King's iron with their eyebrows'.[26] Unfairness bred resentment. Resentment bred unrest.

---

25 *Ibid.*, pp.185ff.

26 Peter Linebaugh gives detailed descriptions of the sort of offences for which those delivered from Newgate had been held, as well as the social background of their liberators (*The London Hanged* (London, 1991), pp.336–56).

CHAPTER 10

Gaol Delivery

As he went through Cold-Bath Fields he saw a solitary cell;
And the Devil was pleased, for it gave him a hint for improving
his prisons in Hell.

Samuel Taylor Coleridge

The universal destruction of the prisons was a vast project, but such
a one as was not altogether improbable to be a favourite scheme with
a lawless rabble.

Thomas Holcroft

Popular detestation of English prisons came to its climax in 1780, one of the last times when they were the direct targets of mob attack.[1] This was during the course of the anti-Catholic Gordon riots, which took place between two Fridays, the 2nd and 9th of June, and caused more damage to London in those few days than was done to Paris in the whole course of the French Revolution.

These citadels of justice – or of oppressive state power – were not alone in coming under attack, and Catholics were not the only objects of ire. There were other grievances mingling with prejudice, as well as soft and lucrative targets aplenty. Foreign embassies and their 'papist' chapels suffered, as did the Irish community whose chapels, schools and houses were all vulnerable. The Bank of England, the embodiment of capital, was another potential victim. The Old Bailey was badly damaged and plans were afoot to destroy the Inns of Court. Specific agents of the law were subjected to rough justice. The house of Sir John Fielding, the magistrate who examined the first rioters arrested and whose brother, Henry, had founded the Bow Street Runners, was besieged, as was that of the Chief Justice, Lord Mansfield,

---

[1] But not the last. In Bristol during the Reform Bill agitation of 1831 the New Gaol (opened in 1820 to replace the infamous Newgate), the Bridewell (where prisoners had cats put into their cells at night to stop the rats gnawing their feet) and Lawford's Gate bridewell would be attacked, breached and fired, and the imprisoned 'liberated'. The devastation would be reminiscent of London during the Gordon riots, the depredations compounded by the unwillingness of the officer commanding the troops to intervene (*The Bristol Riots: Their Causes, Progress and Consequences* by a Citizen [John Eagles] (Bristol, 1832), pp.99–110).

BURNING OF NEWGATE. *(From a Contemporary Print.)*

7. Gaol delivery, the firing of Newgate during the Gordon riots, 1780

whose singular lack of anti-Catholic bigotry made him the most prominent victim of the mob. The latter's property, undefended by the troops nearby, was completely destroyed and with it his vast and irreplaceable legal library. It was 'a martyrdom'.[2]

Prisons proved an irresistible magnet, incarnating popular disquiet. Newgate, the Fleet, Marshalsea, both compters, the King's Bench prison, New Prison, the Clink and the Tothill Fields bridewell in Westminster were all 'liberated' and several were destroyed. Such were the fruits of popular detestation. Newgate was top of the list, the most hated of all, the elaborate ornamentation of its facade mocking the squalor within, the use of leg-irons as a decorative motif on the windows being an abiding provocation. In

2 Ignatius Sancho, *Letters*, Penguin edn (London, 1998), nos.LXVIII, LXIX. As a black Briton, Ignatius Sancho revered Mansfield for his judgment in the Somerset Case. Sancho was owner of a grocery shop on Charles Street, Westminster. He has long been thought an important eyewitness of events but it has recently been argued that he obtained much of his material from news-sheets (Ian Haywood and John Seed (eds), *The Gordon Riots* (Cambridge, 2012), pp.144–61). Of course he did. In his letters he never asserts, although he may imply, that he witnessed all of the events he relates. Some of his news clearly comes from second-hand sources as he refers to 'public prints' as well as to 'meetings in council'. On the other hand, living as he did a stone's throw from parliament and 'in the midst of the most cruel and ridiculous confusion', he must have seen and heard some of what transpired. Curiosity and proximity dictated it. Other information would have come from gossiping with customers and friends.

addition, the prison was already being used to hold four of the rioters who had been arrested and committed there by the magistrates. Justice Hyde,[3] the foremost in making arrests, in the late afternoon of Tuesday 6 June read the proclamation in the Riot Act and ordered Horse Guards to enforce the order to disperse. In retaliation his house in St Martin's Street was burnt to the ground by a crowd led by a big young man conspicuous on a carthorse waving a black and red flag. James Jackson, as he was called, with a voice that 'boomed like the crack of doom', then rallied his followers with the cry 'A-hoy for Newgate'. They were intent on freeing 'their honest comrades' and as many others as they could.[4]

Graphic contemporary accounts exist of what befell the 'English Bastille'. The twenty-three-year-old William Blake was involved in the cataclysmic events that followed that evening. An innocent bystander, or so he claimed, he was drawn into the ferment as he was walking down Long Acre towards Great Queen Street. He encountered rioters, armed with hammers, crowbars, cutlasses and marlin-spikes, who swept him to the fore down Holborn towards Newgate and the Old Bailey. Henry Angelo, the fashionable fencing-instructor, was another curious spectator. He had been walking home after dining with friends when he encountered several groups of people running in the opposite direction who told him that they were going to burn Newgate. Following after them Angelo stopped at the corner of the narrow lane opposite the debtor's door until, for the cost of sixpence, he secured a place at an adjacent garret-window where he had a ring-side view of what was to befall.

Meanwhile, on nearby Snow Hill, John Glover, one of several blacks involved in the riots, was striking the cobblestones with a gun barrel and shouting 'Now Newgate!' Glover was a former slave who had become the servant of a lawyer. He was on an errand when he got caught up in the excitement to such an extent that he was one of those who led the way to the infamous gaol. Standing outside the door, he bellowed at its keeper, Richard Akerman: 'Damn you, open the gate or we will burn you down and have everybody out.' Akerman declined. Known for his humanity and the respectful way he treated his prisoners, and admired on account of how he had dealt with a fire that had broken out in the prison several years

---

3   In the primary and most of the secondary literature Hyde is called 'Justice', although erroneously this becomes 'Lord Justice' on page 6 of Haywood and Seed's introduction. He was not an assize judge but one of the magistrates who were called 'justices of the peace', and whose responsibility it was to read the Riot Act. J.P. De Castro in his index calls him 'William', but not in the text (*The Gordon Riots* (Oxford, 1926)).

4   Sancho, *op. cit.*, no.LXVII.

before, he politely but firmly replied that he was duty-bound to hold those committed to his charge.[5] His friend James Boswell contrasted his 'intrepid firmness' with 'the timidity and negligence of the magistracy' who failed to come to his aid.[6] Stones were thrown at his windows and he was forced to escape over the roof. It was like a siege. Rioting sailors gained ingress into Akerman's house by forcing the shutters and breaking the windows. The place was pillaged, the wine-cellar sequestered, and the conveniently combustible furniture deployed against the prison door. At the same time, while some of the besiegers assailed the entrance-gate of the prison with pickaxes and sledgehammers, others tried to scale its walls with grappling-hooks and ladders.[7]

Entry was gained by another expedient. The keys were eventually found in the ransacked house and when Francis Mockford, a waiter in a Westminster tavern, leeringly brandished them in front of the door, the gatekeeper meekly opened up.[8] Turnkeys were insulted as 'Akerman's thieves' but were not assaulted – indeed the rioters did not kill anyone in the course of the whole week. Buildings were demolished but lives were not lost, except in the repression. Akerman's home was put to flames and reduced to 'a mere shell of brickwork'. The fire spread from the house to the chapel, 'and from thence, with the assistance of the mob, all through the prison'.[9] The prisoners trapped within the two cell-wings shrieked in terror until they were freed by the mob, who clambered up the walls, tore the rafters from the roof, and lowered down ladders. Over a hundred prisoners, including a lucky three due to be hanged, were listed as having been 'delivered from the gaol at Newgate'.[10] Painted on the wall was a proclamation that the inmates had been freed by the authority of 'His Majesty, King Mob'. While

---

5   Christopher Hibbert, *King Mob* (London, 1958), pp.74f.

6   James Boswell, *Life of Dr Johnson*, Everyman edn (London, 1992), II, pp.297ff.

7   William Vincent [Thomas Holcroft], *A Plain and Succinct Narrative of the Late Riots and Disturbances in the Cities of London and Westminster and Borough of Southwark*, 3rd edn (London, 1780), p.27. A shoemaker's son and a radical, Holcroft as an aspiring writer adopted the learned persona of 'William Vincent, of Gray's Inn', under which name the work will be found in the bibliography.

8   Peter Linebaugh, *The London Hanged* (London, 1991), pp.345–9.

9   Vincent, *op. cit.*, p.27.

10   No writer on the subject agrees on the number, and sometimes it varies within the same book – Ian Gilmour is the classic example with three different figures throughout *Riots, Risings and Revolution: Governance and Violence in 18th Century England* (London, 1992). Estimates range from 100 to 300. Vincent, writing a contemporary but novelistic account based on newspaper reports, gives 300, as does Sancho, but this is a suspiciously round number and the same as the official estimate for the number of rioters killed during the whole week.

some 'captives marched out with all the honours of war, accompanied by a musical band of rattling fetters', the dramatist Frederick Reynolds saw others having to hobble or claw their way out, 'blaspheming and jumping in their chains', and being taken by their rescuers to the passage leading to Christ's Hospital, the Bluecoat school, where blacksmiths removed these impedimenta which were then held aloft in triumph.[11] Slaves were being emancipated, their leg-irons were being smote asunder and the cage that had held them was being dismantled by iconoclasts. Flames banished the shadows cast by this edifice of fear, fire purged it of suffering, and awful justice had finally entered its portals.

The 'sublime spectacle' of this iconoclastic carnival could easily be demonised.[12] Reynolds graphically described how 'the thundering descent of huge pieces of building, the deafening clangour of red-hot iron bars, striking in terrible concussion the pavement below, and the loud triumphant yells and shouts of the demoniac assailants on each new success, formed an awful and terrific scene'.[13] The destruction of Troy, the fall of Babylon, Armageddon – no analogy was too extreme for those struggling to express the enormity of it all.

George Crabbe, then twenty-six, was another aspirant poet who witnessed 'this new species of gaol delivery', and wrestled with superlatives. He related how he saw 'twelve women and eight men ascend from their confinement to the open air' and others released from the debtors' prison, the doors of which were forced and fired. In apocalyptic terms he described the hellish appearance of the rioters rescuing prisoners from 'the volcano ... rolled in black smoke mixed with sudden bursts of fire – like Milton's infernals who were as familiar with flame as with each other'. 'Orpheus himself' had no 'more courage or better luck'.[14] By midnight it was over. The prison was left a mere shell, its thick walls alone still standing, and with flames and smoke still 'towering to the clouds', as Lady Erskine recorded.[15] A few hours later Crabbe returned to the scene and found Newgate, once 'very large, strong and beautiful ... open to all; anyone might get in, and what was never the case before, anyone might get out'. He did both.

He was not alone. Dr Burney 'saw the ruins of Newgate, where everyone went in and out as freely as they walk under the Piazzas in Covent Garden'.

---

11 Angelo and Reynolds quoted in De Castro, *op. cit.*, pp.89–92; E.G. O'Donoghue, *Bridewell Hospital* (London, 1923 and 1929), II, p.204.

12 Haywood and Seed, *op. cit.*, pp.125f.

13 De Castro, *op. cit.*, p.91.

14 De Castro, *op. cit.*, pp.91f.; George Crabbe, *Poetical Works* (London, 1884), I, p.83.

15 Hibbert, *op. cit.*, p.80.

Another eminent spectator was Dr Samuel Johnson. He and his friend, Dr Scott, went on an early morning stroll to see the devastation wrought. They observed hundreds of others doing likewise. At 8 am the fire was yet smouldering, as he told Mrs Thrale, and he noticed 'the Protestants plundering the sessions-house at the Old Bailey, working at leisure, in full security, without sentinels, without trepidation, as men lawfully employed in full day'.[16] It is hardly surprising that popular prints produced in the aftermath of the riots concentrated so heavily on the drama of Newgate.[17] So too, later, would Charles Dickens in *Barnaby Rudge*.

Benjamin Franklin, whose country was at war for independence from a Britain governed by arrogance, expressed ironic surprise that instead of replacing the thieves and robbers they had turned out of Newgate 'with an equal number of plunderers of the public which they might easily have found among the Members of Parliament, they burnt the building'.[18] An explanation for this lies in the trial testimony of 'Mad Tom' Haycock who, when asked by his judges why he had participated, said simply: 'the Cause'. Not much enlightened, they asked what the cause was to which he referred, fearing it might be that of Wat Tyler or Jack Cade, the leaders of major revolts during which prisons had been sacked as a precursor to overthrowing the established order. Without setting himself in this historical continuum, Haycock simply and starkly explained his motivation: 'there should not be a prison standing on the morrow in London'.[19]

He had nearly got his wish. Some of the Newgate incendiaries were far from sated. Aiming to 'release all the prisoners in the metropolis', with 'infernal humanity' they sent word to the public prisons at what time they 'might expect enlargement'.[20] Bridewell was spared. Some of its officials could see from its upper windows all that was happening to Newgate and feared the worst. For reasons not entirely clear their fears proved unfounded, as although some rioters broke in and freed those held there they were somehow dissuaded from their destructive intent. Shortly thereafter the South Hants regiment provided a garrison and ensured its safety.[21] Other prisons

---

16 Boswell, *op. cit.*, II, p.296; De Castro asserts that later that day nearly a hundred rioters, attempting to fire the cells at Newgate, were apprehended by a party of soldiers (*op. cit.*, pp.123, 157).

17 Haywood and Seed, *op. cit.*, p.118.

18 De Castro, *op. cit.*, pp.224f.

19 Linebaugh, *op. cit.*, p.347. Two of MacHeath's gang were called Wat and Robin, recalling medieval anti-establishment heroes.

20 Holcroft, *op. cit.*, p.30.

21 O'Donoghue, *op. cit.*, II, pp.205ff.

were not so fortunate. Next on the list were the Clerkenwell bridewell as well as the adjacent New Prison which served as an overflow for Newgate. The former's doors were forced with such ease and the inmates released that the rioters did not bother to burn the building but went on to the latter, which proved an even easier 'delivery' as the terrified gaolers had already thrown open the gates. Lady Anne Erskine, the sister of the famous advocate who would defend Gordon himself, lived in Clerkenwell and could hear 'the mob ... knocking the irons off the prisoners'.[22] Leaving the prison was one thing, entering another. The keeper stood his ground, with a blunderbuss in his hand, warning that 'as many as will may enter but none may return alive'. Why bother to overcome such stout defiance? Why risk bloodshed?

On to the Fleet for 'another gaol delivery', Lady Erskine heard them say. At 1 am on Wednesday 7 June, at the first demand, the great doors of the debtors' prison were pulled back on their hinges by terrified turnkeys. The structure itself was temporarily spared as some of its long-term inmates had no wish to be liberated in the middle of the night and asked 'the compassionate mob' for time to gather their belongings together and find alternative accommodation. It was but a reprieve. Later, when the prisoners had been 'employed all day in removing their goods, preparatory to its being burnt in the evening', accelerants were poured along the floor of the gallery and were set alight.[23] Rioters even tried to push a fire engine belonging to the Royal Exchange Fire Insurance Office into the conflagration. The Fleet burned. A similar fate would befall the Marshalsea, the Clink and the Wood Street compter.[24] Forcible collections were made 'for the poor prisoners'.

The first fatalities occurred at the Poultry compter when three of the crowd were shot dead by troops. The survivors withdrew, but threatened to return with reinforcements. Reluctant to see a pitched battle so close to the Mansion House, the Lord Mayor ordered that prisoners, including rioters held in the compter, be released. The following day, further casualties were occasioned when the military shot or sabred several rioters who had returned to the Fleet to loot or carry the destruction to houses nearby.[25]

To return to 7 June, at about 6 pm Henry Angelo was taking a post-prandial stroll to Charing Cross. Hearing that the King's Bench was in flames and 'I not there!', he 'soon hurried away, and arrived near the obelisk in St George's Fields, the space then before the gaol being quite open with

---

[22] De Castro, *op. cit.*, p.107.
[23] Holcroft, *op. cit.*, p.57; De Castro, *op. cit.*, p.137.
[24] The Clink was never rebuilt. On its site is the Clink Museum.
[25] De Castro, *op. cit.*, pp.121, 154–61.

no houses'. There he gazed for a while on this after-dinner entertainment and 'seeing the flames and smoke from the windows along the high wall' it appeared to him 'like the huge hulk of a man-of-war, dismasted, on fire'. Another pyrophile was Nathaniel Wraxall who with three friends set out from Holborn at 9 pm 'to view the scene' at the Fleet. They could not get very near 'for the showers of sparks and pieces of flaming wood which came falling down' around them.[26] At least the City, rebuilt after the last comparable calamity, the Great Fire of 1666, was not consumed. Damage was extensive but controlled. Fire engines were allowed to do their job, except on buildings specifically designated for destruction, the prisons above all.

Prisoners spilled onto the streets. Bridewell disgorged 119 of them, the criminal prisons in addition to Newgate 100, while some 1,500 were released from the debtors' prisons: King's Bench and the Fleet.[27] In Tavistock Square, and elsewhere, a compulsory collection was made among the householders for 'the poor prisoners' released from the gaols. 'Everybody gave half-crowns and some more.' This was far from being small change. One suspects that some of 'the poor prisoners' would have been among the collectors, giving them added muscle.[28] Others were in dire need of charity. They were bewildered, homeless, hungry and quite possibly afraid. Hundreds tried to give themselves up, but those keepers whose prisons had not been utterly destroyed refused to take them. The keeper of New Prison could hardly be persuaded to lodge a murderer taken in the act and would not accept any of his former charges.[29]

In the days following the riot many of the 'liberated' prisoners surrendered themselves or were easily rounded up, but with the destruction of so many prisons, what to do with them pending rebuilding?[30] Improvisation was called for. They were locked into sheds which had been erected amidst the ruins of King's Bench and the Fleet, as well as in St Paul's churchyard. Hundreds of rioters, however, were put in the more secure accommodation of the Wood Street and Poultry compters, both of which had survived their depredations. Some of the guards who had taken prisoner various suspected arsonists deposited them in the military prison at the Savoy. Tothill Fields

---

26 *Ibid.*, pp.136f.

27 Gilmour, *op. cit.*, p.360.

28 De Castro, *op. cit.*, p.148; Hibbert, *op. cit.*, p.110.

29 Hibbert, *op. cit.*, p.111.

30 The Fleet, for instance, was rebuilt much as it was. Howard's description of it before the fire corresponds closely with later descriptions, the most graphic being that of Dickens in *The Pickwick Papers.*

FLEET PRISON.

8. The Fleet debtors' prison as rebuilt after the Gordon riots, 1780

bridewell took in forty looters arrested in St Giles. New Prison substituted for Newgate as the county gaol for Middlesex, but was hard put to contain its charges who thrice in the subsequent twelve months attempted to escape. A military garrison had to be installed temporarily to forestall any further insurrection, but as soon as they left, trouble flared again in this most volatile of prisons.[31]

The Gordon rioters were not held in prison for long as they were put on trial almost immediately, and under extraordinary security, since fears of organised escapes persisted. By early August 160 of them had been tried and sixty-two condemned to death of whom twenty-six, mainly teenage boys and young men, would hang, enough to set an example but, it was hoped, not so many as would enrage the populace. It was yet another speedy gaol delivery. And it worked. For greater didactic effect exemplary punishment was carried out near the scene of the offence. Felons were hanged outside John Fielding's house in Bow Street and Lord Mansfield's mansion in Bloomsbury Square. Twenty-two-year-old James Jackson was

---

[31] De Castro, *op. cit.*, p. 194; Haywood and Seed, *op. cit.*, pp.190ff.

taken from Newgate and hanged in the Old Bailey, strung up opposite the house of Robert Akerman that Jackson had led the way in destroying. He was a changed man from the firebrand he had been when intoxicated by the excitement of the tumult. His penitence and deportment were such that his 'launching into eternity' was met with weeping among the spectators, but not disapproval.[32] Cruel necessity.

Lord George Gordon, the mainspring of the mayhem, lamented the 'turning off' of so many feckless youths. He himself was lodged securely in the Tower, pending trial for treason and potentially a fate worse than hanging. He was, however, defended by Thomas Erskine, acquitted and set free. It was a respite, as he was to end his days in prison. In January 1787 he was back before the King's Bench on a charge of having written and published *The Prisoners' Petition to the Rt Hon Lord George Gordon to preserve their lives and liberties and to prevent their banishment to Botany Bay*, which was deemed to be a libel against the judges and the administration of justice. He was convicted and imprisoned, appropriately in Newgate which had been rebuilt after the terrible destruction he had inspired. After spending five years there, Gordon died in 1793 aged forty-two, another victim of gaol fever.

One not implicated in, but much excited by, the riots he witnessed as a volunteer with the Lincoln's Inn militia, and who thought himself 'a military hero for a night', was Jeremy Bentham, a young man who would have a considerable effect on the theory and practice of imprisonment. But he would build on the foundations laid by another whom he admired, one less cerebral but just as influential.

---

32 Haywood and Seed, *op. cit.*, pp.206, 211f. Again the numbers vary from book to book but these are the most up to date.

Part III

EXPERIMENTATION WITH IMPRISONMENT
1750–1863

The spotlight shed on gaols by John Howard, Elizabeth Fry and others, and the demand for reform of the old and the creation of something new. The question of the purpose of imprisonment became a major public concern, and for the first time differing ideologies competed about how to achieve the Holy Grail of crime eradication. The temporary nature of the hulks and disquiet about transportation led to the construction of penitentiaries under either the separate or silent systems. Millbank and Pentonville both came under mounting criticism from eminent Victorians, and both were deemed failures. Attempts by Alexander Maconochie to fashion an alternative approach were frustrated.

CHAPTER 11

Diving into the Depths of Dungeons

[Howards's] labours and writings have done much to open the eyes and hearts of mankind. He has visited all Europe ... to dive into the depths of dungeons ... to survey the mansions of sorrow and pain; to take and gage the dimensions of misery, depression and contempt; to remember the forgotten, to attend to the neglected, to visit the forsaken, and to compare and collate the distresses of all men in all countries ... It was a voyage of discovery, a circumnavigation of charity.

Edmund Burke

What he did for the service of mankind was what scarce any man could have done, and no man would do, but himself. In the scale of moral desert, the labours of legislator and writer are as far below his, as earth is below heaven ... His kingdom was of a better world; he died a martyr, after living an apostle.

Jeremy Bentham

In 1777 was published, at a low price to ensure wide circulation, *The State of the Prisons in England and Wales*. It was a Domesday book for gaols, a comprehensive survey of custodial institutions in the British Isles and well beyond. There had been published accounts of English prisons before. In the late sixteenth century John Stow had included those of London in his *Survey*, and reports had been published on the Marshalsea and the Fleet. But there was nothing like this. It took longer to compile than the Conqueror's audit, but it was done not at royal command and by an army of civil servants but by one tireless, middle-aged, and middle-ranking landowner of modest means traversing the country on horseback and in all weather, visiting and revisiting innumerable carceral institutions, gathering a wealth of facts, and writing up his findings and recommendations in a massive volume. He dedicated his great work of benevolence to the members of the House of Commons in gratitude for their encouragement. They, in turn, were duly grateful to him for his extraordinary endeavours.

And extraordinary they were, not only in their extent and detail, but in that they had been undertaken at all. Who would want to spend the last decades of their life in constant travel at home and abroad, and at great personal cost to health and wealth, to visit not the great sites and cities of

Britain and Europe but the dankest, dingiest, smelliest death traps therein, not just prisons but lazarettos and other institutions of confinement as well?[1] The answer was John Howard.

The unlikely hero of this chapter began his great philanthropic work in 1773. He was forty-seven. In that year, after a quiet life as a minor landowner in Cardington, engaging all the while in charitable pursuits, this small and unassuming Dissenter, who worshipped at the Independent chapel where Bunyan had preached, unexpectedly became High Sheriff of Bedfordshire.[2] Unlike others who held such an office he did not shirk his responsibilities, one of which was to visit the gaols in the county. He was appalled by what he found – the squalor, the misery, the venality, the inhumanity and above all the continued detention of acquitted prisoners unable to pay their discharge fees – and resolved to devote the rest of his life to doing something about it. 'The sympathy which all were feeling for the sufferings of mankind he felt for the suffering of the worst and most hapless of men.'[3] Devout, moderate Calvinist as he was, this was to be his divine mission, obeying his Master's injunction to visit those in prison. It may also have been the devil's doing, since Howard, twice-widowed, may have wished to escape his parental responsibilities for his only child, a disturbed and wayward youth who would end his days in a lunatic asylum. Or perhaps it was penance for being a bad parent. Or all three.

Whatever the motivation, Howard set out to transform the lives of debtors, miscreants and felons and in so doing transformed his own. His life had new meaning, and his exertions, perceptions and persistence would fan the faint embers of penal reform and make them glow. The remaining seventeen years allotted to him would be spent in the saddle traversing the British Isles and the Continent gathering the evidence for his great exposé. Despite his own deep devotion he was no bigot in religion and 'would as freely have risked his life to relieve the miseries of a Papist, a Mussulman or an Hindoo, as of a Calvinist, a Baptist or an Independent'.[4] And risk his life he continually did. Never of robust health, for the sake of the common

---

[1]   Lazarettos were hospitals or pest-houses for the diseased poor, especially lepers.

[2]   For a physical description and character assessment of Howard see James Brown, *Memoirs of the Public and Private Life of John Howard, the Philanthropist* (London, 1818), pp. 638–59. Brown was commissioned by his subject's friends to deliver a memoir based on Howard's papers, diaries and correspondence and on personal reminiscences. This task he fulfilled in a substantial volume, published at the height of agitation for prison reform.

[3]   Howard, I, p.1; John Richard Green, *A Short History of the English People* (London, 1874), Folio edn (Avon, 1992), p.752.

[4]   Brown, *op. cit.*, p.656.

good Howard endured a relentless schedule and punishing itinerary. Eventually it killed him. He died on 20 January 1790 in Cherson, near the Black Sea, from a fever contracted during a tour of the lazarettos in Russian Tartary. He is buried there. Given the conditions in which he had regularly immersed himself it is astonishing that he survived for so long. 'Temperance and cleanliness' and trust in divine providence had been his 'preservatives', and seemed to have served him well until his work was well-nigh done.[5]

Hailed throughout Europe as a great philanthropist, his statue was the first to adorn St Paul's Cathedral, Dean Millman declaring that 'perhaps no man has assuaged so much human misery as John Howard'.[6] Howard would not have approved. He had stopped a public subscription to erect a similar 'hasty, sad unkind measure'; he never sat for a portrait, and his last wishes were modest: 'Lay me quietly in the earth, place a sundial over my grave, and let me be forgotten.'[7] Modest but ignored. He did not get a sundial but he has never been forgotten. Among the many statues erected in his honour, two stand out: that in Bedford itself where his great work began, the second in Cherson where it ended. His greatest memorial, however, and a testament to his enduring impact and influence, is to be found not in London's great cathedral but on the entrance to her most famous prison. Howard's head and shoulders, along with those of Elizabeth Fry, are embossed upon the great gatehouse of Wormwood Scrubs. Set in stone, they are head and shoulders above all other prison reformers.[8]

In Howard's day the central government administered neither prisons nor bridewells. They were the responsibility of a variety of authorities from the City of London to local justices of the peace, and those who ran them did so as a commercial concern. Howard had been particularly concerned about the fee system in place in Bedford county gaol, whereby time-expired inmates were not released until they had paid for bed and board and any other bills they had run up while inside. Whereas the chaplain, the Revd Mr Lloyd, was paid an annual sum of £20 for his ministration, and the surgeon, Mr Gadsby, £12 for his work both in the gaol and in the bridewell, the gaoler had no salary but depended entirely on fees extracted from prisoners. Each debtor had to pay a discharge fee of 17s 4d and an additional two shillings

---

5   Howard, I, p.3. When he first visited prisons he had changed his clothes afterwards, but this simple precaution he later laid aside.

6   C.F. Farrar, *Old Bedford* (London, 1926), p.234. John Wesley, who had met him in Dublin in June 1787, thought him 'one of the greatest men in Europe' (*Journal of John Wesley*, ed. Nehemiah Curnock (London, 1938), VII, p.295).

7   Brown, *op. cit.*, pp.483, 489.

8   The Howard Association was so named in his honour.

Ypres Tower; the Prison at Rye

9. A typical lock-up in Rye in John Howard's day

to the turnkey, and the same sums were extracted on the discharge of those committed for lack of sureties or for misdemeanours.[9] Even those acquitted were detained until they had paid their fees. It was all very matter-of-fact and open: there was a table of fees painted on a board for all to see and note. Howard applied to the justices of the county for a salary to be paid to the gaoler in lieu of fees. They were sympathetic but wanted a precedent for such an expense.

Howard sought to find one. He decided to visit sixteen gaols in neighbouring counties to see how typical Bedfordshire was. They were no different, all perpetrated the same injustice, and all harboured 'scenes of calamity'.[10] It was a spur to further action. This proved to be the first of thirty-eight tours in the British Isles and seven on the Continent that Howard would make over the subsequent seventeen years, visiting and revisiting prisons far and wide, penetrating to their furthest reaches, interrogating

---

[9]   Howard, I, p.284. Bedford county gaol was demolished in 1801 and the Great Bridge along with its Stonehouse in 1811. Farrar wrote: 'My grandfather recalled seeing, as a child, the inmates lowering bags through the iron grills for the charity of passers-by' (*op. cit.*, p.233). Gaol fever had raged there twenty years before Howard began his work and had carried off Mr Daniel, the surgeon, most prisoners and many townspeople.

[10]   Howard, I, p.1.

those he found there, and collecting and collating masses of facts and data about them and those who worked therein.

For each institution he recorded the name of the gaoler, chaplain and surgeon, the fees charged by the first, and the salaries paid to the others. The character of the staff was even more important than the state of the buildings. He noted on his visit to the county gaol in Chester castle that the felons' day-room was insecure and the castle walls were decayed, as a result of which there had been a major break-out in 1775, but he commented that 'the keeper, who is careful and humane, was not blameable'.[11]

Albeit in the same dispassionate tones, he revealed the revulsion he felt at what he encountered. On a visit to Cardiff county gaol, for example, he stood appalled in a dungeon recently vacated by a prisoner who, for a £7 debt, had spent ten years there and died of despair. In the bishop of Ely's prison he was outraged by 'the cruel method which, for want of a safe gaol, the keeper took to secure his prisoners'. They were chained to the floor, with a heavy iron bar over their legs and an iron collar with spikes around their neck. In another he found a cell so cramped and filthy that the poor wretch who inhabited it begged rather to be hanged. The more he saw the more the compass of his work expanded. Finding in two or three county gaols that 'some poor creatures whose aspect was singularly deplorable' had come from bridewells, he added those institutions to his tour of inspection. He was as methodical as he was systematic. He was not unfair, praising where praise was due. In the precincts of York castle was 'a noble prison for debtors, which does honour to the county'. He noted that 'the rooms were airy and healthy', perhaps unsurprisingly as this 1705 structure was one of the first specifically designed prisons to be built in England, and resembled a baroque palace.[12]

The conditions he found were noted and his comments on them appended. His recommendations were many and reasonable, especially where the staffing of gaols was concerned. To preclude the exploitation of the inmates he urged that every gaol should have a salaried keeper 'since no office if faithfully and humanely administered better deserves an adequate encouragement'. Similarly a surgeon 'of repute in his profession' should be appointed, as should a chaplain 'who is in principle a Christian who will not content himself with officiating in public but will converse with

---

11 *Ibid.*, pp.438f.
12 *Ibid.*, pp.291, 405ff., 463.

the prisoners, admonish the profligate, exhort the thoughtless, comfort the sick'.[13] For this he should be remunerated to the sum of £50 per annum.

His approach was so thorough and his research so breathtaking that his conclusions about the deplorable state of English prisons were irrefutable. In his wide-ranging travels Howard sought and found alternative models. Scottish prisons proved an oddity as they held 'but few prisoners', attributable to 'the shame and disgrace annexed to imprisonment', to 'the general sobriety of manners' inculcated by good parenting, and to the expedition with which trials and executions were carried out. Although debtors were herded into 'dirty and offensive rooms', and 'poor criminals' were held in close confinement in 'the horrid cage' in the Edinburgh Tolbooth, women were never ironed and the acquitted were immediately discharged from open court, paying no gaoler's fees.[14] Scotland provided not a model of what prisons should be but a lesson that they should be used sparingly.

To find what in his estimation were exemplary prisons Howard had to look further afield. The Dutch won his admiration, and he expatiated at length on what he saw in Holland. Prisons were quiet and clean, the inmates usefully occupied, industrious and orderly. Men were 'put to labour in the *rasp-houses*, and women to proper work in the *spin-houses*'. The rationale was 'make them diligent, and they will be honest'. Moral and religious instruction was paramount. Chaplains were appointed to every house of correction, not only to perform public worship but to instruct and catechise the prisoners. The *Rasphuis* in Amsterdam, founded in 1596, was built in a former monastery as an institute for rehabilitation, though sentences were long, conditions Spartan, and rasping – which involved pulverising logs of Brazilian dyewood to produce a pigment powder for colouring goods – arduous. Over its still-standing gates was a moralising inscription to the effect that 'wild beasts must be tamed by men'. Tamed by men and transformed by Christians. Howard expressed regret at leaving this country 'as it affords a large field for information on the important subject' he had in view. He 'knew not which to admire most, the neatness and cleanliness appearing in the prisons, the industry and regular conduct of the prisoners, or the humanity and attention of the magistrates and regents'.[15] Cleanliness was indeed next to godliness.

It was however in the heart of Catholicism that another 'penitential' experiment took his eye. In Rome he visited the reformatory of St Michelle built in 1703 by Pope Clement XI for 'the correction and instruction of

13   *Ibid.*, pp.26–9.
14   *Ibid.*, pp.196ff.
15   *Ibid.*, pp.44–66.

profligate youth' – refractory boys whose parents paid for their upkeep. Built like the aisle of a church, it had an altar at the east end, but it also had cells (called 'lodging-rooms') built into its walls, and a whipping-post at the west end. In between, seated on (or even chained to) benches, were rows of children spinning wool. Howard approved of what he saw, and was impressed by 'this excellent institution's' 'admirable' motto – 'there is little point in punishing the vicious [*improbus*] unless you render them virtuous [*probus*] by discipline'. He did not see them being whipped or chained. He was told that all were learning 'different trades according to their different abilities and genius', some being educated 'for printers, book-binders, smiths, carpenters, tailors, shoe-makers and barbers'.[16]

Word of his endeavours got around fast and in March 1774, not long after he had begun his visitations and long before he first went into print, he was summoned by the House of Commons to give expert evidence on penal matters. He emphasised that, while British prisons were riddled with abuses and served no penological purpose, a proper prison regime, as existed elsewhere in Europe, could be created here to produce an excellent arena for prevention, punishment and penitence. A prison should be a counterpoint to the disordered society from which crime sprang. A prison should not replicate this fallen world but aspire to a higher ideal. It should generate good and not incubate evil. Idleness, gambling, swearing, drinking and fornicating should not be tolerated, let alone encouraged, but replaced with industry, sobriety, and decency. The raucous autonomy of prison culture, by which prisoners for generations had created their own society within society and found the means to endure, or even enjoy, their incarceration, and where physical pollution and moral contamination abounded, should be suppressed and replaced with external control. Solitude and silence so favourable to reflection leading to repentance should be enforced. Self-control and self-respect would be the result. At a purely practical level there were distinct advantages as strict separation would prevent escapes, protect the weak from exploitation and ensure the safety of those giving evidence against their accomplices.[17] Such was the theory, but the imposition of strict regimes of silence and solitude for prolonged periods would have disastrous results, as their effect on his own son showed and future developments would demonstrate. The best intentions can lead to the worst results, and when theory trumps evidence, unintended evils are allowed to persist. Solitary confinement for social beings was to prove dehumanising and debilitating,

[16] *Ibid.*, pp.113ff.
[17] *Ibid.*, p.22.

and destructive, far worse than the squalor, mayhem and contamination it replaced. This dehumanising regime, however, had not been Howard's intention. Solitude in a single cell should be reserved for the night-time. By day prisoners should work in association.

Even though germination proved slow, Howard sowed his seed on fertile soil. A consensus was growing on the need for major prison reforms. The British, appalled in 1756 with reports of the Black Hole of Calcutta, were being confronted with their own Black Holes, while the idea that imprisonment could serve a deterrent purpose and still have a beneficial effect upon those upon whom it was imposed was taking root. There were several thinkers and writers whose works showed a certain convergence of view which would ultimately give rise to both the panopticon and the penitentiary.[18] In 1771 Sir William Eden brought out his *Principles of Penal Law* in which he propounded the utilitarian argument that 'the good of all is the great object of all', and that punishment should be proportionate to the offence. In 1776 the philanthropic evangelical Jonas Hanway published *Solitude in Imprisonment*. In it he conflated punishment and deterrence with reform, by contending that solitary confinement was 'the most terrible penalty' short of death and 'the most humane'. It removed the prisoner from the baleful influence of other sinners. Left alone to his own remorse, he became his own tormenter, and in his abjection was reduced to calling out for divine forgiveness. This future promise depended on first ending the culture and abuses of the past, and replacing the old penal provision with a 'great number' of 'prisons ... larger, stronger and better calculated for the purpose of a secure confinement and more rational and humane correction'.[19] Although Howard concurred with these sentiments, he latterly, on pragmatic and humanitarian grounds, did not support the complete sequestration that Hanway advocated. Indeed he deprecated the committal of 'petty offenders to *absolute* solitude ... a state ... more than human nature can bear'.[20] Yet it was the practical Howard who provided the facts and figures which would underpin political action which would ultimately lead to Pentonville.

Two salutary enactments immediately resulted from his endeavours, the one to remove discharge fees, the other to introduce sanitary measures to counter gaol fever. Howard personally ensured that they would be enforced

---

18 On these precursors of Howard, and especially on the impact of Hanway's writings, see Janet Semple, *Bentham's Prison* (Oxford, 1993), pp.80–9.

19 Jonas Hanway, *Solitude in Imprisonment* (London, 1776), pp.63, 143.

20 Howard, II, p.169, a note to his 1788 visit to the new prison at Reading.

as he had the legislation printed at his own expense and sent to every county gaol in England.

His influence was far from spent, his enduring aim being the construction of a national system of penitentiaries where convicted criminals would be confined in the privacy, seclusion and safety of single cells at night and be put to hard labour in association during the day, all the while under the influence of a godly and reformist regime. Hard labour was thought particularly apt for those sorts of crimes which were 'the offspring of *Idleness* and *Dissipation*'. Two of his most avid and influential supporters, Sir William Eden, a member of parliament and prominent advocate of penal reform, and Sir William Blackstone, the famous jurist and judge, propelled though parliament the Penitentiary Act of 1779. It attempted to combine the evangelical ideal of silence and solitude being a stimulant to self-reflection, repentance and regeneration, the utilitarian emphasis on social control and scientific observation, and the desire of both for deterrence.[21] Two national penitentiaries were to be built in the London area, one for each sex. Gaolers were to be paid, the keeper's salary being proportionate to the profits made from prison labour. Prisoners were to wear uniforms, and would earn remission by good behaviour and hard work. Howard was appointed one of the three 'supervisors of the buildings' whose initial task was to find a suitable site for the first structure. The supervisors could not even agree on this, and after two years Howard, incapable of compromise, resigned and resumed his travels. Without his hurricane force behind it, with costs mounting, and with the recommencement of transportation imminent, enthusiasm waned and construction stalled.[22]

Despite this setback at government level, notions of imprisonment as punishment and purgation had gained broad acceptance and Howard's penological ideas had percolated far and wide, although his reservations about prolonged solitary confinement seem to have not. A combination of Christian zeal, the belief in the contagious nature of crime, and the hope that the panacea had been found, spawned the investment of time and money in prison construction or reconstruction throughout the land. In 1784 parliament explicitly authorised justices to demolish and rebuild county gaols and to borrow money for this purpose on the security of the rates.

---

21 Bentham influenced aspects of the final legislation but not the name. He had suggested 'Hard Labour Houses'. The appellation 'penitentiary', though he used it himself, had religious connotations 'quite alien from Bentham's thought' (Semple, *op. cit.*, pp.45–50).

22 Eventually Howard's ideas, or a perversion of them, would be put into practice in Millbank and Pentonville. These were his bastards, though he would have disowned them.

The use of dungeons was forbidden and classification was to be introduced. Some, who had been waiting in the hope that the cost of restructuring gaols could be placed on ratepayers, eagerly set to work. The pace of reform was determined in large part by a willingness to pay, and modern prisons were not cheap since the new narrative necessitated new designs. For the first time interiors were given priority. Exteriors had been constructed to over-awe and deter, but behind the intimidating stone screens life had been pretty much unregulated. That was to change.

In 1775 the duke of Richmond began rebuilding the Sussex county gaol at Horsham, and did so 'under Howard's advice and co-operation'. Horsham gaol, opened in 1779, was designed to contain or mitigate the ill effects of communal incarceration, and prevent novices in crime repeating their offences. It was well situated and, on medical advice, built on arches to aid air circulation in an attempt to prevent gaol fever. Debtors and felons were kept apart and each felon had a separate cell. The fear of contagion from disease went hand in hand with fear of contagion from vice, and the old gaols were perceived as having been incubators of both, and proved joint spurs to action here and elsewhere. There were no fees, but a paid gaoler.[23] A salaried chaplain was appointed. The new prison regime was credited with halving the crime rate in the area. It was also credited, along with the Penitentiary Act, as 'incontrovertibly establish[ing]' that 'solitary confinement, modified by well-regulated labour and accompanied with religious instruction' was no nineteenth-century alien import and showing 'that the Separate System [was] British: British in its origin – British in its actual application – British in its legislative sanction'. There would soon be another first for Britain. Richmond's next venture was to rebuild Petworth's house of correction, and this time the aim was as much reformative as preventative. It was said to afford 'the earliest instance of the *complete* adoption of the separate system of prison discipline in the kingdom, and, we might add, in the world'.[24]

Richmond was not the only trail-blazer. Sir George Onesiphorus Paul incorporated Howard's suggestions in his reconstruction of Gloucester prison in 1791. Modelled on the prison at Ghent which Howard had

---

23 It was not until the Gaol Fees Abolition Act of 1815 that fees were totally prohibited and exacting them was made a criminal offence. Garnish was no more. Magistrates suddenly had to pay staff out of public funds and so became directly responsible for the running of gaols. No more shirking!

24 *Extracts*, pp.78, 128. British in origin or not, and the inspectors attributed its first adumbration to a Spital sermon preached by Bishop Butler in 1750, it would be in America, where Howard's researches had great impact, and the influence of Quakers on carceral developments was profound, that the most perfect realizations of this and the silent system would be found in Pennsylvania and New York respectively.

praised, it was designed by William Blackburn, Howard's preferred architect, who saw the main task of prison architecture as the regulation of human sociability. His numerous prison designs drawn up for Liverpool (1786), Manchester (1787), and Preston (1788) had promised to separate the untried from the convicted, criminals from debtors, men from women, men from boys, and so prevent contamination. In Gloucester his ideal of regulated social interaction was put into practice in the world's first example of what would become a rival system, one of separate confinement at night but work in silent association by day. Likewise, Southwell house of correction was built in 1808 along similar lines at the instigation of the zealous magistrate, and Howard devotee, the Revd John Becher.

It is astonishing that in a time of war, high taxation, and national crisis so much money was found to pay for refashioning local prisons. In less than a decade forty-two gaols and houses of correction were rebuilt, many in streets named after Howard and some with busts of the reformer adorning their gatehouses, Shrewsbury being but one example. The fact that they were given such priority in the localities is suggestive that the public conscience, or at least that of the gentry who contributed the most and held the purse-strings, had been pricked to the core. The great expense of reforming prisons and building asylums fell on the landowners and gentlemen who nonetheless, as justices, authorised an expenditure that cost them dearly.[25]

Yet Howard was not satisfied. In the second edition of his great work he recorded with satisfaction that 'from the attention of the magistrates, and the operation of the salutary Act for preserving the health of prisoners' the gaols had been freed from 'that disease which formerly destroyed more persons than the hand of the executioner', and that the public, imbued with a 'liberal and humane spirit', had been engaged in alleviating the 'sufferings of prisoners'. All well and good, but at that point 'the spirit of improvement unhappily seems to stop, scarcely touching that still more important object, the REFORMATION OF MORALS in our prisons'.[26] The Victorian judge and penal reformer, Matthew Davenport Hill, concurred, claiming that 'with the exception of those changes which approve themselves to the common instincts of benevolence, such as cleanliness, ventilation, drainage etc, the seed sown by Howard fell in stony places'. He deplored that 'whatever required the faintest tincture of philosophy for its appreciation was lost, and

---

[25] Margaret DeLacy, *Prison Reform in Lancashire, 1700–1850* (Stanford, CA, 1986), pp.168–70. It was the urban middle class that baulked at the cost.

[26] Howard, II, p.233.

had to be refound'.[27] His reservations, echoing those of Bentham, go too far. Incremental improvements in prison conditions, and above all in sanitation, may have relied on benevolence, common sense or self-preservation rather than philosophy, but were nonetheless desirable. These mundane factors have so often been productive of amelioration while the grand intentions of philosophy have paved the road to hell. So it was to prove with British prisons.

One significant innovation, introduced by the 1776 Criminal Law Act[28] (later endorsed by the 1779 Act), began the temporary and later regular use of prison as a place for punishment, and so reinforced the need for some kind of system, be it penitential or punitive, for all gaols other than the hulks. This was imprisonment with hard labour. It was an alternative to transportation. Over time 'hard labour' would range from the servile if productive – oakum-picking – to the back-breaking but often useless – the crank and the tread-wheel. Oakum consisted of pieces of tarred ropes that had to be unravelled or fluffed for use in caulking the seams between the deck-boards of ships. It was a tedious and difficult task, and beginners would end up with broken nails and blistered and bloody fingertips. The crank was a cylindrical metal drum the axle of which required considerable pressure to rotate. The drum was fitted with a handle and a clock-like device which recorded the number of revolutions made. Prisoners were expected to complete 6,000 revolutions a day, taking from six to eight hours. The warder could make the task harder by tightening an adjusting screw, hence the slang-term 'screws' still applied to prison officers today. The tread-wheel was devised by a Lowestoft engineer, 'Mr Cubitt ... a gentleman of science ... and of gentle and pleasing deportment'.[29] It was first deployed in the Suffolk county gaol at Bury St Edmunds, and in 1821 at Brixton, the Surrey house of correction. Prisoners would enter separate compartments, and mount the steps on a huge revolving drum which sank beneath their feet as pressure was put on it, ever scrabbling to repeat their action and never progressing an inch. Exhausting and stifling, its cant name was 'the cockchafer'.[30]

---

[27] R. & F. Hill, *The Recorder of Birmingham: A Memoir of M.D. Hill* (London, 1878), p.152.

[28] This became known as 'The Hulks Act' or 'The Hard Labour Act'.

[29] M&B, p.288. One is preserved for posterity at Beaumaris county gaol, now a museum. The terms tread-wheel and treadmill are interchangeable. It is sometimes said that there is a distinction in that treadmills served some purpose grinding corn and pumping water. But so too, however, did machines termed tread-wheels, as is evidenced by the prison returns in part II of the Commissioners' *Second Report* (1879).

[30] Kellow Chesney, *The Victorian Underworld* (London, 1970), pp.20f.

TREAD-WHEEL AND OAKUM-SHED AT THE CITY PRISON, HOLLOWAY,
(WITH A DETACHMENT OF PRISONERS AT WORK ON THE WHEEL, AND THOSE WHO HAVE BEEN RELIEVED EMPLOYED PICKING OAKUM.)

10. Hard labour in Holloway

Thus it was 'drudgery', one of Howard's less happy ideas, that was implemented. It was an odd one for him to espouse since the Act's insistence on 'hard and labourious service' had no obviously rehabilitative potential. Coldbath Fields was a case in point. Opened in 1794, it would come to boast twenty tread-wheels. Each inmate became a mountaineer, having to ascend 12,000 feet a day.[31] According to the governor the silent system and 'well-regulated' labour imposed a necessary severity upon a class that was incapable of reform. Howard, while believing that all humans are innately sinful, would have held that no individual was beyond redemption. Indeed 'for Howard, as for Hanway, salvation was the primary end of punishment, as it was of human existence'.[32]

Howard's influence was pernicious on another aspect of contemporary penal policy: the use of hulks to hold excess prisoners stranded in England by the disruption of transportation to the Americas as a result of the outbreak of the revolutionary war. In the first edition of his book Howard had criticised the management of the hulks moored on the Thames. In response, the Commons set up a committee to inquire into their viability.

---

[31] So disabling was this found to be that the daily quota was later reduced to 1,200 feet. The Royal Artillery had refrained from committing their offenders to Coldbath Fields 'owing to the injurious effects observable, on their return to their regiment, from the mischievous excess of tread-wheel occupation' (Chesterton, I, p.156).

[32] Semple, *op. cit.*, p.93.

To their surprise, Howard, who had not only repeatedly revisited those at Woolwich, but had inspected the ones at Plymouth, Gosport and Portsmouth as well, reported that conditions had greatly improved over the decade and pragmatically supported their retention until something better could be found.[33] It was later claimed by James Chapple, keeper of the New Prison in Bodmin, that at least as far as the hulk *La Fortunée* in Langston harbour was concerned, 'the late worthy Mr Howard was deceived when he visited, the overseers etc being present, the convicts were afraid to complain'.[34]

Misled or not, the great man's imprimatur had been bestowed, and hulks were to survive as part of the penal estate well beyond the resumption of transportation, indeed until its demise.

---

[33] Howard, I, pp.465f., II, pp.216f.

[34] James Neild, *State of the Prisons in England, Scotland and Wales* (London, 1812), p.619. This was not entirely true. Howard had noted that while 'the ship was healthy' the convicts did complain 'sadly of the meat, and indeed not without cause' (II, pp.217f.). If he was fooled he was not alone. In January 1778 Bentham visited the *Censor* on the Thames and had found the prisoners well-clothed, the sleeping quarters warm and the food nutritious. This was more than could be said of most prisons, but the hulk he saw may have been unusually 'ship-shape' in expectation of the parliamentary inquiry (Semple, *op. cit.*, p.56).

CHAPTER 12

Flotsam and Jetsam

A sentence of transportation to Botany Bay translated into common sense is this: 'Because you have committed this offence, the Sentence of the Court is that you shall no longer be burthened with the support of your wife and family. You shall be immediately removed from a very bad climate, and a country overburthened with people, to one of the finest Regions of the Earth where the demand for human labour is every hour increasing, and where it is highly probable you may ultimately regain your character and improve your fortune. The Court has been induced to pass this sentence upon you in consequence of the many aggravating circumstances of your case, and the hope that your fate will be a warning to others.

Sydney Smith

In 1584 Richard Hakluyt, drawing attention to 'the many thousands of idle persons' within the realm, 'whereby all the prisons of the land are daily pestered and stuffed full of them where either they pitifully pine away or else at length are miserably hanged', recommended that 'these petty thieves might be condemned for certain years in the western parts' in sawing and felling of timber and 'in the more southern parts' in planting sugar canes and gathering cotton.[1] England was full and overflowing with the workless; the New World was empty and eager for workers. Emptying the former and filling the latter was to the benefit of both. The indolent would become industrious. Prosperity would replace poverty. Everyone would be a winner. It was this beguiling argument that would sustain transportation throughout its history from the beginning of the seventeenth century to America until the middle of the nineteenth to Australia.

England's, and later Britain's, expansion overseas made this suggestion possible. As early as 1598 an Act 'for the punishment of rogues, vagabonds and sturdy beggars' sanctioned it, along with many other measures. 'Incorrigible rogues' were to be banished the realm 'and at the charge of [the] country shall be conveyed unto such parts beyond the seas as shall be ... for that purpose assigned by the Privy Council'. To return without

---

1 Hakluyt, *Discourse Concerning Western Planting*, ed. Charles Deane (Cambridge, 1877), p.37.

licence was death.[2] It took almost a decade to implement. In 1607 transportation to Virginia began and it became the destination of choice. Other American colonies and the West Indies became involved. In 1615 James I offered pardons to felons who agreed to be shipped to the New World. As Shakespeare put it, 'O brave new world, That has such people in't!' In the same year the East India Company took ten condemned felons from Newgate and shipped them to Table Bay on the Cape. They were the first transportees taken to the southern hemisphere and the first colonists of what would become South Africa. They did not take to it, and sought safety on an offshore island inhabited solely by penguins. Later this would be called Robben Island, and develop a fearsome penal reputation of its own. Marooned, and on an unvarying diet of penguin-egg omelettes and penguin pie, the 'colonists' lost heart. They preferred to return to Newgate and were taken back to England. A second group of deportees yet to set sail, getting wind of this, opted for hanging in preference to being abandoned in Africa.[3] These groups' desire for death over exile was to be shared by later generations of transportees. Despite such reservations on the part of felons, the desirability of getting rid of troublesome miscreants was too strong, and the experiment was not curtailed but expanded. During the Commonwealth period political undesirables joined vagrants, rogues and paupers in being sent to the colonies. It was a perfect way to get rid of riff-raff and exile dissent. Transportation was continued and regularised after the Restoration. The first legislation specific to it came in 1662 with an Act providing for the transportation of such 'rogues, vagabonds, and sturdy beggars, as shall be duly convicted and adjudged incorrigible, to any English plantations beyond the seas'.

By 1700 it had become a fairly common form of conditional pardon, particularly for first offenders. Along with the building of houses of correction, transportation was an attempt to find an intermediate punishment between branding and the noose. Both disposals signalled a shift away from penalties that displayed the body to humiliating public spectacle, to sentences during which the body was confined – or consigned – for lengthy periods and subjected to the discipline of loss of liberty and hard labour. Wrongdoers were forcibly removed from the society against which they had offended, temporarily behind bars or semi-permanently beyond the seas, few of the latter, on the expiry of their lengthy sentences, choosing to return. Proponents of transportation believed that prolonged exposure to the severe

---

2   *EHD*, V(a), pp.1143ff. Banishment had existed since Anglo-Saxon times.
3   John Keay, *The Honourable Company* (London, 1991), pp.92f.

conditions of the colonies and 'to toyle in heavey and painefull works' would transform the idle as well as provide them with a new opportunity and a fresh start. For some it did.

A judge could pass such a sentence, or a criminal could even petition for it, as Moll Flanders did. As one justice of the peace put it in 1704 when sentencing two young men:

> I reprieved them because it did not appear to me that either of them had committed any such offence before, or were engaged in any society of offenders ... But they are lewd, idle fellows, and it is fitting the country should be clear'd of them. They are strong, able-body'ed men and may do good service either in Her Majesty's Plantations or army.[4]

The Secretary of State would endorse the reprieve, providing that the felon joined up or agreed to be transported. Until 1718 the costs of passage to the New World had to be borne by the prisoners themselves or by merchants eager to sell them into indenture. Defoe himself took part in this profitable trade in 1688.

This disposal of convicts was finally regularised in 1718 by an Act 'for the further preventing robbery, burglary and other felonies and for the more effectual transportation of felons'.[5] The Transportation Act, as it was called, increased the use of this addition to the penal repertoire. Again it was asserted that there was a double benefit: to the home country because 'the laws now in force' against robbery, larceny and other property offences had proved ineffectual and failed in their primary purpose of deterrence; and to the American colonies which lacked 'servants' to work the land. It stipulated that henceforth 'clergied felons',[6] who had been 'liable to be whipped or burnt in the hand' or ordered to the workhouse, could be transported for seven years, and those convicted of non-clergyable offences could be pardoned and their death sentences commuted if they agreed to be transported for fourteen years. There were no penal colonies in America as there would be in Australia. The transportees would be sold into indentured servitude – a form of time-limited slavery – for the duration of their term. Under contract, three pounds would be paid for each of the convicts transported, and the merchant could make further money on their sale when

---

4   BL Loan 29/369.
5   *EHD*, IX, pp.460f.
6   Offenders claiming 'Benefit of Clergy' for a first felony escaped the noose. This 'benefit' was abolished in 1827 by which time the number of capital offences was being greatly reduced (Harry Potter, *Law, Liberty and the Constitution* (Woodbridge, 2015), pp.59ff.).

his cargo arrived safely on a colonial shore: an unskilled labourer would fetch ten pounds, a skilled craftsman could go for twenty-five. Women were a bargain at only eight or nine pounds.

There was inevitable 'wastage'. Sea journeys were perilous, lengthy ones in old and overcrowded ships especially so. Sickness did for some, shipwrecks for others. The fate of one human cargo provides chilling evidence of this, all the more so since the loss of so many lives would not have happened had they not been transportees. The *Amphitrite* was a two-hundred-ton sailing ship, built in 1804. Under the command of John Hunter, she sailed from Woolwich on 25 August 1833, with 108 female convicts and twelve children on board, bound for the penal colony of New South Wales. While sailing off Boulogne she encountered a gale and was blown ashore. Owing to the fact that the passengers were prisoners under his custody Hunter refused offers of aid. The ship subsequently broke up with the loss of 133 lives. Only three survivors were rescued. Hunter drowned with his cargo.[7]

But misfortunes at sea were not that rare, and were not confined to convicts. They took their chance along with any other sort of passenger. Most got through unscathed. Predictably, critics argued that transportation was not sufficiently deterrent, but more of 'a summer's excursion, in an easy migration, to a happier and better climate'.[8] However it was perceived, it was a cruise that many were to undertake. As early as 1722, the year *Moll Flanders* was published, about sixty per cent of male clergyable felons were transported and forty-five per cent of female. So useful a disposal was it, for England at least, that latterly three-fifths of all male convicts were sent abroad. Between 1614 and 1775, over 50,000 convicts, predominantly young men and boys, mainly vagrants and thieves, were despatched across the Atlantic. Half of them had been sentenced by the courts in and around London.[9]

Some transportees would not go quietly. In 1781 Robert Hill was savagely lashed for threatening to scuttle his transport. Two years later 143 prisoners took over the *Swift* and forty-eight of them got ashore in Kent. A similar insurrection on the *Mercury* in 1784 had to be suppressed violently when the convicts landed at Portsmouth.[10]

---

[7] A detailed account is provided by Andrew Jampoler in *Horrible Shipwreck!* (Annapolis, MD, 2010).

[8] Lord Ellenborough, *PD (Lords)*, XVI (30 May 1810), p.324.

[9] Peter Coldham, *Emigrants in Chains* (Stroud, 1992), p.7.

[10] Ian Haywood and John Seed (eds), *The Gordon Riots* (Cambridge, 2012), pp.191, 196.

11. Portsmouth harbour prison hulk

Not all may have been eager to leave their homeland, but Britain wanted rid of them and America would benefit from their labour. So it was thought. Some of those upon whom they were foisted had reservations. In 1751 a letter attributed to Benjamin Franklin appeared in *The Pennsylvania Gazette*, suggesting that the colonies repay the kindness of Mother England by exporting rattlesnakes to Britain and releasing them in St James's Park.[11] It was hardly a *casus belli*, but it was another irritation caused by the imperious behaviour of the British. When the War of Independence broke out in 1776, America ceased to be a dumping-ground for foreign-born criminals. It was closed, at least for the duration of the war.

What to do until the hostilities ceased or other avenues opened? Prisoners were proliferating; prison spaces were lacking.[12] Eden was instrumental

11 Charles Campbell, *The Intolerable Hulks*, 3rd edn (Tucson, 2001), pp.8f.
12 Such new prisons as were constructed were for French prisoners-of-war: Norman Cross in Cambridgeshire, designed to hold between five and six thousand of these, was opened in 1797. Before its closure in 1816, just after the Napoleonic Wars had ended, 1,770 Frenchmen had died there. Dartmoor served the same function from 1809, as did Perth from 1810. In addition Dartmoor held American prisoners-of-war captured in the war of 1812. Above its entrance was the reassuring injunction from Virgil's *Aeneid*, '*Parcere Subjectis*' – 'Spare the Vanquished' – an inscription that remained when it reopened as a convict prison in 1850 and which mocked the reality that men were immured for 'long silent years in the solitude of granite tombs which were their cells' (Grew, p.43).

in persuading the government to use decommissioned ships – the 'hulks' – to confine convicts sentenced to transportation until some other more effectual means could be found of disposing of 'this criminal sewage'.[13] The ships were redundant and empty. The need for somewhere to house excess prisoners was urgent and pressing. The 'Hulks Act' of 1776 was quickly passed, authorising confinement of convicts on old ships and the use of their hard labour on public works projects – but only for a period of two years. Hulks were meant to be a temporary expedient, a short-term solution to prison overcrowding, pending the resumption of transportation to Maryland and Virginia.

It was the first time that central government had taken charge of part of the prison estate. It had no experience in such a venture and quickly delegated its responsibility to the Middlesex magistrates who in turn contracted the running of the ships to Duncan Campbell, a former transporter of convicts. He took 144 convicts aboard two ailing but commodious vessels berthed at Woolwich: his own *Justicia*, a retired East Indiaman, and the *Censor*, a former Admiralty frigate. More hulks would follow and London would not remain the sole berth for long. There was no shortage of ports nor old warships, too worn-out to use in combat but still afloat, for conversion, such as the *Chatham* and the *Dunkirk* at Plymouth, the *Laure* and the aptly named *Captivity* in Portsmouth harbour, and *La Fortunée* (a captured French frigate) and the *Portland* in nearby Langston harbour.[14] Hulks were also deployed in Bermuda from 1824 and at Gibraltar from 1842 – between them holding 1,800 convicts – and even became an adjunct to the penal colony in Australia. At home this temporary expedient would come to provide the main form of convict custody until 1844, by which time Millbank had been converted into a depot doubling its capacity, and Pentonville had opened.

These were no luxury cruise ships, but floating warehouses for those destined to hard labour on restricted diets in this country or abroad. In *Great Expectations* young Pip was confronted with the terrifying sight of a 'black hulk, lying out a little way from the mud of the shore, like a wicked Noah's Ark, cribbed and barred and moored by massive rusty chains'. Dickens gives no description of conditions aboard but they would have been deplorable, as the memoirs of one who had actually experienced them made clear.

James Hardy Vaux, though of relatively humble origins, was literate, enterprising and charming, thus having all the attributes of an effective

---

[13] Arthur Griffiths, *Memorials of Millbank* (London, 1875), I, p.11.

[14] For descriptions of their condition in 1802 see James Neild, *State of the Prisons in England, Scotland and Wales* (London, 1812), pp.623–31.

CONVICTS FORMING A MORTAR BATTERY IN THE WOOLWICH MARSHES.

12. Hard labour on public works

swindler and thief. In 1809, the twenty-seven-year-old was convicted of stealing jewellery and destined to hang. His sentence, however, was commuted to transportation for life. Before embarking for Australia he spent a year aboard the largest Woolwich hulk, the *Retribution*. A 'floating dungeon' he called it, holding 'nearly six hundred men, most of them double-ironed'. The fastidious Vaux had to contend with 'the continual rattling of chains, the filth and vermin', as well as 'the shocking necessity of associating ... with so depraved a set of beings'. His initial impressions were bad enough but worse was to come when he was put below deck:

> On descending the hatch-way, no conception can be formed of the scene which presented itself ... nothing short of a descent to the infernal regions can be at all worthy of a comparison with it ... If I were to attempt a full description of the miseries endured in these ships I could fill a volume; but I shall sum up all by stating, that besides robbery from each other, which is as common as cursing and swearing, I witnessed among the prisoners themselves, during the twelvemonth I remained with them, one deliberate murder, for which the perpetrator was executed at Maidstone, and one suicide; and that unnatural crimes are openly committed.[15]

If Vaux's depiction of life on a hulk was not vivid enough for taste, or too vivid to be believed, the full reality of the horrors endured would later be made plain to a public avid for such delectation, and prepared to pay for

---

15 *Memoirs of James Vaux* (1819), ed. Noel McLachlan (London, 1964), pp.198ff.

the pleasure. The *Success*, an old East Indiaman, whose torrid history as 'the commodore of the felon fleet' in Hobson's Bay, near Melbourne, was vividly described by Joseph Harvie in his visitors' guidebook, ended its days moored in the Thames by Blackwall as a late Victorian tourist attraction. Festooned with waxwork figures, it vividly displayed the dire conditions under which prisoners were kept in one of the 'floating hells of Victoria'. Cells were built along the sides of her main and lower decks and on each deck there was the 'Tigers' Den', a heavily-barred cage in which the worst characters were herded together, and into which the guards never ventured. The most dangerous prisoners of all were kept on the lower deck, chained in their cells. Heavy 'irons' were everywhere so that recalcitrant prisoners could easily be shackled. They wore them even in hospital, and sometimes they were buried still wearing them. On the upper deck was the salt-water-filled 'compulsory bath', or 'coffin', into which two or three 'fractious prisoners were thrust by the warders, and then scoured with long-handled brushes, to keep them sweet and clean'. It was a punishment and purgation, and for those newly flogged an agony, albeit one that cleansed their wounds.[16]

Despite such bathing facilities and the fresh sea air, hulks were unhealthy and unhygienic. Typhus was as virulent aboard hulks as it was within gaols, or even more so. In the first twenty years of their existence about a quarter of those sent to the hulks died, mostly of 'hulk fever'.[17] In 1811 the House of Commons Committee on Penitentiary Houses, conducting a long overdue review of the hulk establishment, observed the appalling conditions but did not recommend abandonment of the system.

The hulks were not just receptacles for the excess of Newgate and the other London prisons. They were a national resource, serving the provinces too. To give one instance: in 1783 nineteen-year-old Susannah Holmes had her death sentence for housebreaking commuted to fourteen years' transportation to America. As she could not be sent there she was incarcerated in the old Norwich castle gaol for three years, during which time she gave birth to a son whose father, Henry Kable, was also a detained transportee. She and her child were first delivered to the *Dunkirk*, and then in 1787, reunited with the father, transported, not to the New World, but to the even newer colony at Botany Bay.[18]

---

16 Joseph Harvie, *The History of the Convict Hulk 'Success'* (London, 1896); 'A Convict Hulk' in *The Leisure Hour*, 1896.

17 Du Cane, p.119.

18 David Neal, *The Rule of Law in a Penal Colony: Law and Power in Early New South Wales* (Cambridge, 1991), pp.1–4.

During the hulks' further seventy years in service, some, but not all, of their freight was transported. Before their fate was finalised, able-bodied men and boys, and some not so able, were put to labour on public works in Portsmouth and Woolwich. Before being pardoned, skilled workers in particular often served years on the hulks moored there. When hostilities with France broke out again in 1803, for a time prisoners-of-war were held off the south coast on hulks, many of which were French ships captured by the British. Such prisoners proved troublesome and were a constant security risk. In 1809 they were decanted to Dartmoor, construction of which began in 1806 for that very purpose. Nonetheless some hulks were still deployed for fresh – or not so fresh – arrivals. In 1810 thirty-two prisoners-of-war escaped the *Vigilant*, and most were never recaptured. When thirty emaciated French prisoners were deposited at Portsmouth in 1811, the surgeon of the hospital ship *Pegasus* would not allow them aboard unless they were thoroughly washed. They were dunked in the sea and several drowned as a result.

As on land, attempts were made to avoid human contamination – corruption into greater criminality by older and more prolific offenders – as well as rampant sexual exploitation. So far as the former issue was concerned it was largely futile given that the structure of the hulks and the numbers stowed together below deck made contact unstoppable. Although the authorities were loath to acknowledge the latter problem, Vaux saw it with his own eyes, and Bentham asserted that buggery was the routine initiation ritual on the Woolwich hulks, 'stand[ing] in the place of garnish and exacted with equal rigour'.[19]

The young were particularly vulnerable to both contamination and predation. To gain protection, boys would become catamites. Something had to be done to protect their relative innocence. In 1816 the *Bellerophon*, after brave service against Napoleon, ended her hitherto illustrious career as a hulk. Eight years later she was reserved solely for boys, neophytes in crime who should be kept away from hardened adult criminals. The first 350 of its new charges were under fourteen. The Revd E. Edwards, the chaplain, complained that while they worked hard at their trades they had a propensity for lying and that of those who did not respond to religious instruction 'many were very dull and others are reluctant'. Boys will be boys. Cooped up for years in overcrowded hulks with too little food and little to do they quarrelled with each other and fought with the staff. The most recalcitrant

---

[19] Letter to Sir Charles Bunbury in *The Works of Jeremy Bentham* (London, 1843), XI, p.120.

older teenagers were hastily dispatched to Australia. Nor did sequestration insulate those who remained from picking up bad habits. Figures produced before a parliamentary committee in 1835 showed that whereas one in ten of those adults discharged from the hulks re-offended, three-quarters of juveniles did.[20]

At the high-point in 1841 there were 3,552 convicts on hulks in England. Disillusion and decline set in. Joshua Jebb, the creator of Pentonville and the newly appointed prison supremo, was adamant in his opposition to them, preferring the option of land-based, government-run convict prisons. Inquiries in 1847 and 1850 concluded that control of prisoners held on the hulks was impossible and that immorality, especially the unmentionable vice, was as rife as disease. Riots aboard some vessels, requiring the intervention of Royal Marines to quell, added to the unease. Time and decay played their part as the wooden carcasses rotted. By 1854 the numbers on board were down to 1,298, mainly 'invalids' too infirm to be transported to Australia. In 1857 only the *Unite* and the *Defence* remained at Woolwich, until the latter was engulfed in flames, though without loss of life. Their convicts were transferred either to Millbank or as a temporary expedient to the recently opened 'war prison' at Lewes. This left the *Stirling Castle* at Portsmouth until it too was closed down in 1859 when its invalids were transferred to the newly opened convict prison at Woking, ending the era of shipboard confinement in the British Isles.[21]

Despite their diverse deployment, the hulks had primarily floated with the growth, and sank with the demise, of transportation. Despite the hiatus caused by the rebellion in the Americas, transportation was renewed with vigour when an even better depository became available. The government had had its eye on this prospect from the first discovery of New South Wales by Captain Cook in 1770, and necessity quickly turned aspiration into actuality. In 1786 the cabinet decided that Australia was an excellent alternative destination for transportees. The whole vast continent would be designated a prison, the gigantic ancestor of Alcatraz. It was entirely alien and largely arid; it was far, far away; and escape from it and return home was

---

[20] Campbell, *op. cit.*, 129–40; J.R. McCulloch, *A Statistical Account of the British Empire* (London, 1837), I, p.565. 'Juveniles' were defined as being children under the age of fourteen. Many imprisoned were much younger.

[21] Most historians date the end of the hulks to 1857, not 1859. Hulks remained in use in Bermuda until 1862, and one at Gibraltar until 1875 (Sean McConville, *A History of English Prison Administration* (London, 1981), pp.393ff.; J.E. Thomas, *The English Prison Officer since 1850* (London, 1972), p.11; Campbell, *op. cit.*, pp.201f.).

well-nigh impossible. It meant that the unwanted would be removed from British shores, cheap labour would be provided for a new colony, and money would not have to be spent on building penitentiaries. In May the following year a fleet carrying 548 male and 188 female convicts, including Susannah Holmes and Henry Kable – the first colonists – sailed for the antipodes. After eight months at sea they disembarked in Botany Bay to begin a new life of forced labour for the government or a private landowner until finally they won their freedom.

In 1815, after another hiatus, this time caused by the Napoleonic Wars, things picked up apace, and the number of convict ships more than trebled to seventy-eight a year. Numbers swelled in the 1830s and then began to tail off until transportation ended: to New South Wales in 1840; to Van Diemen's Land in 1853; to Western Australia in 1868. In all, around 160,000 convicts, of whom only 25,000 were women, were sent to Australia. These included some 80,000 convicts shipped to New South Wales between 1787 and 1840, 66,000 to Van Diemen's Land between 1801 and 1852, and 10,000 to Western Australia between 1850 and 1868. Their average age was twenty-six, they were disproportionately of English origin, most had trades and almost all were convicted of crimes against property, usually petty theft.[22]

Initially, transportees showed a certain reluctance to acquiesce to their fate, especially when the destination was a strange and unknown land, half a world away. If America was the New World, Australia was *terra incognita*. Fearing the unknown, some preferred death. In 1789 Samuel Burt, a lovesick apprentice who had committed a crime in order to be caught and killed, initially declined the offer of transportation to New South Wales, only changing his mind after the object of his affections died as a result of contracting gaol fever while visiting him in Newgate. In the same year nineteen felons refused to accept transportation to New South Wales instead of hanging.

In time the worst fears were allayed. The crossing to Australia as a convict was safer and healthier than going as a migrant to the newly formed United States. And opportunity awaited those who survived the journey. For some sojourners, release would come after years of enforced labour. For others, after 1845, a period in Pentonville was followed by a free passage and a conditional pardon, the condition merely being that they remain in exile for the duration of their sentence. These erstwhile criminals created a new society, in marked contrast to those who had been shipped to America and

---

[22] James Jupp (ed.), *The Australian People*, 2nd edn (Port Melbourne, 2001), pp.16–21. Since 1856 Van Diemen's Land has been called Tasmania.

had been assimilated slowly into an existing civic structure. As a penal colony New South Wales knew no other settlers than convicts. Exiles from Great Britain were aided in their desire to settle down and start afresh by Lachlan Macquarie, the colony's governor from 1809 to 1821. For him New South Wales had the potential of being more than just a prison. It could be a place of redemption. He turned Sydney into a model city. He built the massive Hyde Park Barracks which in appearance resembled Bentham's panopticon, but in reality was more of a dormitory for workers than a prison for felons. It housed six hundred criminals with artisan skills who slept in hammocks, a hundred to each room. They would provide the manpower to build a great city. They would forge a new nation. In return the governor authorised grants of thirty-three acres of land to convicts who completed their sentences. Few returned to Britain. Many became pillars of Australian society, and by 1828 free citizens outnumbered convicts. The former could prosper in their new home in ways unimaginable in their native land. An illiterate Mancunian, Samuel Terry, freed in 1807 after seven years of hard labour, garnered an estate of 19,000 acres and was known as the 'Rothschild of Botany Bay'. Mary Reibey, who at the age of thirteen had been transported for stealing a horse, became a rich woman, amassing £20,000 by 1820. Freedom and good fortune seemed to go hand in hand in this blessed land. For the poor, transportation was a ticket to a better life. Word soon got back home, and prisoners began to object to having their sentences of transportation reduced to a shorter term of imprisonment. Macquarie rightly claimed that he had 'found New South Wales a gaol and left it a colony'.[23]

And so offenders, transported from out of their old environment, could and did blossom into respectable citizens, without the benefit of new-fangled penological theories. Many observers, including many of those transported, were ready to defend transportation and the opportunities it afforded. They thereby implicitly criticised the alternative being proposed: the penitentiary. Their voices were not heard. Other more strident voices were aghast. Where, amidst all this reform, was the punishment and where the deterrence? The second wave of transportation did not diminish the debate on penal reform. It sharpened it. It polarised opinion. The arguments in favour of hulks and transportation tended to be pragmatic rather than principled and merely fortified the conviction that a more rational form of punishment, based on sound theory, was required. Theory would trump pragmatism.[24] And the leading theorist was one of Britain's most influential philosophers.

---

[23] Niall Ferguson, *Empire* (London, 2003), pp.106ff.
[24] *OHP*, p.85.

In 1802 Jeremy Bentham published a pamphlet entitled 'Panopticon versus New South Wales'. Blind to the evidence, he denounced transportation as an expensive and ineffective device. Good money was being thrown at what he considered to be a futile failure. It was no deterrent, nor was it reformatory, as released prisoners, unlike those earlier sent to America, were not incorporated into an established civil society but created a community of thieves, 'jumbled together in one mass, and mingling like beasts'. Instead, he continued to argue for his penal panacea, his perfect penitentiary, his 'panopticon'. Even those destined for transportation would be better waiting and working in 'an inspector-house' than 'lounging in an ordinary jail, or rotting on board a ballast hulk'.[25]

---

[25] Jeremy Bentham, *Panopticon Writings*, Verso edn (London, 1995), p.76; *Postscript; Part II: containing a Plan of Management for a Panopticon Penitentiary-House* (London, 1791), p.90.

CHAPTER 13

Mr Bentham's Haunted House

If any offenders convicted of crimes for which transportation had been usually inflicted were ordered to solitary imprisonment, accompanied by well regulated hard labour, and religious instruction, it might be the means, under Providence, not only of deterring others, but also of reforming the individuals, and turning them to habits of industry.

Penitentiary Act 1779

Never does the current of my thoughts alight upon the Panopticon and its fate, but my heart sinks within me ... I do not like to look upon the Panopticon papers. It is like opening a drawer where devils are locked up – it is breaking into a haunted house.

Jeremy Bentham

Jeremy Bentham was an odd but eminently consistent man, in this life and beyond. Born in 1748, he died in 1832. Three days after his death on 6 June, and in accordance with his specific instructions, his corpse was dissected before an invited audience. Afterwards his chosen dissector, Dr Southwood Smith, a Unitarian minister and Edinburgh-educated physician, delivered a lecture on the uses of the dead to the living. It took some courage on the part of Bentham to associate his remains with the punishment of criminals or the fate of paupers. But not too much. He asserted that, if embalmed and clothed, his body might be his best representation, his 'Auto-Icon'. So it was. After his public but privileged dissection, Bentham's skeleton was articulated in a sitting position, dressed as in life, his head – which had embarrassingly shrunk – was reconstructed in waxwork, and the whole artifice preserved in perpetuity, still on display in a glass case in University College London, not the fate of an ordinary dissectee.[1]

But Bentham was no ordinary individual. He had a fastidious and orderly mind. He loved italics and the prefix 'pan'. He had opinions on everything, and a philosophical overview that encompassed everything. As his public dissection demonstrated, he was utilitarian to the backbone. He not only

---

[1] This resort to remedial reconstruction might have been avoided if only his embalmer had consulted a treatise on the procedures of head-shrinking among the Maori, written by Bentham himself.

proposed many legal and social reforms, but also expounded an underlying moral principle on which they should be based. His fundamental belief was that pain and pleasure are the 'sovereign masters' of mankind and 'it is for them alone to point out what we ought to do, as well as to determine what we shall do'. His fundamental maxim was the pleasure principle: that the greatest happiness of the greatest number is the measure of right and wrong.

Fastidious to a fault he had an ingrained distaste for disorder and a craving for system. All parts of society should be subject to regularity, rationality and method. The vast vagaries of the common law and the plethora of prisons and penalties irked him. So too did the futile and unproductive labour of the tread-wheel and crank which merely associated industry and hard work in the mind of the criminal with mind-numbing and back-breaking pain. Gaolers blunting saws, in order to 'plague' prisoners sawing wood, were only giving logical effect to the bad system of treatment that was prevalent in those days. And it was misdirected, based on a misunderstanding of the criminal mentality. Criminals were like children whose development had been arrested and warped. They were wilful, lazy, and prone to yield to temptation. They needed a careful eye to be kept on them, a firm hand on their shoulder, and they needed discipline to be instilled if the defective mechanism of their minds was to be re-calibrated, their morality refashioned and strengthened. When they were naughty they should be punished, but parental punishment was designed to improve wayward children not just to hurt them. Let the punishment fit the criminal. Idleness was the most corrupting influence in the lives of the poor that led them into crime, and the cure for idleness was hard work!

Bentham yearned to create a 'Pannomion', a complete utilitarian legal system, and to perfect the pursuit of rational punishment in a 'Panopticon'. All laws ought 'to augment the total happiness of the community' and so 'exclude everything that tends to subtract from that happiness: in other words, to exclude mischief'.[2] Punishments should be no more severe than necessary to attain the end of protecting the law-abiding majority from the depredations of the lawless minority. They should be designed to break the association of crime with pleasure and, working alongside rewards, to recondition the mind of the malefactor, to alter behaviour patterns by creating aversion to the socially baneful and desire for the beneficial, to merge deterrence and reform. A model prison, equipped to monitor every

---

2   Jeremy Bentham, *An Introduction to the Principles of Morals and Legislation* (London, 1789), pp.i, clxci.

movement, and engineered to manipulate minds while minimising pain, could embody all that his ideas entailed. For sixteen years he developed and refined his plan of a far-reaching penological experiment, pursued it more energetically than any other project, and bitterly regretted its ultimate rejection.

He had forebears, as he openly acknowledged, from Leibnitz and his conception of a surveillance society, through Locke and Hume with their associationist theories which explained human conduct as the result of the impact of experience upon the individual, to Priestley, the harbinger of Utilitarianism. Then there was the Milanese Cesare Beccaria who published his seminal work *On Crimes and Punishments* in 1764, the basic premise of which was that 'it is better to prevent crimes than to punish them'.[3] In it he advocated major reform of the continental criminal justice systems, which were savage and arbitrary, inhumane and unfair, irrational and inefficient. Condemning torture and the death penalty, he argued that punishment should be proportionate to the crime and should have a preventive and not a retributive purpose. The certainty, not severity, of punishment would achieve the deterrent effect. His proposals were both humanitarian and utilitarian, and his book was to have a major impact throughout Europe, going through six editions in eighteen months. Within three years an English translation appeared. Four year later Eden, a student of Blackstone and an enthusiast for Beccaria, published his own treatise in which 'public utility' was taken to be the practical measure of punishment. But it was left to the ingenuity of Bentham to draw up a blueprint for the form that punishment should take. He devised a 'mill for grinding rogues honest and idle men industrious' that would put theory into practice. Finally he found in Howard's labours and discoveries the foundation upon which he could build his mansion.

In 1791 he published *Panopticon or the Inspection House etc.* Bracing, confident, italicised assertions prefaced his 'idea of a new principle of construction applicable to any sort of establishment, in which persons of any description are to be kept under inspection, and in particular to penitentiary-houses' – but including prisons, lazarettos, mad-houses and schools – along 'with a Plan of Management':

> *Morals Reformed – health preserved – industry invigorated – instruction diffused – public burthens lightened – Economy seated, as it were, upon a rock – the Gordian knot of the Poor-Laws are not cut, but untied – all by a simple idea in Architecture.*

---

[3]   *Crimes and Punishments*, English trans. (Cambridge, 1995), p.103.

Significantly there is no 'religion instilled' or 'salvation ensured': the panopticon was to be no penitentiary of the sort ardent evangelicals advocated. He found the idea of redemption through suffering meaningless.

Bentham's tract consists of a series of short letters written in 1787 to 'a friend in England' and two much larger modifying 'postscripts' written in 1790 and 1791, advancing and refining a plan he attributed to his younger brother Samuel's inventiveness.[4] The writings were in response to the government's decision, inspired by the work of John Howard, 'to make a trial of the penitentiary system', despite its almost prohibitive cost. But delay beset it. The provisions of the Penitentiary Act of 1779 had been left in abeyance for want of a site. High time they were implemented! Finding a site was just the start. The structure to be built there had to be designed to fulfil its purpose. Bentham, erupting with didactic rigour, hoped to fill a lacuna left by Howard's publications. His 'venerable friend' had afforded 'a rich fund of materials: but a quarry is not a house. No leading principles, no order, no connection.' This befuddled approach was anathema to Bentham's tidy mind. He would rectify it, by prescribing the perfect penitentiary down to the last detail. Perfect and practicable. He believed that his ideas were both economical and applicable to any institution in which persons are meant to be kept under surveillance,

> no matter how different or even opposite the purpose: whether it be that of *punishing the incorrigible, guarding the insane, reforming the vicious, confining the suspected, employing the idle, maintaining the helpless, curing the sick, instructing the willing* in any branch of industry, or *training the rising race* in the path of *education*.

Everyone in such an establishment should ideally be under constant surveillance or at least in practice '*conceive* himself to be so'. Penitentiaries best encompassed 'the objects of *safe custody, confinement, solitude, forced labour* and *instruction*'.

The design of the 'Penitentiary Inspection-House' was of paramount importance: an elegant circular building with cells occupying the circumference and divided from each other 'by partitions in the form of *radii* issuing from the circumference towards the centre' and protruding far enough to cut off each prisoner from sight of any other. In the centre of this 'bee-hive' was '*the inspector's lodge*'. Each cell would have a window large enough to shed light throughout the structure as far as the lodge, and gratings that would not

---

[4] All the quotations unless otherwise noted come from the *Panopticon Writings*, Verso edn (London, 1995).

screen any part of it from the inspector's view. He would see all but be seen
by none other than in silhouette, and where his icy gaze was falling none
could discern. Thus he would become all-seeing. His disembodied voice
would be conveyed to each cell by means of tin speaking-tubes. Illusion was
as good as reality, the illusion of divine omnipresence: 'thou art about my
path, and about my bed: and spiest out all my ways' (Psalm 139:2). Reception
became an initiation ceremony whereby the novice would be baptised into
a carceral cult:

> Thorough cleansing in a warm bath ... clothing new from top to toe ...
> Ablution – regeneration – solemnity – ceremony – Form of prayer –
> the occasion would be impressive – Grave music if the establishment
> furnished it: psalmody at least, with the organ ... To minds like these
> ... what preaching comparable to that which addresses itself to sense?

Bentham goes into every aspect of what was 'more of a contraption than
a building', from reflector lamps to the means of generating economical
heating, from the provision of integral sanitation (for avoiding contact
during ablutions) to the manufacture of prison clothing with sleeves of
different colours to ensure recapture should a harlequin get away.[5] Nothing
escaped his attention, no element of prison life from the smallest to
the largest. 'Hints ... not noble in themselves' are 'ennobled by the end'.
Handkerchiefs for prisoners were a necessity. There should be 'no blowing
of noses but with a handkerchief', and 'no spitting, but in a handkerchief or
spitting-box'. In summer bathing should be once a week, but in winter once
a month. Walking on a wheel would ensure exercise, exposure, seclusion and
economy. Prisoners would participate in 'virtual' worship by observing and
hearing the services 'without stirring from their cells'.

The building should keep prisoners in and intruders out. Only too
cognisant of the fate that befell Newgate during the Gordon riots, Bentham
drew up plans of outward fortification with palisades patrolled by armed
guards. Internally it should be neither too small to afford a sufficient
number of cells, nor too big to exclude light to the lodge. He had done the
calculations and did not stint to give them. For instance, a diameter of 100
feet would allow for '48 cells, 6 feet wide each at the outside, walls included;
with a passage through the building of 8 or 9 feet'. He goes on and on with
every conceivable measurement for penitentiaries from two to six storeys in
height, housing from 96 to 288 prisoners. These dimensions were for each
rotunda, and a single inspector could cover two or even more so long as

---

5   Robin Evans, *The Fabrication of Virtue* (Cambridge, 1982), p.198.

the inspector's windows were not more than '32½ feet from the open light'. Bentham was convinced that 'the business of inspection, like every other, will be performed to a greater degree of perfection, the less trouble the performance of it requires'.

Every exigency is covered; every means of increasing capacity, security, surveillance, and solitude while diminishing expense was considered.[6] Worries that the public might have about cost and 'luxury too great for an establishment of this kind' would be palliated by the need for fewer staff and thinner walls. The essence of the scheme was to combine 'the *apparent omnipresence* of the inspector' with 'the extreme facility of his *real presence*'. The public themselves – 'the great *open committee* of the tribunal of the world' – should be welcomed in, thus becoming unwitting and unwaged inspectors. Such openness reflected the practice of his time and would be in marked contrast to the Bastille-like secrecy of the future when members of the public were rarely invited through intimidating prison gates. The 'principal inspector' should have accommodation in the lodge for a large family, the more numerous the better, 'since, by this means, there will in fact be as many inspectors, as the family consists of persons, though only one be paid for it'. Secluded themselves, they will unavoidably be drawn to 'that great and constant fund of entertainment to the sedentary and vacant in towns – the looking out of the window. The scene, though confined, would be very various, and therefore, perhaps, not altogether an unamusing one.'[7] The pleasure principle in practice.

This was the perfect prison: few staff, many 'solitary and sequestered' prisoners, and the perception of constant surveillance, the essence consisting 'in the centrality of the inspector's situation, combined with the well-known and most effectual contrivances for *seeing without being seen*'. The panopticon was designed primarily for prevention, not detection. It was to police actions, and, despite the God-like nature of the inspector, not to open mirrors into men's souls, 'leaving thoughts and fancies to their proper *ordinary*, the court *above*'. It served a variety of purposes.

Punishment was to the fore and it too served an ulterior purpose. 'All Punishment in itself is evil' and 'ought only to be admitted in as far as

---

6   It is true that in Postscript I he backtracked on absolute solitude except as an occasional punishment, allowing for multiple-occupancy cells in 'mitigated seclusion in assorted companies' but without 'opportunities of promiscuous association'. In this he followed Howard's lead, but he did so as much on the grounds of cost as out of compassion.

7   In Postscript I Bentham abandoned this for domestic accommodation in an adjoining building.

it promises to exclude some greater evil'. Punishment ought not to be inflicted where it is groundless, inefficacious, needless, unprofitable or too expensive. Punishment was both needless and expensive 'where the purpose of putting an end to the practice may be attained as effectually at a cheaper rate: by instruction, for instance, as well as by terror'.[8] Of all the objects of punishment, 'example is beyond comparison the most important'. Punishment must set an example and the setting of an example outweighs reformation. The setting of an example is for the benefit of the many 'innocent', reformation is but for the few who have offended. Punishment was justifiable if it prevented 'all sorts of offences' – if it deterred.

To be a deterrent, it must first and foremost be a spectacle, a dramatic performance aimed not merely at inflicting suffering on the specific criminal but at instilling fear into all those tempted to crime. Appearance was all. The panopticon was the stage. The inspector was a *deus in machina*. Prisoners, like actors in a Greek tragedy – or farce – would wear masks, the grimaces of which would denote the gravity of their offences. They were essential participants in his spectral masquerade; before the curious public they would stage their own guilt and consequent suffering in 'a perpetual pillory'. Guilt could be 'pilloried in the abstract', while the faces of the guilty individuals would be masked from view. As their apparent suffering was magnified, their actual suffering could be diminished. Appearance was paramount and the more who witnessed this charade the greater its deterrent effect.

Such public punishment, primary though it be, need not impair other purposes, and indeed, in Bentham's eyes, they went hand in hand. Every prison would have a hospital but, if his plan was realised, 'the whole prison would be perhaps a better hospital than any building known hitherto by that name'. The mad, many of whom were incarcerated then as now, would be distinguished from the bad. That 'strange and unseemly mixture of calamity and guilt – lunatics raving and felons rioting in the same room' would be ended as 'every vacant cell would afford these afflicted beings an apartment exempt from disturbance, and adapted to their wants'.

Coercion could embrace lenity. The need for punishment would be minimal in this surveillance culture. Whipping was a thing of the past. Gagging could replace fetters for those causing an uproar, and would better ensure silence. Segregation in absolute solitude would be a recourse of last resort. The treatment of those imprisoned would be improved as the abuses of under-keepers would be far fewer since they themselves would be equally under

---

8   Bentham, *op. cit.*, pp.clxvi, clxxiii. He would have thought our current 'war on drugs' an expensive absurdity.

surveillance and the threat of the most severe punishment. This answered 'the most puzzling of political questions – *quis custodiet ipsos custodes*'. It was this circumstance that rendered 'the influence of this plan not less beneficial to what is called *liberty*, than to necessary coercion; not less powerful as a control upon subordinate power, than as a curb to delinquency; as a shield to innocence, than as a scourge to guilt'.

Commendably, Bentham wanted to achieve the greatest apparent suffering with the least actual suffering, the greatest deterrent effect with the best mechanism for reform, and all in the most economical way. Three interlinking 'Rules' governed the whole enterprise. Under the 'Rule of Severity' the 'ordinary condition of the convict doomed to forced labour' ought not to be better – but nor should it be worse[9] – than that of the poorest class of the free population. Tobacco and alcohol should be banned but the food provided should be adequate and wholesome. Under the 'Rule of Lenity' incarceration 'ought not to be attended with bodily suffering, or anything prejudicial or dangerous to health or life'. And then there was the 'Rule of Economy'. Being economical was vital as lack of money had been the main reason why no national penitentiary had yet been built. Political support would depend on the frugality of the scheme and so his third rule was as essential as the first two. Hard work by prisoners would defray the costs of their incarceration, as well as promoting, and providing evidence of, their reformation.[10] Fourteen hours a day of sedentary labour and another hour on wheel-powered machinery would be expected of each inmate – profitable to the person, profitable to the panopticon – very different from the useless hard labour of the crank and tread-wheel. Release would depend on the prisoner enlisting in the army or navy or providing an exorbitant and annually renewable £50 bond for good behaviour from a responsible householder to whom he would be apprenticed. Otherwise detention for the pauper criminal could be for life, in what was a forced labour camp, run for profit. Profits and losses would be farmed out, and private contractors subjected to surveillance and fined for every death in custody or escape, or forced to compensate the victims of unreformed prisoners. Self-interest would promote public good.

His scheme was applicable 'to the joint purposes of *punishment, reformation* and *pecuniary economy*'. But unlike the Christian activists, Bentham said far less about reform than about the other purposes, and what constituted 'reform'

---

[9] In contrast to the 'less-eligibility' principle that would later dominate the penal landscape.

[10] Janet Semple, *Bentham's Prison* (Oxford, 1993), pp.93, 112f.

for Bentham – 'conformity to the pleasure principle' – was very different from the 'repentance and rebirth in Christ' propounded by Howard and Hanway.

His proposal was never fully realised in Britain. Perhaps just as well, although the Christian variants actually realised proved almost as bad. Like its creator his creation was far too prescriptive, intrusive, both coldly rational and utopian. His 'abstract intelligence [was] a coercive instrument ... wilfully rejecting interests and values incompatible with its own assumptions, and thereby depriving itself of the co-operative and generative functions of life – feeling, emotion, playfulness, exuberance, free fantasy'. His utopia, like all others, would have been 'a sterile desert, unfit for human occupation'.[11] An ever-open eye was its emblem. Reactions to it abounded in animal and insect metaphors. Bentham's 'penal panorama' was a zoo or circus, its exhibits in cages or performing to instruction. It was a goldfish bowl upon which light was constantly shone. When Edmund Burke was shown a plan, he remarked, acidly and aptly, 'there's the Keeper, the spider in the web!'[12] Or it was a hive for worker bees.[13] It was a factory for automata not a house for human beings with all their vagaries and variety. It was a travesty of a model prison as he was a travesty of a model reformer. It would have been an atheist's answer to Pentonville, but as demoralising. The work Bentham thought pleasurable would have been monotonous and time on 'the wheel' would have been drudgery. His scheme lacked essential humanity, but then again, for all his good intentions, so did Bentham.[14]

At first the founding of New South Wales as a penal colony did not seem to threaten the future of his obsession. He almost succeeded in getting his project approved. In 1793 William Pitt, then Prime Minister, inspected a model of the panopticon at Bentham's home and authorised him to proceed with his project. Pitt's attentions, however, were soon diverted to foreign and domestic crises, and the scheme languished for a while. Then it revived. It necessitated a further Act of parliament, a new Penitentiary Act which would reverse the whole thrust of the previous one for public management

---

11   Louis Mumford, 'Utopia: The City and the Machine' in F.E. Manuel (ed.), *Utopia and Utopian Thought* (Boston, 1966), p.10. See also Semple, *op. cit.*, pp.299–304.

12   Quoted in Gertrude Himmelfarb, *Victorian Minds* (London, 1968), pp.58f.

13   Bentham used the same analogy but maintained none was a drone.

14   Bentham was not devoid of imaginative sympathy, but lacked empathy. 'For all his lip-service to the welfare of humanity, Bentham's benevolence lacked passion, dedication and the courage of the ultimate sacrifice.' Howard had expended his own fortune and forfeited his own life for the sake of his sacred calling. Bentham admired such dedication but knew he could not emulate it (Semple, *op. cit.*, pp.76f.).

and inspection. Under the 1794 Act the Treasury could acquire land and contract for a private profit-making prison. The entire responsibility for 'the care, management, superintendence and control' of the prison would be put into the hands of a single 'contractor-governor'.[15] Although there were no statutory safeguards for the welfare of prisoners and no restrictions on the powers of the governor, both of which Bentham had urged, in this one essential it conformed to his proposals for a privately-run enterprise – as well it might, since he had pressed for it.[16]

It was this element that most distinguished Bentham's scheme from those of other reformers. Contractors in the past had exploited prisoners and had run prisons as profitable private enterprises. The onus more recently, under Howard's urging, was on public ownership and government oversight. Why was Bentham running against the whole trend of penal reform? Why was he vesting such power and authority in one individual? Ethical and incorruptible as he believed himself to be, he was surely the obvious choice as the first such contractor-governor. It should be a job for life, and one for which he would be well remunerated. Self-interest married megalomania. But worse, a charge of venality could be levelled against Bentham. His collusive correspondence with a friend in Scotland showed how he would cut corners on food, clothing and bedding to maximise profits.[17] Presumably the pleasure he would thereby accrue to himself would outweigh the misery he would inflict on others.

A contract on the above favourable terms was in fact drawn up and all it needed was a signature. It was to be ratified once a suitable plot of land was found. This proved difficult and time-consuming. Landowners did not want a prison built near their estates, depreciating property values. The most influential objector was Earl Spencer whose salubrious land at Battersea Rise, earlier earmarked for a national penitentiary under the 1779 Act, Bentham coveted for his panopticon. Yet Spencer would not sell and could not be made to. Nor could the law be changed to allow for the land's compulsory purchase. Spencer, as a member of the administration, had easy access to Pitt. All the lobbying powers of Bentham would crash

---

[15] The term 'governor' was given statutory basis in 1839 by the Act for the Better Ordering of Prisons which provided for the appointment of governors with all the powers and duties of the gaoler or keeper. The new designation denoted an enhanced status for the role of running the new prestigious prisons and penitentiaries, and soon the positions were filled almost entirely by governors who were former army or naval officers. At the same time 'warders' replaced the old 'turnkeys' and were largely recruited from the ranks.

[16] On the history of the Act see Semple, *op. cit.*, pp.166–91.

[17] Himmelfarb, *op. cit.*, pp.62f.

upon this rock. In itself that was not fatal, and other ground was eventually found in the far from salubrious Millbank, but it contributed to the final demise of the scheme. The initial high costs of construction which the government would have to front in time of war, the provision already made in the counties of prisons in accordance with Howard's principles, and the availability of cheaper alternatives such as hulks or transportation resulted in those in power getting cold feet. The plan, shunted from one department to another, was continually delayed and ultimately thwarted.

In March 1811 a committee of the House of Commons was set up 'to consider of the expediency of erecting a Penitentiary House or Penitentiary Houses' under the Acts of 1779 and 1794. It called Bentham to give evidence, but his desire to protect the profit potential and his refusal to be bound by anything but the literal sense of the contract damaged his cause. It also did little to allay the committee's fears about private contractors running prisons, and the private contractor Bentham had in mind was himself. He defended the unfettered powers of the governor. He was opposed to official inspectors, preferring the unofficial 'promiscuous assemblage' of the public, attracted to visit the prison by 'curiosity and love of amusement', who would act as unpaid overseers. He dismissed the unspoken fear of homosexuality in shared cells by his insistence on constant inspection. Fatally, before such a committee, he downplayed the role of the chaplain and, as he was 'no searcher of hearts', doubted the possibility of inducing genuine repentance. All the while Bentham remained blithely confident of success, but George Holford, who chaired the committee, showed his disgust: 'For such inventions was it gravely proposed to us in the nineteenth century to abandon the ordinary principles of prison management.' Other witnesses, notably Paul from Gloucester and Becher from Southwell, both disciples of Howard, sealed the project's fate. They were as scathing in their criticism of the panopticon as they were staunch in their support for solitary confinement.

The report, published in May, compared Bentham's proposals unfavourably with earlier measures prohibiting keepers from profiting by the sale of commodities in prison. It preferred the example of the prisons recently established in Gloucester and Southwell, which were publicly managed and provided individual cells, moderate seclusion and hard labour. Public management, they concluded, would better serve the interests of the physical and moral welfare of prisoners than a reversion to the older, wholly discredited model of private contractors who had run prisons in their own pecuniary interests rather than for the public benefit or along penological principles. It thought that the 'institution contemplated by Mr Bentham was merely a great manufactory, without regard being had either to the penal or moral objects of a prison'.[18] It proposed instead that a 'National Penitentiary-House' be built in London and managed in accordance with the principles of the 1779 Act, the very penal experiment that Holford would be paid to oversee. With one stroke Bentham was felled and Holford energised.[19]

Bentham's panopticon was never to be realised,[20] but had it been it would, in all probability, have become a standing refutation to the ideals behind it and a reproach to its deviser, just as Millbank and Pentonville would be to their proponents, Holford included. Bentham bemoaned its passing, bewailed its fate, and found the reason in a far-fetched conspiracy on the part of rivals and latterly even of a vengeful monarch. He was, however, compensated for his efforts and expenses to the sum of £23,000. He had asked for £689,062 11s.[21]

His dystopian scheme may have been stillborn, but the notion of the philanthropic prison predated it and survived it. Its time had come. Between 1775 and 1850 a new philosophy of punishment emerged in England. England was a manifestly Christian country and, after the evangelical revival led by the Methodists, an ardent one, more attuned to the moral fervour of John Howard than to the utilitarian zeal of Jeremy Bentham. The ideas of the two men coalesced in many ways, and their vision in its effect was bi-focal and powerful. They agreed on many aspects of prison reform, including the separation of sexes, the division into classes of criminals, and the provision of better sanitation, warm clothing and a nutritious and adequate diet. Their writings, taken together, along with those of James Neild, whose comprehensive survey of British prisons published in 1812 complemented Howard's, had a vast impact. A form of carceral discipline directed at the mind – through religious exhortation, honest labour and contemplative seclusion – would replace a cluster of punishments directed at the body – whipping, branding, pillorying, hanging. This, if implemented,

---

[18] *Extracts*, p 88.

[19] In a third report the committee, forgetting its apprehension about shared cells, endorsed the use of the hulks, and dismissed the fear of unnatural congress below decks where guards were afraid to go by asserting that the prisoners 'do not often ill-use each other' (Semple, *op. cit.*, p.278).

[20] The two American attempts to construct panoptica – the Western penitentiary at Pittsburgh and the Statesville near Chicago – were disasters.

[21] Semple, *op. cit.*, pp.280f.

would mark a decisive transformation in the nature of punishment, if not quite in its strategy.[22]

Deterrence and rehabilitation were non-identical twins, whose parents passed on their respective traits, and who would grow up together and never leave each other's side. They needed each other, yet they were Romulus and Remus, suffering from sibling envy. Their aims were different, and an emphasis on one could have a deleterious effect on the other. In the mind of the public and of politicians, punishment had to serve several competing ends: retribution – punishing the individual malefactor; deterrence – preventing the offender re-offending and would-be offenders from offending in the first place; containment – caging the dangerous; and rehabilitation – redeeming the sinner or re-forming the maladjusted. This last was a point of convergence. Criminals could be considered as sinners needing salvation, or as a malfunctioning machine needing repair. England was not only a Christian country; it was an industrial country. It knew all about sinners and all about machines.

The increasing need for secondary punishments, Enlightenment thinking and Christian concern converged to bring about innovation. Considerable thought and energy were put into devising a rational prison system and a rationale for it. Penal change would be a complex affair, full of contradictory impulses and policies. Reform would come in waves, often the product of compromises between competing ideas and between abstract schemes and practical limitations.[23] Experiments would be made and failures would be discarded. From this period until the present day the varying purposes of imprisonment have clashed and collided, and usually the demands of security and safe custody have overridden the other purposes vested in imprisonment. All prisons were designed to prevent escape, but within those inescapable parameters could they also be designed to promote reform? They would no longer be warehouses storing vice, but become factories manufacturing virtue. Their condition must first be rectified, but thereafter their very nature must be revolutionised. Above all, popular perception of prisons had to change from seeing them as penal dustbins on the one hand or citadels of oppression on the other to perceiving them as pinnacles of progress.

---

22 *Contra* Foucault and others whose cynicism about the motives of reformers such as Howard and Fry betrays a lack of understanding of the moral power of religious conviction. They were not waging class war but fighting the Devil and his works.

23 *OHP*, p.80.

Thus towards the end of the eighteenth century and into the nineteenth, divergent influences converged to bring about a transformation in penal thinking. Evangelical Christians, appalled by the state of ordinary gaols, were attracted to the possibility of inducing repentance in criminals rather than merely punishing their crimes. Stressing the identification of all men in sin, they believed that criminals were not intrinsically different from the rest of society. They too were children of God and, if of infinite worth, worth saving. They too could be redeemed and, if redeemed, reformed. True regret at past conduct was far more likely to lead to a lasting change of behaviour than mere fear of the consequences. Faith grew with time, while the pains of past punishment receded. Utilitarians, on the other hand, considered that the purpose of punishment was not to avenge crime but to prevent it, and the way in which it was administered should reflect the social good and the offender's needs. Criminals were merely sick, not wicked. In so much as they were rational beings they could be deterred by severe punishments; in so much as they were defective machines they could be repaired by social engineering. This dual purpose could best be served by a prison system designed to mould and change character as well as to deter offenders. It was carrot and stick deployed simultaneously and to the same end: the diminution of criminality.

The time was opportune. Other institutions of social benefit and social control were coming into being at the same time, constituting what has been somewhat erroneously called 'the great confinement'.[24] Red brick schools and colleges were springing up to educate and train the upper and middle classes in muscular Christianity and their God-given duty to rule. Gothic revival churches with their ranks of dark hard pews were being consecrated to ensure Christian conformity among the urban poor. 'Lunatics' were being controlled and isolated in asylums; the destitute in workhouses. Workers were being employed – or enslaved – in factories. The political radical, Josiah Dornford, wrote in 1785: 'Nothing but a *real reform* can save us from ruin as a nation. Were our prisons new-modelled, it would be one considerable step toward reform of the lower orders of the people.'[25] It was in keeping with these sentiments that from the 1840s the great penitentiaries, Pentonville *par excellence*, were built to isolate, employ and recreate the criminal. With their single cells, strict silence and regulated regimes these were to be 'virtue

---

24 The title of chapter 2 of Foucault's *History of Madness*.

25 *Seven letters to the Lords and Commons of Great Britain, upon the impolicy, inhumanity, and injustice of our present mode of arresting the bodies of debtors; shewing the inconsistency of it with Magna Carta and a free constitution* (London, 1786).

factories', where errant humanity, left to repent and inspired to work, could be saved or salvaged or both.

This reforming zeal on the part of philosopher and philanthropist influenced the public mind and led to a transformation in both the rationale for, and architecture of, prisons. It was a disaster built on the best of intentions. Even efforts at better hygiene added to the degradation. Enforced bathing, the imposition of uniforms and the shearing of hair may have kept disease at bay, but they stripped inmates of their personal identity. They became numbers. Thus 'the price of these improvements was a different kind of misery: solitude, minutely measured labour, food that preserved life but gave no pleasure, sleep regulated and restricted ... they designed, implemented and constantly refined a system of hygienic suffering'.[26]

But one person, by dint of personality and compassion, did have a transformative effect on the lives of prisoners. That person stood out against the rigours of the separate and silent systems, knowing from personal experience the efficacy of being alone at times for private contemplation but equally believing that enforced isolation for prolonged periods for social beings was utterly destructive of mind and body, and ultimately counter-productive. There was 'a vast difference between useful and improving reflection, and the imagination dwelling upon guilt or prospective evil'.[27] Education, instruction and useful employment were essential to any prison regime, but not so the back-breaking futility of the tread-wheel. The person with those humane and sensible insights and the ability and energy to put them into practice was not a philosopher nor a politician, but a wife and mother: Elizabeth Fry.

[26] *OHP*, p.308; Michael Ignatieff, *A Just Measure of Pain* (London, 1978), pp.100f.
[27] Fry, II, p.253.

CHAPTER 14

The Angel of the Prisons

[Mrs Fry] then told [the women] that the ladies did not come with any absolute and authoritative pretensions; that it was not intended they should command, and the prisoners obey; but that it was to be understood, all were to act in concert; that not a rule should be made, or a monitor appointed, without their full and unanimous concurrence; that for this purpose, each of the rules should be read and put to the vote; and she invited those who might feel any disinclination to any particular freely to state their opinion.

Thomas Fowell Buxton

The better the actual state of our prisons is known and understood the more clearly will all men see the necessity of those arrangements, by which they may be rendered schools of industry and virtue, instead of the very nurseries of crime.

Joseph Gurney

While some prison reformers, following Bentham's lead, stressed impersonal, disciplinary techniques of reform, Quakers laid their trust in empathy, example and the power of the gospel. The redemption of sinners lay at the heart of Holy Scripture. For Quakers the seeming incorrigibility of the criminal was the result not of human nature but of a mistaken view of punishment. Not deterrence, not retribution but reformation was the prime purpose of imprisonment: 'punishment is not for revenge, but to lessen crime and reform the criminal': and to achieve the former you must do the latter. But to do anything you had to have first-hand knowledge of prison conditions and not just a penal theory. Quakers had long acquaintance with the reality of imprisonment and knew how that reality militated against the attainment of rehabilitation. Howard's reforms had had an effect but too often they were not implemented at all, or their effect soon wore off. Newgate seemed untouched by reform. Overcrowding was a major culprit. James Neild recorded that in 1811 there were 396 felons and 233 debtors in the gaol.[1] Worse, there were hordes of children. When George Ellis MP 'went all over Newgate' he found scenes of 'youthful depravity'. One boy

---

[1] James Neild, *State of the Prisons in England, Scotland and Wales* (London, 1812), p.417.

'named Leary of thirteen [had] been in Newgate twenty times, and been four times under sentence of death'. Another four boys ranging from nine to fourteen 'have been altogether in Newgate between 70 and 80 times' and 'all [kept] their women'![2] Thus when Stephen Grellet, a French *émigré*, American citizen and Quaker convert, visited Newgate and told his 'much-valued friend', Elizabeth Fry, what he had found there – 'blaspheming, fighting, dram-drinking, and half-naked children' – she decided to see for herself, as he knew she would.

If Quakers have an aristocracy then Elizabeth – or Betsy – was born into it. Her mother was a Barclay. She herself was a Gurney by birth, and a Fry by marriage. Her husband John was one of the wealthiest and most eligible bachelors in Quaker circles, and heir to the family estate of Plashet, near Epping Forrest. Samuel Hoare and Thomas Fowell Buxton were her brothers-in-law. From childhood she had yearned to 'lessen the sorrows of the afflicted'. In adulthood she had the means to do so. At the age of thirty-two she was well-off, well-placed, well-educated and, most of all, well-suited to the task. She radiated goodness, and her kindly sanctity was something all observed. An old sea-dog put it simply: 'to see her was to love her'. Much of her success was 'based upon that awe which such a presence inspired'.[3] The work of 'the angel of prisons' was about to begin.

In January 1813, accompanied by Anna Buxton, Thomas's sister, she went to Newgate prison.[4] First they had to get in, along with all the other visitors who were hoping to see loved ones. The turnkeys had learnt from past mistakes. All visitors were searched, and those suspected of concealing either spirits or instruments of escape could be subjected to a strip-search. Those found with prohibited items would be taken before a magistrate and committed to Newgate themselves. The ladies had indeed 'instruments of escape' on their person – Bibles.

Once inside, Mrs Fry and Miss Buxton were appalled at what they found: weeping women in a 'deplorable condition ... dwelling in a vortex of corruption', partitioned off 'in that part known as the untried side', but the partition was of insufficient height to prevent the male 'prisoners from overlooking the narrow yard and the windows of the two wards and two cells of which the women's division consisted'. Into this small space nearly three hundred women along with their numerous children were crowded,

---

2   *EHD*, XI, p.384.

3   Fry, I, p.427.

4   Fry, I, pp.201ff. The first reference to visiting Newgate in Fry's journal is dated 16 January – or as she puts it, 'the first month'. She mentions, however, two earlier visits they had made.

without differentiation, without employment and without supervision other than that given by a man and his son who had charge of them night and day. They lacked sufficient clothing and that which they had was so ragged as to leave them half-naked. They had no bedding to put on the floor, and in dirt and squalor they lived, washed, and cooked. What money they could get by begging they spent in the tap on alcohol. Drinking, gaming, fighting and swearing were universal. Some women even dressed in men's clothes. The stench was atrocious. The keeper was reluctant to enter this section of his gaol, and advised the genteel visitors to leave their valuables in his house, advice they ignored.

After a four-year hiatus, during which she gave birth to her ninth and tenth child, Fry sprang into 'a whirlwind and storm' of philanthropic activity. She was not alone, as others in her milieu, inspired by her endeavours, had become involved in prison reform themselves, the Society for the Improvement of Prison Discipline and Reformation of Juvenile Offenders being founded by Thomas Buxton and Samuel Hoare in 1816.[5] The name was significant: *prison regimes* should be improved; *the young* should be reformed. The same hope was not initially or specifically extended to adults, at least until Mrs Fry came along.

In March 1817 she began her mission to Newgate. What she had seen there was but 'an atom in the abyss of vice' in the 'vast metropolis', but it was the place to start. She was convinced that women prisoners in particular needed something more than the ministrations of a male ordinary. 'Woman has a voice for woman, to which she only can respond.'[6] But there was also the moral dimension. No man, not even the chaplain, should have unsupervised contact with women prisoners. It was a matter of decency and dignity and decorum. She believed that the women could be helped to help themselves: it would be a collaborative effort. This inclusive approach would prove the key to success. Courtesy was her calling-card. She brought hope and left self-confidence.

Although her involvement in Newgate was approved by the sheriffs of London, the ordinary, Dr Horace Cotton, and Mr Newman, the keeper, they were pessimistic of success. She persisted, Newgate becoming 'a principal object' for her. Until she had made 'some attempt at amendment in the

---

5 Thomas Buxton, *Memoirs*, 4th edn, ed. Charles Buxton (London, 1850), p.54. An Anglican, he visited many prisons and had seen for himself the wonders of the silent system in the Maison de Force in Ghent. His essay on prison discipline, published in 1818, which commented approvingly on the submissiveness of prisoners under the silent system, made quite a stir.

6 Fry, II, p.365.

plans for the women' she would not 'feel easy'. 'Feeling' was a strong, driving emotion among Quakers. She, as a mother ten times over, was much moved by ministering to a woman condemned to death for murdering her baby, and noted with alarm that, as she witnessed more hangings, their impact upon her feelings was dulled, but not quenched.

There was much to do to make the 'prison a religious place'. And an improving one. She formed a school there – the first in British penal history – 'for the children of the poor prisoners, as well as the young criminals' under twenty-five. An unused cell was put into service as a classroom and Fry – remarkably – invited the women to appoint their own schoolmistress from among themselves. They chose a young woman called Mary Connor who had recently been committed for stealing a watch. She proved ideal for the task and performed it with such zeal and integrity that she was pardoned, although she died of consumption before her release could take effect. Mary had become 'one of the first-fruits of Christian labour in that place'. And fruit there was in abundance. 'Already, from being like wild beasts, [the women] appear harmless and kind.' One reclaimed sinner wrote a letter of thanks, blessing 'the day that brought me inside of Newgate walls, for then it was that the rays of Divine truth shone into my dark mind.'[7]

Introducing employment was another important innovation. It would keep idle hands busy and provide the means of making an honest living on release. Initially it was thought by sceptics and supporters alike not only visionary but wholly impractical because of the character of its beneficiaries, its unfavourable locality, and lack of jobs. Even Buxton and Hoare dismissed the notion. Fry would not be swayed, 'but amidst these discouraging views our benevolent friend evinced that her heart was fixed; and trusting in the Lord, she commenced her work of faith and labour of love'. In April, eleven Quaker ladies and a clergyman's wife formed an 'Association for the Improvement of the Female Prisoners in Newgate', to provide for 'the clothing, the instruction and the employment of the women', to introduce them to 'a knowledge of the Holy Scriptures, and to form in them ... those habits of order, sobriety and industry which may render them docile and peaceable while in prison, and respectable when they leave it'.[8] Self-discipline and self-respect were at the heart of this experiment. So too was the unparalleled and revolutionary idea of prison democracy. Fry was not imposing her views on reluctant inmates; she was encouraging their active participation in their own self-improvement.

---

[7] Fry, I, pp.252–6.
[8] Fry, I, pp.261–3; Gurney, pp.151–66.

To their credit the sheriffs and magistrates thought her scheme admirable, if impracticable. Mrs Fry invited them to a meeting with her charges one Sunday afternoon. The women were assembled and asked if they would abide by the rules necessary to attain the great ends of education and employment. The women complied; the authorities approved. More than approved. They enthusiastically adopted 'the whole plan as a part of the system of Newgate', paid part of the expenses 'and loaded the ladies with thanks and benedictions'. They had seen for themselves what could only be described as an astonishing 'transformation', more, a miracle:

> Riot, licentiousness, and filth, exchanged for order, sobriety, and comparative neatness in the chamber, the apparel, and the persons of the prisoners. They saw no more an assemblage of abandoned and shameless creatures, half-naked and half-drunk, rather demanding, than requesting charity. The prison no more resounded with obscenity, and imprecations, and licentious songs ... this 'hell upon earth' exhibited the appearance of an industrious manufactory, or a well-regulated family.[9]

The Ladies' Committee appointed a resident matron to superintend the prisoners at work and at prayer. Up until then some of the ladies had undertaken the task, bringing in provisions and spending whole days mingling among the women and exhorting them. A matron was a new departure. Her salary was paid in part by the Corporation of London while the Association made up the rest. She was provided with accommodation and was regarded as the principal staff member. A yards-woman was also appointed, as was a sub-matron who 'superintended a little shop ... where tea, sugar, a little haberdashery and other equally harmless articles were sold to prisoners'. This was no 'tap'. Alcohol was not for sale.[10]

One of the members of the Association had the idea that 'Botany Bay might be supplied with stockings, and indeed all articles of clothing, of the prisoners' manufacture'. A local supplier whose own trade would be affected was approached for advice. The owners said that they would 'not in any way obstruct such laudable designs, and that no further trouble need be taken to provide work for they would engage to do it'.[11] Not just the school but the manufactory was soon up and running, the latter in a converted laundry. One clerical visitor was astounded at the calm and propriety of all those gainfully employed, and 'observed upon their countenance an air of self-

---

9   Thomas Buxton, *An Inquiry whether Crime and Misery are Produced or Prevented by our Present System of Prison Discipline* (London, 1818), p.142.

10 Fry, I, p.322.

11 Buxton, *op. cit.*, pp.137f.

respect and gravity, a sort of consciousness of their improved character, and the altered position in which they were placed'.[12]

The initial beneficiaries of the scheme had been convicted women prisoners. Six months after it began, the untried petitioned the newly-established Ladies' Committee that 'the same might be done among them, and promising strict obedience'. Their wish was granted but there was less work, and prisoners preparing for trial or hoping for release were less apt at what there was. An important lesson was learnt by the philanthropists: 'that where the prisoners ... did no work, they derived little if any moral advantage; where they did some work, they received some benefit, and where they were fully engaged, they were really and essentially improved'.[13] Employment, Fry concluded, was essential to reformation, but the employment must be remunerated.

Fry was becoming celebrated throughout Britain and beyond, but celebrity was not a status she courted or relished. This most modest of women was doing God's will, and to God be the glory. But her fame helped swell the coffers. Money poured in, and not just from Quakers. Letters arrived from numerous admirers, many of whom wished to emulate her efforts in their own localities. Magistrates wrote for advice on how to improve the prisons under their control. Others were anxious to witness and learn from what was being done in Newgate. Statesmen and civic functionaries, foreign travellers and clergy of all denominations 'flocked to witness the extraordinary change that had passed over the scene'. The Revd D.B. Taylor attended one of the services Fry led in Newgate chapel, and recorded his impressions in his journal:

> Never till then, and never since then, have I heard anyone read as Elizabeth Fry read [from the Bible] – the solemn reverence of her manner, the articulation, so exquisitely modulated, so distinct, that not a word of that sweet and touching voice could fail to be heard.

He had experienced many eloquent preachers but had never 'listened to one who had so thoroughly imbibed the Master's spirit, or been taught by Him the persuasive power of pleading with sinners for the life of their own souls'.[14] Oftentimes she would reduce audiences to tears.

She had become an expert and an icon. Her views could not be ignored. More, they were solicited. The time was ripe. Public interest in the subject

---

12 Jean Hatton, *Betsy* (Oxford, 2005), p.181.
13 Fry, I, pp.268f.
14 Augustus Hare, *The Gurneys of Earlham* (London, 1895), I, pp.283–6.

of penal reform was growing, 'the true principles of prison discipline [were] beginning to be generally understood', and a consensus was forming that 'if we would diminish crimes, we must give to our punishments a tendency to reform criminals, and that in our prisons in particular, this tendency can be no otherwise promoted than by a regular system of inspection, classification, instruction and employment'.[15] Mrs Fry was the very embodiment of enlightened prison reform, 'a type of her times, an illustration of the benevolent and enlarged philanthropy, which [was] diffusing its influence throughout all classes'.[16]

In February 1818 she gave evidence to a committee of the House of Commons on the Prisons of the Metropolis. She described the conditions she had found, the initiatives she had instigated, and the impact Christian teaching had on those utterly ignorant of it. She went further, advocating a prison solely for women, staffed by women and inspected by women volunteers. It would be cost-effective. Women's prisons would be less expensive as they need be less secure, and women staff would be paid less than men. She also urged paid employment, provided by the government. Mindful that her experiment could not be universally deployed in the myriad of prison establishments dotting the country, and that current success depended on the dedication of a few philanthropic amateurs, she believed that only state control and regulation could effect permanent and universal betterment. Her conclusions were confident and emphatic:

> In a prison under proper regulations, where [prisoners] had very little communication with their friends, where they were sufficiently well-fed and clothed, constantly employed and instructed, and taken care of by women, I have not the least doubt that wonders would be performed, and that many of these, now the most profligate and the worst of characters, would turn out valuable members of society.

The Committee commended her endeavours but shrewdly attributed her success at least in part to the personal touch: it was love that worked miracles. Love and charisma. But could it be replicated elsewhere? Some doubted it:

> The benevolent exertions of Mrs Fry and her friends in the female department of the prison have indeed, by the establishment of a school, by providing work and encouraging industrious habits, produced the

---

15 Gurney, p.99. Fry considered classification – keeping disparate groups apart – vital. In many ways we still do.

16 Fry, II, p.519.

most gratifying change. But much must be ascribed to unremitting personal attention and influence.[17]

Yet if so much could be achieved by a few philanthropists working in Newgate, others thought so much more could be achieved in prisons designed for the very purpose of reform: penitentiaries. Fry was one of them and her successes gave impetus to the enormous expenditure that their construction would entail. The initial cost would be great but would be more than compensated by the resulting diminution in crime. The marquis of Lansdowne, in an address to the Prince Regent on the state of the prisons, urged sceptics to witness what was happening in Newgate. The scenes they saw there would change their opinion. Even 'the hardest hearts could be softened and disposed to reform'.[18]

Like Howard and Neild before her, Fry decided to see other prisons for herself.[19] Accompanied by her brother, Joseph Gurney, in August 1818 she set out for the north of England and Scotland, visiting far-flung Friends' meetings and inspecting prisons in the towns through which they passed. In some places they witnessed improvements on that which previous reformers had seen, or at least they encountered a local enthusiasm to eradicate abuses and instigate the building of new prisons for new penological purposes. Lessons were being learnt, but much remained to be done. As ever, efforts were enervated by the numbers imprisoned, and those numbers had increased as former soldiers who had fought in the Napoleonic Wars were disbanded and joined the increasing numbers of the unemployed rendered redundant by machinery. Many of the poor, hungry and jobless became vagrants or turned to crime and many ended up in prison. What they experienced there varied enormously.

Fry and Gurney discovered Doncaster gaol in a deplorable state, with poor lighting and ventilation, no segregation, no employment, and at times with fifteen 'poor wretches' sleeping in a room measuring thirteen square feet. But the 'intelligent magistrates' had plans afoot to close it down and start anew. York had 'some excellencies and great capacities' but its 'evils [were] very conspicuous'. Its deficiencies included insufficient food and

---

[17] Fry, I, pp.288–96.

[18] *Ibid.*, p.322.

[19] While Fry was aware of Howard and his work, his name is never mentioned in her journals and his book was not included in her reading lists.

clothing, lack of employment and instruction, and 'want of cleanliness'.[20] All could be remedied at modest expense, but when the siblings returned a month later they discovered nothing changed. Quakers, once they perceived evils, were intolerant of any delay in addressing them. Durham was much more promising with a new felons' prison under construction, although they expressed concern that the keeper's fine house might 'elevate him above his true station'. Berwick had no redeeming feature other than the religious instruction provided by the unpaid kindness of a local clergyman.[21]

In Scotland they found Dunbar gaol in a state of extreme filth but empty. By contrast Haddington county gaol was filthy but full. The inmates were confined to their communal cells, without exercise, medical attention, or spiritual comfort. Most concerning was a young man 'in a state of lunacy' who had been consigned to solitary confinement for eighteen months. This was the norm in Scotland: another story they heard was of a young lunatic incarcerated for six years in Kinghorn borough gaol who ended his miserable existence by swallowing molten lead. The Quakers took up the Haddington case with the local sheriff and implored the magistrates to do away with their present prison which violated 'the common principles of justice and humanity'. Overall Scottish prisons were pretty deplorable but still largely underpopulated. Perhaps disgusting prisons deterred. Gurney did not think so, but attributed the lack of crime in Scotland, as evidenced by the dearth of imprisoned criminals, 'to the universal religious education in Scotland and to the general dissemination amongst them of Holy Scriptures'. Aberdeen, a haven of Catholicism, proved an exception, having sixty criminals in its prisons, compared with none in the whole of Forfarshire. The county gaol had poor accommodation and inadequate food, and was both overcrowded and insecure, four prisoners having escaped in one year. It failed even in its primary function of secure detention. The bridewell was an exception, its standard of excellence being rivalled only by the houses of correction in Preston and Liverpool. As a result of their inspection, the county gaol was so improved that when Fry revisited it twenty years later she found it 'in excellent order', with employment, instruction and separation all in place.[22]

---

20 Lack of food was a perennial problem, In 1642 a local worthy petitioned Sir Robert Heath, a judge of assize, on the part of 'the great many poor, distressed people that are now prisoners within the castle of York, that have nothing to subsist withall but the charity of well-disposed persons' (A.W. Twyford and Arthur Griffiths, *Records of York Castle* (London, 1880), pp.138ff.).

21 Gurney, pp.2–17.

22 Gurney, pp.28–34; Fry, II, pp.246ff.

The Scottish capital and its main manufacturing centre were different. In Edinburgh they found the 'new and extensive' Calton gaol very similar to Horsemonger Lane prison in London. The rooms were airy, the bedding plentiful and the food excellent. There was porridge and beer for breakfast and barley, vegetable and ox-head broth for dinner. Every night-cell had a Bible and medical attention was exemplary. Its one major failing was the lack of provision for employment, leaving the inmates in total idleness, prey to corruption. No such defect afflicted the even more impressive bridewell. Its effectiveness was, however, somewhat vitiated by overcrowding which gave rise 'to much evil communication'. Both gaol and bridewell had assiduous and humane keepers. The lock-up and the old Canongate gaol, then serving as a debtors' prison, were also up to scratch. The same could not be said of the bridewell in Glasgow. Opened only in 1798 it had already been censured by Neild who had found prisoners sleeping on boards raised four inches from the floor with an uncovered tub in each cell serving as a sewer. Fry and Gurney found it 'teeming with mischief'. Poor ventilation rendered 'the sickly stench ... so excessively offensive that entrance into the cells was nearly impossible'. 'Idleness, clamour and dissipation prevailed on every side', and Gurney had never witnessed a 'more melancholy spectacle'.[23] The town magistrates, well aware of the problems, were intent on doing something about them, and in William Brebner, the recently appointed keeper, they had found a willing and energetic reformer. Before leaving Glasgow, Mrs Fry set up a Ladies' Committee to visit prisoners and to advocate reform. Overall her effect in Scotland was profound and the harvest she garnered considerable. The Scots, like the English, were eager for prison reform.

On their return journey through England the pair continued their tour of inspection. They noted 'the uneven distribution of punishment', a problem which they thought could only be obviated by the imposition of national standards. Carlisle, on the one hand, was a disgrace, with four felons to a cell, 'heavily ironed', unemployed and inadequately fed. The most remarkable feature was the 'total want of classification'. The convicted and untried, serious and petty offenders, men and women, debtors and criminals, young and old, were not separated, and promiscuous association went unchecked.

---

23 Gurney, pp.41–50. He would in America when twenty years later he visited the state penitentiary at Sing Sing, 'a scene of wondrous industry but the stimulus, alas! is that of the whip, in the arbitrary hands of overseers ... I deplore this mode of government, which cannot possibly fail to harden and degrade those who are subjected to it.' He noted that a fifth of the prisoners were black (*Memoirs*, ed. Joseph Braithwaite (Norwich, 1854), II, pp.169f.). Such penitentiaries perverted their intended purpose. You can beat into submission but not into contrition.

The amount of ale getting into the gaol was 'almost incredible'. The old and decrepit prison building stood in stark contrast to the splendid, new court-house standing opposite it. On the other hand, Lancaster castle, which served as both a county gaol and a house of correction, was clean, the bedding good, and the infirmary excellent. Prisoners were unfettered, well-clothed, and fed on bread, gruel – a thin porridge of oatmeal boiled in water – and potatoes, with meat broth a reward for good behaviour.[24] The visitors noted that no escape had taken place for many years and attributed this more to 'the kindness as well as the vigilance of the governor, than to the security of the building'. The gaoler was Thomas Higgin and a John Higgin had been in the same post when Howard visited in 1787. Howard had described him as 'humane and attentive'.[25] The keepership as well as the benevolence had passed from father to son. Nonetheless, due to overcrowding, the housing of prisoners in single cells which had been planned in Howard's day was not yet implemented, and employment was restricted to serving prisoners. Those untried or sentenced to death or transportation were left idle. If numbers decreased and employment increased, 'this castle would become, in an eminent degree, a house of reformation'.[26] Manchester, Sheffield, Wakefield, York, all were visited, or, in the case of the last, revisited. The governor of Preston house of correction, William Liddell, 'by his kindness gained the hearts of his prisoners'. He kept them all well and productively employed, the consequence being that 'he governs with comfort to them and facility to himself'. Liverpool house of correction was of particular interest as it had been built 'upon the plan recommended by Howard', with the keeper's house at the nub and surrounding it six uniform buildings, each with day-rooms, sleeping-cells and airing-grounds. There was a commodious chapel and good infirmary. The food was nutritious, and instruction and employment were provided, and involved prisoner participation along the lines Fry had introduced into Newgate. As a result inmates were less troublesome and more productive. They earned money and were better equipped for life on release. Once again the gaol was blessed with a good governor who was 'truly zealous to promote, by every means in his power, the well-being of his prisoners'. He was also keeper of the adjoining borough gaol where the old system of prison discipline was 'pursued without alteration or amendment'.

24 So identified was porridge with incarceration that 'doing porridge' became the slang term for serving prison sentences.
25 Howard, II, p.201.
26 Gurney, pp.62–6.

Thus the old and the new ran side-by-side under the superintendence of a single individual.

Time and again the Quaker visitors commented not merely on the material conditions but the good effect a benign keeper might have on his charges. The right environment was important; the compassion of staff vital. Prison visitors were another force for good advocated by the Quakers:

> By the magic force of Christian kindness they will obtain a powerful influence over the objects of their care, and they will exert that influence in discouraging the rapid progress of evil and in fanning the feeble flame of expiring virtue.[27]

They would get to know the prisoners and their backgrounds and would care for them on release. One cannot but wonder, if the whole prison estate, its management, and aftercare had been handed over to Quakers how different the history of British prisons would have been.

Gurney's account of their travels published in 1819 was much admired, and read by the most elevated in society, the duke of Gloucester, Princess Augusta and even George, the Prince Regent, among them.[28] This was important. Quakers, wanting substantial reform, needed social clout. They had long come in from the cold. Indeed they had become the conscience of the nation. Remarkably, no one resented them for it.

Elizabeth Fry moved with as much ease among the political and social aristocracy as she did among the inmates of Newgate. One day she would be conversing with convicts, the next with courtiers. Doors opened for her everywhere. She and her old friend, William Allen, were cordially received by the future Queen-Empress, paying 'a very satisfactory visit to the Duchess of Kent, and her very pleasing daughter, the Princess Victoria'.[29] They took with them some books on slavery in the hope of influencing the 'sweet, lovely and hopeful child' in that cause. Leading aristocrats and senior members of the royal family were all on easy terms with Mrs Fry and indeed eager to talk to her. She had star quality. She also had qualms at being 'cast among the great of this world'. She had fears for herself 'in visiting palaces rather than prisons, and going after the rich rather than the poor', lest her eyes be blinded or she should fall away 'from the simple standard of truth and righteousness'. She wondered if it was right to walk among the upper strata of society, and how others would judge her for it, but her anxiety was

---

[27] Gurney, p.147.

[28] Fry, I, pp.338f.

[29] Later Prince Albert would become an admirer.

assuaged by the belief that from such openings great and good things would accrue.[30] They did.

For her great work to succeed Mrs Fry needed the help not just of other Quakers, not just of other like-minded women and men, but of persons of social and political stature. They had the power and influence to elevate her personal philanthropy into something of permanence: the transformation of the prison estate from local lock-ups run for private profit into a nationalised prison system with reform and rehabilitation at its heart. By her enterprise and persistence and holiness she touched the hearts of those in high places. Kind hearts and coronets could conquer all. Many people of influence joined the SIPD including the leading Whig politicians, Lord John Russell, Lord Stanley and Sir James Mackintosh, and the banker, Sir Thomas Baring. Gloucester was its president, while his wife became patron of the Ladies' British Society for Promoting the Reformation of Female Prisoners, an umbrella group established in 1821.

Fry's great redemptive work was a fashionable sight to see. Clergy, sheriffs, even members of the nobility visited Newgate to experience for themselves Mrs Fry at work and in prayer. The effectiveness of her Friday readings 'arose from her peculiar voice and manner, her skill in arresting the attention of her auditors, and her power to touch their hearts', her daughter observed. Londoners flocked to see Fry's ministrations, hear her speak, and, she hoped, imbibe her belief that religion alone could not only reform but produce a lasting alteration in character. She did not welcome people into Newgate for prurient reasons but for educational ones. As her daughter put it: 'during the infancy of prison reform, whilst public interest had still to be aroused, she believed it a useful and allowable means towards a desired end'.[31] Along with the adulation of the rich, Mrs Fry received even more gladly the pittance of the poor. On one occasion in 1819 she gladly accepted an elaborately embroidered counterpane from the women in Kirkdale bridewell. When she suffered a prolonged period of illness her spirits were lifted by touching letters she received from her flock in Newgate.[32]

---

[30] Fry, II, pp.85–9, 440f.
[31] Fry, II, pp.27, 181, 230.
[32] Fry, I, pp.349–51, II, pp.68f. Another Fry-inspired breakthrough came in 1819 when the Devon and Exeter Female Penitentiary was instituted for 'the rescue, reclamation, and protection of betrayed and fallen women'. It was one of the first of such institutions working with prostitutes and abused women outside London.

Another letter, received at the same time, from a protégé of William Wilberforce, the Revd Samuel Marsden, the chaplain at Parramatta, the penal colony near Sydney tellingly known as 'The Factory', had the reverse effect although it did galvanise her into action. Marsden had met many of Fry's former charges who mentioned her 'maternal care with gratitude and affection'. But their lot was a piteous one and the conditions in which they had to live militated against all the good work that she and others had put into them. The promised accommodation blocks had not been built, food was rationed, and clothing for the women and their children was so sparse that many had resorted to prostitution just to make ends meet. Either the British government had not ordered better provision or the local authorities had not implemented the orders. In short all the good work done in Newgate was being undone in New South Wales. He wrote to her as a last recourse. She took up his concerns with flustered officialdom.

Mrs Fry could not go to Australia but she could do more at home to drum up further support for prison reform in Britain and her colonies. Taking her husband and her two elder daughters with her, in September 1820 she again set out to tour England, visiting many of the major prisons and establishing Ladies' Associations. Later in 1827, 1832 and 1836 she would do the same in Ireland. Indeed over the succeeding years in almost every trip she took she would visit a prison along the way – such as Derby which was 'vile' – recruit helpers to the cause, and energise those already recruited. Her Ladies need not wait for perfect prisons to be constructed. They could transform those that already existed. Much might be done by 'kindness and moral influence, without authoritative enactments'. Such sentiments she expounded in *Observations on the Visiting, Superintendence and Government of Female Prisoners*, the manual she published in 1827.

Her endeavours in Newgate had shown this to be true, as had those of Sarah Martin in Yarmouth whose work in the town prison from 1819 until death ended it in 1843 closely mirrored that of her better-known contemporary, and the wonderful results of which taught an admirable lesson 'of what might be effected by kindness, perseverance and discretion'. This, despite the fact that Martin was of humble origin, had little income or education, and had been repelled by the infestations of vermin and the prevalence of skin disease among her charges. Faith, hope and charity forced her forward in her twenty-four-year ministry to prisoners who were the 'first place' in her 'concern and regard upon earth'. She taught them to read and write. She gave them paid work to do. She helped them during their incarceration and on discharge, a service just as valuable. Fry was the most prominent, but not the sole 'angel of the prisons', as she would be the first to admit.[33]

Like that of John Howard, Fry's interest in places of detention was not confined to prisons nor was it confined to her native land, nor was it narrowly sectarian. Her concerns were extensive, her outreach international, and her outlook ecumenical. The treatment of lunatics vexed her greatly. Visits to asylums were also on her itinerary and her Associations took on their oversight in addition to their prison work. She was cheered that her endeavours prospered abroad. In Berlin and Potsdam they were emulated. She corresponded with prominent Orthodox women in St Petersburg who wanted to follow her lead in prison visiting and reform, and with an English friend who persuaded Czar Nicholas himself to order a complete reform of the management of the insane. The Dowager Empress went on to visit the new asylum and dine with the inmates, while her son would later visit the New Litoffsky prison. The Greek government sought her advice. Fry also kept up a correspondence with Protestant reformers in Amsterdam and Catholic ones in Turin, and Paris.[34]

Later, in the course of several trips to the Continent, Fry, again following in Howard's footsteps, would visit a large number of prisons throughout Holland, Switzerland, Belgium, Prussia, Brandenburg, Denmark and France. Among those in France were Paris's St Lazare for women, La Force for men, and La Roquette for boys – the first was another Newgate, projecting 'a scene of disorder and deep evil', while the last – opened in 1830 – was 'a very fine establishment'. But it was in Geneva that she found the exemplification of her ideals. The prisoners were classified into four groups, worked and

[33] Fry, II, pp.80f, 181; Sarah Martin worked wonders among the inmates of Great Yarmouth gaol. It was typical of many other provincial towns: debtors and felons lived cheek by jowl in squalor, with no employment, no religious instruction, and in conditions much the same as those found by Howard in 1776 and by Neild in 1808, the one major improvement being to the gaoler's pay which rose from £15 in 1776 to £40 by 1808 (Howard, I, pp.299f; Neild, *op. cit.*, pp.603ff.; Sarah Martin, *A Brief Sketch of the Life of Sarah Martin with extracts from her Writings and Prison Journals*, new edn (London, no date), pp.13ff., 21–33, 81; George Mogridge, *Sarah Martin, the Prison-Visitor of Great Yarmouth* (London, 1872), pp.44f., 61.

[34] Fry, II, pp.48–51, 58. Her ecumenism was not purely pragmatic. It was deeply personal. Her acquaintances ranged from Jews to Jesuits and she very much admired the devotion of Catholic nuns. Her own son, Joseph, left the Society of Friends but not the Body of Christ. Other of her children followed. She was intimate friends with her Catholic neighbours, the Pitchfords. She cared not what denomination people adhered to so long as they served Christ and proved their 'faith by love and good works'.

exercised in association, but slept alone in individual cells, each of which had a bed, chair, desk and shelf full of books.[35]

Everywhere she went she was treated as a celebrity, and everywhere she inspired emulation. She would discuss prison reform with princes, politicians, prefects of police, and the general public. Such was her international renown that an engraving of her was included in an 'Almanac for the Beautiful and Good' published in Hamburg in 1830, she was visited at her home in Plashet by the Princess Royal of Denmark, and the king of Prussia in 1842 asked her to escort him round Newgate.

Fry was also keen to increase her knowledge of, and involvement in, the London prison estate, and in early 1822 she visited the long-established Clerkenwell, Coldbath Fields and Tothill Fields prisons, and the Giltspur Street compter as well as the radically new and recently finished Millbank penitentiary. Soon members of the Ladies' Association were regularly attending both the Borough and Giltspur compters, and intermittently the Whitecross Street debtors' prison which had been built in 1815 and was to be the last of its kind in the City. Under her aegis a Mrs Caroline Neave set up the Tothill Fields Asylum, the first ever attempt to give shelter to discharged prisoners, while a School of Discipline for the reception of neglected girls was opened in Chelsea by a Mrs Shaw. The exertions of those visiting Newgate and the Borough compter were rewarded, they claimed, with a forty per cent decrease in the number of female prisoners recommitted, although a benign critic, Sydney Smith, found this assertion 'scarcely credible'.[36] He was almost certainly right, but exaggerated or not, the impact of the philanthropists on the lives and expectations of those among whom they ministered was considerable. The reconviction rate is only one measure of success. When Mrs Fry attended a meeting of the British Ladies' Society in June 1845, just months before her death, she was gratified to hear that Newgate, Bridewell, Millbank and other London prisons 'were all in a state of comparative order ... and the prisons generally throughout England much improved, and in the greater number ladies encouraged to visit the female convicts'. Her sanguine view of their work in Millbank was not shared by its then chaplain-governor, Daniel Nihil, who in his journals constantly deplored 'the behaviour of the female pentagon' where 'bickering, bad feeling, disputes' were increasing among the women 'although to the ladies who visit them (disciples of the estimable Mrs fry) the females quote scripture and speak piously'.[37]

---

[35] Hatton, *op. cit.*, p.300.

[36] Smith, II, p.90.

[37] Fry, II, p.518; Arthur Griffiths, *Memorials of Millbank* (London, 1875), I, pp.258–63.

Women were not Mrs Fry's only concern: she feared for young people of both sexes. Imprisonment tended only to harden them and crime was often increased by punishment. Magistrates had much discretion over the disposal of young offenders. When her son John was appointed to the magistracy she advised him that wherever possible boys and girls should be sent to refuges and not to prisons.[38]

She was also much exercised by the state of the convict ships used to transport women to Australia. She wanted matrons appointed to them, conditions improved, better clothing supplied, and employment and education provided. She very much took female transportees to heart, regularly visiting them, encouraging them to set up schools for the children aboard, and providing them with materials for patchwork which they could sell when the ships docked in Rio de Janeiro *en route* or in Sydney on arrival. Her very presence quietened fears. Before their departure she would sit on deck reading to them and praying for them. Sailors on passing vessels would climb their rigging to witness this bizarre but moving sight.

She had been appalled that women, chained to each other and with heavy irons on their legs, some carrying 'their little nurslings', were brought to London from as far away as Lancaster castle. Nearby Newgate also provided cargo, but of a very different order. This was Mrs Fry's doing. Rather than truculent transportees being fettered and taken to the docks in open wagons, and exposed to public derision, her women were taken there in closed Hackney coaches, all the while accompanied by their champion. Soon it became illegal to put women in irons during their transfer from prison to transport. On one occasion her women so impressed the surgeon of the *Brothers* that he wrote to Mrs Fry praising the exemplary conduct of those who had been 'under moral discipline in Newgate'. Not all her wards were so dutiful, and Fry was sorrowed to hear that those aboard the *Janus* were disorderly. This disappointment merely reaffirmed her belief in the necessity of 'patience and perseverance'. Reform takes time to take root.

To take root in foreign climes also required proper provision, and mindful of Marsden's letter, she wrote to the colonial under-secretary asking that a building be provided for their reception in Van Diemen's Land, a matron be appointed and a school set up. She also suggested that if 'some of the regulations mentioned in the new act of parliament relative to prisons were enforced' there and in New South Wales 'much benefit might result'.[39]

---

[38] Fry, II, pp.438f.
[39] Fry, I, pp.429ff., 435ff.

Meanwhile in England, although the excitement generated by her early work had subsided, it had been replaced 'by a steady, resolute spirit of improvement' which imbued men and women from all classes of society. Prison reform was mainstream, and Robert Peel who became Home Secretary in 1822 was just the man to implement it. He, like Fry – with whom he discussed the matter – believed that the role of the state was crucial. He was determined to bring all prisons under a degree of central government oversight or direction, particularly by imposing uniform minimum standards which had hitherto eluded local government. His Gaol Act of 1823, with its aim 'to improve morals' as well as ensuring the 'proper measure of punishment', incorporated many of the principles that Mrs Fry advocated, to such an extent that in 1831 she recorded with satisfaction that 'the improved state of the prisons, female convict-ships, and the convicts in New South Wales' was beyond her most sanguine expectations.[40] Nonetheless, in many places safe custody seemed to be the only purpose of prison, and the persistence of irons and dungeons reflected that purpose.

The following year she was called upon to address the House of Commons committee on Secondary Punishments. She reiterated her mantra: the necessity of matrons, women staff for women's prisons and convict ships, compulsory instruction for the illiterate, social employment by day, separation at night, and the importance of 'Ladies' visiting and superintending prisoners. She admitted that there were relapses. She admitted even to defeats. But the successes outweighed the failures. She was pressed on the issue of complete separation, a system promoted by American Quakers, based as it was on their own habit of silent reflection, and very much coming into vogue. For Mrs Fry theory had to be leavened by reality. Based on her own experience she had reservations about seclusion. Among young, uneducated girls in particular she had seen signs of depression and even severe loss of mental faculties, and doubted that separation and strict discipline prepared them for a return to social life. Resort to solitary confinement should be made 'only in very atrocious cases', and never for long.[41]

In 1835 it was the House of Lords select committee on gaols that required her evidence. This was a major opportunity for putting her views before a most influential forum. Self-possessed, in melodious tones she expatiated on

---

[40] Fry, II, p.87. The Channel Islands proved an intractable problem until major reforms, including the erection of a house of correction next to an existing gaol, recommended in 1836 by Dr Bissett Hawkins, the inspector for the Southern District, were implemented (pp.193f., 219).

[41] Hatton, *op. cit.*, p.315; Averil Opperman, *While It Is Yet Day: The Story of Elizabeth Fry* (Leominster, 2015), p.194.

her usual themes with simplicity and clarity, and ended with an encomium to the power of Holy Scripture as the greatest agent of reform:

> I have seen (in reading the scriptures to those women) such a power attending them, and such an effect on the minds of the most reprobate, as I could not have conceived. If anyone wants a confirmation of the truth of Christianity, let him go and read the scriptures in prisons to poor sinners; you there see how the gospel is exactly adapted to the fallen condition of man.[42]

Religion, of course, was a powerful factor for all those involved in prison administration. Indeed one member of the newly created prison inspectorate was the chaplain of Millbank penitentiary, Whitworth Russell. He was a separate system zealot, and it was his uncle and Home Secretary, Lord John Russell, who appointed him to the post. His colleague, William Crawford, held similar views. Rightly, the two inspectors were no respecters of persons. They began an investigation into the state of Newgate and found it very wanting, a very 'nursery of crime'. It was distinguished by every quality that a prison ought not to have and by the absence of all it ought to have. In their report they condemned the men's section as deplorable, and although they thought the women's much better, they implied that the members of the Ladies' Association – some of whom had worked there for twenty years – were rather naive and lacked competence. They also criticised aspects of Mrs Fry's labours there, and especially the admission of members of the public to witness her Friday readings, as tending 'to diminish the necessary gloom of a prison'. This criticism riled, as it was always Mrs Fry's view that this was a temporary expedient justified on the grounds that it gained public support for more wide-ranging reform of the prison estate. She was taken aback that the first report of an inspectorate whose creation she had long advocated should undervalue her work and denigrate her experience. 'Amateurs' were being displaced by 'professionals' they had helped call into being.[43] They were doing themselves out of what they considered a vocation. The inspectors would later modify their views and welcome the advice, assistance and cooperation of Mrs Fry and her Ladies. It was the high-point of the involvement of philanthropists in prison reform, before 'professionalism' reduced their role.

Ireland beckoned Fry away from controversies over Newgate and she wanted to see Britain's first all-female prison which was completed in 1837 at Grangegorman in Dublin. Fry provided the matron upon whom the

---

[42] Fry, II, p.169.
[43] Hatton, *op. cit.*, pp.276f.

entire responsibility of the interior management devolved. Mrs Rawlins, the appointee, was also a devotee of Mrs Fry whom she consulted on a weekly basis. The penal experiment and the matron's appointment were both great successes and ten years later were specifically commended in the twenty-fifth report of the Inspectors-General of Prisons in Ireland, which also declared that 'in this prison is to be seen an uninterrupted system of reformatory discipline, such as to be found in no other prison'.[44] As a result several prisons solely for women were opened in Scotland and Australia. For Fry the outcome of this prototype was a prayer manifestly answered, although she never actually saw the fruits of her labours ripen.

Fry's credo was born of Christian compassion and of hands-on and hard-won experience. She believed that clean, warm and orderly surroundings should be provided, as should decent clothing. She did not demand luxury, but did want decency and a well-regulated and compassionate regime. To avoid both contamination and the destruction of reputation, untried prisoners should be held separately from convicts. So too should men from women and children from adults. Every prisoner should have a single cell, for reflection but also for privacy. In this sense a separate system was to be welcomed. She had grave reservations, however, about the solitary and silent systems, 'imported from America', which seemed to answer the need for classification and separation, but which were essentially inhumane, striking at the very essence of what it is to be human, social interaction. Prisoners must be barred from bad influences, but allowed, under supervision, to associate with each other and eat with each other, but also to encounter the beneficial effect of interaction with teachers, clergy and philanthropic visitors. There should be 'tender and gentle treatment' of inmates which would encourage cheerful submission to a regime of work, education and religion, very unlike the rigid and uniform treatment being proposed for the new prisons being set up for men. She viewed prisoners as sinners to be loved and tutored into reform, and not brutes to be driven to submission, broken and reconstituted.

For Mrs Fry 'Christian principle is the only sure means of improving practice'. The Bible was her manual; faith was her rock; and rebirth as the reward of repentance was the hope she held out to the outcasts of society, in whose hearts the divine spark lay dormant. Love was the key that would unlock the heart. Love must impregnate all the regulations, manifest itself in every arrangement, and guide all the persons connected with prisoners. The state should be as a loving parent and not, as others urged, an engineer: 'no

---

[44] Fry, II, pp.186f.

delusion did she consider greater, than that man can be treated as a machine, and remodelled, through having his conduct bent to obedience by strong coercion and dread of punishment'.[45] She was no utilitarian.

Her views, and above all her widely publicised evangelical exertions in Newgate, struck a mighty chord in that age of resurgent religiosity and leant lustre to a campaign that demanded a wider role for religion in prisons, although, just as with the inspectors, the appointment of paid chaplains of the Established Church was destined to engender friction with, and undermine the role of, visiting dissenting evangelists such as Mrs Fry. Not all who would follow her had charisma, let alone tact. Even she had put some snooty clerical noses out of joint. Many chaplains thought the ingress of Christian philanthropists both irksome and unnecessary. Even the innovative and effective John Clay, who had been chaplain of Preston prison since 1823, deprecated the activities of Fry and her Quaker visitors. He believed that chaplains alone, not earnest amateurs, had the necessary insight into the true character of the offender to do any good. For others, less conscientious than Clay, a saint in their midst was a constant rebuke. Sydney Smith archly observed that Mrs Fry was 'very unpopular with the clergy: examples of living, active virtue disturb our repose and give birth to distressing comparisons: we long to burn her alive'.[46]

CHAPTER 15

Mr Holford's Fattening House

The walls of the prison will preach peace to the soul and he will confess
the Goodness of his Maker and the wisdom of the laws of his country.

Jonas Hanway

One penal development that initially met with Fry's approval was
Millbank penitentiary. More than thirty years after the passing of
the Act that first sanctioned their construction, the Holford committee
concluded that 'many offenders may be reclaimed by a system of Penitentiary
imprisonment by which [we] mean a system of imprisonment not confined
to the safe custody of the person but extending to the reformation and
improvement of the mind and operating by seclusion, employment, and
religious instruction'.[1] The committee's report recommended to parliament
the building of penitentiaries first in London and then throughout the
country. Howard had advocated them and Bentham had agitated for his
bespoke model to be built. Finally, what had eluded them, would be realised,
although not according to either of their prescriptions.

Where the Tate gallery now stands at Millbank on the north bank of the
Thames, once stood the General Penitentiary. It was the first panopticon-
type prison to be built, but was under state control, and not the private
venture Bentham had envisaged. With one exception, Millbank marked
the beginning of government incursion into penal administration. It was
very much a national resource, a prestige project rather more befitting an
imperial Britain than the other state resource, the dismal and decaying
hulks. Unlike them it would be no transitory expedient but a permanent
part of the penal estate and the flagship. It had no problem in constituting
its superintending committee from the great and the good. Dukes, bishops
and members of parliament were only too eager to be associated with
this grand endeavour, none more so than George Holford himself. The
country was convinced that, straddling the twin objectives of individual
reform and general deterrence, Millbank was the answer to crime. Money

1   *Report from the Committee on the Law relating to Penitentiary Houses* (London, 1811), p.4.

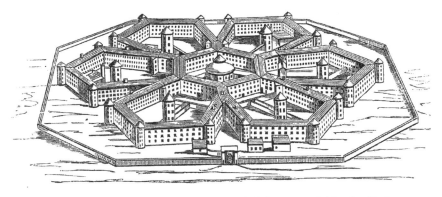

13. Bird's-eye view of Millbank penitentiary, copied from a model by the Clerk of the Works

was lavished upon it, money the increasingly rich country could afford. The nation deserved the very best in carceral innovation. The monetary outlay was more impressive than the ugly edifice it bought. At half a million pounds, more than twice its original estimate, it was one of the costliest public facilities ever built in England, and vastly more expensive than any other prison before or since. It was to prove a very expensive flop.

Designed by William Williams, and begun in 1813, it was 'a monstrous carbuncle', ill-thought-out and over-elaborate in detail, the building frustrating, rather than promoting, its purpose, the very opposite of clarity and utility of design envisioned by Bentham. Set in fourteen acres of marshy land close to London that the philosopher had bought from Lord Salisbury, it resembled a star fort, with six five-sided bastions thrown out from a central hexagon. The architect's aim had been to construct separate and independent prisons, radiating from a central rotunda and under central control. Its very appearance was to denote deterrence, but its object was to promote reformation. Religion was to be at its heart, but religion, or the place of its public profession, proved a major problem. The huge vaulted chapel, 'the centre and omphalos' of the whole edifice, dominated the rotunda and blocked off all vision down the massive pentagons.[2] Christ may have been the light of the world but his temple cast a long shadow over this purgatory.

Though still unfinished, Millbank opened two of its pentagons with a flourish in 1816, under its governor, a forty-four-year-old solicitor, John Shearman. The first batch of convicts – thirty-six women from Newgate

---

2   Arthur Griffiths (*Memorials of Millbank* (London, 1875), I, pp.27–47) provides both a first-hand description and the ground plan, and Norman Johnston (*Forms of Constraint: A History of Prison Architecture* (Illinois, 2000), p.63) the bird's-eye view.

– arrived on 27 June.[3] More followed, male convicts first being introduced in 1817, until subsidence caused by the influx of water from the Thames through the poorly constructed sewers put a temporary halt to admissions. The structure was finally completed in 1821, and, with salaried staff and capacity for 1,200 men and women from throughout the United Kingdom, it was the largest prison in Europe.[4]

Problems proliferated. The ground sank repeatedly under the weight of the edifice and more money had to be expended on stabilising it. Each pentagon contained a labyrinth of corridors, stairways and subterranean passages giving access to indistinguishable cells. The governor had to have a large ground plan of the prison hung on the wall of his office. No one without much study and a prodigious memory could master the intricacies of the place or safely traverse the miles of its walkways. One old warder placed chalk marks on the walls in order not to get lost while doing his rounds. It was the very opposite of Bentham's conception. Surveillance, control, security, all were undermined by the maze-like structure. But the evil above all, in its advocates' eyes, was that clandestine communication between prisoners was prevalent. Not that strict silence let alone rigid separation was imposed. Solitary confinement in the 'dark cells' was reserved for misconduct.[5] The early discipline designed for Millbank was based on the principle of constant inspection and regular employment. Even the initial stage of separate confinement was punctuated by periods of 'working at the mills or water-machines or while taking exercise in the airing-yards' when prisoners would congregate and communicate.[6] Thereafter prisoners would be out of their cells most of the day, working and eating together, but forbidden to be disruptive or abusive, to curse or to swear, to talk loudly or converse with prisoners of another division, to shirk work or chapel. And there was to be no graffiti defacing the walls.[7] In return, work was well-remunerated and the turnkeys were told to treat their charges with consideration but not familiarity.

Practice, however, did not always comply with theory. Prisoners hated Millbank and even preferred the hulks. Riots beset it. During one of them, in 1818, the governor was assaulted. Another 'mutiny' occurred in the chapel

---

3   Griffiths, *op. cit.*, I, p.43, but on p.48 he states it was 27 July.

4   George Holford in his *Account of the General Penitentiary at Millbank* (London, 1828), pp.33ff. It rarely housed more than 800.

5   For a description of these 'fearful places', see William Hepworth Dixon, *The London Prisons* (London, 1850), pp.142ff.

6   *Extracts*, p.90.

7   Griffiths, *op. cit.*, I, pp.55ff.

on a Sunday when the Chancellor of the Exchequer was in attendance, with prisoners loudly demanding their 'daily bread'. When in 1822 it attained full occupancy, disruptions among inmates reached near crisis. Not the claustrophobic conditions, but undue laxity was thought to be the culprit. The then chaplain, Whitworth Russell, complained bitterly that the governor was too generous and slack. The Committee of Management was accused of being over-interfering in the day-to-day running of the establishment and too 'tender-hearted'. Its future deputy-governor and historian, Arthur Griffiths, described Millbank as a 'huge plaything; a toy for a parcel of philanthropic gentlemen, to keep them busy during their spare hours'. The most prominent of them, George Holford, admitted that for a considerable time he did everything but sleep there.[8]

They may have been busy, but to little effect. Their efforts, such as they were, were undermined not just by the design but by so much else. Staff were low-grade, untrained, poorly paid and often brutal. Medical care was inadequate. The building was ill-maintained and rapidly deteriorated. One contemporary thought it constituted a death-trap. 'Built on a swamp, in the midst of damps and smoke', with 'exhalations from the Thames mud, and circumambient stenches from neighbouring gas-works, bone-houses, etc', there was always a potential epidemic lurking in the prison, 'ready on very little provocation to break out into actuality'. Another asserted that 'if an epidemic visit London, Millbank prison is one of the first places in which its presence is detected'.[9] Tuberculosis had displaced typhus as the biggest killer. Whatever the causes, diseases were prevalent, and their incidence aggravated by attempts to curtail 'luxury'. To counter the ridicule heaped on 'Mr Holford's fattening house' and the outrage caused by the perception that prisoners were living too well, in 1822 the medical superintendent of Millbank recommended a restricted diet devoid of potatoes. Scurvy ensued until better doctors were brought in who ensured that potatoes were returned and oranges were added to the diet. The symptoms vanished. Then dysentery broke out. It was decided that the whole place had to be 'fumigated' and its ventilation problem addressed. In the interim, the inmates were evacuated to the hulks. Onboard these less than salubrious vessels they rapidly recovered their health and were returned to Millbank the following year.

The fabric was failing, and the regime promising much and delivering little, even under the auspices of the most avid enthusiast for the whole project, Daniel Nihil. He had succeeded Whitworth Russell as chaplain,

---

8   *Ibid.*, pp.59–65.
9   Clay, p.77; Dixon, *op. cit.*, p.133.

and two years later, in 1837, was appointed governor. Under this chaplain-governor, attempts at deploying religion as a force of reformation came to their apogee. Warders were expected to patrol their wings with a stave in the one hand and a Bible in the other – from which duality the term 'Bible-basher' derives. Walter Clay, John's son, and another critical cleric, portrayed it thus:

> The terrors of the law were abundantly preached in the chapel, tracts were diligently circulated in the wards, and the turnkeys transformed into Scripture-readers, and sent on pastoral visits from cell to cell. Of course, all the readiest rogues played the inevitable game, donned a sanctimonious demeanour, and curried favour by hypocrisy; while a few of the weaker sort went mad under the combined influences of solitude, malaria, and Calvinism.[10]

For Griffiths, its later governor-historian, 'the prayers, expositions, and genuflections, were more in keeping with a monastery of monks than a gaol full of criminals'.[11]

Millbank was doomed from the start. It never worked, and despite twenty-seven years of trying, and with an expenditure that was almost unlimited, it was proved at length to have been an 'entire failure', as the eighth report of the inspectors of prisons put it. In 1843, five years after the establishment of a juvenile penitentiary at Parkhurst and months after the opening of Pentonville Model Prison, it lost its penitentiary role when the Home Secretary, Sir James Graham, decided to cut the state's losses and transfer the reformatory endeavour elsewhere. He introduced a Bill into parliament to end Millbank's time in the limelight and to degrade its status. No longer a penitentiary, there was no place for, nor need of, a 'clerical governor'. Nihil agreed and resigned.[12] Renamed Millbank prison, it became a convict depot, a mere clearing-house for prisoners to be transported to Australia or dispersed to the newly established convict prisons. When transportation ended, it became redundant. After a temporary reprieve when it served as a military prison, unlamented it closed in 1890, and was demolished three years later.

National penitentiaries were expensive experiments. They were necessarily a tiny percentage of the penal provision, and they were very different from

---

10 Clay, p.77.
11 Griffiths, *op. cit.*, I, p.195. Alexander Paterson would write of imprisonment that 'even at its best it is a monastic life for men who have not chosen to be monks' (Introduction to William Douglas Home's *Now Barabbas* (London, 1947), p.ix).
12 Griffiths, *op. cit.*, I, pp.307–10.

the rest. Although, on the conflicting statistics, the actual number of prisons is hard to fathom, there were in 1818 well over three hundred locally-run gaols and houses of correction of all shapes and sizes in England and Wales. Provision was haphazard, and standards varied wildly.

All that changed when the energetic and interventionist Home Secretary, Robert Peel, took a hand. To a mind such as Peel's, disarray was offensive and simply would not do. A wrongdoer's lot should not be determined by the geographical accident of whether he lived in Shropshire or Surrey. And as he was in the process of restricting the ambit of capital punishment, the very apparatus of deterrence, at a time when crime was increasing and more were being convicted, Peel knew that he had to provide adequate alternative secondary punishments – in practice prison or transportation – in which the public would have confidence. He had to give consistency and 'some degree of salutary terror' to both. One reason why Peel was so effective in all he undertook in public office was that he was always well-primed. He was one of the first politicians to lay great store on the accumulation of accurate evidence and statistics. Policy should be dictated by the facts, not facts bent to policy. There was a corollary to this: once the State possessed accurate information about such matters as working conditions, child labour, the price of food, the state of the roads or of prisons, it acquired an obligation to act on that information. Knowledge empowers but it also impels. Peel, one of the midwives of modernity, made the first steps towards the nationalisation of prisons. He began the process which would see the State take over the entire penal estate.

He set about standardising the conditions of imprisonment. The Gaol Act of 1823 was a considerable achievement and constituted the first general prison reform measure enacted by any British government. It also served another purpose, one dear to Peel's heart, that of tidying up the clutter made by earlier piecemeal legislation. Its full title was 'An Act for consolidating and amending the Laws relating to the building, repairing and regulating of certain Gaols and Houses of Correction in England and Wales', and it dealt with previous legislation going back to the fourteenth century, as well as acceding to many of the demands made by a generation of penal reformers. It decreed a common gaol or house of correction in every county, administered by local magistrates and financed by local rates. To prevent contamination it proposed a system of prisoner classification and segregation, dividing, for example, felons from misdemeanants, and, at Fry's urging, required that women be held apart from men and be supervised by women. It set down regulations concerning health, hygiene, and apparel, education and labour. It forbade alcohol, called for the appointment of a surgeon and a chaplain, and ordered regular inspection. Although local control would remain, parliament would dictate the framework, and the inspecting justices would report back to the Home Office on an annual basis, providing the facts and figures which would enable further moves towards centralised control.[13]

The Gaol Act introduced very major reforms, but it would take time, money and energy to implement and refine them. Initially its application was limited to 136 gaols: those under the county justices, those of London and Westminster, and those of seventeen provincial towns. It did nothing to reform the three major debtors' prisons in London or the 150 or so prisons and bridewells in the franchises and the minor municipalities, which constituted 'the filthiest and most abominable in the kingdom'.[14] Further, there was as yet no national inspectorate to ensure compliance, as Peel thought that such an extension of government bureaucracy would have been a step too far for public opinion at that time. Two other Acts remedied some deficiencies. The 1823 Male Convicts Act authorised the employment of transportees on public works in the colonies, while the following year another Gaol Act extended government scrutiny to those penal establishments in the smaller towns not covered by its predecessor. A lack of an inspectorate, however, militated against the full implementation of Peel's measures.

Despite the limitations of the legislation, most county prisons were rebuilt or remodelled, and classification and employment were introduced. Borough prisons on the whole, and prisons in Scotland and in the Channel Islands in particular, continued in their former state of neglect. But there were exceptions such as Derby and Leicester where the magistrates bought the old redundant county prisons for borough use. At Barnstaple the old gaol was rebuilt, Penzance constructed a new town gaol, and the authorities in Norwich tore down the thirty-year-old county gaol and replaced it with a much larger edifice.

There were problems everywhere with developing adequate secondary punishments. The hulks held four or five thousand convicts employed in public works but their numbers could not be expanded. The deployment of what we would now call 'chain gangs' would revolt the British public. Solitary confinement was too expensive to be readily available. Penitentiaries

---

[13] Norman Gash, *Mr Secretary Peel* (London, 1961), pp.315ff.

[14] Clay, p.98; Webb, p.75. Franchise prisons were abolished only in 1858 when the Franchise Prisons Abolition Act was passed.

were always susceptible to the criticism that their occupants were living more comfortably than the non-offending poor.

Conscious of the need to maintain a consensus for lasting and incremental reforms, Peel was quick to disassociate himself publicly from undue lenity, and from the City alderman's jibe of providing 'Turkey carpets in jails'. He defended the tread-wheel and opposed the abolition of whipping (which he thought far less detrimental to health than solitary confinement), saying 'it was incumbent upon those who advocated the necessity of mitigating the severity of the criminal code in respect of capital punishments to beware of rendering such an experiment impracticable by narrowing too much the scale of minor punishments'.[15] In this Peel associated himself with the 'enlightened severity' advocated by his old friend, the Revd Sydney Smith, Whig, wit and wiseacre.

---

15 Smith, II, p.65; Letter from Peel to Smith, 24 March 1826 (*EHD*, XI, p.388).

CHAPTER 16

Goodies and Noodles

There are, in every county in England, large public schools ... for the encouragement of profligacy and vice, and for providing a proper succession of housebreakers, profligates and thieves ... The moment any young person evinces the slightest propensity for these pursuits, he is provided with food, clothing, and lodging, and put to his studies under the most accomplished thieves and cut-throats the county can supply.

Sydney Smith

Solitude, silence and Sydney Smith were not usually words found in conjunction. Indeed it would be hard to think of anyone who would suffer more under a regime of muffled seclusion than he. He was an irreverent and voluble Anglican clergyman, not a Trappist monk. He was also a delightful and amiable companion, effervescent, garrulous, gregarious, mischievous, a great gossip, an inveterate talker, a socialite and wide-ranging social commentator, animated in all by 'a passionate love for common justice and common sense', as he wrote in his *Letters of Peter Plymley*. As a magistrate he blithely disregarded legislation that he considered unjust, most especially the Game Laws which imposed harsh penalties on the poor who poached the pastime of the powerful so that 'for every ten pheasants that fluttered in the wood, one English peasant was rotting in gaol'. Similarly he could not bear to commit young delinquents to custody. Instead he would give them a stern lecture and call for his private gallows, reducing them to tears. At that he would pardon them and 'delay the arrival of his private gallows'.[1]

Like so many others he had strong opinions about secondary punishments. He had visited prisons, he had thought about prisons, and finally, between 1821 and 1826, he had written extensively about prisons, not in pamphlets, tracts or reports but in several lengthy and well-researched articles published in the influential, Whig-supporting, *Edinburgh Review*. Smith wrote with wit and verve and what he wrote the public would eagerly devour. His was no voice crying in the wilderness, but one heard far and wide throughout the land and in the recesses of power.

---

[1] Lady Holland, *A Memoir of the Rev. Sydney Smith* (London, 1869), pp.117f.

He was much exercised by the fate of those in confinement, be it for their iniquities or their infirmities. But he drew a distinction between them, and advocated different ways of dealing with them: cruelty and kindness. In an 1814 article, ironically entitled 'Mad Quakers', he publicly championed the revolutionary 'moral treatment' of the mentally-ill devised by Samuel Tuke, a Quaker tea-trader from York, and close associate of Fry and Gurney. Quakers had long impressed Smith as they always seemed 'to succeed in any endeavour which they undertook'. He considered that the gaol at Philadelphia would remain 'a lasting monument to their skill and patience' and 'in the plan and conduct of this retreat for the insane, they ha[d] evinced the same wisdom and perseverance'. Uncluttered by medical training, in 1796 Tuke had set up 'the Retreat' as a safe and tranquil place for the mentally disturbed. Set in extensive grounds, with gardens for patients to tend and animals with which they could interact, it was a home not a custodial institution, not a Bedlam, not a York Asylum. There were no bars on the windows and little use of restraint. There he pioneered occupational therapy, open wards, and family excursions for his patients, patients he treated as friends and neighbours. This approach horrified the medical establishment who were wedded to harsh confinement and brutal coercion. Smith uncompromisingly declared the Retreat 'the best managed asylum for the insane that has ever been established'. The public agreed and Tuke's methods were adopted far and wide until they later gave way to the regressive prison-like county asylums.[2]

Smith's influence on public attitudes to imprisonment was also extensive. He was a reformer, a rationalist, but could never be written-off as being a 'sentimentalist' or 'do-gooder'. Anglican cleric though he was, Smith acknowledged that it was Dissenters who had taken the lead in penal reform. He genuinely admired 'the advocates of prison-improvement', John Howard, Thomas Buxton and Joseph Gurney, 'men in earnest – not playing at religion, but of deep feeling, and of indefatigable industry in charitable pursuits ... men of the most irreproachable veracity'. When Buxton said he had not found 'Turkey carpets' in Newgate but 'scenes of horror, filth and cruelty', Smith believed him.[3]

Smith deprecated 'the malice and meanness' of those who abhorred not the cruel squalor of prisons but the public revelation of it, and who excited 'horror against' such figures as Mrs Fry who exposed it to public censure. On one occasion he had accompanied 'this holy woman' on her rounds,

2   Peter Virgin, *Sydney Smith* (London, 1994), pp.183ff; Smith, I, pp.313–26.

3   Smith, II, p.65. Ironically Smith's own son was to contract typhus in a carceral institution. But it was not in Newgate prison but in Westminster school.

and was reduced to tears by her compassion and its effect. The 'wretched prisoners ... all calling earnestly upon God, soothed by her voice, animated by her look, clinging to the hem of her garment; and worshipping her as the only being who ever loved them, or taught them, or noticed them, or spoken to them of God' was a 'sight that breaks down the pageant of the world'.[4] He had the highest regard for this 'amiable and excellent' woman whom he deemed 'ten thousand times better than the infamous neglect that preceded her', even though he thought her methods the means to console the incarcerated but not the way to prevent crime.[5] While he approved of her Christian compassion and reforming zeal, he approved even more of Peel's pragmatism and reforming legislation.

Smith neither supported 'pampering' prisoners, nor countenanced the penitentiary system being advocated by some zealots: it was too comfortable to the body and too destructive of the soul, too kind and too cruel. He also doubted its efficacy. With much of what was proposed by the reformers he agreed, and with the humane sentiments behind them. But with much he disagreed, as he did with their earnest propaganda, recounting edifying stories of religion inculcated by devout 'clergymen and ladies', and of 'larcenous lives' transformed by contact with kindness and compassion, dispersed with 'unwearied diligence' by 'the Goodies and Noodles'. Of course there was no place in penal institutions for brutality or cruelty, for heavy irons and manacles (though moderate ones for the convicted were permissible), or for cold, disease and starvation, but the happiness of prisoners was not his concern. He decidedly did not exude tender-hearted empathy with those imprisoned. He supported prison reform, aimed not primarily at amelioration but at humane deterrence, very much echoing the sentiments of the 1822 House of Commons Select Committee on Prisons which declared that prisons should be an 'object of terror, and may operate as real punishment'. 'Now we have made prisons healthy and airy', Smith reiterated, the way to real improvement would be 'to make them odious and austere – engines of punishment, and objects of terror'.[6] The tread-wheel was the vital component and Smith would use no other secondary punishment than it. It filled the imagination with horror and disgust and afforded 'great ease to the government'. As a member of the local magistracy Smith would be instrumental in the construction of an expensive new prison on the

---

4   Holland, *op. cit.*, p.118.
5   While Fry praised Liddell's regime in Preston it was one Smith particularly deplored. He would banish all the looms, and 'substitute nothing but the tread-wheel' or some other 'hard, incessant, and irksome' labour.
6   *OHLE*, XIII, pp.154ff.; Smith, II, pp.86, 102.

silent associated system model within the walls of York castle, and in the deployment there of a tread-wheel. In a scene that he would have relished, some visiting bishops asked to try it out and 'the sight of a dozen or more pairs of black-gaitered legs ascending the cruel staircase was one not to be easily or soon forgotten'. The ecclesiastical volunteers unanimously condemned it as barbarous.[7] Precisely. Smith's views were far from those of 'the benevolent Howard' whose attack on 'our prisons', Smith believed, had led to incarceration becoming 'not only healthy but elegant' and county gaols being turned into retirement homes for paupers eager to gratify their 'taste for magnificence as well as for comfort'.[8]

The governance of prisons, he agreed, should be rectified and regularised. Anglican chaplains were 'of vast importance and utility' and should be better paid, but no Catholic nor Dissenter should be compelled to attend chapel and should instead be able to seek the ministration of a clergyman of his own persuasion.[9] He opposed the appointment of inspectors who would inevitably be well-salaried place-men who would never step inside a prison. Visiting magistrates should fulfil that role and be quizzed on the exercise of their duties by the assize judge or quarter-session chairman. He deplored the lengthy periods between detention and trial. He considered the distinction between those on remand and those convicted as fundamental. The conditions in which they lived and even their diet should differ. There should be a guarantee of a minimum amount of food for all, but alcohol should be excluded except for medicinal use. He urged the separation of the sexes, of men from boys, of criminal lunatics from hardened felons. Female prisoners should be under the charge of a matron with female assistants as otherwise 'the female part of the prison is often a mere brothel for the turnkeys'.[10]

Above all Smith deprecated the numbers committed to prison and the resulting overcrowding, which meant that for months on end the novice

---

[7] Arthur Griffiths, *Memorials of Millbank* (London, 1875), I, p.197.

[8] Smith, I, p.42. Referring to York, Griffiths (p.282) wrote: 'The work was Titanic, Cyclopean; the walls were built of huge blocks of stone, tons in weight ... the whole area was surrounded by a boundary as solid as the great wall of China ... The whole erection was so inordinately wasteful and extravagant, planned on a scale so absurdly out of keeping with the objects for which it was intended, that it was long known as the greatest joke Sydney Smith ever made.'

[9] By 1870 all convict prisons had a Catholic chapel and a salaried priest and provision had been made elsewhere for priestly ministration (W.J. Forsythe, *The Reform of Prisoners 1830–1900* (Beckenham, 1987), pp.106ff).

[10] Smith, II, pp.83f., 113. For instance, in 1700 William Robinson, the deputy-keeper of Newgate, was found to be pimping prostitutes and using the prison as a brothel.

would associate with, and be corrupted by, the inveterate criminal in what were in effect schools of vice. In terms with a strikingly modern resonance, he decried prisons as 'universities of crime', and noted with astonishment that they provided a finishing school for more than 107,000 persons committed to English prisons in 1818, 'a number supposed to be greater than that of all the commitments in the other kingdoms of Europe put together', and a number inexorably rising. Rampant recidivism went in tandem with the building of expensive new prisons along Howard's reforming lines, and 'since the days of their cleanliness and salubrity they have been so managed as to become great schools for crimes and wretchedness'.[11] Gaols and houses of correction too often provided a 'mere invitation to the lower classes to wade, through felony and larceny, to better accommodations than they can procure at home', and a life of luxury, idleness and ease for the better off, the 'dainty gentleman' thief.

> The most vulnerable part of a thief is his belly; and there is nothing he feels more bitterly in confinement than a long course of water-gruel and flour-puddings. It is a mere mockery of punishment to say, that such a man shall spend his money in luxurious viands, and sit down to dinner with fetters on his feet, and fried pork in his stomach.[12]

In Bury, considered by Buxton to be 'a pattern jail' which should be emulated in the new Millbank, sentenced prisoners were allowed to spend 'their weekly earnings (two, three and four shillings per week) on fish, tobacco and vegetables'. This was well-meant, thought Smith, but was no punishment, and should provide no precedent. The increasing annual commitment rate was not solely down to the perks of imprisonment. Population increase, parliamentary legislation, and pheasant proliferation (which led to a multitude of arrests for offences against the Game Laws) all played a part, but so too did prisons and their indulgent regimes. He agreed that the deprivation of liberty was itself a punishment, but a system based on lengthy incarceration

---

11 Smith, II, pp.65, 71, 74, 89. Staffordshire county gaol cost £30,000 to build; Wiltshire £40,000.

12 Smith, II, p.118. Comments later made to one inspector by inmates in Lancaster castle would have confirmed his criticism: 'We are all very comfortable ... My bedding is very clean ... and better than I would get outside ... if I was to work from Monday morning to Saturday night, I could not keep myself ... in the same comfort that I am kept in here ... the officers are all nice and well-behaved men' (*Thirteenth Report of the Inspectors for the Northern and Eastern District*, 1847–8). By way of contrast, the Chartist leader, William Lovett, who in 1839 was imprisoned for twelve months in Warwick gaol, was revolted by the food. Despite his hunger, having found a black beetle in his gruel, he could eat neither (*The Life and Struggles of William Lovett* (London, 1876), p.299).

with education and paid employment acted as a palliative to that punishment, and undermined its deterrent effect.

To be effective, prisons should be places 'from which men recoil with horror ... [places] of real suffering, painful to the memory, terrible to the imagination', and not providers of a boarding-school education which youngsters will commit crimes to attain and will be envied for having 'drawn a prize in the lottery of human life'. Smith thought that the SIPD 'leant too much to a system of indulgence and education in jails'. He would have been glad to 'see them more stern and Spartan in their discipline'. Turning out better-educated, more-employable people is all very well, but turning miscreants away from crime is much better.

> Penitentiaries, in the hands of wise men, may be rendered excellent institutions; but a prison must be a prison – a place of sorrow and wailing; which should be entered with horror and quitted with a earnest resolution never to return to such misery ... this great point effected, all other reformation must do the greatest good.

A prison should not 'lose its terror and discredit, though the prisoner may return from it a better scholar, a better artificer, and a better man'. The test of a good prison system is 'the diminution of offences by the terror of the punishment'.[13] The efficacy of this approach had been proved to his satisfaction by one of his many japes. Farmers in Yorkshire – where Smith had his living – kept huge mastiffs which they made no effort to leash. The owners of these dangerous dogs were deaf to requests or demands and even to preaching. One day a report appeared in the local press about a Northamptonshire farmer being fined and imprisoned for keeping unrestrained dogs. The message was clear: confine your dogs or be confined yourself. The message got through. The deterrent effect of prison was demonstrable. The author of the anonymous article was Sydney Smith.

Citing contribution after contribution made to the Commons' committee in 1819, he asserted that their evidence demonstrated that short, sharp sentences with no work – other than the most 'monotonous, irksome and dull' – and no pay, in darkness for some of the time, in solitary confinement for the rest, and on bread and water throughout, were the obvious means to this end, 'six weeks of such sort of imprisonment' – so long as not to the detriment of mind or body – being 'much more efficacious than as many months of jolly company and veal cutlets'. He believed most firmly that

[13] Smith, II, pp.70–5, 80–98.

whereas 'solitary idleness leads to repentance; idleness in company [leads to] vice'. If this regime was not on offer, the next best would be one of 'severe work, ordinary diet, [and] no indulgences'. Increased severity in prisons could only be justified by decreasing the length of sentences, for otherwise the punishments would be 'atrocious and disproportioned'. He feared that the current 'great disposition, both in Judges and Magistrates', to hand down longer sentences would produce 'dreadful cruelty' if the bitterness as well as the period of incarceration were increased.[14]

Thus, whereas those who 'wisely and humanely' busied themselves about prisons appealed to the rehabilitation or even happiness of the prisoner as the primary justification for reform, Smith appealed to the well-being of society to justify what were essentially similar measures but directed now towards the goal of severity and deterrence. Prisons, he believed, were 'really meant to keep the multitude in order, and to be a terror to evil doers'.[15] Their primary objective should be 'the discomfort and discontent of their prisoners', with reformation secondary and subservient, desirable but not essential. He was on the utilitarian side of the argument. Humane efforts to bring out the best in those who had fallen foul of the law were not high on the agenda.

Peel wrote to him in March 1826, agreeing that the perception that prisoners were being pampered posed a problem. When 'penitents' were given ample food, their lot in winter was 'thought by people outside to be rather an enviable one'. The present prison population was ostensibly living more comfortably than was consonant with strict penitence. There was, however, an even more pressing dilemma: growing numbers. Peel, while admitting that transportation was inefficient, found 'the whole question of secondary punishment ... full of difficulty ... the number of convicts [being] too overwhelming for the means of proper and effectual punishment'.[16] Too many criminals, too few facilities to deal with them and deter them. It is a comment as true today as almost two hundred years ago.

New prisons were needed, but it was not just a matter of their number or size but of their design. Sydney Smith's strictures were prescient but premature. Although other commentators shared his misgivings, philanthropic optimism was still in the ascendancy and no properly constructed penitentiary had yet

14 Smith, II, pp.76ff., 84f., 96.
15 Smith, II, pp.14, 74.
16 *EHD*, XI, p.388.

been built to try out the phantasmagoria of the 'goodies and noodles'.[17] The trouble was there were two contrasting views about how best to proceed, and the architecture of any new prison would be dictated by the sort of regime it adopted.

17 Pentonville would fill this gap but not until the end of Smith's life. He never wrote about it.

CHAPTER 17

Silence or Separation?

Reformers ... understood deviance in irreducibly individual, rather than collective terms; not ultimately as collective social disobedience ... but as a highly personal descent into sin and error ... The appeal of institutional solutions lay in the drama of guilt which they forced the offender to play out – the drama of suffering, repentance, reflection and amendment, watched over by the tutelary eye of the chaplain.

Michael Ignatieff

However managed, we confess, we have but little faith in the anticipations of those who imagine that prison may be converted into seminaries, and made subservient to the moral improvement of those confined in them. At all events, the first thing to be done is to hinder them, in so far as possible, from becoming schools of vice. If we cannot materially improve those that are imprisoned, we are, at any rate, bound to do all in our power to prevent them from becoming worse.

John McCulloch

By the 1830s a sense of crisis over the direction of penal policy prevailed. In his imperial digest the Scottish economist John Ramsay McCulloch produced the statistics and proffered an analytical description along the usual lines.[1] Prisons were chaotic. There was little distinction in their purpose, little coherence, and no uniformity. In 1837 there were 136 prisons in England and Wales under the operation of the Gaol Act, besides a considerable number of prisons belonging to corporate bodies exempted from its jurisdiction. There were in addition 107 county prisons, of which sixteen were exclusively gaols or places for the safe custody of persons committed for trial or confined after conviction; thirty-nine were gaols and houses of correction combined; and fifty-two were denominated houses of correction, being distinct and generally at some distance from gaols. Of the latter, however, only twelve served their original purpose as in the others it was commonplace to confine both those remanded and those convicted. The amount of work provided varied enormously from place to place, and where tread-wheels were installed the severity of labour fluctuated 'from 5,000 to 14,000 feet of ascent per day in summer and in winter from 3,600 to 12,500 feet'. In some gaols women

---

[1] J.R. McCulloch, *A Statistical Account of the British Empire* (London, 1837), I, pp.580–3.

were deployed on the tread-wheels; in others they were exempt. The daily food allowance in one prison could be half that of another. The average annual cost of keeping someone in custody was £18. Prisons in Ireland, still under local control, had improved considerably but from a very low base. Those in Scotland were, with few exceptions, in a worse state than those of England, the exception being the Glasgow bridewell which, with its complete separation and full employment, was considered one of the best-run establishments in the whole of Britain. This was in stark contrast to what Neild and Fry had found in that city, and was due to the labours of William Brebner who since 1808 had been transforming the place, more than doubling its size, enabling him to introduce the separate system many years before America embarked on the same course.[2]

Major unrest was either simmering or boiling over in the first four decades of the nineteenth century as an agrarian society of stable ranks and a widely dispersed population was being replaced by an industrial society of alienated classes and, in the cities, teeming masses.[3] The crime rate soared, inflamed by Chartism and riots over the Poor Laws, and magnified by Game Laws that made many ordinary country pursuits criminal. Crime was being perceived as a national problem, requiring central government intervention. Meanwhile the scope of the noose was being progressively narrowed by parliament, repenting of its erstwhile proclivity to expand it. As a result far fewer felons could be sentenced to death and far fewer were going to the gallows. Consequent upon all these facts the number of prisoners nearly doubled between 1820 and 1840, putting considerable stress on the prison estate. In 1833 the number of cells in the Gaol Act prisons was little over 10,000 while the daily average population was almost 18,000.[4] What was

---

2   Andrew Coyle, *Inside: Rethinking Scotland's Prisons* (Edinburgh, 1991), pp.29–39; *Extracts*, pp.92ff. So concerned was Brebner about the lot of the poor that he allowed into the bridewell 'voluntary prisoners' who were accommodated in ordinary cells and subjected to the same discipline. The Lanark authorities ended this experiment as it would adversely affect the public perception of prison as a punishment. In Scotland the responsibility for prisons lay with the burghs until 1839 when the counties had to share the burden. At the same time a General Board of Directors was established to exercise oversight, encourage uniformity, and rationalise the penal estate by closures, while constructing a national penitentiary at Perth, to which they appointed Brebner as governor.

3   Michael Ignatieff, 'State, Civil Society and Total Institutions', in Stanley Cohen and Andrew Scull (eds), *Social Control and the State* (New York, 1983), pp.75–105, at p.90.

4   McCulloch, *op. cit.*, I, p.581. Although over ten per cent of those were debtors the abolition of imprisonment for debt in the 1860s would prove small compensation for the abandonment of the hulks in 1859, and the end of transportation – the last convict ship would sail in 1867 and its last refuge, the convict prison in Gibraltar, would close in 1875.

to be done to reduce crime and deter criminality? What could be done to suppress the prison subculture and prevent the 'contamination' by which criminality spread?

Millbank was not the answer, but it had deviated not just in design but in purpose. The architects of the building had erred in its construction, and the architects of its regime had groped for a reformatory discipline that eluded them:

> Beyond doubt – and of this there is abundant proof in the prison records – the committee sought strenuously to give effect to the principles on which the establishment was founded. Nevertheless their proceedings were more or less tentative, for as yet little was known of the so-called 'systems' of prison discipline, and those who had taken Millbank under their charge were compelled to feel their way with caution, as men still in the dark. The Penitentiary was essentially an experiment – a sort of crucible into which the criminal elements were thrown, in the hopes that they might be changed or resolved by treatment into other superior forms.[5]

In the face of calls for a more purely deterrent approach to criminals, reformers were unabashed. Millbank had been an experiment from which much had been learnt. Such a regime had failed because it allowed too much human contact and 'frightful contamination'.[6] There had to be a better way.

News of developments in American custodial practice were already having an impact. The United States provided two models, two systems, both of which were up and running and both of which were designed to disrupt prison communication, prevent corruption and bring about reform, but in different ways and at different costs: the silent associated or the silent separated system. The former did have precursors on the Continent, most notably in the Maison de Force in Ghent which in Howard's day had initiated this innovation. The latter too had been trialled in Glasgow in 1826. It was, however, in the New World, where 'improvements are prosecuted with much more zeal and activity than elsewhere', that both systems were most energetically developed.[7] Both had their advocates, both had their detractors, and the advocate of the one was inevitably the detractor of the other. And both had their exemplars: Auburn in New York State where from 1819 the silent system reigned at its most severe; and the Eastern State penitentiary (known as Cherry Hill) in Philadelphia where from 1829 the separate system

---

5   Arthur Griffiths, *Memorials of Millbank* (London, 1875), I, p.58.
6   Joshua Jebb, *Second Report of the Surveyor-General of Prisons* (London, 1847), p.3.
7   Alexis de Tocqueville, *Democracy in America*, English trans, 2 vols (New York, 1976), I, p.258.

prevailed in its purest form.[8] The silent system was the more secular, and involved prisoners working, eating and sometimes sleeping together under strict supervision and rigidly enforced silence. The separate system had religion at its heart, incarcerating each inmate in seclusion day and night in single cells designed as places of habitation, employment and contemplation, where individuals were not just silent but alone, with a Bible as their only companion and consolation.[9] If prisoners were prevented from associating with each other they would be more susceptible to communication with the divine and less able to seduce others into a life of crime.

Britain, reform advocates believed, needed an American-style systematic approach to the problem and not a slapdash experiment like Millbank. But which of the two systems was the more effective? Perhaps an expert seeing them in operation could better advise on the option.

In 1834 William Crawford of the SIPD was sent to the United States by the British government to study 'prison discipline' as practised there. On his return he published a report, providing a survey of the two penitentiary systems whose operation he had witnessed. Unsurprisingly given his evangelical associations Crawford strongly favoured the Quaker-inspired separate system as exemplified in Cherry Hill. What a contrast the placid and penitential atmosphere he found there made to Newgate where misguided lenity allowed prisoners to receive letters from friends and visitors, some of whom were prostitutes and confederates in crime, and where 'hoary offenders, convicted of capital crimes, [were] confined in the same place with young persons committed for some slight offence' and the mad were intermingled with the sane.[10] Crawford conceded that if cost alone was decisive the silent system would triumph, as almost any prison could be adapted for that more secular and pragmatic regime, while the separate system needed extensive and expensive conversion of existing prisons or, even better, new buildings specifically designed for it, with single cells and *en suite* facilities. But cost be damned! It would be mitigated in the short run by requiring far fewer staff since prisoners routinely confined in cells required little supervision, and in the long run by its redeeming impact.

In England a committee of the House of Lords was set up in 1835 under the chairmanship of the veteran prison reformer, the duke of Richmond. Its

---

8   Cherry Hill was built to replace Walnut Street gaol which had been remodelled into America's first penitentiary in 1790 but had become overcrowded.

9   See Norman Johnston, *Eastern State Penitentiary: Crucible of Good Intentions* (Philadelphia, 1994), *passim*.

10 William Crawford, *Report on the Penitentiaries of the United States* (London, 1834), p.30; McCulloch, *op. cit.*, I, p.578.

five reports, based on extensive evidence from individuals such as Elizabeth Fry, proved a watershed in the administration of British prisons, bringing their condition to wider public attention, giving impetus to the development of the separate system within them, and – of longest-lasting significance – beginning the legal process of bringing them under central government control.[11] As a result parliament passed the 1835 Prisons Act which at last instituted national inspection, thereby obliging local authorities to improve prison management, tighten discipline, and improve standards. For the following forty years, county and borough magistrates would continue to administer local gaols, and pay for them out of local taxes, but their autonomy was leaching, and substantial government subsidies would further strengthen central control over the burgeoning prison estate. And the government had the money to build a flagship national penitentiary to encourage emulation. But did it have the motivation? Momentum had to be maintained.

The first appointees to the inspectorate, Crawford himself and Whitworth Russell, were strategically placed to ensure that it was. Over time, not only would their invasive powers and expert strictures undermine the confidence of local administrators, but their trenchant support for the separate system would bear rich fruit. Their *Third Report for the Home District*, published in 1838, was decisive. It was as much advocacy as inquiry. It was far more eloquent than impartial. The two inspectors did not simply describe what they had seen in English prisons but sought to prescribe a particular model of 'a proper and efficient system of Prison Discipline', the 'ultimate success' of which they entertained not the 'slightest doubt'. It alone could prevent the age-old curse of contamination, whereby 'the comparatively innocent are seduced, the unwary are entrapped, and the tendency to crime in offenders not entirely hardened is confirmed by the language, the suggestions, and the example of more depraved and systematic criminals'. 'The novice in crime' too often emerges from prison 'skilled in inequity, hardened in effrontery ... a finished, irreclaimable villain!' It alone could attain 'the purpose of enlightened jurisprudence, – not abstract punishment, – but the prevention of crime'. It alone could impose an 'exact uniformity in every prison' that was essential to expunge the arbitrariness and partiality whereby lenity and severity varied from prison to prison, and some prisoners received undue 'indulgence', either because they paid for it or because they were favoured over others upon whom they could then exercise a 'petty tyranny'. On

---

11   *Reports from the Select Committee of the House of Lords appointed to inquire into the present state of the several gaols and houses of correction in England and Wales; with the minutes of evidence* (London, 1835); Webb, pp.111f.

the other hand, it alone could 'discover the temper and character of the prisoner' and adapt the 'treatment' accordingly, 'without incurring the charge of favouritism to the one or undue severity to the other'. It alone was able to inculcate in prisoners 'permanent habits of useful labour' – which would be solicited by them as an alleviation rather than an aggravation of punishment – essential when they were released back into the world. It alone could 'produce that self-communion, that introversion of mind, which is most favourable to the reception of every useful and serious admonition', the inculcation of true religion and 'the reformation of morals'. It alone would treat 'men as beings who are accessible to reason, and who, in the midst of all their depravity, have secret springs of thought and feeling within them which may be happily and permanently touched'. In short it alone could address 'the futility of the silent system', with its 'penal inflictions and privations' and counter-productive discipline of 'tread[ing] the wheel', upon which the inspectors vented their eloquence and ire.[12]

Although their colleagues, William Williams for the north-east and Bisset Hawkins for the south-west, dissented on the merits of separation, citing the cost of building new prisons or converting existing ones to the cellular plan, and questioning the very morality of strict solitude,[13] and whereas many Quakers, despite their American brethren's Philadelphia scheme, shared the reservations of Mrs Fry, the authors were far from being alone in this view. They had important allies not just among Dissenters but within the Established Church.

A talented group of Anglican clergy would become the foremost proponents, and later staunchest defenders, of the separate system and of their central role within it. Even before 1824 when their appointment was made compulsory, prison chaplains had been coming into their own. Prison was *their* parish. As their influence increased so did that of the penal ideology many of them espoused. Criminals, they acknowledged, were the product of poverty, bad parenting and worse company, but crime was caused by irreligion and immorality among the lower orders. The young were begotten, weaned and trained in vice, and 'instructed to consider vice as their only means of avoiding starvation'.[14] Re-education and the revitalisation of religion, along with education and the acquisition of skills, were the solutions to a host of social problems afflicting English society. The prison

---

12 *Extracts*, pp.1–23, 63, 165–79.

13 Michael Ignatieff, *A Just Measure of Pain* (London, 1978), p.197.

14 *The Times*, quoted in W.J. Forsythe, *The Reform of Prisoners, 1830–1900* (Beckenham, 1987), p.54.

was a central battleground in this struggle where Christian principles, under the right regime, could be applied to the souls of the worst sinners. Sinners could be saved; reprobates reformed; and on release they could redeem their families and friends. The outlaw would become the evangelist.

But these wonders were not achievable under the silent system. It did not go far enough. It was a mere compromise, vesting too much discretion in the governor, relying too heavily on physical coercion to ensure conformity, interdicting only vocal interaction between prisoner and prisoner. Indeed it was deleterious in its effect as it presented 'so many temptations to communication as to render two things absolutely inevitable, both unfriendly in the highest degree to real reformation, – perpetual surveillance and perpetual punishment'.

By contrast, the separate system, a system designed to reform by seclusion, provided the solution by employing the passive weight of architecture to secure its ends. If penitents were confined to single cells there would be no need for surveillance, no infractions to punish, and every opportunity for genuine repentance. Prisoners immured as anchorites would be unable to associate or communicate with each other or with anyone else apart from the chaplain or the governor on an occasional visit to their cells. Solitude reinforced silence and spiritual contemplation replaced physical coercion. The lash would have no more dominion. There could be no riotous assemblies, no mass break-outs, no plotting escapes. 'The stout-hearted can be kept down without brute force; all may be reasoned with, and every single prisoner experience the influence of ... THE LAW OF KINDNESS.' Joseph Kingsmill and John Burt at Pentonville, and John Field at Reading, were all ardent advocates of such a regime whereby 'the will is subdued, bent or broken, and the moral character is made plastic by the discipline'.[15] It promised a true internal transformation, not the temporary docility induced by silent association.

There was also 'the need to keep alive in the heart of a criminal both an invigorating hope and a salutary dread'.[16] What system, if any, could promote these sometimes consonant, but often discordant, ends? The money seemed to be on separation. The propaganda certainly was. It alone could fulfil a number of penological purposes, purposes which were no longer antithetical but complementary and often overlapping: the redemption of the criminal would ensure an agony of remorse (retribution and deterrence),

---

[15] Joseph Kingsmill, *Chapters on Prisons and Prisoners*, 2nd edn (London, 1852), pp.117, 121. All three would pen lengthy defences of the separate system.

[16] Lord Stanley, *Correspondence on Convict Discipline*, PP, 1843 (502), XLII, 451.

a desire to make amends (reparation), and determination to live within the law (deterrence and reform). The tide was high and flowing in separation's favour. Its heyday was about to begin.

Lord John Russell, the Home Secretary, wrote to local magistrates, drawing attention to the 1838 inspectors' report and urging the introduction of the separate system. Yet his urging often fell on deaf ears, many localities opting for the less expensive alternative of the silent system. If his preferred option was to be tried, the State would have to take the lead suggested by the inspectors of erecting 'a Model Prison upon the Separate System, in, or adjacent to, the Metropolis'.[17] It would prove the system valid and provide an exemplar for others to envy and emulate. In 1839 Russell got parliament to pass a Prisons Act, regularising, although not imposing, the separate system throughout the prison estate, and approving a second government-built and administered national penitentiary.

Pentonville was the result. For the proponents of the separate system it was a temple to progress, for detractors it would be a 'palace of felons'. Times would soon change and the tide would recede but for a while it was proclaimed as the 'Model Prison'.

[17] *Extracts*, p.181.

CHAPTER 18

The 'Model Prison'

I repaired to the prison ... an immense and solid building, erected at vast expense. I could not help thinking ... what an uproar would have been made in the country, if any deluded man had proposed to spend one half the money it had cost, on the erection of an industrial school for the young, or a house of refuge for the deserving old ...

It being just dinner-time, we went first into the great kitchen, where every prisoner's dinner was in course of being set out separately ... with the regularity and precision of clock-work ... I wondered whether it occurred to anybody, that there was a striking contrast between these plentiful repasts of choice quality, and the dinners, not to say of paupers, but of soldiers, sailors, labourers, the great bulk of the honest, working community, of whom not one man in five hundred ever dined half so well. But I learned that 'the system' required high living; and, in short, to dispose of the system, once for all, I found that on that head and on all others, 'the system' put an end to all doubt, and disposed of all anomalies. Nobody appeared to have the least idea that there was another system, but *the* system, to be considered.

Charles Dickens

The ever ''umble' Uriah Heep became Pentonville's Prisoner Number Twenty-Seven.[1] He was the very model of a modern penitential. So beneficial had the experience of 'the system' been on his moral character that he wished those benefits bestowed on others, even on his own mother. 'It would be better for everybody', he opined, 'if they got took up, and was brought here.' Before he had been incarcerated, he admitted:

I was given to follies, but now I am sensible of my follies. There's a deal of sin outside. There's a deal of sin in my mother. There's nothing but sin everywhere – except here.

By 1850 when the serialised *David Copperfield* was published in book form none of Dickens's readers would have believed a word of this. They knew the Uriah Heep of old. They knew he had not changed, and could not change. He was rank hypocrisy girding itself in the protective mantle of

---

[1] Dickens does not name the prison where Uriah Heep underwent his penance, but he certainly had Pentonville in mind.

penitence. He was a 'Favourite' of 'the System', and its perverter. He was its most perfect product, and the perfect proof of its ineffectiveness.

Although the danger of holding out a 'bounty to hypocrisy' had been presaged, such cynicism was a later development.[2] It was not cynicism that greeted the creation of the first penitentiary but optimism. In 1839 Captain Joshua Jebb was brought in to provide expert advice on the construction of so novel a prison, and he would eventually progress to oversee the future growth of 'the system' created within it. Born in 1793, he was a professional soldier in the Royal Engineers, graduating from the Royal Military Academy at Woolwich, and serving in Canada and then Chatham, before advising Crawford and Russell on prison design and construction.[3] Like Bentham, Jebb had a healthy dislike of transportation and the hulks, and was a strong advocate of the separate system. In his later published blueprint for, and vindication of, Pentonville, he peremptorily dismissed any system of prison discipline based on association, whether subject to classification or silence, and firmly opted for the more stringent separate system which he denied was 'solitary confinement with a vengeance'. Prisoners were not immured as punishment in 'unmitigated, uninterrupted seclusion' in 'confined, ill-ventilated and dark cells', but resided to their 'moral benefit' in spacious cells with integral sanitation, were provided with work, books and 'the means of moral and religious instruction', were able to attend chapel and school, could exercise in the open air, and, although cut off from fellow prisoners, they were not deprived of 'all human society' as they were regularly visited by 'the Officers of the prison'.[4]

Jebb was the obvious candidate to design, construct and administer the new model prison of which, in December 1842, he became a commissioner. Although he consulted the inspectors to ensure that his design met their purpose, the conception and realisation were very much his own. It was to be a proud structure for a proud project. Built between 1840 and 1842 for the princely sum of £85,000, Pentonville was a monument to faith in an ideal, the apotheosis of the idea that a totally controlled environment could produce a reformed and autonomous individual.[5] It would triumphantly vindicate the proponents of the separate system and would become an exemplar for all future developments. It was designed for a specific end,

---

2   *Extracts*, p.18.
3   The inspectors resented his intrusion into their sphere (Eric Stockdale, 'The Rise of Joshua Jebb 1837–1840', *British Journal of Criminology*, 16, 2 (April 1976), pp.168ff).
4   Joshua Jebb, *Modern Prisons: Their Construction and Ventilation* (London, 1844), p.9; *Extracts*, p.23. It was a distinction with which not all agreed.
5   *OHP*, p.101.

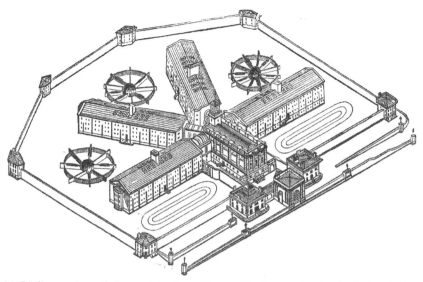

14. Bird's-eye view of the model prison, Pentonville, from a drawing by Joshua Jebb

and would not make the mistakes of Millbank. Or so it was hoped. 'Vulgarly known as "the Model"', it was constructed on a radial plan and 'fitted according to all the refinements of modern sciences', was 'complete in all its appliances', and was of 'wondrous and Dutch-like cleanliness ... utterly free from dust'. It had *en suite* lavatories, 'an unlimited supply of warm and cold water', good cell ventilation and was well-heated. The diet was 'better, richer, than in other prisons'.

'What is there penal in all this?', exclaimed a contemporary observer, William Hepworth Dixon, who 'for his life' could not find out. Yet he was not surprised to discover that 'no prisoner, except in rare cases, likes [Pentonville]. Many fear it worse than they do death.'[6] He was right that each cell would provide all that its single occupant could require – except company. He had entered the prison voluntarily and could leave at will. Prisoners were immured in solitude. That was the rub. Each inmate was the sole inhabitant of a solitary, silent world. Silence was all-pervasive in this well-oiled machine. Since 1839 warders in government-run prisons had been forbidden to talk to prisoners other than when issuing commands, or indeed to each other. Cacophonous gaols holding raucous humanity were being transformed into sepulchral mausolea inhabited by zombies.

Mrs Fry visited this cutting-edge establishment in 1841, before it became operational, and wrote to Jebb, damning it with faint praise. The building,

6   M&B, pp.113, 117, 119; William Hepworth Dixon, *The London Prisons* (London, 1850), pp.150–5.

she thought, did justice to the architect, particularly on important points such as ventilation, the plan of the galleries and the chapel, but there were grave shortcomings in the regime. The pitch-black 'refractory wards' in particular 'should never exist in a Christian and civilised country'.[7] She believed that 'no person should be placed in *total* darkness'; there should be a ray of light admitted. Gloom led to depression and she emphasised the importance of preserving 'the *health of mind and body* in these poor creatures'. She presciently warned that 'separate confinement produces an unhealthy state, both of mind and body', and that everything should be done to counteract this influence which she was sure was 'baneful in its moral tendency'. She perceptively recognised that many of those imprisoned suffered from 'mental derangement as well as bodily disease', and that 'light, air, and the power of seeing something beyond the mere monotonous walls of a cell' were 'highly important'. She did not believe that 'a despairing or stupefied state is suitable for leading poor sinners to a Saviour's feet for pardon and salvation'. Experience had shown that prison warders became 'hardened to the more tender feelings of humanity', judged unjustly, and that 'there are few men sufficiently governed and regulated by Christian principle to be fit to have such power entrusted in their hands'. Prisoners were open to abuse in the future when a less benevolent governor might be in charge or the law became more draconian. Those committed for political or religious reasons would be especially vulnerable to being secluded and ill-treated. Her praise was welcomed; her reservations ignored.[8] The criticism the authorities really feared was that they were pampering prisoners not punishing them, as indeed Pentonville was intended to be a place not of punishment but of probation.

Pentonville opened its 'door of hope' on 21 December 1842, 'the culmination of a history of efforts to devise a perfectly rational and reformative mode of imprisonment', a history stretching back to Howard's 'first formulation of the ideal of penitentiary discipline in 1779'. Combining 'severe punishment with a considerable amount of instruction and other moral influences', it had capacity for 520 prisoners housed in identical and separate cells, with each door under observation.[9] Pentonville was intended to replicate for reformable adults what Parkhurst already provided for

---

[7] They are chillingly described in M&B (pp.135f.), and were a forerunner of the lightless isolation cells which can still be seen in Alcatraz.

[8] Fry, II, pp.386f.; Jean Hatton, *Betsy* (Oxford, 2005), pp.315f.

[9] John Burt, *Results of the System of Separate Confinement as Administered at the Pentonville Prison* (London, 1852), pp.3, 70; Michael Ignatieff, *A Just Measure of Pain* (London, 1978), p.11.

15. The separate system chapel service in Pentonville prison

16. A fully equipped separate system cell in Pentonville prison

17. Convicts exercising in Pentonville prison

juveniles. Originally the intake was restricted to men between eighteen and thirty-five years of age sentenced to at least fifteen years' transportation. They were picked for their youth, health and inexperience in crime. They were deemed ripe for reform and a new life overseas far away from their old associates. For these men Pentonville was to be a portal to a penal colony, the compliant being released soon after their arrival in Australia, the obdurate being held in irons for several years of debilitating toil, harsh living and crushing discipline. The first stage of these penitents' progress was in Pentonville and was to last for a mere eighteen months, a far cry from the lengthy incarceration in Cherry Hill penitentiary. During that period the guards wore padded shoes so as not to disturb the unnatural silence, while the inmates lived in 'a kind of penal purgatory': in separate confinement, in total silence and in complete solitude.[10] They had numbers, not names. They worked alone. They ate alone. They slept alone. They wore masks while exercising or walking to the chapel, so that no communication with other prisoners, even by facial expression, could take place. But at least, unlike in Philadelphia, they were allowed to go to chapel, even if it 'combined the chief architectural features of a theatre and a menagerie'.[11] There they sat in individual cubicles, with high partitions between them, so that their undistracted attention would be on the chaplain in his pulpit, dominating

10 M&B, p.147.
11 Clay, p.192.

them and admonishing them to change their ways.[12] What was being sought was a rebirth, a new being, a person purged of criminal instincts, and ready for the next stage of his redemption in Australia.

For five years there was a rigid adherence to this regime. But at what cost and to what effect? Fear of the birch or the cat or of the refractory 'dark cells' ensured compliance, but not contrition. The loss of the will to resist, 'their wits and their wills' rendered 'limp and flabby', was interpreted as acquiescence in their moral regeneration and not a sign of mental degeneration. Reformation of the soul was often equated with breaking of the spirit. In any case it hardly mattered. Be it moral improvement, be it fear of the repetition of such punishment, be it a combination of the two, the result was the same: reformation and a resolve not to reoffend.[13]

Not all concurred. John Clay of Preston, 'keenly alive to the fact that isolation was as likely to arouse vicious, as to foster wholesome, thought ... shrank from the idea of ministering the Gospel among men languid and listless with the dreary monotony of the cell'. He wanted to help a person reform not to make a puppet perform:

> A few months in the solitary cell renders a prisoner strangely impressionable. The chaplain can then make the brawny navvy cry like a child; he can work on his feelings in almost any way he pleases; he can, so to speak, photograph his thoughts, wishes and opinions on his patient's mind and fill his mouth with his own phrases and language.[14]

Others, less squeamish, were more 'technicians of guilt', pointing the finger of accusation, working on the vulnerable, anxious to find evidence of divine grace at work. For them, outward conformity and tractability – 'yield[ing] to the correction of the place' as John Burt, Pentonville's assistant chaplain, put it – were strong evidence of inward renewal.[15]

It was a distortion of what the Christian reformers had sought. Elizabeth Fry had been right in her concerns about the 'brutality of good intentions'. In prolonged solitary confinement the prisoners were left to their own remorse and became their own tormenters. Some committed suicide. Many more experienced mental illness and those deemed mad were transferred to Bedlam.[16]

---

12 A separate system chapel is preserved in the old gaol in Lincoln.
13 Burt, *op. cit.*, pp.6ff.
14 Clay, pp.196f., 386f.
15 Burt, *op. cit.*, pp.ixf.,4, 80ff. He staunchly defended the original regime and deprecated the 'retrograde relaxations' his own superior, Joseph Kingsmill, supported.
16 Mayhew gave figures for both, showing that the number decreased as the period of strict separation was reduced (M&B, p.115).

Most lost all initiative, and all vitality. They took no responsibility for their own lives and a totally controlled environment proved the worst preparation for eventual release, especially into the wilds of Australia where resilience, self-reliance and initiative were vital. *The Times* was quick to denounce 'this maniac-making system' which sometimes terminated 'in insanity, oftener in idiocy, and still more frequently in permanent weakness and imbecility of mind'.[17]

But the system could not fail: too much money and effort had been put into it for its advocates to concede defeat. Excuses were found, one of the more memorable being that some convicts had been over-excited by the 'somewhat sulphurous earnestness of a too vehement chaplain'. The commissioners of Pentonville were still claiming in 1847 that 'the moral results of the discipline have been most encouraging, and attended with a success without parallel in the history of prison discipline'.[18] The advocates of the separate system were anxious to find living proof of their ideals but instead they encountered Uriah Heep portrayed as *the* model prisoner in *the* 'Model Prison'.

Changes were soon made by those less enamoured of 'success'. Jebb was the most influential. He had been promoted to lieutenant-colonel and since 1844 had been the first holder of two new important posts relating to government-run penal institutions: Inspector-General of Military Prisons and Surveyor-General of Prisons. As such he was responsible for the design and alteration of all state-controlled prisons. He was pragmatic rather than partisan, and having seen it in action began to have qualms about the viability of the system he had helped incarnate.

In 1847 Crawford and Russell both died, the former collapsing during a meeting at Pentonville, the latter committing suicide in Millbank, the desperate act of a disappointed man that would add no lustre to his life's obsession. The demise of these dominant ideologues marked the beginning of the demise of an era in which religious reformation and architectural innovation had been at the forefront of penological thinking. It also made it possible for Jebb, along with Pentonville's chaplain, Joseph Kingsmill, to mitigate the deleterious effects of prolonged seclusion on mental and physical health. If this were seen as an admission of failure the whole project could be compromised. Nonetheless, meliorative efforts were made. The prison was no longer reserved for first offenders and the period to be served there was reduced from eighteen months to fifteen, twelve and

---

17   *The Times*, 29 November 1843 and 6 April 1844.
18   *Fifth Report*, 5 March 1847; George Ives, *A History of Penal Methods* (London, 1914), p.187.

finally to nine, although, as transportation tailed off, such was the pressure to admit more convicts that some spent only two or three months there. From 1853, prisoners, after their induction in Pentonville into penitential solitude, were sent on to convict prisons such as Portland and Dartmoor to endure penal servitude. Like Millbank it had become little more than a sorting depot. It was a mercy of sorts. Back-breaking labour was preferable to soul-destroying isolation.

Two critics in particular were influential and eloquent, and their strictures completed public disillusionment with the grandiose endeavour. Charles Dickens was one; the other was Thomas Carlyle.

CHAPTER 19

The Universal Syllabub of Philanthropic Twaddle

Howard abated the Jail-fever; but it seems to me he has been the innocent cause of a far more distressing fever which rages high just now; what we may call the Benevolent-Platform Fever. Howard is to be regarded as the unlucky fountain of that tumultuous frothy ocean-tide of benevolent sentimentality, 'abolition of punishment,' all-absorbing 'prison-discipline,' and general morbid sympathy, instead of hearty hatred for scoundrels; which is threatening to drown human society as in deluges, and leave, instead of an edifice of society fit for the habitation of men, a continent of fetid ooze inhabitable only by mud-gods and creatures that walk upon their belly.

Thomas Carlyle

Not all supported penitentiaries; not all shared the humanitarian sentiment behind them; not all were as modulated as Sydney Smith in their critical reflections upon them. The times were a-changing. Expectations of extraordinary transformations had been roused but not realised. Doubt set in, and with doubt, distaste. One eminent Victorian went further than any other in voicing his contempt for the whole reformatory project. Nothing and no one would escape his viper's fangs.

In 1850 the so-called 'Sage of Chelsea', vastly influential social commentator, famed historian, and vitriolic polemicist, Thomas Carlyle, published his *Latter-Day Pamphlets*. These included an essay on 'Model Prisons', a brutal assault on what he called the 'philanthropic movement', members of which 'embark in the sacred cause; resolute to cure a world's woes by rose-water'.[1]

Carlyle came from the Scottish Calvinist tradition, a 'stern child of Ecclefechan'. He was Old Testament rather than New. He had long jettisoned the Christian God, but a rigid predestinarian pessimism and moral authoritarianism never deserted him. Although he knew no gospel, he could preach hell-fire. To be kinder to him than he was to others, the gastric ulcers that plagued him all his life may have contributed to his increasing irascibility. 'Clay was in his blood, Calvinism in his head, dyspepsia in his stomach' was

---

1 All the quotations come from this essay. It had been first released as an independent pamphlet, the second in the series, in March 1849.

one biographer's unkind but not unfair diagnosis. His nature was morose, and self-indulgent misery and hypochondria dogged his steps. The bitter tone of his work was a reflection of an unhappy life. Indeed life for him was a prison, but a prison of his own creation.[2] He divided the world into the saved and the damned. Justice, stern, unbending, unmerciful justice, should be our lodestone. Hatred of 'scoundrels' – all who deviated from Carlyle's narrow path – was a necessary adjunct of any true religion. Hatred was his religion, hatred and revenge. In short he was not awash with the milk of human kindness, had no understanding of, let alone compassion for, human frailty, deemed all law-breakers to be scoundrels, and was excoriating of utilitarians and 'do-gooders'. He was trenchant in style, loud in his opinions, and utterly dismissive of those who held views or values contrary to his own. He was the master of belittlement. A Mrs Fry or Mr Howard he was not.

Carlyle's intemperate polemic on penal reform – 'this beautiful whitewash and humanity and prison-discipline and such blubbering and whimpering' – is a rant, not an argument, and the adjective 'beautiful' is inserted, here as elsewhere, more as an insult than as irony. As with so much of the work of a clever man who lacked 'the wit to write plain straightforward English' it is virtually unreadable today, and surely would never have been published had it not come from the pen of the much-feted historian of the French Revolution and of Oliver Cromwell. It is indeed 'ferocious', but it is no 'masterpiece of invective'.[3] It says practically nothing about prisons but a lot about its author. It is the spleen of a bitter man oozing onto paper. An early biographer refers to 'the acrid mood' which 'envenomed the *Latter-Day Pamphlets*', and describes Carlyle writing 'in his study, alone with his anger, his grief and his biliousness'. A later biographer wrote that 'with him denunciation was a temptation that became wearisome when indulged'. And indulged it was. On and on it rolls, a mere barrage of abuse, 'every semi-colon an insult'.[4] In time it contributed to the wrecking of Carlyle's over-blown reputation. At the time it chimed with what many less articulate citizens thought: the country was going to the dogs, wallowing in sentimentalism, soft on crime and soft on criminals.

2   'Carlyle' in Michael Holroyd and Paul Levy, *The Shorter Strachey* (Oxford, 1980), p.101; Osbert Burdett, *The Two Carlyles* (London, 1930), p.152.

3   George Orwell, *Collected Essays* (London, 1968), IV, p.21; Simon Heffer, *Moral Desperado: A Life of Thomas Carlyle* (London, 1995), p.281.

4   Richard Garnett, *Thomas Carlyle* (London, 1887), p.80; Orwell, *op. cit.*, I, p.35; Burdett, *op. cit.*, p.251.

While sarcastically conceding that 'philanthropy, emancipation, and pity for human calamity is very beautiful', Carlyle denounced 'the deep oblivion of the Law of Right and Wrong; this "indiscriminate mashing up of Right and Wrong into a patent trace" of the philanthropic movement' as by no means 'beautiful' but as 'altogether ugly and alarming'.

Carlyle stated that he had visited one of the capital's prisons, which held 'some thousand or twelve hundred' prisoners. He deemed it a 'beautiful' establishment 'fitted up for the accommodation of the scoundrel-world, male and female!' He described it thus:

> An immense circuit of buildings; cut out, girt with a high ring-wall, from the lanes and streets of the quarter, which is a dim and crowded place. Gateway as to a fortified place; then a spacious court, like the square of a city; broad staircases, passages to interior courts; fronts of stately architecture all round ... surely one of the most perfect buildings within the compass of London.[5]

5 Carlyle does not state which prison this was. A pleasant stroll along the Embankment would take him from his house to Millbank, and both Froude (*Thomas Carlyle*, 2nd edn (London, 1885), II, p.29), his friend and first biographer, and Heffer (*op. cit.*, p.281), his admirer and most recent biographer, state it was that penitentiary he pilloried. According to Heffer, Carlyle visited Millbank in October 1848, just before embarking on the *Latter-Day Pamphlets*. He gives his source as *Jane Welsh Carlyle: Letters to Her Family, 1839–1863*, ed. Leonard Huxley (London, 1924), but both editor and biographer have fallen into error. The letter itself (pp.311ff.), dated by Huxley to the autumn of 1848, states merely that Jane, her husband, and their friend John Forster 'went over Tothill Fields prison'. Huxley erroneously equated this with Millbank, when in fact they were quite separate institutions – though not far from each other. Further, Ryals and Fielding convincingly give the date of this letter as 5 February 1849, and correctly state that Tothill Fields was the Westminster house of correction, the governor of which was a friend of Forster (*The Collected Letters of Thomas and Jane Welsh Carlyle* (Durham, NC, 1995), XXIII, pp.223f.).

   Although the regime, the intake of both sexes, and the large number Carlyle says were incarcerated within his 'model prison' suggest it was Millbank he had in mind, aspects of the description indicate the recently opened Pentonville, which was widely known as 'The Model Prison' and was by 1849 all the rage. Radzinowicz thinks that his 'violent diatribe' is directed against the new system as embodied there (p.504). Ignatieff asserts the same (*op. cit.*, p.3).

   There is a problem here too: Froude's *Letters and Memorials of Jane Welsh Carlyle* (London, 1883) includes letters in which she refers to visiting the King's Bench prison on 27 October 1835 (I, p.43), and Pentonville, but not until 2 January 1851 (II, p.144). A further complication is that one of the 'Chartist notabilities' to which Carlyle refers is Ernest Jones who was imprisoned in Tothill Fields (Jules Seigel, 'Carlyle's Model Prison and Prisoners Identified', *Victorian Periodicals Newsletter*, 9, 3 (1976), pp.81–3). Carlyle's governor is based on either Forster's friend Augustus Tracey of Tothill Fields or Dickens's friend George Chesterton of Coldbath Fields (Philip Collins, *Dickens and Crime*, 3rd edn (London, 1994), pp.64f.). Finally, of the four prisons only Coldbath Fields had tread-wheels.

He protested he had never seen so clean a building and averred that 'probably no Duke in England lives in a mansion of such perfect and thorough cleanness'. His own house was comfortable but made 'no pretension to equal a model prison'.[6] The prison food was 'of excellence superlative', the work such as oakum-picking was light and took place in 'well-lit and perfectly-ventilated rooms'. Peace and tranquillity reigned. The women, 'some notable murderesses among them', were all equally composed as they sat sewing in 'substantial wholesome comfort'. From a gallery he looked down into 'a range of private courts where certain Chartist Notabilities were undergoing their term'. One such he had seen before 'magnetizing a silly young person'. Carlyle had 'noted well the unlovely voracious look of him, his thick oily skin, his heavy dull-burning eyes, his greedy mouth, the dusky potent insatiable animalism that looked out of every feature of him'. He was little different from the generality of these 'miserable distorted blockheads', these 'base-natured beings', the 'ape-faces, imp-faces, angry dog-faces, heavy sullen ox-faces; degraded underfoot perverse creatures, sons of *in*docility ... and of [intellectual and moral] STUPIDITY, which is the general mother of such'.[7]

He admired the governor but pitied him his task. The visiting magistrates 'had lately taken his tread-wheel from him ... and how was he henceforth to enforce discipline?' Hard work and occasional hunger were the sole two penalties, reduced to but one. 'To drill twelve hundred scoundrels by "the method of kindness", and of abolishing your very tread-wheel – how could any commander rejoice to have such a work cut out for him.' The gods would have appointed them 'a collar round the neck, and a cart-whip

---

In short there is no evidence that Carlyle visited Pentonville prior to writing his essay and no evidence he visited Millbank at all. As State facilities neither the public nor the magistracy had right of entry into either. The latter's regime had already come in for much parliamentary criticism, and was generally recognised as a failure. Millbank itself had been downgraded from 'general penitentiary' to 'prison' in 1843. It needed no further demolishing. Pentonville was the new, great hope of finally realising the reformers' dream. It was the edifice at which Carlyle's verbal battering-ram would be aimed. To conclude, Carlyle's target was almost certainly Pentonville but his depiction was a composite creation, a fiction based on his imagination buttressed by visits to houses of correction.

6   Letter to John Eadie, 28 June 1850.
7   William Hepworth Dixon similarly found 'a certain monotony and family likeness in the criminal countenance which is ... repulsive from its rugged outlines, its brutal expression, its physical deformity' (*The London Prisons* (London, 1850), pp.138f.). So too Mayhew assured his readers that the 'brutal-violence class of criminals' were an inbred and atavistic 'refuse race' easily distinguishable by their lascivious looks and bull necks from the rest of the working class (M&B, pp.165, 356f.).

flourished over the back ... in a just and steady human hand'. Instead the governor had to 'guide scoundrels by "love"'.

It is the sort of scabrous bile we may expect to read in the tabloid press. He makes some of the same assertions as are made today. Those who break the laws are treated better than those who obey them. The deserving poor live in far worse conditions than those pampered in prisons, but so too do dukes! The honest hardworking artisan struggles to make ends meet, lives in squalor and in fear of famine, yet is taxed to erect this 'Oasis of Purity intended for the Devil's regiments of the line'. It seemed never to occur to him that the lot of the respectable poor might be improved rather than that of the reprobate worsened. He is thoroughly 'sick of scoundreldom'. It was always detestable to him 'but here where I find it lodged in palaces and waited on by the benevolent of the world, it is more detestable, not to say insufferable to me than ever'. Why do reformers, he asks, 'work only on the rotten material?' For Carlyle criminals were sub-human, a reversion to a Neanderthal past. He goes on and on in similar vein, not an argument but a volcanic eruption of venom, his fury 'shedding even that modicum of shame that others of his class display for decency's sake'.[8] Yet his portrayal of criminals as 'perverse creatures' had resonance with a public concerned about crime and sceptical of reform. Base metal, however, burnished remained base metal.

Carlyle finally turns his 'instinctive sneer'[9] on the epitome of 'the beautiful philanthropist', John Howard, eulogised in the words of Burke into a demi-god. Christianity is 'as good as extinct in all hearts' but Howard has resurrected a 'ghastly-Phantasm' of it and paraded it 'through almost all'. Carlyle professes that 'on the whole' he had 'nothing but respect, comparatively speaking, for the dull, solid Howard, and his "benevolence"'. In words leaden with sarcasm he doffs his hat and humbly salutes this 'dull and dreary man' and pours scorn on 'solid John's' meticulous compilation of facts and concentration on detail. As though it were a disparagement, he characterised Howard as a 'man full of English accuracy, English veracity, solidity, simplicity'. Carlyle was 'most sick ... of this sugary disastrous jargon of philanthropy ... which possess the benighted minds of men and women in our day'. Howard had poisoned a generation.

Poor, pedestrian, pernicious John Howard, seduced by sentimentality, tarnished by a sickly 'love of humanity', how could his reputation survive

8   Review by Marx and Engels, *Neue Rheinische Zeitung*, April 1850, in *Collected Works*, X, p.310.
9   Orwell, *op. cit.*, I, p.35.

such a mauling? It did triumphantly. It was Carlyle's that first crashed and then entered near oblivion. Of all his 'pamphlets' it was 'Model Prisons' and the attack on Howard that engendered the most intense reaction. It was his undoing. He is remembered, if at all, as the enemy of democracy, the hero-worshipper of the superman, and even as a forebear of Fascism. Lytton Strachey is not alone in finding it 'so very difficult to believe that red-hot lava ever flowed from that dry neglected crater'.[10] Carlyle's name is now little known; his writings are largely unread and, as a result of 'prose run mad' as Thackeray put it, are virtually unreadable.[11] But he was widely read in his day, almost as widely as an author who fell under his spell but whose popularity has never waned.[12]

---

[10] Lytton Strachey, 'Froude', in *Life and Letters* (December 1930). For a description of the reaction and a different perspective see Michael Goldberg's 'A Universal "Howl of Execration": Carlyle's *Latter-Day Pamphlets* and Their Critical Reception', in *Carlyle and His Contemporaries*, ed. John Clubbe (Durham, NC, 1976), pp.129–47.

[11] Edgar Allan Poe concurred. In his judgement, if Carlyle meant 'to be understood', he took 'all possible pains to prevent us from understanding'. Poe thought him 'an ass' who would 'be remembered only as a butt for sarcasm', and in 1843 presciently said so in print ('William Ellory Channing' in *Works*, ed. James Harrison (New York, 1902), XI, pp.176f. Despite Heffer's defence it is hard to understand how Carlyle was revered in his own day when to later generations, as Yeats (*Letters*, p.609) put it, 'he is as dead as Macpherson's Ossian'.

[12] Ironically in the Du Cane era, hardly known for its mollycoddling, Carlyle's works and those of his biographer, Froude, were not allowed into prisons. Macaulay's, however, were approved (Radzinowicz, p.541, n.59).

CHAPTER 20

Bleak House

[Mr Chesterton is] the gentleman to whom the public as well as the prisoners themselves, are indebted for the correction of abuses that were a scandal to our country, and who was the first to introduce into [Coldbath Fields] that system of non-intercourse among prisoners, which, at least, if it works no positive change in the criminal character, must be acknowledged to prevent that extended education in crime which arose formerly from the indiscriminate communion of the inmates of our jails.

Henry Mayhew

[Christian] zeal had blinded [reformers] to the ratio of endurance which the human mind and physical frame of man are equal to sustain.

George Chesterton

The *Latter-Day Pamphlets* lost Carlyle a lot of his more liberal friends, John Stuart Mill being the most prominent among them, and even some less liberal who were nonetheless aghast at his tone. One he did not lose was Charles Dickens, whom he had known since 1840.[1] Dickens was no liberal where criminals were concerned and was no great believer in character change, as his novels demonstrate.[2] The author of *Oliver Twist* could not have written *Crime and Punishment*. He shared Carlyle's opinion of the penitentiary system, even if he expressed his distaste with more humour in his fiction and less bile in his journalism. With the exception of Carlyle, it has been said, he was more reactionary than any of his literary contemporaries.[3] This is true to an extent, but only in relation to inveterate criminals, the depraved and not the deprived. And this is true primarily of his later years: he changed his mind with changing times, as many of his contemporaries did, and with age, as most people do. As his arteries hardened so did his heart. He was a

---

[1] Michael Goldberg, *Carlyle and Dickens* (Georgia, 1972), p.2.

[2] Philip Collins, *Dickens and Crime*, 3rd edn (London, 1994), p.82. *A Christmas Carol* is a pantomime parable, not a psychological novel of redemption. Dickens did, however, believe that juvenile offenders and prostitutes could be redeemed if given the right support and 'affectionate kindness'. In prisons and police-courts he was to find many recruits for Urania Cottage, the 'Home for Fallen Women' he founded and sponsored.

[3] Peter Ackroyd, *Dickens* (London, 1990), p.378. Dickens was also a great admirer of Sydney Smith.

man of large heart and little consistency.[4] He was, after all, a novelist, not a criminologist. That is why he is still read.

In his novels Dickens discoursed on the hulks, debtors' prisons, and the penitentiary system. His sympathies lay with neglected and deprived children, those who were put in prison cells for minor offences stemming from need or even ignorance, or street-urchins such as the Artful Dodger, who were seduced into a life and love of crime and exploited by adults such as Fagin, a villain not deprived but depraved, and an arch-corrupter of youth. Dickens could empathise to some extent with the ill-used Magwitch, the old lag who ends up on a hulk before being transported, and illicitly returns to England a rich man. He sorrowed for the prostitute Nancy whose cradle had been the alley and gutter, but for her murderer, the brutal Bill Sykes, he shed no tears. He could identify with the essentially decent but always impecunious Micawber who is incarcerated for debt in the King's Bench prison, reflecting the fate of Dickens's own father who had ended up in the Marshalsea, which itself is vividly described in *Little Dorrit*. The moral reprobate Uriah Heep is another matter, the quintessential hypocrite who conned 'the system' by playing on the naivety and self-delusion of its proponents. He was the epitome of a penitent and a humbug to boot.

Dickens had a fascination with the underworld in general and with prisons in particular. All life was there, from the most pitiable to the most vicious. And change was in the air, penal reform had become mainstream. As a young man he had to see the reality for himself. The first felons' prison he visited was the notorious Newgate, standing, as he put it in *Nicholas Nickleby*, at 'the very core of London, in the heart of its business and animation', a microcosm of all the reformers condemned. He did so in 1835, the same year as the Prisons Act was passed. After a two-hour tour he wrote a short piece on it for his first book, *Sketches by Boz*, which, well-written as it is, unsurprisingly tells us nothing new about conditions in that well-documented institution, nor of the author's penological perspective. It is descriptive, not judgemental, let alone critical. In that respect he is unique since no

---

4   Sometimes, however, his empathy increased with maturity. For instance in his original Newgate sketch he described fourteen boys as 'irreclaimable wretches' but in later editions he changed this to 'creatures of neglect'. Similarly, in the autumn of his life, when he was most trenchant in his writing about criminals, his compassion could be roused when he met examples of them in person. On a visit to Stirling Gaol 'he said kind and comforting words to the prisoners which seemed to be a relief to them in their miserable position' (George Dolby, *Charles Dickens as I knew him* (London, 1885), p.68.

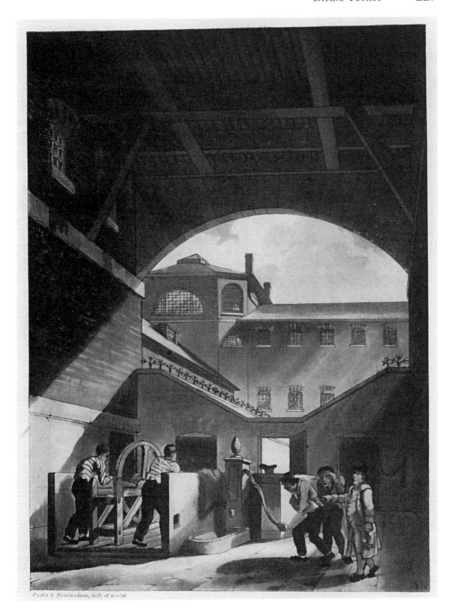

18. The water engine at Coldbath Fields prison

other observer could resist condemning the conditions therein. However, first-hand knowledge of the prison gained on this and subsequent visits proved invaluable to the budding writer. He utilised it in *Oliver Twist* when he described Fagin spending his 'last night alive' in Newgate's condemned cell; in *Great Expectations* when Pip, like his creator, undertook a tour; and in

LARGE OAKUM-ROOM (UNDER THE SILENT SYSTEM) AT THE MIDDLESEX HOUSE OF CORRECTION, COLDBATH FIELDS.

19. Oakum-picking at Coldbath Fields prison

Barnaby Rudge when its destruction by the mob provided the dramatic climax to his depiction of the Gordon riots.

He also wanted to compare and contrast this bastion of the old with a harbinger of the new. He wanted to see the silent system in operation. It was not difficult to do so. Coldbath Fields and Tothill Fields, the houses of correction for Middlesex, were both nearby. They had recently been transformed from a state of chaos and corruption into exemplars of modernity. But it was the zeal of extraordinary governors that provided the compensating metaphorical mortar, as both prisons were badly designed for their task, the detached wings forming almost separate entities rather than a unifying whole. Bad design has been a besetting sin of so many prisons down the ages.

In 1836 Dickens visited Coldbath Fields for an article he was contemplating, a project he soon abandoned as too boring. A year of oakum-picking under a silent regime in a house of correction did not have the same appeal to his public as a day in a condemned cell in raucous Newgate. 'The tread-mill will not take the hold of men's feelings that the gallows does', as he put it.[5] But there he met and befriended someone whose extensive experience undoubtedly influenced his views. This was Captain George Laval Chesterton, the future author of *Revelations of Prison Life*, who in 1829

<hr />

5   Collins, *op. cit.*, p.30.

GIRLS' SCHOOL AT TOTHILL FIELDS PRISON.

BOYS EXERCISING AT TOTHILL FIELDS PRISON.

20. Healthy minds in healthy bodies

had become governor of Coldbath Fields, a post he would hold for twenty-five years.[6]

As we have seen, bridewells, county institutions paid for out of the local rates, had been introduced in the sixteenth century to punish and put to work the idle and dissolute, the 'rogues and vagabonds' of the day, instilling a discipline which would correct their indisposition to honest labour. The punishment was to fit the crime: the work-shy were forced to work hard. Not much had changed by the early nineteenth century, other than that the means existed, by the invention of the tread-wheel and crank, to render penal labour exceedingly onerous and utterly useless. By then local prisons held petty offenders serving prison sentences ranging from seven days to two years, too short to engender reform but long enough to instil dread. It was in such prisons and on such prisoners that the tread-wheel and crank were deployed

Under the inspiration of John Howard, the new Coldbath Fields house of correction was opened in 1794 in Clerkenwell, reputedly the most vicious part of London.[7] The considerable sum of £70,000 had been spent buying land and building a massive structure with high walls 'overloaded with ponderous iron gates' but only 232 cells. Apart from its imposing gateway, the structure was badly designed and shoddily built. Over time, repairs, modifications and extensions were needed, and the number of cells so increased that eventually it could accommodate 'the extraordinary daily average of 1400 souls'.[8]

Degeneration began soon after it opened, and under its first governor, a former baker called Thomas Aris, it became known as 'The Bastille', later shortened to 'The Steel'. During his tenure 'men and women, boys and girls were indiscriminately herded together ... without employment, or wholesome control; while smoking, gaming, singing, and every species of brutalising conversation and demeanour, tended to the unlimited advancement of crime and pollution'. The governor walked around with a knotted rope administering 'summary corporal chastisement'. Aris was replaced, but his next two successors, both former law officers, were little improvement. These 'thief-taking governors held that their primary

---

[6] The tread-wheel, along with the crank and shot-drill, was introduced into Coldbath Fields prior to his arrival.

[7] The site at the north-eastern intersection of Farringdon Street and Rosebery Avenue is now occupied by Mount Pleasant postal sorting office.

[8] Chesterton, I, pp.4,16; for the prison generally see M&B, pp.277–352.

obligation was feathering their own nest and at the same time enriching their subordinates'.[9]

A better class of governor was required and Chesterton, a retired officer in the Royal Artillery, was the ideal candidate. He revered the legacy of both Howard and Fry, and the exertions of the latter's brother-in-law, Samuel Hoare, who as a Middlesex magistrate had been a frequent visitor to Coldbath Fields and who had laboured in vain to put things right. When Chesterton took over, he found it to be grossly overcrowded, with three male convicts to a cell. Worse, it was 'a sink of abomination and pollution'. All manner of illicit items – including 'pickles, preserves and fish sauce' – were smuggled into the prison and traded within its walls. These themselves were porous and prisoners in one cell could easily gain access to the next. Those who could pay got what they wanted and largely did as they pleased. Indigent prisoners endured a different fate, forced to do the most demeaning jobs, punished by turnkey or by prisoner alike for any perceived infraction or for complaining about their lot. In short, Chesterton fulminated, 'there was scarcely one redeeming feature in the prison administration, but the whole machinery tended to promote shameless gains by the furtherance of all that was lawless and execrable'.[10]

Chesterton set to work, gaining the support of Hoare and other magistrates, cracking down on abuses perpetrated by prisoners or staff, recruiting one convict as an informant, replacing the chief turnkey with a sergeant from his own regiment, and dismissing several of the former's underlings. As a reward for his endeavours his life was so repeatedly threatened that he carried loaded pistols in his pockets by day and slept with them nearby at night.

Five years into his tenure he introduced the silent system as an integral part of the discipline of the prison. The 'metamorphosis in discipline' was inadvertently effected through the instrumentality of William Crawford. Having completed his report on penal developments in the United States, Crawford visited a number of prisons in the north of England and in Scotland. Two particularly impressed him: Wakefield in Yorkshire which had introduced the silent system and the bridewell in Glasgow which had introduced the separate system. He strongly favoured the latter, and was confident others would too. Consequently he suggested to Hoare that Chesterton be commissioned to visit the same prisons and to report on the practicability of applying one or other regime to Coldbath Fields.

---

[9]   Chesterton disparaged all his predecessors as venal (*ibid.*, pp.22f.).

[10] *Ibid.*, pp.18, 41–55; M&B, pp.286f.

Upon his return, the strong-willed Chesterton was to prove a disappointment. He concluded that the number of prisoners and the paucity of cells in his establishment prevented the introduction of the separate system, even were that the desired option. But it was not. It was viable neither economically nor psychologically and was predicated on a false premise of Damascene conversion. With some easy alterations, however, the cheaper and more effective 'silent associated system' could be brought in. Once under this discipline his prison could fulfil its ends. These were limited primarily to deterrence and secondarily to reform. Chesterton considered that 'spiritual reformism in general and the separate system in particular were predicated upon an utopian view of criminals and of the working of God in the lives of men'. This was 'doctrinaire sentimentality'.[11] It was naively optimistic about the nature of humanity. He was realistically pessimistic about the achievability of internal reform. A few might be reborn but most offenders in his view were beyond regeneration. They were not, however, beyond associationism. If it were dinned into them that the pleasure they derived from transgression was outweighed by the punishment and that the ineluctable result of crime was pain, then self-interest would make them desist from their criminality. Their souls may not have been burnished but their behaviour could be altered. The dumb ox could easily be restrained. Suffering in silence, it would submit to the halter.

Chesterton imposed his new regime on 29 December 1834.[12] All intercommunication by word or sign was forbidden. Unproductive labour of a distasteful kind was imposed as punishment. The crank, shot-drill and tread-wheel were all deployed 'to apply wholesome severity to the hardened reprobate'. In enforced silence did the prisoners live, work and eat. To break it or any of the other rules was to be immediately punished, and for each infraction the punishment was more severe. By steady repetition the lesson would be learnt, and the association of pain with transgression would be instilled in the mind. Chesterton's retort to criticism was that only three per cent of his charges were disciplined each day, and transitory pain was much preferable to 'the lingering torture', productive at best of a 'fugitive and cloistered virtue', of the separate system. For boys, he thought, 'a very moderate application of the birch-rod is far preferable to confinement on

---

11 W.J. Forsythe, *The Reform of Prisoners 1830–1900* (Beckenham, 1987), p.31; Chesterton, II, p.15.

12 Chesterton, I, pp.294–302.

bread and water'.[13] To make prisoners obedient and docile was his achievable task, not to make them 'effervescently virtuous'.

Silence was golden. Only in chapel, where their attendance was compulsory, could they let rip, as social investigator Henry Mayhew in his *Criminal Prisons of London* chronicled:

> On entering the chapel ... we found the felon congregation already assembled ... The building was silent as a criminal court when sentence is being passed. When the prayer was ended, a sudden shout of 'Amen' filled the building, so loud and instantaneous, that it made us turn round in our chair with surprise; the 500 tongues had been for a moment released from their captivity of silence, and the enjoyment of the privilege was evinced by its noisiness. It was wonderful to watch the men as they made their responses. No opera chorus could have kept better time ... They knew the drill of the service as perfectly as a parish clerk, and appeared to be aware that the only time when they might raise their voices and break through the dumbness men had imposed upon them was when they were addressing their God.

Or each other, as the words of hymns could be altered, and messages conveyed by this means.

Adorning the walls of the central hall were placards displaying admonitions and exhortations. The admonition to 'SWEAR NOT AT ALL' seemed redundant under the silent system, while the exhortation 'BEHOLD HOW GOOD AND HOW PLEASANT IT IS FOR BRETHREN TO DWELL TOGETHER IN UNITY' seemed more appropriate to a monastic community than a prison.[14] Yet in many ways that is what Coldbath Fields had become. Prisoners, like monks, lived in cells, worked in silence and sang in church. This was the system witnessed by Dickens on this the first of many visits he made over the years. He came away impressed by its stern regime. He was aware that the admirable Chesterton had become a vociferous critic of the rival system of prison discipline being widely touted in Britain by men of influence in Church and State. Thus it came as no surprise when Crawford and Russell issued their report championing the separate system, they specifically criticised Coldbath Fields as an example of all they deplored. But it was not alone.

Tothill Fields – dubbed 'The Tea-party' – was a sister house of correction. It too underwent a transformation at the hands of another long-serving governor, the naval lieutenant Augustus Frederick Tracey who was in post

---

13 *Ibid.*, II, pp.10, 23, 137, 158.
14 M&B, p.290. Mayhew researched and wrote most of this work by 1856. Binny's contribution was minimal.

from its opening in 1836 until 1855. Dickens frequented here too, and became an admiring friend of Tracey. Its history was similar to that of its larger comparator, but is less well-documented. In short, the structure Dickens saw had replaced the adjacent seventeenth-century Westminster bridewell. The new prison was built in the 'Devil's Acre', the 'moral plague-spot of the whole kingdom' as it was unkindly called, near the Houses of Parliament.[15] To deal with the miscreants housed there, Tracey also opted for the silent system. The roles of the two houses of correction were later distinguished, from 1850 Tothill Fields taking women and children below the age of seventeen and Coldbath Fields adult males.[16]

Dickens concluded that the success, as he saw it, of these two prisons was largely down to the nature of the regime and the quality of the leadership. The governors of both establishments were 'enlightened and superior men: and it would be as difficult to find persons better qualified for the functions they discharge with firmness, zeal, intelligence and humanity, as it would to exceed the perfect order and arrangement of the institutions they govern'.[17]

A few years later he would use his knowledge of the silent system as imposed in the Middlesex correctional institutions to draw a comparison with its rival alternative, the separate system. To see both at optimum operation would necessitate a voyage of discovery. Anyone who could claim to have anything to say about penal matters had to see them in full swing across the Atlantic. Many who had done so had come down heavily in favour of separation. Some were more even-handed. Alexis de Tocqueville, a close observer of American affairs in the 1830s, having given a balanced appraisal of both, concluded that 'the Philadelphia system produces more honest men, and that of Auburn more obedient citizens'.[18] Dickens would judge for himself. In October 1842, two months before Pentonville opened, he published *American Notes for General Circulation*, a commentary and critique of all that he had experienced on his trip to the United States. The persistence of slavery offended him, and the American propensity for violence amazed him. 'The ideals of liberty and equality seem to include the freedom to shoot or knife any other American' was his gloss on the Second Amendment. But for a British readership most topical and controversial was his attack on the separate system of prison governance which he had seen for himself

---

[15] Westminster Cathedral now stands on that blighted ground.

[16] M&B, pp.353–486.

[17] *American Notes*: 'Boston'.

[18] This comes from a report by de Tocqueville for the French government, and is cited in an article on 'Prison Discipline' published in *The Edinburgh Review*, 64 (1837), p.177.

in its sanctum of Pennsylvania and which was about to be introduced in Pentonville.

Going to Cherry Hill was the culmination of his American prison excursions. Dickens had first visited a House of Reformation for Juvenile Offenders in Boston. He was struck by how 'many boys of colour' it held and thought it bizarre that in their school they 'sang a chorus in praise of Liberty'. However, he thoroughly approved 'the design and object' of such an establishment 'to reclaim the youthful criminal by firm but kind and judicious treatment; to make his prison a place of purification and improvement, not of demoralisation and corruption ... to snatch him from destruction, and restore him to society a penitent and useful member'. Adult offenders were a different matter, and Dickens feared that American benevolence had gone too far with respect to them. They were busily employed in useful labour in the Massachusetts house of correction. It was under the silent system of which he approved but there was no 'ignominious punishment'. Dickens found it hard to believe he was in a gaol and very much questioned 'whether the humane boast that it is not like one, had its root in the true wisdom or philosophy of the matter'. He specifically compared it to Coldbath and Tothill Fields and found it wanting. His criticism was mild and relatively uncontentious.

Not so when his itinerary took him to the much-lauded Eastern State penitentiary. He was granted free rein to go where he would and speak to anyone he wished. The advocates of this monument to Benthamite benevolence and Quaker quietude were proud of their achievement and wanted it to be seen and publicised. Dickens marvelled at the perfect order he found there, but found 'the dull repose and quiet that prevails' awful. The inmates were numbers not names and even the warders who brought them their food did not know their true identity or the nature of the crimes they had committed. They received no visitors, spoke to no one and spent almost every hour of every day alone in their cells, and every day was the same. When let out for daily exercise they wore masks over their faces and felt on the soles of their shoes. So many people; such little human interaction. Criminals were the victims of coercive kindness. For Dickens this system of 'rigid, strict and hopeless solitary confinement' was cruel and wrong in its effect. The excellent motives of those who administered it could not be doubted and the rationale behind it was 'kind, humane, and meant for reformation', but he was persuaded that those who devised such a system did not know what they were doing. Their 'daily tampering with the mysteries of the brain' was 'immeasurably worse than any torture of the body', and there was a 'depth of terrible endurance in it which none but the sufferers themselves can fathom and which no man has a right to inflict upon his fellow-creature'. For the duration of the sentence – and, in contrast to England, the sentences could be very long – the prisoner was 'buried alive' in a 'stone coffin', utterly cut off from human interaction, and 'dead to everything but torturing anxieties and horrible despair'. Dickens was revolted by this imposition of living death. He was sure that 'nothing wholesome or good has ever had its growth in such unnatural solitude'. Those who underwent it were not reformed but cowed and 'MUST pass into society again morally unhealthy and diseased'.[19]

It was also open to rank abuse, and affected the worst criminals the least. He met a burglar who regaled him with racy anecdotes of his past crimes and yet displayed 'unmitigated hypocrisy' by declaring 'that he blessed the day on which he came into prison, and that he would never commit another robbery as long as he lived'. This was playing the system, telling his keepers what they wanted to hear. Dickens was bemused to see children subjected to the same regime, and appalled by the injustice of it, an injustice stemming from America's great open sore. He took pity on 'a pretty coloured boy' he saw in the penitentiary, and asked if there was 'no refuge for young criminals in Philadelphia'. There was, he was told, but only for white children. The English writer's propensity to treat blacks and whites with equal consideration or condemnation would also help to explain the hostile reception *American Notes* received in the land of the select free.[20]

Dickens came away confirmed in his hostility to this trans-Atlantic experiment. It was both cruel and counter-productive. It was also too soft. The short, sharp shock – in silence – was what he preferred. He had written to a friend that he was sure that 'the writers who have most lustily lauded the American prisons, have never seen Chesterton's domain or Tracey's'. He had, and his strictures on separation bore striking similarity to those espoused by Chesterton.[21]

They were also similar to, but not identical with, those of Carlyle.[22] The latter lambasted all philanthropic endeavour. For him any system, be it silent or solitary, predicated on the erroneous belief that criminals could change or be changed, and reform and rehabilitation were at least possibilities, was pernicious bunkum. Prison was for stern punishment, vengeful retaliation,

---

[19]   All quotations are from the chapter 'Philadelphia and Its Solitary Prison'.

[20]   In his rebuttal Joseph Adshead pointed out that two of the women prisoners Dickens had called 'beautiful' were 'Mulattoes, and one of them a Negress!' (*Prisons and Prisoners* (London, 1845), p.115).

[21]   Chesterton, II, pp.9–20.

[22]   Collins, *op. cit.*, pp.88f.

pure and simple. He thought Dickens too accommodating to criminals and too positive about them.

Dickens certainly believed that punishment must predominate, but he was more nuanced. The more punitive silent system had greater virtues, at least in so far as hardened adult criminals were concerned. It was more onerous than the separate system but less destructive. It was workable and much cheaper. It was severe, but so it should be to be deterrent. In 1853 he wrote in his periodical, *Household Words*, that 'it is a satisfaction to me to see that determined thief, swindler or vagrant, sweating profusely on the treadmill or the crank, and extremely galled to know that he is doing nothing all the time but undergoing punishment'.[23] Gruelling useless labour, submissive silence and a Spartan regime would deter inveterate criminals from criminality and were what they deserved. The association between crime and pain would be driven home. But even they should not be broken as human beings. They should be hard-driven but not driven mad. For Dickens while the separate system was not punitive enough it was *more cruel* than the silent and *less effective*.

Separatists were nothing if not vehement in defence of their sacred cause. A local magistrate in his attempt to have Dickens banned from entering Coldbath Fields quoted from *Prisons and Prisoners*, a work published in 1845 by Joseph Adshead, a Manchester merchant, philanthropist, and 'rabid separatist'. Its attempt to blow Dickens's 'statements on the prisons of America ... to the four winds of heaven' proved in vain as the winds of Dickens's reputation had already blown them to the four corners of the earth.[24] Despite his adversary's public lustre as a novelist, Adshead weighed in. He too had visited prisons in Britain and America, but he would offer stolid facts about them rather than florid fictions. He proceeded to do so at considerable length and in considerable detail, taking on first 'the fallacies of "The Times"', another influential critic of the separate system which it denounced as 'maniac-making', and then 'the fictions of Dickens'.[25] Adshead espoused the virtues of 'Separate Confinement', and distinguished it from solitary confinement with which it was often confused. The latter was punitive and deprived prisoners not only of association but of clean accommodation, good food and employment. Bread and water in a damp dungeon was their lot. In contrast the object of the former was 'the permanent moral benefit of the prisoner', and under it 'an appeal is made to the moral sense and understanding of the prisoner' who is 'treated as a man, and with the respect

---

23 'In and out of Jail', *Household Words*, 14 May 1853, viii, pp.244f.
24 Chesterton, II, pp.186f.
25 *The Times* specifically cited Dickens's account with approval.

and benevolence due to humanity, even in its lowest debasement'. A clean, warm cell, adequate nourishment, and opportunities for employment or education were all provided. This system was designed not to punish or degrade, but to redeem and elevate, by quarantining offenders from each other and thus protecting them from 'foul contamination'. Its aims were complementary: 'to prevent the prisoner from holding intercourse with his fellow-prisoners, and to compel him to hold communion with himself'.[26] To equate solitary confinement with separate confinement, in Adshead's opinion, was the root of the problem, and led to unjustified public disquiet about the latter. Superficial journalese coming from the leader writer of *The Times* or from the pen of a famous novelist compounded the problem. Hard facts founded on wide experience and detailed research were the antidote to such pernicious misrepresentations. Dickens, in short, was a fraud.

Well that was one point of view, and one widely shared by many others who rushed into print, including Reading's chaplain, John Field. Dickens, however, as we have seen, was not alone in his denunciations of a well-intentioned experiment that was productive of great evil, an inadvertently inhumane system created by the most humane of philanthropists.[27] In retrospect the insights of a novelist and the instincts of a journalist got nearer to the truth of the matter than the arguments of experts or the encomia of separate system enthusiasts. Odd perhaps that these insights and instincts failed him when assessing the silent system. It is a pity that he did not manage to see the silent system in operation in its citadel of Auburn where criminals were the victims of coercive cruelty, a cruelty exemplified by staff carrying whips and administering savage summary punishment for the slightest infraction of the rules. Perhaps a visit there would have opened his eyes and changed his mind, or more likely would merely have reaffirmed his belief in the superiority of the British way of doing things.

Although it is not certain that he ever set foot in the place, in April 1850 Dickens turned his journalistic fire on the Pentonville experiment in an article entitled 'Pet Prisoners', published a few weeks after Carlyle's 'Model Prisons' and a few weeks before the final part of *David Copperfield*.[28] Dickens accepted official assertions that Pentonville had learnt from the Philadelphia experience and had improved upon it. The regime was somewhat less rigorous and the duration much less long. He agreed that the twelve months of separation by then in force would have no ill effects,

---

26 Adshead, *op. cit.*, pp.viii–x.
27 See the views of Arthur Griffiths in *Memorials of Millbank* (London, 1875), I, pp.185–93.
28 *Household Words*, 27 April 1850.

though he doubted its efficacy. He quoted, in order to ridicule, the literary profusions of John Field who in his book had printed several unctuous letters from penitent prisoners in his care. They could all have been penned by Uriah Heep. What concerned Dickens was not just the severity of the regime or its efficacy, but the disparity between the provision for wrong-doers and the more deserving needy. He repeated the popular refrain that the conditions prisoners endured in penitentiaries were far better than those paupers experienced in workhouses or the honest poor in their hovels. In terms similar to those of Carlyle, whose influence is apparent, he satirised the 'Model Prison' as 'a palace of felons'.

However there was in reality no one 'model' for what the regime in a British penitentiary should be like. Americans tended to go for a pure model, the perfect system. The British tended to muddle through, to compromise, to try out, to adapt or to adopt. Walter Clay pointed out that there were several variations on the separate system, the ways it was put into operation in Pentonville, Reading and Preston being very different. It was 'chiefly in these three prisons that the problem, how to combine reformation with punishment, was worked out', and 'the history of prison discipline in England over the next few years' was bound up with the history of these three institutions.[29] Critics of one might be complimentary of another. Pentonville was not Preston.

In March 1853 John Clay invited Dickens to visit his prison as he wished him to witness the Preston system in operation. He made the point that the writer had accused him of being a champion of the separate system while Russell thought he opposed it.[30] What he had devised in Preston was so modified as to fall neatly into neither of the contending categories. It was *sui generis*. Although he referred to it as the 'separate system', his son called it 'encellulement', with prisoners praying, working, and exercising together. However it was designated, Clay was increasingly confident of its success. As a result he had come to think of prisons as moral hospitals, but where effective treatment took time. It was another instance of liberal aspirations leading to the espousal of longer sentences out of all proportion to the crime.

Dickens does not seem to have taken up the offer. He had little time for chaplains and perhaps no inclination to distinguish the credulous from the credible, John Field of Reading from John Clay of Preston. Partly as a result of his depictions, chaplains became a regular butt of ridicule, and 'a

---

29 Clay, p.188.

30 *Ibid.*, pp.325–46. No reply to Clay's ponderous missive has been found.

felonious hypocrite with his tongue in his cheek, gulling a rose-water chaplain was long accepted by the British public as the symbol of religion in gaols'.[31] It is a pity, as Clay was very different from this caricature, optimistic rather than gullible, conscientious, kind, flexible, intelligent, far more beholden to the statistics he gathered than to sentiment, and wedded not to ideology but to what worked.

The rancour Dickens's writings on prisons produced merely reflected the bitter disputes engendered by the contending views of advocates of the differing carceral systems. The idea that prisons had a purpose above mere detention, although largely accepted, was comparatively new, and the British experience was relatively limited. America was the land in which most experimentation had been done, and there contention also raged over the respective merits of the two systems. Empirical evidence was only one aspect in contention. Penal philosophy was the other, and

> what gave acrimony to the interminable controversy ... was not so much the conflict of evidence as to the efficacy of the particular devices, as the unavowed differences in opinion upon the relative importance to be attached ... to success in deterring, success in reforming, and success in economizing public expenditure.[32]

Separatists, being idealistic and optimistic, emphasised producing a change of heart in prisoners through moral and religious influence. Proponents of the silent system rejected the 'mawkish theory' of 'super-sensitive reformers' that would strip prison of its 'salutary terrors'. They were less enamoured with the concept of 'the perfectability of man', and more cynical of transforming fallen humanity, but they did hold that wrong actions could be restrained, and bad or corrupted people deterred from evil-doing by a regime of 'wholesome severity'. Imprisonment should be unpleasant and prisoners should not be coddled. Prisons were inherently incapable of reforming delinquents, and no amount of tinkering with ethos or architecture would make any difference. All they claimed for their silent system was that it was 'calculated to effect as much good as is derivable from any prison process', although that was not much beyond punishment and deterrence.[33] Less idealism and more realism was their mantra. Sydney Smith and Charles Dickens were of this view, and both had considerable psychological insight

---

[31] Clay, p.265.
[32] Webb, p.77.
[33] Chesterton, I, p.158, II, p.1.

as well as an innate humanity. They would chastise but not brutalise. The more pathological Carlyle demanded severity, or even brutality, alone.

The strictures of *The Times*, the vituperation of Carlyle, the ridicule of Dickens, all had their impact on public opinion and 'a reaction against reformatory discipline set in'.[34] More and more it was accepted that Millbank had failed from inception, and Pentonville had succeeded only in having a destructive effect on the offenders it was designed to rehabilitate. The latter in particular was thought by the critics to have failed in both its aims, and for contrary reasons, being 'at once too well-appointed to deter and too dreadful to reform'.[35] Despite the proliferation of prisons on the Pentonville prototype,[36] and the greater number being incarcerated, the prison remained an institution strangely resistant to the intentions of its designers. Even as it emerged as the central institution in the struggle against crime, the fundamental assumptions that had supported its rise were being questioned. The penological panacea had failed to materialise. Far too much had been expected from a change of system, organisation or architecture. Hope had been boundless, hype had been everywhere. Philanthropists and philosophers had persuaded, parliament had enacted, penitentiaries had been constructed, and yet the wondrous transformation had proved elusive. Reaction was inevitable in the long term. Carlyle's depiction of convicts as dumb animals straining at the yoke and under the lash gained in appeal, but had not yet triumphed.

Penal optimism continued to wane as opposition to penitentiaries grew and their ineffectiveness became more manifest. Some commentators had always been cynical but others had been naively idealistic. Now they were downcast. The legal historian, Henry Maine, ruefully concluded that 'all theories on the subject of punishment have more or less broken down; and we are at sea as to first principles'.[37] Disillusion and disappointment with the reformatory ideal – but not with imprisonment as the prime preventative tool itself – set in, and the disillusioned and disappointed, robbed of hope,

---

[34] Clay, p.255.

[35] Robin Evans, *The Fabrication of Virtue* (Cambridge, 1982), p.386.

[36] By 1848 fifty-four English prisons, new or converted, were being planned on the same pattern as Pentonville and while only a few such as Reading and Winchester would practise separation in its pure form, many others imported elements of it. Its influence was also exported, and Pentonville became the most copied prison in the world. For instance soon after the visit of Frederick William IV to England in 1842, four penitentiaries were built in Prussia, two of them 'exactly like the Model Prison in London, according to the express will of His Majesty' (Fry, II, 445).

[37] Quoted in L. Radzinowicz and J. Turner, *The Modern Approach to Criminal Law* (London, 1945), p.48.

reverted to spiteful retaliation. Punishment replaced penitence, repression reform. The extravagant claims of chaplains and others were found wanting. The penitentiary experiment had failed because it had tried to reform those who could not be changed. They could, however, be deterred. Idealism was replaced with realism.

It was the death of one system, the separate (although vestiges of separation survived the demise), but the rejuvenation of another, the silent. Pentonville had been discredited but Coldbath Fields had not. Silence was retained for the rest of the century and beyond, silence with severity. Such a regime eschewed grand ambitions of making the bad better but was confident it could prevent them becoming worse from contamination, and deter them from coming back. That was what 'reform' – a concept still in currency – was reduced to. Harsh sentences, harsh conditions, harsh treatment was increasingly the mantra. Deterrence was preeminent.

In 1847 Lord Denman, the Lord Chief Justice of England, in answer to a question to the judges by the Select Committee of the House of Lords on Juvenile Offenders and Transportation, had declared that the combination of reform and deterrence as aims of imprisonment was a contradiction in terms and utterly irreconcilable.[38] It is a contradiction we have never resolved. and although we persistently try to amalgamate and reconcile these different aims, the needs of the one always seem to militate against the effectiveness of the other. For a while there was no need, as in the second half of the nineteenth century deterrence had no rival.

There was one aberration from this growing consensus that earned Dickens's approval though it would not win Carlyle's, and it was one well ahead of its time, very different from either the silent or solitary system, totally at odds with the woeful neglect of the past, the wishful thinking of the present or the considered brutality of the future, one which would have little lasting impact on its own time but would resonate in the twentieth-century era of humanitarian reform. It was the 'Marks System', devised entirely by one extraordinary man, the 'saintly reformist', Captain Alexander Maconochie.

---

[38] Evelyn Ruggles-Brise, *The English Prison System* (London, 1921), p.89.

CHAPTER 21

Top Marks

[Prisoners] have their claims on us also, claims only the more sacred because they are helpless in our hands ... We have no right to cast them away altogether. Even their physical suffering should be in moderation, and the moral pain we must and ought to inflict with it should be carefully framed so as if possible to reform, and not necessarily to pervert, them.

Alexander Maconochie

We were relieved by an Angell and Family, the well known and respected Captain Maconochie, Humane, Kind, religious and now Justice stares us in the face, the Almighty has now sent us a deliverance – no gaol, no Flogging.

James Lawrence, convict

In 1849 Alexander Maconochie, a retired captain in the Royal Navy, was made the first governor of the new Birmingham Borough Prison in Winson Green. This would not be his first experience of penal institutions. He was being given a second chance to put his rather unusual ideas on the treatment of prisoners into practice.

Born in 1787, the son of an Edinburgh lawyer, the young Maconochie, upon his father's death in 1796, was brought up and well educated by his kinsman, Lord Meadowbank, a pupil of Lord Mansfield, the revered Scottish Chief Justice of England. Intended for the law, the teenage Maconochie opted for the sea, entering the Royal Navy in 1803 at the age of sixteen. After an exciting and meritorious career he was paid off in 1815. He returned to Scotland before moving to London. During these years he published a number of works on a wide variety of nautical and commercial subjects. In 1830 he became the first secretary of the newly founded Geographical Society, and in 1833 the first professor of geography at University College, London, resigning from both positions in 1836 in order to become private secretary to his old friend, Sir John Franklin, who was replacing Colonel George Arthur as lieutenant-governor of Van Diemen's Land. As such Franklin would have responsibility for the three penal settlements on the island including the one established by his predecessor in 1832 and given his name: Port Arthur. It had acquired quite a reputation, for efficiency but also for inhumanity, and was to give Maconochie a sharp introduction into the ethics, practice and purpose of imprisonment.

Before he left England Maconochie had been asked by the SIPD to report on the 'working of the existing convict system in the penal colonies'. Knowing little about such matters, if anything he was predisposed in transportation's favour, and had he been sent to Sydney his predisposition might have been confirmed. The reality of Port Arthur appalled him. It held hardened recidivists, those who had not been willing or able to grasp the opportunities of transportation to the Promised Land. They had sinned again and again, and as irredeemable sinners had forfeited Paradise and ended up in Purgatory if not Hell. His detailed denunciation of the conditions they endured was based on what he had actually found and not on what he was predisposed to find. What he did uncover was a system whose 'chosen policy was terror' and whose 'predominant feature was misery': labour was unremitting, discipline unforgiving, the lash in constant bloody use. In condemning the penal settlement he condemned 'the whole social edifice of which it form[ed] a part'. He used a verbal lash on the officials who administered it and on the settlers who exploited it. He also made proposals for a markedly different system based on moral training and 'progressive degrees of freedom according to conduct'.[1]

His 'report on the state of prison discipline in Van Diemen's Land' was sent to the Home Secretary, Lord John Russell, who ordered its publication, and passed it on to the Select Committee on Transportation. The committee members, who included Russell and Peel, led by their chairman, the Radical MP, Sir William Molesworth, favoured the separate system – which Maconochie abhorred – over transportation. Reporting in August 1838, they found in Maconochie's strictures much that confirmed their preconceptions and gave substance to their contentions, and they deployed them to condemn transportation in general and Van Diemen's Land and its citizens in particular. The depiction of this antipodean hell-hole so horrified a British public otherwise inured to savage prison discipline, that it was, in the long term, instrumental in the demise of transportation itself.[2] In the immediate term it was instrumental in the departure of Maconochie from his job, as he was dismissed by Franklin when word of his subordinate's exposé got back to the colony. Its reputation had been besmirched.

Maconochie had time on his hands to think, and to think hard about prisons. He would not be idle for long, however. After his initial report had

---

1   John Barry, *Alexander Maconochie of Norfolk Island* (Oxford, 1958), pp.19ff., 41, 46ff.
2   *EHD*, XII(1), pp.513–24; Robert Hughes, *The Fatal Shore* (London, 1987), p.491.

been so well received, Maconochie sent the Home Secretary several lengthy memoranda outlining his radical ideas for shifting the focus of penology from punishment to reform, and asking for a chance to put them into operation. The Molesworth Committee recommended just such a course, urging that his guidelines for a new prison discipline based on incentives and clear future goals 'might in part at least be attempted with advantage'.[3] Who better to attempt it than Maconochie? Where better to try than in the brutal penal colony of Norfolk Island, a lovely but isolated dot in the Tasman Sea, north of New Zealand and east of Australia? It was to there that the most recalcitrant transportees were banished and it had long been notorious for the severity of its despotic regime. Cut off from the Australian mainland by a thousand miles of sea, these doubly-convicted and doubly-damned double-transportees were abandoned to their fate, and could be abused and degraded at will and punished beyond durance and contrary to law. It was 'a place of the extremest punishment, short of death', and from which only death could bring release.[4] For many, death was a blessed resort. Committing suicide or other capital crimes were commonplace, since either act ensured the final end to all earthly suffering. After one bloody uprising among the convicts, a Roman Catholic priest, Dr William Ullathorne, was sent to Norfolk Island to bring spiritual succour to those condemned to death. He found that it was the reprieved who needed his ministrations; it was the condemned who thanked God for their imminent deliverance.[5] Ullathorne was almost unique. Outsiders were rare visitors to this closed community and had to show considerable determination to get there. The Quakers, James Backhouse and George Washington Walker, were two such determined travellers. There were not many others. The sole inhabitants of this island, eleven days by ship from Sydney, were some two thousand convicts along with a large contingent of soldiers, a sprinkling of dependants and a handful of military prison administrators. It was not a fashionable posting.

This British equivalent of Devil's Island was safely far enough away for an experiment likely to end in dismal failure, and already housed the sort of intractable rogues least likely to ensure its success. Let Maconochie try as commandant, and let him fail.

---

3 Hughes, *op. cit.*, p.498.
4 Barry, *op. cit.*, p.90.
5 William Ullathorne, *Autobiography* (London, 1891), pp.102ff. He went on to write a pamphlet called *The Horrors of Transportation*.

He may have been a free-thinker but his whole approach was Christian to its core. Not all are criminals but all are sinners. Many criminals are more sinned against than sinning. Crime has causes other than sheer wickedness, causes such as want, illiteracy, and neglect. No one is irredeemable, no one so debased that they cannot be burnished. Vice is a disease and 'penal science just moral surgery'. The mechanics of imprisonment should be geared towards the enlargement, and not the diminution, of freedom. He stressed the essential worth of each individual:

> A human being is a member of a community, not as a limb is a member of a body, or as a wheel is a part of a machine, intended only to contribute to some general, joint result ... He is an ultimate being, made for his own perfection as his highest end, made to maintain an individual existence, and to serve others only as far as consists with his own virtue and progress.[6]

Maconochie was not averse to severe punishment for serious offences but it had to be merited, proportionate and reformative, very different from 'punitive brutality based on the personal animus of guards'.[7] It should also be a last resort, and in his time in charge he only ordered floggings of 300 lashes on a couple of occasions, and they were administered in private. Prisoners, he emphasised, 'should be *punished for the past* and *trained for the future*'.[8] Punishment must be a preparation for release, and those released should have been improved and not debased by their experience of imprisonment. Reform was of the essence, and to achieve this the dangling carrot was better than the raised stick. Education, the provision of musical instruments, access to the writings of such authors as Burns, Defoe and Shakespeare, practical training in agriculture and cookery, learning to live in, and benefit from, a cooperative community, taking personal responsibility for words and actions, and being rewarded as well as punished were all essential elements in his radical approach, an approach which was 'parental, not vindictive'.

His 'Mark System of Prison Discipline' embodied it. It was the practical 'apparatus' by which the fundamental principles of his penal philosophy would be achieved. Those principles were radical and novel, and were postulated on the startling premise that prisoners should not be given 'favours but *rights*, on fixed and unalterable conditions'. The basic tenet of the system was that criminal punishments should be 'task'- and not 'time'-

---

6   Barry, *op. cit.*, p.71.

7   Norval Morris, *Maconochie's Gentlemen* (Oxford, 2002), p.179.

8   Maconochie's *Report*, in Barry, *op. cit.*, pp.243ff.

orientated. Sentences should not be imposed in terms of years and months but in the number of marks to be achieved. The worse the crime the more marks needed to earn release. Six thousand marks would equate to a seven-year sentence and so on. Every prisoner should be awarded or docked marks depending on industry, behaviour and conduct. Progression through the system should depend on the accumulation of marks, and so should release itself, which should be earned, conditional, supervised, graduated, culminating in full autonomy and reintegration into civil society. A corollary of this was his belief that secondary punishments – imprisonment and transportation – should be indeterminate, their conclusion dependent on the objective criteria of good conduct and the amount of work done, enabling prisoners to secure their release by their own efforts.[9] The more effort put in, the earlier the exit. There was no place for deterrence in this, as sentences disproportionate to the offence should not be imposed on the grounds of deterring others. Similar ideas had been adumbrated at a theoretical level by Backhouse and Walker, the Cambridge utilitarian philosopher, William Paley, and the Oxford professor of political economy, Richard Whately, as well as by Bentham himself, but it was Maconochie who developed them and, above all, put them into practical effect.[10]

He also advocated a revolutionary approach to inter-personal relationships. Prison staff should take an active interest in their charges, and prisoners should reciprocate. Brutality and cruelty should be banished as they debase not just those subjected to them but the society which tolerates their use. Grievances should not fester but be aired and resolved at the lowest level possible, and ultimately prisoners should have recourse, through an ombudsman, to the commandant himself. Nowadays many such notions are trite; in Maconochie's day they were bizarre. His philosophy of punishment was at variance with the weight of contemporary thought, and the administrative methods he devised to put it into operation were unlike anything employed in any contemporary penal establishment.

Not all of his proposals could be implemented on Norfolk Island given the constraints of the existing law, the external restrictions imposed upon him and the brevity of his tenure, and to what extent his considerable success is attributable to the mark system or to his inspirational leadership

---

[9]   In later times this worthy notion would be distorted into release being dependent on the subjective assessment of rehabilitation, leading to prolonged imprisonment for offenders whose offences did not merit it but who were deemed unreformed. Maconochie would have been appalled by this distortion of his views. In the history of prisons bad outcomes often come from good intentions.

[10]   Barry, *op. cit.*, pp.76ff.

and the aura of 'fairness' he created is debatable. Whatever the cause, under his command wonders were worked, 'a living hell [becoming] a conforming prison, relatively safe for prisoners and staff alike', and discharged prisoners earning the epithet 'Maconochie's gentlemen'.[11]

Maconochie had gone well beyond his express mandate, in particular by failing to institute 'a period of punishment before probation', and above all by abolishing the distinction between the two classes of prisoner, the newly arrived transportees from England and the doubly-convicted veterans of Norfolk Island. All were treated in the same way and subjected to the new regime. This included trial by peers, the peers being fellow convicts acting as jurors, and a holiday with rum punch, barbecues, fireworks and amateur theatricals to celebrate the birthday of the young Queen Victoria. The well-deployed gallows outside the barracks was dismantled, the special double-loaded cats used for flogging were discarded, convict graves got headstones, and two churches were built, one for Catholics and one for Protestants. Jews were given a room for their religious observances. His trust was not misplaced and the new arrivals and old hands alike responded enthusiastically. To the former it was a pleasant surprise; to the latter no less than a miracle. They all had a stake in the system and an incentive to shorten their time within it by application and industry. Even the guards were gradually won over.

Their enthusiasm was not shared in New South Wales, the inhabitants of which reacted to reports of these goings-on with a mixture of ridicule and outrage. Although brazen falsehoods were mingled with the truth, the truth was bad enough. Devil's Island should not be displaced by the Isle of the Blessed, Purgatory should not be replaced with Paradise. The locals could not pity those they had oppressed, and reverted to the conventional wisdom that the first object of convict discipline was not the restoration of the fallen but the installation of fear into the heart of the felon. Maconochie's 'whole hog' approach was subjected to 'a wave of execration'. Eleven thousand miles away in London, Russell was having second thoughts. The issue for him was not how well Maconochie's measures were working but their deleterious effect on the morale of the colonists on the mainland and the risks to which they could be exposed if convicts were uncowed by the dread of transportation to Norfolk Island.

---

[11] Morris, *op. cit.*, pp.164, 192; Barry, *op. cit.*, pp.167–75.

In February 1843, after just three years, Maconochie was relieved of his post. Reluctantly he returned to England. Less reluctantly, those to whom he had promised discharge or an 'Island ticket-of-leave' grabbed at the chance to be shipped out. His successor, Major Joseph Childs of the Royal Marines, immediately reversed his predecessor's policies and reinstated savagery, provoking a major revolt in July 1846, as a result of which reproach unfairly fell not on Childs and his incompetence but on Maconochie and his 'over-indulgent' methods. Nonetheless Childs was replaced, but by an even more notorious commandant, John Price, who would be demonised as Maurice Frere in Marcus Clarke's 1874 novel, *His Natural Life*. It was an immortality of sorts for an ogre who in 1857 would himself be murdered by a gang of hulk prisoners in his last job as inspector-general of penal establishments in Victoria. He had lived just long enough to witness, for reasons of cost and not out of distaste for barbarity, the closure of the Norfolk Island colony.

Yet while others criticised Maconochie, Dickens defended him. In 'Pet Prisoners' he declared that the mark system was the only system of secondary punishment of which he knew that was reformatory, even though it would be improved by rigid silence which he considered indispensable. This praise was perhaps odd, given Dickens's other views on imprisonment, but although 'he never repudiated the merely penal and vindictive ideas he had expressed ... he never quite lost faith in the possibility of reforming some criminals'.[12] If a system worked, it should be supported, and Maconochie's seemed to. Dickens had corresponded with him, and may have met him. He explicitly incorporated some of his methods into the work he was engaged in with 'fallen women'. Maconochie's ideas were practical rather than ideological and seemed very suited for the clientele with whom Dickens was dealing. However he did not go along with every aspect of Maconochie's scheme, especially when the latter's zeal for going 'the whole hog' got the better of him. Dickens's was not the only influential voice raised in support of Maconochie. The Recorder of Birmingham, Matthew Davenport Hill, a friend of Bentham and Brougham, a man with great interest in penal reform and a pioneer of probation, also argued strongly in his favour.[13] So too did Mary Carpenter of the Ragged and Reformatory Schools movement.[14]

---

[12] Philip Collins, *Dickens and Crime*, 3rd edn (London, 1994), p.171.

[13] One of his brothers was Rowland Hill, the social activist and inventor of the penny post, and another was Frederick Hill, the penal reformer, author of *Crime, Its Amount, Causes and Remedies*, and Inspector of Prisons in Scotland.

[14] Mary Carpenter, *Our Convicts*, 2 vols (London, 1864), I, p.102; Clay, pp.250f.

For five years after his return Maconochie promulgated his views on prison governance. He rejected both the silent and separate systems and thought Bentham's approach misconceived. None of the alternatives could compare with his mark system. He suggested that a penal colony run along his lines on Chatham Island off the east coast of New Zealand would be economical and effective. He advocated employing convicts under his system on public works. In 1846 he published his most influential work, the title of which tells all: *Crime and Punishment: The Mark System, framed to mix Persuasion with Punishment, and make their effect improving, yet their operation severe.* It was all in vain, as officialdom considered his ideas both idealistic and impractical, the judiciary believed that the dread of punishment should not be diluted, and the separate system in Pentonville and the silent system in Coldbath Fields were still attracting powerful support, particularly in the capital. Fortunately, in the provinces, different methods might be assayed. In October 1849, through the good offices of Davenport Hill and with the strong backing of the newly-appointed Catholic bishop of Birmingham, none other than Dr Ullathorne, he was given a second chance to put his radical alternative into operation, this time in England and on virgin ground, as governor of a new prison.

Birmingham prison, 'a spacious, airy and well-built structure', was to be his laboratory. It was designed for adults and juveniles, and from its opening it was intended that the mark system would be deployed there. This required Home Office approval and since it involved the substitution of task for time sentences that approval was not forthcoming. The separate system was to be enforced for all inmates. With the connivance of the local magistrates, however, Maconochie was able to put in place a makeshift version – of doubtful legality – for boys under sixteen. It may have been merely a pale reflection of what he had envisaged, but 'during its limited operation it was more successful in promoting individual reform than any other system then in use'.[15] He was not allowed to experiment for long. Compromised by his own actions, some of which were strangely at variance with his theory, and undermined by the deputy he had appointed, another naval officer, William Austin, and some of the magistrates whom Austin had influenced, Maconochie was dismissed after only two years in office.

He had been discredited and all his endeavours had come to nought. The great experiment was ended. A bitterly disappointed man, Maconochie died in 1860 at the age of seventy-three, the subject of opprobrium while alive

---

15 Barry, *op. cit.*, p.207.

and of grave misrepresentation when dead.[16] By a cruel irony his eldest son, who joined the Home Office in 1848, would be instrumental in developing the later repressive prison regime that was totally at variance with his father's ideals. Maconochie was a prophet without honour in his own country and in his own time, and even in his own home, but he was a prophet nonetheless. His time would one day come, as Davenport Hill had confidently predicted when Maconochie took leave of Birmingham in 1851:

> Years probably must elapse, and many trials must yet be made before a perfect system can be devised, but we feel assured that no future explorer will act wisely, who does not make himself acquainted with the charts you have laid down before he sails on his voyage of discovery.[17]

And what happened in the Birmingham prison he had left behind? Austin, the usurper who replaced him as governor, had learnt his craft in the hard school of Tothill Fields and 'loved cruelty for cruelty's sake'. He picked on one fifteen-year-old called Edward Andrews. While the chaplain described the youth as 'very neglected ... mild, quiet, docile', Austin considered him to be 'sullen, dogged'. He was put to the crank and on failing to complete the set number of revolutions was put in 'punishment jackets' for hours, 'an engine of positive torture', and dowsed with cold water. He committed suicide in 1853. This and other abuses were uncovered by the assiduous prison inspector John Perry. The government appointed commissioners *to inquire into the conditions and treatment of prisoners confined in Birmingham prison.* Their observations that Austin had imposed a tyrannous regime, 'almost a uniform system of the application of pain and terror', led to him being put on trial and sentenced to three months' imprisonment for his actions.[18] But the savagery perpetrated by one notorious governor did not mean that severity itself in dealing with prisoners was discredited.

Rather, Maconochie's humane approach had little immediate influence in England, although aspects of it were implemented by Jebb whose work in prisons was very far from done. At his instigation a convict service was established by the Convict Prisons Act in 1850, the results of which he carefully documented in a report of that year on the *Discipline and Management of the Convict Prisons.* Two years later he became the chairman of the Directorate

---

[16] It was only in 1958 with Barry's seminal biography that Maconochie was finally and fully rehabilitated. Barry, however, does not shirk from apt criticism: *op. cit.*, pp.202–8.

[17] Matthew Davenport Hill, *Suggestions for the Repression of Crime* (London, 1857), pp.265f.

[18] *Report* (1854), pp.vi–xi, xxxv. The prison under Austin's control is described in graphic detail in Charles Reade's 1856 novel, *It's Never Too Late to Mend.*

of Convict Prisons, which had been set up to oversee the administration of those prisons for which the government was responsible. As this body rose in importance the inspectorate declined. Under Jebb's leadership the emphasis was less on internal reform and more on outward conformity, less on moral suasion and more on military discipline. His experience of Pentonville had led to this change in perspective; the increasing numbers needing to be housed necessitated it. Provision for more women and children had to be made after the refusal of the colonies to take them, and the end of all transportation was on the horizon.

Parkhurst had already been set up for juvenile convicts who were to receive moral, physical and industrial training before being transported to a bright new future in the antipodes, although the reality ultimately did not live up to the rhetoric and the results would not be encouraging.[19] Millbank was designated for convict receptions. Wakefield and Leicester joined Pentonville in housing male convicts in the solitary confinement phase of their sentences. New public works prisons for men were built at Portland in 1848, Portsmouth in 1850, and Chatham in 1856. In 1850 Dartmoor was repaired and enlarged to take older convicts, and ten years later Woking was opened to receive invalids. Innovatively, in 1853 the government paid for two institutions to be used solely for women. Brixton house of correction was bought and expanded to provide a capacity of 780 cells for them, and Fulham Refuge was built as a reformatory for 'Jebb's pets' – well-behaved and well-disposed women who were nearing the end of their sentences. To deter any determined disorder, warders in convict prisons were armed with truncheons, and their superiors with swords.[20] In addition a civil guard, equipped with rifles and bayonets, was created to watch over the gangs of felons who, carrying tools, laboured on public works outside the security of convict prison walls. In Dartmoor, at least, they also mounted guard in the chapel.[21] By 1853, as a result of Jebb's efforts, England at last had a prison establishment capable of housing all her convicts, keeping them securely, and putting them to work.

That very year the penal settlement in Van Diemen's Land was closed, on the fiftieth anniversary of the colony's foundation, and penal servitude was introduced into Britain by the first of five Penal Servitude Acts. Capital punishment was being severely curtailed, the deteriorating hulks were an

---

[19] *OHLE*, XIII, pp.157f.

[20] Anon., *Five Years' Penal Servitude by One who has Endured It*, 2nd edn (London, 1878), pp.77f. The anonymous author remains unknown despite being variously identified as William Thomson or Edward Callow.

[21] *Ibid.*, p.174.

21. Female convicts working in silence in Brixton prison

embarrassing expedient, and the end of transportation was imminent. A new deterrent sentence was needed, one that would reassure the public. The 1853 Act by 'substituting in certain Cases, other Punishment in lieu of Transportation', curtailed the latter's use, encouraged the new alternative, and stipulated that such sentences – which in all their elements had existed in the antipodes prior to the Act – could be served in the United Kingdom but also overseas. From 1 September 1853 no one was to be sentenced to transportation except for fourteen years or more and even they could receive sentences of penal servitude instead. Others liable to less than fourteen years were to be kept in penal servitude, but for a shorter term than they would have received if transported. Instead of sentences of up to seven years' transportation a term of four years' penal servitude would be imposed; between seven and ten years' transportation, four to six years' penal servitude; between ten and fifteen years, six to eight; and over fifteen years, between eight and ten. And this was not all. Under the Act the Crown was given the discretion to grant release on licence in the United Kingdom to those sentenced to transportation, or any punishment substituted for transportation. Thus, in the main the new sentences were shorter than the old, and could be curtailed further by ministerial decree. Soft on crime!

Jebb approved of, and encouraged, this development, and did all he could to ensure it would work. In totality the convict system under him would comprise nine convict prisons, an asylum for criminal lunatics at Broadmoor (designed by Jebb), and a refuge (pre-release prison) for women. Mirroring transportation, sentences of penal servitude were divided into three stages and a Maconochie-type system was introduced, whereby marks for good behaviour were totted up to allow early release when a certain number had been met. Convicts were given conduct badges for each stage in their progression. In theory the stages were supposed to correspond to the different aims of imprisonment, as Edmund Du Cane, a future head of convict prisons, observed, while equating the penal with the deterrent and emphasising the 'pecuniary' aspect – making prisoners pay through labour for the expense of their incarceration:

> The most practical way of carrying out the ... three aims of prison punishment, viz: deterrent, reformatory, pecuniary, is to divide the period of punishment into different stages, during one of which the penal or deterrent object should be considered almost exclusively, and during the other the reformatory and pecuniary may prevail in various degrees.[22]

In practice such clear distinctions were not made. Deterrence overrode all and effectively subsumed reform. The first stage, which could be considered both reformatory and deterrent, was served in either Millbank or Pentonville and consisted of a period of nine months in solitude as a preliminary penance, although the wearing of masks and isolation in chapel, so central

---

22 Edmund Du Cane, *An Account of the Manner in which Sentences of Penal Servitude are carried out in England* (London, 1872), pp.29–33.

to the separate system, were abandoned. Thereafter convicts were sent to the second deterrent and 'pecuniary' stage in the public works prisons to build fortifications, labour in naval dockyards, or reclaim marginal farmland, all of which was done in 'restricted association' and unpaid. Those who so laboured would leave a lasting legacy of their remorseless toil in the reclamation of Dartmoor, the construction of the Portland breakwater, the enlargement of the Warren to accommodate the Arsenal at Woolwich, and the extension of the dockyards in Portsmouth and Chatham (where a civilian convict prison was built on St Mary's Island between 1854 and 1856), along with forts to protect the latter's dockyards. The works in Chatham had been erected under the expert supervision of a military engineer with a penchant for fortifications, one Edmund Du Cane. For those unfit for such arduous employment, some prisons provided more sedentary occupations such as boot-making and tailoring. The third stage was probationary, offering those whose conduct merited it conditional release on 'ticket-of-leave', with the threat of recall for any infraction of the conditions of release.[23]

The promise of remission and the threat of its withdrawal provided a considerable incentive for prisoners to toe the line. But its seemingly arbitrary nature could stoke resentment. One cause of major discontent among convicts was that, for fear of public reaction to the early release of prisoners serving already shortened sentences, 'tickets-of-leave' were, with few exceptions, given only to those sentenced to transportation, many of whom were not actually transported, but whose sentences were lengthy. Another perennial problem was that if the stick greatly outweighed the carrot, discipline could be fatally undermined. In succeeding years sticks got heavier while carrots were in increasingly short supply.

In 1857 the Penal Servitude Act, amending that of 1853, decreed that after its commencement on 1 July no one should be sentenced to transportation, and those who, but for the passing of the Act, would have been so sentenced should be subject to the *same* term of penal servitude, with the sole exception that the court, at its discretion, could impose a sentence of three years' penal servitude where one of seven years' transportation might have been imposed before. The minimum term was three years, the maximum life.[24] Such sentences could still be served overseas (although this recourse would cease in 1867). In short, the Act ended any distinction between sentences of

---

[23] *Ibid.*, pp.13–19.

[24] Under the 1864 Penal Servitude Act the minimum term was raised to five years, and seven years for those who had previously undergone penal servitude. The minimum term was again reduced to three in 1891.

transportation and penal servitude, and lengthened prison sentences for the most serious offenders. It was hoped that this would make more palatable a change in policy that made the remission provisions apply to all convicts equally, albeit not to those sentenced under the earlier Act. In an attempt to maintain public confidence the Home Secretary stipulated a sliding scale for remission, from merely one-sixth for those sentenced to three years' penal servitude, rising to one-third for those serving fifteen years or more. To advocates of deterrence this policy still looked like a dangerous relaxation of prison discipline.

Ireland seemed immune to calls for greater repression. It had been inoculated with Maconochie's ideas to a far greater extent than England. In 1854 Captain Walter Crofton had become the chairman of the Directors of Convict Prisons in Ireland, a position comparable to that of Jebb in England, and in his radical reorganisation of the government-run prisons there had adopted many of Maconochie's principles and produced something extraordinarily progressive. He claimed to have found a way to redeem convicts by reformatory training. Under his scheme, convicts began their sentence, as in England, with nine months' separate confinement. At this point the Irish path diverged, as the initial period was followed by a sequence of 'Progressive Steps' culminating in an 'Intermediate Stage' during which they lived in huts and worked in small groups without supervision. They were then conditionally released into an effective after-care system. A new battle of systems was beginning, but the debate was no longer between the separate and silent but between the Irish and English. Carpenter and Davenport Hill supported the former. Both had gone to Dublin to see Crofton's project in operation in Mountjoy, a radial prison similar to Pentonville (and designed by Jebb) with five hundred single cells each with a flushing lavatory, which opened in 1850, and in Smithfield penitentiary, an old prison converted into a reformatory and used as an 'intermediate establishment between prison and the world'. Given that most of the inmates were Catholics, Crofton considered that religious instruction from priests of their own persuasion was vital to the reformatory project.[25]

The Irish system, in turn, influenced American prison reformers, and in 1870 the Declaration of Principles of the newly formed National Prison Association, with its emphasis on 'moral regeneration', incorporated much of Maconochie's approach and even his very language.[26] Meanwhile after 1865

---

[25] Hill, *op. cit.*, pp.672–6. Crofton's endeavours were related by Carpenter in *Our Convicts*. As the title suggests, she was predisposed to find in his favour.

[26] Barry, *op. cit.*, pp.231ff.

an inferior version of his mark system was introduced in English prisons to regulate remission and encourage progress to less stringent discipline. He is now recognised as a pioneer of prison reform, and one to rank with John Howard and Elizabeth Fry. That was the future. That time of plenty had not yet come.

First there were the years of famine when unremitting severity stalked the penological landscape. The pendulum was swinging not just away from Maconochie's exceptional approach but from any and all high-minded attempts at reform. Not only had penitentiaries come to be seen as an expensive flop, but discipline in the new prisons and the security of the public seemed to have been compromised. Disorder was breaking out in convict establishments where the supposedly deterrent sentences of penal servitude were served. Criminals, no longer exiled, were returning to British streets. As always, released prisoners who made a success of life were ignored, while those who fell back into their old ways were pilloried. Crime scares associated with 'tickets-of-leave' men were seized on by the press and by Dickens himself. Emotive and much-exaggerated reports of a 'garrotting' crime-wave in London by 'prowling gangs of tickets-of-leave men' were grabbing the headlines.[27] It was a perfect storm, resulting in a fresh impetus for repression. Criminals, above all else, had to be contained, controlled and coerced, all the more so if they were working outside prison walls under relatively light supervision and then let loose into the community. They must not be allowed to run riot and frighten the public.

By 1863 when Robert Cecil, the future marquess of Salisbury and Prime Minister, in prose leaden with sarcasm, asked 'whether a criminal should be made to suffer or whether a gaol is a mere House of Solomon for conducting experiments in planting and cultivating exotic virtues in unnatural and uncongenial soils', there was only one answer: suffering was the one inalienable element in punishment, and prisons were there to impose it.[28]

---

27 *Illustrated London News*, 6 December 1862. Garrotting was using an implement temporarily to strangle a person from behind while an accomplice robbed the incapacitated victim.

28 Andrew Roberts, *Salisbury: Victorian Titan* (London, 1999), p.55. Salisbury, an aristocrat of affluence, could make light of sufferings he could not imagine. He once said that the 'treadmill and crank' were mere 'trifles' compared with the treatment government ministers received in the Commons (pp.232f.).

PART IV

PUNISH AND BE DAMNED
1863–1895

Backlash against the reformatory ideal. In the age of Du Cane deterrence takes centre stage, and prisons become places of increasing severity, as evidenced by the experience of women and Oscar Wilde.

CHAPTER 22

Discipline and Deter

> For they starve the little frightened child
> Till it weeps both night and day
> And they scourge the weak, and flog the fool,
> And gibe the old and grey
> And some grow mad, and all grow bad,
> And none a word may say.
>
> Oscar Wilde

> I think it highly desirable that criminals should be hated, that the punishments inflicted upon them should be so contrived as to give expression to that hatred.
>
> James Fitzjames Stephen

Eighteen sixty-three was a momentous date in the history of imprisonment. In that year a death and a birth heralded the end of an era of extravagant optimism based on faith, hope and charity and the start of merciless decades of penal pessimism and deliberately institutionalised cruelty, an era not just of 'grinding rogues to make them honest', but grinding them to make them suffer. Sir Joshua Jebb – as by then he was – suddenly died in office aged seventy,[1] and a House of Lords Committee, chaired by Lord Carnarvon, to examine discipline in gaols, was born.

Fierce debate about the effectiveness of convict prisons and penal servitude had continued throughout the 1850s into the 1860s. Seemingly impervious to it all, Jebb persisted in his benign efforts, and had continued to advocate the humane treatment of prisoners. By treating them with 'firmness and decision united with consideration' he hoped that a 'proper feeling between warders and prisoners [could] be reestablished'.[2] By releasing them without police supervision, he thought that they could better find and longer retain

---

[1] Jebb was knighted in 1859 and rose to be a major-general. Other than an entry in the *Dictionary of National Biography*, there is no biography of this significant but almost forgotten figure. His memorials are Pentonville and the other prisons he built, and the insignificant avenue named after him which leads to Brixton prison in south London.

[2] *Returns Relating to the Recent Convict Disturbances at Chatham*, III, 3.

employment, unfettered by their pasts.[3] His calm determination to weather the storm and not to yield to populist pressure had been maintained even after mutiny had broken out in Chatham. Indeed it had been reinforced, as Chatham was all that Jebb deplored. The extremely harsh conditions experienced by convicts there, coupled with poor governance, had provoked a riot in February 1861 involving 850 inmates who had run amok and gone on a frenzy of destruction. The insurrection had had to be put down by nearby troops and the Metropolitan Police, although the most dramatic intervention came when Captain Gambier, then a Director of Prisons, had gone into the thick of the menacing throng and knocked the ringleader down with his own hands.[4] Jebb had taken moderate action: a general order was posted informing the participants that gratuities were confiscated, remission rescinded, licences cancelled, and warning them that any repetition would be met with far greater severity. For his lenity over this 'outrage' and for his fair-minded approach to prisoners in general he had been savagely lampooned by leader-writers as the 'Convict's Friend'. *The Examiner* had urged him to put on a 'Fat Convict Show' – in parody of 'The Fat Cattle Show' – with prize exhibits reared on 'a generous jail diet' in 'a tranquil confinement' with 'nothing to make them sulky and cross'.[5] To continue the animal analogy, *Punch*, 'the organ of the British middle-class', portrayed a rumbustious feast taking place in 'Sir Joshua Jebb's Pen of Pet Lambs'.[6] Ridicule, not reason, became the most effective weapon against rehabilitation and for repression.

Poking fun at the primary means of punishing criminals and deterring crime would never do. Concerns about the competence of the current prison administration led to the creation of Carnarvon's influential inquiry, and indeed of a parallel Royal Commission into the workings of transportation and penal servitude. Carnarvon had been outspoken on the issue of reformatory regimes. He had long deplored 'the interference of well-intentioned theorists who thought it practicable to make moral influences a substitute for hard labour' as a result of which criminals were free to commit crimes 'in the sure knowledge that there merely awaited

---

3   In 1869 the Habitual Criminals Act was passed to address criticisms levelled against the recidivism of tickets-of-leave prisoners. It introduced a system of police supervision for 'habitual criminals', and those who could not prove they were making an honest living could be returned to gaol.

4   Radzinowicz, pp.521–5; Alyson Brown, *English Society and the Prison* (Woodbridge, 2003), pp.43–54.

5   22 November 1862. Perhaps unwisely he had referred to the imprisoned as his 'family of eight thousand'.

6   13 December 1862. Frank Harris, *Oscar Wilde* (New York, 1916), II, p.375.

PUNCH, OR THE LONDON CHARIVARI.— December 13, 1862.

SIR JOSHUA JEBB'S PEN OF PET LAMBS.

22. Pampering prisoners

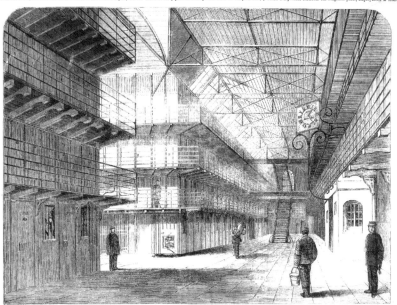

23. Chatham convict prison

[them] a good diet, warm bed[s] and light, often voluntary, labour'. This was an outrage to justice and unjust to 'honest poverty'.[7] It was an outrage he was in a position to end.

The committee began its work in March, took evidence from twenty-seven witnesses, including Jebb himself, and published its findings in July, a month after the sudden death of the Surveyor-General. Just as well. The report was a devastating indictment of the state of prison discipline, a discipline over which he had presided. It was failing in its primary purpose of deterrence, and in its secondary one of reform. The committee members rejected with scorn many of the principles enunciated by the inspectors, and 'especially Mr Perry', the avowed separatist and advocate of the primacy of reformation, and readily concurred with Chief Justice Cockburn's view that 'moderate labour, ample diet, substantial gratuities, with remission of a fixed part of the punishment, [were] hardly calculated to produce on the mind of the criminal that salutary dread of the recurrence of punishment that may be the means of deterring him'. The screw should be turned. Work should and could be back-breaking.

One of the witnesses called before the Lords was Major William Fulford, the governor of Stafford gaol, a county prison which aspired to the separate system but had only 422 cells for the 650 prisoners it held. He reassured the committee that he had all the authorisation he needed, but not all the resources.

> If I were to carry out strict discipline; if I had the means of giving every man who is sentenced to hard labour in Stafford jail the full amount of discipline I am empowered to do by Act of Parliament, for two years, no man alive could bear it.[8]

Indeed the regime he had imposed had reduced 'a muscular individual ... recently one of the strongest men in England' to the status of a baby.[9] Fulford thought that 'the whole machinery of moral reformation' was 'practically thrown away' on most classes of offenders, and especially on thieves and recidivists. Vagrants indeed preferred the comforts of the prison to the inconveniences of the workhouse. This was an observation of some significance as the conditions prevailing in the workhouses built under the

---

7   *PD*, Third Series, vol.169, cols 476–83.
8   *Report from the Select Committee of the House of Lords on the Present State of Discipline in Gaols and House of Correction*, para.1625. Mortality rates were surprisingly low. A single large volume, the 'Death Register', sufficed for the entire prison estate and was thought sufficient to last 1,700 years (Griffiths, p.268).
9   W. Payne, *Stafford gaol and its associations* (Stafford, 1887), pp.13, 19, 22–7.

Poor Law Amendment Act of 1834 were frequently compared unfavourably with those in prisons. The Act ended the practice of parishes having to look after their own poor at the expense of the better-off parishioners. Instead those seeking help could find it only in workhouses, where they would be clothed in a type of uniform and fed on a diet of gruel, mouldy bread and watery soup, but only if they worked for it. Oakum-picking and stone-breaking were the tasks allotted in what were popularly known as 'Bastilles', whose object was 'to establish a discipline so severe which would be a terror to the poor', deterring them from returning. The deterrent effect was such that some even sought food and lodging behind prison walls rather than endure the workhouse. The solution usually proposed to remove this shocking disparity was not to improve the lot of the pauper but to worsen that of the prisoner. This was the principle of 'less-eligibility'. Thus Fulford wanted to substitute a more deterrent element than mere moral instruction and concluded his evidence by agreeing with the proposition 'that if there were severe punishment over all the country there would be greater hesitation about committing offences'. Music to Carnarvon's ears.

Fulford also volunteered his views about juveniles in gaol, of which Staffordshire had a great many. Those who learned to read and write in prison were the 'sharpest of the lot' and the most likely to re-offend. A little learning was a dangerous thing. They should be kept out of prison. More merciful to beat them in the police station than to teach them in a college of convicts. Harsh as it sounds, Fulford was right that momentary violence was preferable to prolonged imprisonment:

> A little boy brought in for stealing a loaf, or a cake ... is sent to prison for 21 days ... I have had them really so small and so tender that I have been obliged to put them in the female hospital to play with the kitten ... Most of these little wretches either have a step-father or step-mother, and they lead the life of dogs at home; and the effect of their coming into prison where they are fed and housed and clothed and treated gently is that they have lost the dread of a prison, and they have gained the swagger of a prison bird, and they come back again. If those little boys were whipped at the police office, instead of being sent to prison, it would make a material difference in the number of our prisoners.[10]

His plea of being cruel to be kind this time fell on deaf ears and the committee made no recommendation about the detention of juveniles. Children who should have been succoured would continue to suffer imprisonment.

---

10 *Report from the Select Committee of the House of Lords on the Present State of Discipline in Gaols and House of Correction*, paras.1582–4, 1613–18, 1672.

Its members had a lot to say about every other aspect of the penal system. In its current guise it was failing by instilling too little dread in the criminal classes. Moral reformation, highly dubious in any case, should lose its primacy. Deterrence should be to the fore throughout. They demanded greater uniformity of labour, diet and treatment, greater centralisation, greater discipline and a more punitive regime, since 'the more strictly penal element of [prison] discipline is the chief means of exercising a deterrent influence' which 'ought not to be weakened, as it had been in some gaols, still less entirely withdrawn'. No one, however poor, should prefer life in prison to life in a hovel. Sparse fare, plank beds and onerous labour were vital to this end. Labour should be devoid of any of the satisfaction of a job well done. The tread-wheel, crank or shot-drill alone merited the designation of hard labour and that was the definition all prisons should adopt. It should be imposed universally.[11] Their conclusions coincided in part with those of the Royal Commission, and confirmed the prejudices and predilections of the press.

The Home Secretary enacted the Carnarvon proposals in another Penal Servitude Act in 1864 and a Prison Act the following year. They laid down a regimented and severely deterrent regime based on harsh treatment and hard labour both in convict and local prisons. Hard labour was divided into two classes. The first class was to be enforced by means that 'quickened the breath and opened the pores', such as the tread-wheel, shot-drill, stone-breaking, the crank and the capstan. The second class was 'such other description of bodily labour as might be appointed by the justices'. Every prison authority was required to provide both. Every male prisoner of sixteen years or older would endure six to ten hours a day of hard labour of the first class for at least three months. Those serving short sentences of over fourteen days would be on first-class labour throughout, although those serving fourteen days or less might be employed in second-class hard labour if the magistrates so decreed.[12]

Again in accordance with the Carnarvon recommendations the Act amalgamated gaols and houses of correction into the designation 'local prisons'. Over the years the distinction had already been largely eroded. The aim was to produce uniformity, and to reduce the numbers by closing down the worst and improving the rest. Many of the old gaols were death-traps, as Captain McGorrery, governor of Springfield gaol, Chelmsford, discovered to his cost. Like many holding that office, he lived with his family within the

11 *Ibid.*, ss.II, III, VI, VII.
12 Du Cane, p.61.

walls of the establishment he ran. In 1862, within weeks of each other, two of his children and his sister had succumbed to disease. Other gaols were unoccupied; one-seventh received fewer than six admissions in a year and one-third fewer than twenty-five. A contracting prison estate under greater regulation was the future, and contraction had already gone on for some time. The number of prisons had dropped from 335 in 1819 to 193 in 1862. Old prisons had been renovated or closed. New large prisons had been or were being built, especially in the major cities, such as Durham in 1819, Wakefield and Leeds (Armley) in 1847, Birmingham (Winson Green) in 1849, Liverpool (Walton) in 1855, Manchester (Strangeways) in 1868, and Hull in 1870, as well as several that had been constructed in London: Brixton in 1820, Wandsworth in 1851, and Holloway in 1852. The land was rid of lock-ups and instead was festooned with great castellated citadels, the like of which had not been seen since the castles of Norman and Angevin times.

For instance Local prisons continued to perform the function of gaols, detaining those awaiting trial, debtors, and the capitally condemned, but they also served as places of punishment for those sentenced to terms of up to two years. The aberrations of Reading were a thing of the past. The regime everywhere was to be deterrent with long hours of hard labour in harsh conditions and on a minimal diet. Prisoners summarily convicted would serve the full sentence without remission.

For instance in 1873, Sabrina Forbes, a thirty-two-year-old prostitute convicted of theft from the person, served her full six months' imprisonment with hard labour in Newcastle borough gaol which, along with an adjoining house of correction, had been constructed fifty years earlier. Here Forbes would endure a Spartan regime whereby she was put to work weaving, washing and cleaning on a diet of gruel, bread and cocoa. Discipline was harsh. Then, as now, the deprivations of prison life would be alleviated by the welcome ingress of contraband such as parcels of cooked meat and tobacco being thrown over the walls. But woe betide you if caught. Even minor infractions merited a restricted diet of bread and water, and for more serious ones Newcastle deployed shower baths and, as recently as 1855, even a scold's bridle.[13] For those convicted of robbery there was a worse fate than mere imprisonment. In 1872 John Smith in addition to four years' penal servitude was sentenced to eighteen cuts with the cat-o'-nine-tails, a sentence that was carried out within the local prison under the watchful

---

13 Such a device was still in use in Preston in 1827, but much to the embarrassed chagrin of the justices (Margaret DeLacy, *Prison Reform in Lancashire, 1700–1850* (Stanford, CA, 1986), p.210).

eye of the mayor, the sheriff, the governor and the surgeon. Two medical students, furthering their education, were also allowed to watch.[14]

Local prisons could serve as places of prurient amusement, the worthies of the area looking upon them as their personal fiefs, a visit to which constituted a diversion for bored house-guests. They were largely financed from the rates – although heavily subsidised by the government after 1842 – and were administered by county and borough magistrates, who to save costs sometimes closed prisons or contracted with others or with the army or navy to take their prisoners.[15] The 1865 Prison Act laid down staffing complements for all establishments, and empowered the Secretary of State to withhold grants to local authorities or even close establishments. In 1867 there were 145,184 committals to 126 local prisons in England and Wales.

Other ancient institutions, redolent of a more haphazard approach to incarceration, were doomed. In 1869, as a result of the Debtors' Act of that year which removed the power of arrest and imprisonment for debtors apart from those who defaulted in paying fines or other sums ordered by courts, the Queen's Bench Prison, the last in England exclusively for debtors, was closed for ever.[16] The House of Detention in Clerkenwell survived a little longer, but it was but a stay of execution. On 13 December 1867 its exercise yard was the target of a gunpowder explosion instigated by Fenians to aid the escape of Richard Burke, an arms supplier. The blast killed bystanders, and the ringleader, Michael Barrett, was the last person to be publicly hanged, outside Newgate. The blast also signed the death-warrant of the prison, although it lingered on for a further decade, succumbing, along with so many other old establishments, to the parliamentary bomb-blast detonated in 1878.

In 1872 a further redistribution of costs from the localities to central government was proposed on the grounds that the economy was booming, the electorate expanding, and criminals were increasingly mobile and hunted far from home. This last argument dovetailed with that propounded by nascent criminologists, largely on the basis of anecdote, that malefactors chose to commit crimes in areas where punishment was less draconian. With the coming of the railway the whole country was being drawn together, and the differences in the effect of sentences in different localities became very

---

[14] Barry Redfern, *Victorian Villains, Prisoners from Newcastle Gaol 1871–1873* (Newcastle, 2006), pp.10ff, 110ff.

[15] Griffiths, p.291n.; *OHP*, p.140.

[16] It had taken on the sole role when both the Marshalsea and the Fleet were closed in 1842.

apparent, a distinction it was feared that the criminal class was exploiting.[17] It was inequitable that geography conditioned punishment. Parity of provision could best be ensured by a greater degree of central direction.

Two years later Disraeli formed his second administration on the promise of reducing local rates and central government taxation. Nationalising prisons, it was thought, would reduce costs as well as induce greater uniformity. It succeeded in the latter but fell far short in the former. No inspection of the prison estate had been done and central government was lumbered with a hopelessly costly encumbrance. Despite earlier closures some of the remaining prisons were run-down or in disrepair, and with nationalisation in the offing, local authorities had little incentive to squander money on that which would soon no longer be theirs. While Newgate dated back to the eighteenth century and Oxford prison was early medieval, Newcastle was modern, but jerry-built and inadequate even from its opening. The 1877 Prison Act transferred to the Home Secretary all the powers formerly vested in local justices in regard to penal administration and brought all local prisons in England and Wales under the aegis of central government.[18] Uniquely, a local service came completely under state control, to the resentment of many magistrates who had been usurped and deprived of their power over prisons which heretofore had been regarded by them as their 'pocket boroughs', almost their private property.[19] Uniformity in the way prisoners were handled would ensure that there would be a minimum standard of treatment for each and every prisoner. The system would be harsh but measured, it would be severe but not savage, and scandals such as had afflicted Birmingham with its sadistic governor would not recur. But there was another perspective, one expressed by William Morrison, a veteran chaplain who had witnessed the transition when he served at Wakefield from 1876 to 1880, that when independent, experienced, and engaged magistrates were replaced by civil servants in Whitehall a more humane approach had been sacrificed on the altar of uniformity and mechanical efficiency. It had, but so too had whimsical cruelty.

---

[17] Du Cane, p.65.

[18] At the same time Irish prisons were placed under a General Prisons Board and the Scottish Prison Commission was set up along English lines. The former came to an end with the 1920 Government of Ireland Act which transferred the administration of prisons in the north to the government of Northern Ireland. The latter survived until 1928 when the remaining twelve prisons in the Scottish penal estate became the direct responsibility of the Secretary of State for Scotland.

[19] Griffiths, p.290.

The Act, which came into force in April 1878, made the national prison system the most centralised public service, and the most secretive. The shutters – which had been closing for some time – came firmly down. The public, which hitherto had almost complete access to gaols and bridewells, was excluded from the newly named Her Majesty's Prisons. Prurience was prevented by this development but so too was vigilance. Further, the Act rendered the erstwhile inquisitive, outspoken and, above all, independent inspectorate an integral part of that system.[20] External scrutiny was replaced with internal oversight. The guards guarded the guards. It was an increasingly closed world. Not entirely. As a fob to local sensibilities the power of justices to inspect prisons within their jurisdiction was retained and formalised in the establishment of Visiting Committees.[21]

The Act also created a Prison Commission to run the new service in tandem with the Directorate of Convict Prisons. The commissioners would be no more than five in number and although they would have considerable autonomy they were housed in the Home Office, their functions were subject to a general supervision, in matters of policy, by the Home Secretary, and he retained the power of appointing their chairman. The first to hold this august office was Edmund Du Cane.

Du Cane had spent a career largely devoted to prison construction and administration, both in military and civilian settings. Of Huguenot descent, he was born in 1830 into a military family. At the age of eighteen, having passed out of the Royal Military Academy at Woolwich, top of the class in mathematics and fortification, he was commissioned second lieutenant in the Royal Engineers and posted to Chatham.[22] In 1851 he had responded eagerly to a request for engineer officers to go to Western Australia to construct a convict prison for transportees. He spent four years there, serving under

---

20 It was not until 1981, after the May Committee had revisited the issue, that the office of an independent chief inspector of prisons was created, and following May's recommendation the appointees would come from outside the prison service.

21 As a result of the 1898 Prison Act these became Boards of Visitors and included non-magistrates in their composition. After 1963 when the prison department was created, members of the boards became appointees of the Home Secretary with a threefold role of being a watch-dog reporting back to the Secretary of State, investigating prisoners' complaints, and adjudicating on disciplinary charges against inmates. In 2003 the boards were renamed Independent Monitoring Boards, and since 2007 members have been appointed by the Justice Secretary. The effectiveness of these boards has long been questioned (J.E. Thomas and R. Pooley, *The Exploding Prison* (London, 1980), pp.86–91), but in recent years they have been outspoken and publicly critical

22 Alexandra Hasluck, *Royal Engineer: A Life of Sir Edmund Du Cane* (London, 1973), p.1. In 1856 the Royal Engineers moved their headquarters from Woolwich to Chatham.

Captain Edmund Henderson, who was yet another officer of engineers, and the first controller-general of convicts in the new penal colony. On his return to England Du Cane continued to prosper in the army, using convict labour to construct barracks and fortifications. Two years later he was promoted captain. Then fate played its part.

In 1863 his old friend, the then Colonel Henderson, also returned from Australia and was invited by Jebb to sit on the Board of Directors of Convict Prisons. Jebb promptly died and Henderson became chairman. On the day he took office, 29 July, and on his recommendation, Du Cane was made Inspector of Military Prisons, and was appointed to the Board. Six years later, at the age of thirty-nine, he in turn replaced his mentor (who had resigned to become commissioner of the Metropolitan Police) as chairman, a role he took on in tandem with being Surveyor-General. He was the obvious choice to chair the Prison Commission in 1878. As chairman of both Directorate and Commission the whole new national system was in his hands. He was knighted the same year.

Du Cane was no penal philosopher and no prison innovator, but he was paramount in giving effect to government policy. He got to work on a task of 'prodigious magnitude', ending eight hundred years of local control and creating a modern, unified prison system and a crushing uniformity of regime. On 1 April 1878 he took over all 113 local gaols, all of which would become Her Majesty's Prisons. Since the 1840s many smaller gaols had already gone, being replaced by fewer, larger institutions, cut off from the communities in which they were placed and making prisoners an alien race. Du Cane accelerated this process. By the end of May a further thirty-eight prisons had been closed, with others to follow, bringing the number down to fifty-nine by 1885.[23] The Treasury would reap some rewards as prisoner numbers fell, excess governors and redundant warders were dismissed, and expenditure on buildings was reduced. In addition a staff whose promotion would be based solely on merit was created, the hierarchical 'paramilitary' staff structure, which had been part of the convict service since its inception, was imposed on the local prison estate, as was the system of prison-warder clerks and schoolmasters – the precursor of specialist civilian staff – enabling Du Cane to discontinue the distasteful deployment of prisoners in those roles. The convict and local services, while retaining their distinctions in uniform, pay and purpose, became two parts of a single state entity of which Du Cane

---

[23] Du Cane, pp.74, 100.

was the linchpin. Without his energy and expertise it would have been all but impossible.[24]

What he created he also moulded, and the mould he made was very different from that of Jebb. Du Cane was the hard man for a hard regime. His influence was as pervasive as it was profound. He left an indelible imprint of his irascible personality on all he undertook. A fellow commissioner acknowledged that he was 'a courteous gentleman of the old school' with 'a hearty and cordial manner to all his colleagues' unless they 'trod on his toes'. He was an intimidating figure. A subordinate who knew him well gives this perceptive pen-portrait:

> Sir Edmund had few equals in the conduct of official business, but his methods in the management of men made him unpopular at times. He was as sharp as a needle, and went straight to the core of every subject he tackled; his mastery of detail was almost phenomenal, his was an exact, mathematical mind, and he could carry an array of figures in his head, and marshal elaborate facts with the utmost precision. His minutes and memoranda were pungent and practical ...
>
> He was easily moved to wrath. At opposition, neglect of orders, stupidity, as he deemed it, the failure to see things from his point of view, he would push his chair back ... and ... jump up to take his position on the hearthrug ... back to the fireplace, his tall, spare figure very erect, his head thrown back, chin in air, his eyes flashing, and his mouth grim ... where he had it out with whomsoever had raised his ire. The best way then was to face him and give it to him back, when, if you had a shadow of a case, and could keep your own temper under control, he gradually cooled down, and quietly dropped the discussion.[25]

He was, in short, a bit of a bully, but a bully in total command, self-reliant, self-satisfied and sure of himself. He was also solitary. He had no advisers, no equals, and would brook no interference. Although there were other commissioners alongside him, he marginalised them. Although he had many able experts under him, he 'completely sterilised them by absorbing all matters, great and small, into his own hands'. He was a master of statistical detail, and could employ that mastery to great effect to counter woolly assertions or nebulous criticism of, or within, his prison system. Public information about prisons would be confined to annual reports to parliament.[26] Governors were appointed by him and bore his imprint. Errant staff who dared to question or undermine his bleak imperium were dismissed. While he could intimidate inferiors – he was once accused, and excused, of assaulting a

---

24   *Report* (1895), para.14.
25   Griffiths, pp.256f.
26   Andrew Rutherford, *Prisons and the Process of Justice* (Oxford, 1986), p.104.

prison gatekeeper who refused him entry – he was not afraid to stand up to superiors. His word was law, and Home Secretaries themselves 'bowed to his decision when any question involving expert knowledge of prison administration was on the *tapis*'.[27]

It was this rigid disciplinarian who developed and refined the uncompromising deterrent approach that would endure until the end of the century. Its rigours were somewhat reduced by the 1877 Act in that no more than the first month of a sentence of imprisonment with hard labour was to be spent in the first class, the punitive and pointless ordeal under which prisoners slept – if they could – on plank beds without mattresses and spent six to eight hours a day uselessly turning cranks. One further amelioration was that the shot-drill, still deployed in Millbank, Chester, Lancaster, Durham, Oxford and Bedford prisons, was abolished except in military prisons. To ensure a healthy work force, adequate medical and bathing facilities were accommodated within the prison estate.[28]

Du Cane had no truck with brutality, and in his day allegations of staff mistreatment of prisoners were almost unheard of, although fear of reprisal may have suppressed many a complaint. Contemporary accounts tend to speak of staff rectitude even if it was frigid and rigid. For a prisoner the severity Du Cane did countenance may not have seemed very different. He boasted of creating a convict system that would serve the purposes of both deterrence and reform, but the former took precedence by far, as he viewed the majority of prisoners as incapable of change. He assumed that crime could be repressed, and the growth of a swelling criminal class reversed, by making imprisonment truly deterrent, which could only be accomplished by making life miserable for criminals of 'low brutish nature'. He was entirely utilitarian. He believed in general rather than specific deterrence. 'Punishment', he wrote, 'is inflicted much more for the purpose of deterring from crime the enormous number of *possible* criminals, rather than for any effect on the criminal himself.'[29] Just deter, not just deserts.

His views reflected the national consensus during the remainder of the nineteenth century. Public attitudes were evolving. The vivid caricatures of debased, dehumanised criminals which had long held sway in the imagination of those who read Carlyle and Dickens were seemingly confirmed by

---

[27] Griffiths, pp.291f.; Shane Leslie, *Sir Evelyn Ruggles-Brise* (London, 1938), p.85.

[28] In 1877 Dr R.M. Gover recorded only fourteen cases of typhoid and enteric fever in the whole prison estate, and two years later he boasted that 'such a term as "gaol fever" might be expunged from the English vocabulary' (Griffiths, p.296).

[29] Edmund Du Cane, *An Account of the Manner in which Sentences of Penal Servitude are carried out in England* (London, 1872), p.7.

positivist Neo-Darwinian social science, 'the hardened criminal character' being increasingly 'perceived as primitive and unresponsive to reformatory opportunities'.[30] Only the most severe of punishments could discourage such lowlife from further criminality.[31] Chaplains were relegated to the periphery, and much less attention was paid to education and moral reform than had been the case earlier in the century.

Harsh measures were applied in all the local as well as in the convict prisons, as Du Cane thought it a waste of time and effort to expend energy on the reform of ordinary prisoners whose sentences were so short. It was the crank and tread-wheel – cheap, easy, and onerous deterrents – for them.[32] In any case all should be treated exactly the same, and individuality ignored. Such 'exact uniformity'[33] was a further reason for nationalisation. The rotation of staff throughout a national institution meant that prisoners were more likely to be treated by the book and less in terms of their individual characteristics, and that warders were more likely to increase severity than to promote lenity. As head of a unified prison system Du Cane could ensure that 'a sentence of penal servitude is, in its main features, and so far as it concerns the punishment, applied on exactly the same system to every person subjected to it'.[34] He could have claimed the same for those serving ordinary sentences. Uniformity and severity were his watchwords.

And severity could be measured to extreme but still safe limits. It could be precision-engineered. The self-confidence of science in the last decades of Queen Victoria's reign encouraged Du Cane to refine the dietary needs, labour demands and living conditions in order to impose the type of savage penal discipline that Carnarvon had envisaged. He had Dr R.M. Gover appointed as the first ever medical inspector. Expertise was now on hand, and committees of scientific and medical experts laid down the quantity of daily hard labour that could safely be extracted on minimal rest and on meagre rations. Prisoners, it was confidently asserted, could work the tread-wheel six hours a day and ascend 8,640 feet, on curtailed sleep and on a diet of 'scientific starvation', consisting of oatmeal, bread and water, prepared in

---

[30] Positivism is an empirical philosophical theory that asserts that all authentic knowledge is verifiable and that the only valid knowledge is scientific. Such knowledge is gained by experiment and inductive reasoning and does not come from juristic or deductive reasoning.

[31] Brown, *op. cit.*, p.118.

[32] These devices were never deployed in convict prisons.

[33] The same as had been urged in 1838 by the inspectors' *Third Report*, but to protect prisoners from the vagaries and petty tyrannies of staff or institution (*Extracts*, p.6).

[34] Du Cane, p.155.

such a way as to make it repellent. This was to be the fate that befell most inmates. Of the 150,000 people imprisoned each year, some 100,000 were sentenced to hard labour in local prisons, three-quarters of whom were declared fit 'to mount the wheel'.

Not just the tread-wheel but the whole system was a machine designed to promote precisely measured misery. 'One who has endured it', a penal-servitude prisoner in Dartmoor in the 1870s noted that if an inmate thought he had been short-served his dinner he could appeal to a warder who would then 'take him to the cook-house where the dinner [was] weighed; if deficient the quantify is made up, if was not the man is reported for giving unnecessary trouble'. Nonetheless, living conditions in convict prisons were markedly better than in local ones. 'One who has endured it' was full of praise for the culinary delights of Newgate and Millbank where he had begun his sentence. The food was good in the former, but even better in the latter where, although plain, it was well-cooked and ample, the gruel being 'very good, thick' and 'sweetened with treacle' and the soup being 'really most excellent, evidently made from heads and shins of beef, well-stewed and thickened with pearl barley and vegetables'. The same prisoner encountered kind warders everywhere he went, and in Dartmoor, where he was confined for most of his sentence, he was full of praise for the comfortable, warm beds, the lovely sunrises he could see from his cell, and the excellent library well-furnished with the works of Macaulay, Froude, Napier and Euclid.[35] His stay did wonders for his rheumatism. Although his are not the norm for prison memoirs, and the writer was a middle-class conformist, well-steeped in, and accepting of, the criminological commonplaces of his time, as well as a model prisoner who earned all his 'marks', his observations cannot be dismissed out of hand. They relate, however, to convict prisons in Du Cane's early years in charge and present, at most, a small flicker of light on an otherwise dismal canvas. Soon it would be snuffed out, and a later commissioner's overall assessment of the Du Cane years was damning:

> In the English prison system the lights that had been lit in Newgate by Elizabeth Fry, on Norfolk Island by Captain Maconochie and at Portland by Colonel Jebb, went out: for twenty years our prisons presented the pattern of deterrence by severity of punishment, uniformly, rigidly and efficiently applied. For death itself the system had substituted a living death. It became legendary ... even in Russia.[36]

---

[35] Anon., *Five Years' Penal Servitude by One who has Endured It*, 2nd edn (London, 1878), pp.83f., 106f., 150, 199.

[36] *EPBS*, p.51.

Politicians and penologists, judges and journalists, accepted this without demur. To the behaviourist the ideal punishment was that which was most deterrent and the most deterrent was likely to be as severe as national, rather than local, sentiment would allow. Retribution, red in tooth and claw, was back in fashion. The prominent judge and eminent jurist, James Fitzjames Stephen, would urge 'the increased use of physical pain by flogging ... together with an increase in the severity of flogging' since, in its present languid state, 'it is little, if at all, more serious than a birching at a public school'.[37] Those who had endured the privations of privilege showed little sympathy for those serving well-deserved prison sentences. If the sons of the upper classes, for mere disciplinary offences, could be made to suffer physical pain behind the closed doors of an educational establishment, the children of all classes – though largely the lower classes – who broke the law must suffer all the more behind the high walls of a penal one.

And, out of sight, out of mind. Howard and Fry had entered any gaol they pleased. The penitentiaries, although not bound to, had positively flung open their gates to welcome visitors such as Dickens. But no longer. The public and even magistrates were increasingly excluded from seeing behind these 'bricks of shame'. This had a double effect. It prevented outrage from 'sentimentalists', and it allowed the myth to continue that prisoners were still being mollycoddled. Even some prison reformers, such as William Tallack of the Howard Association, criticised the regime, at least in convict prisons, as being too soft, and the diet too substantial. The convict got 280 oz. of solids a week while the pauper in the workhouse received only 166 oz.[38] Thus even greater severity was sanctioned throughout the prison system. Tobacco was strictly prohibited but, as would be the case with drugs in later years, found its way inside, often conveyed by prison staff, and at a price which varied, like other commodities, according to the laws of supply and demand.[39] As an added indignity, Du Cane introduced the idea of covering the uniforms of convicts with the broad arrow. He considered this decoration to be both a hindrance to escape and a mark of shame. It was certainly unpopular with the convicts. 'All over the whole clothing were hideous black impressions of the Broad Arrow', wrote one prisoner. Another considered 'the hideous dress to be the most extraordinary garb

---

[37] James Fitzjames Stephen, *A History of the Criminal Law of England* (London, 1883), II, p.80. Prison floggings were carried out by the hangman. The miscreant was secured by his wrists and ankles to the whipping apparatus where he was 'put to the cat' – lashed repeatedly on the back with the cat-o'-nine-tails.

[38] *OHP*, p.151.

[39] Anon., *op. cit.*, pp.120ff.; Griffiths, p.154.

I had ever seen outside a pantomime'. Men sent to public works prisons were issued with cumbersome boots that sported the same device. Jeremiah O'Donovan Rossa left this description:

> Fully fourteen pounds in weight. I put them on and the weight of them served to fasten me to the ground. It was not that alone, but the sight of the impression they left on the gutter as you looked at the footprints of those who walked before you, struck terror to your heart. There was the felons' brand of the broad arrow impressed on the soil by every footstep ... the nails in the soles of your boots and shoes were hammered in an arrow shape, so that whatever ground you trod you left traces that Government property had travelled over it.[40]

The broad arrow markings were in use until 1922, Dartmoor being the last prison to forsake them.

Du Cane took a 'scientific approach' to his vocation and addressed several social science conferences. Science would be his guide, statistics his tool. He had already been interested in the work of the pioneers of Social Darwinism who applied the insights of evolution theory to explain the existence of those above and below the norm, the high-achieving groups and the criminal fraternity. Inherited characteristics were the key, and selective breeding – as with animals – could produce the desired traits and extinguish the less desirable. Genius would expand and criminality diminish.

The man of the moment was Francis Galton, Darwin's half-cousin, founder of the eugenics movement, and coiner of the phrase 'nature not nurture'. In the 1870s and 1880s, deploying his considerable statistical, sociological and anthropological expertise, he sought to demonstrate that the criminal nature, characterised by lack of self-control, ungovernable passion, brute insensitivity, truncated conscience, and imbecility, tended to be inherited, rather than being the by-product of a harsh environment. The criminal was conceived in the womb. It was the scientific equivalent of Original Sin. But from it there could be no redemption, no salvation, just eradication or incapacitation. The mark of Cain was indelible. This was very different from the efforts of evangelicals to convert fellow sinners and restore them to society and even of associationists to habituate them to observe social norms and lead law-abiding lives. In an era of religious uncertainty, positivism and Social Darwinism held powerful sway. Galton and other influential thinkers, such as Herbert Spencer in England and Cesare Lombroso in Italy, denied that reformist endeavours could lead to significant spiritual or moral changes within inferior and atavistic creatures

---

[40] Jeremiah O'Donovan Rossa, *Irish Rebels in English Prisons* (New York, 1882), p.127.

who were at best sub-human. By the 1880s this anthropological pessimism, grounded in seemingly objective research, had pervaded the public mood, confirmed the graphic delineations of Carlyle, Dixon, and Mayhew, undermined Christian notions of common humanity, and explained why reformist endeavour had failed, based as it was on false assumptions about human nature. Further, it had given scientific sanction to Du Cane's Spartan regime. Punish, subdue, incapacitate. These were the ways to protect and preserve society. With the exception of 'occasional criminals' most criminals were beyond reform, and some were beyond deterrence. These inveterate 'habitual criminals', like dangerous animals, should be caged for life. The door of hope leading to Heaven was closed, the gates to Hell thrown open. Science sanctioned savagery.

Du Cane was not entirely of this ilk. He believed in a criminal underclass and thought that a comparison of the prison population with that of non-criminals would shed light on the influence of temperament, health and other social circumstances in developing a tendency to criminality. He encouraged Galton to study the photographs and measurements of criminals. The results did not prove that criminality was innate and inherited but merely showed that many criminals bore the marks of poverty and disease. The eminent and pioneering psychiatrist, Henry Maudsley, in honour of whom the famous London hospital is named, came to a similar conclusion. While never totally abandoning the notion that some personal characteristics could be inherited, he maintained that 'there are no theories of criminal anthropology so well-grounded and exact as to justify their introduction into a revised criminal law'.[41] Scientific research and medicalised approaches to the treatment of prisoners had their place, but they should not undermine the classic English approach to crime and criminals based as it was on moral culpability and proportionate punishment. There was no innate disposition to crime, whatever defects a person might have at birth. Criminals were made in the world, not in the womb.

Galton's failure did not dent Du Cane's belief in a defined criminal group to which most criminals belonged. He liked facts and was never in thrall to scientific fancy. He would draw eclectically from a number of theories. He wanted what worked. It mattered little to him whether criminality's origins lay in the environment or were innate. Maudsley's defence of classicism reinforced his own view of how best to deal with incorrigibles.

But not all criminals were in this category. He knew of youngsters who had been rehabilitated; he knew of adults who had been reformed; he

---

[41] 'Remarks on Crime and Criminals' in *Journal of Mental Science*, 34 (1888), pp.159–67.

knew of those who had made new lives for themselves in the very different environment of the antipodes. There was a place for Howard and Fry in his carceral estate, if not the central one. Chaplains remained, even if their role was diminished. The illiterate were still to be taught to read and write but not to memorise the Bible. Progression through stages as a result of marks awarded for good behaviour was designed to promote 'the formation of ideas and habits which may have a useful reformatory effect on prisoners after their discharge'.[42] But he was never optimistic of success, and knew, as well, that many, if not most, criminals were hardened offenders, immune to the workings of grace and incapable of seizing an honest opportunity. They were identifiable and were listed in a 'Black Book' of his devising, the *Register of Habitual Criminals in England and Wales for the Years 1869–76*.[43] At all costs they must be deterred. He wrote numerous reports and articles boasting of how he was making punishment ineluctable and more onerous, and above all how markedly the prison population had fallen. Where others had failed, his 'huge punishing machine' worked.[44] In 1885 he published his self-congratulatory work, *The Punishment and Prevention of Crime*, to bring his triumph before the public.

Yet two years later *A Description of the Prison at Wormwood Scrubs* was privately circulated. He was proud of this novel creation, one that would show a more humane aspect of his character. It would become his lasting memorial, and the road outside it still bears his name.

Wormwood Scrubs prison in suburban west London was designed by Du Cane himself and built under his oversight between 1874 and 1891 to replace Millbank. He placed another army man in charge of its construction. Arthur Griffiths already had considerable experience in the running of prisons, and would become the first popular as well as a most prolific prison historian, writing a plethora of books on what he called 'the history and romance of crime'.

---

[42] *Report* (1880), p.16.
[43] Hasluck, *op. cit.*, pp.114ff.
[44] The designation was given by Michael Davitt, whose own personal reflections on the 'system of purgatorial expiation ... perfected by Sir E.F. Du Cane' were published the same year as the latter's encomium (*Leaves from a Prison Diary*, 2 vols (London, 1885), I, pp.247ff.).

CHAPTER 23

The History and Romance of Crime

> The gaol and its inmates possess perennial interest for the public, and there may still be something to be said by one who has long made prison matters a business and a study, one who can speak of them from personal observation and a considerable amount of reading.
>
> Arthur Griffiths

In June 1870, almost a decade after the Chatham riots, a tough, young army officer, Major Arthur Griffiths, became deputy-governor of the convict prison there. He was shocked by what he saw, and he was no novice to prison work, having been in charge of the Gibraltar convict establishment. The riots had been caused in part by a sudden reduction in the already meagre diet. Nine years later he could still see men 'greedily devour the railway grease used in the traffic of trucks'. He heard stories that some were driven to eat earth, candles, frogs and worms. He knew of men who would throw themselves under moving trucks, preferring the amputation of a limb to having to endure this sort of existence. Self-mutilation to escape flogging was not uncommon. It was a vain sacrifice since, as the governor told the Royal Commission of 1878–9, 'there was no reason why they should not be flogged because they had only mutilated an arm or a leg'. Griffiths 'could not help commiserating the convicts' yet was 'powerless to mitigate their sufferings'. He thought the system indefensible:

> It was rigorous and relentless, formed by men who thought of deterrence through enforcing a rigid, almost barbarous, rule, from which all solace and alleviation were scrupulously eliminated ... There was no light in the lot of the Chatham convicts, no horizon to which they could look for coming relief ... a dull monotonous round of iron, unchangeable routine ... no creature comforts, no ease, no treats.[1]

Griffiths was a most interesting governor, had a most interesting professional background and would have a most interesting future career as a writer on

---

[1] Griffiths, pp.175ff. Paterson recounts that a colonial official visiting a convict prison in 1887 recommended that a hoarding should be erected a few feet in front of the windows to allow the ingress of air but to prevent the prisoners seeing the 'lovely view of the sea' (p.70).

military and penal matters, as well as being a novelist. He would publish over sixty books, including an invaluable autobiography. Born in 1838 into an army family, he attended one of those public schools which was a 'Spartan institution, run on bare, economical lines', where there was no cosseting and nothing but the plainest food in insufficient quantities.[2] It was a valuable preparation for his later career. At the age of sixteen he was commissioned into the army, and the next year he was deployed to the Crimea, followed by postings to Canada, Ireland and Gibraltar.

Whilst on this last assignment Griffiths paid a visit to Ceuta, the Spanish convict settlement on the north-east tip of Africa. What he saw intrigued him although as yet the direction of his future career was unknown. Ceuta had long been converted into a penal colony, such as the British had developed in Australia. A large proportion of the population consisted of convicts who were employed in public works. After a time they could seek gainful employment, turning themselves into good and useful citizens. Behind the scenes that Griffiths witnessed, things may have been very different, but of those he was ignorant. Ceuta, like so many other custodial institutions, did not wash its dirty linen in public.

After a few years, at the age of thirty-one, Griffiths took charge of the Gibraltar convict prison, locally known as 'the New Mole', where it was feared a mutiny might break out after the previous comptroller had broken down under the pressure of the job. The prison, noted Griffiths glumly, was 'an ancient establishment', consisting of 'a long, low, two-storied wooden shed, of fragile, flimsy appearance', and 'obsolete construction'. The system in force there – 'the congregate' or associated plan, in which all categories and classes were herded together – was no better, being old-fashioned and out of date. The place 'hardly deserved the name [of convict prison] and was but a poor substitute for the imposing edifices that ... were to be met with nearly all over England, embodying the latest principles of prison architecture'. In such conditions, Griffiths concluded, 'it was a mere matter of chance how a prisoner fared, except that he almost invariably deteriorated'. Some of his most difficult and dangerous charges were those 'who had done time in the cruelty and oppression of Van Diemen's Land, or in the foul corruption of Norfolk island'.[3] Griffiths, like Maconochie, thought such treatment unwarranted, immoral and counter-productive.

---

2   Griffiths, p.2. He does not name the school, but as it was one mile from Castletown on the Isle of Man and Dean Farrar was a fellow pupil it must have been King William's College which had opened in 1833 with a complement of forty-six boys.

3   Griffiths, pp.143, 150f.

Griffiths was an astute observer, and when for the first time, in Gibraltar, he became intimately acquainted with members of 'the criminal class', he found nothing in the 'felon faces' to distinguish them from the general population. He never subscribed to the 'ingenious theories' that Cesare Lombroso, the Italian 'father of criminal anthropology', would propound that criminality was innate and that criminals could be identified by their physical abnormalities.

> It would have been impossible for me to say that those before me were all born criminals, a type indeed, the actual existence of which does not seem to me fully proved; but at least they exhibited many of the traits described, which, after long experience, I have found to be largely present in the dangerous classes, and possibly in a large percentage of the general population.

People in prison, adorned in prison garb which 'is, to say the least, unbecoming', naturally looked at their worst. Individuals taken from the stalls of a theatre or from the bar of a gentleman's club and similarly attired and treated, would look just as much the caricature of the criminal. Such physical defects that criminals had were the sort of defects of members of the class from which most had sprung. What Lombroso and other positivists regarded as the anthropology of the criminal class was largely the anthropology of the working class. Griffiths was prescient in his scepticism and, despite the confident assertions of the aficionados of the fashionable and supposedly 'scientific' approach, did not believe that criminals belonged to some sub-human class who needed treatment rather than deserving punishment.[4]

---

[4]   *Ibid.*, p.145. Lombroso, the founder of the positivist school of criminology, spent several years studying the characteristics of criminals in the Italian penitentiaries and along Darwinian lines initially concluded that crime was caused almost entirely by anthropological inheritance. There was a sub-species he called 'Criminal Man', an 'atavistic phenomenon' reproducing a distinct 'anthropological type' which had inherited 'the characteristics of primitive man and of inferior animals'. He enunciated his views in many books and articles, beginning with *L'uomo Delinquente* in 1876 and culminating in *Crime: Its Causes and Remedies* in 1899. In this later work he became more nuanced – or bizarre – emphasising the social, geological, biological, psychological and racial, as well as the anthropological causes of crime. Dark-haired, epileptic gypsies with tattoos, living in hot climes free from malaria, were preordained for a life of crime. They had no moral responsibility for their actions as their actions were predetermined. While some criminals could be reorientated, throw-backs such as these could not be cured but should be caged.

Many studies have debunked these excesses and the pseudo-scientific methodology behind them. In particular, criticism was levelled at the method of analysis, and especially at the failure to compare criminal subjects with the population from which they had come. As the respected prison doctor, James Devon, pointed out in 1912,

He would have extensive experience of them over the succeeding years. In 1870 he left Gibraltar and returned to England. Du Cane immediately offered him a permanent appointment in the prison service, and after some hesitation about forgoing a promising military career, he accepted the post of deputy-governor of Chatham convict prison, at the time the largest in the land with over 1,700 prisoners, and staff and their families numbering close to 2,000. This included five chaplains of various denominations, schoolmasters, nurses, warders and civil guards, with a regiment of soldiers barracked nearby. Griffiths had a lot to learn as Chatham was very different from Gibraltar. The former was a bastion of the associated silent system. Indoors all the convicts were rigidly segregated in their cells; outside they laboured together, but in absolute silence. Discipline was meticulous, and the most minor infringements, or perceived infringements, met with severe penalties: loss of food or of remission. 'It was easy to go wrong, very difficult to do right.' The prison was a well-oiled machine, grinding and pounding those within it. Conformity was the order of the day:

> Everything worked with clock-like precision; the worst that could be said was that it was too mechanical, the inmates were treated too much *en masse*, with no attempt at distinguishing between them. They were as one in the eyes of authority, a single entity, ground under the hard and fast rules of the prison system. The wheels went on and on, round and round, with ceaseless methodic movement, and everyone must conform, and either fall out or be crushed.

Every day the routine was the same. An early rise, a paltry breakfast of bread and cocoa or bread and gruel, a short church service, enlivened by 'the gruesome chorus of so many hundreds of unfortunates expiating their offences against the law', was followed by the working parties being marched out to their respective back-breaking and meticulously enforced tasks which, with a lunchbreak at noon, lasted until 5 pm. The convicts were then marched back to the prison and, but for bathing, were once again kept separate in their individual cells. After a modicum of bread and cocoa or

---

trying to unravel the dynamics of behaviour in the artificial environment of prisons, reformatories or lunatic asylums was 'like writing Natural History from a study of caged birds. Parts will be right but the whole will be wrong' (cited in Radzinowicz, p.15). Apart from its inherent absurdities, perhaps the most telling refutation of his theory is that many crimes are the construct of particular times and particular societies. What is a crime one day, buggery for instance, may not be a crime tomorrow. What was not a crime in the past, non-consensual sexual intercourse within marriage for example, may become marital rape in the future. What is legal in one country or in one era, the consumption of alcohol or of cannabis, incest or female genital mutilation, may be illegal in other countries or in other times.

tea for 'supper' they were left alone and in isolation for twelve hours, after which the same routine was repeated.[5]

The warders, almost all of whom came from service in the army or navy, were accustomed to discipline: to being disciplined and to meting out discipline. The chief warder acted like a sergeant-major, insisting on unquestioning obedience, exacting every due, and punishing every infraction. He and his men were all doing their duty as they saw it, for little pay and meagre thanks, and they were, in the main, upright and hard-working. But, with few exceptions, they were unquestioning of the wisdom or necessity of the regime which they mechanically enforced as the impersonal agents of a higher authority. Griffiths, as an officer and gentleman, was in a rather different position. He could deplore what he could see and give expression to his misgivings, as he would do in a whole succession of books on prisons, the product of his later post-prison-service years.

Meanwhile towards the end of 1872 he was transferred to Millbank. By that time it held both men and women sentenced to penal servitude who were undergoing the first probationary period of nine months in modified solitary confinement, as well as some six hundred military prisoners who had been handed over to the civil authorities for punishment more deterrent than was thought to exist in the army. They were subjected to the same isolation, diet, and work routine of picking oakum, grinding the crank, or engaging in shot-drill, as civilian convicts. The unintended but inevitable consequence, as Griffiths ruefully noted, was to render them unfit for future service. For the remaining two decades of its existence Millbank was to fulfil this dual civil and military purpose.

If the effect on soldiers was deleterious, that on their flabby counterparts from 'civvie street' could be dramatic. Take a case familiar to Griffiths, that of Arthur Orton, who in February 1874 appeared before him. This was no ordinary prisoner, but a pampered imposter, the notorious 'Tichborne Claimant' who, for masquerading as Sir Roger Tichborne, the heir to a fortune, and lying about it in court, had been sentenced to fourteen years' penal servitude for perjury. During his brief time in Millbank, Orton lost nine of his twenty-five stone, one for each month he spent there, and it was a mere shadow of his former self that was transferred to Dartmoor, where

---

5   Griffiths, pp.162–7. The prison was demolished in 1898.

he was held in high regard by the other convicts who deferred to him as 'Sir Roger'. The weight loss may have saved his life.[6]

Back in Millbank, in a locked store room behind his chair, the new deputy-governor chanced upon a chaotic pile of papers and books. These turned out to be the prison's archives, consisting of journals, diaries, architects' plans, cost estimates, parliamentary papers and reports, as well as copies of Howard's and Neild's great surveys. Griffiths ploughed into this fertile field, and his first prison book, *The Memorials of Millbank*, published in 1875, was the early harvest.

It was also a fond farewell as Griffiths was about to be moved yet again. Like a condemned man swinging on the gallows, Millbank's demise was prolonged, but in 1874 vague rumours about a replacement began to solidify, and the word was that land in west London had been secured for its construction. Griffiths was summoned to see Du Cane who told him that he was to oversee the whole enterprise of building Wormwood Scrubs, as the new prison was to be called. He was to use Millbank prisoners for the task, an idea recommended by John Howard when describing his ideal prison, but never before implemented in Britain.[7] When Griffiths arrived on the scene, construction on the temporary prison was well under way. Six months later it was complete and two hundred cells were available for the convict labourers. With an excellent staff headed by a fine chief warder who had been promoted from Dartmoor,[8] work continued apace. Prisoners could be of use other than as mere labourers. On one occasion Griffiths was in a hurry to get into London. He handed his keys to the gatekeeper, but the safe into which they were to be deposited would not open. Worried he might miss the train, he asked for a burglar to be produced with the tools of his trade. The 'locksmith' arrived, and soon opened the safe. Griffiths

---

6   *Ibid.*, p.214. See Rohan McWilliam, *The Tichbourne Claimant: A Victorian Sensation* (London, 2007) for the most recent account of this bizarre affair. Orton survived his incarceration, being released on licence in 1884 and dying in 1898.

7   Howard, II, pp.220–6. There was a notable exemplar of convict construction in America. Mount Pleasant state penitentiary – after 1859 known as Sing Sing correctional facility – in New York State had been built in 1826 by a colony of convicts from Auburn penitentiary, bivouacked on the shore of the Hudson river. Griffiths would visit Sing Sing in 1891.

8   This was a Mr Coffey, who had not come from the services but had been a gardener in civilian life. Good relations between governors and 'chiefs' were vital, the latter being the most experienced and influential members of staff (J.E. Thomas, *The English Prison Officer since 1850* (London, 1972), pp.64f.).

Wormwood Scrubbs Prison.

24. HMP Wormwood Scrubs dominating the landscape, 1891

thanked him, and whispered to the chief warder to do him a good turn at the earliest opportunity.[9]

After two years Griffiths's tenure came to an end, completion of the project being devolved onto others. When finished, Wormwood Scrubs would be something extraordinary, the like of which had never been seen before, and represented an astonishing departure for Du Cane. Not for him the complexity of Millbank or the radial design of Pentonville. This would be a receptacle not of the inner light but of sunshine. He attached particular importance to erecting a soaring gatehouse, flanked on either side by reliefs of Howard and Fry, the prison's guardian angels. In front of the gate were two grand houses designated for the governor and the chaplain. Inside the high walls the layout was utterly novel. Four parallel wings ran on a north–south axis, allowing sunlight into each cell at some point during the day, but also better for segregating different classes of prisoner. There was a fountain behind the entrance, and gardens were placed between the wings. Cloisters connected the wings to the fine central chapel, a Romanesque basilica, built of Portland stone quarried and dressed by inmates there. It was a 'little cathedral' that could seat six hundred prisoners who would be able to gaze at stained-glass windows each depicting one of the Apostles, the models for which were serving prisoners. The very windows reflected redemption. Designed to be a national long-term prison to replace Millbank, Wormwood

[9]   Griffiths, pp.156f.

Scrubs opened in stages, and by the time it was finished in 1891 it had changed to being a local gaol taking short-term petty offenders, including women (whose cells were slightly smaller).[10] Thus cranks and tread-wheels were deployed, though later only for those sentenced to hard labour of the first class.

In 1878, on Du Cane's recommendation, Griffiths was appointed as one of Her Majesty's Inspectors of Prisons. It was a new job for Griffiths in a new era for prisons. As an inspector, his main tasks were to establish uniformity in practice and be 'the "eyes" and "ears"' of the commissioners, 'to spy out everything, and bring all errors and shortcomings' to their notice. For twenty-two years he was to be perpetually peripatetic, on his own estimation clocking up over 20,000 hours of train travel, although as a writer he considered this rather a boon. During this period his official reports were short and anodyne, but he managed to publish a number of books on prisons – *The Records of York Castle* (1880), *The Chronicles of Newgate* (1883), and *The Secrets of the Prison-House* (1894) – as well as others on crime and criminals, and detective novels. In 1890 he won the Czar's gold medal and £80 for the best monograph on John Howard whom he considered to be 'one of the noblest and most illustrious among Englishmen'. Du Cane caustically remarked that 'if the Czar can learn how to reform his prisons at the cost of a gold medal and £80 he will get a good deal for his money'.[11]

On his journeys, in between writing, he visited innumerable prisons throughout the land, from Berwick-upon-Tweed's 'old-fashioned "lock-up" with five and twenty cells, and with a daily average of less than ten [inmates]', to Durham's 'fine, large modern prison' and Armley in Leeds, 'a tall, castellated edifice' rising 'black and grimly forbidding in the prevailing murkiness of the coal-laden atmosphere' and which had cells for 359 males and 142 females. Within thirty years this hodgepodge of provision would, to Griffiths's approbation, be revolutionised, 'the old unsightly and unsuitable "local" gaols ... swept away entirely or converted into places of durance fulfilling the best modern conditions' and 'handsome, new prisons ... built wherever necessary'.[12] Griffiths was impressed by the calibre of wardens in both the convict and local prisons. Coming largely from the services or trades, they were 'honest, sturdy souls', doing their best and doing their duty, and as he put it, with the casual condescension of class and rank, 'excellent

---

10   The last women were decanted to Holloway in 1902.

11   Griffiths, p.400. In 1906 Griffiths agreed to unveil a plaque in Warrington to the great reformer and to give a post-prandial panegyric. This he did after a lunch topped off with a new creation: 'desert a la Howard'.

12   *Ibid.*, pp.279, 284f.

specimens of the subordinate public official'. Most governors were officers from the armed forces, and they too, in Griffiths's estimation, were capital individuals.

As his career progressed, Griffiths seemed less critical of the harsh system and more sure of its efficacy. It was efficient, it was well-run, it was uniform, it was well-provisioned, it was well-staffed. In only one respect did Griffiths find it lacking: it did not deter 'hardened offenders'. Given that deterrence was its primary purpose, it was quite a failing: a well-oiled machine that did not manufacture the goods! For Griffiths, who denied that prisons could reform, it was vital that they should deter. Severity might deter novices, but not 'old hands'. Greater severity might do the job, but 'with due regard to humanity' it could not be imposed. The only solution was to introduce indefinite preventive imprisonment for habitual criminals, to ensure their incapacitation, a device by which the demands of public protection overrode the requirements of justice.[13]

Griffiths had come to the summit of his prison career. He was considered something of an expert. As far back as 1878 he had been a witness called before the Royal Commission on Penal Servitude – the Kimberley inquiry – and he had accumulated a great deal of experience and done a lot of research since then. Perhaps it was no surprise that in 1896 he was appointed to represent England at the Congress of Criminal Anthropology at Geneva University where the central figure was none other than the eminent doctor of Turin, Cesare Lombroso himself. While doubting Lombroso's contentions, Griffiths, in his own contribution to the conference, nonetheless propounded his own decided views on the necessity of indefinite sentences. Acknowledge it or not, he too had been influenced by the new medicalised and pessimistic view of habitual criminals which had emanated from Europe. The self-satisfied rhetoric of British penal exceptionalism sometimes belied the hard reality of Continental influence.

Three years later, Griffiths retired from the prison service that had been his life for half a century. But prisons were in his blood, and he would devote his remaining ten years to continuing to write about them, bringing out a *de luxe* limited edition of his prison works, British and foreign, published in twelve volumes by the Grolier Society in 1900 under the umbrella title *The History and Romance of Crime*.[14] He also wrote an autobiography upon which much of this chapter is based. Griffiths loved a good story, he sought out sensation, but he got a large audience and his books were very popular,

---

13 *Ibid.*, pp.385ff.
14 Reissued as *The World's Famous Prisons* in 1905. Griffiths died in 1908.

in the way that Howard's or Fry's writings could not be. For the first time the Victorian middle classes could feast on prison stories and prison facts. Griffiths wrote to get a readership which he could inform as well as entertain. Posterity owes him quite a debt.

There was another, greater writer, who also had first-hand experience of what he wrote, who would confront the public with the awful conditions prisoners endured, and affect the future development of prison regimes themselves: Oscar Wilde.

CHAPTER 24

Reaping and Sowing

With midnight always in one's heart,
And twilight in one's cell,
We turn the crank, or tear the rope,
Each in his separate hell
And the silence is more awful far
Than the sound of a brazen bell.

Oscar Wilde

Within the circle of the high grey wall is silence. Under a square of
sky cut by high grey buildings nothing is to be seen of Nature but the
prisoners themselves, the men who guard the prisoners, and a cat who
eats the prison mice.

John Galsworthy

Two years' imprisonment with or without hard labour was the maximum
sentence for an offence contrary to s.11 of the Criminal Law Amendment
Act 1885. The Act came into force on 1 January 1886 and for the first
time made 'acts of gross indecency' – any sexual activity short of sodomy
done *in private* between adult men – a crime. Up until then the criminal law
had been concerned only with buggery and acts against *public* decency or
conduct tending to the corruption of youth. Section 11 had been introduced
at the last moment as an amendment to an Act, the aim of which was to
protect vulnerable women and girls from sexual exploitation and to suppress
brothels. It was soon dubbed 'the Blackmailer's Charter'. In the case of one
Oscar Fingal O'Flahertie Wills Wilde it could have been called 'the father's
Fury'.

The father in question was the eighth marquess of Queensberry who
resented Wilde's intimate relationship with 'Bosie', his wayward third son,
Lord Alfred Douglas. His anger wreaking havoc with his spelling, he accused
Wilde of 'posing as a somdomite'. Bosie later admitted in his *Autobiography*
to 'familiarities of the kind common among public school boys' but utterly
denied committing 'the sin which takes its name from one of the cities of
the Plain'. Egged on by his vengeful Adonis, Wilde hubristically prosecuted
the hated father for criminal libel. Belatedly, after admitting assignations
with working-class youths, he dropped the case half-way through the trial.

Too late. The enraged marquess ensured that criminal proceedings were instigated against the man whom he considered to be his son's seducer.

On 5 April 1895 Wilde was arrested at the Cadogan Hotel, taken to Bow Street magistrates' court, and remanded to Holloway prison, pending trial at the Old Bailey on a number of charges relating not to Lord Alfred Douglas but to working-class rent-boys.[1] He was tried twice since the first jury, perhaps influenced by his brilliant defence of Platonic love, failed to reach a verdict. The second jury had no such qualms and on Saturday 28 May Wilde was convicted of eight counts of committing acts of gross indecency. The judge, Mr Justice Wills, was outraged that the penalty was so circumscribed. Had the conviction been for sodomy, a felony, there would have been no limit. Before 1861 sodomy was a capital offence, and thereafter it was punishable with life imprisonment. Gross indecency was a mere misdemeanour, and so two years with hard labour it had to be. Hard labour, however, was a punishment of appalling savagery and two years of such a sentence could break the body and spirit of a stronger man than the 'pampered sybarite' Oscar Wilde.[2]

He spent the weekend in Newgate before being transferred in a 'Black Maria' to Pentonville where he passed through the indignities of reception, being stripped, weighed and measured, bathed in filthy, tepid water, and deprived of all his personal possessions.[3] He was introduced to the harsh reality of prison life in the Du Cane era. 'At first it was a fiendish nightmare', he told his friend, Frank Harris, 'more horrible than anything I had dreamt of'. 'Hate masked in degrading formalism' was the hallmark of what he called '*The System*'. It was designed to 'break you down body and soul and if you resist [to] drive you crazy'. The inhumanity of it all was the worst of it and inhumanity, as he put it, was 'in humanity'. He had never realised how devilish men could be. He had 'never dreamt of such cruelties'.[4] To begin with he could barely breathe the rank air, stomach the food, or tolerate the smell. At unlock in the morning the smell was at its worst, an acrid aroma arising from unwashed bodies and unemptied 'slop-buckets' containing the night's effluence. So bad was the stink occasioned by 'slopping-out' that

---

1   It is a curious irony that 'rent' was slang both for young male prostitutes and for blackmail. It first came to prominence in the 1890s and was famously used, in relation to the Cleveland Street scandal, by Thomas Swinscow who admitted in 1895 to being a rent-boy in a London brothel.

2   Frank Harris, *Oscar Wilde* (New York, 1916), II, p.321.

3   The register, still extant, records that on admission he was six feet tall and weighed fourteen stone (Montgomery Hyde, *Oscar Wilde: The Aftermath* (London, 1963), p.4).

4   Harris, *op. cit.*, pp.331ff., 339.

Wilde witnessed several warders being sick when they opened the cell doors, and they had not spent the night in such conditions. Along with many others, he developed diarrhoea and suffered from insomnia and 'wild delusions'. He was certified as fit only for 'light labour' and so was spared the tread-wheel or the crank. But, clothed in coarse prison garb with its broad arrow markings – 'this livery of shame' – he was to endure solitary confinement in a lime-washed cell where he picked oakum or sewed mailbags.[5] As he would say of Reading, so he could have said of Pentonville, in words that are as frank as they are true:

> Each narrow cell in which we dwell
> Is a foul and dark latrine,
> And the fetid breath of living Death
> Chokes up each grated screen,
> And all, but Lust, is turned to Dust
> In humanity's machine

Of lust he could not be deprived but of books he could, and this proved the greatest punishment. During the first three months of his sentence, a Bible, prayer-book and hymn-book were the only literature allowed. Thereafter he was allowed a book a week from the prison library with its poor selection of mainly religious ephemera. The chaplain provided him with one treasure, written by a fellow jailbird, *Pilgrim's Progress*. Whether Wilde appreciated it, perhaps for its literary value, its spiritual comfort or for the fact that it came from the pen of a fellow sufferer, is not recorded, although it 'did not satisfy him'.[6]

While in Pentonville he received a visit of considerable significance and pregnant with potential. The Home Secretary, Herbert Asquith, who had known Wilde personally and had him to dine at his house, had heard rumours of his mental decline. He directed that the prison doctor report on his condition. The bland assurance that all was well did little to reassure

---

5   Mailbag-sewing, tedious and irksome as it was, would remain a prison industry until 1992. In 1954 prisoners made four million mailbags. When Horatio Bottomley, MP and fraudster, was in Wormwood Scrubs he was visited by the chaplain who found him busy at work. 'Ah', said he, 'sewing I see', to which Bottomley replied, 'No, reaping' (Clayton, pp.90, 136). Or was it a prison visitor at Maidstone? Or an apocryphal tale? John Vidler, a prison governor, was shown the cell in both prisons where the conversation supposedly took place (*If Freedom Fail* (London, 1964), p.121).

6   Richard Haldane, *Autobiography* (London, 1929), p.166. *Pilgrim's Progress* was still being dispensed to prisoners in the twentieth century. Jack Gordon recounts that along with a Bible, Prayer Book and the Prison Rules, it was part of his 'kit' when he was on remand in Leicester prison (*Borstalians* (London, 1932), p.35). So too does John Fletcher when in Durham prison in 1934 (*A Menace to Society* (London, 1972), pp.34f.).

Asquith. At his instigation, or at least with his approval, a meeting was arranged of a rather different type. The lawyer and Liberal member of parliament, Richard Haldane, was a member of the Gladstone Committee.[7] As such he had a warrant which allowed him to visit any prisoner in any prison at any time. He had also encountered and admired Wilde in the past and was 'haunted by the idea of what this highly sensitive man was probably suffering under ordinary prison treatment'. But his was more than a social visit to encourage an old acquaintance. It was also to recruit the famous writer to the cause of penal reform and to help expose the monstrous conditions under which he and others laboured, but of which the public was largely ignorant. Wilde may have been a pariah at that point, but people still flocked to his plays. In two years attitudes would change and sympathy for a broken reed would grow. They would read what he wrote. Wilde had the ability and opportunity to bring the whole system into disrepute, to destroy its moral legitimacy, and to unleash public revulsion. His suffering could be others' salvation. None of this was said so bluntly. It did not need to be. When Wilde was ushered into the room allocated for the interview, 'at first he refused to speak'. Haldane put his hand 'on his prison-clad shoulder', told him that they had met before, and that he had come to tell him something of importance about himself. And an important truth it was, one with which Wilde would later agree when he castigated himself for being 'spendthrift of [his] genius':

> He had not fully used his great literary gift, and the reason was that he had lived a life of pleasure and had not made any great subject his own. Now misfortune might prove a blessing for his career, for he had got a great subject.

Recognising Wilde's potential, Haldane would try to ensure that he had access to books and writing materials. Wilde burst into tears and promised to make the attempt. Books he would dearly love, and, among others, he asked for Flaubert's *Madame Bovary*. Haldane countered that the dedication by the author to the lawyer who had successfully defended him when he had been accused of obscenity made it unlikely to be sanctioned for prison use. Wilde laughed at this and they settled on a number of more suitable works, including St Augustine's *Confessions*, Cardinal Newman's *Apologia pro Vita Sua*, and Pascal's *Pensées*, all of which would have a significant bearing on Wilde's future writing. Haldane got these works for him, and, against the objections of the governor to some of them being 'of a controversial character' and so

---

[7] See Chapter 26.

not in accordance with the Local Prison Code, ensured that Wilde had use of them in Pentonville and could take them with him if he were moved.[8]

Ultimately misfortune did not prove a blessing for Wilde's career but it did do wonders for his posthumous reputation. The conjuror of 'wonder out of nothingness', the mesmerising raconteur, the master of witty repartee and paradox, would of punitive necessity plumb new depths, but from those depths and out of his genius produce works of a profundity that had erstwhile eluded him. He finally recognised that 'the supreme vice is shallowness'.[9] The seed had been sown. The harvest would come.

In July, at Haldane's instigation, Wilde was transferred to Wandsworth prison in south London. Opened in 1851, the impetus behind its construction was a severe outbreak of gaol fever in Brixton, attributed to gross overcrowding. Despite the new Surrey house of correction costing £140,000, externally it had little to recommend it to an aesthete, 'having none of the fine, gloomy character of Newgate, nor any of the castellated grandeur' of Holloway or Pentonville, or even 'the massive simplicity' of Tothill Fields, and its outbuildings exhibiting 'all the bad taste of Cockney-Italian villas'. The 'central mass rising behind the stunted gateway' was 'heavy even to clumsiness', and the whole structure was 'as uncommanding as a Methodist college'.[10] Internally, like the spokes of a wheel, its wings ran from a central hub, making observation easy. Larger than Pentonville, Wandsworth could house over a thousand prisoners in its cells. Unprepossessing as the prison was, it was hoped that detention there would be better for Wilde. In particular, the chaplain, William Morrison, an outspoken critic of the prison system and a proponent of useful employment for raising morale, would provide more congenial ministrations and a watchful eye.[11]

In his new home, however, Wilde's physical, psychological, and, it was suspected, moral condition, deteriorated. A shocked deputy-chaplain claimed to have smelt semen on him and believed he had degenerated into

---

8   Haldane, *op. cit.*, pp.166f. Harris, who believed that Wilde could 'write better things than he has ever done', would later urge him 'to give a record of this life ... and of all its influence on you'. He also encouraged him to 'write the names of the inhuman brutes [among the staff] ... in vitriol, as Dante did for all time'. Wilde declined to do the latter as he had 'neither Dante's strength, nor his bitterness' (*op. cit.*, II, p.340).

9   In *De Profundis* he repeats this refrain time and again.

10   M&B, p.489.

11   Morrison had been in post since 1880. Another bold clerical supporter was Stewart Headlam, a Christian socialist who had brooked condemnation by standing bail for Wilde and who thereafter visited him in prison and waited for him on release (Compton MacKenzie, *On Moral Courage* (London, 1962), pp.61–6).

masturbation.[12] Wilde obviously did not fear going blind but he did fear going mad. He contemplated suicide. What kept him from this was his feeling for his fellow sufferers and the small words of encouragement they sometimes whispered to him. Adversity and 'the community of suffering' made people kind. Many times he was terribly punished for trivial infractions, and he dreaded, and had experienced, what he thought was worse than the rack: solitary confinement in a dark cell which tortured the mind almost to madness. Morrison feared that Wilde, despite his fortitude and apparent resignation, would be fatally ground down long before his sentence expired by 'the great silent machine into whose clutches he had fallen'. Enjoined to be patient, Wilde had exclaimed to him that he could be patient as patience was a virtue but that it was not patience they wanted in prison, but apathy 'and apathy is a vice'.[13] Morrison reported his concerns that Wilde was on the verge of a breakdown and had reverted to 'perverse sexual practices' to Haldane who in turn passed on his comments to Evelyn Ruggles-Brise, whose recent appointment as chairman of the Prison Commission Haldane had helped engineer. Initially Ruggles-Brise was sceptical and defensive, regarding the report as a ploy on the part of 'a dangerous man', who was 'trying to make of Wilde a peg whereupon to hang his theories of the brutality of our prison system'.[14] He would soon change his tune.

Having completed three months of his sentence, Wilde was allowed a social visit, and the friend who came, Robert Sherard, was shocked by his haggard aspect, dishevelled hair and broken nails. Wilde had lost two stone, which, as the doctors observed, was 'not necessarily an unmixed evil'. Finally, after he collapsed in the chapel, he was placed in the infirmary, and, on Home Office orders, seen by two doctors from Broadmoor Criminal Lunatic Asylum. They recommended that he be moved to a more suitable establishment outside London, where he would be away from the influence of those agitating for his release and would have access to invigorating open-air activities such as gardening, even if they were uncongenial to 'a man of indolent and lethargic temperament'. He should also be allowed some association, but given his 'proclivities' and 'avowed love of the society of males' that should always be under strict supervision. Haldane and his new ally, the by then more sympathetic Ruggles-Brise, agreed that Wilde should be moved, the latter authorising his transfer to Reading prison. His trip there on 20 November would be by train, but the journey merely added

---

[12] Richard Ellman, *Oscar Wilde* (London, 1987), p.464.

[13] *Fortnightly Review*, 69 (May 1898), p.781.

[14] Quoted in Radzinowicz, p.589.

to his humiliation. Attired in prison garb, he had to endure a wait at Clapham Junction railway station exposed to the ridicule of all who saw him. One bystander spat in his face.[15]

But why Reading? Ostensibly it was where 'suitable occupation in the way of gardening, and book-binding and library work' would be available to him.[16] Perhaps more pertinently Haldane had a friend on the Visiting Committee there who would look out for Wilde's interests. This was George Palmer whose father had co-founded Huntley and Palmers, the Reading biscuit manufacturers. Palmer *fils* was a man of substance in his own right. He had been mayor of Reading and was the member of parliament. His family had known Oscar Wilde of old and had entertained him at their house.[17] That was in the days of his celebrity. In the days of his notoriety Palmer might be just the man to alleviate the restraints under which his erstwhile guest now had to live.

Reading gaol reminded Wilde of Pentonville, as indeed it should. Completed in 1844, it was reckoned the finest building in Berkshire after Windsor castle; indeed with its turrets and crenellations and fortified gateway it looked like a medieval keep. Its architecture, wrote its chaplain, symbolised its twin aims for 'with the castellated it combines the collegiate appearance', while *The Illustrated London News* thought it 'the most conspicuous building, and architecturally, by far the greatest ornament to the town'.[18] It would remain unchanged until 1969 when the corner turrets and castellated gatehouse were demolished. The prison, with its ornamentation hacked off, was finally closed in 2013.

It was the last and by far and away the most impressive in a line of penal establishments serving Berkshire. The sixteenth-century county gaol in Castle Street was little more than an overcrowded holding-pen with no attempt to segregate the sexes, or the unconvicted or juveniles. To supplement it, in 1785, the county built a house of correction in an area known as Forbury where the old abbey lay in ruins. Shortly afterwards, a larger county gaol was required, but the Castle Street site was deemed

---

15 Hyde, *op. cit.*, pp.35–40; Ellman, *op. cit.*, p.465; Anthony Stokes, *Pit of Shame* (Winchester, 2007), p.82. Wilde in *De Profundis* erroneously gives the date as 13 November.

16 Minute of Ruggles-Brise, 19 November 1895, HO Papers.

17 Stokes, *op. cit.*, pp.81f., 92.

18 Peter Southerton, *The Story of a Prison* (Reading, 1975), p.43; John Field, *Prison Discipline: The Advantages of the Separate System*, 2nd edn, 2 vols (London, 1848), I, p.73; William Hepworth Dixon, *The London Prisons* (London, 1850), pp.392f., 412. Dixon, whom the Berkshire magistrates had welcomed in to see their creation, castigated the exorbitant cost of this 'palace-prison' and deplored the fact that it was seen as a model for nearly all the new prisons which were being 'erected with a similar recklessness of cost'.

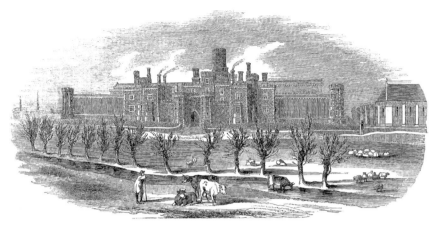

25. Reading gaol as Oscar Wilde knew it

unsuitable for expansion. Consequently it was decided to enlarge and adapt, 'on Mr Howard's plan', the recently built house of correction. The gaol opened for business in September 1793. It was subject to the silent system and later boasted one extraordinary feature: a tread-mill that actually ground grain to supply the prison with bread and for sale on the open market. It had been installed in 1822 at the cost of £1,700 and was powered for ten hours a day by thirty-two prisoners, each of whom would climb the equivalent of 12,000 feet in enforced silence.[19] But the gaol was poorly built and soon became overcrowded. By 1825 the keeper had to accommodate three inmates in cells designed for one, defeating the purpose for which the prison had been constructed. In 1840, the chaplain, John Field, in his first annual report criticised the conditions that he believed prevented any hope of improvement in the morals of the inmates. He advocated, along the lines of the experiment then being conducted at Abingdon bridewell, the solitary confinement of each inmate, combined with labour and instruction. His words hit home and soon moves were afoot to provide something more substantial, as well as being better suited to the separate system. The proposed prison should be modelled on Pentonville, although on a smaller scale. No less an architect than George Gilbert Scott, who had designed the St Pancras Hotel and the Albert Memorial, was engaged, and his plans were approved by Jebb.

Between 1842 and 1844 the not-so-old prison was demolished and the new built in its place. As befitted the partnership recently established between Church and State in the running of penal establishments, and in

---

[19] Southerton, *op. cit.*, pp.11–26.

accord with Jebb's prescription, the governor – as the keeper had been designated since 1840 – and chaplain each occupied large matching houses on either side of the gate.[20] The cost was considerable, the original estimate of £24,000 being half the final bill. The expense was deemed justified, however, as the borough now had a prison worthy of its status and the regime seemed to be working: the number of committals for serious crime dropped, as did the prison population. With an air of self-satisfaction the chaplain observed that 'the separation of the criminals is irksome to many (or to use their own expressive term "very wicked")'. It was obviously doing them good.[21] The justices congratulated themselves on their foresight in introducing the separate system. Their success meant, however, that the prison was underutilised until, in 1847, the government rented forty cells as an overspill for Millbank.

There were concerns that life in Reading gaol was too luxurious as there was lack of hard labour, prisoners being 'employed in nothing but education', though if they tired of their studies they enjoyed the privilege of 'picking a little oakum'. In the House of Lords, Henry Brougham, a former lord chancellor, denounced those responsible for this deficiency:

> The magistrates appeared to glory in their shame. They took credit for their benevolent interventions [and] splendid treatment of criminals, totally forgetting that this was a place of punishment ... [Prisoners are] allowed ten hours sleep ... the gaol might rather be called Reading university, for the only labour expected from prisoners was learning to read.[22]

The report of the inspectorate in 1850 echoed this criticism of 'the burlesque absurdity' of 'Read-read-reading gaol', noting that 'the provisions of the law which require that labour or employment shall be provided for prisoners in separate confinement, have not been complied with'.[23]

Measures were reluctantly taken to remedy this defect and the regime became more punitive, especially after the Prison Act of 1865 came into force with its mantra of 'hard labour, hard fare and hard bed'. With nationalisation, uniform Spartan standards were imposed and, under Du Cane's stewardship, enforced. Amongst other measures designed to remove

---

[20] Joshua Jebb, *Modern Prisons: Their Construction and Ventilation* (London, 1844), p.5.

[21] Southerton, *op. cit.*, p.41.

[22] *PD*, Third Series, vol.106, cols 1368–75.

[23] Dixon, *op. cit.*, pp.400–5. Du Cane related that a felon was said to have been so disheartened that he 'had only got as far as Ephesians' when his sentence ended that he came back (for sheep-stealing) to complete his biblical studies (*The Punishment and Prevention of Crime* (London, 1885), p.57).

'luxury' in Reading, the hammocks that prisoners slept in were replaced by wooden planks for beds. Prisoners would lie down but have little rest. Insomnia by night and diarrhoea by day was to be their lot. And every day would be the same.

The 'reformed' gaol Wilde encountered was cruciform in shape, the four wings radiating from a domed central hall beneath the tower, the hub where staff would assemble for inspection and to receive orders. The north – or D – wing had rooms for the administration of the prison, for the reception of new prisoners, and for visits by family members, lawyers and visiting justices, as well as, for a time, housing debtors in 'sleeping rooms'.[24] The governor had an office there and from it he could command every cell. Above it was the chapel which had been bedecked with individual 'box pews' although these had been removed in 1894 and replaced with bench seating.[25] For male criminals there were three accommodation wings of three storeys surmounted by a vaulted roof. The cells on the ground floor opened onto a central corridor some fifteen feet in width, those on the first and second floors opened onto railed galleries. Stretched across the lower gallery was a net to catch anyone who fell or jumped off, or was pushed over, the railings. Women were housed on the separate E wing and only entered the main prison to attend chapel.

Prisoners were deprived of their personal belongings and almost of their personality. Individuality was replaced by automatism. To preserve anonymity and prevent prison acquaintances meeting up on release, they were known not by their name but by their cell location. Oscar Wilde was prisoner C.3.3 as he was housed in cell number 3 on the third gallery of C wing, the west wing of the prison. His cell was thirteen feet long, seven feet wide and ten feet high. The wall was whitewashed brick, the floor was of red and black tiles, and the sturdy wooden door, studded with iron and with a shuttered peephole, had a lock accessible only from the landing. Food and working materials were pushed through a lockable flap. Daylight could seep in through two high-set windows and gaslight from a nine-inch-square glazed aperture in the corridor wall.[26] There was a wash hand basin, a water closet, a hard plank bed, a stool, a table and a set of shelves. Regular chapel services, daily exercise and infrequent visits alone relieved the monotonous isolation. Wilde could neither lock his own door nor even ensure his privacy from prying eyes. He was an object of surveillance, subject to external control, living

[24] Visiting justices were first authorised by an Act of 1785.
[25] Stokes, *op. cit.*, p.37.
[26] Southerton, *op. cit.*, pp.45f.

in a self-contained twilight world. Locked in his single cell – or 'separate Hell' as he called it – Oscar Wilde was in a prison within a prison. His body was confined within bleak walls and his nails were blunt and bloody from 'tear[ing] tarry rope to shreds', which is what oakum-picking amounted to. He was being ground down. But his imagination could still soar, and his genius could not be held captive. There were no 'mind-forged manacles' for Oscar Wilde. He could, like Bunyan, reach for the stars.

He would not allow 'remorse and hatred to corrupt his very heart' but would 'conquer the prison and possess and use it', as his friends hoped.[27] Out of his debilitating experience, Wilde was to produce his most moving and perhaps most influential works: 'The Ballad of Reading Gaol' and his letters to the *Daily Chronicle* on Warder Martin and Prison Reform, all written and published after his release, and *De Profundis*, written in prison but not published until after his death. His letters to friends and publishers also add to the picture that he gives of *fin-de-siècle* prison life.

Senior staff do not come out well. The governor of Reading prison when Wilde arrived there was Lieutenant-Colonel Isaacson, a harsh disciplinarian with a vindictive streak. His avowed aim was to 'knock the nonsense out of Oscar Wilde' and his delight was to deprive him of his most precious possessions: books. Wilde, sharing the casual anti-Semitism of his time, thought him 'harsh and stupid', 'lacking in imagination', and wrote him off as 'a mulberry-faced Dictator, a great red-faced bloated Jew, who always looked as though he drank ... Brandy was the flaming message of his pulpy face.' The prison doctor also came in for censure, while the chaplain was written off as 'a good-natured fool, one of the silliest of God's sheep, a typical clergyman in fact'.[28]

Lowly prison warders were a different matter, and Wilde got on with several of them. He even helped them win a silver tea service and grand piano in newspaper competitions. He admitted that he libelled them in 'The Ballad', 'but to poetry all must be sacrificed, even warders'.[29] They were only doing their job as best they could, and it was no fault of theirs that their better qualities were suppressed. Some, at risk of severe punishment, defied the regime under which they worked, and brought him 'curious things to eat, Scotch scones, meat pies and sausage rolls, believing that a hungry man can eat anything, just as the British throw Bibles to bears'.[30] One stood out. Tom

---

[27] Harris, *op. cit.*, II, p.321.

[28] *Letters*, p.983; Ellman, *op. cit.*, p.475.

[29] *Letters*, p.987.

[30] Charles Ricketts, *Recollections of Oscar Wilde* (London, 1932), pp.44–9.

Martin, for giving vent to his innate humanity, paid the price for a minor defiance of this unrelenting and dehumanising regime. He gave 'some sweet biscuits to a little hungry child' who had been unable to eat the badly-baked prison bread served for breakfast. He and his two impecunious friends, fined for snaring rabbits, had been committed to prison.[31] The grateful boy told one of the senior warders of the officer's kindness. For this infraction Martin was dismissed the service.[32] Wilde had known Martin as a compassionate warder on C wing who had treated him well and provided him with illicit items such as the *Daily Chronicle*, beef tea, and Huntley and Palmer ginger biscuits. Martin had even made him laugh! In prison!

His letter, under the caption 'The Case of Warder Martin: Some Cruelties of Prison Life', was published on 28 May 1897, less than a fortnight after his release when he first read of the dismissal.[33] In it he defended this act of kindness and condemned sending children under fourteen to prison in the first place. It was an absurdity with tragic results, and their cruel treatment was 'an outrage on humanity and common sense'. To lock them up for twenty-three hours each day was 'an example of the cruelty of stupidity'. It was the cruelty of the system as a whole that was intractable, not the cruelties that the individuals who served it perpetrated. He suggested many practical reforms that parliament could settle in half an hour. Wilde went on to condemn the treatment of the mentally ill in prison, and gave the instance of prisoner A.2.11, a plainly insane former soldier who had been flogged as a result of a report from the doctor that he was shamming mental infirmity and that earlier and lighter punishments had failed to stop his strange behaviour.

As a result of this letter the Irish republican MP, Michael Davitt, who had himself been in prison, asked two questions in parliament about Martin's dismissal and an inquiry was carried out by the commissioners, but Martin was not reinstated. The report concluded that 'to permit warders – even from humane motives – to distinguish one prisoner from another by kindly acts would obviously lead to very serious scandals, and Martin had previously

---

[31] Wilde would pay their fines and so secure their release (*Letters*, p.831).

[32] Disciplinary charges known as 'half-sheets' were given for the most trivial offences such as yawning while supervising prisoners during a chapel service (L.W. Merrow-Smith, *Prison Screw* (London, 1962), p.35). Gerold Clayton, whose father Edward was governor of Lewes prison, recounts that as a six-year-old boy he was 'charged with trafficking' when he gave a piece of bread to a hungry prisoner. His father put him across his knee and gave him six of the best with a ruler (p.13). This did not discourage the youngster from becoming a prison governor himself.

[33] *Letters*, pp.847–55.

been suspected of trafficking with prisoners'.[34] The biscuit to the boy was the final crumb.

Wilde's second letter, on 'Prison Reform', was published on 24 March 1898 at the time when parliament was considering a Prison Reform Bill based on the recommendations of the Gladstone Committee. He put forward additional 'simple, practical and humane proposals', such as the provision of better food, the improvement of ventilation and sanitation, in particular access to lavatories, and the 'adequate supply of good books'. To make these reforms effectual it was necessary to change the attitude of the staff. He concluded that 'the first and perhaps the most difficult task is to humanise the governors of prisons, to civilise the warders and Christianise the chaplains'.[35] This was a rather different emphasis from the stance he took in his earlier letter to the press when it was the whole ethos of imprisonment that needed to be changed first. Staff adapt to the culture. If the culture were kind so too would many of the staff be.

Wilde had encountered one humane governor (though not it seems a Christian chaplain) in Reading. After he had been there for a year, possibly with the connivance of Palmer, and certainly with the intervention of Ruggles-Brise, Isaacson was transferred to Lewes prison and replaced by Major James Nelson.[36] Younger and more enlightened, he was 'the most Christlike man' Wilde had ever met. Though he could not 'alter the rules of the prison system, he has altered the spirit in which they used to be carried out by his predecessor [and] ... quite altered the whole tone of prison life'. Nelson may not have altered the rules generally but he bent them where Wilde was concerned, or, like his namesake, turned a blind eye to their circumvention. Without compromising security the new governor did not stifle creativity. Encouraged by an 'instruction' sent to him by Ruggles-Brise, he proved more than content for Wilde to have ready access to books and even recommended one he had recently read. Wilde was excused oakum-

---

34   Stokes, *op. cit.*, pp.89f. Martin rejoined the army, fought in the Boer War, and ended up as a nurse. He died in 1940, aged seventy-three.

35   *Letters*, pp.1045–9.

36   Stokes, *op. cit.*, p.92; Shane Leslie, *Sir Evelyn Ruggles-Brise* (London, 1938), pp.129ff.; Harris, *op. cit.*, II, pp.327ff. Ruggles-Brise had shown considerable concern for Wilde's welfare and thought an 'exceptional man ought to have exceptional treatment'. Approached by Wilde's friend, Frank Harris, Ruggles-Brise secured the agreement of the recently appointed Conservative Home Secretary, Matthew Ridley, for Harris to report on Wilde's condition and to make recommendations to ameliorate it. Shortly after doing so Harris heard that the governor had been replaced and that books and writing materials had been approved. Ridley thought that it would be 'a great loss to English literature if [Wilde] were really injured by the prison discipline'.

picking and put on library duty. Punishment ceased. Best of all he was given paper, pen and ink and allowed to write. Nelson also sought and got approval for the issuance of a notebook, as he had an inkling that Wilde might compose something comparable to *Pilgrim's Progress*.[37] *De Profundis* was the result of, and reward for, this change in regime. The commissioners would not allow the manuscript to leave the prison during Wilde's sentence but with some prescience did instruct that it be given to him on his discharge. It was as though they had stage-managed the whole relaxation of the rules when it came to Oscar Wilde. Perhaps they had.[38]

To this major work, composed between January and March 1897, largely by gaslight and in his cell, he gave the putative title *Epistola: in Carcere et Vinculis* – 'a letter: in prison and in chains'.[39] On advice he changed the title to the first words of the Latin version of Psalm 130 – *De Profundis* – and it was under this title that it was first published, in expurgated form, in 1905.[40] It is too marred to be a masterpiece, but it is more than just a love-hate-letter to his feckless paramour, Alfred Douglas. It is that, of course, and demonstrates, during the latter half of his sentence, the catastrophic reversal of his feelings for the erstwhile love of his life, 'deep bitterness' displacing infatuation. 'Eighteen terrible months in a prison cell' had done their work and at last he saw 'things and people as they really are'.[41] But it also has a wider audience in mind and a larger time-frame. It is an act of therapy, an elegy for lost greatness, and a many-faceted dramatic monologue. It achieves a cathartic reconciliation with himself and his fate and even, after some very bitter recrimination, with Bosie. It is both an egotistical apologia and an abject apology. Above all it is an odyssey into an understanding of what he had lost and what he had gained.[42] It grows into a meditation on the meaning of life and of suffering, with hints of Newman and some of the soul-searching of Augustine, both of whom he read in prison. In it,

---

[37] Ellman, *op. cit.*, p.479.

[38] Stokes puts forward a convincing argument that influential admirers were at work (*op. cit.*, pp.90ff.). He was not 'forgot' and left to 'rot and rot'.

[39] *Letters*, pp.683–780.

[40] The writer E.V. Lucas claims to have made the suggestion. The whole line is *De profundis ad te clamavi* – 'Out of the depths have I called unto thee'.

[41] See his November 1896 letter to Robert Ross (*Letters*, pp.669f.) foreshadowing the sentiments expressed in *De Profundis*, and compare Wilde's earlier prison letters to Bosie (pp.646f., 650ff.). It was while Wilde was in Wandsworth and his lover was on Capri that the relationship began to unravel and he began referring to Bosie as 'Douglas' (Ellman, *op. cit.*, pp.460, 469). On Wilde's release the affair was rekindled and proved just as destructive.

[42] *Letters*, pp.678, 782.

through it, Wilde's physical hardships and mental turmoil were transformed
into something spiritual, suffused with religious reflection, though blighted
by self-pity. It is a leap from the depths of the dungeon into 'that little tent
of blue which prisoners call the sky'.

> The plank bed, the loathsome food, the hard ropes shredded into
> oakum until one's fingertips grow dull with pain, the menial offices
> with which each day begins and finishes, the harsh orders that routine
> seems to necessitate, the dreadful dress that makes sorrow grotesque
> to look at, the silence, the solitude, the shame – each and all of these
> things I had to transform into a spiritual experience.

Some task. Suffering in prison was unremitting, one long moment when
time itself did not progress but revolved. Wilde experienced 'the paralysing
immobility of a life every circumstance of which is regulated after an
unchangeable pattern ... according to the inflexible laws of an iron formula':

> For us there is only one season, the season of Sorrow. The very sun
> and moon seem taken from us ... It is always twilight in one's cell, as it
> is always midnight in one's heart.

As he wrote to a friend: 'The horror of prison-life is the contrast between
the grotesqueness of one's aspect and the tragedy in one's soul.'[43]

Wilde's most quoted contribution to prison literature, 'The Ballad of
Reading Gaol', was written during his self-imposed exile in France. He had
told Bosie that if, after his release, he could 'produce even one more beautiful
work of art' he would be 'able to rob malice of its venom, and cowardice
of its sneer'.[44] That work of art was published in February 1898, under the
pseudonym of C3.3. It met with his own approbation and great acclaim.
It was in Wilde's opinion and the world's both a great poem and telling
propaganda. It is 'the best ballad in English ... and the noblest utterance
that has yet reached us from a modern prison'.[45] The inspiration behind it
was the fate that befell 'CTW' – Charles Thomas Wooldridge – a trooper of
Horse Guards, for the murder of his wife. He was hanged in Reading gaol
on Tuesday 7 July 1896. Not only is the poem an indictment of inexorable
and implacable justice, and a poignant elegy on one man's fate and the
endless cycle of human misery, but it has provided one of the most telling
phrases we still use about imprisonment – 'bricks of shame' – and one of
the most telling verses about its effect:

---

[43] Ellman, *op. cit.*, p.465.
[44] *Letters*, p.734.
[45] Harris, *op. cit.*, II, p.546.

> The vilest deeds like poison weeds
> > Bloom well in prison-air:
> It is only what is good in Man
> > That wastes and withers there:
> Pale Anguish keeps the heavy gate,
> > And the Warder is Despair.

Wilde found 'describing a prison ... as difficult artistically as describing a water-closet'. 'The horror of prison', he told a friend, 'is that everything is so simple and commonplace in itself, and so degrading, and hideous, and revolting in its effect.'[46] The stark reality, the grinding of humanity, he captures perfectly. It is why the poem still resonates today.

An anonymous donor – probably Wilde himself – sent Haldane a copy of 'The Ballad' which Haldane considered to be 'a redemption of his promise to me'. It was a redemption and a fulfilment. It was his last published work. He had contemplated more but none came, not even on imprisonment. The letters and the poem (which had been quoted in the House of Commons) had proved so powerful an indictment of current penal regimes that prison reformers urged their author to write a lengthier piece on the subject of the prison system. Even his estranged wife thought he should. Wilde himself had declared that he was determined to do all he could to try to alter it, and longed to live so he could explore the whole new world in which he had been living, the world of sorrow and 'all that it teaches'. However, despite buying a copy of John Howard's treatise, he never did. As he said, 'something is killed in me'. That something was his Muse. He had mined what he could from his experience, but the seam was exhausted, as was he. He had 'lost the mainspring of life and art'. 'I am going under: the morgue yawns for me', he told a friend after the publication of 'The Ballad'.[47] He did, however, write to Major Nelson in gratitude, and offer practical assistance to some of his fellow inmates, sending several of them money from his depleted resources, and trying to get them employment.[48]

---

[46] *Letters*, p.957.

[47] *Letters*, pp.736, 754, 1025. There is another explanation for the drying up of his talent. After he regained his freedom, he could not live up to his high-blown ascetic idealism and would suffer 'a second fall' which curtailed any further literary endeavours. He had gorged on his prison experiences and was then left without appetite. He was a Pagan who for a few months became a Christian and then reverted to type, was how Harris summarised it. One warder recollected that in prison Wilde had genuinely tried to lead a new life, 'and if he did not continue that life after he left prison, then the forces of evil must have been too strong for him' (Harris, *op. cit.*, II, pp.364–8, 399). The same can be said today of many a drug-addict who is 'cured' inside and relapses soon after release.

[48] *Letters*, pp.862f., 887f., 897, 903.

Wilde repeatedly assured his friends that he had not come out of prison 'an embittered or disappointed man'. He would have been both had he been released after eighteen months, as the composition of *De Profundis* clearly demonstrated, but the final six months he spent in Reading were so suffused with kindness and humanity as to vitiate the earlier horrors. A little good outweighed a lot of evil. On the contrary his 'life of studied materialism', his 'philosophy of appetite and cynicism' and 'a cult of sensual and senseless ease' were bad for him as an artist. They had narrowed his imagination and dulled the more delicate sensibilities. In prison his life had been enlarged, his sympathies sharpened, and perhaps he would 'be a better fellow after it all'. He had learnt gratitude, and, above all, the meaning of pity. For him, as for Wilfred Owen, the poetry would be in the pity. He had entered prison with a 'heart of stone ... but now my heart is utterly broken – pity has entered into my heart ... what a wonderful thing pity is, and I never knew it'. At least for a while he had 'gained much'.[49]

In his prison books so have we, and in his legacy so had the cause of penal reform. His mantra that 'it is not the prisoners who need reformation ... [but] the prisons' had resonance. He had reaped but he had also sowed. Major changes were afoot, but just a little too late for Wilde. Hard labour was abolished in 1898, a year after his release. A damaged man, a truly tragic figure, Wilde died in French exile on 30 November 1900. His faithful friend, Robbie Ross, had the words of Wooldridge's epitaph inscribed on his grave in Père Lachaise Cemetery, Paris:

> And alien tears will fill for him
>   Pity's long-broken urn.
> For his mourners will be outcast men
>   And outcasts always mourn.

Outcasts could also be women.

---

[49] *Letters*, pp.846, 870, 879f., 891, 894, 911.

CHAPTER 25

Kittle Cattle

I was brought into contact for the first time with those 'kittle cattle', the female prisoners ... Women are more troublesome [than men] ... Their artifice goes deeper; defiance is not less marked, and more prolonged; their misconduct is more contagious, a spark will set it alight; once started it is difficult to extinguish.

Arthur Griffiths

The general impression ... is that these women are so incredibly bad that any attempt to reform them must be hopeless ... It does not appear to me that the women depicted are different in their natures from women who may be met with at large in the world.

Mary Carpenter

As a result of the exertions of Mrs Fry and others, the lot of women in prison had materially improved. They were kept apart from men and they had female warders to guard them. And yet they were to suffer much the same prison regime as the men: solitude, silence and hard labour, although not of the first class, being spared the impropriety of the tread-wheel and the arduousness of stone-breaking and the crank.

In many respects they were considered worse than male prisoners. Their criminality was unnatural, their coarseness unfeminine, their behaviour capricious or hysterical and informed by low cunning, and all the while they were aware of how relatively untouchable they were. In 1862 an anonymous work purporting to be by a prison matron, *Female life in Prison*, was published, followed two years later by the even more lurid *Memoirs of Jane Carpenter, a Female Convict*, emanating from the same hand. That hand, however, did not belong to a prison matron but to the pulp novelist Frederick William Robinson. His sketches and stories, based upon actual records, were so realistic as to be mistaken for first-hand accounts, although some suspected that they came from the hand or artistry of Mary Carpenter who had written extensively on penal matters and who shared a surname with the memoirist. They spoke of 'women harder to tame than creatures of the jungle ... whom physical restraint transforms into a wild beast rather than a human being', but also of the degrading treatment to which they were subjected. The tales were well-told, sensational and titillating. They appealed both to moral superiority and prurient curiosity. Upright Victorians, eager to be improved and excited, bought copies in large numbers, and were captivated. While Mary Carpenter believed that women convicts were made worse by their treatment, the majority of her contemporaries thought them to be feral creatures that should be caged not tamed. Prison officials tended to side with the majority view of these 'kittle cattle'.[1]

There were, however, some genuine accounts by women who had been imprisoned. Two of the best known came from inmates who were hardly typical of the prison population. They could both read and write. Both were well-off, and one was a Lady. Perceptions would be changed when the better off found themselves behind bars and wrote about their experiences.

In May 1889 Mrs Florence Maybrick, a young American living in Liverpool, was charged with the murder of her husband. She was said to have poisoned him, but as he himself was a regular imbiber of arsenic his death may have been an accident. She was remanded to the city's Walton gaol. As a prisoner awaiting trial and having the means to pay five shillings a week, she was housed in a cell with a bed, table, armchair and wash-stand, and was able to have food sent in from a nearby hotel. Just as well she had the means to pay for these little luxuries, as she was locked in her cell day and night and could leave it only for chapel in the morning and for an hour's exercise in the afternoon. Her daily visitors were the doctor and the chaplain but their visits were formal and of short duration. Otherwise she was left on her own and to her own thoughts.

She did not have long to wait as the trial took place in July. The press took against her. So too did the jury who convicted her after thirty-eight minutes of deliberation. The judge, James Fitz-James Stephen, who was going senile and had summed up for a guilty verdict, sentenced her to death, as the law required. Maybrick was returned to prison to await her fate. She stayed in the condemned cell for three weeks, guarded by two female warders. They watched but rarely spoke.[2] There she waited and prayed, hope seeping away. Almost at the last moment she was reprieved, and her sentence was commuted to penal servitude for life.

She was immediately moved from Walton to Woking women's convict prison at Knaphill in Surrey. It had come into operation in 1869 alongside the first convict prison for mental and physical invalids, designed by Jebb,

1   The unpredictable, capricious and difficult to manage.
2   Florence Maybrick, *Mrs Maybrick's Own Story* (New York, 1905), p.58.

which had opened a decade before. She was taken there by train, she and her escort enduring the journey in a third-class compartment.

Worse was to follow. She was dressed in a convict's uniform and her hair was cut off to the nape of her neck. As she observed, 'this act seemed, above all others, to bring me a sense of my degradation, my utter helplessness; and the iron of the awful tragedy, of which I was the innocent victim, entered my soul'.[3] She would need iron to keep going amongst the human automata she found there, prisoners broken by their suffering, from whom 'all will, all initiative, all individuality' had been sucked. She would spend nearly fifteen years in prison.

The first nine months were served in 'voiceless solitude and hopeless monotony'. Twenty minutes of chapel and an hour of exercise in the yard were her only daily respite as even the prescribed work had to be done alone in her cell. The second stage of her imprisonment was nine months' probation, when her accommodation improved as did her social interactions, but silence was still imposed. Once a prisoner had crossed the threshold of a convict prison she was dead to the world and was expected to lose or forget 'every vestige of her personality'. An incautious word or even the turn of a head or a movement of the lips was a gift to a tyrannous warder. Offenders, or even supposed offenders, could be placed in solitary confinement, put on three days' bread and water or – worst of all – suffer the loss of a week's remission. The penal code, she concluded, was doing its utmost 'with tireless, ceaseless revolutions to mould body and soul slowly, remorselessly, into the shape demanded by Act of Parliament'. This was the silent system in operation, destructive of human personality, productive of 'trouble and disaster ... the cause of two thirds of all the misconduct and disturbance that occurs in prison'. It manufactured 'criminals and imbeciles'.[4] Some of its products resided in the Woking invalid prison next door.

Nonetheless, life could have been even worse. As an educated woman of respectable background who had committed but one crime and had nothing in common with the habitual prisoner, Mrs Maybrick was put in the 'star-class', a designation created in 1879 for first offenders in convict prisons, members of which were supposed to be kept apart from the generality of the prison population.[5] Probation completed, Maybrick entered upon the third stage, hard labour. It was hard but not back-breaking and it had utility. Many of the women were employed in the kitchens or laundry, or in needlework

---

3   *Ibid.*, p.64.
4   *Ibid.*, pp.75, 78f., 90ff.
5   This was recommended in the Kimberley Commission report, para.171.

and knitting, while others could earn 1s 2d a day breaking up refuse marble for mosaic floors. After completing the third year of her sentence she was rewarded by being allowed to have a small mirror in her cell. For the first time in three years she would see her own face, and the ravages that prison life had made upon it. In the winter months in an unheated cell she suffered from the cold; in rainy weather after exercise she was soaked through and without change of clothing. She suffered from catarrh, influenza, bronchitis and rheumatism. She arrived at Woking ill, and left it worse.

In November 1895 Woking prison, which was being turned into Inkerman barracks, decanted its prisoners to Aylesbury, England's only remaining national prison for women convicts. Maybrick was taken from the hospital wing, and sent thither by rail. She and the other women were all chained and their prison garb was marked with the 'broad arrow'. They were exposed to the public as 'objects of morbid curiosity'.

Aylesbury had been built as the county gaol in 1847 and converted to its new use in 1890. Its regime was much more enlightened. Prisoners with complaints could see the governor and those with an unresolved grievance would shortly be able to take the issue to the Board of Visitors, outsiders appointed under the 1898 Prison Act to reassure the public that prisons were run humanely and to ensure that the prisoners were treated so. They did much to ameliorate conditions. The women were each given a mat and a stool for their cells. They could sleep in night-dresses and not day clothes. They could keep family photographs in their cells. They could even have toothbrushes. The diet was improved, if the substitution of tea for cocoa and white bread for wholemeal are improvements. The period of solitary confinement was reduced from nine months to four, and probationers could work in association. And work – generally in the tailor's shop – was useful and sometimes even creative.

Such a regime could, and did, come under criticism from those vigilantes who always fret that prison conditions are too good. Maybrick recollected that once, when visitors arrived in the kitchen just as dinner for the hospital patients was being dished up, one of them was 'quite scandalised at the sight of a juicy mutton-chop and tempting milk pudding'. Even after it was explained to him by the governor that this was not usual prison fare but a special diet for a very sick woman, 'he was not satisfied and stalked out, audibly grumbling about people living on the fat of the land and getting a better dinner than he did'. Maybrick thought that he left the prison 'under the impression that its inmates lived like pampered gourmets'.[6] It is an impression that lingers to this day.

She testified to the importance of religion in prisons. She had sought and found solace in the chapel at Woking. She was not alone, nor was solace the only thing sought. Repentance was important to some and resolution to lead new lives to many. When she first arrived in Aylesbury there was no chapel and services had to be held on one of the wings. Matters were rectified by 'the great and the good'. An offer by one of the Board of Visitors, the duchess of Bedford, to construct a chapel was 'graciously' accepted by the Home Secretary. The day of its dedication by the bishop of Reading was a memorable one, and the new chapel was festooned with flowers provided by Lady Rothschild.

Florence Maybrick thrived in this more benign climate. Her conduct was exemplary and she kept her cell in such spotless condition that the matron showed it to trainee warders as a model to be emulated. She was to spend over eight years in Aylesbury prison, being freed in 1904, after she had been visited and interrogated by the Home Secretary and Ruggles-Brise. They approved her discharge.

She returned home to America, having spent fifteen years of her young life in confinement. Prison had left its mark, and, haunted by it as she was, she determined to write about her experience to educate others and to advance the cause of prison reform. In 1905 she published *Mrs Maybrick's Own Story*. She devoted half the book to describing her prison life, and the other half to proving her wrongful conviction, and urging many practical penal and legal reforms, from the provision of newspapers and the appointment of women doctors to the creation of a court of criminal appeal. Most of all she lamented that good governors and decent warders were tightly constrained by rigid regulations which prevented their humanity and creativity from being expressed. Any familiarity on their part with prisoners was strictly forbidden and the slightest manifestation of the sort would entail a fine or even dismissal. The influence for good which a kind, well-disposed warder would exert on a prisoner was denied expression by the spirit of mistrust and suspicion which pervaded the entire prison administration. This she considered to be one of the most regrettable features of the system. She had a high regard for most of the staff, who were doing a thankless task in difficult surroundings, under a regime which sapped their personality as well as that of their charges. Staff and inmates alike were so many cogs in a machine. Her critique mirrored that of Wilde.

---

[6] *Ibid.*, p.101.

Publication saw her lionised and invitations to visit American prisons and to give lectures poured in. She eagerly took them up as a vehicle for change. Through her efforts she exposed the 'disciplinary atrocities' perpetuated in Oklahoma, as a result of which they ceased. She had put her unfortunate experience to good use. Her suffering had to mean something. Here was another instance of prison reform being advocated by one who knew by bitter personal experience what prison was really like. Yet she was never pardoned, never exonerated, never proved to have been the victim of a miscarriage of justice. She died in obscurity in 1941.

Lady Constance Lytton was anything but obscure but she too ended up in prison and was to write about it. She was the granddaughter of Edward Bulwer-Lytton, the author of *The Last Days of Pompeii* and great friend of Disraeli. Her father had been viceroy of India and first earl of Lytton. Her sister Betty had married Gerald Balfour, brother of the future Prime Minister, and her own brother Victor inherited the earldom and was friends with Winston Churchill. Lady Constance was top-drawer. She was also a suffragette, becoming one in 1908 at the age of thirty-nine. It meant 'rejecting her upbringing, abandoning her class and defying her mother'.[7] She never regretted it.

Inevitably her actions led to prison, as she knew they would. For Constance prison usually meant Holloway. Built as a house of correction, its foundation stone had been laid in 1849 and was engraved with the words 'May God preserve the City of London and make this place a terror to evil-doers'.[8] It was a substitute for Giltspur Street compter which although within the City itself was too small and too confined to serve a new purpose and which was closed down completely in 1855. Holloway in nearby Middlesex was the ideal location, where the land was already owned by the City. A large modern prison could be constructed there with far higher specifications and at far less expense, although the authorities did not shirk on the cost which amounted to almost £100,000. Their new prison took three years to build and had 436 cells on five wings. Three wings were for men and one each for women and juveniles. The exterior replicated a medieval fortress, its gatehouse being modelled on Caesar's Tower at Warwick castle. Fantastical gryphons straddled its inner portal. Disraeli in a facetious note to Queen Victoria recounted that when out for a drive one day he 'came upon a real feudal castle, with a donjon keep high in the air. It turned out to be the new

---

7   Lyndsey Jenkins, *Lady Constance Lytton* (London, 2015), p.xxi.
8   M&B, p.535.

26. The City prison, Holloway, 1852

City prison in Camden Road, but it deserves a visit; I mean externally.'[9] Unsurprisingly the gaol was known locally as Camden castle. In 1902 a new extension was built along with an execution shed and the prison became one solely for women. It would become home for many a suffragette.

Constance was one. In February 1909, for marching on parliament, she was sentenced to one month's imprisonment. But she was no ordinary prisoner and received treatment very different from that of others. Because of a heart condition and probably because of her status she was placed in the prison hospital where the conditions were much better than on the wings. The food in particular was reasonably plentiful, of good quality and well-cooked. As a result of her brother Victor's intervention with Ruggles-Brise she was supplied with that ultimate luxury, bed-socks.[10]

Hospital patients were not allowed to attend the daily chapel service but morning prayers were held on the ward. Lytton regretted that there were no hymns, little from the Bible, and that 'the prayers selected were of a dolorous order'. Most of the allotted time was taken up by the chaplain who spoke of how Christ had been tempted in the wilderness in the same way as those imprisoned 'but that He was good and we were bad'. When he said it was wrong of the hungry to steal bread, an old woman stood up, 'tall and gaunt, her face seamed with life, her hands gnarled and worn with work'. With tears streaming down her cheeks she cried out 'Oh, sir, don't be

[9] September 1872 (William Monypenny and George Buckle, *The Life of Benjamin Disraeli*, 5 vols (London, 1910–20), V, p.225.
[10] Constance Lytton, *Prisons and Prisoners* (London, 1914), p.113.

so hard on us.' The chaplain did not answer her, did not even look at her, but continued as though nothing had happened while wardresses bustled the miscreant from the service. Lady Constance was enraged:

> A feeling of passionate indignation took hold of me ... Sympathy for the ejected prisoner, disagreement with the man who represented the teaching of Christianity ... became stored up in a brooding, malignant attitude of resentment towards the whole prison system, its infamous aim, its profound unreason, and the cruelly devitalising distortion of its results.[11]

She pinpointed a genuine problem with chaplains. They were appointed by the government, were part of the regime, and were subject, willingly or not, to its restrictions. 'The combination of the two offices, priest and prison official' seemed to her 'almost incompatible, anyhow while the prison system rests upon its present basis'. She thought visiting ministers with no affiliation to the prison system far preferable. Chapel services were also bizarre, with wardresses seated above the congregation, their backs to the altar and their attention fixed on the prisoners. It gave Constance a strange sensation, taking away all reverence and replacing it with an inclination to laugh. Those who did ended up in cellular confinement.[12]

She was surprised and perturbed when the chaplain later addressed her as 'your ladyship'. His attitude could not have been more deferential. She then for the first time noticed that the dress-jacket she wore was different from that allotted to others. Hers was quite new and without the broad arrow markings. Knives and forks, hitherto never seen on the ward, appeared, and since her arrival, she discovered from other inmates, the food had improved. Evidently prison privileges accrued to the already privileged. She 'resented such favouritism on the part of officials, both as a Liberal in politics, as a believer in the teachings of Christ, and as a woman'. She had thought that after a few days she would be transferred onto normal location. When this did not happen she went on strike, by refusing the 'diet extras' such as the banana and pudding, and insisting on sleeping on a mattress on the floor. When this proved of no avail she scratched 'V' for 'votes for women' over her heart and threatened to extend the phrase onto her face, a drastic act of self-mutilation which finally got her discharged from the hospital and put on normal location with other suffragettes and ordinary prisoners.[13]

---

11   *Ibid.*, pp.120f.
12   *Ibid.*, pp.192ff.
13   *Ibid.*, pp.143, 162–73.

There she and her fellow agitators, by polite persistence, won small improvements in the prison regime. She also came to empathise with the plight of the poverty-stricken wretches with whom she now associated. The prison offered them another sort of misery from that which they endured in the slums. It did nothing to rehabilitate them, nothing to encourage or improve them, and everything to keep them down-trodden, obedient and servile. Votes for women, she realised, was just one important aspect of wider social betterment. She was a socialist in all but name. Those suffragettes who were advocates of social reforms and votes for all women of whatever class saw themselves as following in the empowering footsteps of Elizabeth Fry, and 'like a flame the movement swept through the prisons, purging them and purifying them'.[14]

The more Constance associated herself with the underclass the more she was alienated from her own upper class. And class mattered even in prison as her special treatment had shown. She declared that she had been shown 'every consideration' by the staff and had had 'an exceptionally good time'. She had learnt a lot and had a lot to learn, but she had earned her 'Holloway degree', a term she coined. Having a good time should not be her goal in gaol and she determined to embrace suffering for the cause. And suffering came.

In June 1909 Marion Dunlop was sentenced to one month in prison for defacing the wall of St Stephen's Hall in Westminster. She wrote to the Home Secretary, Herbert Gladstone, demanding to be treated as a political prisoner. But Miss Marion was no Lady Constance and got no reply. Denied her special status she went on hunger strike. When she was asked what she would have for dinner she answered 'my determination'. In one day she threw 'a fried fish, four slices of bread, three bananas and a cup of hot milk' out of her cell window.[15] Others followed suit and all were released after a few days. This subversion of the legal process could not be allowed to continue. The prison commissioners were at their wits' end. The suffragettes' demands for political status could not be met, and they could not go on being released. The authorities would look absurd. But what if one of these women died in custody? In September when Mary Leigh and Charlotte Marsh were imprisoned for four months in Birmingham, Mary immediately went on hunger strike. She was not released but was forcibly fed. Twice a day, while being restrained, two doctors forced a long tube up her nose and poured in liquid food, a mix of milk, gruel, eggs, brandy,

14   Quoted in Jenkins, *op. cit.*, p.93.
15   Sylvia Pankhurst *The Suffragette Movement* (London, 1931), p.307.

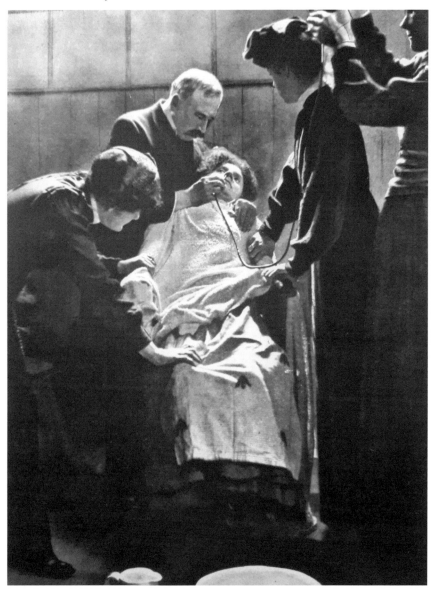

27. Force-feeding of suffragette

sugar and beef tea. This was humiliating, degrading, disgusting, painful, and frightening. Force-feeding was akin to torture. Sometimes the tubes were not even cleaned between feedings. The sensation was similar to drowning in your own vomit. Nearly all the victims suffered severe constipation, and as they struggled many suffered chipped teeth and bruising. The practice received the judicial sanction of the Lord Chief Justice himself, but instead of proving a deterrent it made the suffragettes more determined. Their imprisoned sisters were martyrs, and more martyrs were ready to join them, the older and sicker in particular, the better to embarrass the government. One was Lady Constance.

Her opportunity came in October when she and others threw stones outside the Liberal Club in Newcastle where the Chancellor of the Exchequer, David Lloyd George, was to give a speech. Yet again her status ensured a lighter sentence in the second division than the hard labour that the less well-connected received in the third.[16] Newcastle gaol had more overtly kind staff but worse conditions than Holloway. Constance had to sleep on a plank in a dark, dirty cell. She wrote to Gladstone complaining that there were fleas in her knickers.[17] But there were not yet tubes in her nostrils. She had gone on hunger strike, but, instead of being force-fed, she – along with another well-connected suffragette – was released, on the grounds of ill health. Her heart was too weak for the dreadful 'treatment'. Meanwhile the others arrested with them endured it.

Constance recognised that 'the fact that many educated women were being sent to gaol for a question of conscience must do a great deal for prison reform'. They could articulate their experiences and their voices would be heard. But their experiences were very different from the norm. It was a dichotomy she wanted to expose. She would assume a different persona and become Jane Warton, an eccentric spinster of insignificance. Joan of Arc had inspired the name 'Jane'. She had first thought of 'Warburton' for the surname but decided to discard the 'bur' lest it sound too distinguished. Lady Constance would be pampered; plain Jane would be force-fed. On her release no one would believe a word Jane Warton said. Lady Constance would then expose the double-standards of treating two offenders guilty of identical offences in markedly different ways, dependent not on their constitution but on their social background. She had noticed that prisoners of unprepossessing appearance obtained least favour and so she 'determined to put ugliness to the test'.

She cut off most of her hair and acquired a green tweed coat and a cloth hat.[18] She was ready to act and for action. Thus attired, on 14 January 1910,

---

16 Since 1898 prison sentences had been differentiated. The rigours of the third division made it virtually indistinguishable from imprisonment with hard labour; the second division was somewhat less onerous and was for those who 'were not depraved and not usually of criminal habits'; the first division was reserved for the few prisoners of conscience, such as those who had objected to compulsory vaccination. They could have food sent in, work and earn money in their trades, and have extra visitors. These distinctions were abolished in 1948.

17 Lytton, *op. cit.*, pp.225ff..

18 *Ibid.*, pp.237ff.

she led a demonstration to Walton gaol to demand the release of suffragettes held there. She threw stones at the governor's house and was arrested. She was sentenced to a fortnight's imprisonment in the third division. This time the attitude of prison officials towards her was very different. She repeatedly broke rules and went on hunger strike. She may have dreamt of 'melons, peaches and nectarines', but at last she attained her ultimate dream of being force-fed. This time there was no medical justification for preferential treatment. This time there was no medical examination.

The experience of the procedure was even worse than her imaginings, and as the governor admitted, 'she was practically asphyxiated each time'.[19]

> Two of the wardresses took hold of my arms, one held my head and one my feet. One wardress helped to pour the food. The doctor leant on my chest to get at my mouth. I shut my mouth and clenched my teeth ... The doctor offered me the choice of a wooden or steel gag; he explained elaborately ... that the steel gag would hurt and the wooden one not; and he urged me not to force him to use the steel gag. But I did not speak nor open my mouth ... so he finally had recourse to the steel ... The pain of it was intense and at last I must have given way for he got the gag between my teeth, when he proceeded to turn it much more than necessary until my jaws were fastened wide apart ... Then he put down my throat a tube which ... was too wide and something like four feet in length. The irritation of the tube was excessive. I choked the moment it touched my throat until it had got down. Then the food was poured in quickly; it made me sick and my body and legs double up, but the wardresses instantly pressed back my head and the doctor leant on my knees. The horror of it was more than I can describe.[20]

As a parting shot, the doctor struck her on the cheek to show, Constance thought, his contempt. Every day the force-feeding was repeated. After the sixth time she longed to die. But die she did not.

Just as her cover was blown, she was released from her sentence, and trumpeted as both a martyr and a saint for the cause. Her experiences exposed inexcusable class distinction at the heart of the prison system: as Lady Constance she had been judged too ill for force-feeding; as Miss Warton she had not. As Lady Constance she had been treated with a degree of deference; as Miss Warton with disdain. Her name alone ensured publicity, and her status and connections, as well as political developments, demanded some official response. Churchill became Home Secretary on 19 February 1910, less than three weeks after her release. He was no friend of suffragettes, but he was a great friend of Constance's brother,

[19] Jenkins, *op. cit.*, p.162.
[20] Lytton, *op. cit.*, pp.268f.

Victor, and Victor demanded a public inquiry. Instead he got an internal investigation carried out by Ruggles-Brise. It discovered nothing untoward in her treatment and nothing that merited any 'special or formal inquiry'.[21] Churchill, however, did intervene by removing the discretion that governor and doctors had about the imposition of force-feeding and decreeing that after twenty-four hours of refusing food, all hunger-strikers should be subjected to it, providing that a full medical examination had taken place and the medical officer had signed a certificate stating that no harm would be done by the procedure. He also publicly introduced Rule 243a which did not afford suffragettes recognition as political prisoners, or put them in the first division, for both of which they so strenuously campaigned, but did give them special privileges. It was a sop that put a temporary stop to hunger strikes.[22]

When Constance again ended up in Holloway prison, serving fourteen days there in November 1911, she was amazed by the changed world she found: 'All was civility; it was unrecognisable.' Suffragettes could wear their own clothes and associate together.[23] Indeed later her friend Ethel Smyth, the composer of the suffragette anthem 'March of the Women', conducted her own composition from the window of her cell using a toothbrush for a baton while a choir of suffragettes sang in triumph in the exercise yard below.

Jane Warton and Winston Churchill had worked wonders, if only for a time. In 1912, as a result of the withdrawal of privileges for those convicted of 'serious violence', prison hunger strikes began again. The following year the government passed the Prisoners (Temporary Discharge for Ill-Health) Act, commonly known as the Cat and Mouse Act. Weak or ill hunger strikers were released from prison only to be re-arrested when they had recuperated. As a result of this ploy, except for those few considered too dangerous to be let out, force-feeding ceased.

Too infirm herself to continue with physical activism, Constance instead resorted to writing about her own experiences. The result was *Prisons and*

---

21 Jenkins, *op. cit.*, p.170. Despite this, in October 1911 she wrote to Ruggles-Brise commending him for the tenor of the recent prison commissioners' report which breathed 'a different spirit' from anything she could remember and combined stringent criticism of the past with admirable suggestions for prison reform (Shane Leslie, *Sir Evelyn Ruggles-Brise* (London, 1938), pp.157f.).

22 Having met Churchill many years before in India, she later commented: 'the first time you see [him] you see all his faults, and the rest of your life you spend discovering his virtues'.

23 Lytton, *op. cit.*, pp.329ff.

Prisoners, published in 1914 to great acclaim. It was also her last great contribution not only to the cause of women's suffrage but of wider penal reform. Hers was one voice among many that were applauding reforms that had been in train for twenty years, and were urging reformers on.

PART V

THE AGE OF ENLIGHTENMENT
1895–1965

The great age of penal optimism when Ruggles-Brise, Paterson and Fox, all idealists within the Prison Commission, navigated a new way in the treatment of offenders and especially of the young. The demise of the death penalty dispelled a dark shadow over prisons, while the rise of the borstal, along with innovations in the treatment of the mentally ill and the psychologically damaged, proved to be Britain's greatest contributions to penal progress.

CHAPTER 26

The Sins of Our Fathers

We start from the principle that prison treatment should have as its primary and concurrent objects deterrence and reformation.
Report from the Departmental Committee on Prisons

I learnt of your appointment to the post recently held by Sir E. Du Cane. May the Gods guide you and may the cause of *Humanity* (always remember that a prisoner is still a human being) find in you a merciful and enlightened administrator. Now tis possible to do great things in the interests of your fallen brethren, neglected too long. *Act*, and posterity will, as in the case of the immortal Howard, honour your memory.
Letter to Evelyn Ruggles-Brise from W.F.R., a former convict

In 1892 Herbert Asquith was appointed Home Secretary in William Gladstone's Liberal government. Change was in the air. The attitude of the informed public was moving away from negative, repressive deterrence, and was aspiring to something altogether more positive. They had read with horror the descriptions of 'darkest England' penned by the founder of the Salvation Army, William Booth, and many agreed with his condemnation of 'the rude surgery of the Gaol' which in its sheer punitiveness had ignored 'the first essential of every system of punishment' – reformation – and heeded his clarion call to reclaim the lost and transform the lives of the downtrodden.[1] Those Christians whose faith had been dented by Darwin still adhered to the ethical imperative their upbringing had instilled. Liberals, many of whom had an evangelical background, were troubled in their consciences about what they heard or read of what went on behind prison walls. The extraordinary influence of the Idealist philosopher, the late Thomas Hill Green, was at its zenith, harnessing youthful enthusiasm for self-sacrifice and inspiring many Oxbridge graduates not just to devote their expertise to helping the working-class denizens of London but to engage

---

[1]   *In Darkest England, and the Way Out* (London, 1890), p.73.

with them by living among them.[2] Many of their new 'friends' would end up in prison.

Asquith himself had been at Balliol when Green was a professorial fellow there, and was deeply attracted by his progressive and socially engaged political views. As a politician he had been disturbed by the somewhat overwrought description of a parliamentary colleague, John Burns, of his own experience of incarceration. Burns, an erstwhile firebrand who had participated in an illegal demonstration, had been imprisoned for a short time in Pentonville. More importantly Asquith was convinced by Henry Massingham's 1893 campaigning articles in the *Daily Chronicle*, that prisons had to change, and that they could not change under the autocratic leadership of Du Cane who presided over an administrative machine that was 'cumbrous, pitiless, obsolete, unchanged ... the most conservative, the least flexible and least intelligent department in the British Empire'.[3] Asquith recognised that Du Cane was 'the last of the Bastille-keepers', and the main obstacle to reform. He had to be brought to book.[4]

In June 1894 the Home Secretary set up a Departmental Committee on Prisons under the chairmanship of his under-secretary, Herbert Gladstone. Its focus was on the treatment of prisoners, not on the pay and working conditions of staff who over the years had expressed considerable discontent about their own lot.[5] Thus while it took formal evidence from governors, matrons, chaplains, doctors, ex-prisoners, the Salvation Army and even from the General-Secretary of the National Flint Glass Makers Trade Association, it took none from those with day-to-day, hands-on experience: prison warders. The nearest it got was by examining Mr Charles Hall, a first class clerk acting as storekeeper at Lewes prison, and he was asked about prison industries. The commissioners explained this extraordinary omission

---

2   Green, whose name is all but forgotten, had an influence in Oxford and beyond that is hard to overestimate. For young men in particular, troubled as they were by the scientific and exegetical assaults on the authority of Scripture but still imbued with a strong Christian social ethos, he provided an intellectual impetus, transforming their frustrations into a burning desire for self-sacrificial social service. On this see Melvin Richter, *The Politics of Conscience* (Cambridge, MA, 1964).

3   Massingham was the editor of the paper and author of the articles usually attributed to Morrison. The latter had contributed reviews for the newspaper and may well have influenced Massingham's stance (Sean McConville, *English Local Prisons 1860–1900* (London, 1995), pp.555–64).

4   Shane Leslie, *Sir Evelyn Ruggles-Brise: A Memoir of the Founder of Borstal* (London, 1938), p.90.

5   Committees under the earl of Rosebery and Lord De Ramsey in 1883 and 1891 respectively had looked into pay, leave, hours of work, accommodation, and other gripes of staff.

by stating that whereas during their visits to prison they had spoken to warders, 'the limits of time' had prevented them being called 'formally as witnesses'. In any case they had not been specifically directed to consider the question of prison staff. However, because 'the proper treatment of prisoners is so closely bound up with it', they would go on to express some views 'on its strength and quality' while suggesting some minor ameliorations to conditions of employment.[6] In fact as a result of the changes proposed and later implemented, the role of staff would be transformed, the work becoming more rewarding but considerably more demanding than it had been under the highly restrictive silent system.

Du Cane of course was supposed to take centre stage in the inquiry. He was required by a forty-two-year-old Home Secretary and a Prime Minister's forty-year-old son to give an account of his stewardship and submit himself to interrogation. He became too infirm to appear before the committee, or so he said, but his co-commissioners and subordinates did, torn between their loyalty to their chief and their own desire to disparage his system. For such vocal dissidents as Morrison it was no wrench as he was all too eager to denounce the whole Du Cane imperium. Belatedly Du Cane was cornered into being examined by committee members at his own home, where they questioned him in two short sessions. Given his status, his contribution was absurdly brief, as he could retreat behind infirmity if things got too hot. He was an old soldier in tactical retreat, and had managed to minimise any personal criticism.[7] But he could not stifle it.

He would have been particularly horrified to know that Michael Davitt was to give evidence to the committee. A Fenian activist, in 1870 he had been sentenced to fifteen years' penal servitude for treason-felony. After nine months' solitary confinement in Millbank he had spent almost seven years in Dartmoor and Portland before being released on 'ticket of leave'. He spoke with the voice of experience and authenticity, making the obvious point that 'man is a talking animal and no matter what rules you adopt to prevent talking, if you have a thousand men congregated in a prison they will insist on exercising this natural right to speak'.[8] Human nature would frustrate inhuman ingenuity. So too would humanity, such as the propensity of warders to ignore quiet conversation that did not interfere with work and

---

6   *Report* (1895), paras.21, 99–107; J.E. Thomas, *The English Prison Officer since 1850* (London, 1972), pp.109–22. This omission and concession confirmed the conviction of many staff that prisoners were given more consideration than warders.

7   *Report* (1895), para.21, *Evidence*, pp.361–75; McConville, *op. cit.*, pp.607–14.

8   Rupert Cross, *Punishment, Prison and the Public* (London, 1971), p.73.

'was done in moderation'.[9] Not only was the old regime a stigma on society, it did not even work.

The Gladstone Committee's report was issued in under eleven months. It was to set a novel and liberal trend. While acknowledging Du Cane's 'long and able administration' which had 'achieved a large measure of success' in terms of uniformity, discipline and economy, and which had bequeathed the 'vast machinery in good working order', it proved in effect to be a complete rejection and reversal of his life's work. The prison system was shipshape all right, but the ship had been sailing in the wrong direction. It had lost its moral compass. Du Cane had succeeded in all his aims, but those aims were changing. The report went far beyond its remit to constitute the most considered statement of penal policy ever enunciated in Great Britain. It formulated principles.[10] It placed the reform of prisoners as a primary objective of the prison service as important as deterrence, and questioned whether these disparate ends really created a fundamental and confusing dichotomy of purpose which would be mutually self-defeating, as Denman had long before asserted. It thought that prison conditions could be so altered as to have a reformative effect. It recommended constructive work in association instead of oakum-picking in solitude, and the abolition of the pointless but onerous crank and tread-wheel. Solitary confinement should be reduced, and social interaction allowed. It was concerned at the number of the 'insane and feeble-minded' who entered the prison system, or were created by it, and suggested that they be diverted from prisons and 'sent to some special institution in the nature of an asylum, where they might do light work under supervision'. It wanted an increase in education classes, and the provision of more books. The whole prison ethos would have to change, and to ensure it did the committee urged that provision should be made for 'systematic and scientific instruction' for all grades of staff.[11]

While proposing prolonged or indefinite sentences for habitual criminals, it recommended that there should be indeterminate sentences for recidivists in the making. 'Juvenile-adults' – a term later coined to denote offenders above sixteen but under twenty-three, too old for purely reformatory methods but too young to be treated as fully-formed adults – should be sentenced to between one and three years in penal reformatories, rural retreats intended to be 'a half-way house between a prison and a reformatory'. The committee had been much influenced in this direction by the evidence of a number

---

[9]   Anon., *Five Years' Penal Servitude*, 2nd edn (London, 1878), p.189.
[10]   *Report* (1895), para.14; Cross, *op. cit.*, pp.3f.
[11]   *Report* (1895), paras.102f.

of witnesses, most notably G.P. Merrick, the chaplain of Holloway and Newgate, and John Trevarthen, the secretary of the Redhill reformatory. Founded in 1856 to take up to three hundred boys aged between twelve and sixteen sent to them by the courts, Trevarthen boasted an astonishing ninety-five per cent success rate. A report on the Elmira reformatory in New York State was equally persuasive, asserting as it did that 'probably about eighty per cent of the prisoners are reformed'. Recidivism was to be one of the main gauges of success and the British prison system had a lot to learn from the reformatory movement both at home and abroad. The only way to drain the swamp of recidivism was to cut off the supply of fresh sewage. The members were not sanguine of spectacular results, but thought that 'even a moderate percentage of success would justify much effort and expense devoted to an improvement of the system'.[12]

The bastions of inertia looked askance. The prison commissioners asserted that they would 'be in hearty accord with any *feasible plan*', but were unclear on how to proceed in implementing these recommendations. In particular they were uncertain to what extent the penal reformatory for juvenile-adults was meant to be penal and how far the penal element could be reconciled with the reformatory. And who should be sent to these new institutions? Only first offenders or all in the juvenile-adult age-group? They doubted that 'public sentiment would be favourable to the idea', especially if young first offenders were to receive lengthy sentences as a result, and many of those might well prefer months in prison to years of reformative detention. At most the commissioners wanted 'an intermediate classification, an ameliorated form of "penal servitude"'.[13]

The forces of reaction tried to stem the progressive tide, and sought the support of a public hitherto complacent about, or ignorant of, the fact that British prisons were the harshest in Europe. A *Punch* cartoon famously depicted 'a British convict, with the villainous face of Bill Sykes, lying on a sofa in his cell smoking a cigar with champagne at hand'.[14] This was so far from the truth as to be counter-productive. Liberal sentiment was in the ascendant, and was to grow in strength, inspired and informed by such a luminary as Oscar Wilde, whose poignant and revelatory letters to the press had a major impact on public opinion. The worst of times in prison history were to be supplanted by the best of times. Optimism not seen since the

---

12 *Report* (1895), paras.84f.

13 *Observations of the Prison Commissioners on the Recommendations of the Departmental Committee on Prisons* (1896), pp.27f.; Roger Hood, *Borstal Reassessed* (London, 1965), pp.5f.

14 Frank Harris, *Oscar Wilde* (New York, 1916), II, p.375.

days of the penitentiary movement reigned, and aspects of the former were restored, with chaplains again elevated to a prime position, and with a Lady Visitors' Association reminiscent of that of Elizabeth Fry being established in 1900 by the duchess of Bedford. The shod foot on the head of the malefactor was replaced by a helping hand. No longer to be ground down, the reprobate should be raised up. This was heady stuff.

To implement such a radical transformation in custodial policy an equally radical change in prison leadership was necessary. Du Cane embodied an era that was over. For the first time he would come in for open criticism. Politicians castigated him for the inaccuracies in his annual reports. Reformers directed 'a personal campaign of much fervour and ... much malice against the venerable chairman of the Commission whom they regarded as the embodiment of bureaucratic despotism and arrogance'.[15] The seemingly immovable object had met a truly irresistible force in the Asquith–Gladstone compact. Horrified and humiliated, he was compelled to resign in April 1895, on the very day he reached retirement age and the same month that Wilde began his descent into Hades. His replacement, chosen by Asquith, was one of those commissioners who had given evidence to the committee, Evelyn Ruggles-Brise.

Ruggles-Brise was born into prosperity in 1857. He was educated at Eton and then at Balliol College, Oxford where he was another who imbibed the Idealism of T.H. Green, whose *Lectures on the Principles of Political Obligation*, including 'The Right of the State to Punish', would later inform his beliefs about the proper treatment of prisoners. A near contemporary of Herbert Gladstone at both school and university, Ruggles-Brise entered the civil service in 1880 and, demonstrating his worth and impartiality, became private secretary to a succession of Liberal and Conservative Home Secretaries. The last of these, Henry Matthews, in January 1892 recommended him for a vacant seat on the Prison Commission. Matthews himself left office after the Tories lost the general election in August of that year. His Liberal successor, Asquith, was only too glad to concur in the appointment. The able new commissioner soon discovered that under Du Cane's autocracy the commission had become a cypher.[16] Frustrated and excluded from doing anything worthwhile – he had 'trodden on [the chairman's] toes' to such an extent that Du Cane never spoke to him thereafter – Ruggles-Brise considered quitting public service. As Asquith had anticipated and wanted, his appointee was proving to be a square peg in a round hole. His time would

---

15 Leslie, *op. cit.*, p.86.
16 *Report* (1895), *Evidence*, paras.971–1003.

soon come. The Gladstone Committee called him before it, and Ruggles-Brise, trying to be both loyal to his irascible old chief and at the same time honest with the committee, impressed. He was a new broom, just the man to replace Du Cane and undo his work. The eminent septuagenarian who had spent his life designing prisons and administering the system he had built, was supplanted by a little-known civil servant not yet forty and with no experience of prisons.

Ruggles-Brise was to prove an inspired appointment. He was an excellent executive officer, with the ability and disposition to implement the Gladstone Committee's recommendations. Ironically he had much in common with his predecessor. For him security was paramount, deterrence vital. Reform was incidental to the prison system, 'not its primary or essential condition'. He agreed that penal policy should be based on hard facts and statistics not on soft moralism and anecdotes. He eschewed the latter and acquired the former, although he thought that 'the prevailing scientific habit of ascertaining criminal tendencies through deformities of the body or disfigurement of the head' a fallacy and that there was no evidence of a 'criminal type'. He was also very much a 'doer', in temperament 'an absolute sahib', but he had tact, and charm. He was clever but courteous, autocratic but diplomatic, determined but persuasive. Once he had mastered his brief, however, and come to a conclusion, he swept 'all obstacles out of the way of his will'.[17] His enthusiasm for his new challenge was unbounded, as was his desire both to learn all he could and to teach all who would listen, at home and abroad.

His interest in penal affairs was anything but parochial and expanded with time. He was the British delegate to the International Prison Congress in Paris, becoming President of it in 1910, a role in which he continued until his retirement. Twice he went to America on significant fact-finding tours. On the first of these, in 1897, he visited Elmira reformatory which was inspired by Maconochie's penal experiments and had been designed as an alternative to the Auburn and Philadelphia systems. In turn its apparent success had influenced the Gladstone Committee's conclusions. Elmira was positivist in its approach, being aimed at novice offenders aged between sixteen and thirty who were sent there on indeterminate but not indefinite sentences and subjected to educational classes, vocational courses and sporting activities, following a regime similar to that of West Point.[18] Ruggles-Brise's reaction

---

[17] Leslie, *op. cit.*, pp.158, 164; Rich, p.19.

[18] The idea of passing 'reformative' instead of 'time' sentences originated in the New York Prison Association in 1867, and was incorporated in Elmira. The minimum period was one year, and in 1892 the average stay was twenty-one months. The minimum did not diminish; the average stay tended to increase.

was ambivalent. He was impressed by the enthusiasm of the staff for, and the ingenuity expended on, the reformatory ideal, but found 'much in the system that is extravagant and to English ideas nearly approaching the ridiculous'. In particular he deprecated 'undue leniency and disregard for deterrent influences'. Elmira should not be imported 'lock, stock and barrel' into England. It was a 'bold experiment' but there was no need to imitate its methods. He also thought that, while the British fell short in classifying adolescents as adults, the Americans went too far in 'extending the age of youth as far as thirty'. For Ruggles-Brise the truth lay in between. His long-term aim was 'to take the "dangerous age" – 16 to 21 – out the prison system altogether, and to make it subject to special *"Institutional"* treatment on reformatory lines', those in that age-group being eligible for such novel provision because of their pliable personalities and because they remained susceptible to benign influences. Beyond that age, with their characters 'set', he thought that reformatory methods would be futile.[19]

Meanwhile, his immediate task at home was to implement the committee's wide-ranging and breathtaking recommendations, to transform a system based on savagery into one which grew out of humanity, to find a way to reconcile essential rehabilitation with necessary deterrence, to put prisoners into different grades, and above all to separate the men from the boys, and women from girls. Guiding this 'beneficent revolution' was to be his life's work and mission. It would not be easy. Inheriting a staff deeply schooled in the ways of Du Cane, he would have to re-educate them, motivate them and, in time, even convert them. It would not be quick. In this daunting task he was at least actively aided by the newly appointed secretary to the commissioners, Major Edward Clayton, an experienced governor who had served in Millbank, Chatham, Portsmouth, Wormwood Scrubs and Lewes, and who had helped frame the Prison Act of 1898. Their policy would necessarily be one of *festina lente*.

Ruggles-Brise wanted 'to see the motto of Justice and Pity written upon the gate of every prison'. He tried to bring justice and pity through every prison gate, and wanted the outside world to see the transformation within. In contrast to his predecessor he wanted light shed in dark places and welcomed criticism, so long as it was constructive and informed. To ensure the latter he was quite prepared to grant access to interested parties. One of the most notable was Michael Davitt who asked permission to visit a number of prisons, talk to prisoners there, and inspect the conditions under which

---

[19] Evelyn Ruggles-Brise, *The English Prison System* (London, 1921), p.91; Hood, *op. cit.*, pp.7ff.

they were detained. Despite his controversial past, permission was granted, and the privilege was not abused. He compared what he saw in Bedford, Birmingham, Bristol, Dartmoor, Portland and Wormwood Scrubs with what he had known, and was impressed and surprised by the change Ruggles-Brise had wrought in the short time he had been in charge.[20] However, the chairman distinguished between 'humane sentiment' and the 'feverish sentimentalism' often exhibited by the press. When Lord Northcliffe, the great publishing magnate and owner of many newspapers including the *Daily Mail* and *The Times*, wanted to send Tighe Hopkins into prisons to report on developments, Ruggles-Brise refused 'at any price' to allow in someone whom he disparaged as 'a novelist and a sentimentalist'. No one ever accused Ruggles-Brise of 'sloppy sentimentalism towards crime', one reason he was so effective.[21] By decrying sentimentality he could condemn savagery. Both he thought ruinous. He placed the constituent elements of punishment in the following order if not priority: retributory, deterrent, and reformatory. Thus he could make reform palatable to a public predisposed to be punitive but amenable to change. Like Sir Robert Peel, he proceeded with caution, mastered the facts, mustered the arguments, and implemented changes that would endure.

Legislation, backed by both the main political parties, gave legal sanction to further reform. The 1898 Prison Act, although enacted during a Conservative administration, put Gladstone's proposals into operation. As 'its creator and midwife', it was 'a triumph for Ruggles-Brise and the foundation of his successful career'. He acknowledged with satisfaction that although the changes were far-reaching, 'so ripe was public opinion for a radical departure from the old penal methods, that they met with little criticism or opposition at the time'.[22] The Act empowered the courts to differentiate between offenders and order that those of largely good character who had temporarily deviated from their norm serve their sentences in the first or second division, and abolished cranks and tread-wheels (with the ironical effect of depriving institutions of the pumping apparatus needed to run their previous system of cellular sanitation). It also greatly limited the power to order corporal punishment, introduced remission of sentences on account of good conduct, and enabled fine-defaulters to be released on part-

---

[20] Leslie, *op. cit.*, pp.112–16. In Wormwood Scrubs Davitt was 'extremely pleased with the book-bind industry', an extraordinary endeavour that gave prisoners an apprenticeship in library and antiquarian book-binding. Such craft training took place in other British prisons until, lamentably, it was all closed down in the 1980s.

[21] Leslie, *op. cit.*, pp.153f.; *Vanity Fair*, 10 February 1910.

[22] McConville, *op. cit.*, pp.701, 753, 756; Leslie, *op. cit.*, p.120.

payment of the amount. Before this melioration those who were fined paltry sums for minor offences but who could not pay in full were immediately incarcerated, accounting for half of the local prison population. Turning to the prison system itself, its twin pillars were finally fully fused when the commissioners became, as their chairman had always been, directors of convict prisons, although the bodies would remain separate entities in law until 1948.[23] The least striking but most important clause was not one that sprung from Gladstone but from Ruggles-Brise. It vested powers in the Home Secretary to make rules for the regulation of prisons, which meant that many subsequent developments in the penal system could be made without recourse to parliament. The first Prison Rules, brought in in 1899, made no mention of the objects of prison discipline.

Between 1905 and 1910 Gladstone was Home Secretary in a Liberal government led by Asquith. They had worked together before; they worked in tandem now, overseeing an avalanche of reforming legislation which both restricted the use of imprisonment and – the essential corollary – provided viable alternatives to it. In 1907 the Probation of Offenders Act, championed by Ruggles-Brise, was passed, giving courts the power of binding over offenders to keep the peace instead of fining or imprisoning them, and establishing an aftercare service along lines developed in Massachusetts and pioneered in Britain by the Salvation Army. Probation was the opposite of punitive: it was all about mentoring those released on licence, and helping them find accommodation and employment. This was vital to end recidivism. William Booth described the problem vividly:

> As wounded and sickly stags are gored to death by their fellows, so the unfortunate who bears the prison brand is hunted from pillar to post, until he despairs of ever regaining his position and oscillates between one prison and another for the rest of his days.[24]

---

23 In 1881 the staffs of the Directors of Convict Prisons and of the Prison Commission had been merged.

24 Booth, *op. cit.*, pp.58, 73f. The Army's Prison Rescue Brigades met discharged inmates at prison gates, afforded them food and accommodation in their hostels, and employment in their workshops, actively recruited them into their ranks and promoted some to officer status. This enterprise was so successful in Australia that the Victoria penal code allowed magistrates to put first offenders in the care of the Salvation Army as an alternative to prison. They also offered to supervise 'ticket-of-leave' convicts 'so as to free them from the humiliating and harassing duty of having to report themselves at the police stations' (p.176).

In 1908 the Children Act abolished prison for those under fourteen and permitted imprisonment for fourteen- to sixteen-year-olds only on special certification by the court.[25]

In the same year the Prevention of Crime Act was enacted, coming into force in 1909. Cicely Craven, the Secretary of the Howard League, would later characterise it as 'important in the evolution of a scientific penal system because it contains the germ of a new principle, that the fixed sentence ... must be superseded by a flexible sentence ending at such time as the offender appears able and willing to return to freedom and live honestly'.[26] Divided into two parts, it dealt with the opposite extremes of the criminal spectrum. The first part was concerned with 'the reformation of young offenders', the salvageable novice, the second with 'the detention of habitual criminals', the irreclaimable 'old lag'.

Part I, consisting of nine concise sections, established the innovatory but still experimental borstal system firmly on the penal map. It authorised assize and quarter-session courts, if they concluded that an offender – boy or girl – aged sixteen to twenty-one 'by reason of his criminal habits or tendencies, or association with persons of bad character ... should be subject to detention for such term and under such instruction and discipline as appears most conducive to his reformation and the repression of crime', to pass in lieu of a sentence of penal servitude or imprisonment, 'a sentence of detention under penal discipline in a Borstal Institution for a term of not less than one year nor more than three years'.[27] Encompassing reformation

---

25 Nonetheless the age of criminal responsibility remained very low by international standards: under common law it was seven; in 1933 it was raised by parliament to eight and in 1963 to ten. Children who cannot in law consent to sexual activity can commit rape.

26 Cicely Craven, 'The Progress of English Criminology', *Journal of Criminal Law and Criminology*, 24, 1 (1933), pp.230–47, at p.242.

27 The beginning of the borstal system is recounted in Chapter 28, its development and demise in Chapters 31 and 32. Gladstone, despite recommending an age limit of twenty-three in his 1898 report, thought twenty-one was 'a reasonable age to fix', but that it could be increased by up to two years when more borstals became available. The age limit was raised to twenty-three in 1936, but again reduced to twenty-one in 1948. Twenty-one was Ruggles-Brise's suggestion and was based on nothing more significant than that it was the age of civil majority. Magistrates were given the power to commit suitable offenders to quarter sessions for sentencing to borstal treatment by s.10 of the Criminal Justice Act of 1914. By s.46 of the Criminal Justice Act 1925 they could also commit to assize courts. Before imposing such a disposal the court had first to consider a report by the Prison Commissioners as to 'the offender's health, mental capacity and other circumstances showing whether he is likely to profit by Borstal training'. Candidates were interviewed and assessed 'using Binet-Simon tests of intelligence', and the results incorporated into the pre-sentence report (Craven, *op. cit.*, p.240).

with 'stern and exact discipline', this was a heavy penalty, targeted at those
with 'criminal tendencies', and not those who committed paltry offences for
whom such a sentence would be unnecessary and unfair. Release on licence
was permissible after six months for boys or three months for girls, but the
licence could be revoked. After-care was put on a statutory basis and those
released were put under greater supervision with the sanction of recall.

'Old lags' were another matter. The seven sections which constituted Part
II of the Act introduced 'preventive detention' for those who by their own
admission, or by the verdict of a jury, were deemed to be 'habitual criminals',
defined as those over sixteen years of age who were repeat offenders and
who lived persistently dishonest or criminal lives. After they had served
whatever term of penal servitude had been imposed for an indictable offence
they could be further detained for a minimum of five and a maximum of
ten years, with discretionary release within those parameters. This provision,
while punitive in practice, was protective in its aim. That aim, as Gladstone
put it, was not directed at casual criminals who were reduced or 'drop into
crime from their surroundings or physical disability, or mental deficiency',
but at career criminals, those who 'preferred a life of crime'. Despite this
assurance there was a fear that many Artful Dodgers would join the Fagins
behind bars.

The corollary of this disposal was the danger of totally disproportionate
sentences being handed down by the courts. In the event, classical notions
of English justice were too strong to be overwhelmed by such positivistic
approaches advocated by the Home Office: juries were reluctant to find
offenders to be 'habitual criminals', and judges were loath to deploy their
discretionary powers. Extenuating circumstances could mitigate guilt but all
criminals were free agents responsible for their actions. They were to be
incarcerated because they were culpable not because they were incurable.[28]
The number so sentenced was never great and declined over time, the periods
imposed tended to be the minimum allowed, and finally, the Great War,
which threw the penal system into confusion, destroyed the circumstances

---

[28] The insane were no exception to this as they were not, by reason of their condition,
criminals although they could commit crime – thus Broadmoor at its inception was
for criminal lunatics not mad criminals, although the latter would later be transferred
there from the prison system.

in which such a sentence could be imposed and assessed. Nonetheless it limped on for years to come.[29]

For proponents of preventive detention such as Ruggles-Brise himself, it did not help that Gladstone's successor as Home Secretary had a visceral dislike of the whole concept of indeterminate sentences. Winston Churchill also disliked a lot else about the prison system. He was a zealot for further reform. He had been affected by his own time as a captive of the Boers, and had been appalled by the experience of his friend Wilfrid Blunt, the poet, who in 1888 had 'done time' in Galway gaol. Churchill had promised Blunt that if ever he were Home Secretary he would make a 'clean sweep' of the present system.[30] The biggest influence on both Churchill and the country at large was that of John Galsworthy, the novelist, playwright, and moral crusader, who had campaigned against the caging of wild birds, and had visited several prisons to see the system in operation. The first was Dartmoor to which he went in 1907. The impression he formed there was reinforced by later visits to Pentonville and Chelmsford, and finally to Lewes prison where he interviewed, with the approval of Ruggles-Brise, forty-nine prisoners undergoing solitary confinement. His horrified reaction to what he had seen was expressed first in two sketches published in 1908, 'The House of Silence' and 'Order', then in a published letter to Gladstone,[31] and lastly and most powerfully in his play about Dartmoor, called *Justice*. He was heavily influencing the public and politicians alike against any period of separate confinement.

For Galsworthy six months of this inhumane and pointless isolation meant '4,140 hours of utter solitude and utter silence', conditions 'absolutely opposed to mental, moral and physical health'. In 1909 Churchill, while still President of the Board of Trade, had begun a correspondence with him on this topic and it continued when he became Home Secretary, an appointment the writer applauded. Galsworthy appealed to him as the man

---

[29] Radzinowicz, pp.3–33, 268–78. Although positivist theories were largely rejected in Britain, which has continued to emphasise moral culpability, they persisted for a long time in relation to habitual criminals, and the stress positivism laid on scientific enquiry and medical intervention has never dissipated as the development of criminology as an academic discipline and the deployment to this day of psychiatrists and psychologists within prisons demonstrate. Victorian 'moral imbecility' has metamorphosed into modern psychopathy.

[30] Alan Baxendale, *Before the Wars: Churchill as a Reformer (1910–1911)* (Whitney, 2011), pp.4f.

[31] 'Solitary Confinement: An Open Letter to the Home Secretary', *The Nation*, 1 and 8 May 1909; H.V. Marrot, *The Life and Letters of John Galsworthy* (London, 1935), pp.675–85.

'at the helm' to act, since the indignation that society felt at 'superfluous suffering deliberately inflicted on a free man or woman' did not apply to prisoners who were 'too far out of the line of the public's sight' in prisons 'closed to the public eye'. He was not 'advocating rosewater prisons' but 'strict disciplinary schools ... which should be so contrived as to give in [Churchill's] own words, "some kind of natural life" to the person thus restrained'. Solitary confinement and perpetual silence were 'the two features most hostile to that end'. He could not 'see why education, mental, moral, and physical, should be confined to Borstal establishments; anything that stimulates competition and self-respect must surely be to the good'.

Appositely, *Justice*, which 'gave voice to a dumb thing', was first performed at the Duke of York's Theatre two days after Churchill assumed office in February 1910. Both he and Ruggles-Brise went to see the play on the sensational opening night. According to Galsworthy's notebook, while the former watched it 'with sympathy', the latter did so 'with a sinking sensation', knowing he was losing the battle against growing public concern and the radicalism of the Home Secretary. Audiences were rapturous, the press reports extensive, *The Evening Standard* devoting a leading article to it, and its overall effect was explosive and long-lasting, coming as it did from an author, unlike Oscar Wilde, of unblemished moral authority. The play mirrored reality and realism gave it power. So thought *The Times* and other newspapers. So thought the literati and social commentators. So thought those who should know best. When a prison commissioner said that he would 'resign tomorrow' if what was depicted in *Justice* was accurate, Galsworthy told Churchill of a former prisoner employed at the theatre who, having thanked the manager for putting the play on, when asked if it was true to life had replied, 'every word'.[32]

Solitary confinement would die a death by a thousand cuts. The period to be endured, originally nine months, had been reduced to six by the 1899 Prison Rules. When the new system of classification was introduced in 1905 this was further reduced to three months for 'star-class' offenders but increased to nine months for 'recidivists'. For the 'intermediate class' it remained at six months. In 1909 Gladstone, at Galsworthy's bidding, had changed it to three months for all. Churchill, who had promised the writer that he would act speedily, curtailed it yet again, reducing it to one month for all prisoners, other than recidivists for whom it remained three.[33] All the while Ruggles-Brise seemed to be retarding rapid progress, and he certainly

32 Marrot, *op. cit.*, pp.247–68, 679–82.
33 Radzinowicz, pp.592–5.

had misgivings at the pace of change, and its detrimental impact on the penal aspect of the sentence, misgivings he made known to Churchill.[34] The minister had to assure Galsworthy that his 'external driving-power' was appreciated by the chairman, but, in mild rebuke, Churchill pointed out that 'a man constrained by intractable facts and small resources' may be excused a 'temporary feeling of irritation when he is overtaken and surrounded on all sides by the airy and tenuous clouds of sentiment and opinion'.[35]

Despite Churchill's impatience at the rate of progress in prison reform, he appreciated the achievements of Ruggles-Brise in pioneering an innovative approach to the detention of the young, and championed the patent virtues of 'a man who for ten or twelve years has stood forward at the head of the movement for prison reform', and by whose 'personal exertions, and largely through his own contributions in money and subscriptions' raised by him, 'the noble institution of the Borstal System has been erected, is being expanded and must ultimately cover practically the whole ground'.[36] Churchill also admired a leader who, when faced with an outcry of 'No Pampering for Convicts', had been prepared to resign rather than back down.

A few months after his trip to the theatre Churchill addressed the House of Commons. First of all he lauded the granting of remission on the accession of George V which, without ill effects, 'at a stroke struck 500 years of imprisonment and penal servitude from the prison population'. Then he went on to deliver a clarion call that encapsulated both the Christian insistence on the enduring humanity of the individual and the classic liberal view of the grand rehabilitative potential of punishment:

> We must not allow optimism or hope, or benevolence in these matters to carry us too far. We must not forget that when every *material* improvement has been affected in prisons ... the convict stands deprived of everything that a free man calls life. We must not forget that all these improvements, which are sometimes salves to our consciences, do not change that position. The mood and temper of the public in regard to the treatment of crime and criminals is one of the most unfailing tests of the civilisation of any country. A calm, dispassionate recognition of the rights of the accused, and even of the convicted criminal, against the State; a constant heart-searching by all charged with the duty of punishment; a desire and eagerness to rehabilitate in the world of industry those who have paid their due in the hard coinage of punishment; tireless efforts towards the discovery of curative and regenerative processes; unfailing faith that there is a treasure, if you can

---

34 Baxendale, *op. cit.*, pp.51–63.
35 Marrot, *op. cit.*, p.681.
36 Randolph Churchill, *Winston S. Churchill* (London, 1967–9), II, *Young Statesman 1901–1914*, p.1153.

only find it, in the heart of every man: these are the symbols which, in the treatment of crime and criminal, mark and measure the stored-up strength of a nation, and are sign and proof of the living virtue in it.[37]

Churchill, under the influence of Lloyd George, was at the apogee of his radicalism, and played a crucial role in creating the momentum and appetite for change. While drawing up legislative proposals to reduce radically the prison population, he took what immediate action he could, deploying executive clemency more often than was usual. He introduced regular lectures and concerts into convict prisons, mitigated the lot of elderly offenders, expanded the scheme of correspondence courses already in place for borstal boys to adults serving long sentences, and set up a committee to consider the principles that should govern the supply of books to offenders of all ages. He visited prisons, spoke to inmates and took up individual cases with his officials. He was particularly exercised by the fate of the young. Perturbed to find a number of boys serving sentences in Pentonville for trifling offences he cut the Gordian knot by using his powers to secure their early release. He cast a critical eye on borstals, and sought alternatives to custody for all but the most serious of young offenders.

Both the Home Secretary and the chairman agreed that prisoner numbers had to be brought down. With fewer in prison, more could be done for those who remained. In response to Churchill's 'Prison Reform Minute', Ruggles-Brise asserted that there were '125,000 perfectly purposeless short sentences imposed every year, and of these more than half' were for first offences, tramps and drunkards making up the rest. Churchill agreed and told the Prime Minister so, describing the immense number of petty offenders in prison for short sentences as a 'terrible and purposeless waste of public money and human character'.[38] He also knew that in order to reduce numbers he would have to cajole judges, and that to bring about a transformation of the prison regime it was vital to get a new generation into leadership roles. Ruggles-Brise's efforts were paying dividends, as was evidenced by Frederick Martyn in his teasingly titled memoirs, *A Holiday in Gaol*, published in 1911 after his release. He spoke highly of his treatment when he was in Brixton on remand and in Wormwood Scrubs where he served eighteen months of 'hard Labour'. He found that the labour was light except for the staff, the food good, the chaplain saintly and the warders

---

[37] 20 July 1910. *PD*, HC 1910, xix, col.1354f. In this he echoed Dostoevsky's contention in *The House of the Dead* that 'the degree of civilisation in a society can be judged by entering its prisons'.

[38] Churchill, *op. cit.*, II, Companion, Part 2, 1907–1911, pp.1198–1203.

'jolly decent'. His main disappointment was the library which contained not 'a single volume of Carlyle' and 'practically no standard works of History, Biography and Travel'. Martyn was no ordinary criminal, but a graduate and a model prisoner, but he does provide a refreshingly positive view of prison life in the Ruggles-Brise era.[39] This was what Churchill wanted to hear.

In his meagre twenty months in office Churchill had done more for those in prison than any other Home Secretary.[40] His successor, Reginald McKenna, was less interested in penal reform and much less energetic. The Prison Commission was given a breathing space. Nonetheless his tenure in office resulted in another significant piece of legislation: the 1914 Criminal Justice Act. Among other reforms it obliged courts to allow time for the payment of fines, a measure which went far further than the 1898 Act in dramatically reducing the prison population. In 1909–10 over 90,000 fine-defaulters were imprisoned; in 1919–20 it was less than 10,000.[41] It was a trend that would continue for a long time. Between 1908 and 1939 the daily average prison intake halved from 22,000 to 11,000, making it, per head of the general population, amongst the smallest in Europe. Over that period around twenty antiquated prisons were closed and this when the crime rate was rising.[42] By the outbreak of the Second World War, prisons in England and Wales had contracted to a meagre twenty-two. They provided more than an adequate capacity. In Scotland too the number of prisoners and of prisons plummeted.

Never before had there been such a drop, and never would there be again.[43] It was the 'Churchill effect' writ large, providing a unique opportunity for innovation to take root.

---

[39] Frederick Martyn, *A Holiday in Gaol* (London, 1911), especially pp.161–5, 264–78.

[40] This was recognised even by his ideological opponents. Wilfred Macartney, a Communist, blind as ever to the horrors inflicted by his own creed, considered Churchill to be 'one of the most deplorable exponents of vicious reaction'. Yet he acknowledged that he was 'the only Home Secretary who ever showed the slightest understanding of the convict', cut 'through barriers erected by a stupid bureaucracy', and did so much 'to soften the lives of the most unfortunate and most unhappy people in the country'. 'Many old fellows' had said, 'Well, you can talk Socialism or Communism, Mac, but Winston was the only chap who ever helped the lag or did us any good' (*Walls Have Mouths* (London, 1936), pp.26f.).

[41] *Report* (1920), para.21.

[42] Its cells empty, Reading gaol after the Great War became a secure storage for food and surplus army uniforms, as well as a driving test centre (Anthony Stokes, *Pit of Shame* (Winchester, 2007), p.139).

[43] In direct contrast to the dramatic decline after the First World War, after the Second numbers rose inexorably.

CHAPTER 27

Suffer the Little Children

Foolishness is bound in the heart of a child;
but the rod of correction shall drive it far from him.
... Thou shalt beat the child with the rod and so deliver his soul
from hell.

Proverbs 22:15, 23:14

Churchill and his successors were continuing a trend not creating it. The most symbolic year was 1902: it was an end and a beginning. Newgate prison was demolished, ending an eight-hundred-year history of penal notoriety, and the first institution for juvenile-adults, handsomely funded by Asquith who was then Chancellor of the Exchequer, was opened by Ruggles-Brise on the site of an old convict prison – an annexe of Chatham – in Borstal in Kent, starting sixty years of penal optimism.

He was not the first or only reformer who wanted to divert children from the penal system and help juveniles on the cusp of crime. In the second half of the eighteenth century both the Marine Society and the Philanthropic Society had established schools for waifs, strays and the children of convicts. Their work was preventive. Elizabeth Fry, Charles Dickens, Mary Carpenter, Lord Ashley, and Dr Barnardo are notable examples in the nineteenth century of those concerned about the lot of children both without and within the criminal justice system.[1] Their ambitions were reformative as well as preventive. Ultimately many parliamentarians were persuaded to take action. As early as 1811 and 1819 parliamentary inquiries had condemned the incarceration of young children, but to little effect. Pressure grew especially when reports of a child of three being imprisoned for contempt of court, and a six-year-old homeless vagrant being kept in silent and solitary

---

[1] On the death of his father in 1851 Ashley became earl of Shaftesbury. He campaigned against the employment of young children down the mines, where many were put to 'hard labour' for sixteen hours a day in 'solitary confinement'. Joseph Kingsmill, in a work dedicated to Shaftesbury, said of his labours in this arena that 'our times have more need of an Ashley than a Howard' (*Prisons and Prisoners*, 2nd edn (London, 1852), p.422).

confinement, came to public attention.[2] In 1838 the Parkhurst Prison Act created out of a former military hospital on the Isle of Wight a national 'Reformatory' for 120 boys under the age of twelve and 200 aged between twelve and seventeen sentenced to transportation or imprisonment. The regime was intended to be as reformative as corrective.[3] Ten years later Redhill Farm School was established by the Philanthropic Society as an agricultural colony for boys. The 1847 Juvenile Offenders Act, the 1854 Reformatory School Act ('the Magna Carta of the neglected child') and the 1857 Industrial School Act made provision for the education, training and correction of delinquents under the age of sixteen in reformatories such as the re-designated Redhill, and of truants and neglected children under fourteen in industrial schools. There would soon be sixty-five of the former and fifty of the latter, providing places for 7,500 children.[4] They were established by voluntary bodies but part-funded by the state. Parkhurst was made redundant as a result of a collapse in the number of young convicts and closed for juveniles in 1864.

As the proportion of young people in the population increased, concern about the depredations of out-of-control youngsters grew. Although more and more were placed in these charitably-run institutions, and after 1866 none was sent to a convict establishment, too many juveniles under sixteen as well as young people under twenty-one remained in state-run prisons. Take the case of twelve-year-old Henry Stephenson and his thirteen-year-old friend Michael Fisher. In 1872, despite being of good family and previous

---

2 William Hepworth Dixon, *The London Prisons* (London, 1850), p.349; John Horsley, *Prisons and Prisoners* (London, 1898), p.126.

3 *Extracts*, pp.195–9; Du Cane, pp.202f. Du Cane approved of preventive measures for the young, but cynicism about mollycoddling ragamuffins was commonplace. Chesterton wrote wryly that 'when the juvenile prison at Parkhurst was first instituted, and the superior condition of its inmates extorted the satirical designation of "a seminary for young gentlemen", I was actually importuned by the mothers of boys, frequenters of the prison, to use my influence to procure for their sons, admission into Parkhurst'. It has been a trope for reactionaries ever since. In fact discipline was harsh, food poor and trade training substandard, although the educational provision was very good (W.J. Forsythe, *The Reform of Prisoners 1830–1900* (Beckenham, 1987), pp.125ff.).

4 Industrial schools were of three kinds: the Ordinary where children were detained for several years; the Truant where they were detained for a few weeks; and the Day where they lived at home but got elementary education and industrial training in the school. In 1933 the Children and Young Person's Act abolished the distinction between reformatory and industrial schools and they were renamed 'approved schools'. The normal age of committal was raised to ten, the maximum to seventeen, thus overlapping with borstals by one year and allowing the courts a discretion to send a sixteen-year-old to one or the other. They lasted until 1969.

good character, and despite their offending spree being attributed to the baneful effects of William Harrison Ainsworth's novel, *Jack Sheppard*, which romanticised the notorious felon of that name, these juvenile desperados respectively received two and four months' imprisonment with hard labour, sentences served in Newcastle gaol. At least they were spared whipping, as the Recorder who passed sentence considered it to 'be a terrible degradation'. Many another juvenile offender would be so degraded. In the very same year Durham magistrates ordered three twelve-year-old boys to be birched for petty thieving.[5]

Ainsworth, a prolific and popular novelist, had a lot to answer for. In 1873 'One who has endured it' encountered 'two very decent-looking and respectably-dressed lads' in Newgate awaiting trial for seriously injuring an elderly housekeeper who had discovered the brothers committing a burglary. They beat her on the head with a hammer and left her 'weltering in her blood'. He blamed their schooling. 'Instead of studying Euclid and Delectus' they had been reading penny dreadfuls such as *Jack Sheppard*. This was confirmed when later he shared a cell in Millbank with the elder of the two. He found, from a few questions he asked of the boy, 'that his head had been stuffed with the rubbish he had read of gentlemen pirates, highwaymen and bandit captains'. The thirteen-year-old was sentenced to seven years while his younger brother, whom he admitted coercing into the deed, got two.[6]

Despite the deleterious impact of second-rate literature on unformed minds, the number of juveniles in prison was falling. Contrasting the current intake with earlier times Du Cane could boast that by 1884 in all England and Wales there were '*only* 275 prisoners under sixteen years of age, and 3,226 between sixteen and twenty-one'.[7] Nonetheless he welcomed reducing these numbers further. And so he should as it was still the case in 1885 that children were being sent to prison 'simply for being homeless and friendless, and as such committing the "crime" of sleeping out'.[8] In 1887, at the height of his sway, parliament enacted the Probation of First Offenders Act which permitted the conditional release from prison of well-behaved first offenders 'when expedient', taking into account the 'youth, character and antecedents of the offender and any extenuating circumstances'. In 1850 there were 15,000 juveniles in prison, but fifty years later there were merely 2,000. Yet

5   Barry Redfern, *Victorian Villains, Prisoners from Newcastle Gaol 1871–1873* (Newcastle, 2006), pp.88–91.

6   Anon., *Five Years' Penal Servitude*, 2nd edn (London, 1878), pp.31, 66f.

7   Du Cane, p.201. My italicisation.

8   Horsley, *op. cit.*, p.127.

PRESENTED BY ALEXR. PATERSON (BORSTAL
COMMISSIONER OF PRISONS) TO THE
FOUNDER OF BORSTAL,

SIR EVELYN RUGGLES-BRISE K.C.B.

as a slight tribute to his Faith and Vision in delivering
the Young Offender from the methods of earlier times.

BOYS IN PORTSMOUTH PRISON, 1899 -

(*THREE YEARS BEFORE THE INTRODUCTION OF THE BORSTAL SYSTEM*)

F. P. *Age 11$\frac{10}{12}$*   A. P., *Age 13$\frac{8}{12}$*

THEIR OFFENCE :- *Wilful damage to a door (throwing mortar at it.)*
SENTENCE :- *5 days' Hard Labour, or 7s. 6d.*

[121]

28. Acknowledging a debt

around a quarter of these were imprisoned under the Vagrancy Laws, and for begging or obstructing the highway by selling in the streets. To be poor or homeless was akin to being a criminal. It was rightly feared that out of these indigent urchins the criminal classes were being replenished.[9]

Ruggles-Brise shared this fear but joined it with outrage. He had found it 'a heart-rending sight to go into any prison in those days and see mere lads, almost children, dressed in prison garb, cheek by jowl with the ordinary adult offender, in most cases under very short sentences in lieu of paying a fine for some trivial offence' or for 'sleeping rough'. One fourteen-year-old boy whom Colonel Rich met in Wakefield prison in 1906 had been sent there because he had dropped a banana skin on the pavement. He had been sentenced to a fine of five shillings or seven days' hard labour in default. At the time there was no alternative punishment for this little 'litter-lout'. His father refused to pay, and so his son spent a week in prison.[10] For some this may have been 'the short, sharp shock'; for Ruggles-Brise it was just shocking. Others also found it so. Cosmo Gordon Lang, vicar of Portsea and future archbishop of Canterbury, emulated Oscar Wilde in writing movingly to the press. In 1901 in a letter to *The Times* he deplored incarcerating, for foolish pranks, boys of fifteen or sixteen for days in a prison with felons followed by years in a reformatory with ruffians. As chaplain to the local prison, he had heard the sobs of poor, hungry, bewildered boys, before he had even entered their cells. Was this how we should redeem them from a life of crime?

Ruggles-Brise was sure it was not, and he could do more than deplore. He could act. He modified the treatment of young prisoners held in Holloway, directing more exercise, employment and instruction, and with parliamentary sanction he put an end to children ending up behind bars. He was determined that an alternative to prison for older youths, 'juvenile-adults' as they were clumsily called, one that would mend and not destroy their lives, must be found. In 1900 he had planted the acorn by sending a small group of specially chosen 'London lads' to a separate unit in Bedford prison, one of the smallest local prisons in England, to undergo 'specialised training'. After three months the governor reported that the scheme had exceeded his most sanguine expectations but urged that provision be made for after-care. The experiment had worked, and as a result a juvenile-adult class was permanently established. Ominously the members of a visiting committee at Bedford deprecated 'most strongly' short sentences for juveniles and felt

---

[9]   Charles Russell and Lillian Rigby, *The Making of the Criminal* (London, 1906), p.7.

[10]   Rich, p.84.

that in many cases they were 'worse than useless'. They urged 'that power be given to magistrates to increase the sentences in the case of young prisoners in order that a thorough and efficient training may be given'.[11]

Ruggles-Brise was sympathetic to this plea. Just as he believed that all human beings were unique, Ruggles-Brise believed in the 'individualisation of punishment', a marked break with his predecessor's emphasis on uniformity – all prisoners being treated the same. As a concomitant he also believed in indeterminate (but not indefinite) sentences, a fixation, if taken to extremes, that has bedevilled many a prison reformer. It was first championed in America. The rationale was benign as well as protective. Crime is a disease needing treatment, sometimes lengthy treatment, and to secure a cure the length of time as an in-patient could not be curtailed. Short or even long determinate sentences undermined this treatment model, and would result in re-offending.

The answer for adult 'habitual criminals' was to detain them under sentences of preventive detention until they were 'cured' or too infirm to pose a risk, a move the eugenics movement had strongly advocated. Eugenics, native in origin and thus more palatable in England than positivism, had become increasingly influential since the turn of the century and would remain in vogue for many years to come, spurred on by fears of national decline resulting from the disasters of the Boer War and a 'craving for a scientific treatment of the problems of social life'. To tame the born criminal, the resolute segregation of habitual criminals 'under merciful surveillance' had been proposed by Galton himself.[12] In 1912 Ruggles-Brise opened Camp Hill, a state-of-the-art prison on the Isle of Wight, for the purpose of holding those serving out the second, non-punitive, phase of sentences of preventive detention. Its regime was permissive and relaxed, but survived criticisms of being 'luxurious' by its success in releasing increasing numbers of detainees on licence. The rub was that 'incurables' could be detained for prolonged periods. Injustice could be the bed-fellow of good intentions.

In line with the recommendations of the Gladstone Committee, Ruggles-Brise sought to circumvent this problem with regard to 'young hooligans' habituated to crime. Adopting and adapting its proposal for a 'penal reformatory', he introduced perhaps the most innovative penological development of the twentieth century. Borstal treatment or training, his great creation, was to be primarily reformative and so was suitable for

---

[11] *Report* (1904), p.26.

[12] P. Vinogradoff, *The Teaching of Sir Henry Maine* (Oxford, 1904), p.11; Radzinowicz, p.32.

hardened young criminals but not for those 'who had lapsed into some petty or occasional delinquency'.[13] It was for an undefined but limited period of up to three years. Three years could be far longer than the prison sentence that would otherwise have been imposed for the crime, but was deemed the ideal period for rehabilitative efforts to achieve their ends. Long-term benefit required long-term detention, and, after it, release would be on licence.

On the banks of the river Medway not far from Rochester and Chatham is the village of Borstal. It would be the cradle of, and give its name to, an institution which embodied the ideal of a fresh start, under more conducive conditions than most of the youngsters who ended up there from the London prisons had ever previously experienced. In October 1902 'Fort Borstal', the converted convict prison with its high walls and gates, was opened as the first Juvenile-Adult Prison, the old architecture somewhat at war with the new ethos. Its young inmates were to be smartened up. They were to be given an opportunity to redeem their lives. The regime was based on the reformatory principles of Maconochie and Crofton, and was designed to be 'educational rather than punitive'.

The boys would be instructed in 'useful trades and industries which may fit them to earn their livelihood on release', and were also permitted library books. Arthur Harding, an East End lad and long-term 'villain', would first read Dickens there, the novel of course being *Oliver Twist*. The first governor, 'the immaculately dressed Mr Western', was 'keen to make the new system a success', and would 'visit the lads in their cells and urge them to do well in a trade'.[14]

Nonetheless, in its early days the regime was highly regulated, with a focus on a rigorous routine, strenuous physical exercise, hard work, 'strict penal discipline' and obedience to authority. To convince the public that the worst excesses of Elmira had been avoided it was emphasised and evidenced that deterrence was never neglected and there was 'no undue pampering'.[15] Good conduct won modest rewards; bad behaviour was severely punished. Borstal was not a soft option. Boys were sent there under a sentence imposed by the courts, the first arrivals being taken there in chains, and borstals remained very much part of the prison estate.

'Strict classification', however, was impossible until more borstals came on stream, and so with this experiment successfully underway, the

---

[13] Evelyn Ruggles-Brise, *The English Prison System* (London, 1921), pp.92f. The term 'borstal training' did not get statutory recognition until 1948.

[14] Raphael Samuel, *East End Underworld: Chapters in the Life of Arthur Harding* (London, 1981), p.74. Harding erred. The first governor was Major Blake.

[15] Russell and Rigby, *op. cit.*, p.126.

commissioners, with parliamentary approval, encouraged the sapling to grow into a many-branched tree. In 1903 the scheme was extended in a modified version to young convicts undergoing sentences of penal servitude at Dartmoor – 'the worst that can be found in England and Wales'. The governor reported his 'agreeable surprise' at the outcome. Young criminals in the hardest of prisons, given the right discipline and encouragement, could be changed.[16] It was revelatory. Soon all the 'star-class' juvenile-adults were moved from other convict prisons to Dartmoor. They were put to useful work and given an extensive education in such practical subjects as science, mathematics, geography and drawing, as well as 'Roman history for moral instruction'. From the very beginning, however, the borstal system sat uneasily within the existing penal structure. It allowed for a degree of empathy and individualised treatment utterly alien to the rest of the prison system, and utterly novel to most of the existing prison staff who had previously been forbidden from having any personal interaction with prisoners other than barking orders. Getting to know their charges was unheard of, now it was *de rigueur*. The quality and adaptability of staff would be crucial to success. 'Of all the human factors making for reformation', Ruggles-Brise considered that 'the greatest is the personal influence of good and manly men' who should 'take a keen personal interest in the training and rehabilitation of those placed in their charge'. While disciplinary officers continued to wear uniforms, teachers who were introduced did not. Nor later did 'tutors'. From 1919 they became a feature of the system with the rank of deputy-governors. While expected to be 'an adjutant to the governor in maintaining strict discipline, and a due observance of order and method in every particular', they embodied something new:

> They are in a sense housemasters, or masters of sections or wings of inmates. They are selected for their special qualifications for dealing with lads of this age and character, each of whom it is their duty to 'individualise', i.e. to observe closely.[17]

Tutors had not been shaped by prior experience of prisons. They brought a fresh perspective to an entirely novel role. They were to run the prototype of the quasi-public school 'house system' which Ruggles-Brise introduced in the same year as their deployment, to develop 'the spirit of friendly rivalry and competition among inmates by dividing the establishment into different

---

16 Roger Hood, *Borstal Reassessed* (London, 1965), p.15.
17 Ruggles-Brise, *op. cit.*, pp.98f. 'Lads' is borstal terminology, used, interchangeably with 'boys', even in official reports.

sections or "houses", so that something like the public school spirit may be generated'.[18] While governors and tutors welcomed this novel approach, it could be bewildering and confusing for many of the ordinary disciplinary staff whose role was ill-defined and, they feared, undermined.[19]

Trainee involvement with sympathetic visitors who would mentor them while serving their sentences and assist them on release was also encouraged. To this effect Ruggles-Brise encouraged the formation of the Borstal Association in 1904, under the patronage of the Home Secretary, the archbishop of Canterbury and the Lord Chief Justice, as an organisation for helping discharged 'borstalians'.[20] This was the successor body to the London Prison Visitors' Association, a voluntary after-care scheme that Ruggles-Brise had helped establish three years earlier, the members of which had assisted in Pentonville, Wandsworth and Wormwood Scrubs before being tasked with giving special attention to the boys in Bedford prison who would be discharged to the London district. The Borstal Association would have a long and important part to play in future developments. Its chairman, the barrister Sir Wemyss Grant-Wilson, would put his stamp upon it and shape its future. He was self-confident and outspoken, and so too would be his Association. He was kindly but authoritative, and kindly but authoritative mentoring was what he demanded of his volunteers. Supervision on release as well as gainful employment were thought to be vital factors in preventing re-offending, and providing the one and helping find the other were tasks these 'earnest and philanthropic gentlemen' could perform. They were the social superiors of their charges, and could command respect and deference – or dismay. With patronage coming from the upper echelons of the State, the Church and the Law, the Association also had clout within respectable circles and influence with employers, not all of whom were eager to take on offenders.[21] Emigration for some and seafaring for many seemed ideal alternatives. Both would provide a fresh start, a milder version of transportation. Unfunded and independent, and with growing confidence and reputation, in time the Association would prove a Trojan horse, as its

---

18 *Report* (1920), para.27.

19 J.E. Thomas, *The English Prison Officer since 1850* (London, 1972), p.139.

20 Nor were adults neglected. In 1910 a government-funded umbrella organisation, the Central Association for the Aid of Discharged Convicts, was established to bring cohesion to the myriad of voluntary bodies hitherto involved in aftercare.

21 Sydney Moseley, *The Truth about Borstal* (London, 1926), p.xii. Jack Gordon bitterly contrasted the expectations raised by borstal training itself, and the rosy future promised, with the harsh reality of inadequate after-care, poor lodgings, lack of employment and the stigma attached to being a 'borstal boy' (J.W. Gordon, *Borstalians* (London, 1932), pp.210–17).

members were amongst the first to criticise the prison character of borstal and to question Ruggles-Brise's depiction of the inmates as 'young hooligans advanced in crime'. At present they were content to testify to his creation's success. Low reconviction rates published in its early annual reports provided a 'remarkable justification for the experiment'.[22]

This initial success had exceeded all expectations – and not just the low ones of the Gladstone Committee – and allowed for steady growth. In 1904 the commissioners proposed that the principles of the borstal scheme should be extended nationwide and that all offenders aged sixteen to twenty-one sentenced to twelve months or more – six months was deemed too short to be effective – should be eligible. But not all could be accommodated in Borstal. At least as a stop-gap, prisons would have to be adapted so that the impressionable and improvable young would be separated from adults, live in 'rooms' as their cells were called,[23] be put under a regime where strict discipline, hard work, military drill and physical exercise would coexist with morally improving lectures and talks, and be provided with after-care by the Borstal Association. Within two years this 'modified borstal system' was put into effect, with a wing of Lincoln prison being designated to receive boys from the north of England for training and, as already mentioned, part of Dartmoor being converted to a similar regime for young male convicts sentenced to penal servitude. Liverpool was one of many that followed suit. When the first borstal for girls was opened in 1909 it was within the confines of Aylesbury prison which along with the new intake of borstal girls continued to hold women in a separate wing. In 1910 Holloway incorporated a 'modified borstal' for girls, and at the end of the same year Canterbury incorporated a borstal institution 'for the reception of intractable cases from Borstal and Feltham and for those whose licences had been revoked'.[24] The constant refrain from these prisons was that the sentences were too short to produce the anticipated results.

If the sentences were to be longer, if more young people were to undergo them, then prisons, it was increasingly thought, were hardly the ideal environment for such endeavours. Borstal – or Rochester as it is usually called – should have siblings untarnished by the stigma of prison birth. When Feltham in Middlesex was chosen by the prison commissioners in 1911 as the site of their second boys' borstal institution, the choice was

---

[22] Shane Leslie, *Sir Evelyn Ruggles-Brise* (London, 1938), pp.142f.; Hood, *op. cit.*, p.204.

[23] Some boys called them 'floweries', an ironical term as they were 'so much unlike flower gardens': Gordon, *op. cit.*, p.59. Gordon must be right about the term, but the explanation is unconvincing. Perhaps it was the place where 'lads' were meant to flower.

[24] *Report* (1911–12, part II), p.170.

significant: it had never been a prison but an industrial school. Most of the new buildings would be constructed by borstal boys themselves, and the whole place within a few years would have 'the appearance of a pretty garden colony', with acres of land, a farm, a swimming-pool, playing fields, a broad tree-lined avenue and well-kept flower beds, all surrounded by a wall a mere seven feet high.[25] In the same year Polmont, the first borstal in Scotland, was opened in the former Blairlodge Academy in Stirlingshire. Ireland already had its first borstal – St Patrick's at Clonmel in County Tipperary – in 1906.[26] Foreshadowing future developments, Ruggles-Brise even proposed the creation of an open borstal in pioneer conditions. The outbreak of the Great War in 1914 put paid to this, as it did to many things.

It did not, however, retard the downward trend in prisoner numbers. Whereas in 1883 there were 622 persons in prison for every hundred thousand of the population, by 1914 it was down to 369, and after the war it dwindled to as low as seventy, perhaps hardly surprising as so many young working-class men – prime prison-fodder – had become cannon-fodder in the conflict. Nonetheless this diminution and the apparent impact of borstals in cutting off recidivism at its source created an expectation that the number of prisons would soon be halved, and indeed between 1914 and 1930 fifteen of the twenty-six local prisons were closed. The commissioners were lauded for having produced a system which heralded 'an epoch in the treatment of juvenile crime'.[27] They had found the elusive Holy Grail of penal success. Borstals, after the war, would spring up throughout the British Isles, and would eventually spread throughout the Empire.

During the Great War itself, however, borstals and 'modified borstals' were denuded of their intake as the needs of the armed forces took precedence. With the exception of Feltham which was used for prisoners-of-war, they became in effect short-term training camps rather than long-term rehabilitative institutions, and very early release for those eligible for military service was commonplace. Thus, after hostilities ceased, the borstals had to be revived and their purpose restored. Demobilised army and naval officers, with much experience of training, disciplining, leading and inspiring young men, were ideal recruits to run such establishments, and many wanted to do so. Colonel Charles Rich, who already had extensive experience working in prisons before the war, was one; Major Benjamin

---

[25] Gordon, *op. cit.*, pp.83f.

[26] For the Irish experience see Nial Osborough's *Borstal in Ireland: Custodial Provision for the Young Adult Offender, 1906–1974* (Dublin, 1975).

[27] Lord Yarborough, speaking at Lincoln: *The Times*, 29 January 1906.

Grew another. In January 1920 the former took charge of Borstal itself, with its four hundred lads. The latter joined him three years later as his deputy. Sir Arthur Conan Doyle, who visited Borstal, was very impressed by what he observed there and by Rich himself, 'a tall and handsome' man, with 'a pleasant voice and wise, kind eyes' and with 'more of the university in his appearance and bearing than of the army'. Conan Doyle would have happily entrusted his own son 'to that man's guardianship', a man whom he considered 'hand-picked' for the task.[28]

And it was some task. Post-war disillusionment and lack of opportunity had had a demoralising effect. Absconding was a problem, and the place was porous, but there was worse. Shortly before Rich arrived, the officer in charge of the punishment block had been killed by one of his many charges. Ruggles-Brise urged the new governor to take a firm hand and restore staff confidence and inmate compliance.

This he did by reorganising the institution 'in such a way as to bring up the standard of discipline and to create ... a better sort of "school spirit"'. This involved imposing strict military discipline – but with no flogging although he thoroughly approved of it for adults – and an insistence on 'politeness' and deferential respect to those in authority. 'I impressed upon them', he later wrote, 'that when addressing an officer it was their duty to stand to attention, salute and call him "sir"'. He considered that 'one wholesome thing ... was the uniformed officer', the uniform constantly reminding the 'lad that he was in a penal establishment, and not merely in "a home"'.[29] He was upholding the stated aims of Ruggles-Brise of punishing, deterring and training, and was doing so by combining 'the strictest discipline' with 'a humane inculcation of hard work, obedience, respect, and good manners'. In September the public were invited to a sports day which included 'grenade throwing', 'bayonet display', and a mock infantry battle, culminating in a rendition of 'Rule Britannia' with the daughter of one of the wardens taking the title role.[30] When the Home Secretary, Edward Shortt, visited he was accorded a march-past by the boys and their excellent band, which in musicality and appearance rivalled that of the nearby garrison. Martial music, military manoeuvres and pride in patriotism would make rough lads into loyal men. If this was the inculcation of public school values, it was those of the cadet corps.

---

28 Article in *The Daily Telegraph*, reproduced in Rich, pp.116–20.

29 Rich, pp.214–19.

30 W.J. Forsythe, *Penal Discipline, Reformatory Projects and the English Prison Commission, 1895–1939* (Exeter, 1991), p.54.

To the outside world, Rich 'conveyed the impression ... that he was a military martinet and a perfect terror to those under him who in any way transgressed the rules'. Thus he tranquillised opposition while in reality his regime became ever more benign and therapeutic. The environment of confinement was transformed, as Grew, on his arrival, noted. He had expected 'a much more formidable establishment'. What he found was not 'a training ground to prepare a lad to be a soldier, but a school to help him face the rigours of the battlefield of life':

> Lawns and flower-beds in the grounds were neatly laid out and well cared for by the boys themselves. What at one time had been a sinister prison of narrow galleries and tiny cells had been partially transformed into not unattractive buildings with roomy classrooms, dining halls and pleasant sleeping quarters.[31]

Rich attributed his own success to a combination of laying down strict routine and clear boundaries and encouraging industry and application. It was a classic case of instilling order and then relaxing restraints. He had told the lads to see him as a friend and as governor but never to forget he was both. He received many appreciative letters from his former charges, not all of whom he thought should have been there. He deprecated the tendency of the courts to bend the legislation and send ever more minor offenders to borstal 'for their own good'. He did not think that those who pilfered apples or played football in the street should be associating with criminals or building up resentment at disproportionate punishment. Probation would be better suited for the likes of these.[32]

His reforms included the institution of Ruggles-Brise's innovatory 'House System', whereby boys were allocated to 'Houses' to which they would develop a loyalty and in which they could be closely monitored and counselled by housemasters who knew them well. Those boys who proved themselves trustworthy would be made 'monitors' or 'prefects' and given appropriate auxiliary responsibilities. The old halls which became the new houses were renamed in honour of Borstal's four governors: 'A Hall' becoming Blake House, 'C Hall' Eccles House , 'D Hall' Winder House, and 'B Hall' being named after Rich himself.[33]

---

[31] Grew, p.17.

[32] *Report* (1921), p.51.

[33] Grew, p.22. Maurice Waller regarded Captain W.V. Eccles, who died in 1916, as 'the only real genius' the commissioners had yet found (letter to Herbert Gladstone in 1912, in Alan Baxendale, 'Maurice Wyndham Waller', in *Prison Service People* (Newbold Revel, 1993), p.32).

In 1922 he scored another first when the newly-appointed prison commissioner, Alexander Paterson, suggested that he take some of the better-behaved boys to Deal on a summer camp. Rich complied and 120 boys benefited as a result. The fortnight's excursion was almost without mishap as the camp was run 'on strict military lines', much to the approbation of the locals.[34] It was not quite what Paterson had had in mind, however.

Rich had also established a quarterly magazine called *The Borstalian*, to record notable events and achievements in Borstal and give admonitory advice. In its first issue in July 1923 Rich advised his charges to make the best of their lot but not aspire to higher things, and warned of the dangers of trade unions – 'the workers' ruin and a curse to the country'. As he was about to depart for his new posting in Liverpool's Walton gaol, its October edition gave its originator a fond farewell in an article entitled '*Vale*', in which those he was about to fly saluted him. He was not soon forgotten, as an article in the April 1924 edition indicated. It was simply headed 'Rich':

> There is one thing about the House – no one ever asks us what 'Rich' means. Colonel Rich, our patron, is known to most of the lads of the Institution and to all the staff. We feel justly proud that the founder of the House System in Borstal should grace our House with his name. If the House lives up to the standard he set we shall not do badly.

Rich commented that this was proof 'that strict discipline does not of necessity imply the absence of an affectionate relationship'.[35] Ruggles-Brise would have agreed.

But his era had already come to an end and he knew it. In 1921, with three borstals for boys – Rochester, Feltham and Portland – and one for girls at Aylesbury established as part of the penal landscape, Ruggles-Brise resigned.[36] At a dinner in his honour Asquith presented him with a portrait to which 1,500 people, including three convicts, had subscribed. The former

---

[34] Rich, pp.100f. Of one young university man Paterson had sent along to help, who 'habitually walked about in a rather tight and scanty bathing-suit ... was far too familiar with the lads' and hated them calling him 'sir', he commented acerbically that 'the gentleman in question was later appointed as a housemaster ... possibly his views coincided with those of the high official [Paterson] who was by this time more or less running the prison service'. Paterson certainly did import into the prison service Oxford friends, some of whom had worked with him in Bermondsey (John Watson, *Which Is the Justice?* (London, 1969), p.64).

[35] Rich, pp.82–6, 91, 111f., 122. In Walton, Rich, 'one of Nature's gentlemen', received a similar written appreciation from the 'star-class' for his 'courtesy and kindness' (p.198).

[36] Only one girls' borstal was necessary as far fewer females ended up in custody than males. In the year ended 31 March 1921 there were 568 boys and 73 girls committed to borstal (Ruggles-Brise, *op. cit.*, p.94; H&B, p.415).

Prime Minister looked upon his appointee as a personal refutation of the fallacy widely held that 'the Civil Service was peopled by a pampered brood of idlers fattening on the resources of the exhausted taxpayers', and attributed his success to him being a humanitarian without being a 'sentimentalist'. Herbert Gladstone wrote that he 'had reconditioned the prison service' and would always 'stand in the front rank of prison reformers'. The Borstal Association, long a critic but always a friend, agreed that he could justly claim to have 'made a revolution within the prison system and in the attitude of the judiciary and the public to the treatment of the young offender'. Among the qualities it sought in his successor was a similar 'undaunted belief in progress which has inspired and directed his development of the borstal system'.[37]

Not all were so enamoured. Radicals thought him too reactionary, reactionaries thought him too radical. Of the former, Hobhouse and Brockway gave vent to this sentiment in their magnum opus, *English Prisons Today*.[38] Of the latter, thrice times Lord Chancellor, Lord Halsbury, was scathing of his efforts, while the eminent judge, Mr Justice Darling, mocked them as emanating from some disturbance of the brain he called 'Ruggles-Brisia'.[39] But the critics were outnumbered by his influential friends who recognised his extraordinary achievements and whose support he had assiduously cultivated. Just like Elizabeth Fry he knew the value of ingratiating himself with 'the great and the good'. He also knew the importance of steady but sure. He was a Robert Peel not a Thomas Payne. He was a reformer not a revolutionary.

Just before he retired he published his apologia, *The English Prison System*, which appropriately enough was printed at Maidstone prison by convicts. Detailing the advances made under his leadership, culminating in the borstal system which had converted 'the inveterate gaol-bird of a few years ago to a strong, well-set-up, well-drilled, handy English lad, with respect for authority, with a new birth-right, qualifying him to enter the ranks of honest, industrious labour', it emanated hope, along with faith and charity.[40] It remains a memorial to his life's work. It is not the only one. At his funeral in 1935 when he was borne to his last resting-place by six senior prison officers, among the large wreaths was a bunch of flowers 'to the memory

---

37 *The Times*, 29 August 1921; *Borstal Association Journal* (1921), pp.2f.
38 H&B, pp.74–85.
39 Leslie, *op. cit.*, pp.147, 168.
40 Ruggles-Brise, *op. cit.*, p.99.

of a humane man, Sir Evelyn Ruggles-Brise KCB. He saved me from the cat. Convict No 2148.'[41] Inscribed on the gateway of Borstal is his epitaph:

> He determined to save the young and careless from a wasted life of crime. Through his vision and persistence, a system of repression has been gradually replaced by one of leadership and training. We shall remember him as one who believed in his fellow men.

Despite criticism that he did not go far enough, he went as far as he could, and what he did endured. His colleagues agreed that 'the period of his administration marked a definite epoch in the history of the English prison system – from the purely punitive to the reconstructive and reformative'.[42] Not entirely. Punishment and deterrence remained primary, and for adult offenders reform still had a lesser priority. He had fulfilled the aims set by the SIPD a hundred years earlier. He had improved 'prison discipline' and created the borstal system to reform juveniles. The Great War set things back in that regard, but in the post-war period he went much further in transforming the ethos of borstals. Despite his detractors, his name will long be associated with the rehabilitative ideal and attempting to make it a realistic one in the context of his time. The fact that Du Cane would have been appalled by the transformation his successor had wrought is Ruggles-Brise's greatest vindication.

One group of prisoners were beyond rehabilitation, if not redemption: those condemned to die. Even for them Ruggles-Brise had tried to ensure their ending would be as smooth and swift as possible. The long walk to the scaffold was rendered obsolete by the expedient of building the gallows next to the condemned cell. It was one of the many 'humane improvements' that allowed hanging to persist for longer than might otherwise have been the case.

[41] Leslie, *op. cit.*, p.209.
[42] *Report* (1934), p.46.

CHAPTER 28

Sanitising Death

There sleeps in Shrewsbury jail to-night,
  Or wakes, as may betide,
A better lad, if things went right,
  Than most that sleep outside.

And naked to the hangman's noose
  The morning clocks will ring
A neck God made for other use
  Than strangling on a string.

A.E. Housman

The execution of a murderer is a solemn ritual act and its object is not only to demonstrate that murder does not pay but that it is shameful. The penalty is not only death, but death with ignominy. The death penalty fulfils this role in an unequalled way because of this quasi-religious sense of awe which attaches to it.

Mervyn Haigh, bishop of Winchester

Until 1868 all hangings remained public. That was their point: to punish offenders near the scenes of their crimes or outside the local prison and, by the public and prominent nature of their deaths, to deter others. In practice public executions were popular entertainment, where large festive crowds gathered, much drink was consumed, and pickpockets plied their trade with impunity. A deterrent it was not; a disgrace it was. So thought Thackeray, Dickens, and Hardy, all three of whom witnessed executions and wrote about what they had witnessed. Georgians had been exercised by the proliferation of capital statutes, most of which had been repealed by the mid-nineteenth century. Victorians were exercised by the execution procedure itself and the indecency of what had become an 'open-air entertainment'. Abolitionist sentiment was growing and by the middle of the nineteenth century seemed in the ascendancy.[1]

Anglican clergy were concerned by this development, and none more so than those pioneers of penitence, prison chaplains. The death penalty, unlike transportation for instance, was a sentence of Scripture, ordained of God,

---

[1] On this whole subject see Harry Potter, *Hanging in Judgement* (London, 1993), *passim*.

while the pre-execution period provided a unique evangelical opportunity. The redemption of the worst is the best, and, as Dr Johnson put it, 'when a man knows he is to be hanged in a fortnight it concentrates his mind wonderfully'. To save the soul the noose was necessary. To save the noose it was necessary to sanitise its operation.

So thought the bishop of Oxford, Samuel Wilberforce, son of the great emancipator. He believed that the continuation of hanging was essential to the highest principles of justice, but feared that its continued public manifestation would lead to abolition. In 1856 a report of a select committee of the House of Lords, which he chaired, concluded that the open-air despatch of felons was by no means deterrent in its effect. It hardened those who witnessed it. It made heroes and martyrs out of base criminals. It reduced to drunken merrymaking what should be a most solemn and awful occasion. It brought hanging into disrepute. Wilberforce recommended that public executions be abolished and private ones within the fine, new prisons be substituted. To add to the solemnity a black flag should be hoisted over the gates to indicate to those assembled outside that 'the law had taken its course'. So it was to be. In 1866 a Royal Commission chaired by the duke of Richmond urged the same course of action, and in 1868 parliament passed the Capital Punishment Amendment Act. Public executions were ended and prisons became the places of ultimate punishment, a position they would hold until the demise of the death penalty a century later. On the morning of 13 August 1868, at Maidstone gaol, Thomas Wells, aged eighteen, was the first person to be hanged behind prison walls. Present were sixteen reporters from the press. Hanging might be secluded, but the public were represented by proxy, and in the comfort of their homes upright Victorians could savour in lurid detail the final, fatal moments of the condemned.[2]

Prison governors were unanimously in favour of sequestration. It fitted perfectly with the whole trend of prisons turning in on themselves, of their walls not only keeping prisoners in but increasingly keeping the public out. Even those such as Henry Cartwright of Gloucester prison, who preferred total abolition, were prepared to condone intramural executions 'as being more deterrent ... for greater solemnity, and more humane'.[3] These fortresses for felons, centred around religiosity and decorum, and with all the old riotous cacophony of institutional life suppressed, provided a perfect setting into which executions could be removed from the ribaldry of the street and sacralised behind high walls. These intimidating edifices would provide an

2 *Maidstone and Kentish Journal*, 17 August 1868.
3 *Royal Commission Evidence*, paras.1148–263.

appropriate backdrop to the awe-inspiring execution spectacle and allow for far greater crowd control. Seemly and safe. The ritual itself would be transformed. From then on, street theatre – in theory a medieval mystery play, in practice a 'Saturnalia of Sin' – before an untutored and dissolute audience was replaced by a sequestered morality play, where the condemned would be sacrificed with solemnity and decency and expedition, out of the gaze yet in the presence of their fellow criminals, and before a select group of dignitaries – the chaplain, the governor, and the Lord Lieutenant of the county. The time between sentence and execution was increased from a few days to several weeks. Scaffold confessions yielded to condemned cell confirmations. The quick drop replaced slow strangulation, and death would be as instantaneous as eternal life was assured.

As had been feared, this more seemly display of the ultimate power of the state emasculated further attempts at total abolition. Interest flagged, and the 'storm which once seemed to be gathering has subsided and been followed by a great calm'. Abolition had 'ceased to have a place among the real questions of the day'.[4] To ensure that this happy state continued, successive governments strove to perfect the procedure, to implement best practice and to keep quiet about any mishaps. It was necessary continually to sanitise the procedure to preserve the practice.

In 1886 the Conservative Home Secretary, Sir Richard Cross, set up a departmental committee under Lord Aberdare, a former Liberal Home Secretary, to inquire into existing practice and to ensure that in future 'all executions might be carried out in a becoming manner'. It reported two years later, concluding that if the drop were too short the victim would suffocate slowly, if too long decapitation could result which, though the lesser of two evils, was both 'revolting in itself and affecting the public imagination'. To obviate these problems it recommended the adoption of a uniform scaffold apparatus, a standard length and thickness of rope, and a method of securing the slack. In addition a table of 'drops' was appended. If these measures were put into practice, accidents might still happen but 'this shock to public opinion [would] be an extreme rarity'.[5]

In 1901 the tolling of the bell before, and in 1902 the hoisting of the black flag after, the execution was abolished. It was all too mawkish. Language too became ever more anaemic and formulaic. In 1925 the Home Office instructed prison governors to keep comment brief and stereotyped:

---

4   *The Times*, 14 March 1878.

5   *The Report of the Committee appointed to inquire into the Existing Practise as to carrying out of Sentences of Death*, 1888, HO 144/212/A48697/2, p.vii, and para.87.

every hanging from then on 'was carried out expeditiously and without a hitch'. Two years later chaplains were instructed that audible prayers on the way to the scaffold should be uttered only at the prisoner's request and should never be from the Burial Service since they were conducting not a corpse to a grave but a living being to the gallows. Sensational reporting in the press threatened the decorum. The solemn ritual of the inexorable denunciation of Church and State was in danger of being reduced to the macabre titillation of the breakfast table. Secrecy increasingly joined privacy, and the entry of the press was gradually restricted, 1934 being the last year in which a reporter attended an execution. The camouflage was complete.

The number and nature of those hanged was also curtailed. The number of capital offences had been reduced from over two hundred during the period of 'the Bloody Code' to seven in 1841 and four in 1868. Thereafter, in practice only murderers and traitors died, and there were precious few of the latter. Since 1887 all murderers under eighteen had been reprieved. The Children Act of 1908 merely gave statutory force to this convention. The 1922 Infanticide Act removed this offence from the category of murder, although no woman had been executed for killing her baby since 1849. In 1957 the Homicide Act further restricted the scope of the noose by drawing a distinction between different sorts of murder. Some would merit death, others life imprisonment. It produced bizarre anomalies. Those who shot their victims would die; those who bludgeoned them to death with a rifle-butt would not.

Procedure was perfected. Dynasties of executioners, from which the drunken and dissolute had been weeded, would refine their technique until in its final form the whole process of 'the ceremony' from the entry of the hangman into the condemned cell to the victim being launched into eternity could be measured in seconds. Major Grew, governor of Wandsworth prison, who had officiated at many executions, said he could not ask for a quieter or more merciful death himself.[6]

Death stalked many prisons. Those which carried out executions could not escape from its shadow. It hung like a pall. For many working within the system, capital punishment was corrosive of any rehabilitative purpose. It undermined attempts at turning prisons into centres of enlightened reform. Other prisoners were necessarily neglected as all effort was centred on the condemned, and the salvation of their souls became the primary concern of chaplains. It put them under terrible emotional strain each time a person with whom they had grown intimate was killed, all the more so if they met

[6] Rich, p.190; Grew, p.108.

their end unrepentant. There was no chapel on the day a hanging took place as:

> The Chaplain's heart is far too sick,
>   Or his face is far too wan,
> Or there is written in his eyes
>   Which none should look upon.[7]

Nonetheless they persisted in their ministry, assured that 'in the condemned cell the gospel comes into its own', and supported by their bishops, many of whom took the opportunity to minister to the condemned themselves.[8] Most chaplains acquiesced in the necessity of the retention of the ultimate penalty, but some spoke against it. The Revd S.R. Glanville Murray, a prison chaplain for twenty-eight years, considered it judicial murder and thought an execution to be such a moral shock as to leave a haunting and imperishable memory on the participants. 'No one', he said, 'can leave this slaughter-house without a deep sense of humiliation, horror and shame.'[9] His sentiments were shared by some governors, of whom one had the temerity to go public. On 9 October 1926, Major Wallace Blake, governor of Pentonville for the previous seven years, wrote an article about a notorious murder case in the *Evening News* in which he confessed to feeling 'a bit like a murderer' himself . He was prosecuted under the Official Secrets Act and fined for this indiscretion.[10] On the other hand Colonel Rich, a nostalgic conservative, and an ardent evangelical, had no truck with abolitionists. Even his colleague, the much loved humanitarian Captain Gerold Clayton, despite his physical revulsion at executions and his distaste for the 'calm, cold deprivation of life', believed that capital punishment had to be kept as a deterrent and as retribution in the case of 'the determined, callous killer'.[11]

Dissident governors could be silenced, but the authorities could do little to suppress another blow to decorum delivered to the prison gates by an eccentric millionairess, Mrs Violet Van der Elst. In 1935 she began a campaign of street protests against hanging. She engaged professional publicity agents and proceeded to develop her crusade on sensational lines. The press loved it. First she procured over 100,000 signatories for her petition urging the reprieve of a murderer called Brigstock. When that failed, she hired two

---

[7] Oscar Wilde, 'The Ballad of Reading Gaol', stanza 4.

[8] Canon Hussey in the *York Synod Debate*, 1962, pp.41ff.

[9] 1930 Select Committee Evidence, para.3614.

[10] Blake had been the Borstal governor after whom 'A Hall' had been renamed, and published an autobiography, *Quod*, in 1927.

[11] Rich, pp.180–92; Clayton, pp.72f.

aeroplanes to trail black flags over Wandsworth prison on the morning of the execution, while dozens of men with sandwich-boards patrolled outside the gates. At 9 am, the time of the 'drop', ranks of women knelt in prayer and bared their heads. Promising to get 'worse and worse', she returned a fortnight later for a similar demonstration against another execution. This time the police were out in force and prevented her loudspeaker vans from approaching the prison. Undeterred, Mrs Van der Elst, dressed in full mourning, drove her lemon Rolls-Royce through the police cordon to the gates of Wandsworth, going over one officer's foot in the process. The authorities were horrified by her antics but impotent. Her aeroplanes had committed no flying offences. On another occasion she stopped a lorry and offered the driver £200 to ram his vehicle through the prison gates. The driver agreed, the attempt failed, but the door of publicity was opened to this strange little woman. Buoyed up by this, she capitalised on the attentions of the press – who dubbed her 'V.D. Elsie' – and on and on she would go. Until the late 1950s she was to be seen with her supporters keeping vigil outside prisons on the eve of an execution and singing hymns on the morning of it. She never gave up, she never calmed down. She lived just long enough to see success, dying in 1966. Yet it was this strange woman that Clement Attlee said had done more than anyone else to secure abolition. She had certainly made capital punishment a laughing stock, and an institution that was based on solemnity and reverence could not long survive pantomime. As the 1930s receded and the 1950s advanced, momentum changed.

In the immediate aftermath of the Second World War, many men joined the prison service as governors, chaplains or officers, to be part of an agency of reform. During the war they had served with the sort of men and boys whom they would find within the prison and borstal systems. Change was in the air and they wanted to be a part of it. Few had given any thought to their role in executions. Once confronted with the reality, many felt sullied. In local prisons the care of capital cases was the most important part of the chaplain's job. No one else played so intimate a role. The same chaplain, visiting daily, would deal with the condemned prisoner from the anxiety of remand to the trauma of trial, from the forlorn hope of appeal to the inexorable moment of execution. Rarely did the condemned ask about the actual procedure. Sometimes chaplains would consider it important to say the process would be quick and death instantaneous. Sometimes they placed a crucifix opposite where the condemned would stand so that their last glance would fall upon another executed criminal. Invariably chaplains would spend the final hour with their charges, celebrating Holy Communion for the confirmed, and offering prayers for all. These ministrations were interrupted by the hangman and his assistant, who with unfailing precision at 7 am would enter the cell, pinion the prisoner, march the trussed sacrifice through a hidden partition in the cell wall to the adjacent gallows chamber, place the noose around the neck and pull the lever of the drop. From start to finish the whole process took from nine to twenty-five seconds. The prisoner was literally dead on time.[12]

Chaplains responded in various ways to what was a most traumatic experience, but arguing the rights and wrongs of this punishment does not seem to have been one of them. They were part of the system and it was not their place to undermine it. One governor could not recall ever discussing the ethics of capital punishment with any of the chaplains with whom he had served. The seemingly phlegmatic Baden Ball, in his description of his work at Wandsworth prison, refers in passing to the toll taken on his 'health and well-being'. Doubts as to the legitimacy of the death penalty were no element in this. It was not for him to question the Home Secretary's decision about the hapless Derek Bentley (see below), rather it was his task to prepare the boy to face death with 'sublime faith in God's will'. In its spare record of duties done, the 1952–3 chaplain's journal nonetheless reveals, far more fully than Ball, the crushing burden that a chaplain of a major 'hanging jail' had to carry. Ball was daily visiting two prisoners under sentence of death (Livesey and Alcott) from 19 November 1952. A third (Curtis) was added on 4 December and on 11 December Bentley became the fourth. For one week Ball had to visit four men who were about to die; for two further weeks three. Two executions and one respite reduced the number to one by 19 January 1953. Bentley alone remained. But the strain of such ministry, lasting over two months, was proving too much. His last recorded visit to Bentley was on 23 January. The next day the chaplain fell ill, returning from sick leave a week later, after Bentley's despatch on the 28th. In his autobiography Ball made no mention of this, and indeed strongly implied that he attended the execution himself. He resigned later that year. Traumatised clergy tended to resign rather than rebel. Some felt an element of guilty complicity in their participation. One recorded how he reluctantly agreed to the governor's request to take a condemned man to the chapel so that the hangman, incognito, could observe the specimen and make his calculations. It was all very corrosive, yet they complied and colluded.[13]

---

12 *Royal Commission*, Evidence, paras.8452f.
13 Baden Ball, *Prison Was My Parish* (London, 1956), pp.240–51; Wandsworth Prison Chaplain's Journal.

The ultimate demise of the death penalty is attributable to a transformation in the views of politicians and the press, of church leaders and academics, and even of prison governors and judges. They were a new generation. For the first time, the majority of all elements of the elite class would favour abolition, and so the days of the death penalty were numbered. What brought about this transformation? The year 1953 proved decisive, when the publication of the Royal Commission on Capital Punishment's long-awaited report coincided with two of the most notorious capital cases. The commissioners, restricted as they were by their terms of reference which precluded them from advocating abolition, nonetheless came down as near as they could in its favour. Only with abolition, they seemed to be hinting, could all the anomalies and ambiguities of the present system, which the commission had been set up to rectify, be put right. Perhaps their report's greatest significance lay in the clarity with which it mustered an enormous amount of evidence both for and against the imposition of the death penalty. Such a survey had the power to make converts, the most notable of whom was the chairman himself, Sir Ernest Gowers. He had started the inquiry without any strong feelings either way about the penalty but ended it 'as a whole-hearted abolitionist – not emotionally but intellectually'.[14]

To win over the public, however, appeals to emotion as much as to intellect were necessary. The year 1953 would also provide the emotional stimulus to abolition. Earlier in that year two cases undermined the twin principal pillars upon which capital punishment was sustained: that mercy would always be shown to those meriting it, and that no innocent would ever be sent to the gallows.

In November 1952 two teenagers, Derek Bentley and Christopher Craig, had set out to break into a shop in Croydon. Craig had a gun, Bentley some knuckle dusters. The police were called to the scene. They got onto the roof and quickly apprehended Bentley who shouted to his accomplice, 'Let him have it Chris'. Interpreting this as a lethal command and not a demand for surrender, Craig fired several shots, killing one of the officers, Sidney Miles, and taunting the police in another ambiguous phrase with 'come on you brave coppers, I am only sixteen'. The implication was that they were cowards if they could not take on a boy, or more chillingly that he had nothing to lose because he was too young to hang for killing them. The less than cowardly police did take him on, disarming and capturing him. Both young men were convicted of murder. The jury recommended mercy for Bentley. The trial judge and Lord Chief Justice, Lord Goddard, agreed that he was the lesser

---

[14] Letter to Bishop Bell, Lambeth Palace Archives.

offender. Nonetheless, while the more culpable Craig was sentenced to be detained at Her Majesty's Pleasure (the equivalent of a life sentence for young offenders under eighteen, although Craig spent a little over ten years in gaol), Bentley was sentenced to hang. The murder of a policeman had rightly enraged public opinion, but Bentley's imminent execution in January 1953 generated unprecedented popular and parliamentary agitation for a reprieve. The public's sense of guilt was stronger than its instinct for revenge. As Sir David Maxwell-Fyfe, the Home Secretary, ruefully noted: 'sympathy was abruptly switched from the unfortunate policeman and his family to the youth who faced execution'. Bentley was executed as an example and became a martyr.[15]

Within months the other, even more critical, pillar undergirding the death penalty was to be put under unprecedented pressure. In 1950 Timothy Evans had been executed in Pentonville prison for the murder of his wife and child whose bodies had been found buried in the wash-house at the rear of 10 Rillington Place. Both had been strangled. Evans protested his innocence, and laid the blame on his old landlord and the chief prosecution witness, John Christie. No one believed that this was anything but the last desperate throw of a guilty man. The revelation three years later that Christie was himself a necrophiliac mass murderer, whose six victims were buried behind the wash-house and included his own wife, came as a bit of a shock. He was duly executed in 1953, but not for the murders Evans was alleged to have committed. It was apparent to all but the blind and deaf that a psychopath had been allowed to carry on a killing spree while an innocent man had been hanged for crimes he did not commit.

The execution of the innocent would pose an insurmountable problem to the proponents of capital punishment. The Home Office knew this and did its best to maintain the infallibility of the system. Maxwell-Fyfe had once said that there was no practical possibility of an innocent man being hanged, and he still believed what he said. The problem was that others were losing their faith. In an attempt to quell doubts arising from the Evans case, in July 1953 – the same month that Christie hanged – he instigated a private inquiry by John Scott-Henderson QC. Within ten days his report was completed, concluding that Evans was guilty of murdering his wife

---

15 Viscount Kilmuir, *Political Adventure* (London, 1964), p.207. On the anniversary of his death, flowers were laid outside Wandsworth prison by his family until 1997 when his sister died. In 1993 Bentley received a royal pardon for his sentence, and in 1998 won a posthumous appeal against conviction on the basis of Goddard's summing up which, in the words of Lord Bingham, the then Lord Chief Justice, was 'such as to deny the appellant that fair trial which is the birthright of every British citizen'.

and child, Christie's later confession to being the killer of the former was false, and that there were, by coincidence, two psychopathic murderers living under the same roof at the same time. This conclusion may have assuaged the Home Secretary but it carried little weight with the public or MPs. For them, if not for the Home Office, the case demonstrated beyond reasonable doubt that the possibility of a miscarriage of justice in a capital trial could not after all be wholly excluded and an innocent person might suffer death as a result.

The debate over deterrence would always be clouded in the public mind by seemingly contradictory statistics, but one demonstrable mistake was enough to shake the gallows to its foundations. Thus in one year, a system predicated on infallibility had been smashed. The innocent could die; the venial might not receive mercy. Perhaps in their deaths Bentley and Evans did more to end hanging than any agitator or activist had done or would do. The death penalty had over another decade of life but it was mortally wounded.

The momentum for its demise was quickened by the *cause célèbre* of the Ruth Ellis case. For what in other countries would be described as a *crime passionnel* in which a jilted woman shot her unfaithful lover, this young mother was sentenced to hang. Fifty thousand people signed a petition for mercy, while the *Daily Mirror* led the press campaign against her hanging. In vain! The law would run its course, and Ruth Ellis would die. On the morning of 13 July 1955, in the last minutes of her life, as she prayed before a crucifix, the crowd outside Holloway prison joined with Mrs Van der Elst in the chant 'Evans – Bentley – Ellis'. These were the names of the 'martyrs' – the abolitionist trinity – that would stalk capital punishment in its declining years, and help bring it down.

The moment came in 1965. All three party leaders were abolitionists. The Lord Chancellor, Gerald Gardiner, was a Quaker who had twice declined appointments to the High Court Bench because he might have to pass a death sentence. The archbishop of Canterbury, Michael Ramsey, and a host of newly appointed diocesan bishops were wholeheartedly opposed to the death penalty. Prominent writers and academics wrote books and pamphlets in favour of abolition. Even an erstwhile executioner, Albert Pierrepoint, belatedly denounced his trade as futile. Sidney Silverman, the veteran Labour MP and inveterate campaigner, presented a private member's bill to abolish capital punishment, and the cabinet allowed time for debate. The Murder (Abolition of the Death Penalty) Act became law in November 1965. After an affirmative vote four years later, it remained, and remains, on the Statute Book. Later attempts to revive the ultimate penalty have all come to naught, the last gallows being removed from Wandsworth prison in 1994 and the condemned suite becoming a tearoom for prison staff. Capital punishment in Britain has been consigned to the history books and to Madame Tussauds. Prisons are finally free of this incubus.

Throughout its long history capital punishment has always had its die-hard advocates and apologists, but in the early twentieth century there were some at the forefront of penal reform who, far from being enthusiasts for the ultimate punishment, thought it more merciful than the terrible alternative of prolonged imprisonment. One prominent philanthropist put it pithily: 'it is kinder to break a man's neck in a second, than to spend twenty years in breaking his heart'. The words are those of Alexander Paterson who was not only a moral crusader but a prison commissioner.[16]

---

16 Paterson, p.22. Colin Davies, a lifer, twice given a 'seven-year knock-back' on parole, and who killed himself in Maidstone prison in 1984, would have agreed. He wrote, 'Death must be a fairer place / than this eternal strife, / 'tis better dead and buried than locked away for life. / 'Tis better warm beneath the soil / than waking up alone / to find yourself alive in hell / enclosed in steel and stone' (Mark Leech, *A Product of the System* (London, 1992), p.102).

CHAPTER 29

A Good and Useful Life

Always as we talked there emerged [Paterson's] intense interest and sympathy for the individual ... His sympathy never degenerated into mere sentimentality. He was essentially wise and well-balanced in his outlook.

Clement Attlee

Eventually after he has been in the nick a few times you will decide to give him a chance, so you sentence him to three years Corrective Training. Now this is a real favour for which you think he would be grateful. But he is not on your Nellie. Why? I'll tell you why and I should know, *bird is bird whatever you like to call it, C.T., Borstal, or Remand Home it's all bird. So let's stop kidding ourselves shall we?*

Frank Norman

In February 1922 an inspired but controversial appointment was made to the Prison Commission. Alexander Paterson was the appointee. With enormous reforming zeal and unparalleled experience of working-class life, he would leave an indelible mark on the penal landscape. He was anything but working-class in origin. Born to affluence in Cheshire in 1884 he was brought up as a staunch Unitarian, and his Christian faith suffused his whole life. He went to University College, Oxford in 1902. A contemporary there, and future Prime Minister, Clement Attlee, recalls that although Paterson was 'younger than most of those of his year he very soon became an outstanding influence in the life of the college' owing to 'the power of his personality'.[1] Others testified to his magnetism, humour, originality and determination. He was a moral whirlwind.

At Oxford Paterson was deeply influenced, as had been Ruggles-Brise, by the communitarian philosophy of T.H. Green,[2] and was easily persuaded by Dr John Stansfeld, a pioneer of working with inner-city boys in south London, to visit the Oxford Medical Mission, later known as the Oxford and Bermondsey Club, and to give it a trial 'just for a fortnight'. When he graduated he did. Seduced at once, he stayed in Bermondsey for twenty-one

---

[1] Paterson, p.7.
[2] Radzinowicz, p.598.

29. Alexander Paterson © National Portrait Gallery, London

years, living in a two-roomed flat in a poor tenement block, and accruing a formidable expertise in dealing with difficult and troubled youngsters, in all of whom he found 'natural goodness'. For a while he worked unpaid as an auxiliary teacher in an elementary school where he organised games, instituted 'house colours' and 'achieved among the boys a remarkable *esprit de corps* for their school which he called "Ridley College"'. He pinned a piece of paper over his bed with the names of his ragged pupils written under the caption 'Of such is the Kingdom of Heaven'. He soon came to the attention of Herbert Samuel, the Under-Secretary of State at the Home Office, who consulted him over the provisions of what would become the Children Act of 1908.[3] Paterson contributed over twenty amendments to the draft, all of which were incorporated into the Act.

Consorting with many boys and young men who fell foul of the law, Paterson developed an interest in the criminal justice and prison systems.

---

[3]   Barclay Baron, *The Doctor* (London, 1952), pp.162–6. It was due to Samuel that the new institution for reforming young people was memorably named 'Borstal' and not the more cumbersome 'Juvenile-Adult Reformatory' (Grew, p.16).

As a result of one 'young friend' being imprisoned for murdering his wife, he made monthly visits by bicycle to Dartmoor, and was appalled by what he saw: convicts in broad arrow uniforms, with closely shaven heads and faces covered with a sort of dirty moss, reduced to utter servility, each one pressing his face to the wall as visitors passed.[4] He itched for change. His knowledge of prisons and prisoners increased when in 1909 the eager young optimist was recruited by Ruggles-Brise as assistant director of the newly established Central Association for the Aid of Discharged Convicts. He shared an office with the Borstal Association at 15 Buckingham Street, became a member of its executive committee, wrote articles on its behalf, and greatly influenced the more progressive and critical stance that that organisation would take after the Great War. All the while he remained deeply involved in the Boys' Club, and in 1911 he published *Across the Bridges*, a heart-felt account of life in the area and of his encounters there, and a passionate call to philanthropic action. In this work, long before he could influence the development of the borstal system, he applauded it as 'a great thoughtful plan to save the beginner from a career of crime', providing 'alternative methods of treatment ... for young offenders ... to distract them from the bad and to rebuild the good'.[5] Much of what he would later implement sprang from the insights he gained south of the Thames. His book became required reading for Etonians being prepared for confirmation.[6]

The whole approach to youth justice that would be espoused by Paterson and many others rested on assumptions that wrongdoing was a product of social and environmental factors over which offenders had little control. But they could regain control. They should be helped to do so rather than just be punished for their failure. Although he was influenced by those aspects of European positivism which attributed criminality more to nature than nurture, thought bad behaviour could be eradicated more effectively by internal than external restraints, and so emphasised individualisation of treatment alongside indeterminate sentences and release as a result of administrative decisions made by experts, he never denied free will or

---

4 Paterson, p.11; Grew, on his arrival in 1926 as deputy-governor at this 'most feared and hated prison', shared Paterson's disquiet. He noted the 'pervading atmosphere of gloom and abandonment' and the 'silent and dejected [convicts] trudging along the road ... flanked by two officers carrying carbines'. It was so very different from 'the invigorating atmosphere of optimism' which he had found at Borstal (pp.39ff.).

5 Paterson, pp.130f.

6 W. Eagar, *Making Men: The History of Boys' Clubs and Related Movements in Great Britain* (London, 1953), pp.382f.

moral responsibility and never subscribed to the determinist theory that people were born criminals or had physiological and phrenological traits that disposed them to crime. After all, his Christian faith, emphasising the intrinsic worth of every individual, held that *all* were born in sin, *all* sinned of their own volition, and *all* could be redeemed. This was reinforced by the Idealist view that reformation could only be achieved by impressing on the criminal the antisocial nature of his acts. The dignity of individuals who had erred was preserved by treating them as agents, not as patients.

Thus he shared the scepticism of Du Cane and Griffiths about the more outlandish aspects of positivism, and was buttressed in his view by the findings of Charles Goring, Parkhurst's medical officer, who had been commissioned by Ruggles-Brise to examine the evidence for this alien theory. After exhaustive comparative research which compared convicts with soldiers, undergraduates and schoolboys, Goring published *The English Convict* in 1913 which confirmed Griffiths's hunch and concluded that 'this anthropological monster has no existence in fact'. There was no evidence 'confirming the existence of a physical criminal type', although there were deficiencies in height and weight as well as a greater incidence of defective intelligence. English empiricism had exposed and demolished a fashionable foreign fallacy.[7]

Paterson differed, however, from Goring's other conclusions that crime was 'only to a trifling extent (if to any) the product of social inequalities, of adverse environment, or of other manifestations of … the force of circumstances', and that prisons did no damage. From Paterson's own experience of the slums, poverty – material and emotional – poor parenting, idleness, lack of stimulation and excitement, lack of education and opportunity, lack of self-control and want of guiding principles in life, were at the root of the malaise. These were what deprived poor children of value and worth in their lives. These were what led the young into crime. These were what must be countered. And if they could not be eradicated at source at least they could be compensated for by inculcating in wayward youths a sense of self-worth and achievement, the habits of hard work and industry, and the benefits of discipline and team-working. They could be made to feel part of society and not remain rebels against it. Boys' clubs were instrumental in this, as were the elementary schools, where dedicated teachers could give their charges a second chance, but where they laboured against huge disadvantages and often discipline was imposed with the cane

---

7   Charles Goring, *The English Convict: A Statistical Study* (London, 1913), pp.173, 370f.; Radzinowicz, pp.21–7. Goring did, however, advocate compulsory sterilisation for certain categories of prisoner, very much a eugenicist proposition.

while efforts to instil self-discipline were lacking.[8] Those who fell through these meagre safety-nets should not be outcast and abandoned or further harmed by imprisonment. Never give up.

At the outbreak of the conflict with Germany Paterson volunteered for military service, enlisting with many of his boys in the Bermondsey Battalion. During the conflict he was twice recommended for a Victoria Cross, was badly wounded when rescuing a comrade, and eventually came home with a Military Cross. He had also become a leading member of 'Toc H', a Christian 'Everyman's Club' where soldiers of all ranks could socialise freely and which sought to bring disparate sections of post-war society together in comradeship. Characteristically, Paterson went on to formulate its aims – 'The Four Points of the Compass'.

The start and finish of the Great War marked an end and a beginning for Paterson. The end of being an outsider and amateur; the beginning of a profession and vocation. Although he joined the Ministry of Labour, such work was not to hold him for long. His heart was with his Bermondsey boys, his hope lay in the borstal system shaped as he envisaged it, and his tool was the Borstal Association. He submitted a resolution to its executive committee deploring 'the inadequacy of the present system of training', and proposing the appointment of 'a special Borstal commissioner'. Did he have himself in mind? Probably. He was the ideal candidate. Prison reform and, in particular, transforming its purpose, was to be his forte, but developing alternatives for young offenders was to be his life's work. He would prove to be the right man at the right time, and that time was upon him.

In 1921, the very year Ruggles-Brise retired, the Howard League for Penal Reform was born, a merger between the oldest prison reform organisation in the world, the Howard Association, founded in 1866, and the more radical Penal Reform League which had been in existence since 1907. The latter had been led by Margery Fry and it was she who implemented this happy union. The following year, a friend and fellow Quaker, Stephen Hobhouse, and the socialist, Fenner Brockway, both conscientious objectors imprisoned during the war, edited *English Prisons Today* – 'the Bible of penal reformers' in Margery's view – a report on prison regimes before and during the Great War by the Prison System Inquiry Committee set up by the Labour Party and upon which Paterson had sat. He may have written the chapter on borstals and certainly influenced its content and conclusions.[9] Hobhouse had begun his survey in 1919 but, in the face of obdurate opposition from the prison

---

8 Paterson, pp.57ff.
9 Victor Bailey, *Delinquency and Citizenship* (Oxford, 1987), pp.195f.

commissioners under the 'reactionary autocrat', Ruggles-Brise, and the debilitating effects of his own imprisonment, handed over completion of what would be a massive 700-page work to Brockway.[10] It was in effect a companion volume to *English Prisons under Local Government* which covered the period from the sixteenth century until 1898 and which was published in the same year by Hobhouse's uncle and aunt, Sidney and Beatrice Webb, both leading Fabian socialists. It constituted a damning indictment of the dehumanising system presided over by Ruggles-Brise, arguing that while the 'oppressive weight and mechanical rigidity' of the prison system sometimes made docile prisoners it did almost nothing to make better citizens. Indeed the reverse was true, as 'the cumulative effects of the strain' of being 'in the grip of a huge machine which is felt to be repressive at every point, inhuman, aimless, tyrannical', were 'of the nature of a progressive weakening of the mental powers and a deterioration of the character in a way which renders the prisoner less fit for useful social life'. While an age of penal enlightenment had been proclaimed, according to these influential and well-informed critics, nothing much of real substance had changed, and a far more radical and far-reaching reappraisal was necessary. The Home Office was being called upon to realise in the post-war world the hopes raised by the Gladstone report in the Victorian age.

The academic and even political consensus was moving in that direction. A new vista was opening and the prospect of unending progress was both alluring and seemed within reach. Optimism was in the air. No longer were reformers sweating on the never-ending tread-wheel or vainly pushing, like Sisyphus, a boulder uphill. They, like Bunyan, had at last left the Slough of Despond and were marching invincibly along the King's Highway towards the Celestial City. Paterson wanted to be a pioneer in this triumphant trek.

He got his wish and more when he was invited by the new, reform-minded chairman, Maurice Waller, not just to become one of the three prison commissioners but the one with a new 'special responsibility for borstals'.[11] Paterson would not just join the march; he would lead it. The

---

[10] Enid Huws Jones, *Margery Fry* (Oxford, 1966), p.113. Hobhouse had spent four months in Wormwood Scrubs and eight months in Exeter prison under a regime of solitary confinement and with minimal opportunity to write, commenting that under this 'cruel and stupid prison regime' Bunyan would never have written *Pilgrim's Progress* (*Forty Years and an Epilogue* (London, 1951), pp.167, 175).

[11] Paterson may have asked Lloyd-George to help him secure the post (Bailey, *op. cit.*, p.194). Waller would undoubtedly have supported it as he himself, in his role as one of the prison commissioners, had been primarily responsible for the borstal system from 1910 (Alan Baxendale, 'Maurice Wyndham Waller', in *Prison Service People* (Newbold Revel, 1993), p.31).

appointment of an outsider as commissioner was as unprecedented as it was prescient. In the words of a future chairman, it 'introduced a creative force which was to effect within the next twenty-five years a transformation of the theory and practice of imprisonment, not only in England but throughout the world'.[12]

The appointment of this young, inexperienced 'missionary', as he called himself, was opposed by the *Prison Officer's Magazine*, an organ that well reflected the views of its increasingly dissident grass-roots membership.[13] Nor did it meet with the unqualified approval of governors, all of whom were older than the new commissioner, and most were former military men loyal to Ruggles-Brise and his methods of disciplined compassion. Some resented a 'novice' being put over them; others feared that they would not have the requisite skills to fulfil the new role expected of them. A dedication to 'social service' was displacing 'sterling worth' as the criterion for advancement.[14] Clayton was one ambivalent governor. 'Old One Lug', as he was affectionately called, had joined the service in 1920 when one system was coming to an end and another beginning.[15] His father had been Ruggles-Brise's lieutenant, and the son valued much of what they had done. He thought Paterson 'a remarkable man', but, bearing a grudge for being passed over for the inspectorate in favour of a borstal tutor, he could be scathing about him, especially in his attitude to staff, his disinclination to take advice from more experienced men, the appointments to governorships he made, and the haste with which he acted. Later, undergoing a nervous breakdown, Clayton acknowledged the solicitude Paterson had shown him. Rich was even more antagonistic to someone he considered to be an inexperienced amateur. Although nowhere in his autobiography does he name Paterson, it is quite obvious of whom he writes.[16] These disaffected governors' distrust

---

12 Harold Scott, *Your Obedient Servant* (London, 1959), p.69.

13 This publication, established in 1910, 'marked the real start of corporate consciousness within the service'. It was hostile to 'the autocrats and parasites' who were running the prison service, it opposed direct entry to governor grades, and was dismissive of interfering outside bodies such as the Howard League. It sought pay-parity with the police, and pay rises generally (*Report* (1979), pp.13f.).

14 John Watson, *Meet the Prisoner* (London, 1939), p.75. As late as 1963 a Conservative Home Secretary, Henry Brooke, was heartened by the fact 'that more and more the prison officer is beginning to look on himself as a social worker, charged of course with discipline duties still, but concerned to play a part in helping the individual prisoner to solve his troubles, get more control over himself, and go out of prison equipped to live a good and useful life' (*Report* (1963), p.xi, para.21).

15 Wilfred Macartney, *Walls Have Mouths* (London, 1936), p.57. Clayton had lost an ear in the Great War.

16 Clayton, 19ff., 66, 81, 160–6, 179ff.; Rich, p.279.

of Paterson was mirrored by his distrust of them. He was ever on the lookout for a new breed whom he could inspire and upon whom he could rely.

Major Grew, whom he met by chance at their club later that same year, gave a pen-portrait of the man who would bestride and dominate the penal landscape for a quarter of a century.

> The man I shook hands with was of medium build. He had a kindly face and a most disarming smile. His hair was receding, giving great depth to his already high forehead. His shrewd and penetrating eyes were the eyes of a man of compassion, a man to whom one could appeal and not in vain ... I found him as good a listener as he was a talker.

Paterson told Grew a great deal about life in the slums, and of how he had visited friends in prison and been appalled at what he had witnessed there. He blamed the conditions on the complacency of officialdom and that 'complacency was as bad as neglect and a great deal harder to shift'. Most of all, Grew could tell 'he was concerned about boys ... who had got into ... serious trouble and had no one to help them, boys whose weaknesses led to crime, and crime to despair, misery and ruin'. Yet, Paterson insisted, all bad boys had an element of goodness in them, 'if we could but find it and if we searched hard enough'. They could be redeemed and turned into useful citizens 'if men strong enough in character and patient enough in their ways would be their "schoolmasters" and help them along the way'. Such a vision was, he believed, springing up under the borstal system 'which, as he put it, "sought to teach wayward lads to be self-contained men"'. Inspired by this serendipitous encounter, the following year, having left the army, Grew applied to join the prison service. Paterson was one of his interviewers, and recommended that he be made deputy-governor of Borstal. Thus he embarked on what he believed was pioneering work in 'a great penal adventure', taking to his heart 'the precept that we were no longer trying to make the punishment fit the crime but attempting to make the offender fit into society'.[17]

Another early acolyte was Harley Cronin. Discharged from the army in 1926 he was living with his mother, the matron of Feltham borstal, when he met Alexander Paterson, a 'big, bluff man in his forties, whose charm, wit and affability reflected a career in which he had mixed with "all sorts and conditions of men"'. He encouraged and inspired Cronin to become a prison

---

[17] Grew, pp.13ff., 17, 38.

officer. After a short spell of training at Wormwood Scrubs which, holding mostly first offenders, was then 'more or less a laboratory for Paterson's reforms', he was posted to a very different institution: Horfield gaol in Bristol, where he heard 'one of the older officers mutter to a companion, "Ha, another of Paterson's Light Horse."' Despite the initial hostility towards him as one of 'the disciples', and his revulsion at the practice of 'slopping-out', which survived all efforts at reform, Cronin would remain in the service until 1963, for the last twenty-five years of which he would be General Secretary of the Prison Officers' Association, a quasi-trade union which he helped to found in 1938. While always having a high regard for his mentor, by the end of his career in 1963 Cronin had reservations about some of Paterson's ideas, had become more cynical about the 'treatment' model which he thought had gone too far in encompassing 'savage and persistent thugs', and wanted 'to call a halt to appeasement'.[18]

Paterson was part of the liberal, middle-class Christian activism so strong in the inter-war years, that believed in close personal ties between the classes and not in class war, and wanted to reshape society but not destroy it. This was reformation, not revolution. It was an alternative and antidote to the fashionable totalitarianism of Fascism or Communism or even to 'systematic socialism'.[19] Those from privileged backgrounds had a duty to get to know, understand, assist, encourage and rescue the less fortunate, and especially the young, from a life of grinding poverty and crime. In his chosen arena of penal reform he embodied a more imaginative and constructive approach to the treatment of all offenders than had hitherto been countenanced. 'No man is a prisoner and nothing else' was the principle that ruled much of his thinking.[20] And he meant it. No one was beyond redemption.

Imprisonment as then constituted was more of a curse than a cure. He doubted if anyone who had served ten years in prison could leave undamaged, and the longer the term the more damage done. He believed that imprisonment should be avoided wherever possible as 'it is ... a clumsy piece of social surgery, tearing a man away from the social fabric of home and work ... causing distress to others, and rendering his replacement in social and industrial life a matter of grave difficulty'. More alternatives should be found, and more recourse to those alternatives made. He wanted the name 'prison' abolished, and the Prison Commission to be renamed the Board of Welfare. This may have been a fancy too far, but it was not far-fetched.

---

18 Harley Cronin, *The Screw Turns* (London, 1967), pp.13–17, 110.

19 Paterson makes this explicit (*Across the Bridges*, 2nd edn (London, 1912), pp.20, 176–80).

20 John Vidler, *If Freedom Fail* (London, 1964), p.9.

Welfare was a word much in vogue. The ethos of the embryonic welfare state, inaugurated by Lloyd George, was spreading. The young as well as the elderly were prime concerns. The Liberal government, which had introduced juvenile courts and probation, consolidated the earlier provisions of child welfare, notably school meals and medical attention. This whole process would culminate in the 1933 Children and Young Persons Act, which, like its 1908 counterpart, was designed to protect them from abuse, exploitation or harm. In it the duty of courts to have regard to the welfare of the young would be specifically enshrined in law. For Paterson the welfare of prisoners should no more be neglected than that of pensioners. He was to be 'the "Beveridge" of the penal system'.[21]

He was undoubtedly very idealistic, perhaps a little naive, but certainly not ignorant. During his tenure as a commissioner he educated himself about the problems of the prison system and visited a wide variety of penal institutions in England and abroad. In-depth knowledge as much as inexhaustible compassion would inform his actions. He brought to the commission his great understanding of human nature, honed in the slums of south London, yet he was quite able to see through the Uriah Heeps of this world, whose outward conformity, submissiveness and overt penitence were designed to please, and deceive, the authorities. But he knew that Uriah Heeps were made by the prisons in which they lodged, where all self-reliance and initiative were lost, to be replaced with a cloying sycophancy, cloaking 'dishonesty with the paint and plaster of a well-behaved inmate of an institution'.[22]

Hypocrisy created by, and displayed within, the institution was bad enough; hatred engendered by its dehumanising ethos was even worse. He wanted to introduce into the fabric of prisons 'the Christian conception of the value of the individual soul'. This moral imperative was closely allied to a civic duty. It was his duty and the duty of the prison administration itself to provide permanent protection for the public. To release prisoners, unchanged or changed for the worse, back into society provides but temporary respite for the period of incarceration. Long-term safety requires a change for the better. Caging a wild beast, starving and goading it, reducing it to outward submissiveness while it is impotent and at your mercy, and then setting it free, is fraught with danger. Keeping it under humane restraint, while taming it and training it and encouraging it, is the only way to ensure safety on release. Discharged prisoners should be made fit for freedom and not

---

21 Bailey, *op. cit.*, pp.2ff.
22 Paterson, p.62.

made into the implacable enemies of society. Pragmatism is the consort of morality. Doing unto others as you would have others do unto you is not only right, it is sensible.

His stance was summed up in the classic maxim: 'men are sent to prison as a punishment not *for* punishment'. Deterrence and retribution were already achieved by the disgrace of appearing in court and the loss of liberty. That was the punishment. How they were treated within prison had nothing to do with punishment but all to do with rehabilitation. The real purpose of prison was 'to protect society' by making law-breakers 'fit once again for social freedom'.[23] The function of the regime under which they were detained was to educate, train and reform. These assertions inverted late Victorian beliefs, but they had an earlier history. As far back as 1832, another era of penal optimism, the Revd Robert Appleton, chaplain of Reading gaol, had expressed similar views in a lengthy report to the quarter sessions.[24] Yet it was Paterson's great achievement that this neglected and long-forgotten maxim became the norm, 'our guiding principle' as Grew put it.[25] Although he was the only commissioner with no prior official connection to the prison service, and although he would never be chairman of the commission, Paterson would be the dominant figure within it, and his influence would be all-pervasive. It would first be seen in the Prison Commission report of 1923, which Margery Fry lauded as 'a *Howard Journal* in itself'.[26] His tenure was lengthy, his connections excellent, and his personality galvanising and disarming. Above all he was the great motivator. He would motivate his staff and they in turn would motivate their charges. Or so he hoped and believed. While he demanded loyalty to his ideals from them, he was utterly loyal to them. The quality of staff was crucial to Paterson's contention that even if 'we do not have the best prison system ... we have the best prison service in the world'.

His idealised view of prison officers was often belied by their actions and words, and they, of course, were in day-to-day charge. When Giles Playfair, at Paterson's suggestion, visited Wormwood Scrubs in 1934, he was required to keep his hat on because if he took it off 'prisoners would interpret the act as a sign of respect to which they were not entitled'.[27] Not all staff

---

23 *Ibid.*, pp.13, 23ff.,79.
24 Peter Southerton, *The Story of a Prison* (Reading, 1975), p.71.
25 Grew, p.97.
26 Jones, *op. cit.*, p.121.
27 Giles Playfair, *The Punitive Obsession* (London, 1971), p.185.

were or remained true believers. It was the old clash between idealism and experience. As one veteran officer put it,

> it is the shameless and incorrigible ... beastliness of the average jailbird that gives the prison officer, who has opportunities to see this type in the raw, a very different view of the potentialities of prison reform to that held by those who believe all such jailbirds need is 'understanding'.[28]

Paterson, who had never worked in a prison, was thought too optimistic and seemed unwilling or unable to distinguish between 'incorrigibles' and 'redeemables', 'old lags' and one-off offenders.

Backed by his fellow commissioners, and in particular by a succession of forceful and reform-minded chairmen, starting with the remarkable Waller himself, Paterson was the driving-force behind the major changes of the 1920s and 1930s when England became the centre of prison reform. The great aim was to restore humanity to those from whom it had been taken, and to instil humanity into a system hitherto largely devoid of it. This was simple to say but hard to put into execution. It was alien to existing staff, and the antiquated prison estate was not designed for it. But no one and nothing would stand in Paterson's way or frustrate his ambition to convert criminals into good citizens. They were always individuals and never just prisoners, although even he recognised that some were incorrigible. The prison estate could be reordered; the staff regenerated or replaced. If, in the lyrical sentiments of a future commissioner, Du Cane had built a system in 'the powerful and perdurable Norman' style, and Ruggles-Brise in his 'Transitional style' had modified the structural features while retaining the ambience of the old, Paterson had opted for 'Early English ... releasing the true spirit of the structure in a "first fine, careless rapture" of seminal ideas'.[29] Du Cane's anchored-to-earth Durham cathedral was being replaced with soaring-spired Salisbury. That was the grandiloquent optimism shading a harsher reality that prisoners were still housed in decaying Gothic-style Victorian citadels, under the control of staff not all of whom were enraptured by this brave new world of penal practice.

An important innovation intended to counter the ethos of the past and imbue raw recruits with reforming zeal as well as professional pride was the creation at Wakefield in 1935 of the first training school for prison staff, half a century after Sir Walter Crofton had appealed for one in vain.[30] Under the

---

28 Cronin, *op. cit.*, p.55.
29 *EPBS*, p.66; Alyson Brown, *Inter-War Penal Policy and Crime in England* (Basingstoke, 2013), p.40.
30 *Report* (1879), para.148.

old regime, warders had been employed as turnkeys and the enforcers of rigid discipline, while the civil guard, who carried carbines, manned security posts inside and outside convict prisons. They had been poorly paid and heavily fined for any infraction of the rules – such as talking to prisoners – or minor dereliction of duty – such as turning the head away from a party of prisoners. In 1919 the civil guard was abolished – inadvertently weakening perimeter security at the same time as prisoners were getting more freedom – and warders were renamed prison officers as an indication that 'their duty was more than that of mere custody' and that they were 'expected to co-operate in the national work of training and reformation'.[31] Under the new regime their role would be more demanding as well as more rewarding, and training other than in military discipline became a prerequisite, although they continued to wear uniforms and were kept in line by a chief officer, akin to a sergeant-major in the army from which many recruits came. Wilfred Macartney, who was serving a lengthy sentence in Parkhurst when Clayton was governor, encapsulated the change by observing that whereas in 1928 it had been difficult for a 'jailer' who wanted to retain his 'roof and job' to be a 'decent fellow', by 1935 it was easy.[32]

Like the military or the police, prison officers could neither join a trade union nor take their grievances to arbitration. Nor could they strike, and when some had in 1919, all who participated were dismissed, including sixty-eight officers from Wormwood Scrubs, throughout the years the most militant prison.[33] There would be no more strikes, but gripes grew. Some custodial staff resented aloof governors whose social standing marked them out as members of an officer class, as indeed many had been, but whose civilian garb belied it. They also looked askance at the amount lavished on borstals, swimming pools and sports fields when their own quarters were in

---

31 *Report* (1934), p.14.

32 Macartney, *op. cit.*, pp.58, 107f., 148–55. In 1928 Macartney was sentenced to ten years' penal servitude with a concurrent term of two years' hard labour for espionage on behalf of the Soviets. He served seven and a half. Clayton, governor of Parkhurst from 1930 to 1935, had a genuine liking for the 'under-dog', and proved to be the 'most reasonable governor [Macartney] ever did "stir" with'. Assaults and floggings almost ceased during his tenure, and men embittered by harsh handling left prison markedly better adjusted. In short he turned the harshest prison in the system, where talking was absolutely prohibited, men were reported for the 'slightest thing', and a 'reign of terror existed', into one of the most relaxed, allowing the better natures of well-disposed officers to flourish.

33 *Report* (1920), para.97.

urgent need of refurbishment. Many shared the view that lionising prisoners meant demonising prison officers.[34]

An excellent example of a new breed of governor, prepared and eager to initiate the novel, was Paterson's not uncritical protégé, Major Grew. In 1930 he became governor of Maidstone, a former convict prison that was being re-forged into a 'training prison', in an attempt to apply some of the techniques honed among young offenders in borstal to adults in custody. The emphasis was on 'education in its broadest sense ... teaching skills in workshops, teaching the men to take responsibility ... teaching men to think, teaching them arts and crafts which were of general interest rather than directed to a specific use'.[35] As trust and self-reliance were thought essential to such an enterprise, initially only 'star-class' prisoners were considered suitable for Maidstone, and, until the war changed everything, it was only 'stars' who were sent there. These included the usually best-behaved: reprieved killers, ordinary sex offenders, and homosexuals – who despite causing little trouble tended to arouse considerable concern.[36] Into this *milieu* Grew was sent, and proved just the man for the job. He transformed the prison at virtually no cost to the public purse by holding sports days, evening classes, musical appreciation groups (which led to the creation of a prison orchestra), and even a motor-show with a Rolls-Royce. The *Daily Mirror* lampooned this particular enterprise and, although he had official backing for his endeavours, it was not repeated. Significantly his bold initiatives were supported, and not disowned, by commissioners who applauded innovation

[34] Grew, p.64. In contrast to governors, chaplains and prisoners, prison officers rarely expressed themselves in print. The earliest autobiographical account that I have found is that of Cicely McCall who in 1938 published *They Always Come Back*, about her experiences in Aylesbury and Holloway. The next come from the 1960s: Merrow-Smith's 1962 ghost-written *Prison Screw*, and Cronin's 1967 *The Screw Turns*. Both were long-serving, Merrow-Smith for thirty-two years and Cronin for thirty-six. As the educational standard of prison officers improved, more took to writing of their experiences, and even writing histories of the prisons in which they served, until in the last decade or so there has been a plethora of books from ordinary staff, but almost none from governors or chaplains. Many of the histories are well-researched and well-written but the most recent autobiographies are penned by disgruntled novices and are more like 'penny dreadfuls' than informative or reflective discourses on their subject. They confirm public perceptions of what 'screws' are like, and do less than justice to the majority of their colleagues, who are neither as uncaring and unthinking nor as liable to revel in gratuitous violence as the authors seem to have been (see David Wilson, *Pain and Retribution* (London, 2014), pp.144–55).

[35] Vidler, *op. cit.*, pp.93, 112, 115ff. Vidler took over as governor in 1944. He carried on in the same vein as Grew, but tried to import even more of the borstal ethos. He was particularly proud of the evening art and music classes he introduced.

[36] Rich, p.138; Grew, pp.47f., 83ff.; Vidler, *op. cit.*, pp.121, 132–49; L.W. Merrow-Smith, *Prison Screw* (London, 1962), pp.87f.; Cronin, *op. cit.*, pp.62–70.

and who had the confidence to stand up to the press. They also refused to panic. Once when Major Blake, the governor of Pentonville, in some trepidation telephoned Paterson to report an escape, the cool response was 'Dear, dear, what a pity!'[37]

Fortunately, even simple changes could have profound effects, saying farewell to one era and heralding a new. Banished in 1921 was the 'convict crop' and in 1922 the broad arrow. Provision was made for such basic necessities as shaving. The raised daises in chapels for invigilating officers were removed in 1922 and compulsory chapel attendance was suspended in most prisons in 1924, and the use of leg-irons was discontinued.[38] The previous year, a seven-hour working day was implemented, and in 1929, at the urging of the Howard League, the payment of pocket-money wages was introduced into Wakefield – then at the cutting-edge of penal reform – and Nottingham before being extended throughout the prison estate. Hard labour had already been ended by the 1898 Act. The remnants of the separate and silent systems would go the same way. The period of separate confinement was reduced to fourteen days from 1919, had virtually disappeared by 1922, and was removed altogether by the Statutory Rules of 1931, thus ending the separate system. Although as recently as 1922 the Webbs could describe the prisons as a 'silent world', from that date the rule of strict silence, more rigidly enforced in some prisons than others – Hull was relaxed, Parkhurst the opposite – 'became attenuated to the point of non-existence' until it was finally abolished in the 1950s, thus ending the silent system.[39] Instead, 'recreation in association' and 'conversational exercise' were permitted, and led to a healthier atmosphere and markedly better behaviour.[40] 'Leaders' were appointed from among the trusted prisoners to have a limited supervisory role, as were 'red-bands' who with their red arm-bands could move about the prison unchecked and work without supervision. Convicts were allowed, and even encouraged, to have prison visitors and to attend educational classes, some of which were taken by well-educated prisoners such as the disgraced MP Horatio Bottomley until the Home Secretary, William Joynson-Hicks

[37] Paterson, p.143; Grew, pp.91–5; Clayton, p.61.
[38] W.J. Forsythe, *Penal Discipline, Reformatory Projects and the English Prison Commission, 1895–1939* (Exeter, 1991), p.175.
[39] Webb, p.235; Rupert Cross, *Punishment, Prison and the Public* (London, 1971), p.31. The exact date of abolition is hard to determine.
[40] Lionel Fox, *The Modern English Prison* (London, 1934), pp.41f.; Grew, pp.103, 126; Merrow-Smith, *op. cit.*, p.23.

('Jix'), put a stop to it.[41] The reading of books beyond the Bible and religious tracts was actively promoted. Rudyard Kipling, who had been given a tour of Dartmoor by Clayton in December 1929, donated a large number of books written by famous authors, including himself.[42] Wireless broadcasts were allowed, as were concerts, amateur dramatics and films. Wormwood Scrubs allowed volunteers to put on readings of Shakespeare with prisoners as the cast. The director observed that in a performance of *As You Like It* 'a youth with the most acute cockney accent had acquired the part of Orlando, an Indian of ferocious appearance the part of Rosalind, and a guttural gentleman who had lived on the wrong side of the barbed wire during the war was now Jacques'.[43] Thereafter eminent West End performers were welcomed into the prison on Sunday evenings to read plays before a captive audience.

Music was not neglected either in Wormwood Scrubs or elsewhere. Prison orchestras and bands were created for the gratification of their members and the edification and entertainment of their fellows. Their efforts too were supplemented by illustrious outsiders. In February 1922 the band of the 1st Life Guards performed in Pentonville and 'a little later Stainer's Crucifixion was sung there by a well-known choir'.[44] Despite stiff opposition from the staff, Clayton later introduced concerts into Parkhurst. In the 1940s the Huddersfield Choral Society sang Handel's *Messiah* in Wakefield prison.[45] Wormwood Scrubs could even boast its own matinee idol. As a result of a four-week sentence imposed on him in 1944 for fuel-rationing offences, Ivor Novello, the actor, playwright and composer of 'Keep the Home Fires Burning', ended up there. The chaplain took this effete celebrity under

---

[41] Bottomley was serving seven years' penal servitude for the 'Victory Bonds' fraud. Joynson-Hicks's successor, John Clynes, was persuaded to reinstate the practice after he was regaled with tales of illiterate gypsies taught to read and write by other prisoners at Wakefield before the ban (Forsythe, *op. cit.*, p.178).

[42] Clayton, p.139; Thomas Pinney (ed.), *The Letters of Rudyard Kipling, Volume 5, 1920–1930* (Iowa, 2004), p.518.

[43] John Watson, *Which Is the Justice?* (London, 1969), p.48.

[44] Clayton, p.62; Macartney, *op. cit.*, pp.354ff.

[45] Merrow-Smith, *op. cit.*, p.119. He may have been mistaken about this as the Choral Society has no record of such a performance. Their records do show that they performed *The Messiah* in Wakefield prison in 1972. There were, however, other Huddersfield choirs, and so it may have been one of these. Wakefield was only one of several prisons that would benefit from choral singing. In 1971 the Bach Choir gave a Christmas carol concert in Wormwood Scrubs chapel. This became an annual event for twenty-five years. Most poignantly, after prisoners and staff in Gartree had raised money and supplies for the victims of the nuclear disaster, in 1995 the Chernobyl children's choir was allowed into the prison to perform a concert in the chapel (Dick Callan, *Gartree* (Leyhill, 2005), pp.113–16).

his wing, and put him in charge of the choir, a 'cushy number' indeed. In gratitude Novello donated a piano to the chapel (where it is still in use) and arranged occasional concerts by performers from West End shows to bring some light relief from the drab tedium of prison life which he had found so irksome.[46]

Nor was the body ignored. Gymnasia were constructed in male prisons, and all prisoners were encouraged to improve their physiques and to participate in sport. They were also latterly encouraged to smoke. Until 1922 so strict was the prohibition on tobacco that a prisoner would have to get himself sentenced to death to satisfy his craving.[47] Thereafter those serving sentences of four years or more were granted the privilege of smoking, and finally, in 1936, it was extended to all and permitted even in cells.

In May of that year, the world's first 'prison without walls' was established at New Hall in Yorkshire where adult first offenders – the 'star-class' – from Wakefield prison had been housed for the previous three years. Paterson himself joined a party of twenty men and two prison officers sleeping in wooden huts in a forest clearing seven miles from the nearest town. There they would erect the first prison camp in England. It was hoped that this and further open prisons would build up a rapport with the locals and even help revive village life. One camp would go so far as to provide players to fill gaps in their village football team, 'a practice which the commissioners with some regret felt bound to frown on when it came to notice'. The frown was tempered with a smile.[48]

Paterson would have gone further if unlimited funding had been available from the Treasury. Prisons, he believed, should exalt and not degrade, but the current estate was not conducive to exaltation. Although economy favoured a small number of large panopticon-style prisons, holding more inmates and needing fewer staff, Paterson knew that the classification and training of delinquents could not be done in such institutions. Those existing should be torn down and no more should be built. More and smaller prisons, which

---

[46] Paul Webb, *Ivor Novello: Portrait of a Star*, revised edn (London, 2005), pp.166–9.

[47] Or engage in subterfuge. During the Great War, Billy Hill, then 'a tiny kid' dressed in a sailor suit, delivered an aspidistra in a flower-pot to Holloway, where his sister Maggie was incarcerated, 'to cheer the place up'. In the soil were containers holding snuff which was also illegal but less detectable. It was sniffed up the nose, or snout, which is how tobacco came to be called 'snout'. Maggie found out where the pot had been placed so she could relieve it of its stash. That stash was effectively cash, 'the present currency in British gaols' (*Boss of Britain's Underworld* (King's Lynn, 2008), p.16).

[48] Manuel Lopez-Rey and Charles Germain (eds), *Studies in Penology* (The Hague, 1964), p.39; *EPBS*, p.231. Scotland would wait until 1953 to get its first open prison, Penninghame.

would allow for classification and in which the staff could get to know their charges, were a far preferable, albeit a more expensive, option. The maintenance of proper staffing levels was vital but also costly. Reformation of character does not come on the cheap since adjusting 'the perspective of the individual is a costlier task than [reducing] a crowd to uniformity'.[49] To get solid future returns in the form of fewer crimes and lower recidivism, initial investment had to be substantial. He looked with envy at the American exemplars recently constructed at Lewisburg and Wallkill. With their Norman cloisters, leafy quadrangles, and collegiate aspect, they were far superior to the 'great gaols of frozen ugliness' conceived in the Victorian age. 'America', Paterson contended, 'had brought beauty into the prison without shame or apology, and it is to America that the prison-builders of Europe must go for inspiration, as they once went to Pennsylvania for isolation.'[50]

Reconstructing the prison estate on the model of Oxbridge colleges was a fancy too far. The country was in depression, there were many other priorities, and lack of money would curtail Paterson's ambitions in terms both of buildings and personnel. The most that could be done in the 1930s was a massive upgrade: an extensive programme of electrification, the installation of central heating, and the provision of clear glass and sliding panels in some 18,000 cell windows.[51] Hard economic facts trumped high utopian hopes.

Yet the momentum for change seemed unstoppable. In 1932 a wave of unrest affected Dartmoor and elsewhere but even this blow to political and public confidence over the direction of penal policy did not derail the impetus for reform. The 'Dartmoor Mutiny' of Sunday 24 January was the most serious by far. It resulted in the injury of some officers and more prisoners, the burning of records, the gutting of the administrative block, and an attempt on the life of Colonel Turner, a visiting assistant commissioner, an attempt foiled by the intervention of a life-sentence man called Donovan. An inquiry into this grave disturbance was immediately set up under Herbert Du Parcq, the Recorder of Bristol and future Lord of Appeal in Ordinary.

Held in private and taking a mere five days to complete, it placed the blame on the inadequacies of Stanley Roberts, the new governor, who, unusually, had risen from the ranks; on the singularity of the 'dismal, bleak and demoralising' prison itself; and on a number of dangerous 'gangsters' who had 'great powers of evil', exiled as they were to so isolated a place. Riots

[49] Paterson, pp.53, 68; Clayton agreed, p.81.
[50] Paterson, p.70; Hobhouse, *op. cit.*, p.179.
[51] *Report* (1934), p.14.

and unrest were often blamed on internal agitators – 'bandits', 'gangsters' – or external subversives – academics, communists, social scientists – rarely on conditions, whereas in reality leaders tended to arise as a result of disturbances rather than before them. In an early example of its kind, it was also suggested that young prisoners who had seen the 1930 American jail-break film, *The Big House*, had taken their inspiration for a mass mutiny from it. But a mass mutiny could only come about when an inmate community had been formed, able to communicate, able to congregate, and able to take concerted action when conditions were intolerable and grievances ignored. Such a thing would have been impossible under Du Cane's regime. It was a product of reforms which, however necessary or desirable, had compromised the ability of discipline officers to exert control. Nonetheless, Du Parcq specifically dismissed the idea that it was the new emphasis on 'humane treatment' that had led to the trouble.

Significantly, Paterson had been one of the investigators appointed to the inquiry. He was hardly disinterested.[52] Determined to press on with transforming the prison system, Dartmoor would provide the impetus not the brake. For a man on a mission the disturbances were not the result of the changes but evidence that the changes had not gone far enough. It probably helped his efforts to deflect criticism from recent reforms that in his undergraduate days he had worked alongside Du Parcq (as well as with the future archbishop of Canterbury and leading Christian Socialist, William Temple) when they were officers of the Oxford Union. They came from the same enlightened background and, on social questions, held similar views. It undoubtedly helped that Paterson had the full backing of the other commissioners, and in particular Harold Scott, their recently appointed chief, who stood up to the new Home Secretary, Sir John Gilmour, who had 'come to the Home Office well primed by critics of prison reform', and won him over. He would prove a true convert.[53] This was an era when Tories could become liberals.

And so the commissioners continued on the same path. Undoubtedly great progress was made from what was a pretty low base, but it was imperfect, patchy, and inconsistently applied. Cicely McCall, a psychiatric social worker who became a prison officer, in her 1938 exposé *They Always Come Back* complained that women were neglected in the process, and conditions in

---

52 Brown, *op. cit.*, pp.44–7. Some, unconvinced by what they saw as a self-serving report, blamed lax discipline, 'caused by prisons being converted into a species of "homes" or "institutions"' where there were 'too many concerts and too many comforts' (Rich, pp.47, 275–9).

53 Scott, *op. cit.*, p.75.

Holloway, where she had worked in the 1930s, remained largely untouched, with inadequate medical provision, poor clothing, worse food and petty rules persisting. Provision for women lagged far behind that for men. Pay for prisoners, pioneered in 1929, took almost ten years to reach Holloway. McCall was unique. In this period lowly prison officers did not write books, let alone ones criticising the commissioners and mirroring the issues raised in inmate accounts. She was letting the side down.

Nonetheless, reservations apart, and however variously applied, reform continued. By 1938 the commissioners seemed on the cusp of their greatest success. Sir Samuel Hoare was by then Home Secretary. Like Margery Fry he was of Quaker stock, but Hoare, unlike Margery, was in lineal descent from the great reformer herself. Unlike Margery, he was a Conservative, albeit with a strong liberal streak. Sweeping 'away ... the remnants of Victorian melodrama ... that looked at the treatment of crime principally from the angles of retribution and deterrence', he approached the issue 'from the angles of prevention and reformation'. He put forward a Criminal Justice Bill which, if enacted, would *inter alia* have abolished corporal punishment, penal servitude, and imprisonment for all under sixteen years of age and restricted its use for those under twenty-one. For young offenders, Remand Homes, Compulsory Attendance Centres and night hostels called Howard Houses were to be set up. Hoare also proposed a major prison-building programme which would have replaced relics such as Pentonville, Holloway, and above all Dartmoor. The draft legislation 'was essentially an expression of Paterson's aspirations'.[54] The Czech crisis and the build-up to war with Germany scuppered the Bill along with this much-vaunted and long-awaited scheme. Pentonville and Dartmoor survive to this day, while Holloway was closed only in 2016. Herbert Morrison, the war-time Home Secretary, mused that perhaps it would have been better if all the old prisons had been demolished by the Germans, a sentiment shared by one of his department's civil servants, Lionel Fox.[55]

This remarkably able and versatile figure would provide vital support for Paterson throughout his time as a commissioner. Secretary of the Prison Commission from 1925 to 1934, during which time he published *The Modern English Prison*, Fox became chairman in 1942, holding office for eighteen years, his long tenure providing cover for Paterson's experiments and continuity for his achievements.

---

[54] HC debate, 29 November 1938; Playfair, *op. cit.*, p.177.
[55] Hugh Klare in Lopez-Rey and Germain, *op. cit.*, p.113.

Like Paterson, he believed that the objectives of deterrence, punishment and reform could be reconciled by accepting that deterrence lay in the likelihood of detection, punishment in the loss of liberty, and that reform, not further punishment, was the primary purpose of prisons. Believing, like Paterson, that rehabilitation and release should be graduated, he encouraged, in the face of fear and suspicion, the setting up of ten open prisons, such as Eastchurch – later renamed Standford Hill – in Kent in 1950, and established a 'Hostel System' in 1953 whereby long-serving prisoners would spend the night in a unit outside a prison, but during the day do a normal paid job. He also inaugurated two far-sighted 'experiments', the first at Norwich in 1956 and the second two years later at Bristol, whereby inmates were allocated a specific officer and encouraged to take their personal problems to him. Another bold innovation was allowing Yorkshire prisoners to attend adult education courses at Grantley Hall and to socialise and drink with the other students.

Like Paterson, Fox thought that recidivism could be reduced if society was more receptive to the ex-prisoner. Like Paterson he was proud of what the prison administration was trying to do, but knowing that long-term success depended on public support he wanted the public to be fully informed about the changes being introduced and his staff to be fully engaged with them. Judges and magistrates were encouraged to visit the institutions to which they consigned so many of their fellow citizens. Press interest, partisan and sensational as it could often be, was welcomed rather than shunned. In 1956 he would even allow the BBC to make a documentary, *In Prison*, inside Strangeways. He had nothing to hide but much to expose. Knowledge of the reality of prison life, so long denied, would be a tonic for reform, or so he hoped.

Like Paterson he went into print. In 1945 a cheap illustrated booklet on prisons and borstals was issued, while an in-house organ, *The Prison Service Journal*, was first published in 1960. Fox himself in 1952 – while still in office – would produce his second major foray into penology, *The English Prison and Borstal Systems*. Significantly the text was prefaced with a number of quotations demonstrating the progress of criminological purpose, from Livy's dispiriting *Carcer ad terrorem aedificatur* [a prison is built to instil fear] to Paterson's pessimistic truism that 'it is impossible to train men for freedom in a condition of captivity',[56] but ending with the optimistic declaration in the Prison Rules that custody could be deployed to establish in prisoners

---

56 *Principles of the Borstal System* (Prison Commission, Home Office, 1932), p.12.

the will and ability 'to lead a good and useful life' on release. This was the culmination and very pinnacle of penological theory, and it was realisable.

Like Paterson, Fox would become 'a penological figure of international significance'. Indeed he would become a vastly influential chairman of the United Nations European Consultative Group on the Prevention of Crime and the Treatment of Offenders, renowned for his judiciousness.[57]

Secure in the knowledge that with his friend Fox at the helm his work would endure and even expand, Paterson retired as commissioner in 1946, 'utterly worked out in body and mind'. He received a knighthood in 1947, shortly before his death in November of that year. Alexander Maxwell, a former commission chairman, eulogised his former colleague, attributing 'to his imagination and inventive force ... almost all the schemes of penal reform which have been developed in the last twenty-five years'.[58] Certainly he had overseen a considerable improvement in prison regimes, but above all he had brought about a transformation in the attitude and aptitude of staff, and in the aspirations of the errant young. As his old friend Attlee wrote, 'if his truest memorial is to be sought, it will be found in the hearts of many hundreds of men and lads who had the good fortune to come under his influence and enjoy his friendship'.[59]

Paterson's long-lasting epitaph was the 1948 Criminal Justice Act, and the 1949 Prison Rules. The former, passed shortly after his death, although less radical than the abandoned 1938 Bill, provided a coherent code for the treatment of criminals, and enacted many of his ideas. At long last the redundant additional designation of Directors of Convict Prisons was removed from the prison commissioners. More significantly, hard labour and penal servitude were abolished, only sentences of imprisonment remaining. While corporal punishment was removed entirely as a judicial sentence, the use of the 'birch-rod' and 'the cat-o'-nine-tails' was merely prohibited for all prison offences other than mutiny and 'gross personal violence' on staff.[60] The Act also revived the use of preventive detention from five to fourteen years for 'incorrigibles', those repeat offenders over thirty from whom others had to be protected. Younger recidivists would be subject to a new sentence of 'corrective training' with a minimum term of two years

---

[57] James Bennet in Lopez-Rey and Germain, *op. cit.*, pp.42–9.

[58] Cross, *op. cit.*, p.32.

[59] Paterson, p.7.

[60] The last time corporal punishment was deployed was the birching of a thirty-three-year-old man in HMP Hull in 1962. Flogging for women had been ended in 1820.

and a maximum of four.[61] Thus in both cases the length of sentence was determined, at the discretion of the court, not by the severity of the crime but by the supposed efficacy of the training or supposed need for public protection, classic examples of sentence inflation for the sake of providing 'a benefit', either to the individual concerned or to society at large.[62] No one under fifteen could be sent to prison, and unless there was no alternative nor could anyone under twenty-one, the hope being that alternatives would soon be in place to make the dream of decarcerating all young people a reality. The emphasis, however, was changing from carceral rehabilitation to keeping them out of custody in the first place. Detention Centres, imposing a decidedly deterrent 'short, sharp shock', were introduced for young offenders aged between fourteen and twenty-one whose petty crimes merited no more than six months' detention and who could no longer be subjected to the short, sharp shock of whipping.[63] Howard Houses, the community-based hostels for young offenders proposed in the 1938 Bill, were not.

The Prison Rules had as great an impact, enshrining Paterson's belief in the reformation of offenders. Prefacing them was the statement that would define the very ethos of the prison estate: that 'the training and treatment of convicted prisoners shall be to encourage and assist them to live a good and useful life, and to fit them to do so'. This declaration was embossed on every prison gate.

The impact of the Act and the Rules was soon felt. John Fletcher, one of those 'incorrigibles' who had been in and out of custodial institutions most of his troubled life, was returned to Durham prison to begin a sentence of eight years' preventive detention. He had last been in Durham some eighteen years earlier, and noted the changes:

> After the 1948 Prison Reform Act [as he called it] it was different from before. Smoking was allowed and the no talking rule had been done away with. They didn't shave your head. Tobacco was available from the day a prisoner was sentenced, and the grip of the barons was broken. Wardens were coming into the service now from Prison Colleges. They were civil servants and had to pass civil service exams.

---

61 The Criminal Justice Act 1967 abolished both corporal punishment in prison and preventive detention.

62 Frank Norman provides a first-hand account of corrective training in the 1950s. He found the Camp Hill regime no different from that of any ordinary prison and resented the fact that judges, by giving repeat minor offenders 'a chance', gave them much longer sentences than would otherwise be merited by their crime (*Bang to Rights* (London, 1958), p.140).

63 Radzinowicz, p.719.

> They had to prove that they were interested in human beings and not just in bashing a bloke.

Despite these differences, conditions remained pretty appalling, and with a more relaxed regime came greater opportunity for the weak to be intimidated by the strong. For protection some of the former prostituted themselves. Things had improved, but from a low base.[64] It was amelioration, but was it yet transformation?

After the end of the Patersonian era the thrust of his work was carried on by the Prison Commission under Fox's leadership. The year he published his *magnum opus, The English Prison and Borstal Systems*, saw the passing of the 1952 Prison Act, a consolidatory measure which laid the statutory foundation of the modern prison system, while conferring as much discretion as possible on the Secretary of State. The 1961 Criminal Justice Act, dealing with young offenders and the treatment and supervision of adults, enacted shortly after Fox retired, would continue in the same optimistic mode. Meanwhile, there were improvements in library provision and medical care, there were exciting developments such as the opening of Grendon therapeutic prison, and by the end of Fox's career the English prison system seemed very different from that which he had described in 1934. At his memorial service in Wormwood Scrubs chapel in November 1961, the Home Secretary, Rab Butler, giving the eulogy, said that Fox, having 'succeeded to a great tradition, enhanced it and passed it on embellished to the present generation' and 'at the latter end of his life he achieved many of the reforms to the perfection of which he had devoted long years'.[65]

Yet the high aspirations and benign intentions written on the page or embossed on prison gates did not necessarily accord with the reality experienced inside those prisons. Hopes were dashed on the hard stones of post-war austerity, and institutional inertia. With more people being sentenced to imprisonment, with sentences getting ever longer, with far more habitual criminals to cater for than the 'thirty or so ageing nuisances then serving their sentences under the Act of 1908', the prison population grew inexorably larger and more complex.[66] At the same time staff numbers had not even returned to the pre-war level let alone increased. Control, security, and treatment were all compromised. In crowded prisons with little direct staff supervision vulnerable prisoners were constantly at the mercy of unrestrained bullies and rapacious 'barons', or the casual brutality of unregulated officers.

---

[64] John Fletcher, *A Menace to Society* (London, 1972), pp.84, 133.

[65] A.W. Peterson in Lopez-Rey and Germain, *op. cit.*, p.193.

[66] *Report* (1955), p.24.

The buildings, many of them condemned before the Great War, continued in use and continued to deteriorate. They had in any case been designed for a highly controlled prison system and their very structure militated against more relaxed regimes. With the post-war increase in numbers, the depletion of resources, and the priority given to borstals, two or even three adult inmates being housed in cells built for one became commonplace so that by 1961 over 8,000 were so 'accommodated'. Fox thought this 'doubling-up' and 'tripling-up' the most pressing problem threatening the system. It further undermined the still important aim of preventing 'contamination of the better by the worse'.[67] 'Slopping-out' remained the demeaning early morning means of getting rid of night-time effluvia. Most prisons remained dank and smelly, and over many of the larger ones still hung the shadow of the noose. Life was at best dull and depressing, food was still dreary and unappetising, and work was repetitive and unrewarding. Fox planned for the construction of new prisons, but they would not be opened until after his death when no fewer than eight came on stream. Blundeston in 1963 became the first secure prison built for men since Camp Hill in 1912. Worst of all, despite the declaration of Fox that prisons provided the training and treatment to establish in convicted prisoners the will and ability to lead a good and useful life on discharge, only one in six received any training at all.

Chaotic and sclerotic, the prison service in practice was failing to live up to its own lofty aspirations and proud professions. A mentality that maintains the letter of the law can easily frustrate its intent, and so it could be with prison rules and regulations. Harry Woods, who published the letters of E.W. Mason, a conscientious objector imprisoned in Northallerton, had been appalled to see the deterioration in his friend after four months of solitary confinement in breach of the rule that after twenty-eight days he should have been put to work with other prisoners. This was 'ingeniously surmounted by the official pretense that a man working in his cell with the door open is performing the associated labour prescribed by the regulations'. He acidly commented that it was 'remarkable how efficiently the official mind can neutralise reforms intended to benefit prisoners, so that the prisoner continues to suffer that which the reform was intended to remove'.[68] Woods was writing of events in 1917. Wilfred Macartney and James Phelan were both imprisoned in the 1930s and both made the same observation that

---

67 *Report* (1955), p.15. By 1980, 17,000 or 40 per cent of the prison population would be 'doubled-up'.

68 E.W. Mason, *Made Free in Prison* (London, 1918), pp.210f. Mason had found conditions in Durham, where he had earlier been held, none too arduous, the food satisfactory and the warders kindly, particularly to 'C.O.s'.

while it was illegal to punish prisoners for talking, 'what happened was that if a man spoke, a warder told him to stop, he spoke again, and was reported: not for talking, but for disobeying orders'.[69] Similarly, even if there were bells in every cell, they need not be working or they could just be ignored by staff.

We get an insight into this dichotomy between aspiration and reality from the accounts of well-educated inmates who had the intelligence to analyse what they saw and the ability to put it down on paper. They would not experience or describe the worst as they were mostly 'stars', bound for Brixton or Wormwood Scrubs, not Dartmoor, and so their criticisms are all the more telling. In an attempt to 'rid England of a plague of male vice', as Maxwell-Fyfe, put it, the 1950s saw an increasing number of middle-class homosexuals being imprisoned in an all-male environment for their inability to conform to the sexual mores of the age. Those mores are vividly demonstrated in the prison commissioners' report of 1955 which stated, without differentiation, that the previous year there had been 781 men imprisoned for 'homosexual offences and bestiality'.[70] Peter Wildeblood was one of them. In March 1954 he was sentenced to eighteen months' imprisonment for homosexual offences, arising out of what was known as the 'Lord Montagu Case'. Because the acts had been committed in Hampshire, Wildeblood, on conviction, was admitted to Winchester prison.

Opened in 1849, it was a classic Victorian star-shaped building of red brick which at the time was described as 'a model establishment almost too comfortable for the purpose of correction'.[71] Each wing consisted of three landings traversed by iron staircases, with wire netting stretched between each floor to prevent suicides. They were illuminated by large windows at each end as well as by skylights. Each cell had a gas burner for artificial light. The ventilation system was so good that the temperature inside the wings remained much the same throughout the year. The prison had been designed for the silent system and was equipped with tread-wheels and hand-cranks to keep the mute inmates occupied. It was also a 'hanging gaol', and in its time had seen the execution of thirty-eight men, but no women other than the fictional Tess of the d'Urbervilles. Running water was installed in 1896, but there was no integral sanitation until the 1990s. Constant scrubbing kept it clean. To Wildeblood it looked 'as though it had been carved out of

---

69   Macartney, *op. cit.*, p.78; James Phelan, *Jail Journey* (London, 1940), p.16.
70   *Report*, p.39.
71   Alan Constable, *Five Wings and a Tower: Winchester Prison, 1850–2002* (Winchester, 2002), p.1.

carbolic soap'. It probably smelt of it too. Better than the alternative, given that 'slopping-out' each morning was the only way to get rid of bodily waste.

Wildeblood quickly learnt that prisons were 'the most snobbish of institutions and anyone whose name has appeared in the headlines is a constant source of awe and interest to staff and prisoners alike'.[72] He was a curiosity because of his celebrity, but he was well treated by other prisoners who put being a 'perve' on a totally different level from being a 'nonce' (sex offender) or 'grass' (informer).[73] The tolerance was made more explicable by 'the relaxed moral atmosphere of prison', and the fact that many of the inmates had romantic same-sex attachments with each other or with prison officers. Indeed homosexual relationships flourished in a single-sex world, although so too did sexual abuse and exploitation. Prison, thought Wildeblood, was an odd punishment for those of his sexual preference, and no deterrent.[74] For those in authority, however, he was an aberration, almost a freak, and he was interrogated in turn by governor, chaplain and doctor, to all of whom he was a source of appalled fascination. They may have been crass, but they were not unsympathetic as they sought to encourage within him a desire to be cured. Prison governors had always found homosexuals perplexing. They were often well-educated, intelligent men who caused no trouble, but the effects of imprisonment on them could be severe. Sympathetic governors tried to help them with their 'problem'. When Vidler was governor of Maidstone in the late 1940s, in order to ensure propriety, he sent 'a party of passive homosexuals, all otherwise non-delinquent' to work at the girls' open borstal at East Sutton Park. Later he was delighted to discover that one of the girls had married one of his men.[75] Wildeblood, a self-confessed homosexual, and would-be campaigner for the decriminalisation of homosexual acts, was not susceptible to change, fearing that it would alter his personality and he would lose his all-important ability to write.

In any case his time in Winchester was too short-lived for anything other than a miracle cure. After five weeks he was transferred to Wormwood

---

[72] Peter Wildeblood, *Against the Law* (London, 1955), p.95.

[73] The etymology of 'nonce' is disputed. 'Grass' is short for 'grasshopper', rhyming slang for 'shopper'.

[74] Wildeblood, *op. cit.*, pp.108, 187. Macartney (*op. cit.*, pp.418–26) evidenced the commonplace expression of homosexual relationships between long-term prisoners, many of whom were heterosexual, and between prisoners and officers. He admitted that 'gradually a homosexual shadow obscured the normal picture' and he began to have 'definitely homosexual dreams'.

[75] Vidler, *op. cit.*, p.101.

Scrubs to complete his sentence. Again he was taken through the imposing portico of a Victorian prison, again he was stripped and bathed, clothed in prison attire, and taken to 'D' Hall, which took 'corrective trainees' and 'star-class men', whose numbers were increasing. Wildeblood was one. He was put in a single cell indistinguishable from the one he had left hours before. The prison, however, was very different and he enjoyed the Cockney patter and the larger than life characters he met there, from the neurotic principal officer who worried about what Wildeblood might write about him to the little Londoner who told a dazzling array of mother-in-law stories. Funniest of all was Basil, a Wykehamist blackmailer who told outrageous jokes in French. He also met with unrelenting kindness among his fellow 'cons'. On his first arrival, to supplement the marmite he had brought with him from Winchester, a prisoner bought him a luxury, a jar of marmalade. Another placed a sprig of lavender in his cell. The account he gives of his time in Wormwood Scrubs suggests that even with the indignities, the awful smell, the squalor, the poor food, and the monotony of the routine, life was endurable if on hold, especially as friendships among prisoners of all social classes, forged in adversity and honed in 'association', were prevalent and important.

So far as the staff were concerned he was surprised to find so many decent, good-hearted men among them. In addition to 'the bullies and the robots there exists a small body of warders – almost one might say, an underground movement – which contrives to take a real interest in the prisoners, and which is perhaps the most potent force for the reform of criminals which exists today'. He does not relate instances of staff brutality, although others do, and Wormwood Scrubs officers had a reputation for it. He does refer to the indifference of the senior management to complaints, and their incredulity when complaints were made about staff.

He was less complimentary about the array of governors he had encountered, all seemingly middle-aged military men. In Wildeblood's time, the governor of Wormwood Scrubs was Major Grew, who in February 1945 had 'left the stern and heavy atmosphere of Wandsworth prison for Wormwood Scrubs with its more hopeful approach to penal problems, and its feeling of cloistered serenity'. He prided himself on being an ardent reformer in the Paterson mould and saw the 'architecture of its entrance' as representing 'the open door to new and bolder experiments in reform'. That was not how Wildeblood viewed it or him. In his opinion Grew ran the prison as 'a kind of caricature of military life', was responsible for the dump it had become, and along with his subordinates exhibited a casual condescension to prisoners, especially 'of colour'. Indeed Wildeblood considered that 'the colour discrimination in the prison was one of its most nauseating features'. He found it odd that when the praises of Maidstone were sung, the credit was given to Vidler, but 'when the stink of Wormwood Scrubs reaches the nostrils of the House of Lords it seems to be generally assumed that no blame can be attached to Major Grew'. Grew in his account of his time as governor paints a positive picture of a good prison getting even better under his care, blames the state of the sanitation on the actions of a few 'uncooperative' prisoners who deliberately blocked the lavatories to cause 'inconvenience' – presumably to themselves! – exonerates the staff, and extols the quality of the workshops, the evening classes, and the provision made for books, all things Wildeblood had criticised.[76]

He was not the only critic and not the harshest one. The writer Rupert Croft-Cooke was at Wormwood Scrubs at about the same time as Wildeblood, serving a sentence for a similar offence. He entered the prison unprejudiced and unafraid, having heard of enormous improvements and that inmates were really 'helped towards reinstatement' after discharge, but he was to be sorely disappointed. The food lauded as 'appetising' in the reports of the commissioners he could barely swallow. Nor could he swallow their other rosy assertions. Although he took a more charitable view of the governor, he described conditions in 'D' Hall in similar terms to Wildeblood. There were 'decent screws', odd-ball inmates, and governor grades who treated him impeccably, but even they were second-rate, the one exception being 'Ben Grew' who 'had a conscience and was a man of breeding' but whose efforts at improvements were vitiated by his lack of 'knowledge of what went on in his prison'. With a higher calibre of senior staff, supported in their efforts by the Prison Commission, so much more could be made of the 'superb opportunities' for rehabilitation. Incompetence and laziness were a major part of the problem. Petty restrictions, irksome routines, little indignities, daily humiliations, unthinking adherence to 'rules': these were his gripes. The whole system was second-rate, inefficient and nit-picking, but it was neither particularly arduous nor designedly cruel. As a single man serving a short sentence, working in the library and relishing the solitude in which to write, Croft-Cooke could cope with imprisonment. Others – the illiterate, the bread-winner, the gregarious – were made frantic with worry or loneliness or rendered 'listless and eventually worthless', all worse-equipped on release to resume ordinary life than when they had first come in. His final verdict was damning: 'the thing is rotten throughout, a mosquito-swamp of evil in which crime breeds crime, in which clean minds fester,

---

[76] Wildeblood, *op. cit.*, pp.154–8, 161f.; Grew, pp.128–72.

and all hope of resurrection is lost'. It could not be 'saved by piddling small improvements' but had to be 'changed in spirit wholly, made to serve and protect society, not to germinate enmity, to foster crime and to encourage vice'.[77] Prison as presently constituted could not produce the goods. Paterson and his colleagues would have agreed with these sentiments but would have been horrified at the conclusion. They believed that they had wrought not 'piddling' but substantial changes to the very ethos and purpose of prisons. Grew was not alone in being blinkered.

On his release Croft-Cooke fled the country for Morocco and wrote in exile, while Wildeblood stayed put and took a public and well-publicised stand, giving evidence before the Wolfenden Committee 'on Homosexual Offences and Prostitution'. Its 1957 report resulted in the decriminalisation of private consensual sex between two men aged twenty-one or over, apparently reducing the concern the prison authorities had about 'homosexual behaviour arising from two prisoners sharing a cell'.[78] Wildeblood also wrote his celebrated and influential book, *Against the Law*, which despite being described as 'the noblest, and wittiest and most appalling prison book of them all', did more for legal than for penal reform.[79] Things were to get much worse in future decades.

Had Paterson devoted more time to prisons perhaps things would have been different and the reality would have more lived up to the 'good and useful life' rhetoric, but no one however energetic would find it easy to overhaul the long-established prison estate, especially when money was short, and the exigencies of war interrupted the progress made. The direct results of the reformatory efforts since 1895 were nonetheless considerable, and far ahead of most other countries. The Du Cane era was well and truly over. The whole rigid and authoritarian apparatus he had erected had been dismantled. A 'great relaxation' had occurred.[80] Regimes and the way prisoners were treated had greatly improved. There was no institutionalised brutality. But the prison system had not been revolutionised as Paterson had hoped.

Prisons, important as they were to him, always took second place to the provision of alternatives to them for young offenders. Such provision as existed was still in its infancy and could be nurtured, developed, and

---

[77] Rupert Croft-Cooke, *The Verdict of You All* (London, 1955), pp.61ff., 119, 253.

[78] Andrew Rutherford, *Prisons and the Process of Justice* (Oxford, 1986), p.100.

[79] C.H. Rolph in *The New Statesman*. Rolph cannot have read many books on prison, if he thought Wildeblood's the most appalling.

[80] Forsythe, *op. cit.*, p.211.

expanded. With his prior experience of working with deprived young people, Paterson saw a great opportunity to do something extraordinary for the worst of them, to give working-class delinquents the advantages of aspects of the public school experience, albeit with more manual work and fewer Latin gerunds.[81] Paterson both championed and transformed Ruggles-Brise's creation. Existing custodial institutions for the young would become reformative academies. Borstals would have a rebirth.

---

[81] Neville Staple recounted an amusing anecdote about a friend of his accused of smuggling aftershave into Hewell Grange borstal. When asked to plead, he floored the governor by answering '*nolo contendere*' – 'no contest'. Staple thought it a sad reflection on the prison service that the governor's command of Latin was inferior to that of a borstal boy (*Original Rude Boy: From Borstal to the Specials* (London, 2009), pp.70f.).

CHAPTER 30

The Pioneer Spirit

If the institution is to train lads for freedom, it cannot train them in an atmosphere of captivity and repression.

Alexander Paterson

He had heard of borstal boys who had been asked 'are you Christian?' and had replied: 'No, Church of England.'

Peter Wildeblood

Paterson exaggerated when he told a friend that he had found borstal 'little more than a boys' prison' and re-founded it on educational lines. In truth he would build on his predecessor's work. Evolution, not revolution, even though the evolution was rapid and the transformation considerable. As borstal boys after the Great War were no longer being released directly into the armed forces, the institutions could be thoroughly 'civilianised', becoming almost entirely therapeutic, the emphasis being on individualised treatment, education and industrial training. It was the means to achieve the end that differed between the borstal system devised by Ruggles-Brise and that developed by Paterson, not the end itself which for both men was to turn wayward youths into conforming members of industrious working-class society. Character-building measures aimed at instilling 'stern and exact discipline' through external controls were replaced by methods aimed at changing attitudes through personal example and developing self-respect and self-discipline.[1] Paterson was Elizabeth Fry reincarnate. Rather than re-founding the system as he boasted, he reanimated it and rededicated it to the reformatory ideal. This was just as Hobhouse and Brockway had recommended: taking away the military and disciplinary element and distancing the whole borstal system from the penal.[2]

Paterson learnt a lesson from the most recent acquisition to the borstal estate: Portland in Dorset. In August 1921, the same month as Ruggles-

---

[1] Evelyn Ruggles-Brise, *The English Prison System* (London, 1921), p.99; Roger Hood, *Borstal Reassessed* (London, 1965), p.94. All these principles can be found in *Across the Bridges*, 2nd edn (London, 1912), pp. 41–68.

[2] H&B, p.440.

Brise's resignation, the old convict prison was reopened as the third borstal for boys, although Edward Shortt, the Home Secretary, admitted that had money been no object he would have preferred a custom-built establishment on a different site to this 'great grey stone fortress', frowning 'from its rocky eminence over the English Channel'.[3] The number of convicts at Portland had shrunk to around 250 and they could easily be assimilated at Dartmoor. Phantoms of its past haunted the deserted prison. Sentry-boxes lined its grim walls and 'it was not difficult to imagine that the ghosts of old warders with carbines still kept an alert eye open for escapes'.[4] The buildings with their iron-barred cells, however well they served their old purpose, frustrated their new, until the interiors were transformed by the labour and ingenuity of borstal boys. Apart from a few officers transferred there from Rochester, most of the staff were hangovers from the old convict service. Many of the boys sent there were rejects from Borstal or Feltham. Discipline suffered, and corporal punishment and close confinement were both deployed on the unruly.[5] After one boy killed himself and several escaped, public concern was roused by allegations of staff brutality. There were demands for an inquiry. The Home Secretary himself paid a visit. So did Sir Arthur Conan Doyle. Both luminaries were reassured. The public and the press were not, and their fears went unassuaged until a well-known journalist and erstwhile critic called Sydney Moseley, who had visited Portland and the other borstals and been converted, published his reassuring vindication of them, *The Truth about Borstal*, in 1926.

Yet so far as Portland was concerned, little had changed, as the accounts of former borstal boys show. The most positive was Mark Benney, who arrived there in 1926 at the age of sixteen. He wrote that, despite its prison-like appearance, the ethos of Portland was different. 'The oppressive sense of social disapprobation was several degrees removed. In prison one is always intensely aware of the world beyond the walls and therefore aware of one's criminality. In borstal you could frequently forget both'. Yet on release he would graduate to prison. John Fletcher went there in 1933. He found it far less harsh than Durham, and noted that 'the staff were

---

3   John Watson, *Which Is the Justice?* (London, 1969), p.65.
4   Mark Benney, *Low Company* (London, 1936), pp.217f.
5   Clayton, pp.55f. Clayton was deputy-governor at Portland when the transformation took place. He thought it 'a perfect example of how things should not be done'. He had personal experience of borstal failures when he had been assaulted by a youth in the convict prison who was serving a life-sentence for murdering an officer in Rochester. To his credit Clayton refused to report this incident, saving the lad a flogging (pp.122f.).

picked for the job, they were youngish or out of the army and specially trained'. Nonetheless 'we lived a military life' and gangs proliferated, and he concluded that 'every one gets out of borstal worse'. The epitome of this was Billy Hill who was to become a major-league career criminal. In 1927 after three months breaking stones at Wandsworth reception centre he was allocated to Portland borstal. He was sixteen. Put to work carrying baskets of stones up a steep quarry face, or harnessed to a truck which he then had to pull along, each night, to prevent infection, iodine was applied to the cuts and sores on his back. After an escape-bid during which he committed an aggravated burglary he was sent back to borstal to be whipped and subjected to nine months' hard labour. The Home Office dispatched a birch – three-and-a half feet of twigs tied together into a bundle into which a handle of similar length was fitted – for the punishment. It was first soaked in brine to make it more pliable and then applied to the bare backside of the boy. His wounds dressed, he was sent back to pounding stones or, worse, evil-smelling bones into powder, all the while confined in a cramped cage-like structure. He would later give his professional opinion of this Fagin's kitchen. There could be no better academy for breeding hardened criminals. If a boy was lacking in essential criminality on arrival, that deficiency would soon be made up; if he had a 'spark of honesty', it would be snuffed out; 'if there was a remote hope that he might degenerate into an ordinary dull citizen', it would be 'killed stone dead'.[6]

Paterson sensed that all was not well and knew that the Portland model was not one to be emulated. Although he did not close it he tried to alter its ethos. A high-school for criminals was not what he wanted. The whole sorry saga merely confirmed his conviction that borstals were not only not boys' prisons but they should not be created in existing or former prisons. He was determined to distance his conception of a completely reformatory system from any penal associations. Within months of his appointment he had done away with the term 'modified borstal'[7] which to him was more like

---

6   Benney, *op. cit.*, p.218; John Fletcher, *A Menace to Society* (London, 1972), p.47; Billy Hill, *Boss of Britain's Underworld* (King's Lynn, 2008), pp.20–4. Hill was moved to Rochester where, despite having lost all remission, the governor wanted to give him a fresh start, which he took, excelling in sports and being top boy in his house. It was to no avail. Had they given him 'six, short, hard months of glasshouse treatment' he might have tried to go straight, or so he said. But that was what he had had at Portland. It did not work, nor did the more positive approach of Rochester. Before becoming a borstal boy he was already beyond hope, and yet blamed the institutions for making an animal out of him. Hill was as guilty of self-deceit as he was of self-glamorisation. He was the sort for which preventive detention was designed.

7   *Report* (1922), p.10.

'modified prison', and he would encourage the growth of new establishments 'on modern lines', either camps constructed by borstal boys themselves or country-house conversions. Whereas early borstals were supposed to represent a quasi-military model of discipline and authority, exemplified in Rich's regime in Rochester, Paterson effectively re-modelled them on public school lines with their 'muscular Christianity' and 'house' affiliations, and implicitly advocated the inculcation of middle-class values of honesty, self-reliance, and gentlemanly competitiveness. *Esprit de corps*, a term he much used, was not the preserve of the elite as he had found it in working-class boys' clubs and among the ranks in the army. Borstals were not to be replica public schools but all that was best in terms of character-building that those schools provided should be incorporated into them for the benefit of the less-privileged youths sent there. Public school pupils, through team-spirit and camaraderie, through loyalty to individuals and the institution, through self-discipline and sense of duty, acquired the self-confidence, ingenuity and determination to run an empire. Give such an opportunity to wayward working-class youths, build up their moral sense along with their physique, imbue them with self-worth and ambition, and they too could play the game and go on to better things. Similarly there should be no 'caste system' in education, and all should be 'subjected slowly to the unconscious discipline which should be the chief instrument of every educational establishment'.[8] Education in life and literature would go side by side. Borstal boys should be weaned off 'drivel that once enslaved' them, and be introduced to a higher culture of which they had been deprived, but they were to be encouraged to explore and discover for themselves and find the level appropriate to their varying abilities: 'the intelligentsia play chess and proletariat argue about the Arsenal'.[9] Civic responsibility rather than class identity was inculcated.

Borstal training has been damned as patronising and worse, an attempt to 'prise working-class boys from their indigenous values', but this latter criticism can be taken too far since, as it has been pointed out, 'a concerted assault on proletarian values would hardly have countenanced pigeon-fancying!'[10] Patronising it may have been, but for a while, under inspiring leadership and the spirit of eternal optimism, at least for many it gave a fresh start, and cut down recidivism.[11] As one working-class youth put it,

8   Paterson, p.61.

9   *Principles of the Borstal System* (Prison Commission, Home Office, 1932), pp.11, 54; Erica Stratta, *The Education of Borstal Boys* (London, 1970), p.9.

10   Victor Bailey, *Delinquency and Citizenship* (Oxford, 1987), p.203.

11   In the 1930s the borstal system's re-offending rate was around a third, as opposed to a current rate for young offenders of three-quarters.

'critics of the public school may contend that a better objective could have been found; but it cannot be denied that, for all social purposes, its spirit is an immeasurable improvement on the spirit of the panopticon'.[12] In a quintessentially English way it was a beacon of hope, and there has been a sad lack of these in the history of imprisonment.

Paterson knew, however, that he had to reassure the fickle public, whose concern over brutality was matched by its disapproval of 'mollycoddling', that borstals were not boy scout camps, and that the expense lavished on juvenile delinquents was justified. For this audience his refrain was that 'punishment and reform are not antagonistic. Borstal is for the adolescent offender at once more deterrent and more reformative than prison.'[13] It was certainly the latter, but given the many 'graduates' who looked back on their time in borstal with gratitude, it is not obvious that it was the former. To Paterson it did not matter, for it was a distinction without a difference, as the effect of internal reform was the same as external deterrence. Reformed individuals had no desire to re-offend and so no need to be deterred.

In the face of escapes and re-offending, he also had to persuade the courts to make more use of borstals. They seemed to prefer 'a short, sharp dose of imprisonment' for the errant adolescent to a more prolonged period in borstal. For many judges two or three years in borstal for a minor offence meriting two or three months in prison was plain unjust. Paterson thought otherwise. The sentences were not comparable. Borstals were not prisons. Borstal training was an opportunity that should not be thrown away. All training took time, and the time it took depended on the individual. Thus borstal should be for a minimum period as punishment and have a maximum extent for training. The sentence should be tailored to the offender and when the offender was fit to return to the community he should be released. Thus the period in detention need not be justified by the gravity of the offence, although it should never be out of all proportion to that offence.[14]

His fellow commissioners, rather than resenting an 'outsider' in their ranks, were largely supportive. This was vital as, however charismatic,

---

[12] On the other hand while reviving his 'schoolboy values of fair-play and team-spirit' and eradicating 'resentment from [his] criminal attitude' it did nothing to dispel his attraction to crime. Indeed it equipped him for it by building up his physique and giving him the opportunity to study engineering and chemistry, thereby enhancing his skills as a safe-blower (Benney, *op. cit.*, pp.218, 236–9).

[13] Rupert Cross, *Punishment, Prison and the Public* (London, 1971), pp.36, 130.

[14] Paterson, pp.63f. He thought minima and maxima should also apply to prison sentences, and that 'incorrigibles' should be detained indefinitely. Gordon, an ex-borstal boy, thought that borstal sentences were too short to be effective and that the period should be extended to five years (J.W. Gordon, *Borstalians* (London, 1932), p.239).

Paterson could never succeed alone and in opposition to the others. The backing of successive chairmen was especially important. A fortuitous encounter proved propitious for the future. When Harold Scott, an eager young civil servant at the Home Office, received Paterson's draft of revised borstal regulations, he 'fell on it and cut it to pieces'. He was confronted in his office by 'a stocky, cherub-faced, quick-speaking enthusiast' who had bounded up the stairs three steps at a time 'to find out who had handled his work so roughly'. When the pen-pusher had to concede he had not actually seen a borstal institution, Paterson rectified that omission and took him on a tour. Scott was enraptured with this 'strange world' so different from what he had expected, and 'caught from the young governors and their deputies something of the crusading ardour with which they had been fired by that pioneer of prison reform'. He acknowledged that Paterson was one of the most remarkable men he ever met, had had a decisive influence on his life, and to whose ideas he became 'wholly converted'. Just as well, since in 1932 Scott would become chairman of the Prison Commission, and would continue to give his subordinate full backing in the face of influential detractors and 'a good deal of misrepresentation in the popular press'.[15]

Meanwhile it was a mark of Paterson's initial success that by 1925 there was 'a general rise in prestige for borstal training'. The public and press were reassured. The judiciary, by and large, were won over, and the few dissidents cajoled into submission.[16] Expansion could begin. Paterson would transform the borstal estate in number as well as nature, with a diversity of provision to cater for all, from the 'rougher types' to the 'trustworthy boys'.

Paterson represented the very best in privileged paternalism – or benign condescension – but 'do-gooding' was surely better by far than disdain, neglect or indifference. He genuinely wanted to bring out the best in the least-privileged but at the same time he thought he knew what the best should be. His attitude was very much of its time and of his class and was suffused with Christian, middle-class, public school and even imperialist values. It was the same attitude that could be found in officers for their men in the army, or among school-boys or undergraduates who devoted their holidays to running youth clubs for urban working-class youngsters or soup kitchens for the homeless, just as Paterson had done. In a pamphlet issued by the prison commissioners in 1932, following on from his 1925 articles in *The Times*, he asserted that the principles of the borstal system were 'based

---

[15] Scott credited Paterson with his appointment as chairman (*Your Obedient Servant* (London, 1959), pp.65, 71).

[16] Hood, *op. cit.*, pp.35f.

on the double assumption that there is individual good in each, and among nearly all an innate corporate spirit, which will respond to the appeal made to the British of every sort, to play the game, to follow the flag, to stand by the old ship'.[17]

Lads brought up in 'the school of hard knocks' were re-schooled in borstal. They wore shorts and flannel shirts, the games kit of the school-boy, but were allowed to wear a brown and grey jacket with lapels instead of the more institutional high-collared jacket. They lived in buildings which were designated as 'houses', presided over by 'housemasters', many of whom were scions of public schools and Oxbridge. As 'adjutants' or 'auxiliary officers' they had 'house-captains', chosen by them or sometimes elected by the inmates themselves. On his appointment to this highly privileged and powerful post, Mark Benney 'felt as Hitler must have felt when he became Fuhrer'. The bully may have been brought out in some, but, despite his analogy, not in Benney. But 'if the object of this distinction was to induce a sense of responsibility, the experiment was singularly unsuccessful', he concluded.[18] According to his account, he carried out his prefectorial duties with sufficient application to retain his post but with insufficient rigour to alienate his peers. Hard work and strenuous outdoor activities were encouraged, so that borstal boys would go to bed healthily tired out after a long day's exertions. Cross-country rambles and camping trips began in 1922. Team games in particular were emphasised as was inter-house rivalry, culminating in an annual sports day with a cup presented to the winning house. Paterson was to the fore in encouraging this and he himself arranged and refereed matches with outside clubs including his beloved Bermondsey Boys.[19] Borstal teams would play home and away matches against public schools, and individual athletes would compete against public school boys.[20] The captain of a cricket team from Eton told the opposing Feltham side that he envied them for being allowed to smoke, whereas if he were caught smoking he would be beaten or even expelled. Expulsion would break his parents' hearts whereas their early discharge would delight their parents. Another, 'much annoyed at this display of freedom was overheard to remark

---

[17] *Principles of the Borstal System, op. cit.*, pp.8f.

[18] Benney, *op. cit.*, pp.240–3. Benney was made house-captain in 1927 but wrote his account in 1936.

[19] Gordon recalled the excitement when Paterson refereed a match at Feltham, and how he was cheered at tea (*op. cit.*, pp.134f.).

[20] Alan Sillitoe's 1966 short story, *The Loneliness of the Long Distance Runner*, immortalised one such encounter.

"I say what cads!'"[21] One poignant cricket match was played between the boys in Borstal and those from Howard House in Maidstone prison. The latter were either reprieved murderers or those whose offences were so grave that they had been given long sentences of penal servitude. With Paterson's warm approval Captain Clayton took eleven of them in a coach to play the Borstal boys. They won. It was confidently predicted that such an ethos was growing among the trainees that the time would soon come when the 'traditions of Borstal would be at least equal to those of Eton and Harrow' and the Borstal 'Blue' engender as much pride as a Varsity Blue.[22]

At the heart of the system was the recognition of the individuality of all those sent there. Where the prison system in the past had been expected to crush individuality and had prohibited social interaction between the keepers and the kept, Paterson's vision was the reverse: the task was 'not to break or knead [the lads] into shape, but to stimulate some power within to regulate conduct aright, to insinuate a preference for the good and the clean', to make them want to use their lives well 'so that they themselves and not others will save them from waste'.

> [They] are not raw recruits of a conscript army to be arranged neatly in rows according to their physical stature, to be swung rhythmically in a mass across the parade ground to the beat of a drum. Each is a different and difficult problem. It is because they must be handled individually with sympathy, firmness and discernment that those who handle them must be rare individuals. The strength or weakness of the borstal system lies in the strength and weakness of the borstal staff.[23]

As in prisons, chaplains were integral to the regime and had the vital role of trying to make religion pivotal to the many youngsters who entered borstal with only the most basic understanding of Christianity or of other faiths. Every boy had to attend services, however rudimentary their commitment. Reformation and religion were conjoined twins. As priests, chaplains took services and administered the sacraments; as preachers they enjoined repentance and rebirth; as pastors they befriended their charges and provided an ever-open ear and ever-empathetic counsel. On the whole

---

[21] John Vidler, *If Freedom Fail* (London, 1964), p.63; Richard Maxwell, *Borstal and Better* (London, 1956), pp.147f.

[22] Clayton, pp.101f.; Hood, *op. cit.*, p.54. 'Blue boys' were the best behaved of the borstalians and were in their second year, having spent their first in brown clothes, and having passed through all four stages or 'grades'. With the colour came perks, such as having a pipe or going on summer camps. They were frequently given 'staff' jobs in their house and reputedly lived up to the responsibility (*Report* (1934), p.61).

[23] *Principles, op. cit.*, pp.12ff.

they were highly regarded.[24] Matrons on the other hand were a novelty when they were introduced in 1923 and ideally became mother-figures to the boys in this very masculine environment. They too were popular. Uniforms for custodial officers were abolished in 1924, and instead staff donned sports jackets and flannels, along with the dark blue, light blue and brown 'borstal tie', 'the colours of Oxbridge and Dartmoor'.[25] This civilianisation indicated a transformation in their ethos as well as their role.

Their ethos was that of a vocation and not just of a job. Staff were being professionalised in the highest sense. Paterson believed that they should be carefully selected, thoroughly trained and well-remunerated as it was 'men and not buildings' who would 'change the hearts of misguided lads', but money must not be their motivation. 'Better an institution that consists of two log-huts in swamp or desert, with a staff devoted to their task, than a model block of buildings, equipped without thought of economy, whose staff is solely concerned with thoughts of pay and promotion.'[26]

Their role was the crucial one of 'strong men' helping, teaching and training 'weak boys', and they needed to have a triptych of qualities: 'a wise head, a kind heart, a firm hand'. They were to be moulders, not breakers. As the first of the borstal rules set down, they were to influence their young charges 'through their own example and leadership and by enlisting their willing co-operation'. All the staff, not just pastoral and vocational, but custodial as well, were supposed to get to know their charges and use their initiative, a volte-face from the normal role of the prison officer, a much more demanding one but a much more rewarding one as well. Jack Gordon, who was at Feltham in the 1920s, could 'not help admiring the borstal staff' and knew that they were following in Paterson's steps in 'revolutionizing lads' minds' by trusting them and leading them. He 'saw the methods of curing crime and [he] wanted to be cured'. That was one response. The much more criminally-minded Billy Hill was sent to borstal in 1927 'when borstals were the finest finishing-schools for criminals any underworld could wish for'.[27]

---

[24] Gordon, *op. cit.*, pp.136ff.

[25] Grew, p.22. The headmaster of a leading public school twice wrote complaining that the tie bore a resemblance to that of his former pupils, and implying that it would be demeaning for them to be confused with borstal officers. Paterson took no notice of the first missive but replied to the second, assuring the headmaster that the commissioners had no objection to his old boys continuing to wear those colours (Watson, *op. cit.*, pp.71f.).

[26] Grew, p.19.

[27] Grew, p.24; Gordon, *op. cit.*, p.135; Hill, *op. cit.*, p.20.

Paterson knew that vital to the success of his venture was leadership, leadership after his own image. Borstal governors who adhered to the more military model and strongly opposed 'the soft, sloppy, "sob-stuff"' that was creeping in and which, in their view, was ruining the chances of making borstals effective as places of reform, were shunted off to prisons where Paterson thought their talents would be better utilised.[28] In their place he appointed a new breed of what he considered to be inspirational leaders. Some were Oxford graduates who had experienced life in Bermondsey or the East End. One of these was Stansfeld's own son, Gordon, who became an outstanding housemaster in Borstal itself before, at Paterson's bidding, going to Burma to establish a 'training-school for young offenders' there, only to drown 'pursuing a runaway' in 1931. Paterson wrote an article on both 'Father and Son' for *The Times*.[29] Some were fellow members of 'Toc H'. Others, like Grew, he met by chance and encouraged to join in an idealistic venture. These disciples in turn recruited like-minded subordinates. Paterson's unique contribution was not just making changes but 'in finding and inspiring the men through whom the change was to work'.[30]

For instance, at the end of 1923 Rich was posted, against his will, to Liverpool. Despite his success at Rochester, and although he firmly believed in the borstal ideal as espoused by Ruggles-Brise, his stern disciplinarian reputation, his increasing conviction that his chief's retirement marked the beginning of the rot, and his concerns about Paterson's dominance, the intrusion of inexpert inspectors and interference by inexperienced commissioners, put him in opposition to the prevailing *Zeitgeist*.[31]

Rich's successor at Borstal, his erstwhile senior medical officer, Dr J.C.W. Methven, was very much of the modern stamp, so much so that in 1930 he would become an assistant commissioner (as inspectors were renamed that year) and a full commissioner in 1938, replacing in that role the equally progressive Dr Norwood East. Meanwhile he was to initiate and establish the new training principles that Paterson advocated. Methven recruited by direct entry like-minded individuals to the key posts of housemaster, in which they were to both provide inspiring leadership and set an example of gentlemanly conduct. They were young men with little or no prior prison experience, poorly paid, over-worked and utterly committed. Two were churchmen: the

28 Rich, pp.96f., 105–8.
29 Barclay Baron, *The Doctor* (London, 1952), pp.131f.
30 Hood, *op. cit.*, p.109.
31 Rich, pp.128f. Ex-borstal boy Jack Gordon took this 'military man' to task in a book published the same year as that of the governor (*op. cit.*, pp.281f.).

chaplain, the Revd James Butler, who took over 'D' Hall, and a future priest, Paul Leavey, who was put in charge of C' Hall. The other two, Gilbert Hair of 'B' Hall and Frank Ransley of 'A' Hall, were future prison governors of Wormwood Scrubs and Wandsworth respectively.[32]

Grew remained as deputy-governor and enthusiastically embraced innovation. In 1924 he led a summer camp on the Isle of Sheppey, where the boys nearing release lived alongside staff in disused army huts. This was despite the fact that six boys had absconded from the second Feltham camp the previous year, it being generally recognised that such ventures were a risk worth taking and a test of trust worth setting. The first Labour Home Secretary, Arthur Henderson, visited the camp and had his picture taken sitting on the grass with the lads.[33] So successful had this expedition been that the following year Grew got approval from the commissioners to go one step further and, without discipline officers, take a group of trainees on a week's walking tour during which they would be allowed to associate with boys of their own age from the nearby towns and villages. By bringing his charges into direct contact with the outside world he wanted to dispel myths that had accrued about borstals, and better inform the public of the aims and methods of these institutions. It was an unalloyed success.

John Vidler was another enthusiastic recruit. He had come under the influence of Paterson as the older man was a college friend of his father-in-law and had become a frequent visitor to his own home. There 'the broad-shouldered, dynamic personality ... enlivened our evenings ... with talk that showed a depth of feeling and a fund of creative ideas'.[34] Vidler proved a receptive audience. He too, during his Oxford days, had devoted time to working in boys' clubs, and had thought that trying to help wayward youths back to a normal life would give meaning to his own. Twenty years later Paterson asked him to become a borstal governor. To do so he had to join the prison service, which he did with reluctance as he never wanted to be a gaoler.

In 1932 Vidler was appointed deputy-governor of Feltham, arriving there a complete novice. He rapidly acclimatised to the Patersonian ethos

---

32 Grew, p.21. For some prison officers it was with the introduction of amateurs from outside the service, enthusiasts for the relaxation of all restraints, that the rot set in. And the rot would spread as they were promoted to governor grade, and brought their borstal ideas into the prison system (Harley Cronin, *The Screw Turns* (London, 1967), p.72).

33 Grew, pp.35ff. He and many other writers following him state that this was in 1923, but as Henderson was in office only in 1924 it must have been that year.

34 Vidler, *op. cit.*, pp.8f.

as exemplified in the governor, Captain James Holt, a man who never gave up on the high proportion of 'dull and backward lads ... born invertebrates, instinctively taking the part of least resistance' that he was sent. Like so many he found the 'process of vertebration a slow and painful one', and considered that two years was too short a time to train such unpromising material.[35] His methods were unconventional. On one occasion when Vidler asked to put an abusive runaway in a canvas restraint jacket, Holt refused outright and told his deputy to kit the boy out in oversize shorts and slippers so that he would have to waddle around hitching his trousers up. Immobilising him, and making him look ridiculous, rather than putting him in restraint was the Feltham way. Even the boy could see the funny side.[36] Vidler himself put in ninety hours a week, and testified to the equal dedication of the other staff.

Moving to Portland in January 1934 he succeeded by trial and error in putting his mark on the place. He in turn encouraged his subordinates to plough their own furrow in their own way. Initiative and independence were traits to be cherished in disciplinary officers and especially in housemasters. There was no one way of doing things. There was no *modus operandi* imposed from above. There should be no mould into which to put a creative maverick. The individuality of the staff was as important as the individuality of the trainees. Let them get on with it. Vidler himself employed 'training by paradox', paradoxically with considerable success. One example involved a truculent youth of Italian extraction. Every sanction having failed, Vidler, aware that he was dealing with a staunch Catholic, informed him that the only punishment he received in future must be self-imposed in the form of penance. The lad promptly gave himself fifteen days on bread and

---

35 *Report* (1934), p.63. Richard Maxwell thought that 'if there were more like Captain H in those responsible positions then one of the country's most pressing problems would be viewed with a more humane understanding, and there would be far fewer habitual criminals'. During his stay Maxwell escaped, got into more trouble, yet Holt had him back. On his release Maxwell reverted to a life of crime. Looking back he thought most boys were given a fresh start, but for a minority, of which he was one, it was just temporary respite from a life of crime. Borstal carried a stigma and it required determination to make good. The easier course was to relapse (Maxwell, *op. cit.*, pp.109ff., 148f.).

36 Vidler, *op. cit.*, pp.13f. It had not always been thus. In the 1920s escapees were stripped of their borstal clothes, put in the penal class and, like Victorians undergoing hard labour, had to smash stones during the day and in the evening pick coir – coconut fibre – for mattresses (Gordon, *op. cit.*, p.171). Richard Maxwell testified to Feltham's transformation under 'the gentleman governor'. When the boy arrived in 1934 he was astonished by his reception and the plentiful meal that welcomed him, with real cutlery, china soup bowls, salt and pepper, and large helpings, much better fare than he would enjoy at home (*op. cit.*, pp.109–19).

water, never caused any more trouble and went on to become a successful businessman. Another tearaway testified to the success of Vidler's methods in a lengthy article published in *The Spectator*.[37]

For many of the boys the 'grey fortress' had become 'the jam factory' and fun was in favour. The governor rather admired the survival instinct of one quick-witted lad who had been allowed out on a day's boating trip. When asked what HMBI on his life-belt stood for, he replied 'Harry Mason's Boxing Institute, of course'.[38] Surviving, standing on their own two feet, was what the training was all about. Vidler set up a discharge house in which the boys looked after themselves. This was later turned into an open camp at Bovington, albeit short-lived, as it was closed with the outbreak of war.

Lilian Barker was an equally inspired appointment. She had worked with Paterson at the Ministry of Labour. In 1923 he asked her to become governor of Aylesbury, the sole borstal for girls. He knew she would be 'mother, father, brother, sister, uncle and aunt to everybody'.[39] Since its inception the borstal had been housed in a disused institution for inebriates within the women's prison. It had been hoped to move it to buildings outside the austere walls, but this had never happened. Although the prison and borstal existed side by side, were under one governor, and shared staff, there was no contact between the adult women – 'star-class' convicts convicted of murder or infanticide and another group serving sentences of preventive detention – and the youngsters. All 150 or so girls deemed suitable for borstal disposal could be accommodated there and further provision would be made later, if needed.[40] Given that Aylesbury was the sole girls' borstal, classification was impossible and so first offenders were lumped in with recidivists, and soft girls with tough. One commissioner thought them so rough that if you struck them sparks would fly off. Barker's two predecessors had been rigid disciplinarians and the regime they had created was repressive, with too easy a resort to solitary confinement and even handcuffs and straight-waistcoats, as the report of the prison commissioners for 1921–2 revealed. Those sentenced to two to three years in borstal for an offence that would

---

[37] The article can be found in Vidler, *op. cit.*, pp.45–8.

[38] Watson, *op. cit.*, p.68.

[39] Elizabeth Gore, *The Better Fight: The Story of Dame Lilian Barker* (London, 1965), p.166.

[40] Lionel Fox, *The Modern English Prison* (London, 1934), pp.189f. In comparison with the plethora of material on boys' borstals there is scant information on those for girls. Aylesbury is the exception. In 1922 Hobhouse and Brockway devoted five pages out of 700 to Aylesbury borstal (H&B, pp.435–9). In 1926 Moseley included a chapter on 'Amazing Aylesbury' in his book, as did Gordon in 1932. In 1965 Barker's niece, Elizabeth Gore, published her biography. A brief account of a girl's life there in the fifties was penned by Eileen MacKenney in *Borstal Girl* (London, 2011).

30. A girl's room at Aylesbury Borstal

merit two to three months in prison expected better than this. Resentment was building up among the inmates who, if they were united in anything, it was in hatred of the staff.[41]

Into this stepped Miss Barker, a small but formidable middle-aged woman with a stentorian voice, and 'an iron grey Eton crop'. Always dressed in tweed under a pork-pie hat she had an aversion to make-up. 'Charming, kind, and cheerful', she was 'possessed of great sympathies and a wonderful personality'.[42] Importantly, she had a lot of relevant experience of social and educational work and was an able administrator. She also had decided and vocal views on imprisonment: it should be curative not punitive. She was quite prepared to make an immediate impact and pick up the pieces thereafter. She demanded, and got, a free hand.

Finding the staff dispirited and the girls regimented, she cajoled the former to treat their charges as individuals, and gave the latter greater responsibility, the whole point of borstal training. She improved the quality of the food, the cut of the uniform, the décor of the cells. Too much,

---

[41] Gore, *op. cit.*, pp.116f., 124.
[42] Cicely McCall, *Looking Back from the Nineties* (Norwich, 1994), p. 48; Gordon, *op. cit.*, p.246.

too soon. The 'old guard' among the staff felt that their previous efforts were being depreciated. They did not want to be pioneers in a 'wonderful experiment' but to go back to the old regimented ways. Gradually she won them over, if not to her way of thinking, at least to carrying out her plans, since she would brook no dissent. She cared deeply for her staff, and would let no one other than herself criticise them. They got used to her 'mood swings, the furious condemnation one moment and the slap on the back the next'.[43] She was also kind to, and supportive of, the adult prisoners under her charge.

The girls were harder to bring into line. Kindness could be seen as weakness. Reform and a relaxation of rules were repaid by revolt, when a number of girls on successive nights resorted to 'smashing up' their rooms, an activity which had an addictive quality akin to cutting themselves.[44] Others, having been given more freedom and trust, ran off. The Borstal Association, while noting that under Barker Aylesbury 'was alive – moving, not a valley of dead bones as so many girls' institutions, as contrasted with boys', seem to be', concluded that the changes had produced 'slackness', and found that the regime as it was currently constituted was unsuited to the needs of the inmates, many of whom seemed 'deficient in physique, intelligence and will-power'.

Barker took these comments to heart, learnt from her mistakes, and changed her approach to training – in style but not in purport. 'When I began there', she told the Young Offenders Committee, 'I was far too sentimental and soft; I find now that I get far better results from the girls ... by having a really strict discipline but with really a great deal of affection behind it.'[45] Her sentiments echoed those of her 'esteemed friend', Colonel Rich, who decanted many of his 'star-class' girls from Walton to Aylesbury 'to work out their salvation'.[46] Punishments – usually the loss of some privilege or spending time in the Spartan cells on 'D' Block inside the old prison – became more severe but were often imaginative and invariably just. They did not engender resentment, and rewards there were aplenty. Within a year it was a happy place. Flowers had grown in abundance, behaviour was good, and the staff understood how to go about their jobs. The purpose of training remained the same: to keep girls away from crime and to prepare them for the respectable womanly role they should lead on release, either

43 McCall, *op. cit.*, p.49.
44 Gore, *op. cit.*, pp.128f.
45 Quoted in Bailey, *op. cit.*, p.209.
46 Rich, p.150.

as servants, shop-assistants or house-wives. They should have a place but they should know their place. This would be the Achilles' heel of the whole borstal system: it incorporated assumptions and inculcated values that dated.

As the 'House System' had never been introduced into Aylesbury, there was a lack of the *esprit de corps* commonly found in boys' borstals.[47] Borstal girls were somehow different from borstal boys. They were less enthusiastic, less able and less tractable, or so they were perceived. Consequently they did not benefit from borstal in the way boys did, or seemed to do. Miss Barker did her best to change that. Keeping them constantly occupied in improving pursuits was key. Organised games became integral to the regime, as well as group discussions about the Christian faith and moral issues. Farm work was made readily available, along with training in the sort of skills deemed appropriate to fit girls for domestic service: laundering, gardening, cooking, needlework. But there were also picnics, holidays to Littlehampton, fancy dress parties, New Year's balls. Rapport between staff and their charges improved enormously, and Barker herself inspired both loyalty and devotion among her trainees. She took pains to get them good positions on discharge, told them they could write to her for advice, and took them back if they were recalled. She was a friend and confidante. She would invariably end her letters to them with 'always your friend', and she meant it. As one of her former charges appreciatively put it, 'we started as prisoners living in a prison and we ended as citizens living in a community. Miss Barker gave us responsibility and made us feel we had something to contribute; even expected us to make our own decisions.'[48] With her no-nonsense approach and constant refrain of 'my girls', she was a Miss Jean Brodie in her prime.[49]

In 1935 Harold Scott, a regular and appreciative visitor to Aylesbury, invited Barker to become an assistant commissioner with responsibility for women's prisons as well as for Aylesbury borstal.[50] She was reluctant to take up the post – and her young charges were disconsolate at the news – but Scott persuaded her. The Home Secretary, Sir John Gilmour, almost put her off when he wrote saying that he felt that there was 'room for the advice of a woman on matters not only dealing with staff but also cooking and domestic economy generally'. She replied that while she was quite willing to

---

[47] Gore, *op. cit.*, pp.71f.; Vidler, *op. cit.*, p.34.

[48] Gore, *op. cit.*, pp.161f.; *Report* (1955), p.4.

[49] One half-admiring assistant house-mistress nonetheless noted a 'sadistic trait' which could produce 'a highly unstable atmosphere' (McCall, *op. cit.*, p.51).

[50] A great strength of the commissioners and their assistants was that they each were given specific aspects of the prison estate to look after rather than regions, as would be the case after the commission was abolished.

visit the kitchens she had 'no intention of staying there'. Nonetheless she fulfilled the role until her retirement at the age of sixty-nine in 1943.[51] Her rapport with her colleagues was close, and her opinions were valued. One of her first achievements in office was to decant the adult women still held in Aylesbury to Holloway. Her main disappointment was not being able to inaugurate an open borstal for girls. Another world war put paid to that.

Another much-heralded example of charismatic leadership was that shown by William (Bill) Llewellin, the 'outstanding disciple' who 'played a big part in making Paterson's theories work'.[52] A captain in the Dorsetshire Regiment during the Great War, and an experienced deputy-governor of Feltham borstal, he was a big, shy, solitary figure with a pince-nez on the tip of his nose and a firm belief in the 'sense of honour and loyalty inherent in every British boy'.[53] He would put both to the test when, in May 1930, along with a small group of staff and forty boys, he marched 162 miles from Feltham to Lowdham Grange near Nottingham in ten days. Llewellin chose a Sunday to begin this 'pilgrimage' and it began after a special chapel service to fortify them and sanctify their endeavour, a service Paterson attended. Then off they marched to the promised land, spreading the borstal gospel on the way. There was no need to impose discipline *en route*: 'the boys followed where Bill led'.[54] The 'pioneers' were cheered throughout by well-wishers and honoured by local worthies. The mayor of Granby 'raised a titter' by declaring that had he been younger he would have liked to be in their place. Passing boy scouts saluted their peers.

Accompanying them was Jack Gordon, who only wished that such an enterprise had been undertaken during his own time in borstal. He had gone to Feltham in 1923 as a sixteen-year-old and stayed for two years. To counter the criticisms made of borstals and the misinformation spread about them he determined to write a book about his own experience. After he approached

---

51   Gore, *op. cit.*, p.208. Barker's successor at Aylesbury, Molly Mellanby, a former Roedean house-mistress, replaced her as commissioner for all women's establishments.

52   Scott, *op. cit.*, p.77.

53   'Lowdham Grange – a Borstal Experiment', *Howard Journal*, 3, 4 (1933), p.36.

54   Scott, *op. cit.*, p.70. For first-hand accounts of the march see Gordon, *op. cit.*, pp.267–76; and Jeremy Lodge, *Lowdham Grange. Borstal!* (Nottingham, 2016), pp.57–67. Llewellin would go on to lead a march from Lowdham Grange to found North Sea Camp, and to become the first governor of Usk. A devout Christian, he was utterly devoted to his task, and insisted on sharing the same rigours and food as his boys. They reciprocated his affection for them. In addition to letters, over the years he received so many visits from his former charges that he provided 'a bedroom for such in the old cottage, near Ploughman's Wood'. Visits from 'Old Boys' were commonplace in several borstals, while others wrote to staff or sent Christmas presents (*Report* (1934), p.67, (1955), p.136).

Llewellin, his former housemaster, about the project he received a letter from Paterson suggesting they meet. When they did, the commissioner told him that he fully approved of his literary proposal, exhorted him to be frank and honest about what he wrote, and granted him permission to visit any borstal he wished. Gordon took him at his word. When he returned to his *alma mater* the governor himself put him up. Gordon found Feltham much improved. He went on to Portland, and then Aylesbury where he stayed with Miss Barker before joining the Lowdham 'pilgrimage'. He was an outstanding example of what borstal could do for a wayward youth – 'it lifted me from the dregs of humanity' – and he believed it could do the same for many others. He put pen to paper and, in a much-reviewed book he dedicated to Llewellin, produced the first ever autobiographical account of life as a borstal boy.

On their arrival at the Lowdham estate the enthusiastic team – still 'happy as sand boys' – proceeded to begin to build from scratch the fourth, and the first open, borstal, achieving at last something Ruggles-Brise had merely envisaged. Nothing would be stinted on what was to be 'an advertisement to the world of what borstal boys are capable of doing and of the progress and development of the borstal system for training young criminals into good law-abiding citizens'. The whole enterprise, from its inception to execution, demonstrated that 'young delinquents [could] be trained above crime and folly without walls or bars, without rigorous routine and ... without stern supervision'.[55] To cap it all, on 26 July an inaugural ceremony took place. One foundation stone was laid by the Labour Home Secretary, John Clynes, who professed his faith in the 'inestimable worth of borstals ... the finest of our present-day state services' and his conviction that the 'essence of borstal work is a profound belief in the ultimate goodness of the English boy'.[56] Another was laid by Sir Evelyn Ruggles-Brise. He and Paterson had finally cemented their relationship.

Paterson's vision for open borstals was fully shared by Alexander Maxwell who in 1928 had succeeded Waller as chairman of the Prison Commission.

---

55 Gordon, *op. cit.*, pp.197, 219, 228, 230, 271, 276f.

56 Quoted in Lodge, *op. cit.*, p.70. Clynes's judgement came into question when, after a one-hour visit to Dartmoor months before the mutiny, he declared that the English prison system had reached 'the acme of perfection'. He was not only purblind to reality, he was also 'the harshest and most unsympathetic' Home Secretary of the five that Wilfred Macartney experienced while in prison (though given his predecessor was 'Jix' this is hard to believe). Clynes, who condoned flogging, would have no 'coddling of convicts' and ordered all cell decorations to be removed. No exception was made for a photograph of the Prime Minster, Ramsay McDonald (*Walls Have Mouths* (London, 1936), pp.160f.).

It was also supported by successive Home Secretaries, Conservative and Labour (despite some Labour MPs demanding that local tradesmen be employed in the construction instead of borstal boys), and the fourth borstal had received its initial funding in 1929 from the then Chancellor of the Exchequer, Paterson's old ally Winston Churchill, despite his doubts about the 'tendency to impose unduly long sentences in the belief that it is so bracing'.[57] Paterson had been eager to secure a virgin site upon which the new philosophy of trust and training could be put into practice, unrestrained by the debris of the past, and well away from the prying eyes of the national press who would seek only to disparage the 'pampering', especially in a time of severe economic depression. Conditions at Lowdham Grange were impressive and so it was a jibe with some justification.[58] Public acceptance of the experiment was vital. Although the initial intake had been specially chosen for their proven trustworthiness, there were to be no walls or fences to prevent escape, and while it was desirable for trainees to interact with local host communities, it was essential that they did not steal from them, damage their fences or maim their livestock. Paterson himself, and at his invitation Harold Scott, had accompanied the 'pioneers' on parts of the way to this 'land flowing with milk and honey', handing out bananas and giving the full seal of official approval to risky but rewarding undertakings. The prison service is usually 'risk-averse', but in Paterson's time prison staff knew that they would be supported if they went out on a limb to secure some great good. He adopted the novel proposition that prisons and borstals should be judged not by their failures but by their successes.[59] It was a giddy time.

It was also a time of rapid expansion. The 1929 commissioners' report had envisaged a growth in the number of borstal institutions to cope with rising demand, especially as the courts, encouraged by the commission, began giving minor offenders the 'benefit' of such a sentence. Paterson's tenure saw new ones springing up everywhere. To the closed borstals of Rochester, Feltham and Portland were added Camp Hill in 1931 and Sherwood in 1932.

---

57 Bailey, *op. cit.*, pp.228f.

58 See, for instance, 'He Who Doesn't Get Smacked' (*The Sunday Pictorial*, 3 July 1932), an article denouncing 'how naughty boys are treated by an indulgent State. Broad playing fields, a gymnasium, large open-air swimming bath ... some 350 youths and young men playing cricket, swimming or sparring in the gymnasium ... a stranger would take this as a public school.' Inevitably, it was reported, some parents hoped that their younger sons would soon join their siblings there ('Bad Boy's Paradise', *Sunday Dispatch*, 17 July 1932).

59 Paterson wrote that 'the prison record that shows no escapes and no assaults is too often counted a record of success. It is the record of many receptions but few returns that is the triumph of a good prison administration' (Paterson, p.29).

More open borstals were created to supplement Lowdham Grange: North Sea Camp in 1934; Hollesley Bay Colony in 1938; Usk and Prescoed Camp in 1939. From 1923 Wandsworth housed a reception centre or 'sorting station' where the boys were given a medical examination, and assessed by volunteers who would interview them, read their school records, and visit their homes where possible. Once all the available information had been collated, the lads would be classified and allocated to the appropriate borstal – Feltham for the physically and mentally subnormal and neophytes, Portland for 'toughs and recidivists', and Rochester for those in between. Wormwood Scrubs adopted a dual role: it replaced Canterbury as the recall centre for those who broke the terms of their licence, and served as a correctional centre for those who seriously flouted the rules while serving their sentences. In 1931 the two London prisons switched functions, the reception centre moving to Wormwood Scrubs, and Wandsworth becoming the recall centre.

The outbreak of the Second World War reined in the steady progress of the borstal which until then had 'generated unalloyed admiration throughout the world'.[60] Two-thirds of the trainees were discharged, many of whom along with many of the staff joined the armed forces. Five borstals were taken over for use by the War Office or as adult prisons. The entire intake at Lowdham were either released or transferred to Hollesley Bay. In 1940 Sherwood became a stop-gap recall centre, until replaced by Chelmsford in the following year. While both Borstal and Feltham were hit by bombs, Portland, because of its location, suffered the worst, being repeatedly subjected to bombing and machine-gunning by the Luftwaffe, which damaged buildings and killed or wounded several boys. They got their revenge when one of the German planes crashed and the lads, rummaging through the wreckage, made off with the pilot's ear as a trophy.[61] On the other hand a rash escapee

---

[60] Radzinowicz, p.397.

[61] Vidler, *op. cit.*, pp.58ff. In London, Wandsworth and Pentonville prisons were badly damaged during the Blitz, perhaps being mistaken for factories. Grew, the then governor of the former, the first prison in England to be hit by bombs, described the destruction and havoc wreaked by three German planes, but, as a result of a well-honed procedure for prisoners dispersing and taking cover in the virtually bomb-proof cells, there was no fatality. Despite air raids, each night the prisoners, other than the few chosen for fire-watch duty, were kept locked in their cells with strict instructions to observe the black-out. Executions continued throughout the war, for spies and traitors as well as murderers (Grew, pp.118–22). Pentonville was not so fortunate when on 10 May 1941 it was hit by a large incendiary bomb and seventeen people, staff as well as prisoners, lost their lives. Bristol and Hull and, in particular, Walton in Liverpool were also badly damaged during air raids.

was blown to pieces on a minefield while another had to be guided back to safe custody.

The structure erected during the inter-war years was undermined, not so much by German bombs, but by other effects of the war. Experienced staff were lost, and, overcrowded and under-manned as they became, the few remaining borstals were unable to provide the same quality of training as heretofore. War-work took precedence over everything, and borstal boys were not exempted. Life for them would be taken at a brisker tempo. During the war the number of young offenders increased and they seemed more difficult and disturbed, an aberration occasioned by the turmoil, disruption of family life, and privations of war-time, or so it was thought. One such was Andrew Russell who at the age of eighteen was sent to Portland borstal where in eighteen months he 'learnt nothing and did not try to'. He was released in June 1947 and when asked could recall neither the name of the governor nor that of his housemaster 'and very little indeed of what he did there'. Indeed there was little to do as there was no real vocational training as the governor believed that as 'the lads had failed when their country needed them they would be given the chance to work all hours on war work, so as to regain their self-respect'.[62] As training was in retreat, birchings as well as committals to prison were on the increase. It was assumed that things would gradually return to normal, borstal would be resurgent and its success consummated.

Certainly after 1945, and with the demand for places rising, Paterson wasted no time in repairing the damage, reviving his dream and adding to his empire. Former army camps and government-owned country houses were commandeered. In late 1945, while provision was being created in Durham and Exeter prisons for closed girls' borstals, East Sutton Park, an Elizabethan manor house in Kent, was transformed into the only open borstal for girls, who would be trained in 'housecraft' and 'poultry and rabbit-keeping'. The first governor, Elsie Hooker, served there from 1946 until her retirement in 1963, refusing promotion. Motivated by her Christian faith, and supported by Fox and Mellanby, she ran the country house as though it were a home for a large family.[63] Also in 1946, Latchmere House, the first reception centre with no connection to a prison, and the open borstals of Gaynes Hall, Huntercombe, Hewell Grange and Gringley were all up and

---

62 Leo Page, *The Young Lag: A Study in Crime* (London, 1950), pp.76, 204. Page interviewed many young offenders, all of whom had gone to borstal during or just after the war, and all of whom had re-offended.

63 *Report* (1946), pp.58f. Joanna Kelly, 'Elsie Hooker', in *Prison Service People*, ed. Kenneth Neale (Newbold Revel, 1993), pp.79–89.

running. There was one backward step, when, in the same year, part of Dartmoor prison was designated a closed borstal. This was a recourse born out of necessity but it caused controversy as it again associated borstal with prison, and stood for a 'moral contamination and social isolation' totally at variance with 'the reformative ideals on which training had been developed in the open institutions before the war'.[64] Borstals were a unique part of the rehabilitative landscape. Their post-war resurgence also suggested that they were an indelible part.

Just as borstal boys and girls varied enormously so did the institutions themselves. The few closed borstals were much more restrictive than the more plentiful open ones, and with their very different atmosphere and ethos were almost a reproach to the borstal ideal. Camp Hill, formerly the preventive detention prison, took young boys with bad records, and likely absconders who would at least have barriers to surmount and a sea to cross, while Sherwood housed older, tougher and rougher young men in a former prison with wings and cells and locks. In the open variety, absconding would not be prevented by high walls and iron bars but by inner restraint born of training and trust. These establishments had a style appropriated from, or adapted to, their environment. North Sea Camp on the Wash had no prison officers, only housemasters, and emphasised the outdoor pioneering ideal and socially useful manual work in reclaiming land from the salt-marshes. Gaynes Hall in Cambridgeshire was more cerebral than manual, becoming known as 'the thinking man's borstal' as it housed, among others, Cambridge undergraduates sent there for drug offences or for stealing and gutting antiquarian library books.[65] Hollesley Bay Colony on the Suffolk coast introduced young men to the joys of country life, specialising in market gardening, dairy farming and running the world's largest stud for Suffolk Punch horses. Because of its name, its beautiful seaside location, and the outdoor pursuits it provided, it was dubbed 'Holiday Bay'. One well-known 'alumnus' wrote a best-selling account of his time there. He was the famous Irish writer and infamous Irish drunk, Brendan Behan. His book was *Borstal Boy*.

---

[64] *The Times*, 26 November 1945.

[65] Gaynes Hall in the 1970s is described with some affection by a reformed borstal boy, Kris Gray, in *Two's Up!* (Calne, 2010).

CHAPTER 31

Borstal Boy

I, as an ex-Borstal Boy, will never regret or forget that I experienced borstal training. It was from that period of disciplined training that I derived certain advantages and knowledge which have served substantially in improving my chances of success. It was from that same training that my young, undeveloped mind was influenced from the lower things of life to higher and nobler ideals.

Jack Gordon

Brendan Behan was born in Dublin in February 1923 while his father was serving a term of imprisonment in Kilmainham gaol for IRA activities. His son would surpass his father in fanaticism. It was hardly surprising that he had been radicalised, as many of his family were die-hard Republicans. His mother, in particular, was an inveterate hater of the English and of England. So too was his grandmother. Indeed in 1939 she and his two aunts journeyed to England with the specific intention of carrying out terrorist attacks. A detonation in the house they were renting in Birmingham led the police to their door and to them being imprisoned for conspiring to cause explosions.

The young Brendan, who at the age of sixteen was already a fully-fledged member of the Second Dublin Battalion of the Irish Republican Army, decided to follow their example and go to England to take part in a bombing campaign instigated by the IRA, which had 'declared war' on Britain at the moment the British were fighting for survival against the horrors of Nazi Germany. He had tried twice before to sail to Liverpool but had been deterred by the police presence at the Dublin docks. Third time lucky? In November 1939 he succeeded in making the crossing. The police were already on his tail, and within ten hours of landing on English soil the aspiring would-be murderer was arrested with a suitcase full of gelignite and remanded in custody. Fortunately, following in the family tradition, he was useless at his vocation. His saving grace was front, or so he would have us believe. According to his account (in a letter to a friend) he told the police he was forty-nine years old, his name was Lord Rosebery, he worked as private secretary to the Aga Khan, and had been thrice arrested for bigamy.[1] He was better at the blarney than at bombing.

On 4 December he was remanded to Walton gaol ten months after the IRA had attempted, but failed, to breach a wall in 'this nineteenth-century lavatory', as Behan called it, during the bombing campaign he had come to join. The Roman Catholic chaplain was no terrorist sympathiser and when confronted by a young and mouthy recruit was direct. Father Lane, 'a stout block of a man', bluntly asked him when he was going to give up his 'membership of this murder gang', and told him that unless he did so, condemned as the IRA had been by the English and Irish hierarchy, he could not partake in the Mass. Excommunication touched a particularly raw nerve as Behan was a devout Catholic and, all his life, never broke free from the church's influence. According to his own account, he retaliated with a hectoring lecture on the church's betrayal of the people of Ireland and shouted 'to hell with you, you fat bastard, and to hell with England and to hell with Rome'. At this point two prison officers intervened, dragged the boy back to his cell where they punched him in the ribs and face, splitting his lips and fracturing his left collar-bone, and told him that 'a half-starved Irish bastard had no right to insult a minister of religion'.[2] The insulted priest, in his report on the encounter, disparaged the youth as coming under very evil influences and producing 'with great fluency the communistic and IRA arguments against Church and State'. The governor, James Holt, erstwhile of Feltham, concurred that he was 'a precocious and conceited lad who finds in political fanaticism an easy relationship of wild and undisciplined impulses and who is sustained in his anti-social attitude by the designs to show off as a hero and a martyr'.

Within weeks Holt, ever-positive about the borstal system, modified his view of someone he described as 'an honest youth who will have time in borstal to think of his many problems'. There were to be no more beatings, and Behan himself admitted that his treatment could have been much worse, especially as he was 'about as popular here as a dose of V. disease'.[3] When his case came to court on 8 February 1940, because he was one day short of seventeen, he was sentenced to three years' borstal detention.[4] Mr Justice Hallett's hands were constrained and he remarked that parliament had taken an extremely lenient view of what ought to be done to young

---

1   Michael O'Sullivan, *Brendan Behan* (Colorado, 1999), p.46. *Borstal Boy* differs.
2   Behan, pp.69ff.
3   O'Sullivan, *op. cit.*, pp.49f.
4   The Criminal Justice Act 1948 would change this to 'borstal training'.

people convicted of serious offences. Had he been an adult the maximum sentence of fourteen years' penal servitude would have been imposed.[5] Given the choice, Behan who knew nothing of borstals, would have opted instead for two years' imprisonment.

The way he had been treated by the police, the overall fairness – and food – he found in prison, coupled with the lenity of the sentence, had its effect and he began to re-evaluate his extreme views and alter his attitude towards his erstwhile enemies.[6] His ultimate placement would continue this process. First he was dispatched to Feltham which by 1940, for fear of bombing in London, had to serve a number of different roles: as a remand prison instead of Brixton, as a boys' prison, and, replacing Wormwood Scrubs or Wandsworth, as an allocation centre for newly sentenced borstal boys. As a result it was overcrowded and chaotic, but the food was good and plentiful and Behan was there only for initial assessment and classification. He was in transit. His final destination, he hoped, would turn out to be one of the innovatory open borstals, of which there were three: Lowdham Grange in Nottinghamshire, North Sea Camp in Lincolnshire, and the newest, Hollesley Bay Colony in Suffolk. In mid-March Behan was interviewed by a panel consisting of a prison commissioner, the Feltham governor, and the new governor of Hollesley Bay, 'a stout gentleman with his hair split in the middle like an English soccer player ... and the look of a British army officer about him'.[7] After a perfunctory appraisal the IRA bomber was selected for the Colony, and on 21 March he was transferred there, along with some of his 'chinas'.

When they arrived they were ushered in to meet the governor and were rather surprised when he greeted them with 'gentlemen, you are very welcome'. He prefaced his pep talk with a request that they show courtesy to each other, to the staff and to himself. If they had a problem with each other or with staff they should talk to an officer, housemaster or padre about it. Most issues could be resolved to everyone's satisfaction. He pointed out that if they ran away and had to break in somewhere to get money or clothes, it would make it very difficult for others, as initially some of the local people had not wanted a borstal in their locality, and it had taken some

---

5   Extraordinary as this disposal may seem for a terrorist offence, at the other extreme boys and girls were sent to borstal for attempting to commit suicide, which remained a criminal offence until 1961. Paterson had tried and failed to get a change in the law that would have prohibited the courts sending anyone under twenty-one to prison, except for murder.

6   Behan, p.132; O'Sullivan, *op. cit.*, p.58.

7   Behan, p.159.

31. Hollesley Bay borstal in 1955: the Young Farmers' Club and cadets in training

time to gain their goodwill. Escapees committing burglary would not go down well and would result in restrictions being placed on innocent boys. 'So don't sneak off without telling me', he requested in a matter-of-fact avuncular way.[8]

Cyril Alfred Joyce, 'the old man' or 'the Squire', as he was affectionately known, was a remarkable governor, and was to have a profound impact on his new recruit. Intended for holy orders, Joyce had served as an officer during the Great War, after which, having met Paterson and been inspired by 'his infinite vision', he decided to work with young offenders.[9] He joined the prison service in 1922 when the new, optimistic humanitarian approach, of which he was a disciple and would become an apostle, was all the rage. His first posting was to Portland borstal. In 1927 he was transferred to Wakefield as a housemaster where he remained for three years, during which time he introduced flowers, gardens and an indoor aviary. After three months at Durham prison he was sent to Wormwood Scrubs to take charge of the boys' prison there, a transit point for those *en route* to borstals. It may have been with his regime in mind that Rich's strictures on treating offenders 'like spoilt children' who thought they were 'little tin gods on wheels' were made.[10] The commissioners did not share these concerns, and Joyce was appointed governor of Camp Hill borstal, where he remained for six years.

Supported by Paterson, who was less concerned about the security which came from walls and wire and more about that which came from the creation of mutual trust, it was his idea to establish a third open borstal. He did so in 1938 after Hollesley Bay, a labour colony for the metropolitan unemployed consisting of a large amount of farmland and several buildings, was bought from the London County Council. Fifty boys from Camp Hill volunteered to go with him, walking all the way, and camping as they went. None absconded. Some even prolonged their sentences to see the project through. As one young man put it, he 'could not refuse the honour'. It was also a testament to Joyce's popularity and to the loyalty he could command. Behan, in *Borstal Boy*, testified to it too:

> He was a fair man, and though [the boys] were afraid of him to an extent, they knew that, no matter what they did, he would do anything rather than send a bloke back to Sherwood Forest or Wandsworth.

8 *Ibid.*, pp.197ff.
9 C.A. Joyce, *By Courtesy of the Criminal* (London, 1955), p.17.
10 Rich, p.109.

He was all for giving young people a second or third chance. Other governors got rid of trouble by sending a boy off to a local prison or transferring him to Sherwood borstal. Joyce resolved problems 'in house' and escapees were merely held in detention, not sent into exile. During his benign rule, Hollesley Bay took in some of those who had failed elsewhere or whose original borstal refused to have them back after they had completed their punishment. Boys with a 'B.B.B. crop – the haircut they gave "Bad Borstal Boys" at Sherwood Forest' could be seen redeeming themselves in the Bay. No one was beyond redemption. No one was written off.[11]

Joyce believed that personal relationships were vital, that all were individuals who could be helped and who could help themselves, that punishment must be deserved and reserved for bad cases, and that recognition of the fault and restitution for it was a far more effective means of preventing repetition than the deterrent effects of pain and suffering. He was an advocate of what we would now call 'restorative justice'. He was also an advocate of 'courtesy', a social virtue that he applied to everybody equally. While working in prisons he would always knock on a cell door and say 'good evening, may I come in' and had never met with anything but 'please do'. In borstals he maintained that if boys should not walk on the grass neither should staff. He expected boys to stand up when he entered their rooms, just as he would stand up if they brought their parents into his. The staff, all volunteers, shared his vision and during the early years there were no arguments about overtime, as 'everyone was prepared to give their own time and knowledge to the building of something that we felt was worthwhile'.[12]

Just like Paterson, Joyce took the public school system as his model. The colony, set in extensive farmland, consisted of a clock tower and four 'houses', each with a housemaster, a house-captain elected by the boys, and a matron. St Andrew's and St Patrick's were new-build camp-style one-storey structures with central heating, games rooms and thermostatic showers. The other two, St David's and St George's, were rambling mock-Tudor edifices dating back to the late Victorian period, quaint but cold. Each housed around a hundred boys, mostly aged between sixteen and eighteen, although the colony could take young men up to the age of twenty-three.

---

[11] Behan, pp.240, 247. 'Sherwood Forest', as Behan calls it, was notorious. In March 1930 all the adult prisoners at Bagthorpe gaol in Sherwood were removed and it became the first Young Adult Offenders' prison for twenty-one to twenty-five-year-olds. In October 1932 it became Sherwood borstal, soon gaining a reputation for being the hardest borstal in England and with the unique stigma of having its matron murdered.

[12] Joyce, *op. cit.*, pp.24, 74.

It was to St George's that the young Irishman was allocated. His house-captain, Neville Heath, a 'strongly-built' young man easily shocked by any homoerotic innuendo, was not to prove one of Joyce's more successful protégés, being hanged for the sexually-motivated and sadistic murder of two young women.[13] St George's was considered the finest of the houses, having period charm and the aura of a gentleman's club, with a well-stocked library and an open fire to warm the readers. Behan was impressed to see how well used it was. There he encountered a winsome youth, 'altogether as decadent as our means would allow', who was reading Frank Harris's biography of Oscar Wilde and who seemed to identify with the subject. In 'a languid, elegant accent' he explained to Behan why Wilde had been imprisoned, and offered to lend him the book.[14] Not all borstal boys were working-class kids; some were discards from the public schools. One old Harrovian said he preferred borstal as the food was so much better.[15] Fresh fruit and vegetables, dairy products and prime meat were all sourced from the extensive borstal farm.

And so it went on. Behan was enjoying himself, making friends with the cockney lads and public school boys alike, and spending a lot of his spare time reading. He did as the other boys did: took vocational courses, worked hard, gardened, played sport, and during the autumn abandoned everything else to pick fruit. Rather than rebelling against the system he was conforming to it.

Diversions there were aplenty, and there was something for everyone. In May, Joyce put on what he called an 'Eisteddfod'. There was a boxing tournament, cross-country racing, a tug of war, gymnastic events, an essay competition, gardening and handicrafts. When Colonel Craven, a local landowner and magistrate who had led the opposition to having a borstal in their locality but had been won over, was asked to hand out the prizes, he addressed the 'dear boys' as though they were at public school. Behan got the prize for his essay and, along with his team, for the tug of war. Afternoon tea with bread and jam and treacle duff was served and an ounce

---

13 On 8 October 1946, while in Pentonville awaiting execution, Heath wrote to Joyce, with whom he had stayed in touch, saying that he would always remember the happy year he had spent at Hollesley Bay Colony, and the ideals that Joyce had espoused, and regretting that he had forgotten the many lessons he had learnt there, for which he would pay dearly (Sean O'Connor, *Handsome Brute* (London, 2013), p.149).

14 Behan, pp.226ff.

15 Stephen Fry made a similar point when in 1974 at the age of seventeen he was on remand for theft at Pucklechurch. He described life in prison as a 'breeze' because he had spent most of his life at boarding school. He knew how to survive both (*Moab Is My Washpot* (London, 1997), p.324).

of tobacco dispensed. The event culminated in the performance of a play and a concert in the evening. And, of course, there was a nativity play each Christmas as well as other seasonal treats. All this could be subject to sniping from those who thought that life for offenders was a lot better than for their conforming peers. In many ways it was.[16]

There were diversions of another kind also. His latent homosexuality found physical expression in borstal. You did not have to be 'King Lear' [queer] to get amorously involved with another boy, but Behan was very definitely bisexual. According to his early unpublished manuscript, significantly called *The Courteous Borstal*, homosexual practice was commonplace among the lads, especially the 'good-looking and well-built' ones such as he:

> I loved borstal boys and they loved me ... Our lads saw themselves as beautiful and had to do something about it. About a third of them did. Another third, not so influential or less good-looking would have liked to ... Without women it could not be a pattern of life, only a prolonging of adolescence – it was as beautiful as that.[17]

To Behan it was yet another way in which borstals resembled boarding schools.

Joyce considered Behan, or 'Paddy' as he and everybody else called him, to be one of the most lovable and remarkable boys he had ever known in the system. He also thought that while not abandoning the Republican cause the boy had come to see that violence was wrong, and would be 'clearly and outspokenly pro-English for the duration of the war'.[18] When one Scottish lad remonstrated with him for liking the English despite what they had done in Ireland, Behan rejoined that the English people were not to blame, but imperialism was, and pointed out that the Scots had been

---

16 Behan, pp.247–60. Rich relates that the mayor of Maidstone, on an inspection of the facilities, remarked that he was paying over a hundred pounds a year for his son's education, and it was no better than that provided free for miscreants. The father of one inmate wanted to ensure his other son got there too (p.88).

17 Quoted in O'Sullivan, *op. cit.*, p.69. Trusting borstal boys could lead to trysting borstal boys. On one occasion in 1926 a Feltham officer entered a garden shed to discover it being used 'as a brothel, by a youth who was placing his body at the disposal of all-comers, on payment of a few cigarettes' (Harley Cronin, *The Screw Turns* (London, 1967), p.68). In Benney's experience the allure of cigarettes overcame the most averse, and for protection 'queenies' would become eager catamites (*Low Company* (London, 1936), pp.220–8). Gordon wrote at length about a rent-boy called Monty who was both bullied and exploited (*Borstalians* (London, 1932), pp.100–7). In contrast a purblind medical officer trying 'to tackle the problem of homosexual lads' asserted that 'a borstal institution provides a good place to turn the balance towards the male side' (*Report* (1955), p.151).

18 O'Sullivan, *op. cit.*, p.67.

enthusiastic participants in the imperial venture and in the subjugation of Ireland. 'Fair play' was what had impressed him most about the English, and Joyce embodied it. His influence on a young man finding his way cannot be exaggerated. They even prayed together. Another whose impact was considerable was Ann Halfpenny, the chain-smoking Roman Catholic matron of St George's House.[19] Beloved by all the boys she took a particular shine to Behan who would often take tea with her, and discuss the literary heritage of the surrounding area. She was the only woman with whom the boys would have regular contact, although Joyce's wife, an accomplished sculptor, also took a great interest in Brendan and offered to sculpt his 'lovely head'.[20]

His last months were not so happy. In July 1941 Joyce left the prison service to become headmaster of Ashton Keynes, a new approved school in Wiltshire. Both boy and governor were sorry to say farewell and both would later record their appreciation of each other. Behan was also hoping for early release, although when it finally did come in November 1941, after a six-month delay, it was with mixed emotions that he left the Bay. His account of his time there would have long gestation, being finally published in 1958, to great acclaim.

By way of postlude, the reformatory effect of the borstal had either always been illusory or soon wore off, as within six months of his release Behan was back behind bars for attempting to murder two members of the Irish constabulary. He had reverted to being an IRA activist, even if he was still not very good at it. At the Special Criminal Court, presided over by Colonel John Joyce – 'Hangman Joyce' to the IRA – a very different man from his namesake in Hollesley Bay, Behan was sentenced to fourteen years' penal servitude. It began in Mountjoy gaol, to which many an IRA 'martyr' had been sent and in which he would later set his play, *The Quare Fellow*. Chameleon-like, he assimilated to his new surroundings, impressing the governor Captain Kavanagh as a well-behaved, 'mild-mannered boy' who 'in his senses would not hurt a fly'. Whether this was arch-duplicity or whether there were two very different Behans depending on the environment he was inhabiting, is hard to say. Imprisonment seemed to bring out the best in him. He was released in 1946. Two years later he ended up once more in Mountjoy. For the first time Behan was imprisoned not for his political convictions but merely because he had been sentenced to one month for participating in a drunken street-brawl. Drink was getting the better of him

---

[19] Called Anne Lafeen in *Borstal Boy*.
[20] Behan, pp.252, 332f.

and drunken fights were a commonplace for the rest of his short life. He died in 1964. Twenty years later so too did borstal.

In the 1930s borstals had reached the apogee of success. They had exceeded all expectations, surmounted all challenges, and become an integral, and the most innovative, part of a great movement for penal transformation. The prison commissioners believed they had found the secret of ending recidivism and hoped that they could soon begin closing many of their prisons. Many staff found working in borstals both rewarding and inspiring, which cannot be said for many initiatives in the prison service. A large number of young people benefited from them: some gained literacy; others learnt trades and became employable; and many who experienced borstal training praised it. Joyce in his biography reproduced a lengthy appraisal sent to him by one of his former charges for whom the worst aspect was the lasting stain attached to the appellation 'borstal boy'.[21] These sentiments were similar to those of Jack Gordon a generation before.

The war dealt the maturing system a severe blow, destabilising borstals by mobilising the inmates and removing experienced and dedicated staff, some of whom would be killed, some of whom would never return. To make matters worse, after the war the number of those sent to borstal increased sharply. It took time for the system to recover its old *élan*, if ever it really did. Paterson with his usual vim had begun the process, as we have seen, but his time was short and he was irreplaceable. Gradually, however, things seemed to be back on course and the institution seemed still to be a supreme success. In 1949 it won the accolade of a laudatory feature film, *Boys in Brown: Can Bad Boys Make Good?*, with screen legends Richard Attenborough and Dirk Bogarde playing borstal boys, and that quintessence of reassurance, Jack Warner, the progressive governor.

But there were clouds gathering. The national mood was changing and becoming antithetical to anything akin to appeasement. There were judicial misgivings about early release undermining the deterrent effect of the sentences. There was increasing public unease about the types of offenders being sent to borstal and the adequacy of the sanctions imposed on them there.[22] Of course, the press concentrated on failures and not successes; those who had been reformed and become respectable rarely publicised their borstal beginnings, while the public heard of instances of seeming

---

21 Joyce, *op. cit.*, pp.120–34.
22 Observing borstal boys in Wormwood Scrubs, Rupert Croft-Cooke thought many of them 'semi-imbeciles' (*The Verdict of You All* (London, 1955), pp.70f.),

lenity and laxity, of lawless youths absconding and re-offending, all of which brought discredit on the institution. One such instance, which became a leading case in the law of tort, was in 1962 when seven borstal trainees, working under the supervision of three officers on Brownsea Island in Poole harbour, in what the papers called a 'daring escape', wandered off one night after their supervisors had gone to sleep, leaving the boys to their own devices. The youthful marauders stole a yacht and collided with another one. The owners of the stolen and damaged vessels were angry; the public was outraged. Joyriding on yachts was not how young hoodlums should be allowed to behave.[23]

Nonetheless, the borstal system survived until 1983. For all the tabloid griping, and the often justified criticism, it proved to be a penal experiment that actually worked, at least when the social mores were conducive and when the right staff were in place. The 1930s in particular seemed to have an excess of optimism, a plethora of pliable youths and a surfeit of exceptional governors, self-sacrificing housemasters, and custodial staff who were largely converts to the borstal ideal and all of whom had known Paterson and imbibed his charisma. They met with such success that before the Second World War only some thirty per cent of borstal boys re-offended. Thereafter, with Paterson dead and gone, the raw energy invested in, and the enthusiasm for, borstals slowly dissipated. This despite repeated assurances that the system was working well, and that the number of licence revokees was low as was the reconviction rate. Both had been true in the 1930s, but both increased in the post-war years. So too did the number of absconders, almost doubling from 542 in 1946 to 1,071 in 1947. Society had changed for good and not just temporarily during the war, and trainees were more truculent and less tractable. There was less deference to authority, and more hostility to a 'middle-class moralising system', whereby boys and girls were trained 'in the habits of work and obedience'. There was more resistance to a 'carry on camping' culture, and less enthusiasm for 'following the flag'. It was noted that 'lads now coming into borstal do not speak the same kind of language as the staff'.[24] There was a distinct generation gap as well as a social discontinuity. No longer was there the same steady, comprehensible working-class persona which had apparently been found in the youths of earlier generations. With unconscious symbolism the shorts worn by borstal

---

[23] *Dorset Yacht Co Ltd v Home Office* [1970] AC, 1004. The owners of the damaged yacht sued the Home Office. The case went all the way to the judicial committee of the House of Lords which held for the plaintiffs.

[24] Cicely Craven, 'The Progress of English Criminology', *Journal of Criminal Law and Criminology*, 24, 1 (1933), pp.230–47, at p.241; *Report* (1957), p.117.

boys in the 1930s were replaced with long trousers. Boys had become young men. They had also become alien beings.

In the 1950s as the prestige of borstals continued to tarnish, attitudes to the treatment of wayward youth hardened. At the beginning of the decade a departmental committee concluded that, since discipline had deteriorated and absconding and the reconviction rate had increased, 'the policy of leniency, appeasement, or soft treatment as at present interpreted is not having the success expected or desired'. The commissioners, still under the influence of Paterson's spirit, had swung too far from the more military model established by his predecessor. If this was sweet vindication for Ruggles-Brise's approach, it was a severe blow to the 'Patersonian ideal'.[25] Detention centres, with their brisk and exacting regimes, were coming increasingly into vogue. The young hooligan needed a short and economical dose of discipline. There would be 'no sort of long-haired business' even in open borstals.[26] Punishment became synonymous with training. Security was a much higher priority. Even Fox had to admit that he had too many open borstals and too few closed. It was in the best interests of the public and of the boys themselves that a greater proportion of young offenders be kept in secure establishments. As the era of the expansion of the open borstal ended the number of closed borstals rapidly increased. In the 1951 a correction centre for absconders was set up at Reading, and although it was described as the borstal 'Glasshouse' it still aimed 'to be positive as well as deterrent' and return boys 'to training not only chastened but measurably improved'.[27] In 1962, at Bullwood in Essex, a second girls' secure borstal was opened. Ominously, North Sea Camp became a detention centre in 1963, and a new borstal was created within Hull prison for those serving second sentences and for those who had been 'seriously subversive of the morale of their houses'.[28]

It was deliberate regression to a more disciplinary model. The borstal and prison systems were once again becoming fused, their fundamental distinctions eroded, and the more borstals became like prisons the less relevance they had, although the prison commissioners in their swan-song remained convinced of their effectiveness. They would not be around for much longer to protect their creation, and politicians and civil servants would be less resolute in its

---

25 *Report of the Committee to Review Punishments in Prisons, Borstal Institutions, Approved Schools and Remand Homes*, 1950–1, II, para.33; Roger Hood, *Borstal Reassessed* (London, 1965), p.138.

26 *The Times*, 13 November 1959.

27 *Report* (1955), p.96.

28 *Report* (1963), p.63.

defence, especially when incidents with yachts 'rocked the boat' in 1962 and the reconviction rate doubled by 1965. Nonetheless, in that year the eminent Cambridge criminologist, Sir Leon Radzinowicz, judged the borstal system to have been 'one of the most significant contributions made by this country to the penological theory and practice of the twentieth century'.[29] Indeed it had been, but the century had seen profound social changes and was drawing to a close. Borstal would not survive the century of its birth.

In the 'swinging 60s' the breakdown of social restraints undermined the paternalism inherent in borstals, the craze for the comprehensive school led to the denigration of the public school model as the ideal, and the attitude of inmates was becoming more truculent. In the 1970s, films such as *Scum* graphically depicted borstals as sinks of sin and depravity. In reality they had regressed to the pre-Patersonian model, as Mark Leech recounts of his time in Portland, 'the Colditz of the borstal service, where brutality was an everyday occurrence and the majority of the staff seemed to have been chosen for their arrogance and physical size: bullies employed by the State'. He thought the whole philosophy flawed as it taught skills but did not address offending behaviour.[30] His experience of borstal in the 1970s stands in striking contrast to that of Jack Gordon or Mark Benney fifty years before. The rehabilitative ideal was dying, philanthropic paternalism was going out of fashion, and embarrassed cynicism was replacing naive optimism. It was not necessarily progress, however, when borstal training, after a cursory debate in parliament, was nonchalantly abolished by the Criminal Justice Act of 1982 and replaced with youth custody, and borstals were replaced by young offender institutions, which, despite their name, were most definitely prisons.[31] Punishment had displaced welfare.

---

[29] Hood, *op. cit.*, p.ix.

[30] Mark Leech, *A Product of the System* (London, 1992), pp.42f.

[31] Sharing this view is Simon Barlow, an officer in Rochester borstal and its replacement YOI from 1980 until 1988. He was friends with respectable tradesmen who had been saved by the borstal system, and he thought it 'a shame that this system doesn't exist now, as it offered vocational training, education and a huge lesson in self-discipline'. Nonetheless he deprecated his first governor's desire to replace all prison officers with social workers (*The Self-Tapping Screw* (Brighton, 2013), pp.21, 63, 101). Some attempts have been made to resurrect the educational model, and not just for youngsters. In 2006, The Creative Prison, a project of the radical arts organisation Rideout, published a blueprint of a 'super-enhanced' prison functioning like a 'secure college' for adults and operating on a hundred per cent education or training. It was named HMP Paterson. In 2014 the Coalition government announced its intention to build a 'Secure College' for young offenders with education at its heart. Condemned by many groups as a 'modern day borstal', and facing tight budgetary constraints, the scheme was abandoned by Michael Gove the following year.

One relatively late development in borstal training had been the introduction in 1957, at Pollington borstal in Yorkshire, of group therapy and counselling run by the discipline staff themselves. Although psychotherapy proper was not introduced, this was an early amateur attempt to establish the place of sociological and psychological theory in what was being thought of as a therapeutic community.[32] The concept of such a community has had a long history, and was first expressed in nascent and rudimentary form in the treatment of the insane.

---

[32] Hood, *op. cit.*, pp.142f.

CHAPTER 32

The Nutcracker Suite

Many men who came in here
    Were crimeless in their former sphere,
Perhaps too long were on the dole –
    One tragic day 'went up the pole'.
But they can rise again and win
    Their freedom from this 'looney-bin'
And in nine cases out of ten
    Nevermore go 'queer' again.

The Broadmoor Chronicle

Truth and Goodness, strangers banished from my life, awaited me at Grendon. With their recognition came a new fear; were they only to be found at Grendon? Would they be with my possessions the day of my release. Would *Freedom* mix well with Truth and Goodness? Would they still remain my friends?

Christopher Finlay

Under the category 'Tolerated prisons' Defoe numbered Bedlam and fifteen private 'mad-houses'.[1] Despite being places of confinement he was drawing a distinction between them and ordinary prisons. Although from early on the distinction between the mad and the sad and the mad and the bad has been maintained, the mentally ill and those with a criminal mentality have always been linked. Both groups were detained in coercive institutions, be they gaols for criminals where the ill were cast in with the evil, hospitals for 'lunatics' (as they were called) such as Bedlam, asylums for the criminally insane such as Broadmoor, therapeutic centres within prisons for violent sociopaths, such as the Barlinnie Special Unit, or the only entirely therapeutic prison for the socially and psychologically disturbed, HMP Grendon.

The priory of St Mary of Bethlehem – or Bethlem – was founded in 1247 outside Bishopsgate but just within the City. It existed for prayer and to raise alms for the crusades, but soon took on the roles of caring for the poor,

---

[1] Defoe, I, p.356.

providing lodging for travellers and offering hospitality to visiting dignitaries. It thus became a hostel or 'hospital', but not in the clinical sense of being a specialised institution for the care of the sick. After a century of obscurity it was taken 'under the protection and patronage' of the mayor and aldermen of the City of London.[2] Financially more secure and having survived the ravages of the Black Death, around 1400 it first began taking in 'distracted persons' and has continued in this task to the present day, making it Europe's oldest extant psychiatric hospital. It would become the most famous lunatic asylum in the world and a contraction of its name would give to the English language a word synonymous with noise, uproar and confusion: Bedlam.

In 1547 Henry VIII ceded to the City the custody and governance of Bethlem, the administration of which, a quarter of a century later, was put into the hands of the governors of Bridewell.[3] So began an overlap between those admitted to the one or the other. In 1574 a man was charged at Bridewell with sending his wife to Bethlem without cause. Six weeks prior to her committal he had tied her to her bed until she was 'well-nigh famished'. Others, it was thought, feigned insanity to escape whipping at Bridewell. It did not always work. One woman who 'seemed to be mad' but was still deemed a rogue was first whipped before being sent to Bethlem. Whatever the truth of her condition, and she could have been both, it received appropriate treatment. The conditions of confinement were not dissimilar. Inmates of Bethlem were routinely called prisoners, put in cells and provided with inadequate rations, while those deemed dangerous or out of control were put in chains or locked away amidst 'cryings, screechings, roarings, brawlings, shaking of chains, swearings, frettings, chaffings'. Lady Eleanor Davies, who had been sent to prison before being confined in Bethlem, thought that she had exchanged 'the grave for Hell, such were the blasphemies and the noisome scents'.[4] There was one crucial difference. Patients were being detained not as a prelude to punishment but for cure. They may have been out of their minds but they were not out of sight. They could be seen wandering in the open grounds, and visitors were allowed to come into the asylum to see the lunatics held there. The mad as well as the bad could be objects of public curiosity and philanthropic concern.

---

2   E.G. O'Donoghue, *The Story of Bethlehem Hospital from its Foundation in 1247* (London, 1914), p.37; Jonathan Andrews, Asa Briggs, Roy Porter, Penny Tucker and Keir Waddington, *The History of Bethlem* (London, 1997), pp.55ff.

3   Andrews *et al.*, *op. cit.*, p.62.

4   O'Donoghue, *op. cit.*, p.128; Andrews *et al.*, *op. cit.*, pp.51f., 118.

The original building was old and became ruinous, and was in any case too small for the increasing demand on places. The governors decided to rebuild Bethlem at Moorfields, just north of the City proper. Between 1675 and 1676 the new hospital was constructed on a lavish scale and at great expense by none other than the scientist and City surveyor, Robert Hooke. It was determinably very unlike a prison, with its single-pile structure, palatial dimensions, long and elegant facade and gateway crowned by recumbent figures representing 'melancholy and raving madness'. Its large rooms opened onto well-lit galleries, and all was set in expansive grounds. It was said that it did not go down well at the French court that this 'palace beautiful' took its inspiration from Versailles but cost only £17,000. Defoe considered that it was 'the most beautiful structure for such a Use that is in the World'. He also commended the new rules for the government of the hospital, especially the one stipulating that 'no person, except the proper officers who attended them, be allowed to see the lunatics of a Sunday', and that 'no person be allowed to give the lunatics strong drink, wine, tobacco or spirits' at any time.[5] This was not a zoo, but a refuge. These were not criminals to be execrated but unfortunates deserving of pity and protection. These were distinctions the public increasingly recognised.

The problem was that not all the mad were obviously so. Socially troublesome individuals were not initially presumed to be mad. Time would tell. In 1598 a Joseph Crich was put in the Aldermandbury 'cage' or lock-up to determine his true state of mind. When it was determined that his mind was in a state he was sent to Bethlem.[6] Those who were not 'idiots', those whose insanity was intermittent, those who could engage in seemingly normal social intercourse, those not banging their heads or screeching hysterically, those whose delusions seemed more seditious than insane, were not recognised as mentally ill. Those of them who committed crimes had no legal defence. Not all needed one as those who committed minor offences or made a nuisance of themselves would be subdued, 'beaten with a rod', and confined at home under the care of family members. Serious offences were a different matter. Perpetrators would end up on the scaffold, or in prison. Gradually the perception of mental illness enlarged, and more and more individuals fell into the safety-net of lunacy. Yet before parliament legislated in 1809 for the establishment of county asylums and until those asylums could be built, those deemed lunatics who had committed offences could be held in county gaols just like common criminals. For instance it

---

5 Defoe, I, pp.371f.
6 Andrews *et al.*, *op. cit.*, p.118.

was not until 1816 that most lunatics were removed from Lancaster castle, and Preston still held them in 1846.[7]

In the first half of the nineteenth century, evangelical and Benthamite reformers were active in efforts to improve the lot and treatment of those incarcerated, lunatics as well as criminals. At the same time several well-publicised criminal cases broke new ground in the definition of insanity and an increasing number of offenders were judged not guilty of their offences by reason of that condition. Some were deemed homicidal maniacs. Dangerous though they were, their fate would be to be confined indefinitely not in a prison but in an asylum. But no ordinary asylum. Security would be the primary concern, and so such an establishment would have to have high staffing levels and strong walls, to keep order within the institution and to prevent escape from it. Such an asylum did not yet exist and so resort was made to the short-term expedient of utilising the existing estate for the insane.

Bethlem, which had long prioritised the admission of those deemed dangerous to themselves or others, was to bear the initial brunt, but, following an Act in 1808 'for the better care and maintenance of lunatics', wards could also be made available in newly-built county asylums to accommodate the increasing influx of 'criminal lunatics', a designation indicating both their legal and medical status. Fisherton House in Salisbury, for instance, would provide space once Bethlem was full. This recourse would not suffice for long. With a burgeoning population the number of criminal lunatics grew and by the 1850s it was apparent that more capacity and a specially dedicated facility were essential, especially for the most dangerous and notorious cases. Three mentally disordered individuals in this period were responsible for offences of the utmost seriousness: James Hadfield for the attempted regicide of King George III in 1800; Edward Oxford for shooting at Queen Victoria in 1840; and Daniel M'Naghten in 1843 for killing the Prime Minister's secretary, having mistaken his victim for the true target of his paranoia, the Prime Minister, Robert Peel, himself. Maniacs such as these had to be held in the most secure conditions.

Hadfield, whose case had led to the speedy enactment of the Criminal Lunatics Act of 1800 whereby those tried for treason, murder and felony but found not guilty by reason of insanity could 'be kept in strict custody in such place and manner as to the Court should seem fit, until His Majesty's pleasure be known', was committed to Bethlem. He would be detained in

---

7 Margaret DeLacy, *Prison Reform in Lancashire, 1700–1850* (Stanford, CA, 1986), pp.117, 198.

that asylum until he died in 1841, although his later years were spent in its new site at St George's Fields, Southwark to which it had relocated in 1815. This move allowed for a state-financed wing for the criminally insane, with a capacity for forty-five men and fifteen women, to be constructed in the grounds, a development for which Hadfield's case was again directly responsible and of which he was one of the first beneficiaries. It opened in 1816. Oxford too was sent to Bethlem's new wing for what would be a lengthy interlude of twenty-four years. He was a model patient spending his time wisely in learning modern languages, reading, drawing and playing the violin. In April 1864 he was moved to the newly-erected and purpose-built Criminal Lunatic Asylum, Broadmoor, where he would remain for three years, before being discharged on the condition he emigrated to Australia. During his relatively brief period in Broadmoor he continued to thrive. Finally, M'Naghten followed the same route: twenty-one years in Bethlem, and then a move to Broadmoor. Presumably having been patients concurrently in both Bethlem and Broadmoor, these would-be killers of a queen and of a prime minister would have known each other well. Their acquaintance was cut short by M'Naghten's death in 1865.

Built by convict labour on Crown land near the village of Crowthorne in Berkshire, perched on a ridge within Windsor Forest, Victorian Broadmoor was a monument to the progress in the treatment of mentally-ill offenders, as well as a reassurance to the public that they were safe from that very group. Throughout its history, however, Broadmoor has struggled both to confine its inmates and define its ethos. It was an asylum for the criminally insane and uniquely admission was given only to those who were both criminal and lunatic, but it was also a prison in the sense of being a place of secure confinement. Keeping the dangerously mad under lock and key was its primary purpose, although one not always achieved.

From the outside it was an imposing, red-brick fortress-prison. Indeed it had been designed by Joshua Jebb himself and would be his final project, as he died weeks after Broadmoor admitted its first patients. Constructed over three years by convict labour in the 'Prison-Romanesque' style he favoured, its high, unadorned boundary walls with their spikes, and the long, grim cell-blocks with their serried ranks of barred windows, indicated that security was its prime function.[8] Inside the walls and blocks, however, the atmosphere was far from punitive and very different from the penal regimes being imposed in the convict prisons. The inmates may have been

8   Ralph Partridge, *Broadmoor* (London, 1953), p.67.

32. Broadmoor then

placed in cells, but at least all the cells, other than those in the 'refractory' or 'Back Blocks' where the dangerous and violent were kept in stringent conditions, afforded enchanting views over the Hampshire and Surrey countryside, a sylvan delight deliberately denied ordinary prisoners. There were no padded cells, and any use of 'mechanical restraint' – strait-jackets – had to be recorded, as had the use of 'seclusion' – locking patients in their rooms during the daytime. The asylum was under the charge of a medical superintendent, the first being Dr John Meyer who remained in post until 1870. Another doctor, William Orange, was his deputy. Both men came from the Surrey asylum in Wandsworth. They, along with an assistant, made up the entire medical team. 'Attendants' – neither quite gaolers nor quite nurses – formed the uniformed staff, although, untrained as they initially were and coming mainly from the army or prisons, they often acted as little more than turnkeys, despite the fact that the rules specified that 'kindness and forbearance are first principles in the care and management of persons of unsound mind'. Rather than 'hard labour, hard fare and hard bed', Broadmoor would provide educational, vocational, and recreational facilities, four meals a day and a good diet. It boasted its own kitchen garden to provide locally grown produce and owned 170 acres of farm land to provide recuperative and productive agricultural work.

On 27 May 1863 the asylum, although still under construction, received its first patients, eight women, six of whom had attempted or effected infanticide, sent from Bethlem. More would soon join them as the first block to be finished was for women. The following year, male patients arrived from Fisherton House and Bethlem, Edward Oxford, Daniel M'Naghten and one Richard Dadd among them. By the end of 1864 there were some 200 men and 100 women resident in Broadmoor. The full complement of the hospital – reached by 1870 – would see the number of men double, while the number of women remained the same. The men were ultimately housed in six blocks, the women in two, one for the more passive patients, the other for the more aggressive.

There they would undergo 'moral management', a regime of strenuous exercise and steady occupation in a clean, healthy environment with lots of bracing fresh air complemented by sustaining meals with a high provision of home-grown rhubarb, a purgative thought conducive to mental recuperation.[9] The motto was *mens sana in corpore sano* – a healthy mind in a healthy body. As to the latter, Broadmoor's annual death-rate was merely three per cent, and it continued to decline. Not gaol fever, but 'consumption' – tuberculosis – was the main killer and the inevitable consequence of close confinement in an asylum. Improvements in mental health, however, were harder to gauge and seemed few and far between.

The Broadmoor regime was modelled on that of Tuke's York Retreat and the similar approach of the Hanwell Lunatic Asylum, and was far from the coercive methods of restraint used in Bethlem and elsewhere that had caused a national scandal in the first two decades of the nineteenth century. Meyer had occasionally deployed the strait-jacket, but the practice was so inimical to the Commissioners in Lunacy that it soon died out. Internal restraint was to be inculcated, not external restraints deployed. The inmates would be helped to suppress their inner demons and reforge their own innate humanity. Classification – just as in prisons – had not previously been done, but would be done in the future. The noisy, violent or disruptive would be kept separate from the quiet and introverted, the dangerous from the vulnerable. Later still, attempts were made to classify the particular forms of mental illness and correlate them with specific crimes. Murder was the most prevalent offence, and there was considerable reluctance to release male murderers. While most of these patients would stay in Broadmoor for the rest of their lives, those who had committed lesser offences would more often be discharged.[10] In the Victorian era this amounted to about a fifth

---

9   *Ibid.*, p.76.

10   By no means all. In 1886, the eleven-year-old Billy Giles was sent to Broadmoor for arson. He died there in 1962 (Harley Cronin, *The Screw Turns* (London, 1967), pp.158f.).

of men and over a third of women. Discharge could be to another asylum, or home or even into exile, the fate which befell Oxford.

The character of Broadmoor very much depended on the character of that omnipotent figure, the superintendent. Under Orange, who succeeded Meyer in 1870, it 'passed from its first experimental stage as a concentration camp for homicidal lunatics into a well-run permanent institution'.[11] Orange's aim was compassionate care, but first he had to ensure security. In its early days escapes were fairly frequent as the boundary walls had not yet reached their full height. He ensured that they all attained sixteen and a half feet. Inadequate staff were dismissed and replaced, while those who survived the cull, or came in after it, experienced better terms and conditions of employment, and a happier environment. The asylum settled down to a stable and settled regime. Although the risk to the wider public was reduced, the pent up anger of the paranoid could still burst out within the walls, and the head of a custodial and coercive institution would be the prime target. Just as Meyer had suffered a serious assault, Orange himself was subjected to a murderous attack by a fifty-six-year-old clergyman, the Revd H.J. Dodwell, who as a result of taking a shot at the most senior civil judge, the Master of the Rolls, had been committed to Broadmoor in 1878. Undeterred, under Orange's benign rule, arts, crafts and sports became integral to the institution, patients were integrated to an extent, and interaction between them and attendants encouraged. Orange, to the sorrow of his staff and patients, was eventually replaced by his deputy, Dr David Nicholson, in 1886. He had also been assaulted in his subordinate role and would endure another attack while in charge. He continued to run the asylum along similar lines to his predecessor. He too was caring. Although he was more concerned with keeping patients in than letting them out, the Commissioners in Lunacy criticised his regime as too slack. Nicholson and his predecessors had no experience of prisons, only of asylums.

A new disciplinary broom was needed and in 1895 the new Conservative Home Secretary appointed an outsider as superintendent, the first and foremost of 'the men of iron', Dr Richard Brayn. He came from the prison system, having been medical governor of Woking and Aylesbury prisons. During his stern, authoritarian reign, Broadmoor reverted to being more of a prison than an asylum and its inmates were treated more as criminals than as patients. Inflexible discipline was imposed. Life was severely regulated. Privileges were curtailed. The number of staff and the levels of security and surveillance were increased. Interaction between attendants and inmates

---

[11] Partridge, *op. cit.*, pp.77f.

was discouraged. Although brutality was not condoned, seclusion – inmates being locked alone in their rooms like naughty children – became a routine resort. In Brayn's first year 159 men and 39 women were subjected to periods of seclusion totalling 200,000 hours, and he successfully resisted calls to reconsider this ploy. In one paramount aspect he had succeeded where others had not: there were no escapes in his time. He was also the first superintendent to escape physically unscathed. His reward was a knighthood. Yet as prison shades closed in on Broadmoor there were some ameliorations made even by this Spartan superintendent. He redecorated the tired buildings. A cricket pitch was laid out within the walls in 1903, and 'outside entertainments' began.

After Brayn retired in 1910, and under a succession of more compassionate superintendents, the 'asylum spirit' increasingly pervaded 'the administration while the need for safe custody [was] by no means lost sight of'.[12] More freedoms were allowed, sporting and theatrical activities were increased, patient initiatives were encouraged (such as the publication of a monthly magazine, *The Broadmoor Chronicle*, from 1944), occupational and recreational therapies were extended (including amateur theatricals by 'The
' from 1939), parole within and without the asylum's grounds was introduced, and the all-important discharge rate crept up. Yet, inevitably, the press portrayed the life of criminal lunatics as luxurious. Broadmoor was slowly being transformed from a gaol into a hospital, with patients rather than criminals as its residents. By 1938, when it became a prerequisite that all new entrants to the staff must have passed a nursing examination, the transformation was largely but not entirely complete. In 1945 the name 'attendant' was changed to 'nurse', although, significantly, the nursing staff were affiliated to the POA.

Just as Bethlem became the most famous lunatic asylum in the world, so Broadmoor rapidly established itself as the best-known criminal lunatic asylum specialising in the most dangerous and intractable of mentally ill offenders. Many patients admitted there had been found by juries to be unfit to plead or to be not guilty by reason of insanity. Others, deemed too mad to be brought before a jury, had been sent there by the Home Secretary. The rest were those who had become insane while in prison and had been transferred to Broadmoor to serve out their sentence or to recover their sanity and be returned whence they came. They proved a never-ending source of anxiety to the staff and other patients, being the most violent, most likely to act in concert and most likely to escape. The escape of four

12 *Ibid.*, pp.89–96.

convicts in 1873, two of whom were never recaptured, one of them, William Bisgrove, being the only murderer in the history of Broadmoor to make a complete getaway, roused considerable public disquiet. As a result, in 1875 the bulk of this troublesome convict class was transferred to Woking prison where it remained until the remnants were returned to the asylum in 1888. Their behaviour was bad, but their numbers were small and Block 6 wherein they dwelt had been strengthened and enlarged for their reception. Prison transfers have remained a part of the Broadmoor intake ever since.

Larger than the number of escapees was the number who clamoured for readmission after discharge. They had coped admirably with the structure and routine of Broadmoor but could not retain their sanity in the rough and tumble of life outside its sheltering walls. One was a murderer called Kelly who escaped from Broadmoor in 1888 and made for New Orleans. In 1927 an old man knocked at the door of the asylum and asked to be readmitted. It was Kelly, who wanted the comforts of Broadmoor in his dotage. He got his wish.[13]

Notable alumni were two who would have an enduring impact in the arts, and both were resident together in Block 2 where patients had most freedom and more privileges. The first was Richard Dadd, the patricidal artist, who for over forty years continued to produce notable paintings, first in Bethlem and later in Broadmoor, until his death there from tuberculosis in 1886.[14] The other was the American Civil War veteran, Dr William Minor, who was sent to Broadmoor in 1872 for the murder, under paranoid delusions, of a young man in London. 'The Surgeon of Crowthorne' spent thirty-eight years there as Patient Number 742 , in the course of which, with plenty of free time and ready access to books, he became one of the most prolific and celebrated contributors to the *Oxford English Dictionary*. He had been encouraged in this by both Orange and Nicholson, and indeed in 1876 when Orange managed to get most of the convict patients removed, Minor was given a second cell to store his private library. Under the rather spiteful Dr Brayn, obstacles were put in his way and finally all his privileges were peremptorily removed.[15] It was a relief then that, in 1910, Minor was

---

13 *Ibid.*, pp.78–85.

14 He was one of the last group to be relocated. The day he left was the day the old criminal lunatic asylum at Bethlem ceased to be.

15 They were not the only things removed. In 1902 Minor amputated his own penis 'in the interests of morality'. His lexicographical prowess remained unimpaired. For an account of his time in Broadmoor see Simon Winchester's *The Surgeon of Crowthorne* (London, 1998).

granted a conditional discharge by Winston Churchill and deported back home. Both patient and superintendent left Broadmoor in the same year.

There were also psychopathic killers whose legacy was nothing more than notoriety, such as John Straffen, the child murderer who in 1952 escaped from Broadmoor and during his brief time at large killed again, and Ronnie Kray, one of the twins who for years had dominated London's gangland until they were convicted of murder in 1969, his sibling Reggie spending the rest of his life in prison. Other inmates of note were two schizophrenic mass murderers: Peter Sutcliffe, the 'Yorkshire Ripper', sentenced to a 'whole life' term for the murder of thirteen women, who was transferred from the prison system in 1984 and when deemed 'no longer mentally ill' was returned to it thirty-one years later, and Kenneth Erskine, the 'Stockwell Strangler', who murdered at least seven elderly people and remained in Broadmoor until recently.

The Criminal Lunatics Act of 1860 – known as 'The Broadmoor Act' – had placed all criminal lunatic asylums under the jurisdiction of the Home Secretary. To accommodate an increasing number of patients, greater provision had to be found. In 1910 Rampton in Nottinghamshire was opened as an adjunct to Broadmoor. After the Great War it was converted into a Mental Deficiency Institution for criminal imbeciles while all criminal lunatics were returned to Broadmoor, which had previously found 'the compulsory mixing of ... the mad and the half-witted who do not thrive in each other's company or require similar treatment' a major problem.[16] Rampton fulfilled this skimming role until 1920 when the Board of Control took it over for the confinement of 'dangerous and vicious' mental defectives. A second overspill for Broadmoor was Park Lane in Merseyside, which later amalgamated with Moss Side House to become Ashworth. Together, they made up the trinity of 'Broadmoor asylums' holding criminal lunatics under maximum security.

The Criminal Justice Act of 1948 made both significant and cosmetic changes. Their management was transferred to the Board of Control for Lunacy and Mental Deficiency under the Ministry of Health, while their inmates were no longer called 'criminal lunatics' but 'patients', and the term 'asylums' was replaced with 'institutions'. The 1959 Mental Health Act changed their designation to 'special hospitals', placed them under the management and control of the Ministry of Health, and allowed them to take dangerous patients who had not been through the courts. Nonetheless, until 2001 these high-security psychiatric hospitals were not part of the

---

16 Partridge, *op. cit.*, p.100.

National Health Service but were, like prisons, directly administered by the Home Office, and their nursing staff dressed like prison officers. Only since that date have the hospitals been fully integrated into the NHS and the nurses fully civilianised, although to this day some staff remain members of the POA, and it is the Home Secretary who has the final say on the release of their patients.

Removing the insane from prisons to hospitals did not, however, mean that prisons were cleared of the damaged and disturbed. What to do with them? In 1939 a report on the psychological treatment of criminals by two eminent forensic psychiatrists, William Norwood East, a recently retired prison commissioner, and W.H. Hubert, a pioneer in the use of psychotherapy in prisons, recommended the creation of a penal institution of a special kind to deal with 'abnormal and unusual types of criminal'. War intervened, and nothing was done until 1946 when the first full-time prison psychologist was appointed. The following year the first experiment in group psychotherapy in any prison in the world began on the psychiatric unit at Wormwood Scrubs. Ten selected prisoners lived in community and underwent individual treatment. In addition to psychodrama, group therapy and occupational therapy – especially bookbinding – there was electrical shock treatment.[17] This was a ward, not a wing let alone a prison, but it was a start and a prelude to greater things.

Holloway, Wakefield and Feltham followed suit in setting up similar units within their walls, but the most daring innovation was the construction of a psychotherapeutic prison at Grendon Underwood in Buckinghamshire. The plans were laid in 1956 and the prison opened in August 1962, very much part of the Lionel Fox legacy. Its remit was to investigate and treat 'mental disorders generally recognised as responsive to treatment', to investigate 'offenders whose offences themselves suggest mental morbidity', and to explore 'the problems of dealing with psychopaths'. At one time it had been thought that it would be a special hospital called the 'East-Hubert Institution', but that was not to be. Being a prison and not a hospital it was complementary rather than supplementary to the special hospitals.

When it first opened, Grendon was, like Broadmoor, under the direction of a medical superintendent, and in its early days it had about 150 prisoners and a similar number of staff. The population was to be built up gradually. Initially many of the offenders sent there were recidivists serving relatively short sentences for property offences, but over time this proportion virtually

---

[17] Grew, pp.194f.; *Report* (1955), p.17.

vanished and Grendon became largely the preserve of those serving lengthy or life sentences for violent or sexual offences. Drug addicts were not usually deemed suitable unless they were abstinent, nor were those aged over forty. Whatever the character of its intake, however, it housed only offenders with psychopathic traits or other personality disorders – initially including under this heading 'homosexuality' – as opposed to mental illnesses.[18] Nor could it take those requiring the highest security – soon to be called 'Category As'. It was not a dispersal prison. Nor would it take 'highly disturbed' prisoners who needed psychiatric treatment. It was not a special hospital.

It was a medium security prison, with four wings for men and a single wing for boys, but within its high prison walls and within the constraints of security, its buildings and well-tended, colourful gardens presented a college-like appearance, its décor was bright and cheerful and it 'actually smelt clean and fresh'.[19] Its regime was far more relaxed and permissive than elsewhere in the prison estate, as were relationships between inmates and staff. As a psychiatrist working there put it, this was a deliberate attempt to break down what was perceived as 'the greatest bar of all to rehabilitation': a hatred of authority and a deep-grained loyalty to fellow law-breakers known as 'prison culture'.[20] Everyone living or working there – not just the medical staff – had a role to play in its therapeutic endeavour. They were all 'in it together'.

Prisoners were not sent to Grendon by the courts but, on the recommendation of doctors, probation officers, psychologists or even uniformed staff, were transferred there from other prisons or borstals or, later, from YOIs. Only those who admitted their offence or offences were eligible for Grendon. Only those who consented could be transferred there. And a transfer did not ensure automatic admission. There was a rigorous eight-week initial assessment, and a tremendous culture shock. Leech arrived in the Assessment Unit in 1989. He had come from Dartmoor knowing that there was 'no such thing as a good screw', and yet the day after his arrival he attended the tri-weekly wing meeting, chaired by a fellow prisoner. Leech was 'totally dumbfounded by it all'. It was 'outlandish' seeing a 'group of forty prisoners sitting in a room with three officers and a female [wing tutor] ... chatting away as if they were the best of friends ... The system was turned

---

[18] *Report* (1962), pp.3, 59f. By 1989 when Mark Leech reached Grendon, homosexuality *per se* was no longer a therapeutic issue (*A Product of the System* (London, 1992), pp.135f., 161ff.).

[19] Leech, *op. cit.*, p.123.

[20] Tony Parker, *The Frying-Pan* (London, 1970), p.213.

on its head.'[21] It took some adjustment. Only those prepared to cooperate in determining and engaging with their own treatment, to demonstrate commitment to the therapeutic process, and 'to learn to communicate openly within a group without recourse to physical violence' were assessed by Grendon as suitable for admission.[22] Motivation was the primary criterion. Not all showed it. Some feigned it. Ultimate release from indeterminate sentences could be the spur to simulate motivation. If the 'lifer division' of the Prison Department recommended admission for detailed appraisal, most life-sentence prisoners would agree to go, hardly an exercise in real choice or a demonstration of real commitment. Those accepted but who proved disruptive to the therapeutic environment, especially those who resorted to bullying or violence, would be quietly whisked away to another prison by an early-morning procedure known as the 'Ghost Train'.[23]

Those who survived assessment stayed in Grendon for one to two years before returning to an ordinary gaol or being released. During that time they each kept the same uniform – a uniform that actually fitted – lived on therapy wings they thought of as home, slept in colourfully painted, well-furnished 'rooms' – the Grendon euphemism for cells – with large windows overlooking beautiful countryside, from which they were unlocked during the day to work, exercise, play sports, engage in artistic pursuits and drama, and above all attend therapy. Group therapy was Grendon's forte, its be and all. To begin with, a doctor was in charge of each group but later it could be led by a psychologist or probation officer. Uniformed officers fully participated. Therapeutic feedback – 'grassing is what anyone else would have called it' – was integral to the ethos. An inmate found to have broken the policies fixed by the community was invited to speak of what he had done to the group meeting and if he failed, he would be brought before the whole wing. The result could be expulsion and return to the prison whence he came. The aim, however, was not so much disciplinary as to enable individuals to recognise where they had gone wrong, to learn from their mistakes, and not repeat them. It was the same when talking of their offences: those who came up with excuses, justifications, blaming parents or victims, received tongue-lashings from members of their group. Criminals

---

21 Leech, *op. cit.*, pp.126f. For a detailed account of the assessment process see Elaine Genders and Elaine Player, *Grendon: A Study of a Therapeutic Prison* (Oxford, 1995), pp.47–78.

22 HO (1987), PD CI 21/1987.

23 Frances Finlay, *Boy in Prison* (London, 1971), p.95.

were being held accountable to their peers, peers who knew whereof they spoke! The savaged were then offered support.[24]

Most surprisingly for a prison, staff and inmates were on first-name and even nickname terms, good relations were valued, apologies were made from both sides in a falling-out, and there were even elements of democratic decision-making when the whole community met together at the weekly 'Forum' where inmates could make suggestions, air grievances and even criticise the staff or the institution itself. Similarly young prisoners elected 'group foremen' and 'under-foremen' from their own ranks to perform a prefectural function for a month at a time.[25]

Custodial staff, unlike inmates, did not volunteer for Grendon, and they do not seem to have been hand-picked or even to have received training for such a posting. Some prison officers posted or seconded to Grendon from prisons such as Wandsworth or from closed borstals thought they had arrived 'on another planet'.[26] As one put it: 'I feel like I've been trained as a plumber and given a job as an electrician.' Some, just like some prisoners, would never fit in. Others did and attributed their wholehearted adoption of the rehabilitative model to the culture of the prison and not to their own predisposition. Almost all thought that working in Grendon was much more difficult than working in other prisons, that different skills were required, and that empathy, tact and persuasiveness were prerequisites, and that they had to rely on 'the force of their own personal resources, rather than upon the authority of their uniform'. It was, however, much more rewarding, as they were valued rather than ignored or resented.[27] They also found that trust between staff and prisoners enhanced security. These insights they would carry with them when the time came for them to be transferred to work in other prisons. Consent rather than coercion, cooperation rather than confrontation was the Grendon way. Heady stuff!

Heady stuff, but integral to what Grendon was trying to achieve: trust and openness. In the view of Ian Pickering, the Director of Prison Medical Services, good relationships between prisoners and all members of staff were vital to producing 'a supportive and permissive environment in which the inmate is encouraged to express his inner feelings, his doubts and difficulties,

---

[24] Leech, *op. cit.*, pp.142–5.

[25] Finlay, *op. cit.*, p.142.

[26] Simon Barlow, *The Self-Tapping Screw* (Brighton, 2013), pp.76f.

[27] Genders and Player, *op. cit.*, pp.123ff. Problems they would face would come from prison officers in other penal establishments who had their own prejudices against such rehabilitative efforts or had been fed myths by the POA.

without fear of retaliation from others'.[28] And relationships could run deep. Nineteen-year-old Christopher Finlay bonded with E.F. Turner, the hospital principal officer and trained nurse in charge of the unit. 'To me', he said, 'he was a man, a father-figure with an understanding of my generation's problems.' He revered him as 'a man of honour'. Another kindly, paternal figure was the rotund Catholic chaplain, Father Paddy Glynn, who had a profound influence on the young man. Finlay would 'always remember Grendon, the prison where inmates are treated as individuals, the prison where I was happy'.[29]

Although the modification of behaviour while in prison and on release was a specific aim of the Prison Department, therapy in Grendon was not primarily directed at the prevention of, or reduction in, crime. That was a secondary effect to the goal of improving well-being, enabling offenders 'to re-evaluate their circumstances and to develop alternative ways of responding to them'.[30] It was all about relieving distress, exercising self-control, making sound choices and taking responsibility for actions. The danger was that the public, whose support was all-important for the continuation of this project, might perceive it as being 'soft on criminals'. This is a danger that throughout penal history has bedevilled efforts at reform either of conditions or of individuals, especially when there was no or little evidence of crime reduction as a result. Early studies of Grendon concluded that while there had been a marked increase in self-confidence and self-esteem, a striking reduction in anxiety and depression, and a decrease in the antagonism felt by inmates towards each other and those in authority, therapy appeared to have no greater effect on subsequent patterns of offending, both in frequency and severity, than ordinary prison regimes.[31] Producing happier, better-balanced criminals who still went on happily to re-offend was not the result the public expected or the government wanted to proclaim.

---

[28] Parker, *op. cit.*, p.xii. This important work contains first-hand accounts of how men and boys responded to the therapeutic regime in its early days. From the same period came Frances Finlay's *Boy in Prison* which recounts, in his own words, her public-school-educated son's transition from borstal boy to young prisoner, first in Aylesbury (which in 1962 had become a prison for male young offenders) and latterly in Grendon in the early 1960s. Grendon changed his life, in the way borstal, where he first encountered empathetic staff, had tried and failed to do. Although he initially fell back into crime, by 1968 he had finally kicked the habit. What befell him afterwards is not recorded.

[29] Finlay, *op. cit.*, pp.85, 139–45, 188.

[30] Genders and Player, *op. cit.*, p.12.

[31] John Gunn *et al.*, *Psychiatric Aspects of Imprisonment* (London, 1978), and 'A Ten Year Follow-Up of Men Discharged from Grendon Prison', *British Journal of Psychiatry*, 151 (1987), pp.674–8.

Grendon operated out on a penal peninsula, around which cold winds were blowing. Whereas there had been *ad hoc* therapeutic initiatives within other prisons, this was the only prison the *raison d'être* of which was therapy. It was unique. It had a unique ethos, and a unique management structure until 1985. Then things began to change. The medical superintendent was replaced as supremo by a governor, although the managerial accountability remained bifurcated: the governor being responsible to the Prison Department's regional director, the senior medical officer reporting to the director of the prison medical service. Three years later the senior medical officer was subordinated, and made accountable, to the governor. It was the same old story of security trumping treatment, or not quite. Grendon was still unique but less *outré*, and all was not lost by any means. Its special qualities were preserved by a succession of governors, and it continued to affirm the rehabilitative ethos in times when that ethos was looked upon with cynicism. And it could convert the sceptical. In the early 1990s two Oxford researchers, who began with a predisposition to denounce as futile the idea of a therapeutic prison, were soon confounded in their expectations and decided that the issue they had to study was 'not whether custody and treatment were antithetical, but how these unconsenting bedfellows were being accommodated within a single institution'. They were persuaded that 'a therapeutic prison [was] not only possible but ... desirable'. Their research, unlike that of their predecessors, showed that the reconviction rate of those who had undergone therapy had reduced, and the longer the period spent in therapy the greater the reduction. Those released directly from Grendon, and those deemed a 'success' in therapy, were the least likely to re-offend.[32]

Against all the odds and in dark days for rehabilitative models Grendon has survived and flourished. It is that precious thing: something of a success story. Its success may be its undoing. The more other prisons adopt Grendon's methods, the less need there might be for Grendon itself. What was once unique may become universal. At the very time prison ivy was beginning to creep up the walls of Grendon, the government was determined to rationalise, regularise and increase therapeutic provision within the wider prison estate, and to utilise the methods pioneered in Grendon. The rising number of those convicted of sexual offences, of those sentenced to indeterminate sentences and of those languishing on 'Rule 43' – segregation for their own protection – required it. Sex-offender courses were set up in a number of prisons, and other initiatives trialled. The so-called 'second Grendon', HMP Dovegate, was opened in 2001 in Staffordshire as a privately run prison.

---

[32] Genders and Player, *op. cit.*, pp.5ff., 17, 156.

33. Staff–inmate conviviality in the Barlinnie Special Unit

Unlike Grendon it serves several general penal purposes, only one of which is therapy, and only a fifth of the thousand or so adult male prisoners are placed in the purpose-built therapeutic facility. They are all repeat, serious offenders and are subject to daily group therapy for between eighteen and twenty-four months. Another mainstream prison which has incorporated a therapeutic community is Gartree in Leicestershire which did so in 1993.

Some brave therapeutic initiatives have not survived, the most notable being that inside the austere walls of Glasgow's Victorian prison, Barlinnie. It housed an innovative experiment that burst briefly into radiant bloom: the Special Unit. Initiators and supporters confidently predicted that it would 'take a decade to win acceptance and a further decade for [its formula] to be put into general practice'.[33] In the event it was never fully accepted and after two decades 'the experiment' would be killed off.

The first-fruit of a Scottish Office report on the treatment of long-term and violent prisoners, the tiny Special Unit was opened in February 1973. Although it acknowledged its debt to Grendon, its unacknowledged progenitor was the therapeutic ward in Wormwood Scrubs, the regime of which the Unit largely mirrored.[34] Three key individuals in Scotland

---

[33] Christopher Carrell and Joyce Laing (eds), *The Special Unit* (Glasgow, 1982), p.6.
[34] Grew, pp.195f.

inspired its creation and ethos: Alex Stephen, the influential Controller of Operations for the Scottish Home and Health Department, who had chaired the working party that had produced the report; Ian Stephen, a forensic psychologist; and Ken Murray, an executive member of the Scottish POA. At this point prison officers, worried about the violent potential of those who could no longer be hanged, were supportive, but not for long. The Unit's ethos, as it developed, went against the grain. It was not merely to solve the problem of violent prisoners but to resolve their problems. It replaced solitary confinement and brutality with arts and crafts. It permitted inmates to wear their own clothes and read their own books or even to write them. Within the confines of the Unit prisoners were given freedom, responsibility and choice. There were no allocated duties. They could do what they wished and were allowed to develop their own work and study programmes. One result was a news-sheet tellingly called *The Key*. Inmates and staff were encouraged to establish close and cooperative relationships and talk to each other man to man and on first-name terms. The weekly meeting provided a forum for discussion and comment on how the Unit was running, and recommendations by the prisoners were often put into effect. Those who abused the trust given them or whose actions or behaviour were undermining the cohesion of the community ended up not in a segregation cell but in the 'Hot Seat' where they would be grilled by other inmates and by staff. It evolved into a miniature therapeutic community along the Grendon lines. One noted difference was that the seventeen discipline and nurse officers staffing the Unit had all volunteered and were carefully vetted by a selection panel. Their initial training took them to Broadmoor and Carstairs state mental hospitals as well as to Grendon itself.

The Unit had provision for only ten men, but usually held no more than seven. In its first eight years it admitted, on the recommendation of governors of long-stay prisons, nineteen prisoners, twelve of whom were serving life sentences They were the very worst in the prison system: the most violent, the most disruptive, those immune to the deterrent effect of penal sanctions, those without hope of early release, those with little to lose by refusing to conform. The worst of the worst was Jimmy Boyle.

Boyle was a Glasgow gangster who had survived the most feared of all of Scotland's prisons, Inverness and Peterhead. Born in 1944, he had graduated from approved school and borstal to prison. In 1967, after the abolition of capital punishment, he was sentenced to life imprisonment for the murder of a gangland figure, William 'Babs' Rooney. The press labelled Boyle 'Scotland's most violent man'. He was a 'no-hoper', as were many others who had escaped the noose only to receive interminable sentences –

bad men with nothing to lose. They posed a new problem: how could they be tamed? And if not tamed, caged?

The normal recourse was for violent and dangerous prisoners to be sent to 'the Siberia for prisoners in the Scottish penal system', the northern Gulag of Inverness (Porterfield) and Peterhead, the latter being a grim granite fortress overlooking the North Sea with a notoriety all of its own. Boyle and his fellow 'hard men' belied the first and modified the second part of the Nietzschean dictum that 'punishment tames a man but does not make him better'. They were not tamed. They were made worse. Repeated transfers between the two prisons did nothing to dampen their resort to insubordination, dirty protests, and riots, during which they were the recipients of greater violence than they managed to inflict. But they were incorrigible, and encouraged others to emulate their stance.

The Scottish Prison Department resorted to a draconian solution. When Boyle, after five years yo-yoing between prisons, ended up once more in Inverness, he was put in one of the new 'cages' in 'The Special Unit'. These consisted of cells subdivided by iron-barred enclosures to ensure that there would be minimal physical contact with prison officers and no contact with other prisoners. The only movable objects therein were a plastic chamber-pot, a blanket and a book. The only human interaction was with staff carrying out their thrice-daily searches of the armpits and anus. Those who had engaged in 'aggravated disobedience' were to be kept in these humiliating and degrading conditions for between two and six months, although the maximum was often exceeded. At times they were kept naked, three times a day they were searched, once a week they got a book to occupy them. Boyle read Dostoevsky's *Crime and Punishment* as well as works by Hugo, Tolstoy, Dickens and Steinbeck.[35] He was in the company of great authors, but they were his only companions. There was little other human interaction. Eventually the place erupted, and six officers and three prisoners were badly injured, Boyle being one. Such was the beating he received, that at one point it was thought he would not survive the night. He lived. The governor of Inverness, despite believing that Boyle was too dangerous ever to be set free, recommended that he be transferred to another newly opened 'Special Unit', in Barlinnie. At least he would no longer be the governor's responsibility. The expectation was that at best it would contain the problem that was Jimmy Boyle, not that it would transform him, release his considerable potential, and turn him into a celebrity. Boyle, after all, was the worst of the worst. He was above all others irredeemable.

---

35 Jimmy Boyle, *A Sense of Freedom* (Edinburgh, 1977), p.171.

On his arrival as one of its first intake in 1973 Boyle found the Barlinnie Special Unit disorienting. It was the opposite of the one with the same name at Inverness. Was it a 'con-trick'? Was it a 'launching-pad for Carstairs'? Here were staff addressing him on first-name terms and trying to be pleasant! He could cope with brutality but did not know how to handle consideration.[36] Nor did he know how to react to the very strange behaviour of one of the 'screws'. Boyle was awaiting trial for the attempted murder of six prison officers, victims of the events in Inverness, and this officer gave him a pair of scissors to cut the string holding his possessions! It proved a 'Road to Damascus' experience, as Boyle recounted:

> That was the first thing that made me begin to feel human again. It was the completely natural way that it was done. This simple gesture made me think. In my other world, the penal system in general, such a thing would never happen.

It was another officer he met later that day who would have the greatest effect on Boyle – Ken Murray:

> A tall striking man, he emanated an aura of sincerity and integrity ... He stood out above the others because he spoke his mind, often to the acute discomfort of his colleagues. He was also a very sensitive man and articulate with a keen interest in politics ... [and] was the one person amongst the staff who was idealistic in viewing the true potential of the Special Unit as a meaningful alternative to the old penal system. Never at any time did I doubt his sincerity, but I had a lot of problems dealing with it.[37]

That night Boyle was in turmoil. Scissors! Scissors, in the wrong hands, were weapons. Scissors could kill. Yet they were allowed in the Unit, as were metal utensils and tools and even razor blades. There were bound to be problems and how then would the 'screws' react? He would soon find out. Within a month of his arrival he saw a fellow prisoner and friend from Inverness – Larry Winters – holding a pair of scissors to the neck of an officer. The other staff did not intervene but let Boyle do the talking. He and another prisoner persuaded their friend to hand over the scissors and the incident was defused. Later a Unit meeting was held, the issue thrashed out, and the staff member and prisoner shook hands. Had the officers gone in with batons the inmates would have turned on them. Had Larry been beaten up or had he been put in the punishment cell it would have reinforced

---

[36] *Ibid.*, pp.229ff.
[37] Jimmy Boyle, *The Pain of Confinement* (Edinburgh, 1984), pp.7f.

all the old stereotypes about authority and 'screws'. It was make or break for the Unit. By trusting them, by trying to understand them, by putting it behind them, the 'screws' brought out the best in their prisoners and demonstrated that they were all in it together and for the long haul.[38] The inmates were learning from experience, taking responsibility for their actions and committing themselves to the Unit. Out of crisis came cohesion. Boyle endured mixed feelings about what happened and his role in it. Defending a prison officer against a prisoner, and berating that prisoner publicly looked like 'selling out'. In fact Boyle was 'buying in' to the potential of the Unit, and distancing himself from group loyalty, but instinct was still at war with evidence. He, Larry and another prisoner, Ben, asked for a transfer back to the system from which they had just been plucked. Murray told them that as the Unit had been set up for the likes of them, permission would be refused. In fact their request was not even answered. They were stuck in the Unit, and decided to test its credentials. When, at Boyle's instigation, a discussion and vote took place about the continuing existence of a punishment cell in the Special Unit, prisoners and prison staff, armed with chisels and hammers, dismantled it and turned it into a weight-lifting room. In a cooperative venture the last vestige of the old system was removed from the Unit. It was another telling moment.

But for many of those working within the prison system, this was not supposed to happen. The Unit was a means of getting rid of troublesome prisoners, if only for a short time, or, at best, reducing them to some semblance of compliance, after which they could be handled safely in a normal regime. More likely, these uncontrollables would riot, smash the place up, attack staff and the whole venture would be discredited within weeks. But as weeks grew into months, peace reigned. No one was hurt. No one was ejected. The project was surpassing all expectations, leading to enormous hostility among prison staff throughout Scotland whose whole way of working was being undermined. The 'cage' had not controlled the likes of Boyle but kindness could! Absurd! The staff in the Unit had gone soft, or were afraid, or were being fooled. Their crimes forgotten, prisoners were being coddled and placated, and even getting breakfast in bed, brought to them by prison officers, so it was rumoured. Unit officers were heckled by their former colleagues as they went to work, and they and their families were cut dead in their quarters.[39]

---

[38] *Ibid.*, pp.9ff.
[39] Boyle, *A Sense of Freedom*, pp.244–7.

Journalists, however, took a different tack – at first. In July 1974 they had been invited to meet the prisoners, and came away not just impressed but in many cases converted. The press coverage was more than positive, it was rapturous. As a result, interest in the Unit became extensive, at home and abroad. Both the BBC and ITV were given permission to film inside it.[40] The optimism exuding from it was encapsulated in a lavishly illustrated book spawned by an exhibition in 1980 of prisoners' paintings, drawings, sculpture, ceramics and photographs. *The Special Unit – Its Evolution Through Its Art* was published in 1982. In a preface Ludovic Kennedy described it as celebrating 'the birth, and growth, of a paradox: that a country such as Scotland with its traditions ... should have spawned one of the most imaginative and enlightened experiments in penal history'. The Scottish Office, however, seemingly embarrassed by its success in setting up something that was receiving international acclaim, declined an invitation to contribute to the publication, refused permission for any serving member of the prison staff to do so either, and put severe constraints on the ambit of any comments by inmates or photographs of them.[41] Within these strict parameters the 'celebration' went ahead, showcasing the work of several prisoners. A lot of attention was given to one in particular, the star pupil, Jimmy Boyle. He had developed an artistic and literary bent. More than that, he had become a fine sculptor and was even having his work exhibited at the Edinburgh Festival. He was the celebrity criminal.[42]

But celebrity came at a cost. He, a murderer, while in prison had published a book and seen plays he had co-authored performed,[43] and had twice been allowed out on parole to attend his own art exhibition! A local MP, Teddy Taylor, an enthusiast for capital punishment, was aghast at the thought of the worst of criminals getting the best of treatment. Boyle should have been hanged, not given perks. Taylor was vocal in his denunciation, and his voice

---

40 Carrell and Laing, *op. cit.*, pp.113ff. Two films were subsequently made that featured the Unit: 'A Sense of Freedom', based on Boyle's autobiography, which was aired on ITV in 1981, and 'Silent Scream', about the troubled life of Larry Winters, which came out in 1990.

41 Carrell and Laing, *op. cit.*, pp.3ff.

42 Another was Hugh Collins whose most famous piece of sculpture, 'Christ the Sinner', was commissioned by St Columbus Church in Glasgow, but rejected because it depicted Jesus's genitalia. Collins spent two years of 'punishment and penance' on his creation, and was vilified for it (Robert Jeffrey, *The Barlinnie Story* (Edinburgh, 2009), pp.196f.). It was, he said, 'saturated with [his] personality' and was his 'guilt crystalized in stone', but he acknowledged that merely because he had poured the 'horrors of [his] guilt' into it did not make it a work of art (*Autobiography of a Murderer* (London, 1997), p.174).

43 *A Sense of Freedom* and *The Hardman*, both in 1977.

was heard. Rumour and exaggeration and distortion were all mixed together. By 1977 the press had changed tack. Reverting to salacious scaremongering, journalists were running stories of orgies in the Unit – variously dubbed the 'Wendy House' or the 'Nutcracker Suite' – of a social worker impregnated, of drink and drugs openly imbibed, and other such calumnies. Or at least exaggerations, as Boyle admitted that, in clear breach of trust, drinking behind the back of staff did take place, and Larry Winters did die in his cell of a drug overdose. He had acquired his dependency earlier in his imprisonment, and it had decreased in the Special Unit. That he was 'the last victim of the old system rather than the first of the new was not, however, a view widely held by the press'.[44]

Leading staff were also under fire. The executive committee of the POA had issued a press release asserting that inmates in other prisons were assaulting staff to get a transfer to the Unit. Murray knew that this was a deliberate lie and had the statistics to prove it. He appeared on television with the official figures which showed that the amount of assaults on staff had decreased since the opening of the Unit. He had publicly undermined his colleagues on the committee, exposing them as inept or worse. For his integrity, and because of their lack of it, he was expelled from their number, and shortly afterwards was put on the transfer list by the unsympathetic Labour Under-Secretary of State for prisons, Harry Ewing.[45] Ian Stephen was moved. The sharks were circling. If blood entered the water there would be a feeding frenzy.

In fact the Special Unit was never ripped to pieces, but over the years the nibbles taken out of it had the same effect. Controversy dogged its history. It was soft on the hard men who should have been made to suffer for their sins. It provided criminals with more advantages than they would have had if they had remained law-abiding. It gave too much stress to the artwork of killers and too little concern for the anguish of their victims. It may have rehabilitated some by enabling them to make more money legitimately than lawlessly, but they were neither reformed nor repentant.

---

44 Carrell and Laing, *op. cit.*, p.116. The worst offender was *The Daily Record*, a Labour-supporting tabloid which was praised by Teddy Taylor, a Tory MP, for its 'revelations'. 'The prostitute cannot be selective about bedfellows', as the Scottish Council for Civil Liberties commented in *Scottish Prisons and the Special Unit* (Glasgow, 1978), pp.12–15.

45 In 1981 the by then former minister and 'political opportunist of the worst kind' would claim that Boyle was running and dominating the Unit. Ewing in turn was controverted by Malcolm Rifkind, the Conservative Home Affairs Minister at the Scottish Office, and by a fellow Labour MP, Neil Carmichael, who pointed out that during his time as Minister responsible for the Unit Ewing had spent only twenty minutes there (Boyle, *The Pain of Confinement*, pp.294ff.).

Look at Jimmy Boyle! Since his release from prison in 1982, he had married, divorced and remarried, was feted by the art world, had made a mint out of his sculptures and books, and yet never disowned his past and continued to deny that he was guilty of the murder of Babs Rooney. He was living *the* good life but not *a* good life. The only Christian minister allowed to visit the 'clergy-free zone' of the Unit, Ron Ferguson, was convinced that members of the church hierarchy wanted Boyle to re-offend since 'his redemption wasn't according to church formulae': 'He didn't grovel enough, didn't show enough self-loathing, didn't use the right coded language. Somehow a changed, articulate Boyle was more of a threat than one who lived like a caged animal.'[46] The church hierarchy would have put this in theological terms and more accurately: he had not repented of his sins, he did not seek divine forgiveness and he was not reborn as a Christian. He had been 'redeemed' not by chaplains and the Bible but by psychologists and art-therapy. It was rehabilitation without repentance. Another long-term member of the Unit, and another murderer, Hugh Collins, marked the decline of the Unit as beginning with the departure of the charismatic Boyle, and attributed its demise to his success.

> The Special Unit had become a political embarrassment over the years ... What the prison authorities hated was that they had been proved wrong on the question of treatment. Prisoners like myself had shown that we were not animals: we had shown that if we were treated properly, then we in turn could respond, possibly even change. But what they despised most was the success of one man, Jimmy Boyle.[47]

There were, of course, failings and faults in the running of the Special Unit, and abuses accumulated over the years. There were also failures, and not all inmates survived the course. There were incidents involving visitors bringing in drink and drugs. There were the occasional outbursts of violence, although the most serious, in which one prisoner stabbed another thirteen times, was as far back as 1976.[48] Artistic endeavours had given way to indolence and ease. All imaginative projects tend to decline when their originators and first recipients are replaced. Time tends to erode. The energy and enthusiasm of its begetters was lost on their successors. Fewer charismatic and committed staff encountered fewer charismatic and

---

[46] Letter published in Jeffrey, *op. cit.*, pp.203–7.

[47] Collins, *op. cit.*, p.162. Once when Collins had been given day parole to attend the Glasgow Art School a malicious hoax was perpetrated alleging he had £10,000 and a gun and was heading for London. He was in fact having tea in Sauchiehall Street, and returned to Barlinnie as soon as he heard on the news of his 'escape' (pp.158–61).

[48] Andrew Coyle, *Inside: Rethinking Scotland's Prisons* (Edinburgh, 1991), p.137.

committed inmates. The Unit lost some of its vitality. But its virtues greatly outweighed it vices, problems could have been rectified, excesses eliminated, myths countered, and the Unit allowed to survive. Instead, in the face of constant criticism in the press, relentless opposition from prison officers, and as a result of a critical report into its culture, the Barlinnie Special Unit was closed down in 1994, the same year as the Inverness 'cages' were dismantled.[49] The opposite poles, the 'soppy and stern' extremes of Scottish prison regimes, were simultaneously eradicated.

Rehabilitation, in the form of borstals or psychotherapeutic units, socialisation in the form of improved relations between prisoners and staff, were all very well, but they had always to take second place to the security of the public and the standing of the Home Office. The public perception of a crime-wave, an increase in the reconviction rate, particularly for young offenders, or the escape of a notorious prisoner could have a chilling effect on the rehabilitative ideal. *Salus populi suprema lex*, the safety of the people is the highest law. The early 1960s saw a spate of high-profile escapes. None was of higher profile than that of George Blake whose 'great escape' was both absurdly amateurish and entirely successful.

---

[49] Jeffrey, *op. cit.*, pp.198–202. In 1994 Leech wrote his autobiography while serving in Barlinnie, although not in the therapeutic unit.

PART VI

SAFE AND SECURE?
1965–2018

The prison system in crisis as security concerns and numbers threaten to overwhelm it. With increasing political involvement in the running and management of prisons, and ever-increasing pressure to be tough on criminals, rehabilitation takes on a secondary role. Does prison work and to what end?

CHAPTER 33

The Search for Security

> The dispassionate observer, considering the enormous effort put into this complicated system of security, and its effects in adding to the repression and artificiality of prison life, may well wonder if there may not be more sorrow over one offender who escapes safe-custody than over ninety-and-nine who escape reform.
>
> Lionel Fox

In December 1966 the *Report of the Inquiry into Prison Escapes and Security* by the Admiral of the Fleet, Earl Mountbatten of Burma, was presented to parliament. Two months earlier, and two days after the escape of George Blake, Mountbatten had been appointed by the Home Secretary, Roy Jenkins, to conduct an inquiry and to make recommendations. Having accepted the task on condition that his findings would be acted upon, as he was not prepared to waste his time otherwise, he performed it without fuss and with becoming promptitude.[1] This was all the more impressive as, in addition to Blake, he had to deal with twenty other newsworthy escapees, including two of the most notorious – and admired – criminals of the day who in April 1964 had been sentenced to thirty years' imprisonment for their part in the 'Great Train Robbery': Charles Wilson, who three months later had escaped from Birmingham after his accomplices broke into the prison; and Ronald Biggs who had been whisked away from Wandsworth in 1965. Mountbatten also took evidence from a wide variety of sources, visited seventeen prisons, made detailed proposals, and even gave some consideration to Scotland which was outside his official remit.[2]

George Blake was a spy for the Soviets and traitor to his adoptive country. After his conviction in May 1961 under the Official Secrets Act 1911 he was sentenced to forty-two years' imprisonment – supposedly a year for every agent his betrayal had compromised – the longest determinate sentence ever handed down by a British court. Had he been charged with treason he would

---

1 Conversation with Terence Morris (*Crime and Criminal Justice since 1945* (Oxford, 1989), p.131).
2 *Report* (1966), paras.3–5.

have hanged. This was in effect a slow death sentence. He was allocated to a cell in 'D' Hall of Wormwood Scrubs where well-behaved long-term prisoners were housed. There this most serious of offenders, and national security risk, was left for five years. He was not kept for long on the escape list; he was not subjected to more than routine surveillance; and, even after the escape of six prisoners from his wing in June 1966, he was not moved to a more secure location elsewhere, despite the governor, Leslie Newcombe, the previous January having advised such a transfer.[3] On a Saturday evening in October, when a hundred prisoners were on association, supervised by only two staff, Blake made his way to the second floor landing of 'D' Hall, broke one of the cast-iron frames, and got out of a window. Dropping to the ground he scaled the wall with a rope ladder thrown over not by Soviet agents but by his amateur accomplices, Sean Bourke, a petty criminal from Limerick, and Michael Randle and Pat Pottle, anti-nuclear campaigners, all three having met Blake when themselves serving sentences in Wormwood Scrubs.[4] Then he was away, never to be recaptured.

These events were hugely embarrassing to the government, compromised public or national security and brought the prison service into disrepute and even ridicule. One newspaper published a daily 'score-card' of escapes. This was all the worse in that, three years before, the Prison Commission had been peremptorily abolished by the government for no obvious reason and against almost universal opposition. It was replaced by a Prison Department firmly within the Home Office, and under a Chief Director who was a career civil servant. In the culmination of 140 years of centralisation, politicians and their underlings had finally taken full control over what seemed to be an uncontroversial portfolio just as it exploded in their faces. Commissioners such as Paterson and Fox may have seen escapes as the price to be paid for a more reformative and less restrictive regime and had the courage to say so, but for government ministers faced with the escape of notorious criminals who, as a result of the abolition of the death penalty and the imposition of very long sentences, had nothing to lose, it was political dynamite.[5]

---

3   Nonetheless Newcombe was retired from the service.

4   All three would write about it. Bourke, safely back in Ireland, published *The Springing of George Blake* in 1970. Randle and Pottle waited until 1989 to publish *The Blake Escape* in which they too admitted their offence. Living in England they were put on trial, defended themselves on the non-legal ground that they thought Blake's sentence inhumane, and were the beneficiaries of a perverse verdict.

5   Since 1963 prisons have never ceased to be a political headache for the Home Secretary or, since 2007, the Justice Secretary. Perhaps they should have left the Prison Commission and its expertise well alone.

Nothing like this should ever be allowed to happen again. Mountbatten was to try to ensure it did not, although towards the end of his inquiry another life-sentence prisoner, Frank Mitchell, the 'mad axeman', made off from Dartmoor. Mountbatten made the point that there were no really secure prisons in existence in England. Most were Victorian and in Victorian times security primarily depended on keeping prisoners locked in their single cells all night and working on their own or in silence most of the day, with a large staff to monitor them and armed guards to maintain security and control. The buildings remained, the staff levels were reduced and prisoners were out of their cells far more of the time, working, talking, associating with others. Prisons designed to keep prisoners safely in seclusion were unsuitable for a more liberal regime. In 1895, with a daily average prison population of 15,000 there had been nine escapes; in 1964, with a daily average of almost twice the size there were over 2,000. The escape rate had soared as greater freedom had been accorded. 'Treating prisoners by modern methods in out-of-date buildings inevitably means that some of them can escape', he concluded. Where perimeter security had replaced cellular it had to be incorporated into the old design. Maximum security could not be obtained in the twentieth century using nineteenth-century structures.[6]

Mountbatten recommended that prisoners be divided into four categories: Category A for those whose escape would be highly dangerous to the public, police, or state; Category B for those whose escape must be made very difficult; Category C for those who could not be trusted in open conditions but who lacked the ability or resources to make a determined escape attempt; and Category D for those suitable for open conditions. This novel categorisation was implemented in 1967 when 138 men were designated category A. It persists to this day, although, after a high-profile escape of two highly dangerous prisoners by helicopter from Gartree in 1987, the first category suffered 'grade inflation', being subdivided into 'standard risk', 'high risk', and 'exceptional risk'.[7]

Similarly Mountbatten's recommendations to improve the morale and calibre of prison officers were taken up: the creation of a 'Senior Officer' grade; promotion more on merit; the ending of night patrols by untrained watchmen; the introduction of specialised training with particular emphasis on security; and the appointment in every establishment of a qualified security officer directly responsible to the governor. He also made many enlightened proposals for improving existing regimes.

[6]   *Report* (1966), para.202.
[7]   The helicopter escape is recounted in chapter 9 of Dick Callan's *Gartree* (Leyhill, 2005).

More controversially he wanted the appointment of an 'identifiable professional head of the service' who should have greater command responsibilities, give personal leadership and have a much higher public profile. A new title would be needed for this commander-in-chief, since 'Chief Director' carried the connotation of a desk job. The new office-holder should have the grander Victorian designation, 'Inspector-General'. Such a prominent figure should be away from Whitehall most of the time, inspecting, commanding and leading in the field, and when back at base 'advising the Home Secretary on all professional matters'. It was almost a reversion to the old office of chairman of the Prison Commission – a recognisable, identifiable, autonomous head who reported directly to the Home Secretary. Such a post was created in 1967, and Mountbatten's nominee, Brigadier Maunsell, was appointed. He proved a little too assertive for the Home Office to accommodate. Charisma was not an attribute appreciated by civil servants. Within a few years this unnerving experiment was eviscerated, the post was down-graded to chief inspector, separated from any executive functions, and given to a former governor. The claws had been drawn. No more independent-minded commanders, no more trenchant reports, no more rocking the boat.[8]

Equally controversially, Mountbatten advised that a new fortress facility for Category A prisoners should be built. He recognised that some prisoners posed a serious risk and realised that 'the policy of giving very long sentences up to and including the full life of a prisoner [introduced] a new type of imprisonment, bringing with it human problems which [would] have to be faced'. The likes of Frank Mitchell being left in an ordinary prison could produce a tyranny. There was substance in the allegation that in Dartmoor 'Mitchell was the "boss", that he terrorised prison officers and prisoners and had a retinue of servants'. In short he was in control of the prison and out of control of the staff. This could no longer be countenanced, but the small maximum security blocks recently established in Durham, Leicester and Parkhurst prisons could be no more than a temporary expedient as their restrictive and oppressive regimes were 'such as no country with a record of civilised behaviour ought to tolerate any longer than is absolutely essential as a stop-gap measure'.[9] The solution lay at hand. Mountbatten chose the Isle of Wight – of which he was Governor – for his new prison, possibly the first of two. An island had security advantages, and with three other prisons

---

8   *Report* (1966), paras.236–56; J.E. Thomas and R. Pooley, *The Exploding Prison* (London, 1980), pp.47f.

9   *Report* (1966), paras.23, 154–63, 205, 212f.

already there, staff could be rotated so that the rigours of working in a maximum security facility would not take an undue toll. He had found the ideal site which would allow prisoners a view over the countryside, it being especially 'desirable in common humanity' that those who would spend a large part or even all of their lives 'in an establishment from which there was no hope of getting out should be able to see the sky and surrounding country'. With a Bentham-like enthusiasm he went into every detail of the design and even gave it a name: 'Vectis', the Roman name for the island. It should house no more than 120 prisoners,[10] and within its secure confines there should be a liberal and constructive regime. It would have been no English Alcatraz.[11] But it was not to be.

Although governors and even prison officers were enthusiastic about this proposal, the Home Office was less so, and having taken advice from Radzinowicz and the three other members of a sub-committee of the Advisory Council on the Penal System, opted for their alternative recommendation of a 'dispersal system'.[12] This conclusion was reached not by an impartial consideration of the evidence but by subterfuge and by the manipulation of the committee by one of its members, Leo Abse, a colourful and eccentric left-wing MP obsessed with sex and psychoanalysis. With extraordinary and blatant candour, he boasted in his strange, rambling autobiography that he had come to the issue with a closed mind and was 'totally prejudiced'. Fearing that demands for greater security would make prisons 'still more primitive, still more destructive, and ... still more useless', he had 'one objective ... how to use our terms of reference to circumvent the implementation of the Mountbatten recommendation'. He was determined to disperse 'Category A prisoners into liberal prisons rather than concentrating them into a oppressive fortress that would cast a shadow over the whole prison system'. To achieve this end, he 'cynically' embarked 'upon a diversionary tactic':

---

10 If the number of Category A prisoners had been determined by the size of Vectis it would have necessarily been restricted to 120. With dispersal prisons there was no such restraint on capacity. By 2017 there was almost ten times that number.

11 Nor was it entirely novel. Du Cane and Crofton, confronted with the prospect of murderers whose death sentences had been commuted spending the rest of their days imprisoned, had proposed that a separate establishment to hold them be built where 'the severity of their punishment [could be] relaxed'. This was rejected for fear that those without hope would kill warders (*Report* (1879), para.89).

12 In contrast to the expedition of one man, it took over a year for the 'gang of four' to publish their report. They did so in April 1968.

to shift attention from the real issue of dispersal or concentration to another issue which would rouse the hostility of all the liberals, and place me on the side of the devils. It would provoke great controversy and, by riveting attention upon an irrelevancy, enable our sabotage of the main Mountbatten proposal to go unnoticed amidst the clamour. I put to my committee colleagues that perimeter security should be enforced by the use of guns.

His stratagem worked, Radzinowicz and Robert Mortimer, the bishop of Exeter, were conned into concurrence, while the other member of the committee – the 'kind psychiatrist' – was loud in his denunciation, the predicted furore erupted, and the Home Secretary accepted the recommendations with the exception of guns.[13] 'Wickedness triumphed', he gloated. He was 'shamelessly pleased' with his 'misbehaviour'. Abse, however, had wilfully misread Mountbatten's proposals, and his own chicanery created the shadow he had sought to dispel. Instead of building a special provision for a new group of prisoners serving lengthy sentences who within secure confines could have a tolerable life, and leaving the other prisons to proceed with their efforts at reform and innovation, the decision to confine some securely in select erstwhile 'liberal' prisons, suitably upgraded, would mean that those prisons became less liberal and that all those imprisoned there would be subjected to security constraints that were unwarranted and have their regime severely restricted. Abse was right: rehabilitation was sacrificed to security, but his actions facilitated rather than retarded this process. It was asking for trouble, and trouble would beset the dispersal prisons he did so much to secure.[14]

By 1969 there were four such prisons holding Category A prisoners, one of which was Wormwood Scrubs itself.[15] No longer would a rusty bar be the only thing between a dangerous criminal and freedom. Surveillance there was improved by the introduction of dog patrols, installing cameras, and shearing it of its ornamental fripperies – the flower-beds, fountain, cloisters and garden allotment provided for lifers. It became more desolate but more secure. Mountbatten's inquiry, if not his intention, had begun the move to security becoming central to the system, a very different response from that to Du Parcq's inquiry three decades before.

---

13 Leo Abse, *Private Member* (London, 1973), pp.116, 121–34.

14 For a detailed assessment of Mountbatten's report and of that of the Advisory Committee, which rightly comes down heavily in favour of the former, see Roy King and Kenneth Elliott, *Albany: Birth of a Prison – End of an Era* (London, 1977), pp.9–21.

15 The others were Wakefield, Hull and Parkhurst. Gartree and Albany joined them in 1970 and Long Lartin in 1973.

The great reformative hopes of the first half of the twentieth century were seriously injured by security concerns in the 1960s, would be mortally wounded by outbreaks of collective disorder by prisoners and the increased militancy of prison officers in the 1970s, and would be finished off with the demise of borstals in 1983.[16] It was the age of penal pessimism, when doubts were cast on the possibility that prisons could be reformative, fears were expressed that the belief that they could had had 'a baneful influence on the length of prison sentences', and calls were made that all efforts should be directed at minimising the harm they did, at damage limitation.[17] With the collapse of the rehabilitative ideal there was a crisis of legitimacy. Prison either did not work or worked against its own *raison d'être*.

Harm was a reality of prison life. It was possibly increased by such negativity as it seeped into the penal system, although other factors played a greater part. In particular a major objective of the past three-quarters of a century, to keep as many offenders out of prison as possible, was abandoned. As a result, the number imprisoned began its inexorable rise while many of the prisons were becoming increasingly decrepit. New prisons did not replace the old so much as supplement them. The seventy-seven institutions in the prison estate in 1960 became 123 by 1985, yet overcrowding on an unprecedented scale persisted in local prisons. This could not but affect the regime and hamstring any efforts still being made at rehabilitation. Despite increases in both manpower and resources, the morale of custodial officers plummeted as their role diminished to

---

[16] This, despite the effort that had been made to revive it on innovative lines with the opening in 1969 of Coldingley as the first 'industrial prison'. It aimed so far as was possible within secure confinement to be relatively relaxed – 'good morning' from the staff and tea and biscuits in the evening – and to mimic the working conditions and provide the ordinary challenges and choices of life outside. The work-ethic instilled, that elusive goal of a 'good and useful life' could be achieved, or so it was hoped. In addition productive labour could make the whole project self-financing. Could this be the carceral panacea? (Rod Caird, *A Good and Useful Life* (London, 1974), pp.140ff.). Not for long, if the description of it in 1995 by John Hoskinson, the professional golfer who served most of his sentence for causing death by dangerous driving there, is to be believed. It was awash with drugs, exacerbated by mandatary drug testing which overnight turned cannabis users into heroin users; concessions were made to the worst bullies, who roamed in gangs around the wings; 'ghetto-blasters' at ear-splitting volume were in constant play; and officers were unwilling or too fearful to exercise control. Referring to his first Christmas there, he wrote 'All Coldingley had in common with the outside world, during the festive season, was huge quantities of "cold turkey"' (*Inside: One Man's Experience of Prison* (London, 1998), pp.111f., 117, 128ff., 165f.).

[17] McCulloch had made the same point in 1830. The corollary of this, one usually neglected by policy makers, was that sentences should be shorter, and certainly never increased for the sake of 'reform'.

once again being turnkeys.[18] Obduracy replaced it, and their outlook increasingly diverged from that of governors who still harboured liberal sentiments. While industrial unrest grew among staff, unrest and mutiny grew among prisoners, especially those held in the dispersal system. It was hardly surprising, as the most dangerous prisoners were subject to the most restrictive regimes and had the least hope of release. As the press grew more prurient, and as politicians grew more anxious, the number put into Category A rose. All of a sudden England seemed to have acquired a very large number of very dangerous people. Should such criminals escape, public concern and political flak would be considerable. Cabinet ministers could lose office, civil servants could be demoted, or, more likely, prison governors could be sacked. Maintaining control within prisons, and preventing escapes from prisons, became the primary concerns of the prison service. Lip service would still be paid to rehabilitation but the over-arching primacy of security was the reality.

There was little sympathy from the public for hardened criminals held in maximum security conditions. There was even less from prison officers. The purpose of prison was to keep these dangerous people in custody and keep them there under strict control. The emphasis was on suppression, and Mountbatten was deliberately misinterpreted to justify petty tyrannies and casual brutality.[19] It proved to be the modern equivalent of bear-baiting. But beware if the bears got loose. They did several times in the late 1960s and 1970s when riots broke out in several dispersal prisons – Parkhurst, Hull, Gartree, Albany and Wormwood Scrubs. Other prisons were affected as well. The result was the same. Dissent as well as disruption, recalcitrance as well as rioting, were met with brute force: officers in riot gear storming wings, and segregation units filled to capacity were supplemented by the introduction of 'cages' and control units.

Deflecting blame from themselves, the POA was quick to attribute the trouble to the malign influence of an organisation set up in April 1972 called Preservation of the Rights of Prisoners – PROP for short. It, however, was a product of the discontent rather than the cause, but as a quasi-trade union whose executive committee and membership consisted of former or serving prisoners it gave to prisoner protests greater cohesion and a

---

[18] Caird, *op. cit.*, p.24; Morris, *op. cit.*, pp.136f.

[19] He would be unfairly vilified for the destruction of many of the constructive programmes that had been built up over years and for the unnecessary fortification of prisons such as Pentonville which held minor recidivists serving under twelve months. It was not what he wanted but the result of the rejection of much he had recommended.

collective purpose. Its stated aims were to 'preserve, protect and to extend the rights of prisoners and ex-prisoners and to assist in their rehabilitation and re-integration into society so as to bring about a reduction in crime'.[20] Benign enough, one might think. But inmates organising, unionising, and concerting their efforts was something new, and something that could not be left unchecked for long. It was all the more frustrating that most of the prisoner protests and 'sit-downs' were non-violent, although the reaction to them was often not. PROP even announced a national strike for 4 August. Prisoners in Albany, one of the dispersal prisons, were unanimous in their support, and Gartree took part, as did 250 prisoners in Dartmoor. In all there were protests by almost 10,000 prisoners in thirty-three prisons. In the first official acknowledgement of PROP's existence, a Home Office minister appeared on television to talk about it. PROP 'had pulled off the largest concerted prison action in the history of the world', its exultant press officer, Douglas Curtis, wrote.[21]

In swift reaction the POA seized the initiative, imposed a recriminatory crack-down in the gaols and began a campaign of misinformation and exaggeration. A combination of bad press generated by reports of mass violence and destruction of property – provoked by officers – at Albany – 'the jail of fear' – and elsewhere, a work-to-rule and threats of mutiny by prison officers, and the marginalisation of, and internal dissent within, PROP itself, took their toll. A broad-based, widely supported 'Prisoners' union' had been a mirage, and the mirage dissipated. As its chronicler summed up: 'By the end of September 1972 PROP was not merely a dirty word amongst the prison staff; it had become one amongst the prisoners.'[22] It struggled on for a few more years, having diminishing impact on the penal scene, apart from providing an alternative inquiry and prisoner perspective on the Hull prison riot in 1976, and publicising the excessive force used on prisoners in Wormwood Scrubs three years later, before finally petering

---

[20]　On PROP's rise and fall see Mike Fitzgerald, *Prisoners in Revolt* (London, 1977), ch.5.

[21]　*Dartmoor to Cambridge* (London, 1973), p.174. The thirty-six-year-old Curtis, who came from a working-class background, was a Cambridge undergraduate who had won his place at Trinity Hall while a serving prisoner. He would shortly leave PROP when protests turned violent, the press claimed that he was 'behind the jail revolt', and he had a blistering row with the principal spokesman, Dick Pooley, whom he had first met in prison (pp.175ff.).

[22]　Fitzgerald, *op. cit.*, p.188.

out.[23] Its significance had been greatly exaggerated both by its own deluded leaders and by the POA's more savvy ones. It was, however, a harbinger of greater activism on the part of prisoners and their increasing recourse to legal remedies, a development that would be encouraged by the growth of judicial review, the greater willingness of judges to hold the organs of the state to account, the impact of judgments by the European Court of Human Rights, and the provisions of the 1998 Human Rights Act.

PROP had inadvertently 'played a crucial part in generating a more militant mood among prison officers'. By the late 1970s and early 1980s, when custodial staff militancy fully emerged, it would be they, and not prisoners, who would pose the most serious threat to Home Office control over the prison system.[24] Having seen off the threat they had largely created, the POA was jubilant, the position of their members was enhanced, and their policy of repression could be re-imposed. Some were even openly supportive of the National Front and picked on and abused ethnic minority inmates. Governors and their political masters lay prostrate before them. Control of the prisons fell more and more into the hands of the POA. As was said of Hull by a senior governor seconded to that inquiry, 'the corporal[s] had taken over the army'.[25] They demanded greater discipline of everyone but themselves. They took all sorts of obstructive action, falling short of any that 'would adversely affect the level of overtime, and thus take-home pay'.[26] They demanded 'uniformity', which to them meant stripping

---

[23] Thomas and Pooley, *op. cit.*, pp.55–62, 136f. The violence and 'orgy of destruction' carried out by staff in the aftermath of the Hull riot led to a number of prison officers being convicted at York crown court of conspiring to assault prisoners. In response, select officers were specially trained in riot control and were known as MUFTI (Minimum Use of Force Tactical Intervention) squads, which could be deployed quickly to any prison. 'Minimum use' was certainly put to maximum effect when MUFTI teams were deployed to considerable but controversial effect to suppress a major incident in the dispersal wing of Wormwood Scrubs in 1979. Fifty-three prisoners were injured as a result of their intervention. In the aftermath, probation officers, teachers and even chaplains were excluded from the wing, and psychologists, for asking awkward questions, were banned – not by the government, not by the governor, but by the POA – from entering the prison in its entirety.

[24] Andrew Rutherford, *Prisons and the Process of Justice* (Oxford, 1986), pp.83ff.

[25] *Ibid.*, p.99.

[26] *Report* (1979), para.10.9. As a result of a long period of deteriorating industrial relations Mr Justice May was asked to chair an inquiry into the United Kingdom's prison services. It reported in 1979, concluding that the causes were profound, having their origins in 'a general dissatisfaction with the way the prison services were organised and run, with the state of prison buildings, and with the conditions in which staff and inmates alike [were] required to live and work' (para.1.1). Although he agreed that 'the rhetoric of "treatment and training" had had its day and should be replaced', he warned that 'mere "secure and humane containment" was not enough' as prison

away the idiosyncratic privileges which governors had permitted in their establishments and which, without infringing any regulations, made life inside slightly more tolerable for prisoners and slightly more onerous for staff. As a result, little perks would be prohibited, prisoners would remain locked up longer, visits would be curtailed, those inmates resorting to violence would be punished severely, and the incorrigible and the unmanageable would be segregated or sent on a temporary basis to local prisons such as Wormwood Scrubs.

To support the dispersal structure, in 1974 the segregation unit at Wakefield was chosen to house a 'Special Control Unit' modelled on such exemplars as Peterhead and Inverness. 'Intractable troublemakers' transferred there were subjected to a regime of prolonged solitary confinement, sensory deprivation and, from their point of view, psychological manipulation. Its purpose was to break their spirit of defiance and to convey a message to malcontents generally that this is where they would end up. It didn't pay to cause trouble. This little experiment did not last long as it had to be closed after an exposé by *The Sunday Times*.[27] The segregation unit, however, continued to be used to house those too disruptive to be managed elsewhere in the prison estate. As their numbers increased, the attitude of staff towards them became correspondingly more unyielding and hostile. In 1982 two high security cells, known as 'cages', were constructed for the long-term containment of those considered to be the most dangerous and unmanageable of all. More suppression led to more disruption, just as it had in Scotland. Protests broke out that would seriously undermine the confidence of Wakefield officers and headquarters staff in their ability to manage troublesome prisoners there and in such conditions. By 1983 at least ten major disturbances had rocked the dispersal system to its core.

In 1984, following major trouble at Albany which had dispersed its difficult and dangerous prisoners among the general population and had run a liberal regime of free association from unlock to lock-up, the Conservative Home Secretary, Leon Brittan, set up a committee 'to review the maintenance of control in the prison system ... with particular reference to the dispersal system, and to make recommendations'. Its report, published in July 1984,

staff could not be asked to work in a moral vacuum, and the absence of 'purposive objectives in imprisonment' would in the end lead 'only to the routine brutalisation of all the participants' (paras.4.27–8). He was prophesying what had already happened. One important development did come out of the May report. He had argued that an independent and external inspectorate was vital. Despite Home Office opposition, this recommendation was accepted.

[27] 6 October 1974.

concluded that the problem of most long-term prisoners could be contained without recourse to such units, but there would remain a residue who would continue to pose a serious control threat. For them it recommended that small specialised units (SSUs) be set up, not punitive in purpose, but where prisoners could be helped to find ways of coping in a more supportive environment in preparation for return to ordinary location and where the exceptionally dangerous could be assessed as to what level of freedom they could safely be accorded. As a result, three special units were established for 'persistently troublesome prisoners': in Parkhurst in 1985 for those with a history of mental disturbance; and in Lincoln in 1987 and Hull in 1988 for those with no such history. The Parkhurst regime in particular was to be therapeutic. The experience of Grendon, Barlinnie and the Wormwood Scrubs annexe was to be their inspiration.[28] It seemed to work as major disturbances ceased.

Adapting old prisons to perform a new purpose was far from ideal, however, and it became clear that a new generation of purpose-built SSUs was needed. Following the Gartree escape, and the subdivision of Category A inmates, such units were established for those posing an exceptional risk. In 1988 the first was opened at Full Sutton, the new maximum security prison near York, and due to increasing demand, a decision was made to have a second constructed within the confines of the next dispersal prison to be built. That prison was HMP Whitemoor.

Located on open fen-land just north of March in Cambridgeshire, the new prison opened in 1991 and was regarded as escape-proof. Many security measures had been incorporated, including an inward-protruding 'beak' on top of the outer wall to frustrate climbers. The SSU was the most secure part of all, a prison-within-a-prison situated behind a second concrete security wall and a fence, all under CCTV surveillance. In March 1994 the label of 'impregnable' was assigned to it by the former circuit judge and chief inspector of prisons, Stephen Tumin. It needed to be more than that as it housed ten Category A prisoners whose desire was to get out, not in. Even if it was 'impregnable' it was certainly not escape-proof, as events six months later were to show.

On Friday 9 September five IRA prisoners and a London gangster escaped from the SSU. Although, in contrast to Blake, they were soon captured, the whole episode was a major embarrassment. Because of Tumin's unfortunate accolade, the inquiry into the fiasco that was immediately set up was placed

---

[28] Despite some success they too were to be brushed away in the mid-1990s by Michael Howard's new broom – see below.

under Sir John Woodcock, a former chief inspector of constabulary. He rivalled the expedition of Mountbatten, publishing his report three months later on 12 December. It was utterly damning in its assertion that while it had been 'very easy to find evidence of many loopholes in the adopted practices and procedures', it had been 'difficult to find something being done in accordance with the manuals'. Its detailed findings beggared belief, and brought opprobrium upon the prison service.[29]

Woodcock revealed that the escapees had all the resources and equipment they needed: almost £500 in cash, bolt-croppers, rope-ladders, a torch, a screwdriver, two maps and, most disturbing of all, two loaded pistols with one of which during their bid for freedom an escapee shot a prison officer. Some items had been manufactured in the Unit itself, presumably in the workshop and with woodworking materials helpfully provided in abundance and unaudited by the authorities, all under the noses of, but unnoticed by, the staff. There was worse: money, maps and even firearms had been imported into a Category A prison, and into the SSU within it, where they were kept for some time completely undetected! When the Unit was searched after the escape, along with knives and razor blades found in transistor radios, Semtex, fuses and a detonator were discovered in the false bottom of an artist's paint box.

Woodcock uncovered massive shortcomings, not just in the security of the place but in the whole culture that had grown up there and which had contributed to the ease with which some of the most dangerous criminals in the country had plotted and executed their escape. The Whitemoor SSU was a little world of its own, and within its walls the inmates ruled the roost. Gone was the brutality, the solitary confinement, the degrading treatment. They had been replaced with appeasement. In the light of Lord Justice Woolf stressing the importance of positive inmate and staff relationships, and on the basis that these men were cut off from ordinary prison life and were serving very long sentences, it was thought by the prison authorities that they should be given special privileges, even indulgences.[30] Probably it was intended to give them inches, but soon they were conceded miles.

What they got was quite astonishing. Unlike any ordinary prisoner, these Category As could have twice-daily visits, and when they protested that their visitors were being bodily searched, and threatened to damage the Unit and assault the staff if their complaints were not met, the 'rub-down' searching

---

29 The following is all taken from that breathtaking document, *The Report of the Inquiry into the Escape from Whitemoor Prison*.

30 On the Woolf Report see Chapter 34.

was suspended for seventeen months. A mandatory search of a visitor was replaced with a request, a request which could be refused. Visitors could also bring in foodstuffs, including 'take-aways' in foil containers, and staff claimed that they were instructed by the governor to give food only a cursory glance. Small wonder that guns and Semtex got into the SSU. Bang Bang Chicken took on a whole new connotation. Prisoners were allowed an extensive range of specified items for their own use, and had so much brought in that it cluttered up their cells, and crates of excess property littered the Unit. No inventory was kept, and the amount of stuff meant that rigorous searching was impossible. Cell searches were cursory, nor were they made until the afternoon so as not to disturb those having a long lie. Venetian blinds already obscured the television room, a large refrigerator and clock the gymnasium, and the inmates demanded – and got – two layers of net-curtains for the hobbies room's windows so that staff could not see in. Supervision did not make up for the lack of monitoring. Prisoners were unescorted when on exercise. Patrolling was neither regular nor extensive nor unannounced as staff did not want to upset the inmates or 'rock the boat'.

Most shocking was the fact that inmate demands, no matter how unreasonable, were usually met, with prison officers doing the bidding of prisoners. They could make international calls and would use the principal officer's telephone to do so at the expense of the prison, compromising security and decommissioning a prison utility for extensive periods. Inmates drew up shopping lists and each Wednesday two officers were sent out on day-long expeditions, not just to the local village but up to twenty-five miles away to get the items requested. These were mainly foodstuffs, including fillet steak and smoked salmon. The prisoners insisted that bread be bought after 10.30 am so as to ensure that it was freshly baked. Once when an officer returned with new potatoes that the purchaser considered too small, he threw them at this 'errand-boy' who was then told by his supervisor to go back and get bigger ones. Anything for a quiet life. Or a down-trodden one. The self-esteem of staff must have been seriously eroded. If ever the charge of prisoners being 'pampered' had traction, it was here. Edmund Du Cane would have been as incredulous as he would have been incandescent, and he would have been right to have been both. The penal pendulum had swung too far.

Woodcock concluded that 'the string of concessions to inmates all combined to produce a sense of resignation amongst SSU staff and a feeling that it was not worth confronting any abuses'. Nor was it worth complaining about them. When officers, members of the Board of Visitors and even an MP expressed concern about the lavish provision and the compromises of security, they were overruled by the governor or fobbed off with excuses. A warning from Full Sutton in February 1994 that escape equipment including a ladder made from cell furniture had been found, was ignored. On 9 August – exactly one month before the escape – an internal memorandum was circulated in Whitemoor by a concerned governor grade in which he pointed out many of the shortcomings Woodcock later identified, and presciently asked in light of the fact that '£500 had recently been smuggled into the Unit ... what else? – a gun next?' It is apparent that while his concerns, and assertion that contraband had been smuggled in by visitors, were discussed, no remedial action was taken. He got an answer to his rhetorical question soon enough.

It is a torrid tale, from which no one emerges well. Prison officers were bullied or intimidated by inmates, brow-beaten by governors, or merely rendered quiescent by the prevailing do-nothing culture of the place; senior management was compliant and complacent; and the prisoners were allowed to do pretty much as they pleased. What they pleased to do was to plan and execute an armed escape, from an SSU within a maximum security prison! It was, as Woodcock commented, 'a disaster waiting to happen'. His criticisms and recommendations caused 'severe reverberations throughout the prison service, in parliament, and across the country'.[31] The fear was that the problems identified at Whitemoor would be replicated elsewhere in the dispersal system.

As a result, on 19 December 1994, seven days after the Woodcock Report's publication, the then Home Secretary, Michael Howard, appointed General Sir John Learmont to conduct a comprehensive review of security throughout the entire prison system of England and Wales, while the director-general, Derek Lewis, summoned all the governing governors to London and ordered them to ensure that security was given the top priority and that all procedures were implemented fully and followed. There should be no repetition of the Whitemoor débâcle. Before the governors' New Year's resolution could take effect and before the inquiry team could begin its work, the issue of security was thrown into even sharper focus by another escape by Category A prisoners. This time from Parkhurst.

On the evening of 3 January 1995 three Category A inmates slipped out of the sports hall, cut through the inner perimeter fence, climbed over the outer wall and made off into the dark. Somehow they had managed to get hold of £200 in cash, fashion tools, manufacture the parts of a ladder,

---

31 *Review of Prison Service Security in England and Wales and the Escape from Parkhurst Prison (Learmont)* (London, 1995), p.1.

which they had dispersed innocuously around a welding workshop, and arm themselves with a gun, all rather redolent of Whitemoor. One had even made a key that would open all the doors and gates that stood between the hall and the outer defences of the prison. No officer noticed them missing. No CCTV operator picked up their movements. They were on the loose on the Isle of Wight for five days.[32]

Learmont had co-opted Woodcock onto his team. They found in Parkhurst the same problems as had existed in Whitemoor: low morale; inexperienced staff intimidated by career criminals and too prone to conciliation; lax procedures during visits; reluctance to carry out rub-down searches; cursory cell and communal area searches, hampered as ever by the large amount of personal property allowed; inadequate CCTV coverage; the lack of an inventory of tools and equipment; and so on. In addition Parkhurst, ostensibly as a result of building works going on, was the only prison holding high-risk Category A prisoners without geophones affixed to the perimeter fences which would detect vibrations. The governor had specifically requested them but, despite their feasibility, his request was ignored. Their planned installation was no earlier than 1996. Learmont noted that the Woodcock Report had accurately foreshadowed the events at Parkhurst, and concluded that the escape there

> was not based on any new or ingenious plan but simply on the ability of prisoners to follow a well-trodden path through loose and ineffective security. The alarm bells should have been constantly ringing throughout the prison service; some heard but did too little, too late; others showed a reprehensible complacency and false sense of invulnerability.

Parkhurst, he said, should be removed from the dispersal system and alternatives, such as Belmarsh, be considered.[33]

More widely, Learmont was concerned that while the fabric of old prisons was inadequate, the design of modern prisons had serious deficiencies, particularly in line-of-sight and opportunities for comprehensive surveillance. He had reservations about the very viability of the dispersal system and suggested that Mountbatten's proposal for a single fortress prison be reconsidered. Similarly he recommended that a prison be built specifically to hold highly volatile and disruptive inmates of whatever category and

---

[32] In 1991 there had also been an escape of a Category A prisoner from Parkhurst.

[33] *Review, op. cit.*, pp.72f. Belmarsh opened in 1991, the first adult prison to be built in London since Wormwood Scrubs a century before. It was joined on the same site by Isis in 2010 which is both a YOI and a Category C prison for men up to the age of thirty, and nearby by Thameside, a privately-run Category B prison for men, in 2012.

whether mentally ill or not. He predicted that in a society becoming more violent, and with drug-related crime expanding, the difficulties were unlikely to subside, and that failure to produce a realistic resolution of the control problems raised by difficult prisoners would result in the prison service having immense problems in carrying out its responsibilities in the twenty-first century.

But it was not all stick. Learmont wanted every prisoner to have a personal officer, a sentence plan, and incentives such as home leave and earned early release. He was particularly impressed by a Catalan model whereby prisoners earned a day's remission for every two days of work. Work itself was a privilege to be won by good conduct and the system produced a very high degree of work attendance and exceptionally good behaviour. Life in prison was constructive from the outset and staff morale was high.

There was another issue concerning the very governance of the prison system: the problem of disconnect between headquarters management and staff working in prisons. This was a real enough concern and one that had also exercised Mountbatten twenty years before. Learmont, however, saw only half the picture. He never levelled his sights at the Home Office, he never visited the prison service headquarters, but he did direct much of his ire at senior office-holders personally. The most senior, Derek Lewis, the director-general, had been recruited from industry and was assisted by civil servants and a few governors promoted into the civil service structure. For Learmont, they were managing a nationalised industry rather than motivating a service. A dynamic leadership was alien, a clear purpose was gone, the almost missionary zeal that had galvanised staff in the first half of the twentieth century was lacking. The prison service had lost a sense of purpose. Much of this was true, and much the same had been said by Mountbatten. Nonetheless, it was unfair to the individuals concerned, as Learmont took no account of the long history of neglect and underfunding, the continual political interference, and the efforts recently made by Lewis to put the prison service on a sure footing, efforts that would take time to come to fruition. Learmont took aim at the wrong target, just as Howard hoped he would.

Heads had to roll, but not the Home Secretary's. John Marriot, the humane and innovative governor of Parkhurst from 1990 to 1995, who had already been removed from his duties, was dismissed, a sacrifice demanded by a Home Secretary anxious as ever to deflect blame and quite prepared to interfere with operational matters when it suited. Although he had been hung out to dry, Marriot was not without fault, especially as he had failed to act on the security deficiencies identified by Tumin the previous October.

When dealing with the very dangerous, all precautions must be maintained. Clever prisoners, with time on their hands, and escape on their minds, will understandably exploit each and every lapse.[34] Howard later sacked the director-general himself, who had stood his ground in refusing to suspend or dismiss Marriot, and was another convenient scapegoat.

Perhaps with more justification, Learmont emphasised the discontinuity between the twin penological poles of custody and care. The prison service's 1988 statement of purpose itself embodied this duality between keeping convicts in custody and looking after them with humanity. The humane approach advocated by Woolf and adopted by many governors and other staff eager to find some higher purpose in their work and anxious to have a sense of vocation, and the requirement to keep increasingly ruthless and dangerous offenders safely behind bars, were at variance. These were different aims, and the problem was to keep them in balance without compromising either.

For thirty years or more, the prison service had walked a tight-rope juggling two balls. Somehow it had lost its footing. Learmont sought to find a solution, to 'achieve balance', and to put it back on its feet.[35] He emphasised a third 'C': control. Control in harmony with care and custody could, he believed, provide a well-balanced regime. He may well have been right about this, although Woolf had said much the same, but he made one other pronouncement: the *primary* purpose of the prison service was to keep in custody those committed by the courts; the duty to look after them with humanity and help them lead law-abiding lives was secondary to this.

It was a far cry from Paterson uttering 'what a pity' when told of an escape from Pentonville.[36] It was also a very different emphasis from that of Lord Justice Woolf.

---

[34] The removal of a governor was an operational matter, and Howard claimed to have no involvement in such matters, implying Marriot's fate was decided by Lewis, which it patently was not. Marriot, a broken man, died prematurely in 1998 at the age of fifty-one.

[35] Alison Leibling in Anthony Bottoms and Michael Tonry (eds), *Ideology, Crime and Criminal Justice* (Cullompton, 2002), p.118.

[36] When Pentonville had been a penitentiary and each prisoner had been immured in a single cell there had been no escapes. Since 1995 no Category A inmate has escaped from a prison.

CHAPTER 34

Crying Woolf

As the manager of a large penal dustbin I am driven to write as my patience and tolerance are finally exhausted. I did not join the prison service to manage overcrowded cattle-pens, nor ... to run a prison where the interests of the individuals have to be sacrificed continually to the interests of the institution, nor did I join to be a member of a service where staff that I admire are forced to run a society that debases ... I am aware that any gesture I would make would in all probability be futile, but if I do not stand up I shall be like a political party putting pursuance of power before humanity.

John McCarthy, governor of HMP Wormwood Scrubs

Woolf's inquiry was a model of thorough, objective investigation, reaching sound conclusions based on intelligent consideration of the evidence ... The first comprehensive statement on prisons for decades ... it created new hope for prison governors as well as providing inspiration for those who had been brought up in the reformative tradition of borstals ... who had been recruited with a mission to rehabilitate, but had found themselves thwarted by overcrowding, poor conditions and an increasing sense of hopelessness, made worse by an intransigent Prison Officers' Association determined to obstruct.

Derek Lewis, Director-General

In April 1990 a series of riots convulsed several penal institutions. Some of the worst features of the prison system were beginning to be tackled and intransigent problems were at last being confronted. As often happens in times of change, improvements engendered increased instability which made prisons particularly vulnerable to disturbances. The six most serious took place in two YOIs, Glen Parva and Pucklechurch, and in four prisons, Dartmoor, Cardiff, Bristol and, first in time and most serious of all, Manchester Strangeways.[1]

A fine construction when it was opened in 1868 as a local prison, Strangeways reflected the confidence so characteristic of Victorian England. Of radial design with a central rotunda from which emanated six spokes, five wings containing the cells, and a sixth housing the administrative offices

---

[1] The following account is based on *The Report of an Inquiry into the Prison Disturbances, April 1990.*

and the chapel, it was monumental, the largest British prison and one of the largest in Europe. By 1990 it was dilapidated and overcrowded. With accommodation for 970, it housed 1,647 adults and young prisoners. Some were segregated for their own protection, others in the interest of 'good order and discipline'. All lived in insanitary and degrading conditions and remained locked in their cells for prolonged periods, soaking in the aroma of sweat and grime and piss.

The riot began in the chapel. Where else? It was the one building where enough men could congregate together to constitute a mob. Victorian prisons were designed to have religion at their core, and at the centre of most of them stood a chapel large enough to accommodate all Anglicans, who, until 1976, were compelled to attend. It was also the one place to which prisoners had ready access that was clean and open and welcoming, and in Strangeways the congregation usually numbered several hundred. It was in the chapel, during a Sunday service on April Fool's day, that the trouble began. One prisoner grabbed the microphone from the chaplain and incited his flock to seize control. Pandemonium ensued. Prisoners grabbed keys off an officer, and barricaded themselves in the chapel. Some got through a gap in the eaves of the roof, enabling them to break through into A Wing. Premature staff evacuation allowed inmate access to be gained to all the other wings, where prisoners were unlocked to join the fray, or, if sex offenders, subjected to violence. The majority of the inmates had no desire to get involved in the disturbances, and were evacuated, many helped to safety by other prisoners. Keys were given by staff to a Category A prisoner on his promise, which he kept, that he would return them once he had released other inmates. Officers were also protected by some of their charges. The hard-core remnant of the rioters – down to a mere twenty-five by the evening of 5 April – were allowed to retain control of a prison under siege, generating enormous publicity and inspiring copy-cat outbreaks elsewhere, until 25 April when finally an incursion was ordered and the prison retaken. No one had died, but fear had been generated, and damage was extensive.

Lord Justice Woolf, as he then was (he had earlier been in-house counsel to the Prison Department and would become Lord Chief Justice in 2000), was asked, along with Tumin, to undertake a far-reaching inquiry, one that would prove to be the most important into the prison system since that of Gladstone almost a century before. They wanted to hear opinions from a wide variety of sources, including prisoners, and their investigation was thorough, comprehensive and authoritative. Implicitly rejecting the *canard* that a 'toxic-mix' of lifers with nothing to lose and psychiatric cases was a major cause of unrest,[2] they found that while there were reasons specific to each disturbance there were several factors common to all: appalling living conditions; poor quality food; gross overcrowding; prolonged cellular confinement; staff attitudes; but above all something hitherto largely ignored in a prison context: an all-pervading sense of justifiable grievance at the 'absence of justice'.[3] Prisons which in the eighteenth century had embodied injustice in the perception of the lower classes now lacked legitimacy in the eyes of the imprisoned. Criminals had become victims.

The Woolf Report, as it became known, was almost six hundred pages long and was published just nine months after the riots. The two judges understood the competing demands on the prison service, the tension between security and control and humanity and justice, and between prisons as carceral cages and rehabilitative spaces. They emphasised the importance of maintaining standards of dignity and fairness if prisons were not to become nurseries of violence. 'Slopping-out', the daily and smelly reminder of degrading treatment, contributed to prisoners' sense of injustice, and should be ended forthwith. A 'Complaints Adjudicator' to hear prisoner grievances and ensure their just resolution should be appointed.[4] Respect had to permeate the system: the respect of management for their staff, and of the staff for their charges. Better relationships between prison officers and prisoners should be encouraged, both improving security and reducing the need for coercion.

The judges championed a rehabilitative approach which was based not on the old model whereby offenders were sent to prison for reformative treatment but on self-help: providing the educational, vocational and therapeutic opportunities for prisoners to address their offending behaviour and to prepare themselves for release and reintegration into society. Reiterating Mountbatten's view, they also praised Grendon as a model for emulation. They did not forget the importance of security and control, in particular with regard to really disruptive and difficult prisoners. Prisons had to be well-run, officers had to be in charge, and prisoners had to be treated fairly but firmly. As the Barlinnie Special Unit and Grendon showed, fair treatment and constructive and respectful social relationships between staff and inmates were more important than the architecture of the prison

---

2   For a succinct debunking of this myth see Michael Cavadino, James Dignan and George Mair, *The Penal System: An Introduction*, 5th edn (London, 2013), pp.18f.

3   Similarly in his 1986 report (p.xiii) into the Brixton riots Lord Scarman had concluded that 'public disorder usually arises out of a sense of injustice'.

4   In 1994 the post of Prison Ombudsman, with just such a role, was established.

confining them. Justice above all was the bedrock upon which effective security and control must be built.

Wolff was severely critical of the dichotomy between the high calibre and deep commitment of most staff and the 'dissension, division and distrust' that existed between them and Home Office ministers and headquarters' managers. The problems of Strangeways during the riot had been exacerbated by the governor having constantly to consult his superiors in London, many of whom had no experience in running prisons. Above all, the director-general should have such experience, be given greater autonomy, act as the visible head of the service, provide 'clear and visible leadership', call the shots and carry the can. Prison officers, who felt their role was undervalued by managers, undermined by the incursion of professionals such as probation officers and psychologists, and unappreciated by the public, should be better trained and their skills better utilised. The best should be brought out of them, not the worst.

The prison service at all ranks welcomed what was hoped would be a long-term, coherent strategy for change. Woolf attempted to instil a sense of purpose which for a quarter of a century or more had been atrophying, perhaps even absent from the prison system. For a time, at least, he brought back hope.[5] The government accepted almost all of the recommendations and incorporated them in a White Paper called 'Custody, Care and Justice'. His proposals for enhanced security and control – such as metal detectors – were rapidly adopted, but those meliorative measures he thought vital

---

5   By way of a coda to this tale, strange things can happen in prison chapels, not just riots. Only months after the trouble at Strangeways, on Saturday 14 July 1990, an opera was performed in the chapel of another 'penal dustbin' – Wormwood Scrubs. The members of Pimlico Opera, founded in 1987, were inspired by the idea of performing in unusual places and moulding the performance to the setting provided. In the great Romanesque basilica which is the chapel they performed *The Marriage of Figaro* in Italian and without interval before an audience comprising 150 prisoners and an equal number of invited guests. To reassure the rather nervous performers (and governors) a cordon of lifers was placed around the orchestra and in the front stalls, lifers, contrary to the misconception that they have nothing to lose, invariably being the most responsible and responsive of prisoners. For two and a half hours, men, few of whom would have heard or been to an opera, and fewer still who could understand Italian, sat motionless and silent. So relaxed were two of them that they lit up cigarettes while one meditatively ate an apple. They watched intently as a young and animated cast – which included inmates in the chorus – performed a sublime work with verve and rapport. As the opera ended with its poignant scene of forgiveness, the audience erupted into a rapturous and spontaneous standing ovation, and all departed with a benediction. The following year *Sweeney Todd* proved a particular success with the lifers. Another planned performance of the macabre musical in Kingston prison in 2008 was cancelled. It did not pass the 'public acceptability test' brought in by Jack Straw, the new Labour Home Secretary, ever-anxious about bad press.

would never be implemented. Money for the former was forthcoming, for the latter lacking.

There was one short window of opportunity but it was soon firmly closed. Kenneth Clarke, who became Home Secretary in 1992, was pragmatic and undoctrinaire, irreverent and genial. He was sympathetic to Woolf's proposals and wanted to shake things up, and get things done. In particular he strongly backed eliminating 'slopping-out', increasing educational provision, and getting prisoners out of their cells and engaged in purposeful activities. He also supported the 1991 Criminal Justice Act which had been devised by one of his equally pragmatic and liberal predecessors, the urbane Douglas Hurd. The end was to bring down prisoner numbers. The means was to sound tough – they would get what they deserve (or more in the case of really serious offenders) – but get soft – fewer would be sent to prison as punishment. The philosophy behind this legislation was that of 'just desserts', as the illiterate writer of the White Paper had it, turning punishment into pudding, which for the first time removed deterrence as a factor that sentencers should take into account. Giving offenders their due did not mean giving them disproportionately long sentences to satisfy deterrent ends, and retributive punishment as a result was less onerous than rehabilitative treatment. When the Act was implemented in October 1992 prison numbers plummeted. The proof was indeed in the pudding, but the pudding proved politically unpalatable, especially for an ageing government approaching a general election. The whole radical 'justice' approach to sentencing whereby punishment in the community would be expanded and imprisonment restricted was immediately controversial and inevitably short-lived. It would not outlast its mentor, and at the end of Clarke's short tenure it was amended to remove the clause restricting courts from taking previous convictions into account when sentencing.

Clarke was also concerned about the capacity of the Home Office to administer its peculiar inheritance. Following the initiative of his immediate predecessor, Kenneth Baker, he championed the involvement of the private sector in running prisons both for remand and sentenced prisoners. It would increase capacity and would provide an interesting contrast, a challenge and a threat to the existing set-up, just as he wanted. The POA was aghast, cladding their fear of loss of power with moralising about the iniquity of profiting out of punishment. Clarke's point was that if private prisons could provide better conditions and results for less money, both prisoners and the public would be well served. It did not matter who ran prisons; it mattered that they were run well. The state sector had nothing to brag about. Nonetheless privatisation was a reversal of the 1877 settlement, by which the state had taken control of the entire penal estate. The Wolds, the first privately-run prison, opened coincident with Clarke taking office in April 1992. It spurred the state sector into action by emulation. Innovative managerial techniques were employed in HMP Woodhill, another new-generation prison, with similar results in terms of improved regime and the number of hours inmates were out of their cells. The private sector vindicated its role in the eyes of both Conservative and Labour Home Secretaries, and currently there are now fourteen prisons in England and Wales under its aegis, although controversy about their efficacy and the ethics and economics of privatisation continues.[6]

Clarke also commissioned Sir Raymond Lygo, a retired admiral and chief executive of British Aerospace, to look into the management structure of the prison service. He was to find the state system the most complex organisation he had ever encountered and 'its problems some of the most intractable'. His views were similar to Woolf's, that 'unless there was a preparedness on the part of the Home Office to take its hands off the management of the prison service in its day-to-day business, and allow itself to be constrained by matters of policy only, then it would not be possible to effect' the necessary changes. The '"confetti of instructions" and the over-large headquarters from which they descended' should be reduced.[7] Clarke concurred and in April 1993 gave the prison service greater operational autonomy with the status of an executive agency under a director-general appointed by open competition. Derek Lewis, a Granada television executive, got the job and was left alone to get on with it. Ministers would be responsible for policy, setting performance targets and monitoring results, while Lewis and the Prison Board would have operational autonomy, or so they thought.[8]

---

[6]   The difference in culture between the public and private ethos and the threat the latter posed to the former is illustrated by an anecdote told by Derek Lewis (*Hidden Agendas: Politics, Law and Disorder* (London, 1997), p.45). Having sent headquarters staff into Blakenhurst prison to carry out a security audit, he was amazed that, whereas most public sector prisons would have struggled to produce a plan to remedy deficiencies, Blakenhurst rectified them within twenty-four hours of having them pointed out. Ramsbotham was similarly impressed by Wolds, and even more by Altcourse, which he called 'far away the best-run prison in the country'. Simple improvements such as flexible shifts had been introduced, and simple techniques such as being courteous had been deployed (Lewis, *op. cit.*, pp.93f., 106f.). Blakenhurst, reverted to state control, was merged with two other prisons on the same site to become HMP Hewell, and in 2018 was deemed the worst prison in the country.

[7]   David Ramsbotham, *Prisongate* (London, 2003), p.77.

[8]   He described the farcical selection process, and the political and civil service manoeuvring around it, in *Hidden Agendas*, pp.1–16.

Lewis had been brought into the service by a Home Secretary who very much shared Woolf's views, but shortly afterwards Clarke was replaced with a man of a rather different ilk: Michael Howard. A reactive right-winger eager to embrace a populist 'Law and Order' stance, when he addressed the Conservative Party conference in October 1993, he told them that the government's criminal justice policy should not be judged by a reduction in the prison population, but rather the reverse.[9] In contrast to his predecessors' views, and in the face of two decades of penal pessimism and two years of Woolf optimism, he declared that 'prison works' by keeping 'murderers, muggers and rapists' off the streets and by 'making many who are tempted to commit crime to think twice'. Prisons were no longer described as 'an expensive way of making bad people worse', as Hurd had put it, but as the solution to the problem of crime. They should hold greater numbers not fewer, and the conditions of detention should be more austere not less. Justice was subordinated to law and order, and the justice model yielded before the punitive imperative. Containment, punishment, deterrence: these three were all back with a vengeance, but there was no mention of rehabilitation or fairness. It was Du Cane redivivus, a complete volte-face, the demise of Woolf, and its effect was dramatic and immediate: home leave was halved, privileges curtailed, and security tightened.

In addition, as a result of the moral panic which had ensued after the murder of the toddler, James Bulger, by two ten-year-olds, Robert Thompson and Jon Venables, the forthcoming Criminal Justice and Public Order Act began to reverse the trend of keeping children and young people out of custody by creating Secure Training Centres for twelve- to fourteen-year-olds, and enacting other measures allowing for the detention of more youngsters for longer periods.[10] The 1994 Act also placed restrictions on the right to bail, and changed the rules of evidence to ensure a higher conviction rate. From 1993, according to Lord Bingham, the then Lord Chief Justice, the

---

[9] Howard's speech came ten years to the day after Leon Brittan, a previous Home Secretary, had announced at a similar party conference a severe curtailment of parole for those serving five years or more, an action which had led to protests and work-strikes throughout the dispersal estate, culminating in a roof-top protest at Long Lartin where prisoners displayed a banner with the truism emblazoned on it: 'NO PAROLE = NO CONTROL (Mark Leech, *A Product of the System* (London, 1992), pp.78–81).

[10] David Wilson, *Pain and Retribution* (London, 2014), pp.162–6. By way of contrast, the killing by Mary Bell of two younger boys, one the day before, the other a few months after, her eleventh birthday in 1968 had no long-term impact. She was convicted of manslaughter on the grounds of diminished responsibility and initially sent to the Red Bank secure unit, the same facility which would one day house Venables. Her case was seen as an aberration, theirs as a trend.

use of custody increased 'very sharply in response (it would seem likely) to certain highly publicised cases, legislation, ministerial speeches and intense media pressure'.[11] A higher proportion of those convicted were imprisoned, and the length of sentences imposed increased. In consequence the daily average prison population rose from 40,000 to 47,000 in less than a year, an ever-rising trend that has bedevilled the prison service ever since, and the primary cause of the penal chaos of today. Money, resources, and energy were all dissipated on building more prisons rather than on improving existing ones. The sad irony was that Howard would prove not to be the successor to previous Tory Home Secretaries but the precursor of future Labour ones.[12]

Howard had undone his predecessors' work, and would, as we have seen, undo his predecessor's appointee. In October 1995 Lewis, who would not go willingly, was dismissed. The Parkhurst escape, the Learmont Report, and the desire of a Home Secretary to shore up his own position had led to the downfall of a figure who, despite their initial reservations about an outsider taking over the service, had won the overwhelming support of senior governors. They had come to recognise his merits and the improvements he was making. In his time 'slopping-out' had been all but abolished, the practice of putting three prisoners in a single cell had ended, and rehabilitative programmes had been introduced.[13] He had also taken on the powerful POA, one of the few remaining bastions of 1960s neanderthal trade unionism. Its Achilles' heel was that it was not actually a trade union, and since prison officers had the power of constables they were not legally entitled to go on strike. Their representatives could be sued if they did. In a number of legal blows the stuffing was knocked out of them, and their leader, John Bartell, resigned, a broken man. The power of the POA was diminished; the power of governors enhanced.[14] Lewis had achieved almost all his targets and overseen a reduction in the number of escapes, though not alas those in the most newsworthy category. Howard sacrificed him on

---

11 In an appeal against sentence, *Brewster* [1998] 1Cr App R(S), 181.

12 Both parties would compete in being 'toughest on crime' – which meant being 'toughest on criminals', and for once Labour (under Blair) would win.

13 'Slopping-out' ended in England and Wales in 1996. In Scotland budget constraints delayed abolition, and in 2004 it still persisted in five of its sixteen prisons. When it ended in Polmont in 2007, only Peterhead, because of the difficulty of installing plumbing there, lacked integral sanitation, and chemical toilets had to be used until it closed in 2013, being replaced by HMP Grampian, a modern facility which had never known the practice.

14 Lewis, *op. cit.*, pp.130–42. A resurgence in obduracy soon recurred and staff unrest has failed to evaporate.

the altar of political expediency. Ann Widdecombe, who had been minister for prisons at the time, would memorably characterise her senior colleague as having 'something of the night' about him, and Lewis ably defended himself and savaged his executioner in a book called *Hidden Agendas*. He also took legal action, until accepting an out-of-court settlement of £280,000.[15]

Within six months of his dismissal, and with prisoner numbers rising ever higher, much that had been achieved had been lost. Lewis believed that unless the prison service achieved statutory independence from the Home Secretary in the same way as the police force, it could not fulfil its task. In short he advocated a return to the old days of prison commissioners who were allowed to get on with the job and when other countries had learnt 'from Great Britain how to prevent the infiltration of partisan politics and ulterior influences into the administration of criminal justice'.[16] An unnecessary and retrograde change in the 1960s was still having repercussions in the 1990s.

But Lewis was no more, and another liberal thorn in the Home Secretary's side, Stephen Tumin, retired at the same time. Hoping to put more grit into the inspectorate, in December 1995 Howard appointed a retired general, David Ramsbotham, to the post of chief inspector. He could not have made a worse – or better – choice.[17] As the appointee later wrote:

> Those who thought that I would not follow the example of my predecessors in openly criticising poor treatment and conditions clearly had not read my remit or understood soldiers. Soldiers are taught to obey orders. My orders were to report what I found. I could only assume that those who were disappointed that I did so neither understood my orders, nor wanted them obeyed.[18]

If anything Ramsbotham, although full of praise for the professionalism and dedication of the vast majority of staff working in prisons, was even more scathing of the prison system, of the appalling conditions he found almost everywhere and particularly in the publicly-run prisons, of the lack of imagination and enterprise of some demotivated officers, of beneficial

---

15 Howard had form for high-handed and low-principled behaviour. When he arbitrarily and illegally increased the 'tariff' of Venables and Thompson from ten to fifteen years, a former senior judge condemned his action as 'institutionalised vengeance by a politician playing to the gallery'. He also rescinded an early release scheme that resulted in expectant prisoners being 'knocked back' yet again.

16 Sanford Bates in Manuel Lopez-Rey and Charles Germain (eds), *Studies in Penology* (The Hague, 1964), pp.30–41, at p.32.

17 He had even offered Ramsbotham the post of director-general, but he had declined (Ramsbotham, *op. cit.*, p.47).

18 *Ibid.*, p.50.

local initiatives snuffed out by senior management or the intervention of the POA (which he considered to be an unrepresentative and selfish body), of a slavish adherence to 'key performance indicators' irrespective of their worth, and of the distant, complacent governance by civil servants who could produce an avalanche of circular instructions, targets, and directives – focusing on procedures rather than results – but had little or no idea of the extraordinary institution they were administering. Under the Prison Commission a headquarters staff of 168 had sufficed to run the system well; by 1995 it took 1,800 to run it badly. While such staff had proliferated, their effectiveness had diminished and their interventions were often counter-productive. With the recent exception of high security prisons which, as a result of Learmont's recommendation, had their own director, no one was responsible for prisons of a particular type, such as those holding women, or the group to which Paterson had devoted so much of his energy, young offenders.

Above all the leadership put politics and self-preservation above principle. Ministers and the director-general reacted with surprise to Ramsbotham's damning reports, refusing to take responsibility and blaming prison governors for their own failings. Nor would area managers or regional directors support governors such as Joe Mullins who had recently been appointed to Wormwood Scrubs. He took on the obduracy and obstructiveness of the POA in an attempt to make staff turn up when they were most needed rather than to suit their own convenience.[19] Rather than face confrontation, Mullins's superiors caved in. Courage and leadership, at all higher levels, were absent. The whole thing was a shambles. Ramsbotham was not the malleable tool Howard had been hoping for. Instead, he was savaging the system he was inspecting, and so undermining the Home Secretary and his populist rhetoric.

He would prove just as discomfiting to Howard's Labour successor, Jack Straw. In 1999 Ramsbotham criticised him for compromising the new and hard-won independent agency structure by appointing a career civil servant, Martin Narey, director-general. He also forced the Home Secretary to explain to parliament why nothing had been done to implement the recommendations he had made in his report on Wormwood Scrubs three years earlier in which he had drawn attention to persistent allegations of staff brutality and management indifference, and had described the prison as 'a flagship dead in the water'. Since then things had deteriorated. Ramsbotham summed up his despair by asserting that 'none of this would have happened had there been

19 *Ibid.*, pp.103ff., 163–75.

a proactive, responsible and accountable management system, stretching from the Home Secretary down to every individual prison officer, that had taken the appropriate and required action years before'.[20] And Wormwood Scrubs was just the symptom; the disease had infected the entire prison system. The politico-management structure was not up to the task. There was lack of direction and no coherent strategy.[21]

And there was worse, an inability at the highest levels to support, let alone nurture, best practice. The most graphic example took place in May 2000 when, with the collusion, or at least the acquiescence, of the director-general and the minister for prisons, one particularly overbearing and bullying area manager who seemed to think all efforts at rehabilitation a waste of time set out to destroy the extraordinarily successful and universally praised resettlement work being done by Eoin Maclennan-Murray, the governor of Blantyre House, by removing him from post and sanctioning an overnight raid by eighty-four prison officers, who during their extensive search could find virtually nothing amiss. What was amiss was the action taken in the first place, as a result of which the prison lapsed 'from its previous excellence not through any fault of its own but because the fall was initiated and driven by those supposed to be responsible for raising standards'. Despite a highly critical report into the raid on one of the country's best-regarded prisons, no action was taken against those who had instigated and authorised it.[22] Defend the indefensible, justify the reprehensible, penalise initiative, and abdicate responsibility: the perfection of inadequacy, the production of malignity. In the chief inspector's eyes the prison service was not just failing in its professed task of treating prisoners with humanity and preparing them for release, it was actively preventing that task being fulfilled. As one perceptive prisoner put it, 'slowly the knife was being turned on any institution that offered hope'.[23] The man who wielded the knife was the Home Secretary.

---

20 *Ibid.*, pp.104–9.

21 In 2001 at the annual prison service conference Narey surprised his audience by seeming to break ranks in saying that he had had enough of trying to justify the immorality of the treatment of some prisoners and the degradation of some establishments. He specifically said that Ramsbotham's recent strictures on Wormwood Scrubs came as no surprise as he had made them all back in 1996. However, he never blamed the inadequacies of anyone above 'middle management'. Governors could take the blame, not ministers, not the members of the Prison Board, and certainly not the director-general.

22 Ramsbotham, *op. cit.*, pp 159ff., 163–75. The same year the same area manager wrecked the good work being done in Ford open prison.

23 John Hoskinson, *Inside* (London, 1998), pp.165f.

Ramsbotham would not have his tenure extended when it ended in 2001. He had been a thorn in the side of too many powerful people, exactly as a good inspector should be. He went on to write a passionate and withering account of his experience in *Prisongate*, with its subtitle, *The Shocking State of Britain's Prisons and the Need for Visionary Change*. He names names and is trenchant in his criticisms, many of which mirrored those of Mr Justice May in 1979 and Lord Justice Woolf in 1991. While Ramsbotham's was yet another voice crying in the wilderness, he did not cry alone. Anne Owers who replaced him, and those who succeeded her, echoed his cries and proved equally independent-minded. Those who acquire extensive knowledge of the reality of the prison system cannot and will not paper over the cracks. They see their task as saying it as it is and not as others would have it be. The Home Office just cannot find a chief inspector to its liking. Perhaps if more ministers and civil servants spent a day or a week with their inspectors in the prisons they control, the reason would be obvious.

Despite his tough talk on deterrence and penal austerity, Howard did not put an end to one of the most enlightened measures which had benefited numerous prisoners for a quarter of a century. The year 1970 had witnessed an entirely benign innovation: prisoners being given the opportunity of studying at degree-level through the newly established Open University. It began on a small scale in two men's prisons, Wakefield and Albany. The Home Office paid the fees, and provided the books and other necessary equipment. Although courses had to be approved – chemistry was not one of them – and applicants vetted by the prisons, the selection of candidates was the responsibility of the university. Twenty-two students were admitted in 1971 and three years later Wakefield produced the first graduate. The experiment was extended to other prisons in subsequent years and by 2011 there were nearly 1,800 prisoners from 150 British prisons studying over 200 courses across all faculties.[24] In addition the Prisoners' Education Trust finances Open University and other educational projects, and the Longford Trust funds scholarships for those in or about to leave prison, many of which are awarded to OU applicants.

The most notorious beneficiary of the scheme was Myra Hindley, 'the most evil woman in Britain'. She was certainly the most infamous prisoner of her day, the 'Moors Murderess'. Along with her lover, Ian Brady, she had sadistically killed and sexually assaulted a number of children, sometimes

---

[24] Another survivor is the Koestler Award scheme, set up in 1962 by the writer of that name to encourage and reward the creative arts in prisons.

tape-recording their entreaties and frequently picnicking on their burial sites on the bleak Saddleworth Moor near Manchester. Tried in 1965 just after the abolition of the death penalty, they were both imprisoned for life. For both that was what it would ultimately mean. Hindley, despite her contortions to secure release, would never be freed, dying in prison in 2002. Twenty undertakers refused to bury her. Brady, who always said he had no desire for any release other than death, lived longer, expiring fifteen years later, having been in Ashworth secure psychiatric hospital for thirty-two years.

Not all murderers die in prison, not all 'lifers' are Category A, and not all Category A prisoners remain in that category for long. Those for whom there is most hope are young offenders, even though some of them have committed the most atrocious crimes and are serving lengthy sentences. The most serious are kept in Aylesbury Young Offender Institution, the former women's prison and girls' borstal in Buckinghamshire. At one time, under effective and imaginative governance it provided a blend of 'discipline with affection' that echoed that of Miss Barker, or, in more modern parlance, 'custody, control and care', which both Woolf and Learmont would have lauded.

CHAPTER 35

Tea-Bags for the Chaplain

Imprisonment is a family event ... Deprivation of one's personal liberty is part of the punishment, but the destruction of family ties is surely not? ... The role of the personal officer – a creative and heartening concept – might formally embrace prisoners' families and not prisoners alone.

Robert Runcie, archbishop of Canterbury

Whatever the complexion of the government or the public mood, the rehabilitative ideal within a carceral setting still survives, sometimes wilting, sometimes reviving, but always showing persistence and tenacity in the face of adversity. Challenging but rewarding, it motivates staff as much as inmates. It is always under threat from gross overcrowding, longer and longer sentences for more and more people, budgetary constraints, overworked staff, anachronistic buildings, and an ever-increasing emphasis on security.

In the 1980s Aylesbury Young Offender Institution held around three hundred male offenders aged between eighteen and twenty-one serving from five years' imprisonment to detention for life, for serious offences including armed robbery, aggravated burglary, rape, and murder. It was, and still is, the only YOI able to house those considered to be the most dangerous in their peer group. These were officially known as 'restricted status', the equivalent of Category A, an anodyne term which would not alarm local residents. It was not, however, part of the dispersal system, and managed to avoid the worst restraints of that system.

It had undergone a turbulent few years. Serious disturbances and escapes had taken place, officers and inmates had been assaulted, and many youngsters had been isolated for their own protection. Then a new governor, John Dring, arrived in the late 1980s and everything changed. It was a propitious time as prisoner numbers began to drop dramatically and Aylesbury was soon well below capacity. The 1991 Criminal Justice Act would reduce numbers further; the Woolf Report would encourage better relationships.[1] It was an opportunity for a fresh start, an opportunity already enhanced

---

[1] These expectations were dashed by Howard's futile but draconian measures.

by a reorganisation that had been introduced in 1987, aptly called 'Fresh Start'. Intended to simplify the labyrinthine complexity of staff working arrangements, increase job satisfaction and improve the relationship between prison officers and management, it involved a fundamental reorganisation of those arrangements and structures. It was an attempt to create a more unified service with everyone potentially able to rise from prison officer to governing governor, although with the chief officer becoming a junior governor and wearing a suit there was a danger of further delineating the divide between the uniformed staff and governors. There was no longer a sergeant-major between officers and their troops. While the number of prison officers was increased and pay was improved, lucrative payments for working overtime, which had been milked for years, became a thing of the past, being replaced by time off in lieu. Despite the opposition of the POA, the wheel was turning in a progressive direction.

First of all, order had to be restored. Prisons run by prisoners are run by bullies and it is far preferable for prison officers to be in control. In Aylesbury a stick and carrot approach was introduced. Troublemakers were shipped out to other institutions to mend their ways before returning, and it was made clear that anyone causing mayhem in the future would be transferred or placed in segregation. The bullies would be locked in cells, not the bullied. Those conforming would have enhanced opportunities. A new and much larger segregation block was built to house malcontents. When it opened it was filled to capacity but within weeks it was, and for a long time remained, largely empty as trainees realised the benefits of life on normal location. As staff took control, inmates acquiesced. All or most benefited from working or living in a safer as well as more secure prison.[2] Within a short time no one needed to be isolated for their own protection, and even sex offenders could safely mingle with other prisoners. Uniformed staff had regained both control and self-confidence. The way Aylesbury was run in the late 1980s and early 1990s prefigured Learmont's emphasis on keeping custody, care and control in balance. It provided the right circumstances for innovation.

It was not status but contribution that counted. That is how it should be, and applies to all staff in a well-run prison. Too often chaplains, in particular, had been of poor calibre, unable and unwilling to take a larger role in the prison system, yet craving status and recognition. Time and

---

[2]   This was replicated in the dispersal system where the atmosphere since 1995 has been calmer (Alison Leibling in Anthony Bottoms and Michael Tonry (eds), *Ideology, Crime and Criminal Justice* (Cullompton, 2002), pp.97–150, esp. pp.126–39).

again the prison service chaplaincy has not contributed to issues of prison reform, parole, privatisation or the Woolf Report. When the House of Lords reported on life-sentence prisoners there were representations from Buddhists and Quakers but none from mainstream Christian denominations. Chaplains fail when they are perceived to be 'screws with dog-collars' by the prisoners, or undisciplined anachronisms – 'sky-pilots' – by the officers. A cell left unlocked after a visit, a refusal to inform officers when on the wing, a confidence betrayed, a bit of prison gossip being spread, and a chaplain is distrusted, disliked or dismissed as irrelevant.

In the last quarter of the twentieth century the long-cherished centrality of Christianity within the prison system was fading. Aylesbury epitomised the decline. The Anglican chaplain, the only full-time religious appointee, drew key number eight, not two; his accommodation was no longer one of the grand houses outside the prison gates but a bungalow in Bierton village; his department was no longer dominant in the area of welfare and education, but just one among several that came under the disheartening heading 'Inmate Activities'. The chaplain was no longer second only to the governing governor but was answerable to one of his juniors. Perhaps the greatest symbol of the declining role of established religion was the size and situation of the chapel. It was more a room than a temple, perched atop the hospital block, off one of the wings, access to it being via a converted cell. It was not always so. The original chapel was prominently placed, and imposing, part of it being large enough to serve as the present visiting area. Religion had been moved from the centre of prison life to the margins, an optional 'activity'.

Prisons are no longer places where religion is predominant but they are places in which it still plays a vital part, at the heart rather than the centre. Christianity speaks a language which can be understood only too dramatically in a carceral context where there are many 'prodigal sons' and a few 'good Samaritans'. Theological concepts such as guilt, sin, repentance, forgiveness and redemption are common currency, all made alive in a place where humanity is in the raw, and where experiences so often really are matters of life and death. From a prison perspective the Bible takes on a radical dimension. God seems hell-bent on choosing the deviant to be the instruments of his purpose. Cain, the first murderer, is not executed but given a life sentence, for ever bearing the mark of conviction and protection, a fratricide who is the founder of urban civilisation. Jacob was a conman, who defrauded his own father and brother. Moses was a terrorist prepared to murder to engineer a prison break. David instigated a contract killing of a faithful servant to cover up his own adultery. The Jews, God's chosen people, were prisoners first in Egypt then in Babylon. Jeremiah the Prophet was a political prisoner left to die in solitary confinement. John the Baptist was imprisoned and executed in prison. At the beginning of his ministry, Jesus announced that he had come to set the prisoner free. Three years later, wanted by the authorities as a subversive, he is betrayed by one of his disciples, the 'supergrass' Judas. Taken before a kangaroo court, arraigned on trumped-up charges before false witnesses and condemned to death, Jesus was another victim of a gross miscarriage of justice and the irreversible finality of capital punishment. He was judicially murdered: in prison argot, 'grassed up, stitched up, strung up', not in a cathedral between two candles but on a cross between two thieves. In his death agony, deserted by his friends, rejected by his people and abandoned by his father, he can still forgive those who crucify him and speak words of comfort to the thief who asks for it, reassuring him that the first Christian in heaven will be a common criminal, like himself.

Chapel was surprisingly well attended and challenging. Order had to be maintained. A few disruptive inmates were periodically banned, an action that merely induced penitence and increased the allure of the chapel as the 'in place' to be. Audience participation was frequent and novel. Being challenged on points in a sermon was a commonplace. The chapel was also a place to relax over tea or coffee, biscuits and cigarettes. Sunday afternoons saw it hosting another self-selecting society – 'Culture Club' – for those interested in watching 'improving' films and operas. Few realised they had this interest before they joined, but attitudes soon changed, and applications for membership always outstripped places.

Local involvement was encouraged. The chaplain was responsible for recruiting, appointing and regulating prison visitors, volunteers from the community of any religion or none who, after vetting and a little training, were asked to befriend prisoners who requested their services. Although the scheme greatly expanded, the demand always outstretched the resource. Students from theological colleges did placements. Once a month a Pentecostal choir took part in the Sunday service, their singing reverberating round the whole prison, officers standing in the yard below enraptured. Members of other denominations took groups and occasionally led worship. The Buddhist minister was allowed to use the chapel for meditation classes to which any prisoner might go. A Sikh minister made regular visits and always sent Christmas cards of the Nativity to the chaplaincy team. When no orthodox rabbi would visit a boy whose father was Jewish but whose mother was not, a liberal rabbi was found instead. There was no imam to care for the Muslims and so the Anglican chaplain organised Friday prayers in the chapel. The first Rastafarian visiting minister was appointed, chaperoned by an Ethiopian Orthodox Archimandrite. The Catholic and Methodist chaplains worked closely with the Anglican and shared many responsibilities, and the Ash Wednesday and Christmas Carol services were ecumenical.

Working closely with all disciplines was the key to success. In cooperation with education staff, probation officers and psychologists, the chaplain helped initiate and organise regime improvement. Restricted category prisoners were locked up for twenty-three hours a day and denied access to education, recreation and work. No one knew why. A committee was set up, recommendations were made and largely accepted, and their lot was markedly improved. One result was a prison newspaper produced in 1991 by an enterprising and well-educated prisoner serving seven life sentences. It was not the first such publication – that had been *The Weekly News-Sheet* produced in Maidstone in December 1929 – but it was the quirkiest and had the drollest title – *The Informer*.[3]

Aylesbury housed many young men serving life sentences, usually for murder. Along with colleagues in other disciplines, the chaplain had to write regular reports on the progress of these prisoners – or 'trainees' as they were called – and attend their review boards. Chaplains have a unique opportunity to get to know their charges. They alone among the civilians in a prison have a cell key. They sometimes are the only member of staff trusted with confidences, confidences it is assumed will not be betrayed. They may be able to form a fuller and rounder picture of the particular prisoner than anyone else. Their opinions, if respected, and the quality of their advocacy for a 'parishioner', may profoundly affect that parishioner's progress through the prison system and beyond. And progress through the system was what lay heavy on the minds of all lifers and their loved ones.

Perhaps the most important innovation was that of 'Lifer Family Days'.[4] Among no group is the sustaining of family connections more important than among young offenders, and among young offenders those serving indeterminate sentences occupy a uniquely vulnerable position. They have no release date; they are liable to serve a substantial fraction of their young lives in detention (the average 'tariff' at that time for lifers in Aylesbury was

---

3   Informers or 'grasses' rank with paedophiles in the inmate hierarchy. The editor, Matthew Williams, having been transferred to Parkhurst, was one of the three Category A prisoners who later escaped using a counterfeit key in the process. As he later wrote to the author, since they had thrown away the keys on him he had manufactured his own.

4   A full account of this initiative can be found on pp.63–73 in vol. 9 (1992) of *New Life*, the Prison Service Chaplaincy Review.

over ten years); and they are often ignorant of the nature of the lifer system itself. If they knew little, their families knew less. They could not understand the implications of such a sentence, their expectations of early release might be too high or their fears for those imprisoned might be exaggerated. At the same time the support of the family could be crucial for the young lifer, and ultimate rehabilitation could depend on continuing support. Since the day of their arrest such inmates had seen their families for short, fraught periods in sterile visiting areas. In addition families had little or no accurate information about how the sentences would be progressed. A 'circular instruction' sent by headquarters recognised this:

> The support of the family will be important for a young offender lifer ... The family can continue to play an important role in supporting him, and can help focus his thoughts constructively on his future ... [The] family also needs to understand the key features of a life sentence. Staff should place importance in getting this across and on developing a positive relationship with the family ... Some establishments have found it useful to hold an information session comprising the lifer, institutional staff, the home probation officer and members of the family. It is striking how the provision of information can both resolve concern and inform staff about the needs of the lifer.[5]

As a result of a conference on this issue held in Feltham YOI, a working party at Aylesbury consisting of the Lifer Liaison Officer (LLO) – the governor in charge of lifers – a psychologist, a probation officer, and the chaplain drew up a proposal to go one step further and to invite the parents, siblings, and friends not merely to an 'information session' but to spend a whole day in the institution. For those lifers with no family, or no family interest, prison visitors or other concerned parties could be substituted. It was to be as domestic and intimate and enjoyable as possible. First the all-important security department had to be won over. This was easily done. They were involved from the start and were confident that no breach of security would ensue. None did and the event would prove a considerable success.

The first 'Lifer Day' involved twelve inmates and eighteen visitors – one of the twelve had no one to invite but such was his enthusiasm that he attended alone. In addition about a dozen uniformed and specialist staff were involved throughout the day, with other officers dropping in as they were able. On the whole they embraced the chance to show their human

---

5 Family visits had been proposed by the Woolf Report and endorsed by prison service headquarters. In 1995 Learmont recommended that they be stopped in all dispersal prisons.

"You've read your page, now it's my turn!!"

34. An example of prison humour presented to the author by the artist, who was serving a life sentence at Aylesbury YOI

and humane side, and welcomed the opportunity to do something more constructive than merely locking people up. Four members of headquarters staff attended as observers.

It began at 9.30 am in the chapel. After refreshments the governor welcomed the participants and set the tone. The showing of a short film by Aftermath, an organisation set up to support the 'carers' of long-term prisoners, was followed by an introduction to the lifer system by the LLO. Each participant was given a detailed dossier containing all the relevant material and taken through it step by step, giving them an accurate and honest overview of the system, one that was being described but not necessarily defended. Most interest revolved around the issues of 'tariffs' and the assessment of risk. The level of ignorance was shocking and surprising: some three-quarters of the visitors attending thought that a life sentence meant that their boy would never be released. Such ignorance and despair had to be dispelled. One mother wrote afterwards:

> The information about the structure of the stages of life sentences was beyond anything I could have hoped for. I have tried for over two years to gain access to this kind of information with very little success.

Another said that the main benefit of the day had been 'the opportunity to meet other parents also coming to terms with the loss of their son, to know they shared the same experiences and sought the same information'.

Thereafter discussion groups continued until lunch, which had been prepared by trainees on the vocational catering course and was provided for all the participants. A post-prandial tour of the prison took place, the visitors being accompanied around the wings by their particular 'trainee', being introduced to the staff looking after him, being shown the cell in which he lived, and seeing the workshops and education classes he attended. Comments by staff who conducted the tour proved particularly enlightening to the visitors. As one wrote, 'a statement that the lifers' wings were the least disruptive and that first-time offenders other than lifers were placed in these wings because of this ... added to my growing peace of mind during the day'. Even decaying Victorian wings and cells were a considerable improvement on what had been anticipated. The fact that conditions were less awful than they had imagined proved a great relief. One said that seeing where her son 'lay his head was like a dream come true'. For another, it was 'like visiting a shrine':

> We can only imagine what is going on behind the high walls, heavy barbed wires or doors. Now that we have seen it the fear of the unseen and doubts have been removed and replaced with hope.

In the afternoon session, specialists introduced the work of their departments, after which tea was served, allowing some time for the lifers and their family members to socialise and say farewells. The boys left at 3.30 pm but the families stayed on to raise further questions and make suggestions.

The whole venture had cost little and had been productive of considerable good, and the benefits to all concerned were soon apparent. Family members were tearfully grateful for the occasion, having for the first time in years been able to spend a relaxed and lengthy period of time with their loved one, being provided with invaluable and erstwhile inaccessible information as to how the lifer system operated, and finding that the reality of prison was not as bad as the image they had formed in their minds. The reality of what had brought their loved one there in the first place also struck home for some visitors, who perhaps for the first time had broached the subject of the offence. One trainee who had reacted strongly against the showing of the Aftermath tape which stressed the importance of families 'knowing the worst', shortly afterwards requested a special visit in order to tell his parents the full facts of his offence. Knowing the truth instead of guessing the worst enabled them to be more supportive, not less. One mother wrote to the chaplain, 'it was a special moment when you stated that love meant all of him, including knowing what he did'.

Improvements in relationships between staff and inmates were striking. It was not just that the latter knew that officers could contact their parents – with whom some were on first-name terms – if they misbehaved. It was also a growth in trust. For instance, a prisoner who had been uncommunicative to the point of refusing to be interviewed for long-term training boards began to open up to staff. Another who was almost constantly in trouble became calmer and more settled. A third who regularly spent time in the segregation block rarely returned after participating. There were also instances of simple practical kindness. One visitor sent the chaplain a package of 500 tea bags as a small contribution to future events, while a mother who had expressed a desire to watch her son play rugby was telephoned by the governor and invited to do so the following weekend.

The experiment was so successful that it was repeated, improved, and extended to restricted category lifers, while special extended visits were introduced for fixed-term prisoners, with a buffet provided and 'personal officers' in attendance. Perhaps the most successful innovation in subsequent lifer days was jettisoning of the rather formal afternoon 'brains trust' in favour of inviting along a lifer from Sudbury open prison and another who had started his sentence at Aylesbury over ten years before and had been released on licence. The real value of their contributions was not so much what they said as who they were: fit, healthy young men who had survived prolonged incarceration without becoming cabbages. They constituted symbols of hope, and hope is a scarce and valuable commodity in a prison holding long-term inmates. The relief they brought both to visitors and young lifers was tangible.[6] The cost was no more than £120 for lifer days and £50 for the special visits afternoons. Cheaper than Strangeways.

Another successful initiative came from the prisoners themselves and was warmly adopted by the institution. Young men in the community whom it was feared would resort to a life of crime were invited into the prison, and were spoken to and engaged by a number of inmates, mainly those serving indeterminate sentences. On the same wave-length as the visitors

---

[6]   Hospitality could be reciprocated. Once when the chaplain of Aylesbury was visiting Lewes prison he was tapped on the shoulder by a young inmate who told him that Reggie Kray invited him to afternoon tea. This was an offer that could not be refused and the chaplain proceeded to the immaculate cell – reminiscent of that of 'genial' Harry Grout in the celebrated seventies BBC sit-com *Porridge* – holding Britain's most notorious gangster. There he was served refreshment from a silver teapot.

the 'trainees' could talk directly to them, engage them in role play and show them the sort of life they could expect if they got into major criminality. Similar projects were being done elsewhere, but ultimately would fall foul of the new punitive ethos of the mid-1990s.[7]

No prison is a happy place but Aylesbury at that time had many positive features. This was largely a result of being a small, niche institution, with a long-term and stable group of young offenders, numbers below the maximum, and a regime that was structured, innovative and fair. There was a team spirit among staff and a degree of optimism that was inspiring within those bleak walls. Probation officers, psychologists, the visiting psychiatrist, the chaplaincy and the education staff all worked well together alongside supportive governors and highly motivated uniformed staff, many of whom as 'personal officers' would get to know their charges well and were prepared to fight their corner when necessary. And the relationship could be reciprocal. One night a popular officer was taken hostage by two prisoners, broken glass held to his neck. The other staff had to restrain some lifers from going to the assistance of their colleague! Fortunately their intervention was not needed as he himself, a former member of the Royal Marines, disarmed both of his assailants, and was back at work the following day, to the dismay of some of the officers who would have been tempted to recuperate at home. When a particularly popular lifer governor was transferred, his charges raised money to buy him a leaving present, while the chaplain was presented with a very fine satirical painting done by a young man serving life.

A positive ethos within prison is transitory, and subject to many vagaries: changes of governor, changes of staff, changes in the nature of the inmates, changes in government and in prison service policy. A television documentary on Aylesbury YOI in 2013 showed a dismal, strife-torn, violent place, plagued with gangs, awash with drugs – very different from twenty years before – and the 2017 inspectorate report showed a prison dangerously out of control with a fatalism on the part of prisoners and staff alike that

---

7   One such was instigated by a prisoner at Coldingley and was so successful that it received praise from the Metropolitan police to whom a number of those attending had handed in knives and other weapons. On the verge of expansion, the Home Office starved it of publicity and denied its replication elsewhere. It would have shown prison conditions at their worst and prisoners at their best, the inverse of Michael Howard's agenda (John Hoskinson, *Inside* (London, 1998), pp.171–9).

'Aylesbury will always be a violent place'.[8] Prisons in general were entering a dark era from the shades of which they have yet to emerge.

---

[8] *The Prisons Handbook 2018*, pp.16, 46–52. Perhaps the Home Office should have continued a cheap little experiment that had taken place in Aylesbury in the mid-1990s which produced a thirty-seven per cent reduction in violent behaviour among a group whose diet was supplemented with vitamins, minerals and fatty acids. Presumably this was deemed to be 'pampering'.

CHAPTER 36

The Old Imprisonment Blues

What people do not seem to realise is that by sending a man to nick for a few years they are punishing him for doing wrong: Yes! but they are also doing there selves [*sic*] a great wrong, for as sure as Hells [*sic*] a mousetrap, when that man gets out he will rob someone else, and if he looks like getting captured again he may kill.

Frank Norman

Gaol is our specific for despair.

William Booth

As we have seen, the 1991 Criminal Justice Act, based on the just deserts theory of punishment as espoused by C.S. Lewis and other ethicists in reaction to the prevailing positivist treatment model, had led to a decline in the prison population. This was not to last. Howard put paid to that, and his Labour, Coalition and Conservative successors continued the same upward trend in numbers. This was unprecedented, and bucked the hopes of earlier generations.

In 1900 there were roughly 14,500 men and 3,000 women daily in prison in England and Wales. By the outbreak of the Great War it was 13,500 and 2,500 respectively, and numbers dropped during the course of the conflict to 9,000 and 2,000. By the outbreak of the Second World War the total was around 10,000 men and a few hundred women. Then, with the peace, began the 'Age of Expansion', an epoch from which we have not yet emerged. By 1949 the number of men had risen to 19,000 and women to 1,000. By 1964 the totals were 29,000 and 1,000; by 1974, 36,000 and 1,000; by 1984, 42,000 and 1,500. This was bad enough, but twenty years later the numbers had jumped to 70,000 and 4,500, culminating in 2014 when approximately 82,500 men and 4,000 women were in prison at any one time in England and Wales.[1] Of these one in ten is under the age of twenty-one, a proportion greater than in any other West European country. Despite attempts to halt the upward trend by ministers worried about the capacity of prisons to cope

---

[1] In Scotland there are approximately 7,500 people in prison excluding those released on home detention curfew.

and the cost to the public purse – Hurd in the late 1980s and more recently Clarke who during his time as Justice Secretary expressed his dismay that the prison population had doubled since his days as Home Secretary – they have remained stubbornly at this level ever since. Over a hundred years the number of men imprisoned has increased eight-fold while the number of women has fluctuated but remained relatively low.[2] In the worst decade in penal history – 1995–2005 – the prison population increased by sixty per cent.

In 1975 the Labour Home Secretary, Roy Jenkins, said that should the prison population rise to 42,000, conditions in the system would approach the intolerable. We have now reached double that figure, and although new prisons have been built, they have been filled, compromising educational and employment provision, sports and recreational diversions, endangering familial contact and preserving the degrading conditions that perpetuate a sense of injustice. This exponential rise is a result of policy, of succeeding parliaments being ever more determined to imprison ever more offenders for ever-increasing periods. This is done by introducing minimum, or raising the maximum, terms for certain offences as well as by making aggravating features such as previous convictions statutory. Political rhetoric and press clamour do the rest. Short-term political gain by the two main political parties vying for votes by 'populist punitiveness' has had the effect of driving prisoner numbers inexorably up. As a result, Britain today imprisons a higher proportion of its population than any other West European country.[3]

Incapacitation has again come to the fore, climaxing in 2003 when the Criminal Justice Act of that year brought in imprisonment for public protection. This led to an enormous leap in the numbers serving indeterminate sentences, many of whom would massively exceed their 'tariff' – the minimum period to be served. Although this form of preventive detention was abolished in 2012, many of its 'victims' still languish in prison, unable to access the courses that would facilitate their release. The 2003 Act also prescribed 'starting points' for the minimum term for murderers, resulting in almost a doubling of the 'tariff'. Britain today has more prisoners serving mandatory and discretionary life sentences than all the other countries of the European Union put together.

---

[2]   Prison service statistics. The better the conditions or the greater the 'humanity', the longer the sentences. When birching was prohibited, the length of sentences increased. Some consider it a poor trade-off.

[3]   The USA, however, imprisons a proportion around five times that of Britain.

The number of those prisoners deemed high risk has also increased. In 1998, in a continuation of Howard's repressive policies, the system of special units developed in the late 1980s to manage disruptive prisoners had been replaced by close supervision centres – almost a reversion to the discredited and disgraceful control units of the 1970s. By aggravating feelings of injustice and unfairness they would prove counter-productive, as Woolf had predicted and Ramsbotham witnessed. The punitive conditions in the first of these new centres at Woodhill appalled the chief inspector. He thought it incredible that anyone could justify them and that Philip Wheatley, the director of high security prisons who had created and monitored them, should end up as director-general of the prison service in 2003.[4] By then England had eight prisons in its maximum security estate, five dispersal prisons – Wakefield, Frankland, and Full Sutton in the north; Long Lartin in the west; and Whitemoor in the east – and three local prisons – Belmarsh in south London (replacing Wormwood Scrubs), Woodhill in Buckinghamshire, and Strangeways in Manchester. Belmarsh and Whitemoor have High Security Units or 'prisons within prisons' where 'super Category A' prisoners such as terrorists or traitors are held in 'cramped and claustrophobic' conditions.[5] More positively, specialist units were set up in Whitemoor and Frankland – as there were in Rampton and Broadmoor – to provide lengthy treatment programmes for those with dangerous and severe personality disorders. By 2007 there were almost 3,000 prisoners held in conditions of high security.

In 2004 the Prison Service was subsumed within the National Offender Management Service and the whole put under a Chief Executive. Sceptics initially referred to it as Nightmare on Marsham Street (where its headquarters was based) due to the confusion that ensued on its creation. The Prison Commission lasted for almost ninety years and since its abolition a sense of coherence as well as purpose seems to have been lost. Unlike peripatetic and often maverick commissioners, civil servants or others managing a public service, as the new nomenclature acknowledged they were, tended to stay put in Westminster and continued to be focused on 'key performance indicators', efficiency savings and 'best value', the everyday jargon of a

---

4   David Ramsbotham, *Prisongate* (London, 2003), pp.116–20.

5   Belmarsh has twice held, if not political prisoners, politicians who were imprisoned, both for perjury. In 2000 Jeffrey Archer, the popular novelist and Conservative peer, spent the first three weeks of his four-year sentence at what he called 'Hellmarsh'; and five years later Jonathan Aitken, a former Tory cabinet minister, followed in his footsteps. Both wrote accounts of their time in prison, the latter's rather better than the former's (Archer, *A Prison Diary* (London, 2002); Aitken, *Porridge and Passion* (London, 2005)). Aitken makes no mention of his predecessor.

business. Managerialism concentrates on the way things are done and not on what is achieved. It prefers labels to leadership. It may pull up the worst but can de-motivate the best.

The setting up in 1970 of four regional headquarters to bridge the gap between central administration and the field proved no substitute for commissioners with responsibility for specific aspects of the system and who regularly visited their respective establishments. Staff felt ever more isolated and ignored. The Home Office, which, despite supposedly ceding operational control, could not resist micro-managing or meddling, seemed distant, out of touch, ignorant of the problems facing staff and prisoners alike, and unable or unwilling to solve them. Instead of determined action, reports and inquiries, so beloved of ministers and civil servants, proliferated and their recommendations were adopted or ignored. In any case these were commissioned in response to crises – riots or escapes – or to perceived deficiencies in management; they were not, with the exception of Woolf, the careful, sweeping reviews of penal policy that had taken place in 1865 and 1895.[6] Changing names is not the same as changing direction; commissioning inquiries is not the same as initiating wide-scale reform. The 'constitutional relationship between politicians responsible for formulating the overall direction of prison policy' and those charged with implementing it is unresolved. This is encapsulated in the dictum that 'ministers continue to wield authority without responsibility while the prison service has responsibility without authority'.[7]

The Home Office finally rid itself of this incubus when the new Ministry of Justice took over responsibility for prisons in 2007. With the financial crisis and austerity budgets, funding for prisons was drastically cut. Kenneth Clarke, who became Justice Secretary in 2010 to be faced with a cut of twenty-five per cent in his budget, proposed closing some prisons and reducing the prison population. He proved too liberal for the Coalition government and was replaced in 2012 with yet another 'law and order' hard-liner, Christopher Grayling. To achieve further cost savings without cutting prisoner numbers, he ordered a reduction in staffing levels, a cut in pay for new recruits and a curtailment of the privileges of prisoners. It was an explosive mix as events would show. Michael Gove succeeded him in 2015 and, bucking the trend, evinced a determination to make rehabilitation

---

[6] Mountbatten (1966), May (1979), Woolf (1991), Lygo (1991), Woodcock (1994), Learmont (1995), and Carter (2007) are just the major ones.

[7] Micheal Cavadino, James Dignan and George Mair, *The Penal System: An Introduction*, 5th edn (London, 2013), p.193.

the primary purpose of the prison system, and wanted to close down and sell off some of the dinosaurs of the prison estate. He left office before this could be actioned. The current Justice Secretary, David Gauke, and his prison minister, Rory Stewart, want secure, safe and decent prisons and are aiming at ultimately bringing prisoner numbers down, while immediately recruiting more staff.[8] Too little, too late? Numbers are still astronomical and the experienced officers who left the service in droves are being slowly replaced by neophytes and not in the numbers needed.[9]

A constant state of crisis pertaining over many years and its more recent escalation, aggravated by the never-ending changes in policy and direction made by politicians whose tenure in office has proved short, has damaged the reputation of the prison service and rendered the prison estate barely able to cope. It is surviving – just – but not thriving. At one point police station cells were being used as an overspill, and there was almost a revival of the hulks when from 1997 *HMS Weare* operated as a prison ship at Portland to relieve overcrowding, until it was decommissioned in 2005, mainly due to cost. To provide greater capacity and allow for the closure of some old gaols, Lord Carter's review of prisons called 'Securing the Future', instigated by Straw, recommended the construction of three 'Titan' gaols housing 2,500 inmates each. By contrast Wandsworth, the largest prison at that time, had a capacity of around 1,500. This proposal was much criticised, not least by the chief inspector of prisons, Anne Owers, on a wide variety of grounds, including a concern that one or more could be designated maximum security prisons of the Vectis type, but on an unprecedented and gigantic scale. The idea was put on hold during the remaining years of the Labour government but was revived under the Coalition, leading to the opening of HMP Berwyn in Wrexham, north Wales, in February 2017 as a Category C establishment holding over 2,000 men. England and Wales today have 121 prisons, Scotland has fifteen and Northern Ireland five.

With ever-increasing inmate numbers have come other problems. There seem to be more prisoners with mental health problems, drug-induced or otherwise, and they can erupt into violence directed towards themselves or

8   See the former's March 2018 speech reproduced in *The Prisons Handbook* (High Peak, 2018), pp. 20–4. A magnificent achievement, *The Handbook*, an annual publication by the former prisoner Mark Leech, offers easily the most accessible, comprehensive and up-to-date information on the prison service, its individual establishments and the inspectors' reports on them. It has become the vade-mecum for all interested in the current prison system.

9   Over a third of prison officers have less than three years in the job, while the level of staff leaving is around three times the 2010 rate (*The Prisons Handbook 2018*, p.12).

others. There are certainly more ethnic minority prisoners and they constitute a disproportionately large part of the prison population. So too by far do the disadvantaged, economically, educationally, and socially. Prisoners are less integrated with each other and more alienated from staff. The ghetto has come to gaol, warring factions have proliferated, and with them an increase in violence, riots and fear. Race, religion and radicalisation go together. Prisons may long have been universities of crime, but now they are becoming madrassas of Islamicist extremism, particularly in maximum security prisons such as Whitemoor, and YOIs such as the aptly named Isis. 'Contamination' is just as much of a problem as it always has been. In November 2011, the Cambridge Institute of Criminology published disturbing findings. A number of prisoners had told researchers that they had converted to Islam for protection or because they were bullied into it. Reasons given for conversion included 'seeking care and protection', 'gang membership', 'coercion', and 'rebellion'. Non-believers would not dare confront Muslims in case it led to retribution from the wider group, and would avoid cooking pork in communal kitchens or undressing in the showers in case it caused dangerous offence. A number of non-Muslims and prison officers claimed that many who converted did so to join an 'organised gang' and a 'protection racket' which 'glorified terrorist behaviour and exploited the fear related to it'. Non-Muslims would be visited by inmates with Islamic literature, told to read it and promised that they would be safe from physical assault if they changed faith. In its conclusion, the report noted:

> The new population mix, including younger, more black and minority ethnic and mixed race, and high numbers of Muslim prisoners, was disrupting established hierarchies in the prison. Social relations among prisoners had become complex and less visible. Too much power flowed among some groups of prisoners, with real risks of serious violence. There were high levels of fear in the prison. In particular, there were tensions and fears relating to 'extremism' and 'radicalisation'.

Converting criminals into terrorists is the most disastrous result of contemporary imprisonment.

Other major challenges facing prisons in the twenty-first century – inmates getting their hands on psychoactive drugs, including erstwhile 'legal highs' such as 'Spice' and 'Mamba', mobile phones, and weapons – are primarily down to loss of control, as Learmont pointed out. And loss of control is accentuated by increasing prisoner numbers, savage staffing cuts, decreasing inmate–officer ratios, and severe restrictions in funding. Money is tight while expenses are high. The average cost of keeping someone in prison for a year is about £40,000. The material crisis of resources is flanked by the ideological crisis of legitimacy. The prison system is perceived 'as being simultaneously ineffective in controlling crime, inefficient in its use of resources, insensitive in dealing with staff at all levels, and, all too often, downright inhumane in its treatment of offenders'.[10] The last, in particular, does not seem to worry the general public or their elected representatives. The nation is singularly failing Churchill's 'civilisation test'. Prisons are inexorably becoming dangerous warehouses rather than places of penological purpose. Hardly surprisingly, suicide and assault rates have shot up over the last fifty years, while riots and other disturbances have become almost routine. To cope with outbreaks of violence, Tornado teams and a National Tactical Response Group were set up. The latter were deployed 118 times in 2010 but 580 times in 2016, along with 19 deployments by the former. Prisons are out of control.

Rehabilitation within the present prison structure is possible but extrinsic and cannot be engineered or imposed. It has now been generally recognised that 'we cannot wrest grace from providence', but we can facilitate its action.[11] Thus, despite the recent emphasis on 'humane containment' in which the prison service has veered away from the moral message to a concentration on the technical problems of making things work, residues of the rehabilitative intention remain. To this day prison chaplains remain an integral part of the service, psychologists and probation officers continue to walk the wings, and the first prison rule still states that the aim of imprisonment is that the 'training and treatment of convicted prisoners shall be to encourage and assist them to live a good and useful life', while the 1988 'statement of purpose' encapsulates the dual role of 'look[ing] after' prisoners 'with humanity' and helping 'them to lead law-abiding and useful lives in custody and after release'. Most recently the Prison and Courts Bill reiterated the primacy of rehabilitation for the newly named Her Majesty's Prison and Probation Service which replaced the National Offender Management Service on April Fool's Day 2017.[12]

As ever, the proof will be in the pudding. Another change of name does not portend much, but the retention of Michael Spurr as Chief Executive Officer does. He has a deep commitment to the rehabilitative ideal having joined the prison service in 1983 in the hope of working in borstals, a hope frustrated by their abolition that very year. Nonetheless he

---

10 Cavadino *et al.*, *op. cit.*, pp.30, 226f.

11 Margaret DeLacy, *Prison Reform in Lancashire, 1700–1850* (Stanford, CA, 1986), p.13.

12 The Bill failed to pass before the calling of the 2017 general election and its future is uncertain. Part 1, s.1 set out the purpose of prisons as being fourfold: to protect the public, reform and rehabilitate offenders, prepare prisoners for life outside prison, and maintain a safe and secure environment.

served as deputy-governor of Aylesbury under John Dring, and replaced him as governor in 1993. In 2010 he was put in charge of NOMS and his reappointment ensures much-needed continuity and stability. The challenges he and his newly named service have to meet are perhaps the greatest that have ever faced the prison system.[13] At the beginning of 2018, overcrowding and appalling conditions were again highlighted in reports that found that Swansea, a gaol designed to accommodate 268 men, was being forced to hold more than 400, and that Liverpool prison was so squalid, with broken windows, blocked toilets, cockroaches and rats, that parts of the gaol were too hazardous to clean. *Squalor carceris* has reasserted its proprietorial rights.[14]

In 1993 a Home Secretary asserted that 'prison works', and his successors have largely repeated the same mantra. But does it, and in what ways and to what ends? It still fulfils adequately enough its original role of confining securely remand prisoners pending trial. By loss of liberty imprisonment satisfies retribution or punishment. By containment it incapacitates offenders for prolonged periods or indefinitely, protecting the public from them just so long as the sentence lasts, although crimes are committed, or organised, within prison. Thus it still has a function which high walls and locked doors can satisfy. In these negative senses prison may be said to 'work', but it aspires to being more than just a cage. At the stick level it has long been assumed that prison is the great deterrent, at the carrot level the last hope. Yet even its value as an individual or general deterrent is highly questionable.[15] As for reform and rehabilitation, over the years there have been many disappointments and some successes, such as the special unit at Barlinnie or the specialist prison, Grendon. The reality is that in the wider prison estate far more inmates are made worse than are made better. And this to protect the public!

Retribution, deterrence, reformation: punishment, protection, penitence. The modern history of our prison system has been a mismatch of these three predominant justifications for imprisonment, but while retribution and deterrence go hand in hand even if the latter is ineffective, there is

---

[13] As this book went to the publisher, news broke that this dedicated public servant has been told he must relinquish office in March 2019. Spurr, an exceptional individual who has dedicated his life to improving the prison service, stayed in post as circumstances became ever more dire to try to ensure that a catastrophe not of his making, and of which he warned, was as contained as it could be. An impossible task, perhaps, but an honourable one. Displacing him now is likely only to exacerbate the prison crisis, not rectify it.

[14] *The Prisons Handbook 2018*, p.17.

[15] Cavadino *et al.*, *op. cit.*, pp.33–6.

a strong possibility that punishment and rehabilitation are irreconcilable. As George Bernard Shaw put it: 'If you are to punish a man retributively you must injure him. If you are to reform him you must improve him. And men are not improved by injuries.' Prison is a paradox, but can it ever be a purgatory? At different times and for different groups the emphasis changes. Sometimes deterrence is to the fore, sometimes reform. For some very dangerous individuals containment and control must always be of the essence. For others prison is hardly needed and punishment could be imposed in the community. In general we imprison too many and for too long. Those for whom imprisonment is necessary should not be made worse. To punish those who have committed crimes by imprisoning them and then return them more damaged, more delinquent, more disaffected, and more dangerous to society is a calamity. Attempts to improve, to educate, to reform, or at least not to injure, still have to be made, but the best remedy is for the courts to remand fewer defendants, to imprison fewer of those convicted, and to sentence them to shorter terms. This primarily requires political will, but that will has so far been largely lacking, and parliament rather than applying the remedy has let the wound grow gangrenous.

Since the abolition of the prison commissioners in 1963 the pendulum has very much swung away from the hope and innovation of the first half of the twentieth century or, for that matter, the first half of the nineteenth. Both were eras that emphasised the common humanity, infinite potential, and intrinsic worth of all. Both were eras where dedicated individuals gave their all to better the lot of their fellows. High-minded reformists undoubtedly were, misguided they may have been, but how much more life-affirming and inspiring was the missionary optimism of John Howard, Elizabeth Fry, Alexander Maconochie, Alexander Paterson and all those ordinary prison staff who over the years have tried to make things – and people – better – and make themselves better human beings in the process – than the dispiriting penal pessimism and punitiveness of Thomas Carlyle, Edmund Du Cane and Michael Howard.

And where has the punitive emphasis, the assertion that 'prison works', led? To the highest prison population in Europe, to the longest prison sentences in our history, to an ever-ageing population, with one prison being designated for geriatrics and many more holding elderly and often infirm prisoners, to overcrowding in prisons, many of which were built in different times for different purposes, to increasing violence within prisons and to stubbornly high crime rates without, to a collapse in morale, and to a moral as well as a material crisis. And what is the answer? More of the same: more prisons, more prisoners, lengthier sentences, less justice, shorter fuses. It cannot go on like this. But it does, until the system explodes or implodes, or politicians act to reduce the use of imprisonment and inject more resources and justice into it. A failure to do so will ultimately be more costly to our society and to our humanity.

The last lament I leave to an eloquent old lag, Frank Norman:

> I've got the old imprisonment blues
> > Right down to my shoes.
> Will I ever get away one day
> > Or will I always have to stay
> With these imprisonment blooooooows?[16]

---

[16] *Bang to Rights* (London, 1958), p.111. In January 2019 to widespread acclaim, Rory Stewart announced that prison sentences of under six months would be abolished – if Parliament agrees!

Bibliography

Single citations are not included here, full bibliographical details being given in the footnotes.

Adshead, Joseph, *Prisons and Prisoners* (London, 1845).

Andrews, Jonathan, Asa Briggs, Roy Porter, Penny Tucker and Keir Waddington, *The History of Bethlem* (London, 1997).

Anon., *Five Years' Penal Servitude by One who has Endured it*, 2nd edn (London, 1878).

Babington, Anthony, *The English Bastille: A History of Newgate Gaol and Prison Conditions in Britain 1188–1902* (London, 1971).

Bailey, Victor, *Delinquency and Citizenship: Reclaiming the Young Offender 1914–1948* (Oxford, 1987).

Ball, Baden, *Prison Was My Parish* (London, 1956).

Barker, Juliet, *England Arise: The People, the King and the Great Revolt of 1381* (London, 2014).

Barlow, Simon, *The Self-Tapping Screw* (Brighton, 2013).

Baron, Barclay, *The Doctor* (London, 1952).

Barry, John, *Alexander Maconochie of Norfolk Island* (Oxford, 1958).

Baxendale, Alan, 'Maurice Wyndham Waller', in *Prison Service People* (Newbold Revel, 1993).

—— *Before the Wars: Churchill as a Reformer (1910–1911)* (Whitney, 2011).

Beccaria, Cesare, *Crimes and Punishments*, English trans. (Cambridge, 1995).

Behan, Brendon, *Borstal Boy* (London, 1958).

Bell, Walter, *The Great Plague of London in 1665*, revised edn (London, 1951).

—— *The Great Fire of London*, revised edn (London, 1951).

—— *Unknown London*, revised edn (London, 1951).

Benney, Mark, *Low Company* (London, 1936).

Bentham, Jeremy, *An Introduction to the Principles of Morals and Legislation* (London, 1789).

—— *Panopticon Writings*, Verso edn (London, 1995).

—— *Postscript; Part II: containing a Plan of Management for a Panopticon Penitentiary-House* (London, 1791).

Booth, William, *In Darkest England and the Way Out* (London, 1890).

Boswell, James, *Life of Dr Johnson*, 2 vols, Everyman edn (London, 1992).

Bottoms, Anthony and Michael Tonry, *Ideology, Crime and Criminal Justice* (Cullompton, 2002).

Boyle, Jimmy, *A Sense of Freedom* (Edinburgh, 1977).

—— *The Pain of Confinement* (Edinburgh, 1984).

Brown, Alyson, *English Society and the Prison: Time, Culture and Politics in the Development of the Modern Prison, 1850–1920* (Woodbridge, 2003).

—— *Inter-War Penal Policy and Crime in England: The Dartmoor Convict Prison Riot, 1932* (Basingstoke, 2013).

Brown, James, *Memoirs of the Public and Private Life of John Howard, the Philanthropist* (London, 1818).

Brown, John, *John Bunyan*, Tercentenary edn, revised by Frank Harrison (London, 1928).

Bunyan, John, *A Relation of the Imprisonment of Mr John Bunyan*, in *The Pilgrim's Progress and other Select Works by John Bunyan* (London, 1874).

Burdett, Osbert, *The Two Carlyles* (London, 1930).

Burt, John, *Results of the System of Separate Confinement as Administered at the Pentonville Prison* (London, 1852).

Buxton, Thomas Fowell, *An Inquiry whether Crime and Misery are Produced or Prevented by our present System of Prison Discipline* (London, 1818).

—— *Memoirs*, 4th edn, ed. Charles Buxton (London, 1850).

Caird, Rod, *A Good and Useful Life* (London, 1974).

Callan, Dick, *Gartree: The Story of a Prison* (Leyhill, 2005).

Cameron, Joy, *Prisons and Punishment in Scotland from the Middle Ages to the Present* (Edinburgh, 1983).

Campbell, Charles, *The Intolerable Hulks: British Shipboard Confinement 1776–1857*, 3rd edn (Tucson, 2001).

Carlyle, Thomas, *Latter-Day Pamphlets* (London, 1850).

Carpenter, Mary, *Our Convicts*, 2 vols (London, 1864).

Carrell, Christopher and Joyce Laing (eds), *The Special Unit, Barlinnie Prison – Its Evolution Through Its Art* (Glasgow, 1982).

Cavadino, Michael, James Dignan and George Mair, *The Penal System: An Introduction*, 5th edn (London, 2013).

Chesterton, George, *Revelations of Prison Life*, 2 vols, 2nd revised edn (London, 1856).

Clay, Walter, *The Prison Chaplain* (London, 1861).

Clayton, Gerold Fancourt, *The Wall Is Strong* (London, 1958).

Cohen, Stanley and Andrew Scull (eds), *Social Control and the State* (New York, 1983).

Collins, Hugh, *Autobiography of a Murderer* (London, 1997).

Collins, Philip, *Dickens and Crime*, 3rd edn (London, 1994).

Coyle, Andrew, *Inside: Rethinking Scotland's Prisons* (Edinburgh, 1991).

Craven, Cicely, 'The Progress of English Criminology', *Journal of Criminal Law and Criminology*, 24, 1 (1933), pp.230–47.

Creighton, Charles, *A History of Epidemics in Britain* (Cambridge, 1891).

Croft-Cooke, Rupert, *The Verdict of You All* (London, 1955).

Cronin, Harley, *The Screw Turns* (London, 1967).

Cross, Sir Rupert, *Punishment, Prison and the Public* (London, 1971).

Davitt, Michael, *Leaves from a Prison Diary*, 2 vols (London, 1885).

De Castro, J.P., *The Gordon Riots* (Oxford, 1926).

Defoe, Daniel, *A Journal of the Plague Year* (1722), Norton edn (New York, 1992).

—— *Tour of the Whole Island of Great Britain* (London, 1724–6, reprinted in two vols, ed. G. Cole, 1927).

DeLacy, Margaret, *Prison Reform in Lancashire, 1700–1850* (Stanford, CA, 1986).

Denholm-Young, N., *Collected Papers on Mediaeval Subjects* (Oxford, 1946).

Dixon, William Hepworth, *The London Prisons* (London, 1850).

—— *William Penn* (London, 1851).

Dobson, R.B., *The Peasants' Revolt of 1381*, 2nd edn (London, 1983).

Du Cane, Edmund, *An Account of the Manner in which Sentences of Penal Servitude are carried out in England* (London, 1872).

—— *The Punishment and Prevention of Crime* (London, 1885).

Dunbabin, Jean, *Captivity and Imprisonment in Mediaeval Europe, 1000–1300* (Oxford, 2002).

Ellman, Richard, *Oscar Wilde* (London, 1987).

Ellwood, Thomas, *The History of Thomas Ellwood Written by Himself* (London, 1885 edn).

Emmison, F.G., *Elizabethan Life: Disorder* (Chelmsford, 1970).

English Historical Documents I, *c.500–1042*, ed. Dorothy Whitelock, 2nd edn (London, 1979).

—— II, *1042–1189*, ed. David Douglas and G.W. Greenaway (London, 1953).

—— III, *1189–1327*, ed. Harry Rothwell (London, 1975).

—— IV, *1327–1485*, ed. A.R. Myers (London, 1969).

—— V(A), *1558–1603*, ed. Ian Archer and F.D. Price (London, 2011).

—— VIII, *1660–1714*, ed. Andrew Browning (London, 1966).

—— IX, *American Colonial Documents to 1776*, ed. Merrill Jensen (London, 1964).

—— XI, *1783–1832*, ed. A. Aspinall and E.A. Smith (London, 1969).

—— XII(1), *1833–1887*, ed. G.M. Young and W.D. Hancock (London, 1956).

Evans, Robin, *The Fabrication of Virtue: English Prison Architecture 1750–1840* (Cambridge, 1982).

Extracts from the Third Report of the Inspectors of Prisons for the Home District (London, 1838).

Farrar, C.F., *Old Bedford* (London, 1926).

Fennor, William, *The Counter's Commonwealth or a Voyage Made to an Infernal Island* (London, 1617).

Field, John, *Prison Discipline: The Advantages of the Separate System*, 2nd edn, 2 vols (London, 1848).

Fielding, Henry, *The Life of Mr Jonathan Wild the Great*, Folio edn (London, 1966).

Inquiry into the Causes of the Late Increase of Robberies etc, in *Works*, XIII (London, 1903).

Finlay, Frances, *Boy in Prison: A Young Offender's Story of Grendon* (London, 1971).

Fitzgerald, Mike, *Prisoners in Revolt* (London, 1977).

Fleta, 4 vols, ed. G.O. Sayles (London, 1984).

Fletcher, John, *A Menace to Society* (London, 1972).

Forsythe, W.J., *The Reform of Prisoners, 1830–1900* (Beckenham, 1987).

—— *Penal Discipline, Reformatory Projects and the English Prison Commission 1895–1939* (Exeter, 1991).

Foucault, Michel, *Discipline and Punish: The Birth of the Prison*, English trans. (London, 1975).

Fox, George, *The Journal of George Fox*, ed. John Nickalls (Cambridge, 1952).

Fox, John, *The Third Volume of the Ecclesiastical History Containing the Acts of Monuments of the Martyrs* (London, 1684).

Fox, Lionel, *The Modern English Prison* (London, 1934).

—— *The English Prison and Borstal Systems* (London, 1952).

Froissart, John, *Chronicles of England, France Spain, and the Adjoining Countries*, trans. Thomas Johnes, 2 vols (London, 1855).

Fry, Elizabeth, *Memoir of the Life of Elizabeth Fry with extracts from her Journals and Letters*, edited by her two daughters, 2 vols, 2nd edn (London, 1848).

Garland, David, *Punishment and Welfare: A History of Penal Strategies* (Aldershot, 1985).

Genders, Elaine and Elaine Player, *Grendon: A Study of a Therapeutic Prison* (Oxford, 1995).

Gordon, J.W., *Borstalians* (London, 1932).

Gore, Elizabeth, *The Better Fight: The Story of Dame Lilian Barker* (London, 1965).

Grew, B.D., *Prison Governor* (London, 1958).

Griffiths, Arthur, *Memorials of Millbank and Chapters in Prison History*, 2 vols (London, 1875).

—— (with A.W. Twyford) *Records of York Castle* (London, 1880).

—— *Chronicles of Newgate* (London, 1884).

—— *Fifty Years of Public Service* (London, 1904).

—— *The History and Romance of Crime*, 12 vols (London, 1905).

Gurney, Joseph John, *Notes on a Visit made to some of the Prisons in Scotland and the North of England in company with Elizabeth Fry* (London, 1819).

Haldane, Richard, *Autobiography* (London, 1929).

Hanawalt, B.A., *Crime and Conflict in English Communities, 1300–1348* (Cambridge, MA, 1990).

Hanway, Jonas, *Solitude in Imprisonment* (London, 1776).

Harding, Christopher, Bill Hines, Richard Ireland and Philip Rawlings, *Imprisonment in England and Wales: A Concise History* (Beckenham, 1985).

Harris, Frank, *Oscar Wilde: His Life and Confessions*, 2 vols (New York, 1916).

Harvey, I.M.W., *Jack Cade's Rebellion of 1450* (Oxford, 1991).

Hasluck, Alexandra, *Royal Engineer: A Life of Sir Edmund Du Cane* (London, 1973).

Hatton, Jean, *Betsy: The Dramatic Biography of a Prison Reformer* (Oxford, 2005).

Haywood, Ian and John Seed (eds), *The Gordon Riots: Politics, Culture and Insurrection in Late Eighteenth Century Britain* (Cambridge, 2012).

Heffer, Simon, *Moral Desperado: A Life of Thomas Carlyle* (London, 1995).

Hibbert, Christopher, *King Mob* (New York, 1958).

Hill, Billy, *Boss of Britain's Underworld* (King's Lynn, 2008).

Hill, Matthew Davenport, *Suggestions for the Repression of Crime* (London, 1857).

Himmelfarb, Gertrude, *Victorian Minds: Essays on Nineteenth Century Intellectuals* (London, 1968).

Hobhouse, Stephen, *Forty Years and an Epilogue* (London, 1951).

Hobhouse, Stephen and Fenner Brockway, *English Prisons Today* (London, 1922).

Hodges, Nathaniel, *Loimologia or An Historical Account of the Plague in London in 1665* (London, 1665, English trans., 1720).

Holland, Lady, *A Memoir of the Rev. Sydney Smith*, new edn (London, 1869).

Holmes, Richard (ed.), *Defoe on Sheppard and Wild* (London, 2004).

Hood, Roger, *Borstal Reassessed* (London, 1965).

Hoskinson, John, *Inside: One Man's Experience of Prison* (London, 1998).

Howard, John, *Prisons and Lazarettos*, 2 vols, 4th edn (London, 1792).

Hughes, Robert, *The Fatal Shore* (London, 1987).

Hunnisett, R.F., *The Mediaeval Coroner* (Cambridge, 1961).

Hyde, Montgomery, *Oscar Wilde: The Aftermath* (London, 1963).

Ignatieff, Michael, *A Just Measure of Pain: The Penitentiary in the Industrial Revolution 1750–1850* (London, 1978).

Jebb, Joshua, *Modern Prisons: Their Construction and Ventilation* (London, 1844).

—— *Report of the Surveyor-General of Prisons on the Construction, Ventilation and Details of Pentonville Prison* (London, 1844).

—— *Second Report of the Surveyor-General of Prisons* (London, 1847).

—— *Report on the Discipline and Management of the Convict Prisons, 1850* (London, 1851).

—— *Reports and Observations on the Discipline and Management of Convict Prisons*, ed. by the earl of Chichester (London, 1863).

Jeffrey, Robert, *The Barlinnie Story* (Edinburgh, 2009).

Jenkins, Lyndsey, *Lady Constance Lytton: Aristocrat, Suffragette, Martyr* (London, 2015).

Jones, Enid Huws, *Margery Fry: The Essential Amateur* (Oxford, 1966).

Joyce, C.A., *By Courtesy of the Criminal* (London, 1955).

Judges, A.V. (ed.), *Key Writings on Subcultures 1535–1727*, vol. I, *The Elizabethan Underworld: A Collection of Tudor and Early Stuart Tracts and Ballads* (London, 2002).

Kingsmill, Joseph, *Chapters on Prisons and Prisoners*, 2nd edn (London, 1852).

Leech, Mark, *A Product of the System* (London, 1992).

Leslie, Shane, *Sir Evelyn Ruggles-Brise: A Memoir of the Founder of Borstal* (London, 1938).

Lewis, Derek, *Hidden Agendas: Politics, Law and Disorder* (London, 1997).

Linebaugh, Peter, *The London Hanged* (London, 1991).

Lodge, Jeremy, *Lowdham Grange. Borstal!* (Nottingham, 2016).

Lopez-Rey, Manuel and Charles Germain (eds), *Studies in Penology* (The Hague, 1964).

Lytton, Constance, *Prisons and Prisoners* (London, 1914).

Macartney, Wilfred, *Walls Have Mouths* (London, 1936).

McCall, Cicely, *Looking Back from the Nineties* (Norwich, 1994).

McConville, Sean, *A History of English Prison Administration 1750–1877* (London, 1981).

—— *English Local Prisons 1860 to 1900: 'Next Only to Death'* (London, 1994).

McCulloch, J.R., *A Statistical Account of the British Empire*, 2 vols (London, 1837).

Marrot, H.V., *The Life and Letters of John Galsworthy* (London, 1935).

Maxwell, Richard, *Borstal and Better* (London, 1956).

Maybrick, Florence, *Mrs Maybrick's Own Story: My Fifteen Lost Years* (New York, 1905).

Mayhew, Henry and John Binny, *The Criminal Prisons of London* (London, 1862).

Melossi, Dario and Massimo Pavarini, *The Prison and the Factory: Origins of the Penitentiary System*, English trans. (London, 1981).

Merrow-Smith, L.W., *Prison Screw* (London, 1962).

Mirror of Justices, ed. W.W. Maitland (London, 1895).

Morris, Norval, *Maconochie's Gentlemen* (Oxford, 2002).

Morris, Terence, *Crime and Criminal Justice since 1945* (Oxford, 1989).

Moseley, Sydney, *The Truth about Borstal* (London, 1926).

Neild, James, *State of the Prisons in England, Scotland and Wales* (London, 1812).

Norman, Frank, *Bang to Rights* (London, 1958).

O'Donoghue, E.G., *The Story of Bethlehem Hospital from Its Foundation in 1247* (London, 1914).

—— *Bridewell Hospital, Palace, Prison, Schools*, 2 vols (London, 1923, 1929).

Oliver, Lisi, *The Beginnings of English Law* (Toronto, 2002).

Orwell, George, *Collected Essays*, 4 vols (London, 1968).

O'Sullivan, Michael, *Brendan Behan: A Life* (Colorado, 1999).

Oxford History of the Laws of England (Oxford, 2003–)

—— ii, *871–1216*, John Hudson (2012).

—— xiii, *1820–1914: Fields of Development*, William Cornish *et al.* (2010).

Oxford History of the Prison, ed. Norval Morris and David Rothman (Oxford, 1995).

Page, Leo, *The Young Lag* (London, 1950).

Parker, Tony, *The Frying-Pan* (London, 1970).

Partridge, Ralph, *Broadmoor* (London, 1953).

Paston Letters, 6 vols, ed. James Gairdner (London, 1904).

Paterson, Alexander, *Across the Bridges*, 2nd edn (London, 1912).

Peare, Catherine, *William Penn* (London, 1956).

Penn, William, *A Collection of the Works*, 2 vols (London, 1726).

Pepys, Samuel, *Diary*, ed. Robert Latham and William Matthews, 11 vols (London, 1970–83).

Phelan, James, *Jail Journey* (London, 1940).

Playfair, Giles, *The Punitive Obsession* (London, 1971).

Porter, Stephen, *The Tower of London: The Biography* (Stroud, 2012).

Potter Harry, *Hanging in Judgment: Religion and the Death Penalty in England from the Bloody Code to Abolition* (London, 1993).

—— *Law, Liberty and the Constitution* (Woodbridge, 2015).

—— *Principles of the Borstal System* (Prison Commission, Home Office, 1932).

—— *The Prisons Handbook 2018*, ed. Mark Leech (Southampton, 2018).

Pugh, R.B., *Imprisonment in Mediaeval England* (Cambridge, 1968).

Radzinowicz, Leon, *A History of English Criminal Law and Its Administration from 1750*, vol. 5: *The Emergence of Penal Policy* (with Roger Hood; London, 1986).

Ramsbotham, David, *Prisongate: The Shocking State of Britain's Prisons and the Need for Visionary Change* (London, 2003).

Redfern, Barry, *Victorian Villains, Prisoners from Newcastle Gaol 1871–1873* (Newcastle, 2006).

Report of the Commissioners of Prisons [and Directors of Convict Prisons] (annually).

Report from the Select Committee of the House of Lords on the Present State of Discipline in Gaols and House of Correction (Carnarvon) (1863).

Report of the Commissioners on the Workings of the Penal Servitude Acts (Kimberley) (1879).

Report from the Departmental Committee on Prisons and Minutes of Evidence (Gladstone) (1895).

Report of the Inquiry into Prison Escapes and Security (Mountbatten) (1966).

Report of the Committee of Inquiry into the United Kingdom Prison Services (May) (1979).

Report of an Inquiry into the Prison Disturbances, April 1990 (Woolf) (1991).

Report of the Enquiry into the Escape of Six Prisoners from the Special Security Unit at Whitemoor Prison (Woodcock) (1994).

Review of Prison Service Security in England and Wales and the Escape from Parkhurst Prison (Learmont) (1995).

Reynolds, Andrew, *Anglo-Saxon Deviant Burial Customs* (Oxford, 2009).

Rich, C.E.F., *Recollections of a Prison Governor* (London, 1932).

Roberts, John, *Memoir of John Bunyan* (London, 1874).

Ruck, S.K. (ed.), *Paterson on Prisons* (London, 1951).

Ruggles-Brise, Sir Evelyn, *The English Prison System* (London, 1921).

Russell, Charles and Lillian Rigby, *The Making of the Criminal* (London, 1906).

Rutherford, Andrew, *Prisons and the Process of Justice* (Oxford, 1986).

Salgado, Gamini, *The Elizabethan Underworld* (London, 1977).

Sancho, Ignatius, *Letters*, Penguin edn (London, 1998).

Scott, Harold, *Your Obedient Servant* (London, 1959).

Semple, Janet, *Bentham's Prison: A Study of the Panopticon Penitentiary* (Oxford, 1993).

Sharrock, Roger, *John Bunyan* (London, 1968).

Slack, Paul, *The Impact of the Plague in Tudor and Stuart England* (London, 1985).

Sloane, Barney, *The Black Death in London* (Stroud, 2011).

Smith, Sydney, *Works*, 4 vols (London, 1839).

Southerton, Peter, *The Story of a Prison* (Reading, 1975).

Stockdale, Eric, *A Study of Bedford Prison 1660–1877* (London, 1977).

Stokes, Anthony, *Pit of Shame: The Real Ballad of Reading Gaol* (Winchester, 2007).

Stow, John, *A Survey of London* (1603), 2 vols, ed. Charles Kingsford (Oxford, 1908).

Thomas, J.E., *The English Prison Officer since 1850* (London, 1972).

Thomas, J.E. and R. Pooley, *The Exploding Prison* (London, 1980).

Twyford, A.W. and Arthur Griffiths, *Records of York Castle* (London, 1880).

Vaux, James Hardy, *Memoirs* (1819), ed. Noel McLachlan (London, 1964).

Vidler, John, *If Freedom Fail* (London, 1964).

Vincent, William [Thomas Holcroft], *A Plain and Succinct Narrative of the Late Riots and Disturbances in the Cities of London and Westminster and Borough of Southwark*, 3rd edn (London, 1780).

Wakefield, Edward Gibbon, *Facts Relating to the Punishment of Death in the Metropolis* (London, 1832).

—— *The Hangman and the Judge or a Letter from Jack Ketch to Mr Justice Alderson* (London, 1833).

Watson, John, *Meet the Prisoner* (London, 1939).

—— *Which Is the Justice?* (London, 1969).

Webb, S. and B., *English Prisons under Local Government* (London, 1922).

West, Richard, *The Life and Strange Surprising Adventures of Daniel Defoe* (London, 1997).

Wilde, Oscar, *Complete Letters*, ed. Merlin Holland and Rupert Hart-Davis (London, 2000).

Wildeblood, Peter, *Against the Law* (London, 1955).

Wilson, David, *Pain and Retribution: A Short History of British Prisons 1066 to the Present* (London, 2014).

Ziegler, Philip, *The Black Death*, Folio Society edn (London, 1997).

Index

Numbers in bold refer to illustrations and their captions. Individual prisons and gaols are listed alphabetically by names, but other custodial institutions are to be found under bridewells, borstal institutions, counters and hulks. The dates of their opening and closing (where ascertainable) are given.